ADULT DEVELOPMENT AND AGING

FIFTH EDITION

K. WARNER SCHAIE
The Pennsylvania State University

SHERRY L. WILLIS
The Pennsylvania State University

Prentice Hall

Upper Saddle River, NJ 07458

Library of Congress Cataloging-in-Publication Data

Schaie, K. Warner (Klaus Warner),
    Adult development and aging / K. Warner Schaie, Sherry L. Willis.—5th ed.
      p. cm.
    Includes bibliographical references and index.
    ISBN 0–13–089439–7
      1. Adulthood.   2. Life cycle, Human.   3. Adulthood—Psychological aspects.   4.
    Aging—Psychological aspects.   I. Willis, Sherry L., 1947–   II. Title.

    HQ799.95. S33 2002
    305.24--dc21

                                                                    00–053729

VP, Editorial Director: Laura Pearson
Senior Acquisitions Editor: Jennifer Gilliland
Assistant Editor: Nicole Girrbach
VP, Director of Production and Manufacturing: Barbara Kittle
Managing Editor: Mary Rottino
Production Editor: Randy Pettit
Prepress and Manufacturing Manager: Nick Sklitsis
Prepress and Manufacturing Buyer: Tricia Kenny
Director of Marketing: Beth Gillett Mejia
Senior Marketing Manager: Sharon Cosgrove
Cover Design Director: Jayne Conte
Cover Design: Bruce Kenselaar
Director, Image Resources: Melinda Lee Reo
Image Specialist: Beth Boyd-Brenzel
Photo Researcher: Julie Tesser

For permission to use copyright material, grateful
acknowledgment is made to the copyright holders listed
on page 603, which is considered an extension of this
copyright page.

This book was set in 10/12 Baskerville by Pine Tree Composition, Inc.
and printed and bound by R.R. Donnelley & Sons Company, Harrisonburg
The cover was printed by Phoenix Color Corp.

 © 1996, 2002 by K. Warner Schaie and Sherry L. Willis
A Division of Pearson Education
Upper Saddle River, New Jersey 07458

Printed in the United States of America
10 9 8 7 6 5 4

ISBN 0-13-089439-7

Prentice Hall International (UK) Limited, *London*
Prentice Hall of Australia Pty. Limited, *Sydney*
Prentice Hall Canada Inc., *Toronto*
Prentice Hall Hispanoamericana, S.A., *Mexico*
Prentice Hall of India Private Limited, *New Delhi*
Prentice Hall of Japan, Inc., *Tokyo*
Pearson Education Asia Pte. Ltd., *Singapore*
Editora Prentice Hall do Brasil, Ltda., *Rio de Janeiro*

BRIEF CONTENTS

DETAILED CONTENTS

PREFACE

The "graying of America" proceeds at a rapid pace. The post-World War II baby boom generation, comprising 1 out of every 3 people in the United States, is now at middle age. One out of every 4 Americans is already 50 years of age or older. By the year 2025, 64 million Americans will be 65 years of age or older.

We are finally beginning to come to grips with the implications of the burgeoning population of older people. Our increasing longevity and the need for understanding its ramifications have also resulted in considerable scientific research, especially during the last four decades. The demand has grown on college and university campuses for courses that focus their attention on the broad period of adulthood. Exploring the development of an individual's career, marriage, family life, and psychological functioning as he or she is affected by a rapidly changing society have become vital issues.

Th objective of this textbook is to encourage the student to consider the phenomenon of adult development and aging from a behavioral point of view in a readable but comprehensive and scientifically well-documented manner. We introduce current theory and research on the major psychological issues, and we provide background on those social and biological aspects of development that are essential to understanding behavioral age changes.

We continue to believe that the study of adult development is best served by using a combined chronological and topical approach that we have consistently used in previous editions and the sequence of presentation first introduced in the third edition has been retained. *Adult Development and Aging*, fifth edition begins with an introductory chapter that sets the stage for our study. This chapter examines demographic changes in our society and the current state of research in the field. To provide an overview, we next consider the broad issues of adult development in three chronological chapters: young adulthood, middle age, and late life. We then provide a research methods chapter that focuses on the quasi-experimental methods prominent in the study of devlopment, and also provides a brief exposition of relevant experimental deisgns. Our experience in teaching earlier editions of the text suggested that students were often overwhelmed when research methods were introduced in the first chapter before some substantive material was covered. The methodology chapter is now placed at the point where that material seems to be needed for a proper understanding of the topical chapters that follow.

The topical chapters are placed roughly in the life-stage order at which particular developmental processes become most salient. First, we consider topics that are important in young adulthood: families, gender issues, and careers. The gender issues chapter comes immediately after the family chapter because issues first raised under the rubric of the family are considered further in the chapter on men and women. The second group of topics consists of personality development, motivation, learning and memory, and intellectual development, areas in which age changes become important as people move from midlife into old age. The final three chapters cover lifelong processes that become most salient in old age: biological aging, mental disorders associated with old age, and bereavement.

The material that we cover in the topical chapters, however, is not limited just to the life stage within which it happens to be particularly relevant. The flow of human lives can not be segmented that easily. Initial career choices, for example, may be of paramount importance to young adults, but matters relating to career development permeate much of adulthood. Although our chapter on careers is placed early in the book, it also includes material on occupational development in middle age, career reevaluation, change in later life, and the retirement experience.

What we hope to accomplish is to present an integrated picture of the psychological processes involved in adult development and the stages of human experience. We therefore, whenever appropriate, use a life-span approach in following psychological processes as they develop from young adulthood to the end of life.

During the five years since the fourth edition of this book was published, research on aging has continued at a furious pace. In this fifth edition, we have attempted to incorporate new findings that occurred during the previous decade as well as to provide further documentation for our discussion. Unfortunately, much of the newly added material can not always replace older findings. Thus the research literature cited in this volume keeps expanding and now numbers over 2,000 references. In order to understand behavioral aging, we continue to provide limited discussions of the necessary context to be found in concurrent biological and societal changes. We have further updated the material on family relationships in rapidly changing circumstances, such as the increasing number of women in the workforce and the increasing frequency of dual careers. And we continue to monitor the recent advances in work on Alzheimer's disease and the relationship between cardiovascular disease and behavior.

The methodology chapter covers design issues important to descriptive studies of human aging, but it also summarizes principles of research employing experimental paradigms. A thorough understanding of human development requires data that are collected over time on the same individuals, the longitudinal approach. Wherever possible, we therefore present data from at least short-term longitudinal follow-up studies. We have tried to present a sound and thorough review of scientific research methods that avoids jargon and unnecessary technical detail while providing the student with the essential details needed to understand the studies described in this volume as well as other relevant research literature.

Tables and graphs have been updated wherever more recent information was available. However, the reader should note that the results of the 2000 census were not available at the time this edition went into production, and population figures must therefore rely on census publications from the 1990s. The illustration program was also reviewed and substitutions were made where we thought improvement was indicated.

In order to keep the size of this textbook manageable, we have once again tried to make room for the most recent work by trimming some older materials that are now primarily of historical interest or material that is not directly essential to an understanding of the aging processes. For students who wish to pursue major issues in greater depth, we continue to include suggestions for further reading at the end of each chapter and a listing of major reference volumes and journals at the end of the book.

We are pleased to know that previous editions of *Adult Development and Aging* have had wide circulation outside of North America. But we must admit that the book retains a somewhat "Americanocentric" orientation and content. Although the great bulk of the psychological aging literature continues to originate in North America, there has been a steadily increasing amount of work on aging in Europe and elsewhere. In the present edition, we continue our attempt to overcome our past avoidance behavior by including materials on international studies in each chapter whenever possible and by including citations to books and journals published outside of North America. This effort was enhanced by the fact that significant portions of this edition were written in Berlin, Germany, while we were guests of the Max-Planck-Institute for Human Development and the Division of Geropsychology of the Geriatric Klinikum at the Free University of Berlin. We would like to thank our hosts Paul Baltes and Jacqui Smith as well as the many researchers and students who were stimulating conversation partners during our stay in Berlin.

Creating and revising a textbook requires the harmonious efforts of many skilled professionals. We would like to acknowledge the contribution of reviewers who read all or part of the manuscript and helped to improve both coverage and clarity: Marion Beaver, University of Pittsburgh; Joan Erber, Florida International; James Blackburn, University of Wisconsin at Milwaukee; Marion Hunt, Dakota Wesleyan University; Dale Lund, University of Utah. We wish to thank our editor Jennifer Gilliland and her assistant Nicole Girrbach. Anna Shuey handled the clerical and technical details associated with revising the manuscript, with assistance from Judy Davis who assembled the indexes.

Much remains to be learned about adult development and aging, but a clearer picture has begun to emerge as the results of intensive scientific research accumulate. The picture that we present is as comprehensive and accurate as we could make it at this point in time. It may often differ from some of the common stereotypes about adult development and aging. Our interpretation of the research literature is somewhat more optimistic than many popular, often erroneously held beliefs, but it also conveys a realistic appraisal of the many problems the elderly must face in today's society. It is our view that the life course from young adulthood to old age is not so much a series of "life crises" as a progression of gains and losses, of challenges and of opportunities. We hope to convince you that even the final years of life can be filled with substantial personal creativity and satisfaction. We will be gratified if this book can help you to see the potential richness of your own life in the years to come as well as to understand the lives of those older adults you may love and/or care for. We hope, therefore, that you will find *Adult Development and Aging*'s contents both enlightening and encouraging.

K.W.S.
S.L.W.

CHAPTER 1

Adult Development and Aging

An Introduction

This is a book about the psychology of adult development and aging. However, behavior always occurs in context. We therefore also provide the necessary background materials concerned with the demographic facts of aging, those biological factors whose aging affect behavior, and the societal influences that provide the context for our inquiry. Although we now know much about human aging, the reader will find that time and time again we encounter a question about adult development—a reasonable question, a researchable question, one whose answer would have social as well as scientific value—and find that, if it has been investigated at all, the studies are few, they use uncertain measures of concepts that have been too broadly conceived, or they are based on inadequate samples drawn from a population too narrow for meaningful generalizations. Popular, sometimes contradictory notions abound, and sometimes data are still lacking that would allow us to distinguish between correct beliefs and unfounded myths.

A PREVIEW OF THE TEXT

The purpose of this text is to examine the available research evidence and to formulate the most plausible conclusions about adult development and aging. Research findings in developmental psychology can be presented in two ways: chronologically and topically. A chronological presentation uses the life span as the organizing principle, covering in the case of adult development, first young adulthood, then middle age, and then old age. The biological, cognitive, and social processes that occur in a particular period of life are discussed together; the same processes are then discussed again, in reference to later age periods. A topical organization, in contrast, follows a process throughout the life span. A particular topic is discussed as it applies to several age stages, in our case, to young adults, the middle aged, and the elderly. Instead of finding chapter titles such as "Young Adulthood," there would be chapters on "Biological Development," "Personality Development," "Families," and "Careers." In a chronological organization "starting a career" would be one of several topics discussed in the section on young adulthood, and "retirement" would be discussed many chapters later, in the section on old age. In a topical organization, the initial choice of a career, midlife career changes, and retirement would all be located in a single chapter.

Each type of organization has advantages and disadvantages. A chronological organization seems more "lifelike"; a book organized in this way reads like a biography or a collection of biographies. Each chapter would have a mixture of biology, intellect, personality, and society, just as in real life. But one of the disadvantages of this kind of organization is that many of the issues of adult life do not change significantly from one age to another, and thus one section often repeats what was already said before. Another disadvantage of a chronological organization is that it "chops up" the processes, making it difficult to get a full picture. You might read in the section on middle age, for example, that measured IQ tends to be stable during this period. You try to remember what you learned chapters back about intellectual development in young adulthood: Did it decrease during this period? Increase? And what, you might wonder, will happen in old age? Does IQ remain stable throughout life?

The topical approach presents the full picture of each process throughout the life span. In addition, many of the theories that are most helpful in understanding adult development are often limited to a single topic: a theory of intellectual development, a theory of personality development, a theory of careers, or a theory of the family life cycle. These theories are difficult to present in a chronological organization, because they are constructed from research that crosses different chronological stages. The principal disadvantage of the topical approach is that it tends to fragment the individual. It separates personality from intellect; it pays little attention to family concerns as it discusses careers. The topical organization might therefore seem more abstract than the chronological organization; hence it may not feel quite as "lifelike."

A chronological organization makes a book more interesting, but a topical organization makes it more informative. We would like to make our text both interesting and informative and have therefore combined the two organizing principles. As befits a scientific textbook whose primary purpose is to inform, our basic organization is topical. Nevertheless, we begin our account with three chronologically organized chapters; they cover some of the most salient issues in the three major stages of adult life: young adulthood, midlife, and old age. These chapters are then followed by an overview of the methodological problems of studying changes across age and time. Contrary to some other textbooks, we elected not to put this chapter at the very beginning, because it is difficult to talk about methodology before some substantive content has been covered. Needless to say, however, an understanding of how researchers design studies of aging is essential for an understanding of the topics that follow.

Each of the topical chapters that follow covers the entire life span from young adulthood to old age; for example, careers are followed from the first job to retirement and beyond. The topical chapters are arranged roughly in the order in which their content begins to be of major concern to adults. Thus, the first group of topical chapters considers issues that must be attended to in young adulthood, such as intimacy and marriage, career choice, and personal identity.

The next group of chapters cover issues that become important in midlife, such as the role of motivation and the question of continuity or change of personality as the individual matures. Middle age is often a period of reevaluation. Many middle-aged adults reevaluate their marriages and other aspects of man–woman relationships, such as perceived loss of sexual attractiveness. Middle-aged people often fear that decreased "drive" will make it difficult to escape from a career that no longer remains interesting to them. Fears and uncertainties related to these issues may precipitate a midlife transition, whether there is a true "midlife crisis" or not.

The remaining chapters concentrate on developmental changes that become of greatest concern in old age. These chapters in large part deal with the experience of growing old: Does intelligence decline at age 13 or 18 or some other ridiculously young age, or is it maintained throughout adulthood? Can old dogs learn new tricks? What happens to memory? What sensory losses occur in vision and hearing? What exactly is "aging"? What is the probability of becoming demented? What exactly is dementia? And, finally, what do we know about the process of dying?

There has been an exciting explosion of knowledge in gerontology in general and the psychology of aging in particular. The publication rate of research specifically relevant to the psychology of adult development and aging has grown to thousands of articles and chapters a year (Birren and Schroots, 1996, 2001), and the number of research publications that peripherally discuss aging, old age, and the elderly now exceeds over ten thousand a year. Hence, it would be impossible to discuss the thousands of new studies that have appeared since the fourth edition of this text was published. What then, are the principles that we have applied to decide which old material to discard and which new material to include?

A major temptation in revising and updating a text is to delete older studies and replace them with new ones. This temptation must be resisted, for, as the astute reader will realize, the newest studies often tread on uncharted territory. They must be carefully reviewed and analyzed by qualified colleagues to see if they deserve to be accepted. More recent studies may not necessarily be as rigorous and precise as older work; the most recent studies are often premature publications of incompletely digested data, prompted by the "publish or perish" anxieties that plague many promising young academics.

Our decisions have been greatly influenced and made much easier by a careful reading of the recently published *Handbook of Theories of Aging* (Bengtson and

Schaie, 1999), the *Handbook of the Psychology of Aging* (Birren and Schaie, 2001) and of recent relevant chapters in the *Annual Review of Psychology* and the *Annual Review of Gerontology and Geriatrics.* Once again, we found that relatively little material could be deleted but that quite a bit had to be added. Many of the new additions are from primary sources from the mid-1990s, whose relevance and meaning have now become clear enough to be considered a firm addition to the current state of knowledge.

At the end of each chapter, we provide a summary of the information and interpretive statements in the chapter that we think are particularly noteworthy. We conclude each chapter with a list of recent reviews and readable books for those who want more extensive information about the topics covered. These references also provide a good place to start in a search for materials for a term paper.

A BIT OF HISTORY

The field of adult development and aging is a relatively young topic in psychology. Although research in adult development is now booming, a lot of work still remains until we achieve the comprehensive understandings that have been attained in other areas, such as the psychology of perception or child development.

Why is it that a field that covers 75 percent of the human life span has gone relatively unstudied for so long? Adults do almost everything of importance in a society: they work, marry, make war, create art, exercise power, organize religions. Why have developmental psychologists ignored them for so long? Some of this neglect may be explained by the values and theoretical biases of early pioneers in the developmental sciences. Freud, for example, quoting Woodworth proposed that "the child is the father of the man" and thought that most of the events of adulthood could best be explained by an understanding of early childhood experiences. Likewise, many developmental researchers were interested primarily in discovering how individual behavior is acquired in the first place. They moved slowly into the study of behavioral growth through childhood into adolescence and they were even less willing to tackle the complexities of the maintenance of behavior, its change, and decline through adulthood.

Many developmental scientists, until quite recently, considered age-related changes during adulthood to be quite rare. No clear distinctions were drawn between normal aging and the impact of chronic disease. Hence, those aspects of a person that were affected by disease were thought to change with age and everything else was thought to remain stable from the emergence of a behavior until the end of life. It was believed that the individual's personality was well set by the age of maturity and that changes were unlikely and perhaps impossible. When divorce and midlife career changes were much rarer than they are today, it was believed that family and career decisions were made early and then maintained throughout life. Very few people expected to change employers, and even fewer expected to take up new occupational pursuits not learned in young adulthood. Sexual abilities were believed to decline during the adult years, but because sex was a taboo topic, no one knew for sure. Intellectual abilities were also believed to decline, especially toward the end of life, and tests of intelligence were among the first psychological measures used to compare adults of various ages—leading to questionable conclusions, as we shall see. There was interest in intellectual and biological changes in old age, but until the present century relatively few people lived long enough to attain this status and thus become subjects of inquiry.

The Rise of Gerontology

The first beginnings of a developmental psychology for adults came at the far end of the field, in the study of aging (Birren and Birren, 1990; Birren and Schroots, 2001). Advances in sanitation, nutrition, and medical knowledge made possible incredible changes in life expectancy in the United States and throughout the world, providing subjects for study as well as the need to study them. In the United States, only 50 percent of children born in 1900 could reasonably hope to reach the age of 50; life expectancy today is approximately 77 years of age. But note that there is a big discrepancy between males and females, 73.6 years for men and 79.4 years for women. Life expectancy is lower for African Americans; 67.2 years for men and 74.7 years for women (Hoyert, Kochanek, and Murphy, 1999).

The percentage of people over 65 in the U.S. population has risen from less than 5 percent in 1900 to approximately 12.5 percent in 1990 and is projected to reach 22.9 percent by the year 2050 (U.S. Bureau of the Census, 1992b). This growth is even more impressive when expressed in absolute numbers. At the time

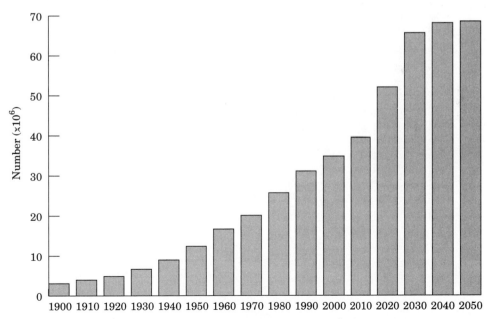

Figure 1-1A Older Populations of the United States from 1900 to 2050 (Actual and Projected). *Source:* U.S. Bureau of the Census (1992b).

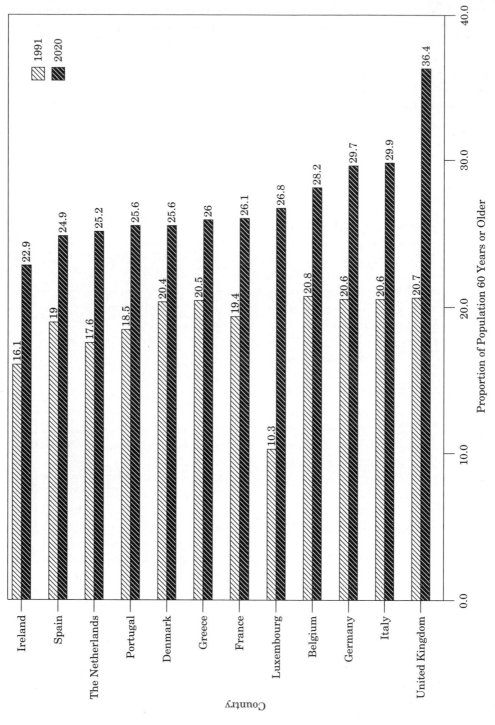

Figure 1-1B Population Aging in Europe. *Source:* Center for International Statistics (1992).

of the first U.S. census in 1790 there were fewer than 50,000 Americans (or about 2 percent of the population) over age 65. Figure 1-1A shows the growth of the elderly population from 1900 to 1990, with projections until 2050. In 1900 there were about 3 million persons over age 65. In 1990 there were over 31 million, and by the time people who were born during the 1970s and 1980s reach old age, the number of old people will exceed 69 million (U.S. Bureau of the Census, 1996). The median age in the United States (half the people are younger, half are older) will be nearly 40 years, compared to slightly above 30 today. In 1995, 85.6 percent of the U.S. population over age 65 were white, 8.1 percent were black, 4.5 percent were Hispanics and the remaining 1.8 percent were other races, including Asians and Native Americans.

The proportion of minority elderly will increase markedly, as life expectancy in nonwhite groups will catch up in the coming decades. By 2050, the distribution of those over age 65 is projected to be 64.8 percent white, 10.7 percent black, 17.2 percent Hispanics, and 7.2 percent others.The explosion of the elderly population is by no means confined to North America. In fact, most industrialized countries show similar population trends. Figure 1-1B shows the proportion of persons over 60 in 1991 and projections for the year 2020 for the member countries of the European Community (Center for International Statistics, 1992).

What is the cause of the population explosion among the elderly? A number of variables affect the composition of a population; the most important are migration, changes in fertility, and mortality. Because most immigrants spend their childhoods in their native country and migrate as young adults, their chief demographic effect is on the average age of the population. But older immigrants may place additional burdens on the health care system (see Ikels, 1998a),

Fertility, the number of babies born in a population, is of much greater importance. Most of us are familiar with one recent period of high fertility rates—the "baby boom" period that occurred in the United States between 1947 and 1967. However, the fertility rate has fluctuated throughout our history. There were relatively few people born, for example, during the years of the Great Depression between 1931 and 1940 and, more recently, during the period from 1971 to 1980. The latter period is sometimes called the "baby bust."

Changes in fertility rates have a profound effect on the age distribution of the population. This can be seen in the population pyramids in Figure 1-2, which show how the age structure of the United States population will change between 1990 and 2060. The data are from the 1990 census. Because everyone who will be age 70 or older in 2060 has already been born, we have accurate knowledge of how large some parts of the population will be many years in advance; indeed, we may err on the side of conservatism because mortality rates will most likely decline even further. Younger age groups, who have not yet been born, are estimated on the basis of current fertility levels.

Several features in Figure 1-2 are worth noting. In the 1990 pyramid, the "depression" cohorts then between the ages of 50 and 70 are quite small. This group has had several advantages. They faced relatively little competition from age peers as they grew up. When members of this group retire between now and 2005, they can

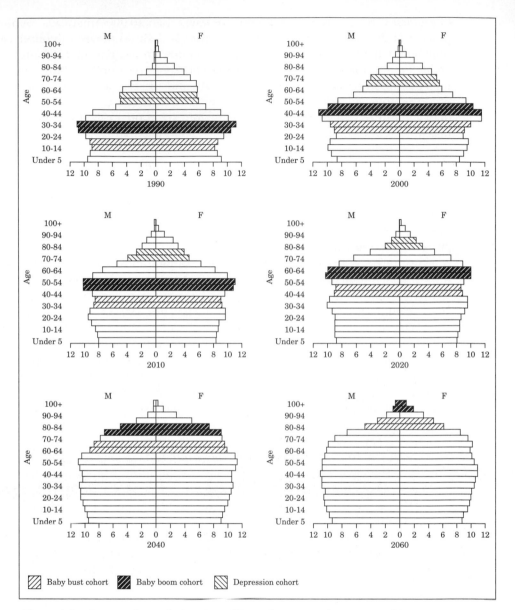

Figure 1-2 Projected Population (in Millions), by Age and Sex: United States, 1990–2060. *Source:* U.S. Bureau of the Census (1992a, 1992b).

rely on the cohorts that follows them, the baby boom group, to provide them with an adequate income. They will face less competition for support and services than either the cohort that entered old age before them or the cohort following them.

The baby boom generation faces a very different prospect as it turns into a "gerontic boom." When its members retire, probably between the years 2010 and

2030, they will have to rely for their income on the relatively small cohorts that follow them. The *dependency ratio* of persons not gainfully employed (children, the retired, and the unemployed) to persons who are in the workforce will be unusually small. That is, the number of persons who pay taxes and contribute into the social security system will be shrinking, while the number of persons receiving pensions and requiring extensive health care will be markedly increasing. That is why Congress, in 1983, decided to gradually raise the Social Security retirement age to 67 years beginning with the year 2000.

The number of persons who become newly available to provide professional and personal care will be small compared to the number of individuals who will require greater support and care by others. During this period there will be a great many old people but relatively few very-old people. Later, this situation will reverse, and there will be many very-old and relatively few young-old people. The baby-bust cohort, when it retires, will have to compete for services with a much larger group of the very-old and increasingly fragile baby boomers.

Over the next fifty years from 2000 to 2050, the U.S. population pyramid will become increasingly rectangular, and the median age as a whole will increase

The baby boom generation is now in midlife; their aging will be somewhat different from that of their parents.

from 33 to 41.6 years, almost a full decade (U.S. Bureau of the Census, 1996). The imbalance between men and women in advanced old age is also likely to increase. This is one of the reasons that we must pay close attention to sex differences in adult development throughout this book. You should remember that when we describe the very-old, we will be speaking of a predominantly female population.

The increase in the older population is, of course, also affected by decreasing mortality rates. These rates are already quite low, and further declines are expected before the end of the century (Smith, Martin, and Ventura, 1999). Progress in preventing premature death has dramatically increased a person's chances of surviving to a very old age. It is currently estimated that by the year 2045, 95 percent of all deaths will occur between the ages of 77 and 93; the average age of death (not including those who die from accidents or violence) is expected eventually to stabilize somewhere around age 85 (Fries, 1985)

Life expectancy figures at birth markedly underestimate life expectancy as figured at later ages. This fact is made clear by Figure 1-3, which charts life expectancy by average number of years remaining at various ages. Note that until early adulthood, on average, it appears that we actually do lose one year for each year we live. As we get older, however, we lose less time for each year we survive. In midlife, we lose only four years for every five years we live. In the five years from

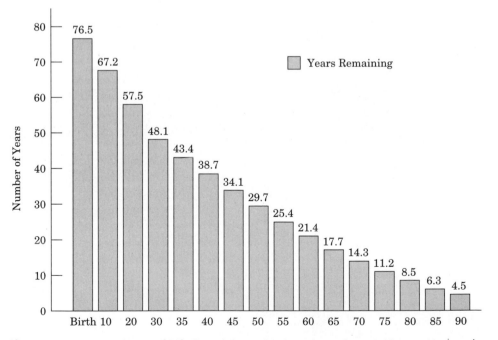

Figure 1-3 Average Years of Life Remaining at Various Ages. *Source:* Hoyert, Kochanek, and Murphy (1999).

age 85 to 90 we lose less than two years! What is happening, of course, is that once we have survived the hazards of late middle age and early old age, reductions in the mortality rate increase the likelihood that we will get to live even longer (Hoyert, Kochanek, and Murphy, 1999).

Life expectancy differs widely across many countries. However, life expectancy at birth is very much affected by infant mortality rates. Hence, a better cross-national comparison may actually be life expectancy among the survivors into old age, perhaps measured from age 65. Table 1-1 shows recent estimates for life expectancy at birth and at age 65 for a selection of industrialized and developing countries.

The rise in the proportion and absolute number of elderly people in the population will force us to make a number of structural changes in our society. The elderly will have to be integrated into the social structure so that more of them can actively participate. Many changes of this sort will generate problems of interest to psychologists and other social scientists (Atchley, 2000; Riley, Kahn, and Foner,

TABLE 1-1 **Life Expectancy at Birth and at Age 65, by Sex and Selected Countries (Latest Available Year)**

| | *Life Expectancy* | | | |
| | *At Birth* | | *At Age 65* | |
	Male	*Female*	*Male*	*Female*
Malawi (1977)	38.2	41.2	10.6	11.4
Rwanda (1978)	45.1	47.7	10.9	11.8
Zambia (1980)	50.4	52.5	11.5	12.1
Nepal (1981)	50.9	48.1	11.0	11.5
Botswana (1981)	52.3	59.7	10.2	12.5
India (1980)	52.5	52.1	11.7	13.2
Guatemala (1980)	55.1	59.4	13.5	14.2
Colombia (1985)	63.4	69.2	14.0	15.8
Ecuador (1985)	63.4	67.6	14.3	15.8
Hungary (1987)	65.7	73.7	12.0	15.2
Ukraine (1986)	65.9	74.5	12.4	15.5
Venezuela (1985)	66.7	72.8	14.2	16.7
Poland (1987)	66.8	75.2	12.3	15.9
Chile (1990)	68.0	75.0	13.8	16.7
United Kingdom (1987)	71.2	77.5	13.3	17.2
Austria (1987)	71.5	78.1	14.2	17.4
U.S.A. (1988)	71.5	78.3	14.9	18.6
France (1987)	72.0	80.3	14.9	19.4
Australia (1986)	72.8	79.1	14.6	18.5
Canada (1986)	73.0	79.8	14.9	19.2
Sweden (1987)	74.1	80.2	15.0	18.9
Japan (1987)	75.6	81.4	16.1	19.7

Source: Atchley, R. C. (2000); compiled from United Nations (1990a).

1994). This consideration in recent years has stimulated scientists to increase their investigations of mature and older persons.

The Study of Adult Development and Aging

Gerontology is the study of the phenomena of the aging process from maturity into old age, as well as the study of the elderly as a special population. (A closely related word is *geriatrics,* which refers to the medical treatment of the elderly; the root word is the Greek *geras,* meaning "old age.") In the United States, the first important psychological studies in gerontology were published in the 1920s, but barely more than a trickle of research can be noted until the 1950s (Charles, 1970). In a review published in 1961, the author remarked, "More research seems to have been published in the decade of 1950–1959 than had been published in the entire preceding 115 years the subject may be said to have existed" (Birren, 1961, p. 131). Reviewers writing in 1980 had seen the trickle of research grow into a stream, almost a torrent; from 1968 to 1979, they computed, psychological publications in gerontology had increased by 270 percent (Figure 1-4A, Poon and Welford, 1980), and thousands of new items are now published annually (Birren, Cunningham, and Yamamoto, 1983; Birren and Schroots, 2001).

Figure 1-4B updates the evidence on an ever increasing volume of research publications. We created this figure by counting the number of publications ab-

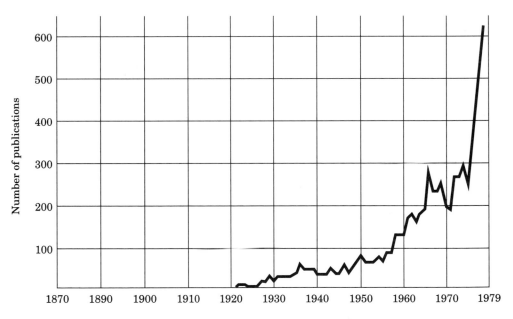

Figure 1-4A   Number of Psychological Aging Publications per Year from 1870 to 1979. *Source:* Poon, L. W., and Welford, A.T. (1980). Prologue: An historical perspective. In L. W. Poon (Ed.), *Aging in the 1980's* (p. xiv). Washington, DC: American Psychological Association. Copyright 1980 by the American Psychological Association. Reprinted by permission of the publisher and author.

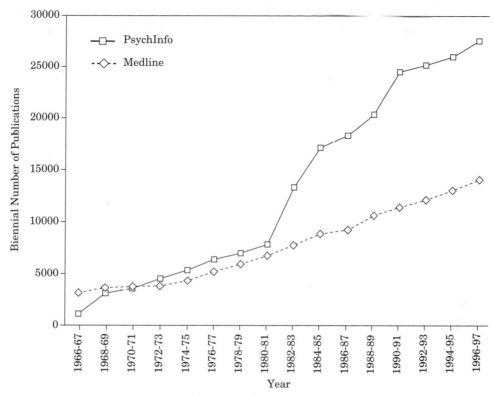

Figure 1-4B Growth in Number of Citations of Gerontological Contributions in the Medical and Psychological Data Bases. *Source:* Authors' compilation of entries in PsychInfo and Medline, see text.

stracted in Medline (biomedical and biobehavioral sciences) and in PsychInfo (the specialized psychological data base) for those years where data were available and which included the words "aging," "aged," "elderly," and "old" after excluding all nonhuman studies, and studies of persons under age 18. These data bases are also better estimates of the worldwide interest in gerontology because they include abstracts of the literature published in many different languages. Certainly, the pace of investigations has skyrocketed, and it becomes more and more difficult to select those items that are worth considering for inclusion in a textbook.

Nevertheless, still much more basic and applied research is needed. Research on human aging in the behavioral and social sciences was stimulated markedly when federal support was included specifically in 1979 as part of the National Institute on Aging (NIA) research program (Riley, 1994). However, a remaining impediment to developing knowledge is the reduction in support for the training of basic and applied researchers. Paradoxically, the passing of the baby boom has reduced the number of students interested in the topics that will become a major social problem in their later adult lives (Knight, Teri, Santos, and Wohlford, 1995).

Besides having an interest in old age, psychologists have begun to investigate the psychological development of adults between the ages of 18 and 65 (e.g., Lachman and James, 1997; Ryff and Seltzer, 1996; Willis and Reid, 1999). A major reason for these new concerns is the disruptive effect that our fast-paced, technologically advanced society has on the lives of adults. Frequent changes in jobs and spouses, for example, create problems and stress. The ability of "old dogs" to learn "new tricks" becomes an increasingly important factor in personal adjustment, so that age-related changes during the adult years in learning ability, memory, and general intellectual competence become interesting to psychologists.

There is also a lot of interest in some of the major transitions in adult life; events that provide great opportunities and great risks. These transitions are often called normative because they are experienced by most persons in our society. Keep in mind, however, that what is considered normative in one culture or one generation may not be perceived as such in another. Nevertheless, there are many examples of what would indeed seem to be normative transitions for most of us—getting married, having children, starting out in a career, losing a spouse, and retiring. Turning 40 years old is viewed by some as a mystical transition, reflecting people's beliefs that it is the midpoint of life and that one is no longer a "young adult" but has certainly entered the life stage that we call "middle age."

Another source of research in adult development emerged almost by accident. In the 1920s and 1930s, several groups of psychologists began long-term studies of children. These researchers observed, tested, and interviewed the same children every few years to assess their physical, intellectual, and personality development. By the 1940s and 1950s, their subjects had reached adulthood. But there seemed to be no good reason for these researchers to abandon their investigations simply because their subjects were no longer children. Indeed, these studies offered rare opportunities not only to study adult development, but also to relate significant events in adult life (such as the breakup of a marriage) to experiences in childhood. Prominent examples of such studies are the Berkeley Growth and Guidance studies (Eichorn et al., 1981). A good deal of the research in adult development owes its existence to the fact that adult subjects about whom much was already known became available for study (Birren J. E. and Birren, B. A.,1990; Schaie,1983b).

Studies that were originally designed to describe the life experiences and growth of children may not be the most satisfactory source of data on adulthood. The appeal of such studies is that they provide more meaningful data on development than do the studies comparing different age groups, which are so common in the literature on adult development and aging. These age-group comparison studies of midlife have yielded little information because behavioral and biological changes occur rather slowly during adulthood. The age differences found in these studies are often the result of generational differences between cohorts rather than individual development (see the discussion of cross-sectional and longitudinal methods in Chapter 5).

A significant number of longitudinal studies, however, have been conducted during the past several decades that represent a proper alternative to age-group comparison studies and studies designed to examine children. These longitudinal studies have been conceptualized explicitly to study individuals from young adult-hood to old age (Migdel, Abeles, and Sherrod, 1981; Schaie, 1983b; 1996b; Schaie and Hofer, 2001). As a result of these studies, we now have a much larger body of data on adult development that actually tracks the development of individuals.

Findings from longitudinal studies have been published in such areas as physiological aging (Shock et al., 1984), health and behavior (Busse, 1993; Palmore, Nowlin and Wang 1985; Steen and Djurfeld, 1993), personality (Costa and Mc-Crae, 1993; McCrae and Costa, 1997; Schmitz-Scherzer and Thomae, 1983), career development (Bray and Howard, 1983; Howard and Bray, 1988), memory (Hultsch, Hertzog, Dixon, and Small, 1998); and intelligence (Cunningham and Owens, 1983; Schaie, 1996b; Rott, 1993; Shanan, 1993; Siegler, 1983).

Several new comprehensive longitudinal studies of old-old persons have been initiated in Europe over the past decade (e.g., the Berlin Aging Study; Baltes and Mayer, 1999; Baltes and Smith, 1997; Baltes, Mayer, Helmchen, and Steinhagen-Thiessen, 1993; and the ILSE Study; Rudinger and Minnemann, 1997). Other studies that focus on the very old include the Lund 80+ study in Sweden (Svensson, Dehlin, Hagberg, and Samuelsson, 1993), which recently has been expanded to Iceland, and the Georgia Centenarian study (Poon, Sweaney, Clayton, and Merriam, 1992).

A final reason for the interest in adult development was that certain issues in the scientific study of psychology required the extension of existing work with children into adulthood. For many years, research on these issues provided the only substantial body of data in adult development and, in addition, clarified the particular methodological problems faced by workers in this area. One of the earliest (and most enduring) of these issues is the topic of intellectual development. Early research suggested that the growth of intelligence, as measured by standard IQ tests, was essentially complete by the age of 13 (Yerkes, 1921). But most adults, including adult psychologists, found these results somewhat startling; they demanded more research. The issue spawned a series of studies and the testing of people ranging in age from 10 to 80 (e.g., Miles, 1931). These studies moved up the peak age a bit, to around 20, but continuing reports of apparent decline of intellectual ability thereafter gave rise to further controversy that is not entirely resolved even today. We will discuss this issue and the related controversies in Chapter 12 on intellectual development; here we merely note the vital historical role that research on specific issues such as intellectual growth has played in the psychology of adult development.

COMMON BELIEFS ABOUT AGING

One of the major purposes of science is to dispel misconceptions surrounding the phenomena under study. Some of these misconceptions represent stereotypes people have formed about the aged and aging. For example, one might assert, "Old people do not engage in sexual intercourse." This statement might be based on jokes heard at work, a general notion of old people as physically incapable (especially of sexual activities), or anecdotal evidence such as the verbal denials of modest grandparents. (Table 1-2 presents some myths on aging.) Such commonly held beliefs are not necessarily incorrect; sometimes scientific investigation turns up evidence of their validity. But they are frequently distorted and often dangerous, to the extent that they dictate social policy or personal interactions. For example, beliefs about old people and mental illness—primarily the assumption that mental confusion in old people means they are becoming "senile"—prevent effective treatment of what in many cases is a reversible condition such as depression or physical

---

TABLE 1-2 Commonly Held Beliefs about Adult Development and Aging

Common beliefs about adult development and aging have been formed without much scientific evidence pro or con. Some, it turns out, are true, some are partly true, and many are mostly or completely false. By the time you finish this book, you will be in a much better position to evaluate these myths. (For true-false answers, see p. 31.)

Chapter Two. Young Adulthood

---

   1. Young, enthusiastic people are more creative than old people.

Chapter Three. The Middle Years

---

   1. Most women experience severe physical symptoms during menopause.
   2. Menopause often results in nervous breakdowns.
   3. Most adult children can't wait to ship their aging parents off to a "home" of some sort.
   4. All men experience a "midlife crisis."
   5. A good leader is one who is able to solve problems effectively.

Chapter Four. Late Life

---

   1. Most people over 65 are financially insecure.
   2. Most people over 75 are in nursing homes or other institutions.
   3. Rarely does someone over 65 produce a great work of art, science, or scholarship.

Chapter Five. Research Methodology

---

   1. Comparing younger and older people at one point in time will tell us what the younger people will be like when they are old.
   2. Studies of aging have the same problems of validity and reliability as those in other areas of psychology.

Chapter Six. Families

---

   1. Nuclear families in today's society have little contact with kin.
   2. Extended families were common in earlier eras of American life.
   3. Mothers commonly experience great distress when the last child leaves home.
   4. Aging parents often reverse roles with their adult children, becoming childishly dependent on them.
   5. Remarriages among old people are generally unsuccessful.

Chapter Seven. Men and Women: Together and Apart

---

   1. Women don't enjoy sex much after menopause.
   2. Old people are not very interested in sex.
   3. Most child molesters and exhibitionists are old men.

4. Impotence is usually psychological, except in old men, when it is more or less inevitable.
5. Men are more interested in sex than women
6. Rape is the result of the intense sexual needs of some men.

Chapter Eight. Careers

1. Most people have the same career for a lifetime.
2. Work is central to an individual's sense of self-worth.
3. The shock of retirement often results in deteriorating physical and mental health.

Chapter Nine. Personality Development

1. Personality is relatively stable during the adult years.
2. People become more conservative and inflexible in old age.

Chapter Ten. Motivation

1. Old people are harder to motivate than young people.
2. Old people get rattled more easily.
3. Achievement motivation is highest in young adulthood.
4. Old people should keep active to keep their spirits up.
5. Old people prefer to reduce the number of their activities and friendships.

Chapter Eleven. Learning and Memory

1. Old dogs can't learn new tricks.
2. A failing memory is the worst intellectual problem in old age.
3. In old age, memories of the distant past are clear and vivid, but memories for recent events are fuzzy.
4. With all their intellectual deficits, old people don't benefit much from education.

Chapter Twelve. Intellectual Development

1. Intelligence peaks around the age of 20 or 30 and then declines steadily.
2. With age comes wisdom.
3. Those who are most able in their youth decline the fastest in old age.

Chapter Thirteen. Biological Development

1. Women live longer than men because they don't work as hard.
2. Soon people will live to 150 or 200.
3. There are certain groups of people in South America and Russia who live to extraordinarily old ages.
4. Elderly patients do not respond well to surgery.
5. After 65, the majority of people are unhealthy.
6. It is possible to "worry oneself sick."
7. Hard work never killed anybody.

Chapter Fourteen. Mental Disorders

1. Most old people become senile sooner or later.
2. Senile old people cannot be helped by psychotherapy.
3. Women are more susceptible to mental disorders than men.
4. Unmarried people are more susceptible to mental disorders than married people.

Chapter Fifteen. The End of Life

1. Most people who are faced with their imminent death try to deny it.

illness. Even senile patients can be helped considerably by proper treatment (Patterson, 1996).

Common beliefs about the aging process result in negative stereotypes— oversimplified and biased views of what old people are like. The "typical" old person is often viewed as uninterested in (and incapable of) sex, on the road to (if not arrived at) senility, conservative, and rigid. The stereotype would have us believe that old people are tired and cranky, passive, without energy (Green, 1981), weak, and dependent on others. Children perceive older people as having some positive personality traits but lower physical capacities. If physical capacities are more important to children than positive personality traits, then elderly persons will be viewed less positively than younger adults (Mitchell, Wilson, Revicki, and Parker 1985; Crockett and Hummert, 1987; Hummert, Garstka, Shaner and Strahm, 1994).

This negative stereotyped image, most of which is either inaccurate or highly exaggerated, affects the behavior of not only the elderly and younger people in interaction with the elderly, but also of young adults and middle-agers. "Growing old" is so negatively valued that many adults will try, often desperately, to preserve at least the look of youth—dyeing their hair, dressing like teenagers, or romancing those young enough to be their children. The effect on the behavior of the elderly is even more pronounced and considerably more malignant. Perceived by others as forgetful, uninteresting, and incompetent, many old people begin to accept the

To prejudge that someone can't handle a job because of age is ageism.

stereotype as an accurate description of themselves. They avoid social interaction because they think they're dull; they refuse to learn a new skill because they believe themselves incapable. Physical symptoms of serious but treatable disease may be ignored because they are viewed as inevitable accompaniments of the aging process (Pasupathi, Carstensen, and Tsai, 1995; Rodin and Langer, 1980).

Discrimination against the elderly simply because of their age is *ageism,* a relatively new "-ism" that is taking its place alongside racism and sexism (Butler, Lewis, and Sunderland, 1991). Like discrimination on the basis of race or sex, ageism in the job market involves rejection of someone as incapable on grounds other than the direct assessment of capability. The employer decides that an old person (or a black or a woman) cannot handle the job and so chooses instead someone else (someone young, white, or male) even though, had the applicants been given a valid test of job performance, the rejected applicant might have scored higher than the accepted candidate.

The increase in affluence in at least part of the elderly population has led to the argument by some sociologists that the status of the elderly and related public perceptions will be upgraded substantially as the baby boomers reach old age (cf. Gergen, K. J. and Gergen, M. M., 2000). This conclusion has been criticized, however, as being relevant only to a small favored portion of the elderly who benefited from the economic boom prevailing during their midlives (Holstein, 2000; Krause, 2000).

The negative stereotypes about aging also have influenced psychological researchers. Studies are often designed and their results interpreted by using ageist language in ways that increase the likelihood that adverse stereotypes are supported even if they are false (Schaie, 1988a; 1993a). The myths of aging lead to negative stereotypes, which in turn lead to ageism and the exclusion of old people from many activities in society. It is an insidious process, one that can be halted and reversed only by solid evidence contradicting or qualifying the mistaken beliefs. We plan to present such evidence, to paint as accurate a picture of "growing old" as is presently possible.

THEORIES OF ADULT DEVELOPMENT

Theoretical models help in understanding and organizing empirical findings. Some fields of study are dominated by elegant theoretical structures that permit formal tests of propositions regarding the body of knowledge that is to be organized. Such a condition does not yet exist in the study of adult development and aging. Indeed, in many areas of adult development, we find little more than a variety of speculative theories; we often cannot choose among them without considerably more research. We shall review the major theoretical contenders in the sections to which they apply, but we need to say a few words about theories in general. How is a developmental theory formulated? What approaches are common? What seem to be the chief explanatory constructs?

Before we proceed further we need to distinguish between *developmental theories* and *models of development.* A developmental theory describes and explains the empirical evidence for changes in behavior with age and also differences in such changes between individuals or groups (Baltes P. B., 1987; Bengtson, Rice and Johnson, 1999; Dixon and Lerner, 1984). A model of development describes how a specific developmental process is thought to occur or how such a process is organized. We first discuss the broad theories and then focus on specific developmental models.

A developmental theory should be able to describe and explain the course o f an individual's intellectual growth or decline over the adult years; it should also be able to do so for groups to which an individual belongs, such as "Americans," "males" or "females," and "middle class" or "lower class." In addition, a good developmental theory should be able to explain why two individuals might change with age in different ways or at different rates, and why different groups might change differently. A developmental theory, in short, is concerned with *age changes.*

Before beginning our discussion of the theories themselves, we should explain the various concepts of aging that have influenced research on adult development. Different definitions come from biology, the social sciences, and psychology. Several biological definitions have been offered. Edmund Cowdry, one of the fathers of biological gerontology, suggested that aging could be viewed as either an endogenous or an exogenous process. In the endogenous view, aging is an involuntary process that operates cumulatively with the passage of time to result in the adverse modification of cells. In the exogenous view, aging is regarded as a consequence of impairments attributable to infections, accidents, or poisons in the external environment (Cowdry, 1942). Theories explaining the biological basis of human aging are either stochastic, postulating senescence as the result of random damage to the organism, or they hold that senescence results from genetically determined processes. Currently popular theories include (1) the *free radical* theory of reactive oxygen metabolites that cause extensive cumulative damage; (2) *caloric restriction* arguing that life span and metabolic potential can be increased by caloric restriction (thus far not demonstrated in humans); (3) *somatic mutation* arising from genetic damage originally caused by background radiation; (4) *hormonal theories* proposing, that elevated levels of steroid hormones produced by the adrenal cortex cause rapid aging decline; and (5) *immunological theories* attributing aging to decline in the immune system. Another prominent view holds that protective and repair mechanisms of cells are insufficient to avoid cumulative damage occurring over time, limiting the replicative ability of cells (see Cristofalo, Tresini, Francis and Volker, 1999)

A biologist's purpose might be served adequately by a definition based on an organism's probability of survival; such a definition would prove frustrating to psychologists, who concern themselves often with outcomes that do not bear directly on the organism's ability to survive. Furthermore, as we shall see, some psychological functions actually increase with age—wisdom is one example—and others show vast individual differences at various life stages. The biological definitions do not adequately reflect these possibilities. They are concerned primarily with forces that result in the organism's deterioration and eventual demise.

An alternative definition has been offered to include the psychologist's concerns that is more satisfying: "Aging . . . refers to an orderly or regular transformation with time of representative organisms living under representative environments" (Birren, 1988, p. 160). Note the stipulation in this definition that changes to be called "aging" must occur in representative organisms under representative conditions. Many animal experiments used to simulate human aging may be misleading because they examine subjects under conditions that have little in common with the natural environment. The age changes in behavior displayed by such animals would probably not reflect what one would find in the wild. For example, a comparison of maze-running speed between young and old laboratory rats might be invalidated by the fact that the old animals have become obese because they do not have to hunt for food and, being confined in cages, do not have the need or opportunity to exercise their muscles as would be the case in a natural environment.

Human laboratory studies may similarly impose conditions that alter the behaviors one might see in a field setting. A further concern in human studies is the distinction between aging and disease. Some of the diseases of old age, such as cancer and heart disease, are not inevitably part of the aging process. Their high incidence in old age, however, may result from adverse changes in the immune system that can increase susceptibility to disease, and these adverse changes may be a normal result of aging (Solomon, 1999).

A definition of aging from the social sciences point of view considers the individual's position with regard to a social timetable consisting of age norms about which there is broad consensual agreement in society, but which may shift due to societal changes (Elder, 1998a, 1998b; Hagestad and Neugarten, 1985; Riley, Foner, and Riley, 1999). In this view, people experience stress when their expected life course sequences and rhythms are upset. Life transitions that are "on schedule" do not seem to elicit psychological dysfunctions (Pearlin, 1982; Pearlin and Mullan, 1992).

Unlike the biological view of aging, in which aging should be impervious to historical developments, the social view suggests that aging is influenced by historical changes in cultural norms (also see Elder, 1979). For example, at the turn of the century, a woman who was not married at age 30 would have been considered "off time," whereas today, when later marriages are more common, such a woman might well be considered "on time" (Neugarten, Moore, and Lowe, 1968). Other changes in the formation and dissolution of the modern family (see Chapters 6 and 7) may also display social timetables. Some predictable events in the life course, such as widowhood for women, are of course less governed by social timetables, although they, too, may be affected by historical events such as wars and changes in public health practices.

How do we apply these perspectives to the study of adult development? We are accustomed to thinking of aging in terms of the number of years that have elapsed since a person's birth, and chronological age is in fact used as a major yardstick in aging research. But we should recognize that there are other ways to denote a person's position in the life span (cf., Schaie,1986, 1994b). Chronological age is an index that has little meaning by itself. What matters is what has happened to the individual as time has passed (cf. Schaie and Hertzog, 1985; Schroots and Birren, 1990; Wohlwill, 1973).

Alternative definitions of aging from a biological, sociological, and psychological point of view lend themselves to the development of nonchronological time frames that for some purposes may be more informative than calendar age. A person's *biological age* is his or her position with regard to remaining life expectancy. The fortunate person whose vital organ systems are in above-average condition would be able to beat the average survival odds expressed in charts such as Figure 1-3. Such a person would have a biological age lower than his or her chronological age. A person's *social age* would be determined by judging his or her position in the life course as compared to the average ages at which various positions are reached (Freund, 1997). These positions are determined by cultural norms. To make such a judgment, one might assess surface characteristics such as manner of dress or speech patterns and more fundamental characteristics such as the life stage of the person's preferred leadership roles (Neugarten, B. L., and Neugarten, D. A., 1986).

Finally, a person's *psychological age* would indicate how he or she functions in response to environmental demands. Depending on one's level of functioning, one could be psychologically younger or older than one's chronological age on adaptive behaviors such as intelligence, learning ability, memory, and motor skills, or on subjective dimensions such as motives, feelings, and attitudes. The biological, social, and psychological age concepts may diverge markedly, converging only during extremes such as young childhood and very old age (Birren and Birren, 1990).

Theoretical Approaches

Why do people change with age? There are many approaches to this question in psychology, approaches that differ in whether they concentrate on the person or the environment, the individual or the social group, and the behavior or its meaning within a repertoire of behaviors (Table 1-3); see also Lerner (1995). The behavioral or *social learning approach* focuses on environmental determinants of behavior and behavior change, in particular, the environmental outcomes of behavior—rewards and punishments (Bandura, 1977). This approach also places great importance on the role of modeling or imitating the behavior of persons to whom we have formed emotional attachments. For example, a social learning theorist might approach the effects of marriage on adult development by viewing it as an interaction in which each spouse rewards certain behaviors and discourages others. Each spouse will encourage the other to express the same view of the world and will punish "heretical" beliefs with silence, dispute, and other forms of behavior that are considered undesirable by the other. Thus, happily married couples

TABLE 1-3   Theoretical Approaches to Adult Development

	Author(s) Associated with Approach	*Topical Area To Which Applied*
Behavioral, social learning	Bandura (1969, 1977) Seligman (1972)	Learning Motivation
Psychoanalytic	Freud (1946) Erikson (1964, 1979)	Personality Motivation
Humanistic	Maslow (1970) Kohlberg (1973, 1981) Magnusson (1998)	Motivation Moral development Holistic
Individual differences	Cattell (1971), Horn (1982) Guilford, Zimmerman, and Guilford (1967) Salthouse (1999) Schaie (1977-1978, 2000) Schaie and Willis (1999) Sternberg (1980)	Intelligence Personality Cognition Cognition Everyday Competence Learning, Memory
Social-psychological	Whitbourne (1986) Blanchard-Fields (1996) M. M. Baltes and Carstensen (1996) Heckhausen and Schulz (1995)	Self-concept Attribution Socio-emotional Control
Dialectical	Riegel (1975, 1976) P. B. Baltes (1997)	Personality, Life crises Lifespan

should become increasingly similar in attitudes and values over the years, as indeed appears to be the case (see Gruber-Baldini, Schaie, and Willis, 1995).

Another traditional approach to human development applies *Freudian* or *psychoanalytic theory*. In general, psychoanalytic theory focuses on emotional conflicts and unconscious mental processes. Emotional conflicts are often triggered by social responsibilities, duties, or realities that do not fit with one's selfish desires (i.e., the id impulses). Hence, psychoanalytic theory is often applied to major transitions in life—parenthood, menopause, or death of a spouse. Erik Erikson, who expanded the psychoanalytic theory of development from childhood to the adult years, describes in his writings conflicts about intimacy, productivity, and integrity that he feels are major themes of adult life.

The *humanistic approach,* taken by authors such as Maslow, focuses on motivation, especially on the higher (more spiritual) motives that distinguish the human species from lower animals. There is an emphasis on personal growth and "self-actualization," which is defined as the desire to become the best person one can be. Humanistic theorists remind us that the "whole person" (rather than "mechanistic" principles of learning) must be considered when trying to predict what an individual will do next in life. To use a humanist's example, human beings who succeed at a fairly difficult task are not likely to try the same task again (as a simple reward theory of learning might predict). Most humans aspire to somewhat more

Happily married couples tend to grow more alike in their attitudes and interests because they tend to encourage one another's similarities and discourage the dissimilarities.

each time; they set their sights higher and higher, until finally their reach exceeds their grasp.

A contemporary holistic person-centered approach is provided by the work of Bergman and Magnusson (1997; Magnusson, 1998). In this view the individual is seen as an organized whole, functioning and developing as a totality. Patterns of factors influencing development are emphasized instead of a concern with singular explanatory variables.

Another approach that turns out to be rather important in the psychology of adult development is the *individual differences approach,* which is most commonly represented in the use of psychological tests such as intelligence tests or personality questionnaires, will also be prominent in our discussions of memory and perception. This approach includes theories of intelligence as well as theories of everyday competence (e.g., Schaie and Willis, 1999).

Cognitive theories of aging will also contribute to our discussions of memory and intelligence. Theoretical perspectives on cognitive aging can be classified into whether the proposed primary causal influences are distal or proximal in nature. Distal theories attribute cognitive aging to influences occurring at earlier periods of life but that contribute to concurrent levels of performance. Other distal explanations focus on social-cultural changes that directly affect cognitive performance. These explanations assume cumulative cohort effects leading to obsolescence of the elderly. Distal theories are useful in specifying why the observed age differences have emerged, since it is generally agreed that mere passage of time can not account for these differences (Salthouse, 1999).

Proximal theories of aging consider concurrent influences thought to determine age-related differences in cognitive performance. These theories do not specify how the age differences originated. Variations of these theories include strategy-based age differences, quantitative differences in the efficiency of information processing stages implicating deficits in specific stages, or the altered operation of one or more of the basic cognitive processes (see Salthouse, 1999).

Social-psychological approaches to aging contribute to the understanding of numerous normal and pernicious age-related phenomena. Theoretical formulations explain how social-psychological processes exert normative influences on life course changes. Recently prominent theories include control theories contrasting primary and secondary controls, coping theories that distinguish between accommodative and assimilative coping, and theories about age differences in attributive styles.

In control theory, *primary* control involves the individuals' belief regarding their ability to change the external world to fit their needs and desires. *Secondary* control is concerned with individuals' ability to adapt or accommodate their goals, desires and beliefs to fit the existing situation (Heckhausen and Schulz, 1995). The latter approach is further expounded as a coping theory by Brandstädter and colleagues (Brandstädter and Grewe, 1994). Here distinctions are made between older people engaging in *assimilative* strategies designed to prevent further losses or substitute alternate activities when encountering undesired life changes, and *accommodative* strategies that adjust goals and expectancies to match unfavorable changes in personal resources and functional capacities.

Age differences in attributional style lead to theoretical formulations (e.g., Blanchard-Fields, 1996). These predict that in ambiguous situations older adults are more likely than young adults to view the cause of an event as a combination of external and internal causes. This is considered to be the result of more mature thinking, defined as *relativistic orientation*.

Socioemotional selectivity theory seeks to provide an explanation of the well-established reduction in social interactions observed in old age. This theory is a psychological alternative to two previously influential but conflicting sociological explanations of this phenomenon. Activity theory considered inactivity to be a societally induced problem stemming from social norms, while the alternative disengagement theory suggested that impending death stimulated a mutual psychological withdrawal between the older person and society. By contrast, socioemotional selectivity theory holds that the reduction in older persons' social networks and social participation should be seen as a motivated redistribution of resources by the elderly person. Thus older persons do not simply react to social contexts but proactively manage their social worlds (see Baltes M. M. & Carstensen, 1999).

A less frequently advocated approach in psychology is the *dialectical approach.* It is well suited to the study of human development because it focuses on change; it focuses on oppositions and contradictions and their eventual resolution and synthesis. In its best-known form, a dialectical process involves three stages: thesis, antithesis, and synthesis. For example, in dialectical reasoning, a thought (thesis) suggests a contradiction (antithesis); the paradoxical truth of both the thesis and its antithesis results in a synthesis, a new level of understanding that somehow combines the truth in both thesis and antithesis. This synthesis becomes a new thesis, suggests a new contradiction, and is itself synthesized into a still higher level of understanding. It is a self-perpetuating, never-ending sequence that can lead to remarkable insights.

In adult development, the dialectical approach views people as active and changing organisms in continuous interaction with an active and changing environment (Riegel, 1975, 1976). Psychologists who take the dialectical view look for incongruities and conflicts. They may be interested in such concepts as the "midlife crisis," in which some people recognize that their hopes and dreams are incongruent with their present lives. These psychologists would consider the potential for growth as well as the threat of depression, withdrawal, and psychological injury during the midlife crisis.

A recent example of the dialectic approach is P. B. Baltes' (1997) theory of selection, optimization, and compensation (SOC). Psychological gains and losses occur at every life stage, but in old age losses far exceed the gains. Baltes considers evolutionary development incomplete for the very last stage of life, during which societal supports no longer sufficiently compensate for declines in physiological infrastructure and losses in behavioral functionality (see Baltes and Smith, 1999; Baltes, Staudinger, and Lindenberger, 1999). Selection, optimization and compensation, however, can also be seen as strategies of life management, and thus may be indicators of successful aging (Freund and Baltes, 1998).

Models of Development

Cutting across the theoretical approaches are certain basic assumptions about the general nature of the developmental changes that occur in adult life. For example, some psychologists prefer to think of adult life as a series of discrete stages, whereas others tend to view the same changes as more or less continuous. To illustrate the stage model in an extreme fashion, we can point to the butterfly, a distinctly different and far more beautiful stage of an organism that once was a caterpillar. In adult psychology, somewhat the same notion is applied by theorists who view the middle-aged person as the butterfly who grew from the larva of a young adult.

Psychologists who prefer a *continuous model* of development claim that much is lost in the broad categorizations of a stage model. The stage approach can indeed cloud the immense changes that occur within a stage and thus distort the picture of the developmental process; this is in a sense the cost of using the stage approach. What one gains from such an approach is a sharper contrast between periods of development that are different in important theoretical aspects. The change from one stage to another may be so abrupt that to define it as merely a change of sizable degree misses the point that a new quality has emerged in the new period. Life after puberty, after menopause, after retirement is qualitatively different from that before these stages. The question thus becomes whether or not the changes are great enough that the benefits of a stage analysis outweigh the costs.

In addition to the distinction between stage and continuous models, there are differences in assumptions about fundamental trends in adult development. *Trend models* are basically of three types: increment, stability, and decrement. Theories of child development, for example, typically use increment models for most variables: Intelligence increases with age and so do social skills and biological capacities. For the description of adult development, decrement models are more common: Certain biological capacities decrease and, according to some theorists, so do basic intellectual abilities. Other variables, such as many personality dimensions, may be considered fairly stable during the adult years (McCrae and Costa, 1997; Schaie, 1996b; Schaie and Parham, 1976).

Distinctions may be made within a model. The *decrement model* is often divided into the "irreversible decrement" model, describing an inexorable, usually biological, decrease, and the "decrement-with-compensation" model, involving decreasing biological capacity that is moderated by social experience to produce stable or even increasing socialized abilities. Vision often follows a decrement-with-compensation model; biological visual abilities decrease but are compensated for by social interventions such as eyeglasses.

Another useful model attempts to summarize the multiple causes that affect adult development. Figure 1-5 lists three major sets of factors: normative age-graded influences, normative history-graded influences, and non-normative influences. These sets of influences interact to produce developmental change over the life span (Baltes P. B., 1979; Marsiske, Lang, Baltes, M. M, and Baltes, P. B., 1995).

Normative age-graded influences are the biological and environmental factors that are highly correlated with chronological age. These are the variables that have traditionally been studied by developmental psychologists. Some, such as menarche, puberty, and menopause, are biological. Others involve socialization and the acquisition of normative age-correlated roles, such as entering schools, marrying, and retiring.

Normative history-graded influences are events that are widely experienced in a given culture at a particular time. These events may be environmental, as with an economic depression, war, or other political dislocation, or they may be biological, as with environmental pollution, malnutrition, and large-scale epidemics. Obviously, biological and environmental events are often mutually influential. In developmental research, these influences are called "cohort" effects if they affect only one generation and "time-of-measurement" or "period" effects if they occur for a limited time

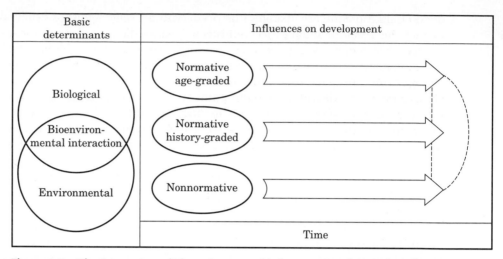

Figure 1.5   The Interaction of Three Systems of Influences Regulating the Nature of Development over the Life Span. *Source:* Baltes, P. B. (1979). Life-span development psychology: Some converging observations on history and theory. In P. B. Baltes and O. G. Brim, Jr. (Eds.), *Life-span development and behavior* (Vol. 2). New York: Academic Press. Reprinted by permission.

but affect the entire population that is exposed to them. For example, the Great Depression in the 1930s was a period effect because it affected virtually all persons then living in our society. By contrast, we can speak of a Vietnam cohort effect, because it was primarily those persons of the right age to be conscripted into military service who were maximally affected. Research designs that differentiate these dimensions are discussed in Chapter 5 (also see Featherman and Petersen, 1986).

Nonnormative influences are factors that may be significant within the life of a particular person, but are not necessarily experienced by everyone. These may be favorable events such as winning a lottery or succeeding in a job or unfavorable events such as unemployment, divorce, or a serious disease (Schaie, 1986, 1994b).

The relative significance of these three types of developmental influence may vary in different behavioral change processes and at different points in the life span. For example, age-graded influences may be especially important during childhood and then again in old age, whereas history-graded and nonnormative influences may predominate in early and middle adulthood. This would explain why child development researchers focus on age-graded influences while those who work on adult life have favored an emphasis on history-graded and individualized nonnormative experiences (Baltes P. B 1979; Baltes, P. B. and Willis, 1978; Marsiske, Lang, Baltes, M. M, and Baltes, P. B., 1995).

SUMMARY

1. The organization of this book is both topical and chronological.

Three chronological periods— young adulthood, the middle years, and late life—are considered as a whole. They are followed by topical chapters on families, careers, relationships between men and women, research methodology, personality, motivation, learning and memory, intellectual development, biological development, mental disorders, and death.

2. The scientific study of adult development and aging has surprisingly recent origins. One reason is that in the past people simply assumed the adult years to be a time of stability. Another reason is that in the past there were very few elderly citizens, so aging was less of an issue.

3. The number of elderly people in the population has increased dramatically since the turn of the century, primarily as a result of decreases in premature death. In the decades ahead, the median age of the population of the United States will increase substantially, which will require certain structural changes in society. Gerontology is the study of the aging process from maturity to old age and the study of the elderly as a special population.

4. One of our major goals in this book is to evaluate commonly held beliefs (untested assumptions) about adult development and aging. Inaccurate beliefs often lead to negative stereotypes of aging and ageism, and unfair discrimination on the basis of age.

5. Theories of adult development attempt to explain changes with age and also differences in such changes between individuals or groups. Different disciplines offer varying definitions of aging. A person's biological age is his or her position with regard to remaining life expectancy. A person's social age is determined by judging his or her position in the life course against the average ages at which various positions are reached. A person's psychological age is how he or she functions in response to environmental demands. The behavioral or social learning approach focuses on the rewards and punishments that people receive from actions in their environment. Psychoanalytic (Freudian) theories focus on emotional conflicts and unconscious mental processes. Humanistic theories stress distinctively human motives, such as self-actualization or take a holistic view of development. The individual differences approach, including cognitive theories of aging, relies heavily on psychological tests (such as IQ and personality tests). The information processing approach tracks information from the environment from perception through learning and memory to decision and response. Social psychological theories explain the psychological processes that exert normative influences on life course changes. Recently prominent theories include control theories contrasting primary and secondary controls, coping theories that distinguish between accommodative and assimilative coping, and theories about age differences in attributive styles. Theories of any type can be classified as stage theories, or as theories that assume incremental, stable, or decremental trends in development. Another developmental approach takes into account three major sets of factors

that influence individual development: normative age-graded life events, normative history-graded life events, and nonnormative life events.

SUGGESTED READINGS

Atchley, R. C. (2000). The demography of aging. In R. C. Atchley (Ed.), *Social forces and aging* (9th ed.) (pp. 23–42). Belmont, CA: Wadsworth. An expanded account of a number of interesting population facts, including distribution by states and mobility patterns of the elderly.

Birren, J. E., and Schroots, J. F. F. (2001). On the history of geropsychology. In J. E. Birren and K. W. Schaie (Eds.), *Handbook of the psychology of aging* (5th ed.).San Diego, CA: Academic Press. A thorough discussion of the early history of psychological gerontology.

Hendricks, J., and Achenbaum, A. (1999). Historical development of theories of aging. In V. L. Bengtson and K. W. Schaie (Eds,), *Handbook of theories of aging* (pp. 21–39). New York: Springer Publishing Co. A review of theories that have influenced research and interpretation of findings in the study of adult development and aging.

Evaluation of the Commonly Held Beliefs about Aging (Table 1-2)

Chapter 2	*Chapter 7*	*Chapter 11*	*Chapter 14*
1. Partly true	1. False	1. False	1. False
	2. False	2. Partly true	2. Partly true
Chapter 3	3. False	3. Partly true	3. False
	4. Partly true	4. False	4. Partly true
1. False	5. False		
2. False	6. Partly True	*Chapter 12*	*Chapter 15*
3. False			
4. False	*Chapter 8*	1. False	1. True
5. True		2. Partly true	
	1. False	3. False	
Chapter 4	2. True		
	3. False	*Chapter 13*	
1. False			
2. False	*Chapter 9*	1. False	
3. False		2. False	
	1. True	3. False	
Chapter 5	2. Partly true	4. False	
		6. Partly true	
1. False	*Chapter 10*	7. Partly true	
2. Partly true		8. False	
	1. Partly true		
Chapter 6	2. Partly true		
	3. False		
1. False	4. True		
2. False	5. False		
3. False			
4. Partly true			
5. False			

2

Young Adulthood

Independence Versus Intimacy

ENTERING THE STAGE OF YOUNG ADULTHOOD

It is not easy to define when a child becomes an adult. No single answer would fit all people. In some cultures, young people barely into their teens assume the full responsibilities and privileges of adulthood, whereas in other cultures, men and women stay with their parents until well into their thirties, struggling to get a start on their own. In our society the age of 18 confers some legal status (e.g., the right to vote). At this age, many young people have finished high school, begun their work lives and become adults in that they earn their own money. Others postpone career decisions for more schooling in college or in vocational training.

Events Marking Entry into Adulthood

The transition to adulthood is marked by a number of events. Five events are defined as hallmarks of the transition to adulthood by social scientists: (1) end of schooling, (2) working and financial independence, (3) living apart from family, (4) marriage, and (5) parenthood. These events involve biological, psychological and social aspects of the person (Lerner 1995). These events are of interest to social scientists because they represent the individual taking on new social roles and responsibilities (i.e., worker, parent, spouse, voter, etc).

The age or stage in the life span at which these events occur is of interest developmentally, and whether these events occur sequentially or simultaneously is significant. The timing and pattern in which these events occur varies considerably for individuals and cohorts. The timing of these events is determined in part by biological maturation, but also by social expectations and historical events (Lerner,

More than half of young adults in the United States now seek some form of postsecondary education.

1995). For instance, as the length of compulsory schooling has increased, the age at which one is expected to enter the labor force has changed. Almost half of the young adults in the United States now seek some form of postsecondary education and thus entry into full-time employment occurs later. In addition, many young women, who throughout much of this century entered the job market only briefly, prior to marriage, are staying in the workplace after marriage and during child-bearing years; these women are juggling multiple social roles involving marriage, childrearing, and a career.

Social expectations have changed about the "normative" timing of these events and the normative order in which these events should occur. Neugarten (1964) has found that most individuals have a social clock that tells them if they are "on time" or "off time" relative to their culture's expectations with respect to a particular event. Disruption of the usual order and timing of transition events can place great pressure on young adults and may pose problems for society as well.

There are also cross-cultural differences in expectations regarding the sequencing of events (Pallas, 1993). Cross-cultural research contrasting the U.S. and Japan indicates that in both societies more recent cohorts of young men obtained more schooling, and thus the age of school completion has increased. There are cultural differences in the implications of additional schooling on entry into other social roles. In Japan, delaying school completion results in delayed entry into the labor force and delayed marriage, while in the U.S. the prolongation of schooling results in more men beginning full-time work and/or marrying while still in school (Hogan and Mochizui, 1988).

Of the five events considered to mark the transition to the independence associated with young adulthood, educational attainment is the event considered most likely to influence an individual's plans and the timing of the remaining events (Alan Guttmacher Institute, 1998; Hogan, 1985; Teachman and Paasch, 1998). Specifically, the young person's aspirations and expectations about their educational achievement were predictive of the timing and sequence in which the remaining events (work, marriage, parenting) would occur. Young persons with higher educational aspirations were more likely to experience the other events at a later age than young persons who expected to end their education at high school or less. Young women's educational aspirations were particularly important in determining the expected age at which they would marry or become parents.

The impact of level of education on delaying childbearing (and sometimes on marriage) is world-wide (Alan Guttmacher Institute, 1998). Delaying childbearing benefits young women by giving them more time to acquire education and develop skills that will enhance their ability to care for their families and compete in the job market. It also can have a dramatic impact on the rate of population growth both within a country and globally. In many developing countries, a woman who has her first child by age 18 will have an average of seven children. Postponing the first birth until her early 20s reduces the average number of births she has to about five. Education is associated with differences in adolescent childbearing in developed countries as well; in the United States, teenagers with less than 12 years of schooling are about 6 times as likely as those with more schooling to give birth by age 18. There are cohort differences in educational gains and reductions in childbearing. Women aged 20–24 years in parts of Asia are about 80 percent as likely as those aged 40–44 years to have had their first child during adolescence.

Given the finding that educational aspirations often impact the timing and sequencing of young person's entry into other roles, there has been considerable interest in what factors influence a young person's educational expectations. Studies suggest that the family plays a major role in determining the individual's educational aspirations. Siblings in the same family have more similar educational aspirations than do individuals from different families. The parents' own education and occupational status certainly impact their children's educational aspirations, but research suggests that more specific factors within the family are also predictive (Teachman and Paasch, 1998). Mothers' expectations regarding the amount of education their children will achieve was significantly predictive both of the children's educational aspirations and the actual level of educational attained. In addition parents' beliefs about sex roles influence their educational and work expectations for their daughters. Parents with more egalitarian sex role beliefs expected their daughters to spend longer in school and to leave home before marriage (Hogan, 1985).

Sociologists have been concerned with the social roles that young persons assume as they make these transitions, and the influence of society on the timing and ordering of entry into these roles. In contrast, developmental psychologists have been concerned with the psychological processes associated with assuming these roles. For example, assumption of all of these roles involves the development and differentiation of one's *identity*—college graduate, worker, spouse, parent. The young adult often sees entry into these roles as a mark of *independence*—of becoming one's own person and separate from one's childhood family. Society expects that as one becomes independent and takes on these roles, one assumes new responsibilities to the family, community, and society. Several of these transitions (e.g., marriage, parenthood) also involve intimacy as an important psychological process. In young adulthood the conflict between independence and interdependence (intimacy) with others is a major one. How well individuals resolve the conflict between maintaining a sense of personal identity and independence and yet developing an interdependent and intimate relationship with another person will influence the level of maturity they reach in this stage of life. In this chapter, we reflect on this dynamic in discussions of personal identity, intimacy, and relationships between the individual and the larger community.

ESTABLISHING PERSONAL IDENTITY

As young adults make the momentous decisions that shape their lives, they more firmly establish their personal identities—their sense of who they are as unique individuals. Formation of a personal identity is a critical aspect of achieving a sense of independence, of differentiating oneself from parents and others. The choices of a career and a mate constitute a large part of personal identity. Children, too, become a significant part of one's identity, in some cases almost an extension of oneself. Several different perspectives have been offered on the nature of identity and how it changes in young adulthood and throughout life.

Identity: A life-long process

The term *identity* is most closely associated with Erikson (1963, 1980), who introduced the concept of the identity to describe the fifth of eight stages of development throughout the life span. The search for one's identity arises during adolescence in response to the rapid physical and emotional changes that occur in combination with increasing social expectations for adult behavior. The young person must integrate into his/her earlier identity as a child such important characteristics as a new physical appearance, new abilities, new feelings, and new roles (Marcia, 1988,1999; Waterman, 1982,1999; Whitbourne and Connolly, 1999). The young person who manages to integrate these characteristics into a consistent whole by questioning and exploring alternative possibilities for adult life achieves a new level of ego identity. The individual who is overwhelmed by the changes occurring and the range of possibilities available experiences identity diffusion.

Erikson's stages and related concepts such as identity and intimacy have been difficult to quantify and study empirically. Recent work by Marcia (1999), Waterman (1999) and Whitbourne (Van Manen and Whitbourne, 1997) have expanded and extended theory and research on identity development. Marcia suggests that identity might be studied in terms of four identity status categories (Marcia, 1988; 1999): identity achievement, foreclosure, moratorium, or diffusion. The individual's identity status is examined in an interview that assesses whether or not an adult has undergone an exploration period and made subsequent commitments in each of five areas: vocational plans, religion, politics, sex-role attitudes, and attitudes concerning sexual intercourse. The individual is classified into one of four identity statuses. The *identity achiever* has explored multiple alternatives regarding identity and has developed some firm commitments about goals, values, and beliefs. The person classified as *foreclosed* has never seriously considered alternatives, yet has made some commitment with regard to his or her identity. Both foreclosure and identity achievement represent states of commitment involving fidelity and clarity about one's beliefs. Foreclosure, however, represents commitment based on adopting roles and values of earlier figures with whom one identified or viewed as an authority figure (e.g., parent, minister, teacher), whereas identify achievement involves commitment based on personal exploration of alternatives. The distinction between identity achievement and foreclosure is important developmentally and possibly clinically. For example, many vocational interest scales would categorize both those in identity achievement and foreclosure as having clear occupational preferences. The developmental processes involved in acquiring these preferences for identity achievement versus foreclosure would be quite different and could have implications for future career achievement.

A person in a state of *moratorium* is actively seeking alternatives in an attempt to arrive at some commitments. It involves a state of exploration and inner struggle; the individual has not yet achieved the level of commitment characteristic of the identity achiever. In contrast, the person in a state of *identity diffusion* has not made any firm commitments and is not seriously seeking to make any. Diffusion is a state of indifference in which the sense of identity is lacking and not sought.

While these identity statuses were originally formulated with respect to adolescent development, they may be useful in thinking of identity across the adult life span (De Haan and Schulenberg, 1997). Across the adult life span individuals may cycle through the four statuses multiple times. There are conflicting findings from prior research whether individuals go though the identity statuses in a particular order. For example, one young person may progress from identity diffusion to a moratorium and finally to identity achievement. Another young person may experience identity foreclosure, then identity moratorium and then identity achievement.

Although the identity crisis is most often associated with the younger part of the life span, Erikson believed that identity continues to be an issue throughout adulthood. It may be more useful to think of the search for identity as a *lifelong process* rather than as a discrete stage or phase (Whitbourne, 1986). The individual may recycle though the different identity statuses as described by Marcia at various phases in the life span or with respect to different domains of identity (e.g., work, political beliefs). For example, the loss of a close relative or unemployment may force a person to reevaluate identity decisions previously made (Waterman and Archer, 1990).

Identity: Global Versus Domain-Specific Perspectives

Discussion of Erikson's formulation of identity has often focused on a global concept of identity, independent of a particular domain. Young persons are considered to be in an identity crisis without specifying a particular domain or are categorized into one of Marcia's identity statuses without indicating a domain. However, Erikson himself did not consider identity as static or unidimensional. Erikson discussed at least five domains of identity including sexual, religious, political, ideological and occupational.

Some recent research has focused increasingly on studying identity with respect to a particular domain. There is growing evidence that young persons are likely to be at different phases in identity achievement for different domains. For example, some studies show that young persons may develop vocational preferences and perhaps a vocational identity earlier than they develop political or religious identities (Skorikov and Vondracek, 1998; De Haan and Schulenberg, 1997). Vondracek and colleagues report the majority of adolescents in both the U.S. and in Germany could state a clear vocational preference, while Schulenberg found that the majority of college students still had not developed clear political belief systems. Vondracek has suggested that formation of a vocational identity may be particularly salient since identity achievement in this domain may occur somewhat earlier than in other domains.

Processes Related to Identity Development

What factors may influence young persons' progression toward identity achievement in various domains? There is some evidence that schooling may influence certain domains such as vocational identity more so than domains such as religion or political beliefs. This may be because a major aim of education is to prepare young persons for a vocation; schooling forces individuals to choose courses related to vocational abilities and interests.

Erikson postulated that two key processes in identity formation were exploration and commitment. Exploratory behavior in childhood has been associated with factors such as internal control, a warm and close relationship with parents and personality characteristics such a curiosity and goal directedness (Schmitt-Rodermund and Vondracek, 1999). Likewise, individuals with wider exploratory behaviors might be expected to develop broader and more varied interests which may be sustained into adulthood.

In support of Erikson, a recent study found that young persons classified as identity achievers rather than identity diffusion reported engaging in a greater and more diverse set of activities in domains including leisure, music, school subjects, movies, and technical interests (Schmitt-Rodermund and Vondracek, 1999). In particular, greater exploratory behavior was associated with young persons' having clear vocational preferences. What were the predictors of level of exploratory behavior in young adulthood? Two sets of predictors were found involving childhood interests and achievement orientation and self efficacy. Young persons who had a greater variety of interests as children also engaged in a wider range of exploratory activities as young adults. Second, high achievement orientation and goal directedness were related to exploratory behavior in young adulthood. Young persons who were achievement oriented had high goals for the future and those with high self efficacy reported having both a greater number of interests and a broader variety of interests (Schmitt-Rodermund and Silbereisen,1998).

Possible Selves

Another approach to the study of self or identity in adulthood has focused on the construct of *possible selves* (Cross and Markus, 1991; Markus and Herzog, 1992). Possible selves include both positive and negative images of self in the future. Hoped-for selves include negative images of self, or feared selves. They are seen as the personal embodiment of one's life goals. Similar to the concept of identity as studied by Erikson and Marcia, the construct of possible selves focuses on the self as developing and changing across the life course and being created by the person, rather than shaped totally by the environment. In contrast to the Eriksonian construct, the concept of possible selves has focused on adulthood rather than on adolescence or earlier phases in the life span.

A very important feature of this approach is that an individual's possible selves are seen as motivating the individual's current behavior. Possible selves reflect goals that are currently important in a person's life and impact one's current behavior. Possible selves are created on the basis of adults' knowledge of themselves—their past and current experiences as well as future expectations and wishes. Thus a possible self may become more salient during a period in the life span when the individual is having personal experiences related to such a self. For example, Hooker and Kaus (1994) hypothesized that a health-related possible self would be particularly salient in middle age (compared to young adulthood). It is in middle age that adults have increasing health-related experiences, such as a life-threatening illness, health problems of peers, declining health of parents, and a sense of less time to live. To examine whether a health-related possible self became increasingly salient in middle age, Hooker and Kaus (1994) asked young adults and middle-age adults to describe how they saw themselves in the future—what they hoped to be like or feared being like—their hoped-for or feared possible selves. As predicted, over half of middle-aged adults reported their most important possible self was related to health issues. In contrast, only one-quarter of young adults described their most important possible self in terms of health issues.

Of interest is that similar processes have been identified as being related to identity development and to activities associated with one's most important possible self. Recall that young adults who engaged in more exploratory activities had a higher level of identity achievement and that processes associated with level of exploratory activities included being goal directed and having high self efficacy. Similar to exploratory behavior, one engages in more activities related to the possible selves that are important to the individual (Hooker and Kaus, 1994). Processes including goal directedness and high self efficacy have been found to predict the number of activities engaged in that are related to one's most important possible self, just as these same processes have been related to the amount of exploratory behavior studied in identity approaches. Specifically, adults who listed a health-related possible self as most important and who were goal directed and had high self efficacy were likely to engage in a greater number of positive health behaviors in their daily lives.

ESTABLISHING INTIMACY

"It's very important for me to share my life," an attractive, single, 25-year-old accountant reported. "When I accomplish something, I want someone to celebrate with. When I have a problem, I'd like some advice from someone who's interested in what happens to me. When I think of something profound or funny, I want to share it. I need to give. I have a lot of talents. I'm a nice person, sensitive, skilled at anticipating the desires of other people. I want somebody to share those talents with."

Like the accountant, most young adults desire an intimate relationship and the opportunity to share experiences with another. However, the need for an intimate relationship may present certain problems. Typically, young adults have just attained independence from their parents, and they are struggling to understand who they are as unique human beings. The need for intimacy runs counter to these identity and independence needs. It calls for giving up some of the hard-won independence and redefining identity, at least to some extent, in terms of the values and interests of a pair of people rather than those of an individual.

To a large extent, maturity in young adulthood is a function of an individual's ability to balance the two opposing needs for independence and intimacy. Without a degree of self determination and independence, the person may find it difficult to identify one's own unique interests and goals and may eventually define his or her identity solely in terms of an intimate relationship; intimacy itself may be threatened, for the spouse may find a mate with no clear sense of self uninteresting and lacking in initiative or direction. Without intimacy, on the other hand, there is loneliness and despair.

According to Erikson, the stage of *intimacy* versus *isolation* marks the transition into adulthood. To achieve intimacy, the individual must establish a close, mutually satisfying relationship with another person. Erikson defined intimacy as "the capacity to commit [oneself] to concrete affiliations and partnerships and to develop the ethical strength to abide by such commitments" (Erikson, 1963, p. 263). In Erikson's view, intimacy need not be physical or sexual. It exists in any relationship involving an emotional commitment between two adults, whether they be

One of the major tasks of young adulthood is to establish an intimate relationship without losing one's independent identity.

family members, friends, or lovers. Intimacy involves a union of two identities, but allows each person the freedom to remain an individual. Isolation occurs when the individual's defenses are too rigid to permit a union with another person. Out of the successful resolution of the intimacy versus isolation problem evolves the motivation for generativity that characterizes the next stage, which is concerned with producing and caring for a new generation and helping to improve society.

Erikson has argued that a successful resolution of the identity crisis in young adulthood may be important in the development of intimate relationships. Differences between men and women in the nature of identity and intimacy and their interrelationship have, however, been given little attention in Erikson's theory. Some have suggested that Erikson's theory focuses primarily on male development, and the concepts of identity and intimacy and their relationship need further study with regard to women (Gilligan, 1982, 1996; Marcia, 1993, 1999). Recent interpretations of Erikson's theory have emphasized autonomy and self-sufficiency as salient aspects of identity; society may give greater emphasis to these characteristics of identity formation in men than in women.

The relationship between development of identity in young adulthood and intimacy as defined by the establishment and maintenance of marital relationships in midlife was examine by Kahn and associates (Kahn, Zimmerman, Csikszentmihalyi, and Getzels, 1985). Students at one of the foremost art schools were assessed with regard to Erikson's identity concept; 18 years later they responded to a questionnaire regarding personal, family, and professional life. Three questions were examined in the study. Was there a relationship between identity scores as college students and marital relationships in midlife? Were there gender differences in the relationship between identity and subsequent marital relationships? Was identity in young adulthood related to life satisfaction and happiness in middle age?

Identity in young adulthood was found to be predictive of future marital status for both men and women, but in different ways. Men with low identity were more likely to remain unmarried. Women with low identity, on the other hand, were just as likely to marry as were women with high identity in young adulthood. The difference was that low identity women were more likely to experience breakups in their marriages. For men, identity bore little relation to the stability of the marriage. Identity was also predictive of self-reported satisfaction and happiness in midlife, particularly for men. Identity in young adulthood was related to men's satisfaction with their occupations and standard of living in middle age; identity was also significantly correlated with happiness in midlife. There were fewer significant correlations between identity in young adulthood and life satisfaction or happiness in middle age for women. The interpretation of findings regarding identity and intimate relationships (e.g., marriage) may be particularly difficult for the cohort of women involved in this study. These women were in college in the 1960s, during the onset of the women's movement, and they entered middle age during the 1980s. Given that identity and intimacy are life-long processes that are influenced by life events and social-cultural trends, further exploration of gender and of cohort differences is needed.

Rogers (1972) took another approach to the study of intimate relationships. Rather than regarding an emphasis on intimacy simply as a stage in development, he analyzed the elements common to intimate relationships at all ages. He found that such relationships had four factors in common. First, he found that there was a mutual commitment—not a commitment to love and honor one another forever, but a commitment to work to keep the relationship growing for both partners. Second, there was communication occurring at a meaningful level. Third, expectations that were not based on the actual desires of the individuals in the relationship were broken down. The goals and needs of the relationship were defined in terms of the partners' needs and desires, for example, not in terms of societal or parental expectations. Fourth, the identities of both partners were developed. Ideally, as the partners grow individually, the relationship itself is enhanced. Each partner encourages and supports the growth of the other.

Love

Intimacy is characteristic of relationships between friends, siblings, colleagues, and others, but the form of intimate relationship of most concern to many young adults is what is sometimes called a love relationship. What is special or unique about this form of intimate relationship? This question has been addressed by poets as well as psychologists; the latter have attempted to define precisely what is meant by "love."

Sternberg and colleagues (Sternberg and Barnes,1988; Sternberg, 1998b) proposed a triangular theory of love in which three components—intimacy, passion, and decision-commitment—are viewed as forming the points (angles) of a triangle. *Intimacy* is the emotional component of love; it includes sharing oneself, being concerned about the well-being of another, communicating intimately with another, and valuing another. *Passion* is the motivational and arousal component, the exact nature of which differs according to the nature of the relationship. In a sexual relationship, it includes desire for romance, physical attraction, and sexual consummation; in a parent–child relationship it involves nurturance, support, dominance, and submission. *Decision-commitment* is the cognitive component of love involving two parts: the initial decision that one loves another and the long-term commitment to maintain that love.

The strength and importance of the three components varies in different relationships. While intimacy is seen as the core of all loving relationships, passion is extremely high in the beginning of romantic relationships. Decision-commitment, which may come and go with friends who also come and go, is important in the love for one's parents and children. The strength and importance of the component may also shift across time within a relationship. For example, in some romantic relationships passion initially draws the individuals together, and intimacy helps to sustain that closeness; in others, intimacy may develop first with physical attraction coming later. And at times, because all loving relationships have their ups and downs, the decision-commitment component is all or almost all that keeps the relationship alive.

Couples may also have different types of commitment to each other (Johnson, Caughlin & Huston, 1999). *Personal commitment* refers to the extent to which one is attracted to one's partner and wants to stay in the relationship. *Moral commitment* is based on feeling morally obligated to stay in a relationship, such as the belief that marriage ought to last "until death do us part." Finally, *structural commitment* is based on the sense of constraints or barriers to leaving a relationship regardless of the level of personal or moral commitment.

The four dissimilar triangles shown in Figure 2-1 illustrate Sternberg's triangular theory of love. The equilateral triangle at the top represents balanced love in which all three components are roughly matched. The triangle on the left represents a relationship in which the passion component is emphasized. In this sort of relationship, physical attraction may play a large part while intimacy and commitment play smaller roles. The middle triangle illustrates a relationship in which intimacy plays the primary role. The lovers here may be good friends and close to each other, but physical attraction and commitment to the future are not so strong. And the triangle on the right represents a relationship where decision-commitment predominates over intimacy and passion. This may be the case in a highly committed relationship where intimacy or physical attraction has waned or never existed. Thus in Sternberg's scheme, by varying the shape of the triangle, it is possible to represent a wide variety of love relationships and to represent the course of a relationship over time.

BALANCED TRIANGLE

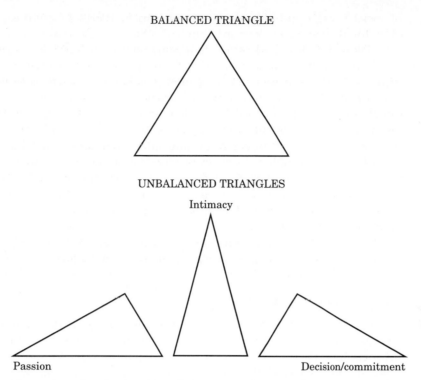

UNBALANCED TRIANGLES

Intimacy

Passion   Decision/commitment

Figure 2-1   Sternberg's Triangular Conceptualization of Love. *Source:* Sternberg, R. J., and Barnes, M. L. (Eds). (1988). The psychology of love. New Haven: Yale University Press; Sternberg, R. J. (1998). Cupid's arrow: The course of love through time. New York, NY: Cambridge University Press.

Love, however, does not involve only a single triangle because there are always two people in a love relationship and each of them experiences a triangle of love. In addition, each person involved has both a real and an ideal triangle of love. Therefore, one could also conceptualize the degree of match or mismatch between the real and idealized triangles of both partners.

Love – Gender and Cultural Considerations

While love for both men and women include each of Sternberg's three dimensions, the relative salience of these dimensions may vary by gender and ethnicity. Dion and Dion (1988, 1993, 1996) have examined styles of love that include dimensions similar to those of Sternberg in college students varying in ethnicity as well as gender. Across a number of studies, women has been found to emphasize emotional and deep caring aspects, similar to Sternberg's intimacy dimension; women also focused on logical and practical aspects of love, in which one's choice of partner is carefully planned on rational criteria, such as social class or similarity of social background (Hendrick and Hendrick, 1988). In contrast, college men often focus on an erotic love style, similar to Sternberg's passion dimension.

Dion and Dion and others have suggested that there may be ethnocultural differences in the social conception of love, particularly for Western versus Asian cultures. In Western societies, love often has been depicted as involving intense emotional involvement and physical attraction, with the couple focusing on each other to the exclusion of others in their social world. It may be that this view of love would be at odds with some aspects of Asian cultural tradition that emphasize the individual's interconnectedness and interdependence on a larger social network. Given this tradition, love may be viewed as developing more gradually, focusing on one's partner as a caring companion, yet remaining mindful of one's larger network of family relationships. Findings from several studies of Asian college students have found a style of love focusing on deep caring and companionship (Dion and Dion, 1993, 1996; Hendrick and Hendrick, 1986). Also, Asian students were concerned with pragmatic aspects of love, reflecting a more planful and rational manner in choice of one's mate and in one's style of love.

Intimacy as a Dynamic Process

As the partners in a relationship grow and change, so does the relationship itself. Two questions are often asked by young adults about the nature of romantic involvements. The first is, "Is what I feel really love?" The second is, "Will our love last?" or, in some cases, "Why did our love die?" We have already addressed the first question in our discussion of the various dimensions of intimate relationships and love. In addressing the second question of will the relationship continue to be happy, it is useful to consider intimacy as an ongoing process rather than a fixed state (Gottman, Coan, Carrere, and Swanson, 1998).

Over the course of an intimate relationship, a couple's patterns of involvement may change because the two individuals continue to develop and because the modes of communication and conflict resolution change. Huston, McHale, and Crouter (1984; McHale and Crouter, 1992) examined changes in the feelings and behavior patterns of newlyweds over the first year of marriage. All the couples were married for the first time. The most striking change was a reduction in the rate at which partners did and said things that brought each other pleasure, for example, complimenting each other, saying "I love you," or doing something to make the other person laugh. The number of pleasurable activities reported declined by about 40 percent overall. Spouses spent less time talking about the quality of their relationship, making efforts to change their behavior, and explaining their desires and concerns to each other.

The importance of positive affect in the continuing happiness and stability of a relationship was also found in a six-year follow-up of newly-wedded couples (Gottman et al., 1998). The newlyweds were observed discussing a problem that was a source of ongoing disagreement in their marriage. The behaviors and emotions recorded during this session were related to the couple's level of marital happiness six years later and whether the couple was still married. The amount of positive affect shown by newlyweds during a conflict situation predicted whether a couple remained married six years later and also discriminated between happily married and unhappily married couples after six years. Though couples who remained happily married became angry and had negative exchanges during conflict as newlyweds, these couples were more likely to use positive affect (i.e., humor, affection, interest) to de-escalate negative exchanges during conflict situations. In particular, the newlywed husbands were less likely to escalate negative exchanges and were more likely to acknowledge the wife's influence or power in the relationship. Wives were more likely to use humor to soothe their husband.

Love Through the Ages

To most Americans today, love relationships seem to develop in a "natural" progression. One develops a liking for someone, which turns into love, which is followed in turn by sexual involvement and, in many cases, marriage. We tend to assume that this has always been the natural sequence for relations between men and women. In fact, however, our current conceptions concerning the relationship between love, sex, and marriage developed rather recently. It is true that marriage and sex have always been linked, but the relation of love to marriage and sexual expression has varied widely throughout history. Although the notion that love should be a primary basis for marriage developed in the eighteenth century, only in the present century has it grown to be the predominant view (Hendrick and Hendrick, 1983).

Development of the modern perspective on love and marriage has paralleled a number of other social developments, especially those that pertain to the role of women in society. In ancient Greece and Rome, women were uneducated and were considered legally and morally inferior to men. A major role of marriage was to provide a social context for producing children; it was also a way for a male to increase his estate. In most societies, marriages were arranged by the parents of the couple to be married.

During the Middle Ages, a new approach to relationships evolved. This new approach, which has come to be called "courtly love," involved emotional exaltation, adoration, and an intensely devoted pursuit of the beloved. The pursuit was highly ritualized. The suitor composed songs, wrote poetry, and fought in tournaments to win the lady's attention and favor, but marriage rarely resulted. In many cases, both the lady and her suitor were already involved in arranged marriages.

Although it was stylized and idealized, courtly love did support the notion that a woman could be intensely loved by a man. It also fostered a range of forms of behavioral expression between men and women. The notion of love marriages developed during the Reformation and Renaissance, although the traditional arranged marriage remained the norm for a long time. At first, love was considered only one possible basis for marriage, and not the most important one. Other considerations, such as status, family alliances, and economic security, were important, and they remain important today in many cases.

Hendrick and Hendrick (from whose 1983 account much of our information on the history of romantic love is derived) suggest that the growth of the concept of love in marriage is related to increasing societal recognition of the value of the individual as a unique and important entity in his or her own right, regardless of status, social class, and other such considerations. A sociocultural perspective, then, would suggest that societal recognition of the intrinsic worth of the individual was a necessary precursor to the concept of love marriages and to the subsequent development of the concept of equity in marriage relationships.

COMMUNITY INVOLVEMENT

In addition to the balancing of identity and intimacy in their personal lives, young adults face the task of determining their relationship with the larger community. No longer does their world consist simply of family and friends in the home, school, and church. The town, the nation, and the world enter their sphere of interest and influence. Young adults become involved in the broader community in many ways: they have legal rights, hold office, and vote; they pay taxes and comply with government regulations concerning work; they take on responsibilities for a family that cannot be fulfilled without community support.

Community involvement for many individuals entails social or political ideologies and becoming active in community organizations. For some people, a religious organization is the primary vehicle of social participation. For others, political parties, unions, or volunteer organizations provide opportunities for community involvement. Some people do little more than contribute to charity now and then.

One of the major factors in the degree of community involvement is the "orderliness" of one's career. Young people who settle down in one location and who embark on a career that promises to move them up the ladder to some higher goal are much more likely than those with less orderly careers to join and participate in community organizations, to get involved in local issues, and to give generously to charities. Perhaps they have the most to gain if the community is healthy and functioning effectively, and the most to lose if the social contract is poorly written and executed. Also, their work organizations may foster and support their involvement in volunteer and community organizations.

The political ideologies and affiliations of many seem to be undeveloped and diffuse, resulting in limited political commitment or identification. Erikson argued that acquisition of religious and political belief systems is particularly important for ego identity development, because it enables an individual to develop a "worldview." Earlier in this chapter we discussed whether one's identity development proceeded at the same developmental pace in all domains. There is some evidence that suggests that development of political or religious identities may develop later than a vocational identity.

De Haan and Schulenberg (1997) examined the relationship between political identity and political involvement; similarly, they studied the relationship be-

During young adulthood one takes on increasing responsibilities including not only those to family but also to the broader community.

tween religious identity and religious beliefs and practices. The relationship of identity status to both intrinsic religious commitment and to importance of the church/temple was examined. Those who had achieved a religious identity were more likely to report an intrinsic religious commitment. Those in identity diffusion were least likely to report intrinsic religious commitment. Similarly, those in identity diffusion were less likely to see the church or temple as important in their lives. Thus, identify diffusion was associated with lower religiosity as measured by intrinsic commitment and salience of the church to the individual. With regard to political identity, those in identity diffusion were least likely to be politically involved. The researchers also examined whether young persons had similar identity status for political and religious domains. The most salient finding was that young persons in identity foreclosure with respect to politics were also likely to be in the foreclosure status with respect to religion.

This delay in achievement of political identity or commitment may be reflected in young persons' voting patterns. In the 1996 elections, only one-third of young adults aged 18 to 24 years reported voting (U. S. Census, 1997). Partially underlying the lack of activism and concern about political issues may be students' beliefs about their inability to "make a difference" and bring about social change.

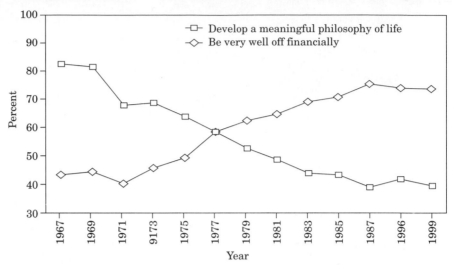

Changes from 1967 to 1999 in Goals that Freshmen Viewed as Very Important

Figure 2-2 Changes from 1967 to 1999 in Goals that Freshmen Viewed as Very Important. *Source:* Sax, L. J., Astin, A. W., Korn, W. S., and Mahoney, K (1999). The American Freshman: National Norms for Fall 1999. Los Angeles: Higher Education Research Institute, UCLA.

There are some recent trends in young adults' goals, values, and aspirations that are disturbing. There are apparent changes in goals and aspirations of college-educated young adults. For over 30 years, the goals and aspirations of college freshmen have been studied by the American Council on Education (Astin et al., 1987; Astin, Korn, Sax, and Mahoney, 1994; Carmody, 1988; Sax, Astin, Korn, and Mahoney, 1999). Figure 2-2 shows changes from 1967 to 1999 in the proportion of freshmen who identified as important goals such things as "developing a meaningful philosophy of life" and "becoming financially well-off." In 1999 almost three-quarters of college freshmen surveyed around the country felt that being financially well-off was an essential or very important goal; only 39 percent felt that developing a meaningful philosophy of life was important. According to Dr. Astin, director of the council's study, these statistics indicate that students see their life as dependent upon affluence and are not inclined to be reflective. Of the freshmen surveyed, the majority stated that a key reason for attending college is to make more money.

SUMMARY

1. The transition to adulthood is marked by a number of events. Those most common events are (1) end of schooling, (2) working and becoming financially independent, (3) living apart from family,

(4) marriage, and (5) parenthood. These events may occur either sequentially or simultaneously, with their timing and pattern varying for individuals and cohorts. They are determined in part by social expectations and historical events. There are individual, social class, and cultural differences in the ages at which people experience events associated with young adulthood. There is some evidence that aspirations and decisions regarding educational level influence the timing and sequence of other events, such as marriage and parenthood.

2. Erikson introduced the concept of the identity crisis to describe the period, which most often occurs during adolescence, in which the maturing individual must integrate new abilities, feelings, roles, and physical appearance into an earlier identity as a child. The search for identity is a lifelong process, not a discrete stage or phase. Expanding on Erikson's work, Marcia postulates four identity status categories: identity achievement, moratorium, foreclosure, and identity diffusion. Much prior research has focused on global definitions and assessment of identity status. There is increasing interest in identity status within specific domains (vocation, religious beliefs, political views). Some research indicates that young persons are not in the same identity status for different domains. Achievement of a vocational identity may occur somewhat earlier than in other domains.

3. For Erikson, the stage of intimacy versus isolation marks the transition into adulthood. The task is to establish intimate relationships without losing identity and independence. Isolation occurs when a person's defenses are too rigid to allow union with another.

4. Many researchers have attempted to define "love." Sternberg has proposed a triangular theory involving intimacy, passion, and decision-commitment. The strength and importance of the components vary across relationships and across time within a relationship.

5. While love for both men and women include each of Sternberg's three dimensions, the relative salience of these dimensions may vary by gender and ethnicity. Across a number of studies, women have been found to emphasize emotional and deep-caring aspects, similar to Sternberg's intimacy dimension; women also focused on logical and practical aspects of love in which one's choice of partner is carefully planned on rational criteria, such as social class or similarity of social background. In contrast, college men often focus on an erotic love style, similar to Sternberg's passion dimension.

6. Intimacy, like identity, can be regarded as a developmental process. Several studies of newly married couples indicated that their feelings and patterns of behavior changed over the first year of marriage; with positive interactions decreasing. In addition, interaction patterns observed in the first year of marriage were predictive of marital satisfaction six years later. Specifically, positive interactions

were related to marital stability and satisfaction over the long haul.

7. Young adults also face the task of determining their relationship with the larger community. Political and religious identity and commitment may be important in becoming involved in the community. There was relatively little relationship between identity status for religion commitment and identity status for political commitment. Political and religious identity achievement may occur later than identity in other domains. A thirty-year study of the goals of college freshmen indicate that being very well off financially is increasing in salience, while developing a meaningful philosophy of life is declining in importance across time and cohorts of college freshmen.

SUGGESTED READINGS

Schmitt-Rodermund, E., and Vondracek, F. W. (1999). Breadth of interests, exploration, and identity development in adolescence. *Journal of Vocational Behavior, 55,* 298–317. Discussion of developmental antecedents of identity achievement in young adulthood. Discussion of role of exploration and family involvement in identity achievement. Particular attention given to vocational development.

Sternberg, R. J. (1998). *Cupid's arrow: The course of love through time.* New York, NY: Cambridge University Press. Updated discussion of Sternberg's framework for the study of love, particularly romantic love.

Van Manen, K J., and Whitbourne, S. K. (1997) Psychosocial development and life experiences in adulthood: A 22-year sequential study. *Psychology and Aging, 12,* 239–246. Update on Whitbourne's longitudinal study of age-related change and cohort differences in identity and generativity during the adult years.

Waterman, A. S. (1999). Identity, the identity statuses, and identity status development: A contemporary statement. *Developmental Review, 19,* 591–621. A recent overview of research and theory on identity statuses and developmental change in identity status in young adulthood.

CHAPTER

3

The Middle Years

Generativity and Responsibility

DEFINING MIDDLE AGE

If you ask a large sample of people what they consider to be middle age, they are likely to say that it begins around the age of 40 and continues to the age of 55 or 60. Although reasonable, this definition leaves the period from 35 to 40 undefined—neither young adulthood nor middle age—and similarly leaves people between 60 and 65 without a proper label. These gaps in our social definitions mark transition periods in which people vary considerably in their attitudes and behaviors. Some people are well into middle age by the age of 35, whereas others are involved in normative tasks of young adulthood (e.g., childbearing) even after 40. Some people seem very old at 50, while some 65-year-olds display the manners, attitudes, and even physical appearance of people a decade or two younger. Perceptions of middle age and health-related events seem to vary with social class (Keyes and Ryff, 1998; Tamir, 1989). Blue-collar workers often consider themselves to be middle aged at age 40, having peaked and begun simply holding onto what they have achieved already. However, for upper-middle-class professionals, that apex may not be reached until the fifties.

In this chapter we will be concerned primarily with social and psychological markers of middle age. Midlife, however, is also of interest from a biological perspective. Finch (1991) has suggested that from a biological perspective middle age is the life phase with somewhat soft boundaries between maturation (menopause and end of reproduction) and the onset of senescence. Senescence may be demarcated from middle age by the onset of sharp increases of morbidity from chronic diseases and mortality rates.

We define middle age as the era that begins between 35 and 40 and ends between 60 and 65. However, we acknowledge the wide variety in attitudes and behavior that exists in our culture, especially in the transition periods, and the limitations in using chronological age as definers of developmental periods.

The difficulty in defining and discussing middle age is partly due to the fact that middle age is a twentieth-century development in the human life cycle (Lawrence, 1980; Moen and Wethington, 1999; Rossi, 1980). Middle age as a period in the life cycle has resulted largely from two major biological and social changes. First, the average life span has increased dramatically during this century, so that now individuals commonly live past the period known as middle age. In 1900, the life expectancy was 50, so that many people died before or during what we now call middle age. The longer life expectancy today influences when people begin to become aware of their aging and mortality; the growing awareness of one's own mortality, typically occurring in midlife, is believed by some to precipitate what has become known as the "midlife crisis" (Jaques, 1965, 1993).

Second, the postparental, or the empty nest phase, occurring after the children leave home, is relatively new in the family life cycle (Huyck, 1989). In 1900, women were, on average, 55 years old when the last child married. Thus, given the lower life expectancy in 1900, the average woman could expect to be a widow before the last child left home. With increased life expectancy, smaller family sizes, and closer spacing of children, the average couple can now expect to live almost 20 years after the last child has moved out.

Thus, the characteristics of the period known as middle age have changed (Willis and Reid, 1999). We may expect that the characteristics will continue to change as a result of future biological advances and social changes. For example, retirement often has been thought of as the event marking the end of middle age, and in recent years, median retirement age has decreased from age 65 to 62. In 2027, however, eligibility for Social Security will be increased to age 67. This leads to the question of whether median retirement age will also rise, causing the period perceived as midlife to be extended. In addition, as the large baby boom cohorts have moved into midlife, the sheer size of these cohorts have draw increased attention to midlife (Morgan, 1998). Many of the popularized accounts of midlife concerns in the 1970s were based upon the midlife experiences of the parents of these baby boomers (Levinson, 1978; Rossi, 1980). However, because the baby boom cohorts had different sociocultural experiences in childhood and young adulthood, their midlife experiences should also be different from their parents (Easterlin, Schaeffer, and Macunovich, 1993; Moen, 1998; Morgan, 1998; Rosenberg, Rosenberg, and Farrell, 1999).

What are the major developmental tasks of the period known as middle age? In Erik Erikson's theory, people at midlife face the dilemma of *generativity versus stagnation* (Erikson, 1963). Generativity is a broad concept encompassing parenthood (both having and educating children) and most of what we consider as "productivity" and "creativity." An individual generates products (works hard, effectively) and ideas (is creative). She or he aspires to be the best that is possible, as parent, worker, spouse, citizen, tennis partner, or vegetable farmer. Erikson has suggested that generativity may also include a more global concern for the environment and the need to preserve rather than deplete the earth for future generations (Goleman, 1988). If the individual fails to "generate," then there exists instead a negative quality that Erikson calls *stagnation*. Erikson (1964) claims that caring is the human virtue that we associate with generativity. Mature adults are those who care for their children whom they have created, for the work that they have produced, and for the welfare of others in the society in which they live.

McAdams and colleagues (McAdams and Aubin, 1998; McAdams, Hart and Maruna, 1998) have extended Erikson's thoughts and have proposed a model of generativity that involves seven components. All seven features are oriented toward the overall goal of providing for the next generation. The first two components of the motivation for generativity include both (a) inner desire and (b) cultural demands. Individuals desire to invest themselves in life and in work that lives after them and they also have a need to be needed. Likewise, societies demand that adults take responsibility for the next generations as parents, teachers, mentors, leaders, and "keepers of the meaning." There appears to be a social clock in many societies with expectations that it is in the middle adult years that individuals assume primary responsibility for nurturing the next generation. The third, fourth, and fifth, components in the generativity model focus on (c) concern for the next generation, (d) a belief in the goodness or worthwhileness of the human experience, and finally (e) a commitment for taking responsibility for others. The sixth component (f) involves action—the behaviors associated with care and commitment. The seventh and final component focuses on the personal meaning of one's generative actions to the individual—individuals' sense of identity is broadened to see themselves as caring generative individuals that have contributed to the development of the next generation.

Robert Havighurst (1972) listed some of the specific developmental tasks faced by middle-aged people in our culture (Table 3-1). In this chapter, we consider some of the issues that have developed from research on middle age—issues that relate rather directly to Havighurst's tasks. For example, we discuss reactions to menopause and other physiological changes in middle age and the psychological adjustments associated with biological change in midlife. We discuss also the experience in middle age of being both a parent and an adult child. In the 1970s, much popular literature on the "midlife crisis" appeared (Levinson, 1978; Farrell and Rosenberg, 1981; Rosenberg, Rosenberg, and Farrell, 1999; Whitbourne and

---

TABLE 3-1   Havighurst's Developmental Tasks Of Middle Age

1. Accepting and adjusting to physiological changes of middle age
2. Reaching and maintaining satisfactory performance in one's occupation
3. Adjusting to aging parents
4. Assisting teenage children to become responsible and happy adults
5. Relating to one's spouse as a person
6. Assuming social and civic responsibility
7. Developing leisure-time activities

Two of the developmental tasks in the middle years are to develop satisfying relationships with one's spouse and with one's aging parents.

Middle-aged parents form the "sandwich generation" with responsibilities toward both their aging parents and their growing children.

Connolly, 1999). Is a midlife crisis a normative experience in middle age or do most individuals perceive themselves to be going through transitions rather than crises? We consider issues related to this debate in this chapter.

BEING A CHILD AND A PARENT

Middle-aged people are in a unique position in their families: They are both parents and children. Not only must they aid their by-now adolescent and young adult children to become reasonably competent adults, they must also help their aging parents adjust to lives that may be changing as rapidly as the lives of teenagers (Penning, 1998; Pillemer and Suitor, 1998). The children are gaining in responsibility and face the prospect of financial independence. The aging parents are adapting to physical, social, and financial changes (for example, retirement, health problems, loss of spouse, reduced income). In the center of these storms of youth and age are the middle-agers, with their own challenges.

The Sandwiched Generation

It is probably in middle age that the adult becomes most acutely aware of being *both* a parent and a child. Prior research in the 1980's and 1990's presented the middle aged adult as simultaneously caught in the middle of multiple roles, as caregiver to an older parent, parent to one's children and a paid worker (Brody, 1990), but demographics suggested in prior cohorts caring for aged parents and one's own children was more likely to occur sequentially than at the same time. Recent findings, however, suggest that being sandwiched between multiple caregiving roles *simultaneously* may become increasingly likely for children of the baby boomers (Morgan, 1998). Since baby boom women had their children in their thirties, later than their own mothers, more of the baby boomer's children will be in their forties and fifties (with their own adolescent children) at the time their baby boomer mothers reach 80. In contrast, parents of baby boomers typically had the boomers in their twenties and thus the parents reached their 80's after the boomers peak childrearing years.

Early studies on caregiving focused primarily on the emotional, physical, and financial strain experienced by the middle generation in giving care to their frail elderly parents (see Chapters 4 and 6). Recent studies have provided a broader and more balanced perspective, in that they consider relationships between middle-aged adults and their young-adult children as well as with their aging parents; more importantly, the dynamic nature of these relationships and the growth and change occurring for *both* parties as a function of the relationship are considered (Penning, 1998; Keyes and Ryff, 1999; Ryff and Selzer, 1996).

Parenting in Middle Age

When children are young and vulnerable, the lives of adults are said to be shaped by a "parental imperative" (Gutmann, 1975). Parents may repress aspects of the self that interfere with the considerable time and psychological and financial resources required for the care and socialization of their offspring. As children mature, parenting has been considered to fade in importance. Two quite different perspectives on the effects of a reduction in parenting responsibilities have been hypothesized. One perspective characterizes the middle-aged adult (primarily mothers) as depressed and lonely, suffering from the "empty nest" syndrome. A very different perspective casts parents as feeling a renewed sense of freedom and potential as children are launched. Both perspectives suggested some closure in the parenting role during midlife. Recently, it has been questioned, however, whether adults ever reach the "parent emeritus" status, suggested by the empty nest perspective (Huyck, 1989; Ryff and Selzer, 1996). Rather, for most adults, parenting is a lifelong role; what does change, often in midlife, are the behavioral requirements of parenting and the nature of the relationship with one's maturing children.

The parenting role may be quite different for parents in early versus late middle age. Many parents in *early middle age* have adolescent children who are in the process of becoming physically mature, socially active, and psychologically independent. These developments in the adolescent have been found to be related to more distancing in the parent–child relationship.

The question arises of whether and how the adolescent's search for identity and struggle for autonomy affects parents' own self-perceptions and personal well-being. Any effects are likely to be moderated by the characteristics of the parents themselves. The empty nest perspective would hypothesize that adults with a strong psychological investment toward their role as parents would be more likely to be affected. Alternatively, parents with a strong psychological investment in roles outside the family (e.g., work or community roles) may be less vulnerable to the transitional stressors of parenting an adolescent.

Silverberg and Steinberg (1990) find some support for the later hypothesis, but not for the former. That is, parents who do not have a strong investment in their paid-work role reported more intense midlife concerns, lower life-satisfaction, and more frequent psychological symptoms as their adolescent children matured and engaged in more heterosexual activities, such as dating. However, those parents with a lower work-role orientation were not necessarily more invested in their parenting role than other parents. Being invested in one's work does not imply being less invested in one's parenting role. The authors' interpretation is that investment in roles outside the family, such as work roles, provides other sources of satisfaction and self-identity that buffer the challenges of their youngster's maturity and expanding social world.

While adults in early midlife are actively involved in assisting with their children's struggle for autonomy and identity, *later middle age* may be a time for beginning to appraise how adult children have "turned out." Parents see before them the accomplishments (e.g., educational attainment, occupational achievements) and adjustment (e.g., happiness, successful marriage) of their adult children. It should be a time not only of reflection about "them" as adult children, but also of "me" as a parent (Ryff, Schmutte, and Lee, 1996; Seltzer and Ryff, 1994). It was hypothesized that parents who think that their children have turned out well would have more positive views about themselves and their past lives; seeing positive products of parenting would be associated with self-acceptance, a purpose in life, and a sense of managing the surrounding world. In addition, positive adjustment and attainment in their offspring would support achievement of the American Dream—that each generation is "better off" than the prior generation.

These issues were examined in studies by Ryff and colleagues (Ryff and Seltzer, 1996; Ryff, Schmutte, and Lee, 1996). The researchers examined whether parents' well being was associated with their children's *adjustment* socially and/or the children's *attainment* in education and occupations. As hypothesized, parents' sense of well being (i.e., self-acceptance, purpose in life, control) was strongly associated with their assessments of their children's social and personal *adjustment;* this was found for both mothers and fathers. Parents who judged their children to be happy and have successful marriages also had higher levels of psychological well-being themselves. An unexpected finding, however, was that a parent's level of well-being was much less closely related to their assessment of children's level of *attainment* in education or occupation. Currently, only cross-sectional findings are available, so that it is not possible to determine the directionality of the relationship between parents' well-being and the adjustment and attainment of their adult children. Parents' sense of well-being may reflect their pride in producing well-adjusted children, or it may be that well-adjusted children are more likely to establish and maintain good relationships with their parents, thus enhancing their parents' well-being.

In addition, parents were asked to compare their children's level of adjustment and attainment (1) to the parents' own adjustment and attainment at comparable ages, and (2) to the adjustment and attainment of friends' or siblings' children. With regard to children's *adjustment,* parents who believed their children were doing better than themselves in early adulthood had lower levels of well-being. Although somewhat counterintuitive, this finding supports prior research on social comparisons that perception of others doing better than oneself has negative consequences for self-esteem. In partial support of the American Dream hypothesis, however, there was higher well being among parents who judged their children to have *attained* more than themselves in educational or work pursuits.

These findings also provide support for Erikson's focus on generativity as the major challenge for middle age. In discussing parenting as one form of generativity, Erikson wrote "it is through reconsidering their children's adulthood successes and failures that they seek, retroactively to validate the responsible caring they themselves provided in their years of active parenting" (Erikson, Erikson, and Kivnick, 1986; see also McAdams and Aubin, 1998).

Aging Parents

There is the myth that the adult child's relationship to his or her parents is extremely difficult, with the aging parents becoming more and more dependent, in effect, reversing previous role relationships (see also Chapter 6 on Family). In this myth, the adult children can hardly wait to ship the old folks off to a "home" of some sort. Such a picture is accurate for only a minority of families.

Caring for aging parents is becoming a normative part of middle adulthood (Penning, 1998). In 1800 a 60-year old woman had about a 3 percent chance of having a living parent, but by 1980 her chances had increased to 80 percent. A relatively small proportion of the elderly are in institutions, but it is estimated that for every disabled person in a nursing home, two or more equally disabled elderly live with or are cared for by their families.

Care of aged parents has only recently become a widespread concern, in part because of demographic changes such as increases in life expectancy (Pillemer and Suitor, 1998). As parents live longer, they are more likely to become dependent on their middle-aged children for care and to need care for an extended period. As we will discuss further in Chapter 6, *filial maturity* involving caring for one's parents while at the same time respecting them as adults with their own rights, has been described as a unique developmental challenge of midlife (Blieszner and Hamon, 1992). Given the smaller number of children produced by the baby boomers, we can expect the ratio of potential adult-child caregivers to elderly parents to decline significantly in the future. The parents of baby boomers have on average three children surviving until age 40. In contrast, baby boomers have under two children reaching middle age.

Who provides care for the elderly? If the older person is married, care is most often provided by the spouse. In this situation, the caregiver is an older person, too. You will recall, however, that the majority of older women are widowed or alone, so they must be cared for by someone else. The task generally falls to adult children, especially adult daughters (Penning, 1998). Cantor (1983) has documented what she calls the "hierarchical compensatory" support system. By this, she means that support for the elderly is activated in order from the closest and most intimate to more distant relationships. This hierarchy progresses from spouse to adult child to distant relative and/or neighbors and finally to assistance from formal agencies (Greenwell and Bengtson, 1997; Walker, Acock, Bowman, and Li, 1996). Because over half of all middle-aged women work, caring for aged parents can be a strain, especially because women in this age bracket must also care for their own families. Working women, however, manage to spend almost as much time helping their parents as nonworking women do, even though they must give up their free time and opportunities for socialization and recreation (Marks, 1998).

What types of support do adult children most often provide for aged parents? First, and most commonly, children provide emotional support—interacting socially, "cheering up" when the parent is depressed, listening to concerns and fears (Blieszner and Hamon, 1992; Ganong, Coleman, McDaniel, and Killian, 1998). Second, children provide direct services such as running errands, shopping, providing transportation, and banking. With more severely impaired elderly, this also includes such daily-care activities as bathing, preparing food, and giving medications. Third, children mediate between the elderly and formal support services and bureaucracies by filling out Medicare forms and arranging for "meals on wheels" and transportation services. Providing financial assistance and taking parents into their homes are two other responsibilities that adult children believe they should assume if needed (Hamon and Blieszner, 1990). The number of older parents' living with their adult children has declined in the last century (Ruggles, 1994). Approximately five percent of adults over age 75 live with an adult child.

What types of strains are experienced by the caregiver? The most universal type of strain is emotional: concern about the health and safety of the older parent and the need to come to terms with changes in the older parent. Most caregivers also experience restrictions in time and freedom; they have less leisure time, difficulty in taking vacations, and more work conflicts. Increased family conflicts may also arise within the caregiver's own family as a result of the need to provide care (Brody, Hoffman, Klehan, & Schoonover 1989; Walker, Acock, Bowman, and Li, 1996). Much less strain is reported to be associated with giving financial assistance to the elderly. Are there also positive consequences to caregiving? Many caregivers report feelings of self-satisfaction and increased self-respect, stemming from the knowledge that they are fulfilling responsibilities and coping with a personal challenge.

Given the increasing proportion of individuals living to very old ages, parental loss is becoming a common experience of midlife (Moss and Moss, 1989; Winsborough and Bumpass, 1991). By age 45, among women, 60 percent have experienced the loss of one parent and by age 55 almost half of women have lost both parents. Loss of one's parents occurs earlier for nonwhite women and those with less education. By age 45, among those with less than a high school education, 50 percent have lost at least one parent and half of black and Hispanic women have lost one parent (Bumpass and Sweet, 1991). Loss of one parent during middle age increases the probability of having an unmarried widowed parent who may need care and assistance. Moreover, loss of a parent in middle age is becoming a significant life-stage transition. The death of the second parent is especially symbolic because it represents the succession to the status of the elder generation within the family. There is also the loss of an important source of emotional support and the recognition that one can no longer return to the parental home (Moss and Moss, 1989).

MENOPAUSE: BIOLOGICAL AND PSYCHOLOGICAL

Physical Symptoms of Menopause

If bearing children is one manifestation of Erikson's notion of generativity, then middle age also brings for women closure of this source of productivity. Is the "closing of the gates" as described by Deutsch (1945) a wrenching and traumatic experience? Although Havighurst (1972) considers adjusting to physiological changes as one of the developmental tasks of middle age, there are few changes that are truly universal in the middle years.

For women, menopause is one of the few biological changes that can be considered normative in middle age. Menopause is defined as the cessation of menses. The standard epidemiological definition in U.S. and European studies is twelve consecutive months without menstruation (Kaufert et al., 1986; Treloar, 1974). The median age for the last menstrual period is between 50 to 52 years and 80 percent of women experience their last menstrual period between 45 to 55 years (Avis, Crawford, and McKinlay, 1997; Brambilla and McKinlay, 1989). The cessation of menses is part of a longer phase in the aging process known as the climacteric, which is the period in which women are making the transition from the reproductive to the nonreproductive stage of life.There are, however, wide individual differences both in the beginning and end of menopause and in women's physical responses to it. Some women begin to experience menstrual changes in their thirties, while others experience no change until their sixties. It is not clear whether age at menopause has changed historically, as has the age of menarche (onset of menstruation), which has gotten lower with successive generations. Based on current findings, age of menarche and age of menopause are unrelated (Avis, 1999; Treloar, 1982).

Some understanding of the menstrual cycle is required in order to consider the menopausal process (Avis, 1999). At the beginning of the menstrual cycle, the pituitary gland releases a follicle stimulating hormone (FSH), which causes the follicle cells surrounding the egg to develop. The egg and follicles produce the hormones estrogen and progesterone. The follicle eventually grows large enough to rupture and the ovum is released. The high circulating levels of estrogen and progesterone produced by the ruptured follicle inhibit the release of FSH. If fertilization does not occur, the production of estrogen and progesterone decline, FSH begins to rise, and the menstrual cycle begins anew.

Menopause is a gradual process that starts long before a woman is aware (Avis, 1999). Beginning in her thirties, a woman begins to have some menstrual cycles in which no egg is produced; women are generally unaware of these nonfertile cycles. As the age of 50 approaches, the follicles become depleted; there are more cycles in which no egg is produced, and hormone production slows. Greater amounts of FSH are released in an attempt to stimulate the follicles, but the follicles do not respond and menstruation stops altogether. Increased FSH is generally seen as a hormonal indicator of impending menopause.

Because menopause is best described as a process, three "stages" of menopause are recognized in the literature: perimenopause, menopause, postmenopause. Perimenopause involves the indefinite phase characterized by irregular flow, reduced hormone production, and increased levels of FSH. The median length of perimenopause is estimated to be 3.8 years (McKinlay et al., 1991), but there are wide individual differences. Length of perimenopause appears to be largely physiologically determined. The length of perimenopause has been found to be related to an earlier age of beginning perimenopause and psychological symptoms reported prior to menopause. Menopause *per se* is defined retrospectively as twelve consecutive months without menstruation. Postmenopause is the state after achieving menopause.

Estrogen production does not stop altogether following menopause. More than 90 percent of estradiol, the most potent naturally occurring estrogen is produced in the ovaries. However, other forms of estrogen, such as estrone are produced by other glands, such as the adrenal, and by peripheral conversion of circulating androgens in some tissues, such as the blood, liver, and adipose tissue.

What factors might be associated with early onset of menopause? The most well-established factor is cigarette smoking, with those who smoke experiencing menopause one to two years earlier than those who do not (Brambilla and McKinlay, 1989; Willet et al., 1983). There is some support to the idea that women who had shorter menstrual cycles in young adulthood and women who have never been pregnant also experience earlier menopause (Whelan et al., 1990).

Although menopause is a normative biological change, it historically has been viewed as a negative event for a woman. Victorian physicians blamed menopausal symptoms on indiscretions of one's youth (Stearns, 1975). Deutsch (1945) described menopause as a partial death. In the late twentieth century, the medical community has characterized menopause as a deficiency disease in which the postmenopausal woman is in an "estrogen deficient" state due to "ovarian failure" (McCrea, 1983; Kaufert and McKinlay, 1985).

In the 1980s, menopause became increasingly implicated as a risk factor for osteoporosis and cardiovascular disease, due to the reduction in estrogen that precipitates menopause (Bastian, Couchman, Nanda, and Siegler, 1998). With the development of hormone replacement therapy (HRT), menopause is viewed by the medical community as something that is treatable and that warrants medical intervention. Some consider this increasing medicalization of menopause to be a reflection of the treatment of menopause, a normative biological event, as a disease (Bell, 1990; Gonyea, 1998).

Menopause is stereotypically assumed to be inevitably accompanied by hot flashes, sweats, prolonged menstrual irregularities, vaginal dryness, and a host of other "symptoms," including depression, irritability, weight gain, insomnia and dizziness (Avis, 1999; Avis et al, 1997). Vasomotor symptoms (hot flashes, night sweats) are the primary symptoms associated with menopause. There has been tremendous variability in reported incidence of hot flashes in the United States and worldwide, ranging from 24 to 93 percent of women reporting symptoms (Kronenberg, 1990).

There have been few longitudinal studies of women beginning prior to menopause and following the women through the menopausal process. The Massachusetts Women's Heath Study (MWHS) has followed a large, representative sample of women across the menopausal process (McKinlay et al., 1991; Avis et al, 1997). Almost one quarter of women in this study did not report hot flashes or night sweats throughout the menopausal process, and of those who did experience hot flashes only one-third reported them to be very bothersome (Avis et al., 1997). Only one-third of the longitudinal sample consulted an MD for menopause-related problems.

What characteristics of women predicted frequency of hot flashes and what characteristics predicted reporting being bothered by hot flashes? Women who reported having physical or psychological symptoms prior to menopause and women who had negative attitudes toward menopause reported a greater number of hot flashes and night sweats. Negative attitudes were associated with agreeing with statements such as "Many women become depressed or irritable during the menopause" and "Many women think they are no longer 'real' women after menopause." The finding that premenopausal symptoms are related to hot flashes suggest that some women may be more sensitive to bodily symptoms and changes and this is a relatively stable characteristic, beginning prior to menopause. Lower education and smoking were also positively related to frequency of hot flashes. Women who reported being bothered by hot flashes reported having more hot flashes,were more likely to smoke, to be divorced, and to have had a benign breast cyst removed.

A persistent belief held by both many clinicians and women is that menopausal women are likely to become depressed (Avis and McKinlay, 1991). In earlier times a form of clinical depression *(involutional melancholia)* was said to be associated with menopause. Support for this belief is inconclusive. Longitudinal data from the MWHS indicated that the majority of depression occurring during menopause could be attributed to women who had first experienced depression prior to midlife (Avis et al, 1994). Onset of menopause was not related to an increased risk of depression. Also, there was a slight elevation of depression for women who had experienced a lengthy perimenopausal phase of over two years duration. The association between a long perimenopause and depression appeared to be explained by a greater number of menopausal symptoms rather than menopause *per se*. The depressive symptoms, however, were transitory and decreased following menopause.

The Psychology of Menopause

Although menopause is a universal physiological event, the cultural and individual variation in women's responses and symptoms is very striking. Cultural variation in menopause symptomatology is evidenced in a study comparing symptoms across three distinct populations of women in the United States, Canada, and Japan (Avis, 1999; Avis et al., 1993). All women were from 45 to 55 years of age, and similar methodology and questions were used across groups. Figure 3-1 shows a cross-cultural comparison of symptoms (hot flashes, depressed feelings) reported by menopausal status for each of the three cultural groups. There are significant differences in frequency of reporting hot flashes and feeling depressed. Japanese women had much lower frequencies on most symptoms studied; these findings held across menopausal status.

Avis and colleagues' findings are congruent with those of an International Health Foundation study on menopause in seven Asian countries, which also found lower levels of vasomotor and psychic complaints among Asian menopausal women (Payer, 1991). It is difficult to determine the extent to which these societal differences are due to genetic, dietary, reproductive, or cultural factors. In addition to different societal views of menopause, countries also differ in the number of children women have, exercise patterns, and diet. Japanese women, for example, may not perceive heat changes as remarkable or they may experience them at a much lower rate, possibly due to the much lower fat content in their diets.

Likewise, in societies in which women acquire social, religious, or political power in postmenopausal years, menopausal symptoms are minimal. For example, women of the Rajput case in India have fewer menopausal complaints than women in the United States (Flint, 1982). This may be a result of cultural differences. Rajput women live in purdah (that is, they are veiled and secluded) prior to menopause. They are not allowed to be in the company of men other than their husband. Once they reach menopause, however, cultural taboos against flowing blood and childbirth no longer apply to them, so they are released from the restrictions of purdah and can talk with men. Because their status increases after menopause, it is not an event that they view with foreboding.

In spite of evidence refuting many of the stereotypes of menopause, they remain strong (Gonyea, 1998). In Western society, which extols youthfulness and sexuality, menopause is feared because it signifies aging—a lack of sexual attractiveness. There is no evidence, however, that women's physical capacity for sex

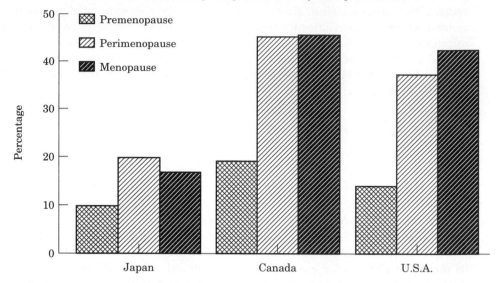

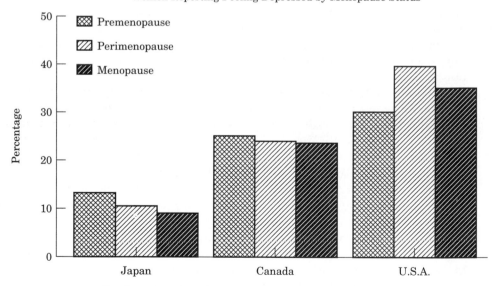

Figure 3-1 Cross-Cultural Comparison of Menopausal Symptoms. *Source:* Avis, N. E., Kaufert, P. A., Lock, M., McKinlay, S. M. & Vass, K. M. (1993). The evolution of menopausal symptoms. In H. Burger (ed.), Bailliere's Clinical Endocrinology and Metabolism, (vol 7, pp. 17–32). London, England; Bailliere Tindall.

declines after menopause. Some psychoanalysts have suggested that the loss of childbearing capacity is especially traumatic, but very few women mention the inability to have more children (at age 50) as a chief concern in menopause. They are much more concerned about aging in general.

The actual experience of menopause is for most women much less negative and, in some respects, much more positive than popular belief would have it (Avis et al, 1997; Gonyea, 1998). The MWHS findings indicate that women's attitudes become more positive as they experience menopause (Avis et al., 1997). Longitudinal change in attitudes from premenopause to postmenopause was overwhelmingly toward positive attitudes. How a woman views menopause appears to be related to several factors, including her prior beliefs about menopause (Avis et al., 1997; Matthews, 1992) and her experience in other psychosocial roles, such as work and family. Women who held negative attitudes prior to menopause were more likely subsequently to report symptoms, such as hot flashes and night sweats.

Menopause occurs at a time when women are also experiencing other life changes, such as children leaving (or returning) home and parents aging and needing assistance (Adams, Cartwright, Ostrove, Steward, and Wink, 1998; Martire, Stephens, and Townsend, 1998). Women who have good social networks and support report fewer menopausal symptoms. On the other hand, stressful life events such as losses in one's social network (e.g., death of parent, widowhood, or divorce) were associated with higher rates of psychological symptoms (Martire et al., 1998; McKinlay, McKinlay, and Brambilla, 1987). Indeed, psychosocial factors have been found to account for more variation in depressed mood among women at the time of menopause than menopause itself.

As indicated in the previous discussion, current menopausal research is beset with methodological problems (Avis, 1999; Goodman, 1982). First, menopause is a complex biosocial, biopsychological phenomenon, but most research deals only with one or two aspects. For example, research that deals with the physical aspects of menopause without taking into account women's socialization experiences, fears, and unfounded beliefs about menopause may inappropriately attribute symptoms solely to physiological variables. Second, cohort and cultural differences probably affect the menopausal experience. Cohorts of women differ, for example, in age at menarche and in the number and spacing of pregnancies, and these factors could affect menopause (Gonyea, 1998). For example, baby boom women who came of age during the 1960's, an era of greater reproductive choice, now are exploring their options (e.g., HRT) as they make the transition to menopause. There are also cohort differences in medical intervention procedures pertaining to childbirth, surgical menopause, estrogen replacement, and other matters, and these, too, may have long-term effects on health during menopause. For example, while women were originally urged to consider the short-term use of HRT to relive the symptoms of menopause, it is now suggested by some that only through the long-term use of HRT can osteoporosis, and heart disease be reduced. Third, there are often sampling problems. The case history approach often used in menopausal research is biased in that only those women who seek professional help for menopausal complaints are represented. The experience of the many women who have few or no menopausal problems is not reflected in case histories. Finally, without cohort-sequential longitudinal research it is difficult to disentangle the effects of aging from those of cohort differences in reaction to menopause. For example, a common complaint of menopause is insomnia, but increasing sleep disturbance occurs with age as well. A menopausal woman's complaints of insomnia, then, may be a function of increasing age rather than menopause itself.

Aging and Menopause

Hormonal changes accompanying menopause are thought to have an impact on other bodily systems, including the musculoskeletal, cardiovascular, and urogenital systems (Avis, 1999; Bastian, Couchman, Nanda, and Siegler, 1998). It is currently unknown, however, to what extent changes in these systems are directly due to reductions in estrogen (as a function of menopause) or whether such changes are primarily associated with aging *per se* (Merrill and Verbrugge, 1999) or with behavioral changes occurring at the same time.

Osteoporosis, involving a loss of bone mass, is a major concern for older women (Center for Disease Control and Prevention, 1998). The most serious consequence of osteoporosis is the increased risk for bone fracture, particularly in the hip. Petite, small-boned, fair-skinned women enter old age with less bone mass and thus are at increased risk as loss of bone mass occurs. Approximately one half of the total loss in bone mass occurs during the ten years after menopause.

It often has been purported that cardiovascular disease in women increases significantly after menopause. Although men develop coronary artery disease one to two decades earlier than women, the incidence of coronary artery disease in men and women becomes equal around age 75 (National Center for Health Statistics [NCHS], 1990). This has led to the belief that estrogen deficiency plays a major role in the acceleration of cardiovascular disease in women. In fact, mortality from heart disease does not substantially increase for women following menopause; the rate of increase from age 40 onwards is fairly smooth (Bush, 1990). The reduced sex difference in mortality associated with heart disease appears to be more a result of a leveling of male mortality rather than an increase in female mortality.

Breast cancer is a disease that can be clearly mediated by hormones (Howe and Rohan, 1993). Factors, such as age of menarche, pregnancy, and age of menopause, that are markers of hormonal status, also affect risk of breast cancer. Menopause is important in that women who experience menopause at a late age are at greater risk for breast cancer (Brinton, 1990); in contrast early menopause reduces the risk. Finally, although the incidence of breast cancer increases with age, the rate of increase is less steep after age 45 to 50 than in the reproductive years (Kelsey and Horn-Ross, 1993).

There continues to be serious debate regarding the benefits and risks of hormone replacement therapy (HRT) for treatment not only of menopausal symptoms, but also of osteoporosis and cardiovascular disease (Bastian et al., 1998; Gonyea, 1998; Kuller, 2000; Meade and Vickers, 1999). More recently, cognitive functioning has also been included in the HRT debate. Although the media and pharmaceutical companies have presented HRT as the first choice for many women in dealing with menopause, and risk of osteoporosis and cardiovascular disease, researchers are more cautious as findings of clinical trials become available (Kuller, 2000; Meade and Vickers, 1999). In particular, there may be an early, short-term detrimental effect of HRT in relation to cardiovascular disease and the long-term effects are still under investigation. HRT use has also been linked to a slight increase in risk of breast cancer.

MIDLIFE: A TRANSITION OR A CRISIS?

For the past twenty years, there has been intermittent debate in the social sciences regarding how to describe and explain the developmental changes occurring during midlife. During the 1970s and 1980s, much of the debate centered around two models for conceptualizing the nature of development in middle age: the crisis model and the transition model (Jaques, 1993; Levinson et al., 1978; Levinson, 1990; Whitbourne and Connolly 1999).

Crisis Model

The crisis model is concerned principally with changes occurring *within* the individual. This model conceptualizes development as passage through a series of stages, each characterized by a particular type of crisis, which the individual experiences and must resolve to advance successfully to the next stage. All individuals are said to experience the same set of stages. Crises are seen as normative developmental events, experienced by all individuals at specific stages of development. Each stage and its accompanying crisis is typically defined as occurring within a particular chronological age range. A major contributor to this developmental model is Erikson. However, interestingly, the Eriksonian stage model does not give special emphasis to middle age and does not single out for special attention the crisis of generativity versus despair occurring in midlife.

The term "midlife crisis" became popular because of an article by Elliot Jaques (1965, 1993) on the career crises of artists. In an intensive review of their lives, Jaques found some kind of dramatic change around the age of 35 in almost every case. He found that in many instances the period of crisis was precipitated by the individuals' recognition of their own mortality. The artists studied became concerned about the time left to live, rather than time since birth. Some artists (Gauguin is a prominent example) began their creative work at this time. Others quit, and many died. The people who were artists before and after this crisis usually demonstrated some significant change in their work. Often the change was one of intensity, as impulsive brilliance gave way to a mellowed and more deliberate form of the art.

Popularized writings on adult development, such as those by Levinson (1986, 1978), Gould (1978), and Sheehy (1976), all emphasize crises occurring in midlife. Levinson's research was based on 10 to 20 hours of interviews with 40 men in the age range from 35 to 45. Four occupational groups were studied—executives, workers, biologists, and novelists. Based on retrospective biographical sketches given by these men, Levinson conceptualized the life course as divided into four eras: childhood and adolescence, early adulthood, middle adulthood, and late adulthood. Bordering each era are times of instability and developmental crisis. Levinson gives particular emphasis to the period of instability during entry into middle adulthood. He suggests that there are three tasks associated with this crisis period: The man must review his life as a young adult and reappraise what he has done; he must move toward entering middle age; and he must deal with four sets of polarities that are sources of conflict. These four polarities are young versus old, destruction versus creation, masculine versus feminine, and attachment versus separation.

Levinson sees these periods of instability as closely tied to specific chronological ages. The unstable period in midlife is said to occur between age 40 and 45, and Levinson argues that it cannot begin before age 38 or after 43. Moreover, these periods of instability are considered to be nearly universal. Levinson suggests that 80 percent of all men experience such a period of crisis in midlife.

It is important to note several limitations of research conducted within the crisis model, because this model has received such widespread attention within the media and popular literature (Rosenberg, Rosenberg, and Farrell, 1999). First, there has been concern regarding the samples used in these studies. In several instances clinical populations have been used. Also, white, middle-class males are overrepresented in the samples. Moreover, as Rossi (1980) has pointed out, the research of Levinson, Gould, and Sheehy is based on the same birth cohort, raising questions regarding generalizability to other generations. To the extent that the problems of midlife are related to specific societal and historical trends and events, we may expect that midlife may be experienced differently by different generations (Bumpass and Aquilino, 1995). A second concern is that midlife-crisis research has been based almost totally on interview data. There has been little attempt to quantify this interview data and subject it to statistical analyses, nor have these researchers crossvalidated their findings by use of standardized instruments (McCrae and Costa, 1984). Finally, the major studies cited to support the crisis model are cross-sectional. It is not possible therefore to compare functioning in early or later adulthood with functioning in midlife and determine whether midlife is indeed marked by a period of greater instability.

Transition Model

A second conceptualization of development during middle age that evolved in the 1970s and 1980s rejected the notion that crises are normative developmental events. Rather, progression across the life course is seen as being predictable and orderly, for the most part. The individual constructs a timetable for when major life events would be expected to occur (Moen and Wethington, 1999). The expected timing of events is based largely on societal age norms. That is, there exists a socially defined timetable for the age at which men and women are expected to marry, raise children, retire, and so on. Much of one's life is construed and evaluated in terms of this social timetable.

Other researchers have also questioned some of the assumptions of the crisis model, including that a midlife crisis is nearly universal, occurs within a limited age range, and results in significant changes in self-perception or lifestyle (Tamir, 1989). Epidemiologists find little support for the proposal that midlife is a time of excessive stress compared to other age periods. Divorce is most common in the twenties (National Center for Health Statistics, 1995, 1999); admissions to psychiatric hospitals peak at 40; suicide is more prevalent in young and old age than middle age. Longitudinal studies of personality characteristics, such as neuroticism, which from a crisis perspective might be expected to increase in midlife, have found that such characteristics are remarkably stable over much of the life course (Chapter 9).

Why do some studies conclude that midlife crises are common while others conclude that they are uncommon? A number of disparities exist between the two camps in methods of research. First, research within the crisis model has drawn more heavily, although not exclusively, from clinical populations, who have sought help because of concerns and problems. Research within the transition model has used nonclinical populations. A limitation of both camps has been the overrepresentation of white, middle-class samples (see Fiske, 1980; Farrell and Rosenberg, 1981, for exceptions). Second, researchers in the two camps have also tended to employ different types of measures. As mentioned previously, the crisis model has been based primarily on interview data. Interviews may be geared to tap "inner turmoil" and may therefore tend to elicit complaints and general concerns. In one major interview study (Vaillant, 1977), many men claimed to be in crisis, but other evidence (for example, radical changes in their careers or marriages) was uncommon. On the other hand, the transition position has supplemented interview data with projective techniques and self-report or self-ratings of life satisfaction and happiness (Tamir, 1989). Those concerned with personality variables (McCrae and Costa, 1984) have also employed personality questionnaires. As a result of using different instruments and asking different types of questions of the data, the outcome measures of the two groups have been different. The crisis group has relied heavily on case-study descriptions. Readers are left to draw their own conclusions from these case studies regarding whether a crisis has occurred or to accept the author's summary statements. In contrast, the transition researchers have sometimes offered global self-ratings of life satisfaction or happiness in support of their positions. The research base of both groups has suffered from a lack of longitudinal studies.

THE BABY BOOMERS IN MIDDLE AGE

The U.S. birth rate plunged to historic lows in the 1920s and 1930s and then rose sharply after World War II and remained high through the early 1960s. A similar increase in births after World War II also occurred in Canada (Foot and Stoffman, 1996) and in western Europe.

These dramatic shifts in birth rates, in addition to increasing life expectancy, resulted in two cohorts that vary significantly in size and in life experiences. The "baby boom" generation is defined as the exceptionally large birth cohorts born after World War II between 1946 and 1964 (AARP, 1998; Easterlin, 1987; Morgan, 1998). In contrast, the parents of the baby boomers were part of unusually small cohorts born in the 1920s and 1930s. The small size of the parent cohorts of the baby boomers as well as their entry into adulthood and the labor market during the economic and technological boom after World War II resulted in their experiencing an unusually favorable labor market as young adults. Given the economic and technical expansion occurring during their birth years, the baby boomers, were better housed, fed, clothed and educated than any previous generation; great things were expected of them.

The sheer size of the baby boom cohorts has impacted almost every aspect of their lives. They grew up in larger families of on average 3.4 children. They attended schools with larger class sizes, straining with the explosion of boomer cohorts into the educational system. The early baby boomers entered adolescence during the socially turbulent 1960's with civil rights and the women's movement. They experienced the national debate of the Vietnam War and many fought in that war. They began their work lives during the 1970's and 1980's a period of slower economic growth. In addition, the upswing in the supply of young workers in the boomer cohorts had adverse effects on relative wages, employment rates, and upward job mobility.

This somewhat pessimistic view, however, does not take into account that the baby boomers' personal and economic future lies, in part, in their own hands. Economists suggest that the competition and economic conditions experienced by the baby boomers may have influenced some significant decisions boomers made in regard to their personal and family lives (Easterlin, Schaeffer, and Macunovich, 1993; Morgan, 1998; AARP, 1994). Boomers have on average achieved higher levels of education than prior cohorts (AARP, 1994). Over half of boomers have graduated from high school and almost a quarter have a college education. Approximately two-thirds of baby boomers have married. However, they have had children at later ages and had fewer children. Compared to the parent generation, more baby boomers have remained single and more of those in unions have remained childless. They more frequently combined childrearing with spouse's work to supplement the family income.

To illustrate these changes in household composition, Figure 3-2 presents the household distributions for the 1935 to 1939 birth cohorts and for the 1950 to 1954 birth cohorts when at the same chronological age (26 to 30 years). The 1935 to 1939 cohorts present parent generations and the 1950 to 1954 cohorts represent baby boomer generations. A comparison of the two cohort groups shows a marked decline from 73 percent to 48 percent in the proportion of households that include a couple with children. Most of this decline is accounted for by a greater proportion of baby boom cohorts remaining childless or single.

A greater proportion of boomers, particularly women, have worked full time; over 90 percent of males and 75 percent of women are in the workforce (AARP,

Household Distribution: 1935-1939 Birth Cohorts at Ages 26-30

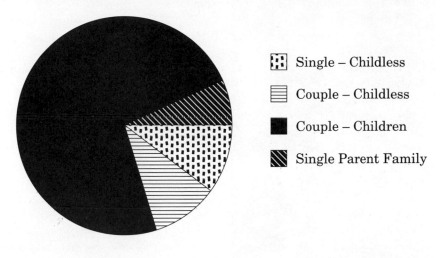

Household Distribution: 1950-1954 Birth Cohorts at Ages 26-30

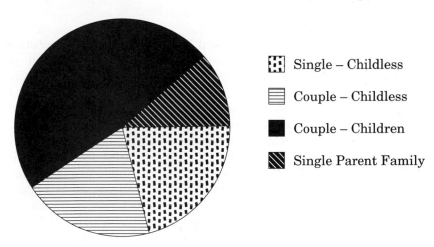

Figure 3-2   Comparison of Household Distributions for Parent and Baby Boom Cohorts. *Source:* Easterlin, R. A., Macdonald, C., & Macunovich, D. J. (1990). Retirement prospects of the baby boom generation: A different perspective. Gerontologist, 30, 776–783.

Baby boomers, like Bill Gates, are now in leadership roles.

1998). Most boomers are now in their prime working years and constitute one of the most vital economic and political constituencies of the adult population (Alwin, 1998). In 1990 almost one third of the U.S. population were members of the baby boom cohorts (AARP, 1994).

An important but less discussed issue with regard to the baby boomers is the increasing diversity in these cohorts (Lachman and James, 1997). The baby boom cohorts are often pictured as a homogeneous mass; however, its diversity is of considerable concern particularly as they age. This diversity is associated with ethnic, socioeconomic, and birth cohort issues. While the dramatic increase in the number of elderly in the population in the first half of the twenty-first century is well known, it is less well recognized that the ethnic distribution of the future aged will shift. While the number of whites over age 65 will double between 1990 and 2050, and the number of older blacks will triple, the number of older Hispanics and Asians will increase by factors of more than five (Morgan, 1998). Many minority and unmarried boomers differ considerably in socioeconomic and lifestyle from the mainstream boomers. While two-thirds of all baby boomers have married, only 40 percent of African-American boomers have married (AARP, 1994). While 25 percent of boomers have a college education, less than 15 percent of blacks or Hispanics have completed college.

Boomer cohorts are diverse not only socially and ethnically, but also in terms of year of birth. The boomer cohorts have been classified into two birth waves with the first wave (leading edge) born from 1946 to 1954 and the second wave (trailing edge) born 1955 to 1964 (Morgan, 1998). This distinction in birth cohorts is important given that economic and social advancement has not been as prevalent for the second wave as for the first wave. For example, educational attainment of the second wave is less than the first wave. This lower educational attainment is accompanied by lower income and rates of home ownership for the second wave. Should the educational and economic differences between the cohorts fail to close in midlife, the second wave may suffer lower lifetime incomes and their standard of living in retirement may be less than the first wave.

A major concern for boomers and for society as a whole is the aging of the baby boomers (AARP, 1998). The Social Security system is based on intergenerational exchanges. The current workforce provides the funding for the social security benefits of the preceeding generation. The much smaller cohorts that followed the baby boom cohorts have shifted the dependency ratio expected when the boomers become old. In 2000 the dependency ratio is 48 children and 21 older adults for every 100 persons likely to be in the workforce (ages 20–64 years). In 2050 there will be 42 children and 37 older adults for every 100 persons likely to be in the workforce. Given this shift in the twenty-first century in dependency ratios, age of eligibility for full Social Security benefits will rise. Beginning in the year 2000, eligibility for Social Security benefits will rise by two months each year. Thus a member of the baby boom cohort who was born in 1946 will not be eligible for full Social Security benefits until age 66. A person born toward the end of the baby boom in 1960 will have to wait until age 67 (Kutza, 1998).

The economic prospects of boomers for the retirement years are mixed. It is estimated that approximately 80 percent of boomers will have some pension benefits in retirement, largely due to a greater proportion of women being in the workforce and in jobs with pension benefits. Although more individuals will have some pension benefits, the median value of pensions is not expected to increase greatly from 1990 to 2030. The upside is that more families will have two pensions of both the husband and the wife. Finally, many baby boomers have limited financial assets and most are not saving the amount needed for retirement (AARP, 1998; Kutza, 1998).

What are the boomers plans for the retirement years? As shown in Figure 3-3, the majority of boomers plan to retire by age 65, although many will not be eligible for full Social Security benefits (AARP, 1998). Approximately 35 percent plan to be retired by age 60. In general, second wave boomers expect to retire earlier than first wave boomers even though their economic situations as a group is somewhat less strong than early boomers and they will receive full social security benefits at a later age. While boomers expect to retire at similar ages to their parents, their view of retirement differs. In contrast to prior generations, a majority (70 percent) of boomers expect to continue working at least part-time after retirement (AARP, 1998). Currently, the workplace is not oriented toward continued work after retirement. This emphasizes the importance of creating more options such as "bridge jobs" that span the transition from full-time career jobs to full-time retirement.

The living arrangements and families of boomers in old age are also predicted to differ from prior cohorts. As the baby boomers come into late midlife (55

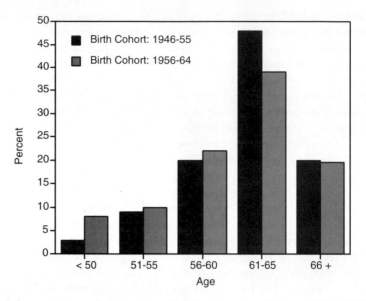

Figure 3-3   Expected Age of Retirement of Baby Boomers *Source:* AARP (1998). *Boomers approaching midlife: How secure a future?* Washington, DC: AARP.

to 64 years), the proportion *not* living with a spouse are expected to reach new co-hort highs. Approximately 30 percent of the first wave and 40 percent of the second wave boomers are estimated not to be living with a spouse in late midlife (Easterlin, Schaeffer, and Macunovich, 1993). This results from an increase in boomers who never married and an increase in divorce rates compared to a de-crease in proportion widowed.

It is estimated that close to 10 percent of the second wave boomers will have never married by age 55 to 64, a proportion almost double to the parent genera-tions, but similar to their grandparent generations. In addition, an estimated 30 percent of trailing-edge boomers will be divorced or widowed in late middle age. Not only are the boomers in late middle age less likely to be married, but they also will have fewer grown children. The 1901 to 1905 cohort (grandparent generation of the boomers) had on average 2.6 children; the 1931 to 1935 cohort (parents of the baby boomers) had 3.4 children on average; the 1951 to 1955 cohort is pre-dicted to have 2.1 children. These projections regarding fertility patterns can be made with reasonable assurance for the first wave boomers because they are at the end of their reproductive years.

Although it is still somewhat early to project the outlook for the trailing edge, based on their fertility to date, the difference between them and their par-ents appears to be even greater than for the first wave. The baby boomers in late midlife (age 55 to 64) are, therefore, likely to appear much more similar to their grandparents' generation than to their parents' generation in terms of the propor-tion never marrying and the percent of childless women. One of the implications of these demographic trends is that a greater proportion of the baby boomers are expected to live alone in old age. It is estimated that 37 percent of the 1946 to 1955 birth cohorts will live alone at age 65 to 74 years.

Based on demographic and economic data now available, the following policy implications for the baby boomers' aging have been proposed (AARP, 1998).

- Given the greater diversity of the baby boom cohorts, the future of the boomers is mixed. Most are expected to do substantially better than their elders. A significant minority will be financially much less secure and vulnerable with continued reliance on public insurance programs, such as the U.S. social securtiy system.
- For most boomers, Social Security, Medicare, and flexible work opportunities in retirement will continue to be crucial to an adequate standard of living in their later years. Boomers are planning to retire prior to being eligible for full Social Security benefits. However, many plan to work part time in retirement.
- Politically, the greatest challenge for boomers will be to keep strong the social insurance contract between the generations. As the proportion of elderly increases, the dependency ratio will increase with approximately four dependent children and elderly for every five adults in the workplace.

SUMMARY

1. The period of life called middle age begins around the age of 35 or 40 and ends around the age of 60 or 65. It is a period that, in Erikson's terms, involves the issue of generativity—creativity and productivity in family life (children) and in career. Stagnation is the opposite.

2. One of the few truly normative biological events of middle age is menopause for women. Women, on average, experience menopause in their early fifties; however, there are wide individual differences in onset and progression through the menopausal process. Smoking is associated with early onset of menopause. Two of the stereotypical symptoms associated with menopause are hot flashes and feeling blue or depressed. However, there are wide individual and cultural differences in women's reports of these symptoms.

Personal characteristics (e.g., prior depression, premenopausal expectations) influence women's experience and reporting of symptoms.

3. There is debate over whether psychological changes in midlife are best represented as crises or as transitions; currently transitions appear to be the more common perspective. Different measures and different types of studies have been conducted to support the crises versus transition perspectives. The nature of the midlife crisis, if it occurs, is probably influenced by the social context.

4. At various times in middle-age individuals are involved both with responsibilities for their adolescent or young-adult children and their aging parents. These three generations are usually in close touch with one another in our society—giving aid and exerting influence. Middle-

age parents' own psychological well-being is related to their assessment of how well their adult children "turned out." Caring for aging parents has become a normative part of middle age. Relatively few elderly are in institutions; most are cared for by family members. The task most often falls to the daughters, who may experience considerable strain if they also have jobs and responsibilities to their own families.

5. The exceptionally large baby boomer generation (cohorts 1946 to 1964) is now in middle age. These cohorts have made a number of decisions regarding personal and family lifestyles that differ sharply from those of their parents and that will significantly influence their experience of middle and later adulthood. They had a smaller number of children and females in these cohorts were more likely to be in the workforce. There are wide individual differences among boomers in rates of marriage, educational attainment, and income—as a result, the boomers cannot be seen as a homogeneous set of birth cohorts.

SUGGESTED READINGS

Avis, N. E. (1999). Women's health in midlife. In S. L. Willis and J. E. Reid (Eds.), *Aging in the middle* (pp. 105–147). San Diego, CA: Academic Press. Thorough discussion of the process of menopause with consideration of both biological and sociopsychological factors.

AARP. (1998). *Boomers approaching midlife: How secure a future?* Washington, DC: AARP Public Policy Institute. Through a series of graphs and figures, issues related to the financial well-being of baby boomers, their attitudes toward work and retirement, social security, and policy implications are considered.

Generations (Spring, 1998). The Baby Boom at Midlife and Beyond. This special issue of *Generations* is dedicated to issues of midlife as it applies to the baby boom cohorts. There are articles on demographics, policy implications, careers, political beliefs, families, health, menopause, and intragenerational equity.

Lachman, M. E., and James, J. B. (Eds), (1997). *Multiple paths of midlife development.* Chicago, IL: University of Chicago Press. An edited volume of research on midlife topics including: changes in self, relations with others, health and stress, and the world of work.

Kalish, R. A. (Ed.) (1989), *Midlife loss: Coping strategies.* Newbury Park, CA: Sage. Midlife is a time of change and challenge. Chapters on changes in midlife, such as loss of one's parents, launching of children, and job turnover.

Ryff, C. D., and Seltzer, M. M. (Eds.), (1996). *The parental experience in midlife.* Chicago, IL: University of Chicago Press. Topics in the edited volume include demographic and economic aspects of midlife parenting, historical and social changes and the parental experience, adolescent transition and their parents, parents and children as adults, and parent-child relations in midlife.

Willis, S. L., and Reid, J. E. (Eds.), (1999). *Life in the middle: Psychological and social development in middle age.* San Diego, CA: Academic Press. An edited volume on midlife issues from a psychological perspective, including theories of midlife, health, work, well being, and identity.

CHAPTER 4

Late Life

Reintegration or Despair

We now come to the last stage of adult life, old age, that part of life when many leave the world of work, assume the status of being a "senior citizen," turn toward coming to grips with the meaning of one's life, and eventually prepare for the end of their physical existence. In the past, old age was a very small portion of the human condition, reached by only a few, but now most of us can expect to reach the advanced years. In fact, for a not-insignificant number of persons, old age may encompass as much as a third of the life span; a fact that the French recognize by calling old age *le troisième age,* "the third age."

Any discussion of old age must immediately stress the distinction between normal, pathological, and optimal aging. The frequency of disease obviously increases with advancing age, but physical and mental decline are not necessarily directly associated with normal aging. Thus, many older individuals are well able to compensate for the minor dysfunctions that accompany the normal aging process. In later chapters, we will describe the facts of normal aging and those physical and mental pathologies that interfere with normal aging. In this chapter, we emphasize the possibility of optimal aging and deal with those aspects of old age that can interfere with or enhance optimal aging. To do so, we call attention to the fact that the aged are not a homogeneous population and distinguish among several stages of old age. We then discuss the problems of diminishing independence and the related fears of dependency that haunt most people as they reach old age. We next examine creativity in adulthood to show that many positive and rewarding opportunities remain until the end of life. Finally, we discuss briefly some of the factors that make for optimal aging.

"Old age" covers 30 to 40 years of the life span; the differences between the "young-old" and the "old-old" can be considerable.

THE YOUNG-OLD, THE OLD-OLD, AND THE VERY-OLD

Old age is often viewed by many as a single stage of life, and all persons defined as "old" are therefore seen with the same mixture of awe and pity. In any life stage, of course, people differ, often radically. But nowhere else in the life span does a single stage provide so inadequate a fit for all those in it as is true in the case of old age. "People over 65" can be divided into at least three stages, the young-old (65 to about 75), the old-old (75 to about 85), and the very-old or "oldest-old" (those aged over 85; Suzman and Riley, 1985).

Comparing someone who is 95 to someone who is 65 is not unlike comparing people 30 years different in age at other points in the life span: a 5-year-old to a 35-year-old, or a 20-year-old to a 50-year-old. Indeed, the physical and mental changes in the 30 years prior to the end of life are, in most respects, far greater than changes over a similar time span at other ages. The probability of physical disease, for example, is much greater for someone over 85 than for someone between 65 and 80. (Bould, Smith, and Longino, 1997). On many aspects of mental and physical performance, the young-old resemble the middle-aged far more than they do the old-old. For bright and well-educated people who continue to work or who maintain fulfilling retirement roles, the seventies can be a rewarding and active period of life. A fulfilling life during this period will become even more likely as our age-differentiated society gives way to a more age-integrated one (Gergen and Gergen, 2000; Riley and Riley, 1994).

The 30,000 or so centenarians, on the other hand, are a very different breed. They are the remnants of an earlier generation who differ from the young-old in virtually all their demographic and personal characteristics. Nevertheless, even the very-old represent a culturally diverse population (Homma, Shimonaka, and Nakazato, 1992; Johnson, 1994b; Poon et al., 1992). It should be noted further that the majority of the oldest-old are women. Some writers consider being old and female as representing "double jeopardy" due to lower income and higher risk of disability than older men. Others suggest to the contrary that premature death is a "man's problem" and that the survival of women should be celebrated (Bould and Longino, 1997).

Erik Erikson (1979, 1982) defined old age as a stage of life during which one must try to balance the search for ego integrity with a sense of despair. Resolution of this conflict may result in the emergence of wisdom, the human virtue frequently associated with old age (see Chapter 12 for empirical research on wisdom). Erikson chose to emphasize those tasks of old age that involve a review of one's life, making sense of it, tying together all the loose ends, integrating its elements. He views despair as a necessary component in this process, for a life's review is bound to turn up ample evidence of human failings; someone who could not remember a single failing would not be called wise but neurotic. The negative emotions associated with this stage, which is the last of Erikson's life crises, are in part a result of the limitations of a person's physical and psychological energy (Butler, Lewis, and Sunderland, 1991; for another view also see Schaie and Willis 1999, and Chapter 12, this volume).

The process of reminiscence and autobiographical writing that may be part of this life review has been found to be particularly useful for well-educated persons in resolving their concerns about old age (Birren, 1993; Kenyon, Ruth, and Mader, 1999). Vivid accounts of this process have been given to us by eminent psychologists reflecting on their own aging, with little difference in emphasis among writers who were active almost sixty years apart (Hall 1922; Skinner, 1983).

Besides being disappointed with one's own failures and those of others, one must also deal with the loneliness that results from the death of people to whom one felt close. But even the despair can be accepted, in an active balance with integrity, which is Erikson's definition of wisdom (Erikson, 1979; Erikson, Erikson, and Kivnick, 1986). This kind of loneliness is particularly likely in the very old. A cross-cultural study of loneliness in centenarians showed that personality characteristics such as apprehension and tension, low social support, and low physical health predicted loneliness in an American sample, while cognitive problems and low social support predicted loneliness in a Swedish sample (Martin, Hagberg, and Poon, 1997).

Many studies have been conducted of psychological well-being in older adults (e.g., Kasper, 1988; Ryff and Essex, 1992; Smith, Fleeson, Geiselmann, Settersten, and Kunzmannn, 1999). Older persons' perceptions of how the important dimensions of well-being change from middle age into old age have also been studied. In a study of 171 middle-aged and older men and women, Ryff (1989) asked her subjects to define well-being. Interestingly, across age and sex, responses had an other-directed orientation. These persons conceived well-being to be related to being a caring, compassionate person and having good relationships with others. However, as criteria of successful aging, middle-aged persons stressed self-confidence, self-acceptance, and self-knowledge, while older persons emphasized acceptance of change, a sense of humor, and enjoying life. Further studies of well-being suggest that this dimension is important in inducing generativity at all adult levels (Keyes and Ryff, 1998).

Psychological well-being may also be related to one's developmental expectations for the self and how one compares oneself to most other people. Most older people seem to have favorable expectations for themselves regarding their old age as compared to others (Heckhausen and Krueger, 1993). While older people, as expected, express less positive attitudes about their body than do young adults (Franzoi and Koehler, 1998), they also believe other problems of aging to be less serious than is anticipated by younger individuals, perhaps expressing a self-protection tendency (Heckhausen and Brim, 1997). It should also be noted that the experience of life crises can actually lead to renewed personal growth regardless of one's age (Schaefer and Moos, 1998).

There are six major developmental tasks that must be faced in late life, one way or another, that have been formulated by one of the early pioneers of social gerontology, Robert Havighurst (1972; Table 4-1). A major theme running through Havighurst's list is disengagement, the voluntary or involuntary lessening of active participation in society. Retirement is seen as part of disengagement; decreasing strength and health make activities more difficult; and the death of a spouse removes one's companion in previous activities and drains remaining emotional resources. Disengagement from the social roles of middle age—the role of worker, for example—is compensated for to some extent by "adopting" new activities and "adapting" old ones. Retired people often take up a new hobby or, as part of their explicit association with those sharing their new life status, join a political action, social, or recreational group. They may expand their home-and-family role (taking the grandchildren on excursions, planting a garden) or develop their role in community organizations (in a church, a club, the neighborhood). Finally, old people must often alter their living arrangements to satisfy their changing needs (easy access to shopping, health care, and other activities) and to avoid becoming a burden to their adult children.

TABLE 4-1   Havighurst's Developmental Tasks of Late Life

1. Adjusting to decreasing physical strength and health
2. Adjusting to retirement and reduced income
3. Adjusting to death of a spouse
4. Establishing an explicit association with one's age group
5. Adopting and adapting societal roles in a flexible way
6. Establishing satisfactory physical living arrangements

These general issues faced by people as they grow old, however, do not distinguish well between the young-old, the old-old, and the very-old. Clearly there are differences, even in the degree to which the tasks in Table 4-1 are relevant to various subgroups of older persons. Past the age of 80, physical decline usually becomes much more evident and may progress rapidly, whereas most people between 65 and 75 remain in quite good health and tend to recover as rapidly from acute illness as do the middle-aged. Adjusting to a reduced income following retirement is a "sudden" task precipitated by the event of retirement; by old-old age, financial adjustments have typically been made. As people reach advanced old age, they may have to rely more and more on support from children and institutions.

Financial problems may once again become quite acute for the very-old, because the financial resources planned for in retirement may have been "outlived." If the very-old person has a fixed income, inflation may well have eroded what may once have been a more-than-adequate income base (Schultz, 1995). People in their nineties may even lose the support of their children because the children have died before them, have experienced declines in their income, or have become too frail themselves to support their parents. Thus, the problem of dependency becomes increasingly serious as one grows older (cf. Horgas, Wahl, and Baltes, 1995). Conspicuous in its absence from Havighurst's list also is the task of facing one's own death (discussed in more detail in Chapter 15), which becomes an increasingly more preeminent concern the longer one lives.

In this chapter, we explore in some detail the concept of *dependency*—the fear of it, and the reality of it. Many old people are afraid, to some extent realistically, that they will become financially dependent on their adult children. They also fear becoming physically dependent, needing help getting around, for example, because of severe arthritis or a broken hip. They fear becoming senile due to brain disease, which might make them dependent on others in all facets of their lives and might even make them dependent in such embarrassing matters as bowel control. Then we turn to a brighter prospect, the creative accomplishments of older adults, many of which may lean heavily on the wisdom born of years of experience.

DEPENDENCY

Virtually every family maintains a reciprocal attitude that permits, even encourages, family members to depend on kin for financial, physical, and emotional support (see Chapter 6). Thus, old age does not bring something new in the sense of dependencies that did not exist before, but there is a change in the direction and nature of the dependencies. Old age upsets the curious but fragile balance between dependence and independence that exists for most of our adult lives (Baltes M. M. and Silverberg, 1994; Baltes M. M. and Wahl, 1987).

The beginning of life is characterized by an almost total dependence on others for survival. We do not begrudge young children their incapacities; we view child care as a natural responsibility of the parents. As children grow, the contribution that they can make to their own welfare increases. In adolescence, the balance of dependency and independence becomes a major source of conflict between parent and child. In marriage, the degree of independence of the two spouses might remain controversial. Another issue in adult life is the relative degree of dependence on and independence from one's employer (consider the "company town," for example, in which employees were paid in company "script" and therefore had to buy from the company-run store). The obligations to one's government and the freedom one should have from its dictates are traditional topics in history and political science.

The balance of autonomy and independence shifts as old age approaches. Older people need to establish a balance between the security provided by a supportive environment and the autonomy that a stimulating environment can foster. In old age, people typically retire from the world of work and face the increasing possibility of disease. To some extent, they must rely on their adult children to provide financial help, emotional support, and physical aid, a reversal in the continuous trend toward increasing independence that they have experienced since birth. Sometimes it may seem as if old people are becoming children again.

The dependencies that old people see developing are not typical "adult dependencies," those that grow from, say, a mutual recognition of the benefits of a division of labor or a mature recognition of everyone's need for emotional support. Instead, they may be seen as "childish dependencies," those that threaten the individual's self-reliance, personal autonomy, and self-esteem (Herzog and Markus, 1999). Old people fear these dependencies, and they struggle against them. Structured dependency is also created through programs of social services provided especially for frail older persons. Although these services are usually designed to maintain autonomy and independent living, they can actually have the opposite effect if the older person's autonomy is extinguished through excessive dependence upon the service delivery system (Baltes M. M. and Silverberg, 1994; Guillemard, 1992).

Financial Dependency

The greatest fears of many old people concern events that actually are very unlikely to occur. These fears, nevertheless, cannot be called unrealistic, because the effects of such low probability events, if they should indeed occur, could be quite devastating (Cutler, Gregg, and Lawton, 1992).

Old people, in a sense, are like persons who live next to a nuclear plant; chances are nothing will happen, but if something goes wrong, it's a disaster. Thus, old people fear crime (and they are indeed prone to certain "highly visible" crimes such as purse snatching), although across the range of criminal activities, they are the least victimized of any age group. They fear senility, although brain disease is not exceedingly common, even in the very-old. They are afraid that something will happen to wipe out their savings, even though the majority of older people live in reasonable financial security. But, this was not always the case. Medicare and

Medicaid have mitigated the economic impact of disease on older persons. The rising cost of health care, however, has increasingly led to political decisions that in the future may require the old once again either to contribute a far greater share of the cost of their health care or to forego quality care.

Over the past decade, however, financial difficulties have been cited as a major problem of old age by only a minority of older persons. For example, a study by Atchley (1993) suggested that only 10 percent of the men and 20 percent of the women in a community-based sample thought that their incomes were inadequate. This optimistic assessment must be interpreted with caution, however, because it has been found that a person's satisfaction with his or her income may be only indirectly related to the actual income. What seems to be most important is whether people feel that they are well off relative to the people they compare themselves to and relative to their own past experience.

Economic statistics provide some support for this favorable self-appraisal. At the same time, however, these statistics reveal that older persons are still less affluent than the average of the population as a whole. In 1998, the median income of families in the United States headed by people 65 or older was $21,729; for all families, the median was $38,885 (US Bureau of the Census, 1999). But there was tremendous variability by family status. Thus, the median income for married couples ($24,814) was more than double that of non-married women ($10,613). It was even less for black elderly ($9,467) or those of Hispanic origin ($8,943). And the income of all household units over age 85 was less than half then that for those in the 70 to 74 years age group (Smith, 1997). The very-old also typically have far fewer assets than do the young-old (Radner, 1993), and the poverty rate was highest for centenarians (Goetting, Martin, Poon, and Johnson, 1996).

People's expenditure patterns shift after retirement, so that older persons' income may be more adequate than it would seem at first glance (Nieswiadomy and Rubin, 1995). For example, there is a decline in expenses related to employment, such as transportation and meals away from home, as well as tools, and union or professional membership dues. In addition, the children have left home, so the average household consists of two or three people rather than the average of four persons for the population as a whole. On the other hand, the physical limitations of many older people may force them to pay for services that they could have performed themselves when they were younger. Few old-old or very-old people can wash windows, do yard work and heavy cleaning, or paint their own houses.

Table 4-2 shows three typical budgets developed by the U.S. Bureau of Labor Statistics for an urban retired couple in 1981 and originally projected by Atchley to1987 levels. Unfortunately, more recent data are not available, because the government stopped publishing these data due to budget cutbacks. We have therefore adjusted these figures by considering changes in the consumer price index. (U.S. Bureau of the Census, 1999) to what these figures would have been in 1998. The low budget is above the poverty line, but it would provide only for the most basic necessities. The moderate and higher budgets would be typical of lower-middle and middle-middle class couples, respectively.

TABLE 4-2   Annual Budget for a Retired Couple, for Three Levels of Living: Urban United States, 1998

	Budget Category Low	*Budget Moderate*	*Budget Higher*
Budget			
Food	$3,882	$5,137	$6,476
Housing	4,228	6,034	9,438
Transportation	984	1,908	3,485
Clothing	433	727	1,109
Personal items	351	516	753
Medical care	1,930	1,939	1,953
Entertainment and recreation	490	814	1,603
Other	553	1,094	1,987
Total	$12,851	$18,169	$26,804

Source: Estimates by Atchley (1994, p. 233) based on U.S. Department of Labor (1982). Amounts updated by authors using 1998 Consumer Price Index (CPI) and U.S. Bureau of the Census (1999).

In 1997, 10.5 percent of older persons had incomes below the official poverty level. Although this compared favorably with the total population poverty rate of 13.3 percent, it should be noted that many more older persons were barely above the poverty line. Thus, while 22.5 percent of the total population had incomes that were below one-and-a-half times the poverty definition, 23.4 percent of older persons fell into this category. And of those over 75, 12.2 percent fell under the poverty level, while a shocking 28.9 percent were below the one-and-one-half times poverty level threshold (US Bureau of the Census, 1998b).

About 92 percent of all older Americans received some income in the form of a Social Security pension (Gratton, 1993; U.S. Bureau of the Census, 1998a). In 1982, on average, Social Security replaced 66 percent of the earnings in the last year of employment for couples, compared to only 44 percent of the earnings of unmarried persons. (This is because Social Security taxes also provide benefits for spouses.) In the past 20 years, these rates have gone up about 60 percent. The ever-increasing Social Security taxes, however, have gone mostly to reduce poverty; they have not provided lavish pensions (Atchley, 2000; Pifer, 1993). In fact, the reason that some retired people do reasonably well is not because of Social Security, but because of the gradual development of private and public pension systems, some people continuing to work, and income from private investments (Ranson, Sutch, and Williamson, 1993). Of the total income of persons over 65, 15 percent comes from private or public pensions, 31 percent from earnings from employment or self-employment, and 15 percent represents income from property rents, dividends, and interest (Schultz, 1995; Social Security Administration, 1998).

The data suggest that although most older couples have incomes large enough to support themselves comfortably, most unmarried older people have financial troubles. In general, financial problems in old age tend to occur most often in certain subgroups, particularly minority men and some women. In 1992, for example, 14 percent of the American older population fell below the poverty line, but the figure for whites was only 12 percent, while it was 35 percent for blacks. Only 6 percent of the families headed by white males were below the poverty line, compared with as many as 43 percent of the families headed by black females (Social Security Administration, 1994). Thus, the people who suffer discrimination during the adult years before age 65 are also most likely to suffer from the income deficits common in the later years of life.

We may conclude then that although most old people are not exactly affluent, neither are most of them living in poverty, and a substantial proportion experience a reasonably acceptable level of comfort. What most old people need in the economic sphere, then, is not so much increased everyday financial support, but rather protection from the devastating effects of huge medical bills, runaway inflation, and similar catastrophes.

Physical and Emotional Dependency

As with financial dependency, physical dependency is a fear not typically realized to any significant degree by the great majority of older persons. Only 5.4 percent of the people over 65 are in institutions because of incapacitating physical or mental illness. Figures on institutionalization differ markedly, however, between early and late old age. As is to be expected, less than 2 percent of the young-old are institutionalized, a proportion not very different from that for the younger population. But of the old-old, those between 75 and 84 years of age, about 7 percent are in institutions, and this proportion grows to 22 percent for the very-old, those over 85 years of age (U.S. Bureau of the Census, 1983, 1992a). Relatively few older people report their health to be poor. Blacks perceive their health as poorer than whites, although they are no more disabled functionally, and have significantly better morale (Gibson and Jackson, 1992; Johnson, 1994a).

Statistics such as these translate into lives in which physical dependency is severe only in relatively few cases. Most older people must depend on others only slightly more than they did when they were younger. They might need a ride at night, help moving furniture, or confirmation of their reading of a blurry street sign. When help is needed, family members are the most likely source. At present, in the United States, social agencies provide only a small percentage of all in-home care for older persons (Hing, 1994). Formal home care systems are much more prevalent in Europe and particularly in the Scandinavian countries, permitting a much larger number of even frail elderly people to continue life in their accustomed environment (for a description of the Swedish system of home care, see Sundström and Thorslund, 1994).

Many infirmities that might make old people more dependent can be handled with compensatory devices (such as eyeglasses) or compensatory techniques (such as paying professional furniture movers). A whole new discipline of gerotechnology is beginning to address the human factors issues that are involved in the effective use of modern technology to provide environmental support and rehabilitation for the physical infirm elderly (Liebig and Sheets, 1998; Schaie and Willis, 2000b; Tesch-Römer and Wahl, 1998).

Physical changes in functioning from the seventies to the eighties, for most elderly, are less severe than might be expected. Little or no decline in social and economic functions and only moderate decline in mental, physical, and activities-of-daily-living functions are observed over this decade. However, impairment in one type of function in early old age predicts greater declines in other functions as people moved into advanced old age. Those at greatest risk of decline in old age are the uneducated, the poor, and those living alone (also cf. Kasper, 1988; Schaie, 1989b).

Although older people need to feel self-reliant both financially and physically, they do not necessarily like to be alone. They are increasingly likely to be alone, however. This fact is reflected in the changes in housing arrangements that occur in old age (Figure 4-1). Between the ages of 45 and 64, over 80 percent of the men and 65 percent of the women live with their spouses. During the young-old stage, the figure for men doesn't change much, but the proportion of women living with their spouses drops to 61 percent. Beyond age 75, about 68 percent of the men still have spouses living, compared to only 35 percent of the women, and wives are the primary caregivers for physically dependent men (Lugaila, 1998;

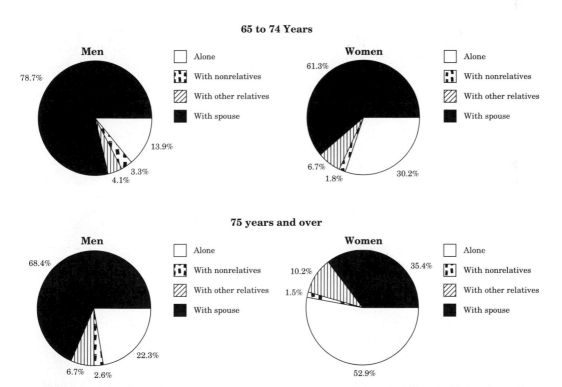

Figure 4-1   Living Arrangements of Noninstitutionalized Persons by Age and Sex in the United States, 1998. *Source:* Lugaila, T. A. (1998). Marital staus and living arrangements: March, 1998. Current Population Reports, P–2, No. 51. Washington, D.C.: U.S. Census Bureau..

Sodei, 1993). Older people of Chinese or Japanese descent who are living in the United States are more likely than their white counterparts to live with their children, suggesting that preferred living arrangements are particularly resistant to acculturation and modernization (Kamo and Zhou, 1994). However, other investigators have presented data suggesting that differential living arrangement for minority elderly may be accounted for by different patterns of marital status and life expectancy (Himes, Hogan, and Eggebeen, 1996).

There is a wide variation in co-residence between generations across different countries. For example, China and Japan still have very high rates compared to the United States and western Europe (cf. Ikels, 1997). But what is perhaps most noteworthy is the fact that there has been an almost worldwide decline over the past 40 years in the proportion of older persons living with their children (Sundström, 1994; see Figure 4-2). This decline has been sharpest in Finland, Poland, and Spain, but it is found in virtually all countries accompanying the move from largely rural to urban environments, which make co-residence more difficult (Gille, 1992). In addition, it has been frequently observed that older adults are more likely to remain in rural environments even when their adult children move to the cities (Norris-Baker and Scheidt, 1994). Acceptance of parental co-residence is also

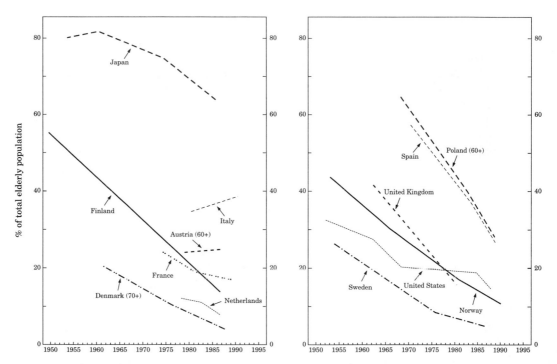

Figure 4-2 Proportion of Elderly People Living With Their Children, 1950–1990. *Source:* Sundström, G. (1994). Care by families: An overview of trends. Social Policy Studies, No. 14, 15–55. Paris, France: OECD.

affected by early childhood experiences, with parental co-residence being more prevalent among men and women raised by single mothers and women growing up in a traditional extended household (Szinovacz, 1997).

Old people, of course, need love, affection, and social interaction just as others do at any age. For many older persons, a marriage may have lasted for 40 years or longer. Men in particular express a great deal of marital satisfaction if their marriages have survived this long (Field and Weishaus, 1992). When a spouse dies, however, it may be increasingly difficult to find substitute ways to meet the needs formerly fulfilled by the close marital relationship. People are typically retired from work, and for one reason or another they often reduce their involvement in community organizations. Their parents are dead, and often brothers, sisters, and friends may also be dead or ailing.

The emotional response to this growing isolation is *loneliness*, and next to physical dependency it is one of the greatest fears that people associate with old age. Loneliness is often greatest following the death of a spouse, but it may also be a result of contextual factors such as the general loneliness of urban existence. It is not surprising that a survey of small-town widows found that only 25 percent considered themselves to be lonely a lot (Kunkel, 1979). Paradoxically, the low level of formal services available in rural areas and small towns may actually lead to greater interaction with neighbors and relatives, who in these circumstances become the primary providers of supportive services (Blieszner et al., 1987). But loneliness is not the same as being alone. It is a psychological feeling associated with being alone, that can either be debilitating or can actually be a strength for people with strong inner resources (Payne and McFadden, 1994).

Loneliness is a dependency issue because, with increasing age, the people upon whom one depends for emotional sustenance are increasingly the members of one's family. In fact, a Dutch study found that the loneliness commonly associated with being old and without a partner seems to be associated with the absence of friendship support rather than with the absence of a marital partner (Dykstra, 1995). But as persons grow older their frequency of personal interactions decrease with friends but increase with family members (Van Tilburg, 1998). Old people like to talk, to discuss current politics, to apply their past experience to current problems. To whom can they talk? As they grow older, they are increasingly limited to their adult children. From the old person's point of view, this is just one more "burden" that their existence puts on their beloved offspring. In their efforts to avoid being a nuisance, they may inadvertently choose loneliness.

Women live longer than men and because husbands tend to be older than their wives, older men may often become dependent on their wives, turning them into part-time (or full-time) nurses. With the increasing mobility of our population and the higher incidence of childlessness, the care of frail older persons also often falls upon younger siblings, typically sisters (Ikels, 1988). This trend greatly reduces the freedom of many older women to continue participating in rewarding activities in the community. Not surprisingly, the life satisfaction expressed by older couples is therefore strongly correlated with health. Interestingly, men seem to be affected more adversely by their wives' poor health than wives are by their husbands' (Atchley and Miller, 1983). This may be because women expect their husbands to become more dependent on them in old age, while men expect just the opposite.

The inevitable physical and emotional dependencies of late life have been alleviated for many older citizens by the Older Americans Act of 1965 (Atchley, 1994, 2000). The act, among its other features, supports senior centers, which provide information, counseling, meals, stimulating field trips, and "plain old getting together" for talk and perhaps a game of cards. Nutrition sites provide good food in a group setting (as well as the transportation to and from the site); for those confined to their homes, there are "Meals on Wheels."

Other services (which may be funded by other local, state, and federal agencies, as well as the Older Americans Act) include visiting nurses, general transportation (for shopping and medical care, for example), legal assistance, day-care facilities for seniors, and a number of telephone or mail "reassurance" programs, which make certain that the individual living alone is all right (by a daily phone call, for example) as well as sending someone to check if there is any indication of trouble. The Older Americans Act also supports home repairs and expansion of supportive housing for the elderly (Liebig, 1996). However, many older persons and their families are quite unaware of the wide array of services for which they are eligible. Consequently, one of the major tasks of agencies serving this population may well be to train them to be more aggressive users of community services (Linsk, Hanrahan, and Pinkston, 1991).

In order to access community services, health care, and other amenities of life, it is also necessary to have access to adequate transportation. Because of the lack of frequent and convenient public transportation in the rural areas of the United States, older persons living in nonurban areas are heavily dependent on the use of personal automobiles. Hence, maintenance of driving abilities (and driving privileges) is a particularly important requirement for quality living. Because of declines in sensory processes and response speed (see Chapter 13) many older persons in their late 70s or 80s either give up driving voluntarily or lose their driving license. The resulting reduction in mobility leads to increased dependence on others. Current efforts to improve the skills of older drivers by training as well as by redesigning automobiles to meet the needs of older drivers promise to alleviate these problems in the future (Carr, Jackson, Madden, and Cohen, 1992; Schaie and Pietrucha, 2000; Yanik, 1994).

Some enterprising older persons have formed *communes* (a living arrangement in which a group of unrelated persons shares their resources) for older persons, helping each other with financial, physical, and loneliness problems (Butler, Lewis, and Sunderland, 1991). Less radical and more common are social clubs of various types. These clubs may be purely social, serving only as a vehicle for getting together, or they may have an additional purpose, such as travel, old movies, charitable activities, or finance. For some older people, however, dependency needs become great enough that more radical solutions are necessary. For some, this involves moving in with children. When this is not possible or desirable, the older person often ends up moving to some kind of assisted living setting. Such settings, in which older persons reside with nonrelatives, range from facilities providing minimum care to those providing maximum services. At one end of the continuum is housing in retirement communities that may provide no more than weekly housecleaning or meal programs. At the other end are long-term care settings that include skilled nursing facilities and hospitals for the chronically ill (Carp, 1994; Morse and Wisocki, 1991; Regnier, 1996).

Retirement Communities.~Some older people deal with their loneliness and the fear that they will become dependent on their children by moving into retirement housing. Others have seen their neighborhoods deteriorate and have moved in the anticipation that they will need more supportive environments as they become more frail (Silverstein and Zablotsky, 1996; Thompson and Krause, 1998). Not all people who move to such housing do so for these reasons. Some individuals simply want to leave the community to which they were tied by their jobs in order to move to some place they like better for their remaining years. Most of the residents of re-

Being able to get around by oneself is a key ingredient for self-reliance at any age.

tirement communities are reasonably well-off people who have decided that they would like to live in a community of people their own age. This age homogeneity facilitates social interactions and the development of new friendships, but it may also generate interpersonal conflict unless the community is well organized (Adams and Blieszner, 1998; Timko and Moos, 1991).

Full-service retirement communities provide a continuum of services, ranging from arrangements for independent living to semi-independent living to nursing homes that provide full-time care. They typically also offer an extensive array of services in such areas as preventive health care, recreation, transportation, and education. Most planned retirement communities are relatively expensive and draw mostly upon the more affluent (Somers and Spears, 1992). Therefore, it is likely that the affluent baby boomers will increasingly be found in such communities as they reach retirement age (Longino, 1998). However, working-class older persons are more likely to move to less expensive mobile home parks or publicly supported low-rent apartments for older adults that offer similar services (Golant, 1992).

Planned retirement communities often include an unobtrusive array of supportive design features that allow for gracious and dignified life styles for older people with differing levels of physical limitations. Such design features often include a barrier-free environment, single-level construction, and user-friendly apartments with physical assistance features (Fernie, 1994; Regnier, 1996; Thompson, 1994; Watzke and Smith, 1994). Well-marked and simple routes through the facility furthermore can reduce the spatial memory load that often reduces neighborhood use in complex environments (Simon, et al., 1992).

An interesting study by Longino (1981) compared the residents of three types of retirement communities: full-service communities, public housing for older persons, and unplanned retirement communities that have arisen in certain areas as a result of the migration of retired people to small communities. In the planned full-service communities, the residents tended to be older (average age 76), more affluent, and interested in obtaining such services as meals, housekeeping, and nursing. In public housing, the residents were predominantly older women (average age 78) who had previously lived in the same geographical area, but who sought the greater security and lower expense of subsidized housing. In the unplanned retirement communities, the residents were typically somewhat younger people (average age 68) whose primary objective was independence and enjoyment of the natural environment.

These findings support the notion that older people seek housing that satisfies some of their dependency needs. These needs can probably be met most effectively by the planned retirement community, which often provides a suitable program for the remainder of the residents' lives (Smyer, 1995). Unplanned retirement communities, on the other hand, may provide only an intermediate solution because the services they offer may be insufficient when dependency needs increase.

The migration pattern of retirees can be placed in a developmental perspective. Three kinds of moves seem to be prevalent. The first occurs shortly after per-

Keeping fit and having fun continues to be important in old age.

sons retire, sometimes to locations to which they have previously flocked for brief vacations chosen frequently to escape an inclement climate (the "nesting" of the snowbirds; Longino, Marshall, Mullins, and Tucker, 1991). This type of move is usually to an independent living situation. A second move often occurs when a moderate form of disability is experienced, often to be near their children, a life-time care facility, or even to return to the community where they have lived most of their lives. The final move occurs when a major chronic disability is experienced, typically to a nursing home setting (Litwak and Longino, 1987). Relocation to a new community does not always occur without a price. A study of relocated women showed that women with greater psychological resources were least impacted by their moves (Smider, Essex, and Ryff, 1996).

Interesting migration patterns in the United States have been shown for black retirees. Because of their strong initial southern settlement and their labor force out-migration patterns in the middle of this century, many physically able black retirees seem to return to their "roots" (Smith, Longino, and Leeds, 1992). This return may also account for the trend of black elders living in larger households (Hays, Fillenbaum, Gold, Shanley, and Blazer, 1995). On the other hand, there is a contrary stream of out-migrants from the South, typically consisting of those who are dependent on relatives living in other parts of the country (Longino and Smith, 1991; Silverstein and Angelelli, 1998).

A particularly interesting (and fairly recent) phenomenon is the return of older migrants to their original communities of residence from retirement communities in areas such as Florida. These return migrants have been found to be older and have greater dependencies than those who remain. Apparently, the amenities of life that prompted the earlier move become less important, as persons become frailer, than are the support systems available in the community in which they have been life-long residents (Longino, Jackson, Zimmerman, and Bradsher, 1991; Longino and Serow, 1992).

Nursing Homes. About half of those older persons who receive care in institutions are in nursing homes. In the United States, there are roughly 1.8 million people in more than 25,000 such homes (Sirocco, 1988; U.S. Bureau of the Census, 1992b). By the year 2010, this number is expected to double, given constant mortality figures and to triple if mortality declines at the same rate as has been the case in recent decades. Nursing homes tend to serve most heavily the old-old and very-old. Currently, three-fourths of their residents are over 75 years of age, and 35 percent are 85 or older. If mortality declines, forecasts for the year 2010 further suggest that at that time almost 87 percent of nursing home residents would be over 75 and as many as 52 percent would be 85 or older (National Center for Health Statistics, 1989).

In the past, nursing homes were operated primarily by governmental units and charitable organizations, but there has been a dramatic shift toward nursing home care becoming largely a for-profit industry. Currently, almost 80 percent of nursing homes have for-profit ownership, while only 4 percent are administered by government units, with the remaining 17 percent being operated by nonprofit groups (Sirocco, 1988). Increasing government regulations have had the effect of significantly improving the quality of nursing home care; however, larger facilities and those operated on a nonprofit basis seem to score higher on many quality indices (Lemke and Moos, 1986). Nevertheless, there is still a dearth of qualified personnel providing services in these homes. For example, while over 100,000 registered nurses are employed in nursing homes, this number translates to no more than 6 nurses for each 100 residents (Strahan, 1988), and the fact remains that the bulk of nursing home care is provided by lowly paid and basically untrained casual help.

In most cases, people move to nursing homes because they or their families recognize a need for a setting that can provide around-the-clock support, and care that can not be provided in the home. If the older person has a severe illness and is bedridden or requires frequent medications, the move is likely to be voluntary. But emotional problems and mental decline are often denied by older people and their families alike, so in some cases, people are placed in nursing homes only when a professional intervention establishes that a person has become a safety hazard to himself or herself or others (Capp, 1996; Jackson, Longino, Zimmerman, and Bradsher, 1991; Wolinsky, Stump, and Callahan, 1996).

Entering a nursing home does not mean that interactions with friends, children, and other relatives come to an end. On the contrary, a regular pattern of visits, letters, and phone calls is often established. Strong ties between relatives usually persist. Although contacts with friends and former neighbors are less frequent than contacts with relatives, they are often continued as well. The extent to which contacts are maintained with people outside the institution may be influenced by whether or not the old person is seen as likely to be discharged. If the stay in the institution is likely to be short, concerted efforts may be made to stay in frequent contact. This continuation of relationships offers several advantages, decreasing the adaptation necessary for both the old person and friends and relatives once the return is made to the community. Long-term residents, on the other hand, may be more inclined to get involved in the life of the institution to fill voids in social areas (Aizenberg and Treas, 1985; Baltes M. M. and Horgas, 1996).

The structural arrangement and management of the nursing home have a powerful influence on the residents' social lives. Interpersonal support and encouragement of self-direction may be directly related to the comforts provided by the facility and the availability of more than minimal staff resources (Timko and Moos, 1990). There is some evidence, for example, that as the size of the institution increases, the communication, satisfaction, and activity of the residents decline. Friendships are more likely to develop among people in facilities that have fewer than 50 residents. It has also been found that residents of facilities for fewer than 100 people are more likely to form "companion" relationships with nurses' aides than are residents of larger institutions. Perhaps smaller facilities resemble the home environment more closely and are therefore better able to meet residents' social needs.

Long-term care has become a major health-care industry as well as a form of humanitarian service. A great deal of thought has therefore been given to the planning of facilities that provide the most economical care while offering optimal services to residents. Most people who enter nursing homes do so because they are no longer completely capable of self-care, but interactions between staff members and patients often encourage unnecessary dependency and discourage independence (Baltes M. M. and Reisenzein, 1986; Wahl and Baltes, 1990). In some cases, this tendency results from the best of intentions, but more often the nursing staff does tasks for the residents because it is more efficient and cost-effective than allowing residents to struggle along on their own. Staff may also have negative attitudes toward older persons, to the extent that they may use "baby talk" in speaking to them and otherwise treat them like children (Caporael and Culbertson, 1986; Caporael, Lukaszewski, and Culbertson, 1983). Some residents may require physical restraints because of severe cognitive impairment, but studies have shown that use of restraints may speed cognitive decline even further (Burton L.C. et al., 1992; Evans et al., 1997). Other effective methods(including drugs and behavior therapy) are also available for the management of verbally agitated or disruptive residents (Burgio, Scillen, Hardin, Hsu, and Yancey, 1996; Cohen-Mansfield and Werner, 1997).

Studies of the social ecology of nursing homes have shown that reinforcing independence reduces dependence, which in turn reduces incidence of disease and death (Baltes M. M. and Horgas, 1996). Current laws regulating nursing homes in the United States in fact require that nursing homes are to permit maximum possible autonomy for their residents (Altman, Parmelee, and Smyer, 1992, Capp, 1996). But changes in nursing home policies are needed to reward staff for positive residents' outcomes and to prevent burnout of staff members (Timko and Rodin, 1985). However, the implementation of an extensive on-the-job training and job redesign program was shown to have little effect in improving performance because of rapid turnover of poorly paid workers and constraints on quality care imposed by supervisors (Smyer, Brannon, and Cohn, 1992).

Although many older persons report high levels of well-being, this is not necessarily true for those in nursing homes and particularly less true for women over 85 (Smith, Fleeson, Geiselmann, Settersten, and Kunzmann, 1999). If it is assumed that the well-being of nursing-home residents can be improved by allowing them more personal control of their lives, it would follow that they should be allowed to determine their daily routines (policy choice) as well as to participate in decisions that determine some aspects of the home's programs and policies. Indeed, higher levels of policy choice and resident control were found to be associated with more cohesive, independence-oriented social environments and with resident activity levels. Most women, in particular, reacted more favorably to the provision of choice over their daily activities as did the other more functionally able residents of both sexes.

ACCOMPLISHMENTS IN LATE LIFE

In some Eskimo societies, people live difficult lives in environments that barely provide sustenance for their small, isolated families. When people in these societies reach an age when they feel that they can no longer contribute to the family's welfare, they go off by themselves to freeze to death on the ice. In one family, a woman went to sit on the ice when her first grandchild was born. She reasoned that the family would have a better chance to survive if her "mouth-to-feed" was subtracted as the new "mouth-to-feed" was added (Ruesch, 1959). The parents, however, had never before seen an infant, as can happen in such an isolated existence. They thought their toothless, complaining newborn was defective, incapable of survival. They rushed to the grandmother, urging her to take the infant with her to the ice. The grandmother realized that she was not yet dispensable. She told the naive parents that she could grow teeth in the infant; that she could teach it to survive. Thus, the old woman returned to her family for a few more years of life and duty.

In other societies, it is not until quite late in life that positions of power and authority are attained. A social system that is ruled by the old is called a gerontocracy (Achenbaum, 1993). Such systems were found in ancient as well as modern times; they occur in different environments and in societies of different degrees of complexity, which subscribe to different political philosophies.

Gerontocrats acquire power in a variety of ways. In agricultural and pastoral societies, ownership and control of property are acquired through inheritance from senior members. Older people are therefore more powerful in family and village affairs than their juniors. In primitive societies, knowledge of technology and ceremonies and the formation of long-standing social bonds tend to enhance the power of the old (Missinne, 1980; Werner, 1981).

Although the industrialized countries, such as the United States, Canada, Western Europe, or Japan are far more complex than pastoral or primitive societies, elite families may still control power in ways that resemble those characteristic of clans in tribal societies (Fry, 1985). Senior family members usually control decisions about economic resources. They determine to which of the younger family members or others they are willing to yield power. Many members of the United States Congress and of legislative bodies in other democratic societies live to an advanced age, and perhaps it is not surprising that most parliamentary bodies have a seniority system that increases the power of older members. This system, again, is not at all unlike the power systems found in primitive societies (Weatherford, 1981).

It should be noted, however, that the existence of a gerontocracy does not necessarily ensure the well-being of older people in general. Government by the older politicians is not necessarily government that ensures the well-being of the old. Success and accomplishment in old age, in general, seem to be determined by four factors: degree of respect attained during earlier adulthood, knowledge, desire to participate, and control of property (Achenbaum, 1993; Fry, 1985).

Research on Creativity

Creativity has been likened to the characteristics and strategies that characterize successful investing. A successful investor who buys an out-of-favor stock may be seen as foolish, but is lauded when that action produces a financial killing. Similarly, a scientist or professional who produces work that is currently in vogue may be viewed as competent, but not as creative. It is the person who advances a new idea in science, who initially may be seen as foolish, but when others recognize the value of the idea, will then be considered as highly creative. The investment theory of productivity proposes that six resources represent the basics of creativity: intellectual ability, knowledge, intellectual style, personality characteristics, motivation, and environmental context. Creativity is rare because most people are not willing to invest in it and because it requires the confluence of so many resources to make it possible (Lubart and Sternberg, 1998: Sternberg and Lubart, 1991, 2001). While an investment theory of creativity is intuitively appealing, much work remains to put all the pieces together. But in the meantime, much can be learned from the historical study of successful scientists and professionals (Csikszenmihalyi, 1991).

The years of young adulthood and middle age are frequently observed to be those of the greatest creativity and productivity. Many people in centuries past never reached the age of 60 or 70. Hence, their greatest works had to be accomplished at an earlier age. Nowadays, people often retire during their 60s and put a deliberate end to striving for creative or productive goals. Illness, increasing in frequency with advancing age, but different from it, can slow and inhibit creative urges. Nevertheless, old age can be a time of significant accomplishments for many. Substantial numbers of people over 60 or 70, and even over 80, have made important contributions to art, science, education, and politics. What is the nature of these accomplishments in late life? Are they age related; that is, do they in some sense depend on the fact that the individual involved is old and wise? Or should they be viewed as accomplishments of creative people who have produced something of value despite their advancing years?

To explore the relationship between age and creativity, psychologists have examined the creative products of scientists, philosophers, artists, business people, politicians, chess players, and other people whose achievements can be said to be important and notable (Mumford and Gustafson, 1988; Simonton, 1990a, 1999). Major creative works—the one or two accomplishments for which a person is best known—tend to occur relatively early in life (Simonton, 1990b). There are, of course, impressive individual exceptions (Goethe completed *Faust* after the age of 80) and major achievements in certain fields, such as philosophy, often occur later than in other fields. But, as shown in Figure 4-3, most scientists produce the works for which they are best known in their thirties and early forties. Considering the years of training often necessary before a major scientific or artistic contribution is possible, these figures suggest that most major creative works come early indeed.

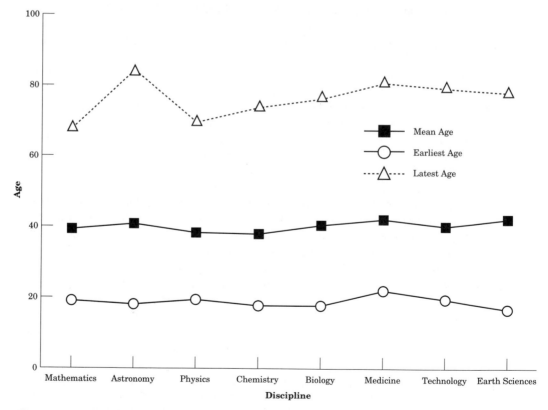

Figure 4-3 Age at Which Scientists Produced Their Best Work. *Source:* Adapted from Simonton D.K. (1991) Career landmarks in science: Individual differences and interdisciplinary, contrasts. *Development Psychology, 27,* 119–130.

But be sure not to ignore the vast amount of individual differences. As also shown in Figure 4.3, while the best work of a scientist can occur in the teens, it can also happen quite late in life (Simonton, 1991a). These findings have also been confirmed in studying lives of classical composers (Simonton, 1991b), and in eminent psychologists, who tend to produce their best work somewhat later (in their late 40s (Simonton, 1992). A number of personal characteristics have been identified for the most prolific scientific contributors. They include intuitive and competitive working styles, not having others set clear goals for their work. They were rated as having inconsistent personality styles, and not being motivated by economic incentives (Feist, 1993).

It is striking that virtually all of the work on creativity reviewed here is confined largely to male samples, even though there are many anecdotal accounts of creative women (see below). Perhaps the opportunity structures for women in the sciences and professions are still too recent to produce meaningful analyses of such work.

The great creative works of young adults are often different in style from those of older people (Simonton, 1988, Wyatt-Brown, 1992). Older adults are known for "wise and mature" works that integrate disparate themes and also for works that depict or elucidate the particular conflicts and problems of old age. Young adults, by contrast, produce works that critics are likely to laud in terms such as "innovative, refreshing, a new look." Young adults tend to play with ideas and come up with new approaches. David Hume contrived some highly original views in *A Treatise of Human Nature,* for example, published before he was 25. Mary Shelley took an even more original look at human nature in her classic novel of horror, *Frankenstein,* written when she was 21. Louis Braille, blind since the age of 3, took a more practical view of human nature and the needs of visually-handicapped persons to create an alphabet of raised dots at age 20.

Critics often use the term "freshness" to describe the works of young people such as Georges Bizet, whose Symphony in C Major was written at the age of 17. "It is a work that abounds in youthful vitality," one reviewer said (Lehman, 1953, p. 201). A fresh look at some ancient literature resulted in John Keats's *On First Looking into Chapman's Homer,* considered one of the best sonnets ever written, especially by a 20-year-old. A new look at the time dimension produced *The Time Machine,* by a 29-year-old author, H. G. Wells.

Willingness to experiment is another characteristic of young adults. Thus, at 28, Sigmund Freud tried a strange new drug called cocaine and was, in fact, largely responsible for its introduction to European society. Sir Humphrey Davy was only 20 when the "intoxicating effects of nitrous oxide when respired were discovered by him on April 9, 1799" (Lehman, 1953, p. 204). These drugs, now predominantly used for thrill-seeking purposes, had at the time important anesthetic uses for surgery and other medical procedures.

The most prominent developmental tasks faced by young adults are decisions about careers and families, but interestingly enough we find very few important works on these topics by young adults. Great discourses, scientific discoveries, and works of art on work and family life seem rather to be the province of older adults, who perhaps have the advantage of having lived through the various stages of processes that only begin, but are by no means completed, in young adulthood. What we do find in young adulthood is a lot of work on love and intimacy. Jane Austen's *Pride and Prejudice,* written when the author was 21, is a remarkably insightful portrayal of the manners and traditions that stand in the way of love. Emily Bronte's *Wuthering Heights,* written at 29, is a brilliant forerunner of the decidedly inferior "gothic romances" that line the bookshelves of our supermarkets today, depicting both the romance (intimacy) and the danger (uncertainty, dependence) that love holds for any young adult.

Creativity in Later Life

Although the major works of creative people tend to occur early in life, their total output is spread far more evenly across their life span. In a study of 738 persons who lived to age 79 or beyond, the 60s were the most productive years for four groups: historians, philosophers, botanists, and inventors (Dennis, 1966; also see Simonton, 1991a). In terms of more general categories, scholars (history, philosophy, literature) were more productive in their later years, including their seventies. Scientists were most productive in their forties, fifties, and sixties. Artists were most productive slightly earlier, in their thirties and forties.

In a highly sophisticated mathematical analysis of the lives of ten of the most famous composers, creative productivity was found to peak between the ages of 45 and 49 (Simonton, 1977, 1991b). Productivity was related to age in what was termed an "inverted-backward-J" curve instead of the "inverted-U" curve that the researcher hypothesized. This means that productivity rose to a peak and then fell, but the decline was considerably less than the initial ascent. This relationship held even when the results were controlled for the variable of physical illness. That is, illness, which becomes more frequent in the later years of life, does *not* fully explain the decrease in creative productivity in the later years (Horner, Rushton, and Vernon, 1986).

Some would argue that productivity in late life may be a function of our society providing opportunity structures that allow for continuation of productive work (Commonwealth Fund, 1993; Riley and Loscocco, 1994), rather than exerting a virtual prohibition of professional participation for older scientists, as is currently the case in many European settings (e.g., Straka, Fabian, and Will, 1990). Nevertheless, some productive older persons manage to create their own opportunity structures. An interesting study of American architects, for example, suggested that those architects who continued to be productive past age 65 were characterized by commitment and drive, overlearned skills, aesthetic sensitivity, ability to be a good salesperson, and ability to delegate responsibility (Dudek and Hall, 1991). Older scholars also express their generativity by facilitating the paths of their students and serving as mentors to the next generation of scientists (Birren, 1990; Simonton, 1998).

Another hypothesis to be considered is that major creative works appear to occur mostly in young adulthood simply because the longer one lives, the more

Pablo Picasso, one of the world's greatest artists, continued to create works of art into his eighties.

competition one has. The number of creative people in any discipline (e.g., art, literature, science) has been increasing at a fantastic rate (Simonton, 1977; 1990b). Consider a hypothetical author—"Anthony Owen Colby," we'll call him—whose work at age 20 is considered to be the best that the world of literature has ever experienced. By the time Colby is 30, two new 20-year-old geniuses have appeared on the scene; the three of them compete for the plaudits of critics. When Colby reaches 40, his "old" (30-year-old) competitors are still around, joined by four new 20-year-olds. At 50, we add eight new 20-year-olds to Colby's previous list of six. At 60, with sixteen new 20-year-olds, Colby is only one of 31 "great writers." He might be writing as well as before, but the competition is now fierce. Centuries later, looking back, we might decide his creativity failed in his later years because he wasn't discussed as much.

Although some creative endeavors require the enthusiasm and high energy levels of youth, there are other areas, such as philosophy and history, that require extensive experience. Contributions in these areas are therefore more likely to peak later, and little decrement in productivity will be seen in old age. This is even more true when experience results in leadership that enhances productivity in others (Simonton, 1988, 1990b). While fluid abilities and divergent thinking diminish with age (McCrae, Arenberg, and Costa, 1987; also see Chapter 12), some age-related increments have been found in dimensions of everyday experience (e.g., Cornelius and Caspi, 1987; Salthouse, 1999). Qualitative changes have also been observed in the work of authors in the direction of greater attention to spiritual issues, and evidence of a "swan song" phenomenon has been found in an analysis of the last works of 172 classical composers (Simonton, 1989). In Simonton's study, it was observed that these last compositions were brief but full of aesthetic significance and reflected a creative wisdom that might have been a function of some kind of "life review" conducted by the composer in proximity of expected death. Some have argued that the products of older persons might be of lesser importance than those of the young. While there is clear evidence of an overall decline in productive quantity, it has nevertheless been shown that the probability of impact of any particular contribution is equally great for the creations of older and younger persons (Over, 1989).

The productivity of creative old people is indeed amazing. In the retrospective studies of Wayne Dennis (1968), the subjects were eminent scholars, scientists, and artists who had lived at least 80 years. Their creative output was categorized into six decades of adult life, ranging from the twenties to the seventies. We are here concerned with the accomplishments of late life, when the subjects were 60 to 80 years old. If 100 percent of a person's works were evenly divided by decade, we would expect 16.7 percent per decade or a little over 33 percent for the two late-life decades combined. By actual count, we find 41 percent for the scholars (historians, philosophers, scholars of literature), 21 percent in their sixties and 20 percent in their seventies. The sixties was their most productive decade! Among scientists, 35 percent of their work was done in late life, 20 percent in their sixties, and 15 percent in their seventies. Famous inventors did well over half their work after 60 (53 percent). Among artists, 20 percent of their work was done in late life, 14 percent in their sixties and only 6 percent in their seventies. The poorest late-life performance was by dramatists, architects, and opera composers (10 to 15 percent after 60).

The first thing to note about these data is the remarkable number of significant achievements after the age of 60. Scholars and scientists seem scarcely to slow down, and artists are productive, though at a lesser rate. Some of the greatest works of art were done by people in the last years of their lives. Michelangelo, for example, finished painting *The Last Judgment,* one of the most famous pictures in the world, at age 66. At 70, he completed the dome of St. Peter's in Rome. Monet painted until age 85, a year before his death (Ravin and Kenyon, 1998). Goethe was 82 when he finished *Faust.* Wagner finished *Götterdämmerung* at 63. Verdi produced *Otello* at 74 and *Falstaff* at 80. Cervantes wrote *Don Quixote* at 68 (Nelson, 1928).

Are the creative productions of old people in some respects dependent on their age? Certainly, there are instances in which the impediments of old age add little. One thinks of a deaf Beethoven composing symphonies, a blind Galileo at 74 working out the application of pendulum movement to the regulation of clockwork. But there are few works of late life that did not benefit in some way from the accumulated knowledge and wisdom of the creator. Late-life works typically have a maturity, a complexity, and an insight into the interrelationships of things that early works lack. It is difficult to define terms such as wisdom and maturity, although it is not difficult to recognize these traits in finished work (Adams-Price, 1998; Birren and Perlmutter, 1990).

Many scholarly and scientific works in late life represent an integration of the observations of a lifetime. Personal memoirs are the most individualistic of these integrations, although memoirs are often personalized histories of a field (e.g., medicine, law, and government). Historians in general produce a high percentage of their best works after the age of 60 (44 percent in Dennis's [1966] study), and many people in other disciplines produce insightful histories of their fields (education, mathematics, psychology).

In similar fashion, many of the great works of late life represent the individual's final attempt to make sense of the often conflicting "facts" in his or her field. The work may be a *magnum opus,* such as the 10-volume treatise on social psychology that Wilhelm Wundt (the father of modern psychology) finished at the age of 88. (Wundt followed this work with his memoirs, which he also completed at 88, shortly before he died, in 1920.) The work may be an important textbook, such as those of John Henry Comstock, who wrote *An Introduction to Entomology* at 71, and Asa Gray, who wrote *Elements of Botany* at 77. Integrative works such as these require wisdom and maturity; it is difficult to imagine their being done by young adults.

Many great works of late life have to do with old age. With intimate knowledge and a vested interest, old scholars and scientists often turn their creative energies to this topic. G. Stanley Hall, twice president of the American Psychological Association in the early 1900s, was one of the first psychologists to examine aging in his book *Senescence: The Last Half of Life* (Hall, 1922; also see Cole, 1993). Hall was 75 years old at the time. In medicine, the first book specifically on diseases of old age was written by a physician at age 75, and the first book on senility as a disease (as distinct from normal aging) was written by a physician at age 71 (Lehman, 1953). Numerous older inventors have turned their talents to the problems of old age. The most famous is perhaps Benjamin Franklin, who at age 78 invented bifocal lenses for eyeglasses because he himself could not see both near and far with lenses of a single focus.

The list goes on and on, and we have not even mentioned leadership positions, which old people could be fairly said to dominate. Among leadership positions that have been filled more than half the time by people over the age of 60 are the popes of the Roman Catholic Church, justices of the United States Supreme Court, speakers of the United States House of Representatives, presidents of France, prime ministers of Great Britain, presidents of major United States corporations, and top-ranking commanders of the United States Army and Navy (Achenbaum, 1993; Lehman, 1953). The world as we know it today has been shaped by such leaders as Charles de Gaulle of France, Winston Churchill of Great Britain, Konrad Adenauer of Germany, Mao Tse-tung and Deng Tsao-ping of China, and Ronald Reagan in the United States; all of whom held the reins of government when they were in their seventies or early eighties. George Meany was head of the powerful AFL-CIO labor organization into his eighties. There are many reasons why older people are generally found in positions of power in a society; among the better reasons are that they commonly display wisdom and maturity, they are not "rash" as younger people tend to be, and they know how to orchestrate the activities of large organizations.

Our discussion of creativity has focused largely on eminent scholars, scientists, artists, and leaders, but only to illustrate by their extreme creativity the kinds of things that are possible in the later years of life—indeed, are made possible by the experiences of many years of life. Mature wisdom, an ability to integrate information, an interest in the aging process, and a talent for leadership are often found in old people eminent only in a small circle of family and friends (Sasser-Coen, 1993). Fine, handcrafted furniture that distills the accumulated knowledge of an old carpenter; a family genealogy written by a retired schoolteacher; a political movement for government policies aiding old people—organized by an old woman such as Maggie Kuhn, head of the Gray Panthers—these too are fruits of old age. Some old people set out in totally new directions, such as Grandma Moses, who took up painting for the first time. But again this type of productivity may require continued good health, marital stability, and a supportive environment (Glass, Seeman, Herzog, Kahn, and Berkman, 1995).

Maintenance of productivity in old age in a changing society will require the willingness and ability to adopt new technologies. The universal introduction of computers, instant communication via e-mail, and access to wide ranges of information via the internet has created many opportunities for societal participation of the elderly. Fortunately, recent studies have shown that older persons are quite willing to become computer literate, although they tend to complain more than younger computer-users about problems of comfort, efficacy, and control over computers (Czaja and Sharit, 1998a, 1998b).

Some researchers argue that we would do well to differentiate between creative productivity, as represented by the leaders in science and the professions discussed earlier, and the creative ability that leads to mature thinking and wisdom, which makes it possible to integrate subjective experience and objective knowledge that can be applied to problems of everyday being and living (Kastenbaum, 1992; Labouvie-Vief, 1990; Sasser-Coen, 1993). This type of creative ability in the past has been represented most often in groups of able women who engaged in generative activities while assuming a primary role as a homemaker (Rodehaver, Emmons, and Powers, 1998; Vaillant and Vaillant, 1990). An alternative model of productivity in the elderly therefore needs to incorporate process benefits of regular and irregular work as well as the benefits accruing from activities that enhance the person's social network and sense of well-being (Jackson, 1996b).

A significant accomplishment of old age, one that may well be related to the resolution of conflict between integrity and despair, is the increase in altruism and humanitarian concerns during the last part of life (Schaie, 1996b). This may to some degree be a compensatory development. Social exchange theory suggests that people in social interactions attempt to increase rewards and minimize costs, thereby obtaining the most profitable outcomes possible. It may be that the majority of older people hold so little power and are sufficiently aware of the limits of

their existence that such motives are less influential. Indeed, a study of old peo
ple's motives in relocating found that they often felt a sense of relief and freedom
once they escaped from exchange-oriented work life (Kahana and Kahana, 1982).
At the same time, however, people still have a strong need to leave a psychological
legacy (Butler, Lewis, and Sunderland, 1991; Schaie and Willis, 2000a), and in
many cases they channel their energies into contributing to the welfare of others
for intrinsic reasons alone. Empirical data do show that humanitarian attitudes
among older persons increase (Schaie, 1996b; Schaie and Parham, 1976). By participating in volunteer and community efforts, the older person may also avoid the
emotional problems that result from dependency and helplessness. Helping others
may provide a sense that one's life is meaningful, leading to a sense of competence
and increased self-esteem (Okun, Barr, and Herzog, 1998).

Old age, properly considered, is a time of great potential. It is, in the words of
Goethe, a time when "knowledge of the world is much clearer. For I am as one who
had in youth many small pieces of copper and silver money, who constantly ex-
changing them for better, beholds now the property of his youth in pieces of pure
gold" (Nelson, 1928, p. 310).

OPTIMAL AGING

Why do some persons age gracefully, experiencing many rewarding retirement
years and maintain full intellectual competence, independence, and good health
almost until the end of their life, while other persons decline early and live out
their last years in misery and as burdens to their families? The reader will need to
explore our discussions of normal age changes in the following chapters to gain a
full understanding of the vast individual differences in aging processes that are implicated in answering this question, but we can preview here some of the factors
that lead to optimal aging.

It has been argued that optimal aging involves a general strategy of being selective in one's efforts and using alternative strategies and activities to compensate
for the losses that the aging processes bring with them. The theory of selection,
compensation, and optimization (SOC) discussed in Chapter 1 provides a useful
model describing the processes involved in successful aging (Baltes and Baltes,
1990; Baltes and Carstensen, 1996; Carstensen, 1992a; Heckhausen and Lang,
1996). An important reason why some older people do so much better than others
is the fact that there is substantial behavioral plasticity at all ages. Throughout life,
many people function below the limits of their "reserve" capacities. This may not
matter in young adulthood, but in old age it is those individuals who manage to
function closer to their limits and who are able to maximize the supportive qualities of their environment who are going to do much better and to appear more
competent than those who do not (Baltes and Kliegl, 1987; Baltes and Reichert,
1992).

Some have argued also that successful aging might be easier in more traditional societies that offer more respect for their elders. Empirical studies suggest
that in developing countries the role of the elder does not necessarily offer great

advantages. In all societies, satisfaction of basic economic and health needs are closely related to successful aging. Hence, a comparative perspective suggests that successful aging requires both reasonable maintenance of functionality and adequate societal supports (Ikels et al., 1995). Successfully aging individual are generally differentiated from those who age less well by having greater social contact, better health and vision, and fewer unfavorable life events. And the frequency of those aging successfully declines from the young-old to the oldest-old (Garfein and Herzog, 1995).

Successful aging obviously does not begin in the sixties. The foundations for a successful old age are laid by lifestyles that maintain a healthy body and a healthy mind through good habits of nutrition, exercise, and involvement in interesting activities that challenge the mind. Conversely, midlife life styles that lead to frailty in old age include heavy drinking, cigarette smoking, physical inactivity, depression, social isolation, and the prevalence of chronic disease (Strawbridge, Shema, Balfour, Higby, and Kaplan, 1998). The development of healthy lifestyles that lead to successful aging, of course, is influenced by education and the attitudes and encouragement of family and friends who value a healthful and productive life. Optimal aging is also encouraged in midlife by learning techniques for stress reduction, developing techniques for coping with change, and acquiring leisure skills that do not require substantial physical strength and endurance (see Schaie, 1984b, 1996b).

Another important strategy is the maintenance of a social support system and the substitution of new relationships for those lost by the death or departure of friends and relatives (Antonucci and Akiyama, 1996; Blieszner, 1995; Jackson, Antonucci, and Gibson, 1990; Lang and Carstensen, 1998). But there are significant gender differences in friendship as people age, with women more likely to retain previous friendship patterns, while in one study men were found to decline in the number of new friends, in their desire for close friendship, and in involvement in beyond-family activities (Field, 1999).

Successful aging also requires a positive self-concept which may be maintained by being able to evaluate one's performance in proper relation to the remaining levels of physical and mental capacity (Brim, 1988). Many older individuals influence their own aging in a positive manner, by not expecting to pursue all possible options, as was possible in their youth, but instead selecting priorities to make maximum use of their motivation and remaining strength, and the increased leisure time now available to them (Mannell and Dupuis, 1994). A positive self-concept at older ages, however, is often found to be mediated by high levels of formal educational attainment (Herzog, Franks, Markus, and Holmberg, 1998).

As the majority of our population can expect to reach old age, there have been significant changes in our society to accommodate this fact, which in turn have had significant impact on the lives and psychological development of individuals (Atchley, 1989b, 2000). As old age becomes an expected life stage, different social norms develop for this stage and people engage in new age-typical patterns, thus actually changing the way in which the aging process occurs. These new behaviors become commonplace, are reinforced by the media and other authorities, and become part and parcel of our institutions (e.g., the role of older persons as the new leisure class). Finally, the changed age norms and their expression in changed social structures alter many age-related behaviors, with further impact on our society (see Riley and Riley, 1994).

SUMMARY

1. Old age is often viewed as a single stage of life, but it can be divided into at least three substages: the vigorous young-old (65 to 75 or 80), the slowing old-old (75 or 80 to about 90), and the frail very-old or oldest-old (85 to 90 or over). The three groups differ in significant ways: The young-old remain active and in many ways behave more like the middle-aged, even though most have left the work of world. The old-old show increasing incidence of physical frailty, but many are still able to live a full life, using both environmental and personal supports. The very-old are frequently physically or mentally impaired and usually require intensive support systems, often within institutions.

2. In Erik Erikson's view, the basic developmental concern of late life is the issue of *integrity* versus *despair*. One of the chief impediments to personal integrity is the fear or reality of financial, physical, or emotional dependency. A great many old people, however, experience reasonable financial security and are in reasonably good health, with friends and family to combat loneliness. Senior centers and other government-sponsored programs have done much to alleviate the problems of dependency in late life. Some older people move to retirement communities or nursing homes. The type of retirement community sought is a reflection of dependency needs. Nursing homes are primarily housing for the old-old and very-old. Moving to a nursing home does not generally involve severing relationships with family and friends. Studies show that nursing-home staff members often encourage dependency among residents.

3. In healthy old people creativity can flourish to a degree not significantly reduced from the levels exhibited by younger adults. Although the majority of the most remarkable works of scientists and creative artists occur during the 30s and 40s there are wide individual differences, and productivity for many continues into advanced old age. The creative productions of older scholars, scientists, and artists benefit from their experience and wisdom. Often works created by older persons represent an intellectual integration of the observations of a lifetime, and many of these works have to do with old age itself. A society ruled by the old is called a gerontocracy. Government by the old is not necessarily government that benefits the old, however. Altruism and humanitarian concerns typically increase in old age.

4. Old age can be a time of great personal fulfillment and can provide

the opportunity to engage in the exploration of options not available earlier in life due to pressures of job and family. Successful aging consists of a process of selective optimization and compensation. This process involves maximizing interpersonal and environmental supports. Most successful older persons function much closer to the limits of their "reserve" capacity than is the case at younger ages.

SUGGESTED READINGS

Butler, R. N., and Kiikuni, K. (Eds.) (1993). *Who is responsible for my old age.* New York: Springer. Reviews the consequences for society of the fact that most individuals now survive into old age and discusses the tension between individual and societal responsibilities for the welfare of older persons.

Regnier, V. (1996). Designing housing that enhances cognitive competence in the elderly. In S. L. Willis, K. W. Schaie, and M. Hayward (Eds.), *Societal processes that affect decision making in older adults.* New York: Springer. A review of specialized housing for older persons, describing methods for assessing the quality of such settings and discussing the relationship between the characteristics of residents and the facilities that serve them.

Schultz, J. H. (1995). *The economics of aging* (6th ed.). New York: Van Nostrand Reinhold. Facts and fictions regarding the actual economic status of older persons, including a review of the adequacy of the money income of older persons and the status of major pension and welfare programs.

Simonton, D. K. (1998). Career paths and creative lives: A theoretical perspective on late life potential. In C. Adams-Price (Ed.), *Creativity and successful aging* (pp. 3–18). New York: Springer. Reviews recent theory, methodology, and substantive developments in the study of creativity in older adults.

5

Research Methodology in Adult Development and Aging

The psychology of adult development is a branch of scientific psychology and thus shares the methodological concerns of the parent field. Adult developmental psychology uses the same kinds of data, generated by the same procedures, as do other fields of psychology. The formal experiment, the correlational study, the use of survey methodology are as much in evidence here as elsewhere. As is true for other areas of psychology, researchers in this field often have trouble finding an adequate control group to which to compare their experimental group, they have problems generalizing their results beyond the particular individuals whom they happened to observe, and they worry about statistical distortions (Birren and Birren, 1990; Birren and Schroots, 1996). There also are additional concerns, not always faced in other branches of psychology, that relate directly to the fact that in the developmental sciences we not only describe static phenomenon, but most importantly are concerned with the measurement of change over time. Finally, there are special methodological problems in doing research with older subjects (Teresi and Holmes, 1994).

CROSS-SECTIONAL AND LONGITUDINAL STUDIES

A central problem, not shared with other researchers, begins with the basic distinction between an *age change* and an *age difference*. An age change occurs in an individual as he or she grows older: At 60, for example, an individual's reactions might not be quite as quick as they were at 25. An age difference is observed when one compares two people (or groups) of different ages. The person in our example at age 60 might have slower reactions than another person of age 25. We are often interested in age changes (what happens as people grow older), but have data only from research on age differences (where the performance of different age groups is compared). In that case we must be quite cautious in not assuming that age differences necessarily reflect age changes. As we shall see, sometimes they do, and sometimes they don't.

The distinction between age changes and differences corresponds to the data generated by two different experimental designs common in the study of development (see Figure 5-1). A *cross-sectional design* compares groups of different people varying in age at the same time. It allows us to record age differences. A *longitudinal design*, on the other hand, involves the observation of the same individuals at two or more different times; these kind of data represent age changes. To illustrate, two researchers might use the different designs to investigate income across the normal working life. One, using a cross-sectional design, compares the average

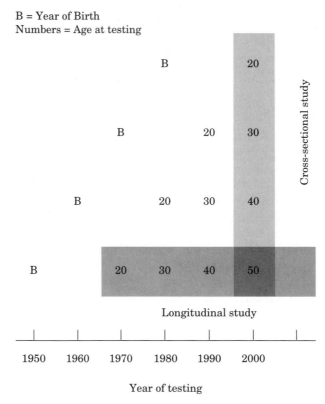

Figure 5-1 Cross-Sectional Studies Test Different Groups of Different Ages, All at the Same Time. Longitudinal Studies Test the Same Group at Different Ages, Requiring Several Tests at Different Times.

income of representative samples of 25-year-olds, 30-year-olds, 35-year-olds, and so forth, up to the age of 65. The second researcher follows one sample of people, checking on their income every five years, at age 25, 30, 35, and so forth.

One major difference in the two experimental designs is immediately apparent. The cross-sectional study can be completed in a single day, whereas the longitudinal study will take 40 years! It is not surprising therefore, that many more cross-sectional studies can be found than longitudinal studies.

Age and Cohort

The differences between cross-sectional and longitudinal designs can best be understood by considering the several dimensions involved. One, of course, is age, which is a variable in both designs. A second variable is *cohort,* which is usually defined as the people born in the same year (or range of years). If you were born in 1980, you are in the 1980 cohort; your parents probably belong to a 1950s or 1960s cohort. Cohort is similar to the concept of generation; it is used to distinguish people by time of birth (for formal distinctions between the concepts of cohort and generation, see Riley, 1992; Riley, Foner, and Riley, 1999).

Now let us consider the two designs in more detail. The subjects in a longitudinal design all belong to the same cohort, whereas the subjects in a cross-sectional design belong to several different cohorts, each representing a different age group. As a result, the age differences produced by a cross-sectional study could be interpreted as being due to age *or* they may be due to cohort differences. Imagine a cross-sectional study of liking Frank Sinatra's music. It would not be surprising to find that older people like Sinatra more than do younger people, but you might be unwilling to conclude that a liking for Frank Sinatra increases as one gets older. Most of the age difference, you would therefore assert in this case, is likely to be an effect of cohort, not of age. People who are old today were members of the "younger generation" who adored Sinatra when he was young. Today's cohorts will grow old and, 40 years from now, perhaps will listen with rapt attention to a gray-haired Jewel!

Cohort effects often become apparent by comparing results from cross-sectional and longitudinal studies. For example, the Census Bureau often publishes statistics on average income in various age groups. Graphs of these statistics usually look like Figure 5-2: showing an increase to middle age and then decline until retirement. These statistics are often interpreted as reflecting the normal course of an individual's earnings over the work life, but they are *cross-sectional* data on *age differences,* subject to misinterpretation. Longitudinal studies typically shows that individuals studied over their work lives almost always increase their earnings right up to the time of retirement (Schultz, 1995). The cross-sectional data mislead us because each new cohort made more money at every stage of life than did preceding cohorts. Thus, though men between 55 and 64 typically earn more than they ever did earlier in their lives, their earnings are less than those of men between 45 and 54 who started at higher salaries and received greater increases than the older men (U.S. Bureau of the Census, 1999).

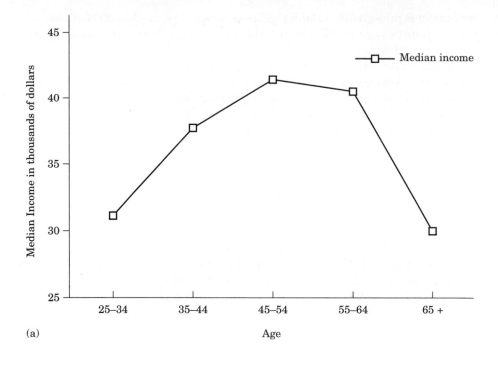

(a)

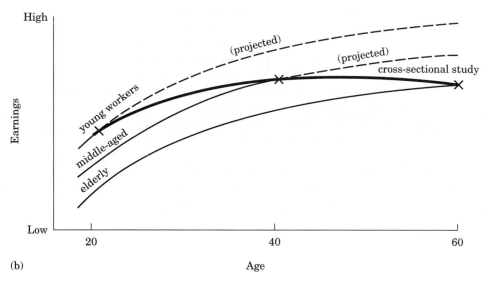

(b)

Figure 5-2   Age and Cohort Effects. (a) Median income of white males by age, 1998. (b) If each generation earns ever-increasing income, but also each generation makes more at each stage of the life span, a cross-sectional study can misleadingly make it appear that income drops toward the end of one's career.

Age and Time

Longitudinal studies observe members of the same cohort at two or more points in time. The data that they produce are *age changes*, and their interpretation is not clouded by possible differences between cohorts. However, longitudinal studies have their own difficulties, not the least of which is the large expense, in both time and money, necessary to mount a well-designed longitudinal investigation. Nor are longitudinal studies free from potential misinterpretation. The external validity (generalizability) of the findings is affected by the time of measurement (i.e., the period of years over which the study is conducted). Findings of change in longitudinal studies can be attributed either to a true developmental change of the sort we want to discover (a change with age in intellect or memory or personality) *or* to something else, some event or societal change that happened between the first and subsequent times that the subjects were observed that has nothing to do with advancing age (Schaie, 1982; 1988b, 1996b).

Suppose you had conducted a longitudinal study of attitudes toward the war in Vietnam during the late 1960s and early 1970s. You might well have found that your subjects, tested first in 1965, then in 1970, and finally in 1975, had become increasingly intolerant of our nation's involvement in Southeast Asia. What does your finding mean? Does it mean that people become less accepting of war as they grow older? (Is it a true developmental change?) Or, as is considerably more likely

Members of a family differ not only in age but also in generational (cohort) membership.

in this case, does it mean that social-historical events occurred between surveys that resulted in a change in many indivduals' attitude toward the war?

Practice effects are also a problem in longitudinal studies. A longitudinal study involving tests (e.g., IQ tests) requires repeated testing with the same measures. What may look like an increase in the skill being assessed over time could be no more than increasing familiarity with the test items.

Cross-sectional studies are not affected by time of measurement issues, because all subjects are observed at a single time. In summary, cross-sectional studies confound age and cohort or generational effects; but longitudinal studies confound age and time-of-measurement effects.

Time-Lag Design

Another type of study, called a *time-lag* design, involves the observation of people of the same age at different times (Schaie, 1977, 1988b, 1996b). Suppose you are interested in the sex life of 20-year-olds and, specifically, in the differences between such activities today and in 1930. Assuming someone had surveyed young people on this issue in 1930, you could survey a new sample of young people today and compare the data. Age is held constant; it is not a variable. The researcher, in this instance, is typically interested in the direct study of cohort effects; that is, differences between generations. The confounded variable is now time of measurement. If you found that today's 20-year-olds report more sexual activity, perhaps generations truly differ; but alternatively it is possible perhaps, between Time 1 and Time 2, that society has become more open and honest about reporting sexual activity.

SAMPLING DIFFICULTIES

One of the chief impediments to sensible conclusions about research in adult development and aging is the difficulty in gathering (and holding on to) appropriate groups of subjects. Subjects are generally presumed to be a *sample* of a larger *population*. The sample that we want to obtain is one that is *representative* of the larger group. But there are many ways a sample can become unrepresentative, making generalization of the results uncertain, perhaps invalid.

A representative sample will produce data that can be generalized to a larger population. The people who run opinion polls have an obvious need for representativeness in their samples, for they wish to generalize to very large groups, often the entire population of the United States, or another country. In voter surveys, the population is often considered to be the "people eligible to vote" or "people likely to vote." The goal of such surveys is to predict the actual vote on election day or at least to determine what the vote would have been, had the election been held on the day the survey was taken. Unrepresentative samples can result in misleading data, showing one candidate ahead when in fact he or she is far behind. In some polls taken in the United States early in this century, Republicans were overrepresented because telephones were used to solicit opinions; in those days, Republicans were typically richer and were more likely to have phones.

In studies of adult development, people with greater income, more education, and better jobs are usually included in samples more often than less fortunate individuals. More affluent people are easier to find (they belong to clubs and organizations) and easier to persuade to participate (they are more likely to believe in the value of research and are proud of themselves and their lives). Thus, many of the samples providing research findings discussed in this book are not truly representative of the adult population in general, but primarily of its middle class. In addition, men also have been more frequently studied than women during young and middle adulthood, although the reverse is true in old age. The debate regarding the factual basis of the so-called midlife crisis, for example, was based almost entirely upon the life experience of middle-class males (Levinson, 1978; see Chapter 3). More recent studies of women, minorities, and the less affluent, suggest that the so-called midlife crisis may be limited to certain historical periods and specific subgroups of the population. We must therefore be cautious in generalizing research findings beyond the population of which a particular sample can reasonably be called representative.

Researchers who do longitudinal studies face particular problems in sampling. Not only do they need to find a representative sample, they also have to keep it—to recover it for each subsequent retesting. Between observations, some people die (especially if the subjects are elderly), some people move away (and may not leave a forwarding address), and some people refuse to participate in the next round of tests. Usually this subject loss makes the sample less representative, for the subjects who die, move away, or become uninterested often have less education, less income, and less prestigious jobs. In short, if the sample was not biased toward the middle class to begin with, it is likely to become so by the time the longitudinal study is completed (Cooney, Schaie, and Willis, 1988; Schaie, 1988b, 1996b; Sharma, Tobin, and Brant, 1986).

Sampling also affects studies that examine the interrelationship of different attributes and psychological constructs. If a sample is very homogeneous (restriction of range) it may be quite difficult, for example, to demonstrate a strong relationship that might readily appear if a more heterogeneous sample had been used. Likewise, the relationship of two variables may differ, depending upon the segment of the population that has been sampled (Maitland, Intrieri, Schaie, and Willis, 2000; Nesselroade, 1988a; Schaie, Maitland, Willis, and Intrieri, 1998). In longitudinal studies, it is particularly important to represent a broad variety of different genetic and environmental conditions, in order to be able to examine a broad spectrum of different aging patterns (see Kruse, Lindenberger, and Baltes, 1993).

SPECIAL PROBLEMS IN THE MEASUREMENT OF CHANGE

If we want to be certain that we know what it is that changes, we must of course have reliable tests. But no test can be designed to be perfectly reliable and not every person will perform reliably at all times on a given test. One of the common critiques of looking at change scores therefore is that the error of measurement for the test given on two occasions is multiplicative, and that change scores consequently tend to be less reliable than measurements taken on any single occasion. In particular, there tends to be regression to the mean. That is, high scores on the first occasion are probably above the subjects' true scores and low scores are probably below the subjects' true scores. As a consequence high scores tend to become lower on the second occasion, while low scores become higher. This problem becomes less severe as change is studied over more than two occasions because observed scores will vary randomly about the true scores (Nesselroade, Stigler, and Baltes, 1980). Other methodologists argue that perhaps we should not look at group differences on two occasions, but rather study individual change profiles over multiple occasions. Such an approach is called "growth curve" measurement and allows individuals to be grouped into types that show similar patterns of change over time (Collins, 1996; Rogosa, Brandt, and Zimowsky, 1982). We can then look for predictors that inform us about the reasons why these patterns of change differ across individuals (Willett and Sayer, 1994).

In many longitudinal studies, however, there are only two data points. Also, in many instances it is indeed the average change over two occasions that needs to be assessed, particularly if we want to measure the effect of some natural or planned intervention into the developmental progress of groups of individuals. In that case, it is important to be doubly certain that our basic measurement tools are as reliable as possible.

SEQUENTIAL STUDIES

Many of the interpretational difficulties that are part and parcel of a simple cross-sectional and longitudinal designs can be alleviated with more complex approaches called *sequential designs,* shown in Figure 5-3 (see also Schaie, 1965, 1977, 1988a,1996b). A *cross-sectional sequence* consists of two or more cross-sectional studies, covering the same age range, executed at two or more times. For example, we might compare age groups ranging in age from 20 to 80 in 1980 and then repeat the experiment in 2000 with a new sample of subjects in each age group, still from 20 to 80. A *longitudinal sequence* consists of two or more longitudinal studies, using two or more cohorts. Suppose we begin a longitudinal study of age changes between 20 and 80 by observing 20-year-olds in 1990 (the 1970 cohort) with the plan of observing each of these subjects again, every 10 years until they are 80. This is a simple longitudinal study. In 2000, however, we begin a second longitudinal study of the same age range, choosing a new sample of 20-year-olds from the 1980 cohort. These two longitudinal studies are the simplest case of a longitudinal sequence.

Schaie's "Most Efficient Design"

K. Warner Schaie (1965, 1977, 1994b, 1996b), who has conducted extensive studies of research methodology in adult development, has proposed a "most efficient design," which generates data that is useful for many informative analyses.

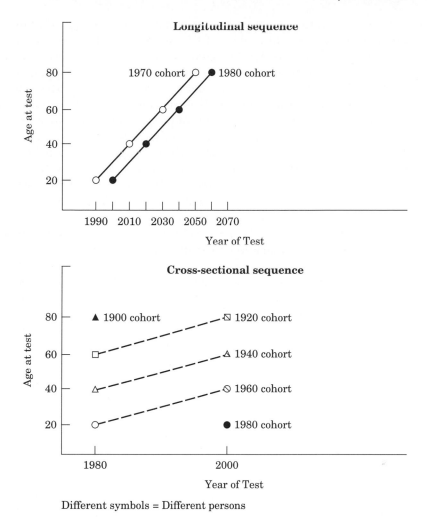

Figure 5-3 Longitudinal and Cross-Sectional Sequences. Longitudinal sequences use two or more cohorts; cross-sectional sequences test the same age groups at two or more times, using independent samples.

The most efficient design is a combination of cross-sectional and longitudinal sequences, created in a systematic way. In brief, the researchers begin with a cross-sectional study. Then, after a period of years, they retest these subjects, which provides longitudinal data for several cohorts (a longitudinal sequence). At the same time, they test a new group of subjects which, together with the first cross-sectional study, forms a cross-sectional sequence. This whole process can be repeated over and over (every 5 or 10 years, for example) with retesting of old subjects (adding to the longitudinal data) and first testing of new subjects (adding to the cross-sectional data).

As an illustration, suppose we were to give IQ tests to four groups of people, ranging in age from 30 to 60 in 1980 (see Figure 5-4). This is a straightforward cross-sectional study. In 1990, we retest as many of these same subjects as can be found. These data will show, for each of 4 cohorts, what happened to average IQ scores as the subjects grew 10 years older. At the same time, we recruit new subjects in the same age groups as the original subjects and test their IQ for the first time. We would probably add a new cohort of people who, at the time of second testing, are 30 years old to make the second cross-sectional study comparable to the first. The second cross-sectional study should yield results similar to the first; if it does not, we will have interesting clues to the nature of intellectual development. In 2000, we retest our first sample (the one that started in1980) for the third time, adding more data to our longitudinal sequence. We also retest the subjects who were new in 1990, adding an entirely new longitudinal sequence. Finally, we recruit new subjects to form a third replication of our cross-sectional study. As you can see, we will have generated a wealth of data.

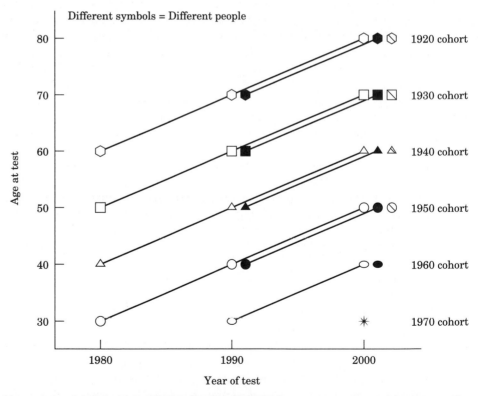

Figure 5-4 Schaie's Most Efficient Design. In 1980 four groups are tested (a cross-sectional study). They are retested in 1990 and 2000 (a longitudinal sequence with repeated measures). New groups from the same cohorts are first-tested in 1990 and in 2000 (cross-sectional sequences, independent samples). These new groups are later retested to form new longitudinal sequences.

Analyses

Data collected by using Schaie's most efficient design or comparable designs can be analyzed in several ways. The approach of greatest interest to developmental psychologists is to contrast age changes against cohort effects (Schaie, 1996b; Schaie and Baltes, 1975). To do this, we need at least two cohorts, and we must observe each cohort for at least two different ages. To simplify our illustration, consider only the changes in IQ scores between the ages of 60 and 70. This analysis allows us to test for the presence of irreversible decrement as contrasted to changes in performance levels across successive cohorts. The people in our hypothetical study (see Figure 5-4) who were 60 in 1980 (the 1920 cohort) and 70 when retested in 1990 are compared to the people who were 60 in 1990 (the 1930 cohort) and 70 in 2000. Do their IQ scores increase, decrease, or remain stable over the 10-year period? If there is irreversible decrement with increasing age, we should find similar decline patterns for both cohorts. In a traditional longitudinal study, we would have data only for a single cohort and would not know, therefore, whether the observed change can be generalized beyond the specific cohort that was studied. For example, one cohort may show an increase while the other shows a decrease, or one cohort may increase at a slower rate than the other. One cohort may have a higher average IQ than the other at both 60 and 70, though the increase or decrease may be similar for the two cohorts. Obviously, a lot of interesting comparisons can be made from this type of analysis, which is called a *cohort-sequential analysis* (Figure 5-5).

Another type of analysis is called *cross-sequential*. As the cohort-sequential analysis contrasts cohort effects against age effects, the cross-sequential analysis contrasts cohort effects against time of measurement. At least two cohorts are compared at two or more times of measurement. This strategy is particularly appropriate for data sets that fit the adult stability model discussed earlier. No age changes are expected, and the primary interest turns to identifying the presence and magnitude of cohort and time-of-measurement effects. The cross-sequential analysis is helpful when the researcher is interested in, say, the effects of some event or sociocultural change that occurs between the two times of measurement and, in addition, suspects that different cohorts might react differently. For example, the effects of the sexual revolution culminating by the 1970s might be compared for a cohort whose members were in their twenties in 1970 and a second cohort whose members were in their early forties in 1970. In addition, if there is reason to suppose that time-of-measurement effects are slight or nonexistent, cross-sequential analysis can be used to estimate age changes because subjects are obviously older at the second time measurement.

If the cohort-sequential analysis contrasts cohort against age, and the cross-sequential analysis contrasts cohort differences against time of measurement, we have one logical possibility left: the *time-sequential* strategy that contrasts age against time of measurement. People of at least two different ages are compared at two or more times of measurement. Consider a study of changes over time in the generation gap; the attitudes of 50-year-olds are compared with those of 20-year-olds, both in 1970 and in 1990. We might find that the difference between the age groups narrows between 1970 and 1990, or perhaps both age groups become more liberal

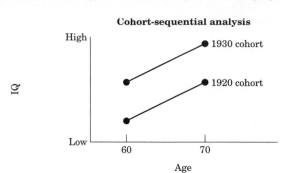

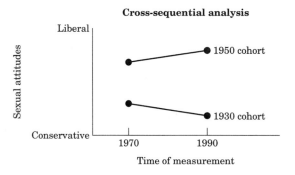

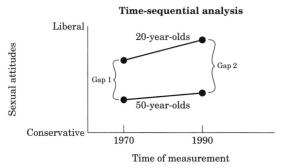

Figure 5-5 Sequential Data Analyses. Analyses of data from cross-sectional and longitudinal sequences can compare two or more cohorts at two or more times of measurement (cross-sequential), or two or more ages at two or more times of measurement (time-sequential). The data in time-sequential analyses must be from independent samples, but data in the other analyses can be repeated measures or generated from independent samples of the same cohorts.

in their attitudes, but the gap between them remains sizable. The time-sequential method is also appropriate for a test of the decrement with compensation model. When a new compensatory method is introduced (for example, a computerized memory prosthesis or a drug affecting declining memory), the time-sequential method would show that age differences over the same age range would be smaller at Time 1 than at Time 2.

Repeated Measures Versus Independent Samples

In a typical longitudinal study, *repeated measures* are taken of the same persons at different times. Another possibility, however, is to use the same research design but with *independent samples* at each point on the longitudinal time scale. If we are interested in intellectual development, for example, we might begin a longitudinal study by testing the IQ of 30-year-olds, with plans to retest these same individuals every 10 years; these would then be repeated measures. The alternative would be to draw a new (independent) sample from the same cohort every 10 years. Thus, in 10 years, when our 30-year-olds are 40, we find a new representative sample of 40-year-olds, instead of retesting the old batch. The independent sampling approach works well when a large sample is drawn from a large population, and is commonly used in large-scale demographic or sociological surveys. If small samples are used it is, of course, necessary to make sure that successive samples are matched on factors such as gender, income, and education to avoid possible differences due to selection biases.

What do we gain from the independent-samples procedure? First, we gain a replication of sorts of the repeated-measures study, a second look at the same trends. If, for example, our typical longitudinal study shows decreases in average IQ from age 30 to 60, the independent-sample study should show the same thing. Of course, we cannot use the independent-sample data to follow a particular individual. We cannot say that Joan Doe increased her IQ scores, nor can we say that 87 percent of our subjects decreased and 13 percent increased. But we can say that the averages for the cohort decreased or increased.

In addition, independent samples allow us to estimate the effects in the repeated-measures study of such problems as losing subjects due to their inability or unwillingness to be retested; practice effects can also be examined. The independent samples are new each time and thus reflect what the composition of the single sample of the repeated-measures study would have been if no subjects had been lost between testing. As a new sample, the subjects have not taken our tests before, so practice effects can be estimated by comparing this "no practice" group with the repeated-measures sample, who practice each time the measures are repeated.

Finally, if the longitudinal study is a longitudinal sequence (that is, if at least two cohorts are studied), then the independent-samples replication will form a cross-sectional sequence, providing valuable information for cross-sectional analyses at each testing period. Suppose we begin our longitudinal study with four cohorts, ranging in age from 30 to 60, retesting each cohort every 10 years. In 10 years, in addition to the retestings, we also test new, independent samples for each cohort. The retestings are longitudinal but the new testings form a neat, cross-sectional study of the age range 40 to 70. One could add a new cohort, a new group of 30-year-olds, and begin a second longitudinal sequence, to be retested for the second time. Thus the independent samples comprise (1) a replication of the original longitudinal study, (2) a new cross-sectional study, and (3) the start of a new longitudinal sequence. It is not surprising, then, that independent samples are included in Schaie's "most efficient design."

EXPERIMENTAL STUDIES OF ADULT DEVELOPMENT

It is not possible to conduct true experiments to assess the aging processes because we cannot assign research subjects randomly to different age levels. Nevertheless, a number of experimental designs (more properly called *quasi-experiments* [Campbell and Stanley, 1963; Cook and Campbell, 1979]; also see Mertens, 1998) can give us important insights and make it possible to examine alternative explanations for a variety of aging phenomena, provided that we keep in mind what such studies can and cannot tell us. As always, we must also be alert to the precautions that are necessary in these and in all experimental studies. In this section, we will briefly discuss three types of research designs that are commonly found in the aging literature and that the reader will encounter in many of the studies discussed in this book: age-comparative experiments, single age group intervention designs, and molar equivalence-molecular decomposition experiments.

Age-Comparative Experiments

One way of identifying the processes thought to be involved in age changes in behavior is to conduct a study in two groups of subjects of different ages that are matched on as many demographic variables as possible. We then assess the performance of the members of a younger and an older group on some behavior, for example, sorting a variety of objects into classes of objects. Suppose we find that the younger persons score higher on average. We now introduce a manipulation designed to improve performance. Perhaps we teach all of our subjects strategies for identifying various aspects of the objects that would make sorting the objects easier. We then retest all of our subjects to see whether there is differential improvement by age. This is what is called a *nonequivalent control group, pretest-posttest design* (Cook and Campbell, 1979).

Figure 5-6 shows the design of a study in which we compare the effects of an intervention on the older and the younger groups. Note that in the age-comparative experiment it is not particularly interesting to demonstrate that there is an age difference; we take that for granted. Neither are we concerned with demonstrating the effect of our intervention; this is also taken for granted, or we have chosen the wrong kind of manipulation. The critical effect that is of interest to us is the age by treatment interaction. If we can show that the older group gains significantly more than the younger group, we then argue that the age difference in the pretest was due to the fact that the older group performed less well than the younger because it lacked the sorting strategies needed to do as well as the younger group. In other words, if we can show age-differential effects of an intervention, we can then argue that we have determined a factor that explains the age difference in behavior.

Single Age Group Interventions

There are a number of instances in which intervention experiments might be conducted in a single age group because it does not make sense to have a younger comparison group (Krauss, 1980; Willis, 1987; Willis and Schaie, 1994b). For

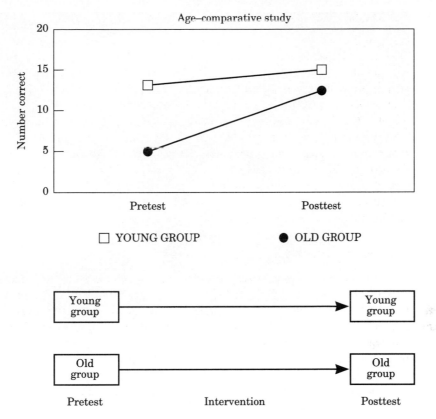

Figure 5-6 Design of an Age-Comparative Experiment.

example, suppose that we are interested in determining whether some educational procedures might be useful to reverse cognitive decline in older persons. In this instance, it would not make sense to have a younger control group, because the nature of the training effects would not be comparable. The training effect for the younger persons would involve enhancement of the initial level of functioning, while for the older persons it would involve the remediation of losses from a previous level of functioning. The most effective design in this case would be to study older people on whom we have longitudinal data over a reasonable period of time. We could then compare the effects of our intervention on individuals who had remained stable over time with the effects on individuals with known cognitive decline (see Chapter 12 for further discussion).

Single age group intervention studies, of course, must have suitable control groups. We usually require two types of control groups. The first receives the pretest and posttest but does not receive any intervention. The second receives the tests and some alternate or neutral procedure to measure the effect of an irrelevant intervention; the latter group is sometimes called a contact control group. A good intervention design, moreover, will assess not only the behavior that we wish

In addition to laboratory studies, field surveys and observational methods are important sources of scientific information in the social sciences.

to modify, but also some other behaviors, which should not be affected by our intervention. This type of assessment is needed to prove that our intervention is targeted to a specific behavior, rather than being a general, nonspecific intervention.

Molar Equivalence–Molecular Decomposition Experiments

Some older people do every bit as well as younger persons on some behaviors, even though they seem to have declined as much as their age peers on other psychological functions that seem superficially to be related to the behavior on which they are successful. The experimenter attempts to discover what it is that these older persons might do to compensate for declines in the basic functions that may have occurred. The experimental strategy is to find groups of younger and older people that can be matched on a complex (molar) behavior, so that the correlation between that behavior and age is zero. The experimenter then breaks down the components of the molar behavior (molecular decomposition) to show that there is indeed age-related decline in some one component, but that this decline is compensated for by enhanced skill in another component of the molar behavior (Charness, 1983; Salthouse, 1979, 1987).

An example of the *molar equivalence–molecular decomposition* experiment is a study by Salthouse (1984) in which he examined the behavior of transcription typists. He investigated typing, because it is a skill that is widely represented over great ranges of ability and age. Moreover, although typing is an integrated activity, some of its aspects can be reliably "decomposed" into distinct factors such as choice reaction time, tapping speed, acquisition of information in one form (reading the text to be transcribed), and transcription of information in another form (the actual typing). Salthouse found that both choice reaction and tapping time were correlated with age; the older typists were slower on these components. However, the older typists were more proficient in acquiring the information to be typed. They tended to pick up (read) larger chunks of information to be transcribed, reducing the time that they needed to acquire the information and thus compensated for their slower motor speed in hitting the typewriter keys.

MEASUREMENT ISSUES IN STUDIES OF ADULT DEVELOPMENT

The concepts about measurement that you might encounter in any tests and measurements course in psychology all apply equally to the field of adult development. We are concerned with the reliability and validity of formal test instruments and we pay attention to the problems of making objective observations and transforming the resultant qualitative data into quantifiable form (Dunn, 1989; Ikels, Keith, and Fry, 1988; Keith, 1988). There are, however, some additional issues that bear on the validity of our research findings when we study changes in behavior over time and across age groups.

Direct Observations and Latent Constructs

Many developmental psychologists are concerned more with studying changes and differences on latent (abstract) constructs, such as anxiety or intelligence, than in the specific behaviors or tests that are thought to represent these constructs. Nevertheless, the only way we can measure constructs is to observe the performance of subjects on tests or to observe their behavior in specific situations, from which we then infer the individual's standing on the abstract construct that is not directly measurable. One of the problems in studies of adulthood is that there is no guarantee that the same observation or test will be an equally valid representation of the same construct over a wide age range. Studies with the Wechsler Adult Intelligence Scale, for example, early on showed that the Digit Span subtest of that scale is related to a general ability factor in young adulthood, but to a memory factor in old age (Cohen, 1957).

More recent work with the Primary Mental Abilities, comparing the relation of observed tests to the underlying ability factors, has shown that there are shifts over the adult life span in the relative efficiency with which specific tests measure the latent ability constructs (Schaie, Maitland, Willis, and Intrieri, 1998; Schaie, Willis, Jay, and Chipuer, 1989). Similar issues arise when we study gender differences across the adult life span (Maitland, Intrieri, Schaie, and Willis, 2000). Unless we can show that relationships between the observables and their latent constructs are stable across age and time, it may be that reported changes in performance levels result from comparing apples and oranges.

These relationships are demonstrated typically by a technique known as *confirmatory factor analysis*. In this method, we specify a model that demands that the regression (correlation) of the observed variables or behaviors with the latent constructs are the same across different ages or different age groups. The fit of this model to a particular data set is then estimated. If the difference in regression coefficients is less than chance, we can accept the equivalence of the measures across age or time. If the equivalence model does not fit, we would then test a weaker model, in which we require that the same observed variables represent the factors across age or time, but do not demand that the values of the regression coefficients be identical (see Horn and McArdle, 1992; Maitland, Intrieri, Schaie, and Willis, 2000; Meredith, 1993; Schaie, Maitland, Willis, and Intrieri, 1998).

Generalizability of Research Findings

Whether findings from research can be broadly applied depends to a large extent upon the representativeness of the sample used. In work on adult development, however, representativeness goes beyond merely seeking a reasonable representation of various demographic dimensions. To generalize across age and time, we need to attend to the fact that populations shift over time and that whenever we compose a sample that differs in age, we are dealing with individuals who belong to different populations (Nesselroade, 1988b; Riley, Foner, and Riley, 1999). The dramatic shifts in levels of education, occupational status, income, and mobility characteristics across successive cohorts affect virtually every behavior studied by psychologists (cf. Atchley, 1989b; Schaie, 1996a, 1996b; Willis, 1989a). Thus, any study that matches these characteristics exactly across age groups will at the same time introduce distortions in the degree to which the subsamples are representative of their cohort.

There are also problems in generalizing from special samples of older people with known pathologies to healthy, community-dwelling individuals. While it is impossible to equate young and old groups in terms of the incidence of certain diseases, it is still necessary to worry about the impact of disease on behavior in age-comparative studies (Bosworth, Schaie, and Willis, 1999; Elias, Elias, and Elias, 1990; Elinson, 1988; Solomon, 1999). In any event, it is always necessary to note the demographic and health status characteristics of the participants in any study, so that we can understand the degree to which findings may be relevant to populations with different characteristics.

DEVELOPMENTAL RESEARCH

The primary goal of developmental psychologists is to describe and explain age changes. To do this within a practical time frame, they often try to estimate age changes by observing the age differences obtained in cross-sectional studies. This approach works reasonably well if cohort differences in the variable under study are slight. The assumption of trivial cohort differences, however, is unreasonable when young adults and the elderly are compared. But it makes sense when comparison is made of relatively small age slices, for example, comparing the late middle-aged with young-old persons or comparing persons in their twenties with those in their thirties. Alternatively researchers use longitudinal studies that directly record age changes for a variety of individuals. But longitudinal studies are expensive and very time-consuming. In addition, the pure effects of age may be masked by social-historical changes between measurements. Large segments of the original sample may die, move away, or refuse to be retested, changing the sample in significant ways that hinder the researchers' ability to generalize their results to a larger population. Tests that were used on 20-year-olds in 1940 may also be considered obsolete by the time the subjects were retested as 80-year-olds in 2000.

Longitudinal studies, nevertheless, have the great advantage of directly measuring changes in characteristics such as an individual's intellect or personality or brain function as he or she grows older. Longitudinal studies produce data that provide at least partial answers to such questions as: Do some people increase in intelligence as they grow older, and some decrease? How much variability is there? What causes the variability? Does intelligence increase for people in "intellectual" jobs and decrease for people in "manual" jobs? Does an increase in blood pressure relate to a decrease in intelligence? As expensive and time-consuming as longitudinal studies are, they provide data that are among the most important for theories in developmental psychology.

Developmental research, which covers the life span, encounters somewhat different difficulties at different stages of life. In a child development textbook, for example, you will find a discussion of the difference between cross-sectional and longitudinal studies, but the sense of drawing dangerous conclusions about maturation from cross-sectional studies will be less. In child studies, cross-sectional and longitudinal studies often produce similar results. One reason is that these studies cover a smaller age range. For example, 2-year-olds might be compared to 4-year-olds, and it is not likely that cohort differences will be pronounced in a span of two years. Also, many of the age changes in childhood are based on biological changes; the maturation of the brain and nervous system or the sexual-reproductive system, for example, accounts for fairly uniform changes in intellect and sexual activity among children. Adulthood, on the other hand, covers 60 years of an average 80-year life span, and social events rather than biological events are often the primary determinants of change (Hagestad and Neugarten, 1985; Riley, Foner, and Riley, 1999). Thus, cross-sectional studies of adults, which confound cohort effects with age effects, are fraught with danger; the time span is longer and the variability of social causes is much greater than the variability of biological causes. Longitudinal studies are much more important, therefore, in the study of adult development than they are in child development.

SUMMARY

1. Cross-sectional designs compare several age groups (cohorts) at the same time. They yield data on *age differences*. Longitudinal designs compare the same cohort at different times. They yield data on *age*

changes. Longitudinal studies suffer from subject loss, practice effects, and historical changes that affect behavior, but cross-sectional studies are more prone to confusion of age effects with differences between generations (cohorts). Difference scores tend to be less reliable than scores on single occasions; alternate methods require three or more measurement points. A major research problem in adult development is finding representative samples; white, middle-class males are generally overrepresented in the research literature, but in advanced old age women are overrepresented. Longitudinal studies also have the problem of keeping the sample representative once it is recruited; lower-class subjects, for example, tend to drop out in disproportionate numbers.

2. Sequential designs are complex combinations of the simple cross-sectional and longitudinal designs. A cross-sectional sequence consists of two or more cross-sectional studies run at different times. A longitudinal sequence consists of concurrent longitudinal studies of two or more cohorts. Schaie's most efficient design includes both cross-sectional and longitudinal sequences formed by retesting the subjects of an earlier cross-sectional study while testing new subjects in a new cross-sectional study. Analyses of the resulting data can be cohort-sequential (cohort versus age), cross-sequential (cohort versus time of measurement), or time-sequential (age versus time of measurement).

3. In repeated measures designs the same subjects are tested at different times. Independent samples designs test new subjects from the same cohort, instead of retesting the same subjects at different times.

4. Many experimental designs (quasi-experiments) may yield important insights and allow researchers to examine alternative explanations for a variety of aging phenomena. Age-comparative experiments compare groups of subjects of different ages to assess their performance of some behavior in order to determine if a particular factor explains the age differences in behavior. Single age group intervention designs study a group on whom longitudinal data is available and compare the effects of intervention on stable individuals with the effects on individuals experiencing decline. Molar equivalence-molecular decomposition experiments seek to discover how the older person might compensate for declines in performance in one area by enhanced performance in another area.

5. In addition to concerns about reliability, validity, and objectivity, several issues bear on the validity of developmental research. Relationships between observables, such as test performance and behavior, and latent constructs, such as anxiety and intelligence, must be stable across time to provide valid representations of performance. The method of confirmatory factor analysis is used to test the equivalence of these relationships across time or different age groups. The generalizability of research findings must also be taken into account. The extent to which research

findings can be broadly applied depends greatly on the representativeness of the sample. It is also necessary to be aware of the demographics and health characteristics of subjects in order to understand how findings may be relevant to other populations.

SUGGESTED READINGS

Hertzog, C. (1996). Research design in cognition studies. In J. E. Birren and K. W. Schaie (Eds.), *Handbook of the psychology of aging* (4th ed. pp. 24–37). San Diego, CA: Academic Press. A more advanced discussion of research designs (focusing on cognition) and particularly of the pitfalls of cross-sectional studies then is covered in this chapter.

Keith, J. (1988). Participant observation. In K. W. Schaie, R. T. Campbell, W. Meredith, and S. C. Rawlings (Eds.), *Methodological issues in aging research* (pp. 211–230). New York: Springer. A systematic presentation of the rules and procedures for implementing qualitative research in aging that can lead to collecting qualitative data suitable for scientific analyses.

Mertens, D. M. (1998). *Research methods in education and psychology: Integrating diversity with quantitative and qualitative approaches.* Thousand Oaks, CA: Sage. A very accessible presentation of research designs and elementary statistics suitable for students who have little or no background in measurement and social science statistics. This text also emphasizes issues in research with minority populations.

Schaie, K. W. (1988). Internal validity threats in studies of adult cognitive development. In M. L. Howe and J. Brainard (Eds.), *Cognitive development in adulthood: Progress in cognitive development research* (pp. 241–272). New York: Springer-Verlag. Provides examples of designs for the control of the validity threats in cognitive aging research.

CHAPTER 6

Families

Interdependent Relationships

From the beginnings of history, families have been the key to civilization and the primary relationships among people. In contemporary Western culture, a family begins with a man and a woman who decide to satisfy one another's sexual and intimacy needs on a permanent basis and to participate in a division of labor to maintain each other and a household establishment. Children add to the size of the family and bring their own needs—they would perish without proper care—but most parents need their children as well, to provide love, respect, a sense of immortality, a view of the world through innocent eyes, and the many other things children can offer their mothers and fathers.

A family serves many functions for its members and can be viewed as a system of *interdependent relationships*. Each family member has a specific role to play in the system, and other family members depend on him or her to play that role. Young children depend on their parents for the basic necessities of life (e.g., food, protection), and sometimes very old parents become similarly dependent on their adult children. Even the youngest and oldest participate to some extent in the division of labor among family members. In addition to these "labor" dependencies, there are also important emotional dependencies between husbands and wives and between parents and children.

When a child becomes an adult, we often think of this change as a shift from dependence to independence. Young adults, even older adolescents, often speak of their newly gained "independence" and what it will mean for them. What in fact it typically means, of course, is an opportunity to explore possible mutual dependencies with other people in a love relationship and, eventually, to have children who are dependent on them (and upon whom they depend in ways that they could never quite perceive when they were playing the child's role). Thus, a better way to conceptualize the changes of young adulthood is to see them as movement from

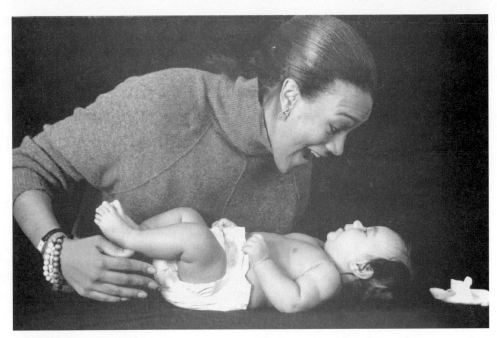

An interdependent smiling contest.

one interdependent system to another. What has happened then is that one family has reproduced itself; a new family has been created.

Consider the interdependencies of family life from the point of view of an individual throughout the life span. One begins life almost totally dependent, relying on instinctive or culturally prescribed nurturing tendencies in parents. Soon after birth, however, parents begin feeling rewarded by certain of their infant's behaviors; a smile, for example, can make a parent's day. The parents become dependent on the child, in a sense, for the fulfillment of their need to be needed. Thus, *inter*dependency begins, even though the most important, the more pressing dependencies are the child's. As the child grows, the balance of the interdependencies shifts, until finally the child becomes an adult, breaks away, and forms a new family. Now the more important, more necessary dependencies become responsibilities, in terms of adults' relationship with their children (and, perhaps, their aging parents). In one's relationship with one's spouse, of course, there is a more nearly equal division of labor and emotional dependencies that must be shared if they are to have any meaning. As one grows older, the balance of interdependencies shifts again; one's children become more self-reliant and one becomes less so.

Households in the United States are classified into two major groupings. Households of *related* individuals include: married couples with and without children, and female-head and male-head households. The second major grouping involves *nonfamily* households, including one-person households and households of nonrelatives. Although in 1998, 69 percent of U.S. households were composed of *related* individuals, the stereotypical family of a married couple with children under 18 years accounted for slightly less than a quarter (24.6 percent) of all households (U.S. Bureau of the Census, 1998a). Figure 6-1 shows the proportion of households in 1998 by membership type: 28 percent involved a married couple with no children or children over 18, 12.3 percent were families headed by females with no husband present, and 3.8 percent were headed by males with no wife present. The 25.7 percent of one-person households includes single young adults, divorced adults, and widows and widowers. Approximately 5 percent of households involve nonrelated individuals.

The proportion of households composed of *related* individuals is similar across ethnic groups: whites (69 percent), blacks (67 percent), and Hispanics (81 percent). However, there are ethnic differences in the type of household in which related individuals dwell. While over half of white and Hispanic households involve a married couple (with or without children), only 31 percent of black households include a married couple; 31 percent of black households involve a female head without a spouse, compared to approximately 10 percent for white households (U.S.Bureau of the Census, 1998b). Thus, there is an equal likelihood that a black child will live in a single-parent family as in a dual-parent family. That one-third of black households have a female head reflects in part the increasing number of black children born to unmarried mothers.

In many cases the modern family no longer follows the traditional linear pattern from marriage and birth of children to the empty nest, retirement, and death (U.S. Census Bureau, 1998a). It is estimated that only 30 to 40 percent of recent first marriages are likely to stay together until widowhood (Bumpass, Sweet, and Castro-Martin, 1990; Castro-Martin and Bumpass, 1989). Of the approximately 50 percent of marriages experiencing marital disruption, the majority of spouses will remarry. Indeed, remarriage has become as common as first marriage. Approxi-

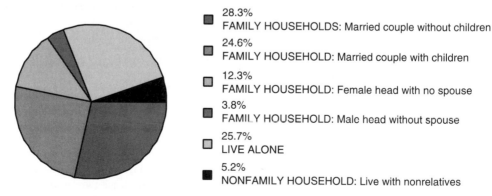

28.3%
FAMILY HOUSEHOLDS: Married couple without children

24.6%
FAMILY HOUSEHOLD: Married couple with children

12.3%
FAMILY HOUSEHOLD: Female head with no spouse

3.8%
FAMILY HOUSEHOLD: Male head without spouse

25.7%
LIVE ALONE

5.2%
NONFAMILY HOUSEHOLD: Live with nonrelatives

Figure 6-1   Proportion of Households in the United States by Membership type. *Source:* U.S. Bureau of the Census, (1998a), Current Population Reports No. 515. Series P20-514. Washington, DC: U.S. Governments Printing Office.

mately 40 percent of all marriages involve a remarriage for one or both partners (Johnson and Booth, 1998).

Through remarriage, interdependencies may develop horizontally across families (Cherlin and Furstenberg, 1998). A child may have a brother or sister from his biological parent's marriage, stepbrothers and sisters from a remarriage, and half-brothers or sisters when the remarried parent and stepparent decide to have another baby—not to mention relatives from the other biological parent's remarriage. It is not unusual for the pattern of relationships to grow even more complicated. Remarriage following the death of a spouse in old age is also becoming increasingly common, particularly for widowers.

Although the structural nature of one's relationships with one's family (or families) may change throughout life, the interdependencies within the family remain more or less the same. If we view the family in terms of the interdependencies among family members, we will have a better perspective on the specific issues that affect families throughout the life span (the topics to be covered in this chapter): choosing a partner, having children, living in a nuclear or extended family, and coping with the empty nest. The concept of interdependence also helps us understand the continuing relationship between adult children and their aging parents, the relationship between grandparents and grandchildren, and the transmission of values and traditions from generation to generation. We will examine a few of the alternative forms of the family (single-parent families and cohabiting couples, for example) that are becoming more common and discuss the possible effects of such alternate life styles on family relationships and interdependencies.

CHOOSING A MATE

How does a family begin? One of the first developmental tasks of young adults is to split apart from one nuclear family (parents and offspring) to set up another (Havighurst, 1972). Thus, the family reproduces itself. The first step in this process of familial reproduction is choosing a mate.

The reasons that people give for marrying are often diverse and complex. They include such obvious themes as falling in love, legitimizing sexual relationships, satisfying needs for companionship and communication, providing security and legal rights for children, and, last but not least, satisfying social expectations and needs for conformity. The marriage decision may also be influenced by the fact that most of one's peers already have married. (See Chapters 2 and 7 for further discussions on male–female relationships.)

Choosing a partner with whom to share life's joys and duties (with whom to establish interdependency) has traditionally been marked by a marriage ceremony. In this chapter, we will discuss the most common pattern; a young man and a young woman meet, fall in love, and get married. Our immediate concern, then, is with the majority of young people who unite in heterosexual alliances formed before the elder of the pair reaches the age of 35 (U.S. Bureau of the Census, 1998a).

Although marriage is still the expectation and norm, the imperative to marry does seem to be weakening and happiness of marriage questioned (Glenn, 1998b). Reservations regarding marriage appear to be particularly notable among black young adults, especially young black males; over 50 percent of blacks who are 25–34 years of age have never married (McNeal, 1998; U. S. Bureau of the Census, 1998a).

Why Marry Young?

Young adulthood is unquestionably the period of a person's life when marriage decisions begin to be made. Women, on average, marry men older than themselves. The age difference between the sexes at time of first marriage, however, has been diminishing since 1950. Interestingly, these trends have also been observed cross-culturally. Age at first marriage in the United States has fluctuated across this century, as shown in Figure 6-2. Age at first marriage was relatively stable from 1900 until 1940, and then dropped in the period from 1940 to 1960; the past three decades have seen a postponement of marriage. The median age of first marriage for males and females in 1990 was higher than the median age in 1900 (U.S. Bureau of the Census, 1998a). There are also ethnic differences in timing of marriage, with blacks marrying at a later age (U.S. Bureau of the Census, 1998b). Reduced social pressure and such alternative lifestyles as cohabitation have contributed to the rise in age of first marriages. In addition, many young women today

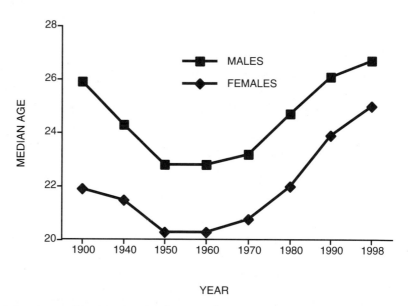

Figure 6-2 Age at First Marriage in the United States. *Source:* U.S. Bureau of the Census, (1998a). Current & Population Reports Series P20-514. Washington, DC: U.S. Government Printing Office.

delay marriage to complete higher education and begin a career. People tend to wait a bit longer during economic recessions, and they marry a bit earlier after a period of unavailability of marriage partners, such as might be caused by war (Cooney and Hogan, 1991). The decrease in age at first marriage in the 1950s, following World War II, illustrates the relationship between age at first marriage and secular trends.

Several explanations have been offered for why most individuals marry in young adulthood. One reason for this is biological. Marriage provides each spouse with a convenient and usually desirable sexual partner at a time when physical health is good, stamina is high, and hormones are raging. Young adulthood is the optimal biological time to have children. Miscarriages, birth defects, and other indications of less efficient biological functioning are more likely to occur with older parents and parents who are in their early teens. Differences in the economic roles of males and females may influence gender differences in age at first marriage. In societies in which the economic role of males as providers is varied and specialized, males who expect to prosper will delay marriage until the evidence of their success allows them to attract more desirable females (Bergstrom and Bagnoli, 1993); delays may also be due to lengthier educational requirements. Males with lower socioeconomic expectations may acquire a job at an earlier age and marry earlier.

Who's the Lucky Person?

Choosing a mate is a process of considerable interest to many people, as any young person engaged in the process can attest. In earlier historical periods and, indeed, in a few societies today, the individuals about to enter marriage had little to say in the matter; their mates were chosen for them, often when they were quite young (Xiaohe and Whyte, 1998). The notion that love is important in a relationship was considered not only to be ridiculous but also dangerous: young people in love were believed to act impulsively without thinking about the economic, political, and social ramifications of the potential union.

Whether based on romantic love or not, the choice of a mate today is left largely up to the individuals involved. This does not mean, of course, that the process of mate selection is unpredictable, governed only by the irrational choices that Cupid makes with love's arrows. On the contrary, the person whom you will choose (or have chosen) for a life's partner is one of the most predictable choices that psychologists have yet uncovered.

Some theories of mate selection view the process in terms of a series of "filters" that screen out unacceptable candidates at various stages of an intimate relationship (Cate and Lloyd, 1992; Feingold, 1992; Udry, 1971, 1974). For example, as shown by the representative filter theory in Figure 6-3, the pool of all possible dating partners is first screened through a *propinquity* filter. Propinquity means closeness in a geographic sense. If two potential mates are close to one another, they are more likely to meet, date, fall in love, and marry. Distance filters out many people. There may well be a perfect mate for you living in Phoenix, Arizona, but if you live in Iowa City, Iowa, the chances are poor that you will ever meet this

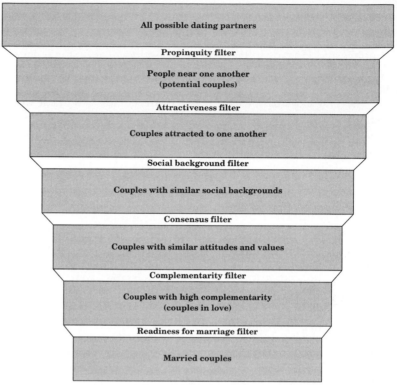

The "filters" represent variables that predict whom one will choose as a marital partner; they do not necessarily reflect conscious decisions.

Figure 6-3   A Filter Theory of Mate Selection. *Source:* From Udry, J. Richard. (1971). The Multi-Stage Mate Selection Filter. In *The Social Context of Marriage* (2nd ed., Fig. 9-1). New York: Lippincott. Copyright © 1971, 1966 by J. P. Lippincott Co. Reprinted by permission of J. Richard Udry

person. Not only are you more likely to meet someone who lives in your own city, but also, once you have met, a romance carried out in person usually wins out over a romance carried out long distance by e-mail, phone calls, and occasional visits.

Next, there is an *attractiveness* filter, which is a screening process that you can appreciate from your own experience. Attractiveness has been a factor of theoretical interest in mate selection for several reasons. First, physical attractiveness is one of the most "accessible" attributes of another person. That is, it is observed very early in the attraction process and is used to screen out potential partners (Feingold, 1992). Less accessible characteristics (e.g., character, disposition), which are time-consuming and more difficult to judge are taken into consideration only for would-be partners who make the "first cut." Highly accessible characteristics, such as physical attractiveness or ethnicity, may exert undue influence because once an individual has invested time in getting to know someone, based on easily accessible features, they may be more willing to overlook or undervalue less accessible characteristics (e.g., attitudes toward gender roles).

Physical attractiveness has been hypothesized to be of more importance to males than females, based on the parental investment model of mate selection (Doosje, Rojahn, and Fisher, 1999; Fletcher, Simpson, Thomas, and Giles, 1999). Evolutionary theories contend that sex differences in mate selection preferences reflect biological gender differences regarding reproduction. Because women have a shorter reproductive life span than do men, men are said to be attracted to the opposite sex primarily by visual cues (e.g., youth, physical attractiveness) that signal the capacity to reproduce. Women invest more heavily in their offspring than men and are said to seek non-appearance-related factors (e.g., financial resources, ambitiousness) that maximize the survival prospects of their children.

Indeed cross-cultural research and research in the United States support these sex differences in mate selection preferences. In a large study of mate selection preferences in 37 cultures, Buss et al. (1990) found within nearly every culture significant sex differences on these two features; males valued physical attractiveness more and females valued economic earning power more.

One rather subtle physical factor that enters the selective process is age. There appears to be cross-cultural agreement that the groom should be slightly older than the bride, although the magnitude of this difference is decreasing. This custom has been based on the notion that the man is the "breadwinner" of the family and should "establish himself" before taking on a young, dependent bride. However, as discussed in the following section, as women become more economically independent, age differences between the sexes may become less of an issue.

The third filter in Figure 6-3 screens potential mates on the basis of *social background*. People tend to marry those who are similar in religion, political affiliation, education, occupation, and social class. Some of these factors (religion, for example) have become less important in recent years, but others (education and occupation, for example) have become more important. Marrying someone "of like mind" (someone who is striving for similar goals in life, someone who has the same basic values that you have) is important, and factors such as related occupations and similar educational level are among the clearest indicators of like-mindedness. The economic resources of both women and men have been found to be important factors associated with marriage opportunities and the attractiveness of marriage. Economic status appears particularly important in understanding marital patterns among African-American adults (McNeal, 1998). When women have greater employment opportunities and higher remuneration, these conditions provide alternatives to marriage and reduce females' financial incentive to marry (Lichter, LeClere, and McLaughlin, 1991). Historically, more African-American women have been in the labor force, and the female–male difference in earning has been smaller for blacks than for whites, providing less economic incentive for black women to marry. Marriage patterns, particularly among African-American women are influenced by the availability of economically viable males (McNeal, 1998; Wilson, 1987). The shortage of black men with adequate employment is one of the most serious impediments to marriage for African-American women (Lichter, McClere, and McLaughlin, 1991).

As the relationship continues, the potential mates learn much about each other's specific attitudes and values and have less need to depend on the broad social background indicators of similarity. Joe and June may both be white Lutheran Republicans with college degrees, but they still might disagree violently on issues such as abortion, the value of money, and the role of women in today's society. Similarity in certain personality traits is also important in mate selection, marital satisfaction, and stability of the marriage (Johnson and Booth, 1998). The *consensus* filter screens people on such specific attitudes. Mate selection may involve consideration of characteristics that are consensually desired, that is, characteristics about which men and women hold common views, and of traits that the sexes view differently.

The large cross-cultural study of mate selection preference conducted by Buss and colleagues (Buss et al., 1990) indicated that there is a core of characteristics that are preferred across many different cultures. Nearly all cultures rated mutual love and attraction as the most important characteristic. Other commonly agreed upon desirable mate characteristics were dependability, emotional stability, kindness–understanding and intelligence. Two clusters of traits differentiated between cultures. The first cluster focused on "traditional" mate characteristics. Foremost in this cluster was chastity and also included was desire for home and children. China, India, Iran, and Nigeria rated high on this "traditional" cluster, while most western European countries rated low. A second cluster focused on high valuation of education, intelligence, and similarity in education, with cultures such as Spain, Columbia, Greece, and Venezuela rating these as highly desirable mate characteristics.

Then comes a *complementarily* filter to indicate that beyond similarity of attitudes, values, and goals, we want a mate to complement us ("complete us"), someone who is strong where we are weak. Finally, there is a *readiness* filter, which is based simply on the fact that people tend to enter first marriages within a limited age range. Thus, individuals will often marry whomever they happen to be dating at the "right time"—when they graduate from high school or college, for example. Graduation ceremonies and similar events often convey the message that it's time to settle down, get a job, and choose a mate. And who is better to fill the role of mate than the person you love at the moment?

An alternative scheme of mate selection was proposed by Adams (1979), whose concepts are based on earlier work by Kerckhoff and Davis (1962). It differs from Udry's filter theory in that it pays more attention to the process of establishing the couple bond rather than emphasizing the elimination of sources of future marital friction. Adams offers the following sequence:

1. Attraction to marriage itself (a conscious desire to marry)
2. Propinquity
3. Early attraction, based on such surface behaviors of the partner as gregariousness, poise, similar interests and abilities, physical appearance and attractiveness, and similarity to one's ideal image
4. Perpetuation of attraction, aided by the reactions of others, including being labeled as a couple; disclosure (opening up to each other); and pair rapport (feeling comfortable in each other's presence)

5. Commitment and intimacy, establishing a bond
6. Deeper attraction, which may be enhanced by (a) value consensus or co-orientation, providing validation of each other's viewpoints; (b) having feelings of competence reinforced; (c) perceiving other similarities in partner, such as attractiveness, levels of emotional maturity, emotional expressiveness, self-esteem, race, ethnic group, religion, and matching birth order
7. Deciding that this is "right for me" or "the best I can get"
8. Marriage

A problem in determining a sequence for mate selection is that most such sequences assume that marriage is the ultimate goal, the validating end state. Yet relationships may develop over time without ending in legal marriage. In fact, the actual decision to get married may be precipitated not by the stage that the relationship has reached, but by such factors as getting a job, pregnancy, parental strictness, or the death of a parent. A domino effect may also be observed. A couple may begin to consider marriage if it seems that most of their friends are getting married. By the same token, a couple who would like to get married may hesitate if most of their friends are still single. Nevertheless, although it may not be safe to conclude that every couple that marries has completed a sequence, most relationships do fall into some variation of this pattern.

HAVING CHILDREN

Although the majority of women become mothers, the timing and family setting into which children are born has changed. Traditionally, a baby was born to a married couple in the United States sometime in the second year of marriage. This pattern is becoming less typical as adults delay childbearing and in some cases have children outside of marriage. A recent large survey studied adults aged 19 to 39 over a six-year period. Over the six-year interval, 45 percent of couples remained childless although stating an intention to have children (Heaton and Jacobson, 1999). An increase in first births for women aged 30 to 34 years, rather than in the twenties, has been found in the U.S. and Canada (Dion, 1995). Black Americans are consistently less likely than whites to postpone childbearing. Furthermore, it is estimated that approximately 15 to 20 percent of white women of current childbearing age will remain childless; this increase in childlessness is less evident in nonwhite women (Heaton and Jacobson, 1999). While involuntary childlessness has decreased, voluntary childlessness has increased in recent decades. Being married and having a strong commitment to one's spouse are two of the strongest predictors for childbearing. Myers (1997) found that childbearing was most likely to occur among traditional homemakers and happily married couples. Higher levels of education increase the chances that people will postpone having a child or remain childless. Surprisingly career goals and concerns about having time and energy for a career have not consistently been found to be strongly related to childbearing decisions (Dion, 1995; Heaton and Jacobson, 1999) In contrast a higher income increases the likelihood of having an intentional birth. Adults concerned about the stability of their marriage were most likely to be childless; as couples age, they are also less likely to have children.

Why Have Children?

Recent research bears on the question of whether parenthood is an imperative or the extent to which it remains a desirable adult role. Although there has been a significant decrease in the idea that parenthood is imperative, still most young adults do expect to become parents and expect parenthood to be fulfilling (Heaton and Jacobson, 1999).

Why do couples have children? The most direct answer to that question, especially if one considers the many centuries before effective contraceptives were developed, is that couples engage in sexual intercourse, and babies appear on the scene soon thereafter. No doubt Mother Nature has made sex enjoyable so that members of our species will reproduce themselves; having children is certainly "natural" in that sense. But what are the other reasons, beyond the instinctive imperative to perpetuate human life?

For most adult humans, parenthood is still the ultimate source of meaning. Gutmann (1975), for example, discussing what he terms the "parental imperative," suggests that parenthood as an activity that is vital to our species exercises a controlling role over the entire life span. Just as our relationship with our parents is instrumental in shaping our childhood, so our adulthood is shaped by the relationship with our children (Huyck, 1989).

Many people express social reasons for having children. In the interdependent system that we call a family, children often contribute their part to the family's welfare, doing chores even when quite young. In less technologically advanced societies, children provide a sort of insurance policy for one's old age. In advanced societies, social security systems represent an intergenerational transfer of resources, with the aggregate of the younger generation contributing the resources that pay the pensions of the current elders .

There are wide differences among nations in terms of family values related to children. A 1997 Gallup (Gallup Organization, 1997a) poll examined international differences related to three questions: (1) For you personally, do you think it is necessary or not necessary to have a child at some point in your life in order to feel fulfilled? (2) Do you think it is or is not morally wrong for a couple to have a baby if they are not married? and (3) What do you think is the ideal number of children for a family to have? Table 6-1 presents findings on these questions for sixteen countries on four continents. Over 1,000 individuals were surveyed in each country.

One sentiment which is generally shared across the globe is the importance of having children. A majority of adults in all countries surveyed except Germany and the U.S. say that having children is vital to their personal sense of fulfillment. In almost all of the countries surveyed men and women were equally likely to say that having a child was vital to their sense of personal fulfillment. The exceptions are the U.S. and Columbia where men are more likely than women to view children as critical to personal fulfillment. It should be noted that most young adults in the U.S. want and expect to have children, although they do not report having children as vital to personal fulfillment.

The findings in Table 6.1 show a wide range of opinions about the ideal family size. The preferred number of children in most nations is higher than the 2.1 children per woman that the Zero Population Growth organization estimates as the replacement rate. The survey found that men and women within each country tend to agree on the ideal number of children for a family. To the extent that there are gender differences, women prefer to have slightly more children than do men. There have been dramatic changes in attitudes about family size in the U.S. over the last half century. In the first Gallup survey of preferred family size in 1937, three or more children were preferred with a mean of 3.6. These preferences held steady until 1973 when the mean number preferred dropped to 2.8. Since the 1980s the mean number preferred has been 2.5.

The most controversial and widely discrepant issue in the survey focused on whether having children outside of marriage was condoned. The most liberal countries on this issue with 90 percent or more of adults saying it is morally acceptable are Germany, France, and Iceland. Very high percentages in countries such as India, Singapore, and Taiwan say it is not acceptable. Interestingly, the U.S. is the country most evenly divided on this issue with 47 percent saying it is wrong and 50 percent saying it is not wrong. There is minimal disagreement between men and women in each country on the issue. In some countries there are generational differences with young adults (aged 18 to 34) expressing greater tolerance than older adults (aged 55 and older). This is particularly true in the U.S. where the majority of adults aged 55 and older do not approve, while the majority of young adults do not consider it morally wrong.

TABLE 6-1　Differences among Countries in Family Values

Country	Fulfillment & Children		Ideal # of Children		Child w/o Wed	
	Yes	No	0–2	3+	Wrong	Not wrong
Canada	59	37	61	33	25	73
Columbia	72	26	77	23	10	87
France	73	26	51	49	8	91
Germany	49	45	77	17	9	90
Great Britain	57	41	67	24	25	73
Guatemala	74	23	35	61	38	56
Hungary	94	6	73	24	16	81
Iceland	85	13	26	69	3	95
India	93	6	87	12	84	14
Lithuania	82	10	63	33	16	75
Mexico	61	38	56	42	31	67
Singapore	81	7	53	47	69	11
Spain	60	35	77	18	21	73
Taiwan	87	3	41	52	55	26
Thailand	85	13	69	30	37	57
U.S.	46	51	50	41	47	50

Source: Gallup Organization, (1997a) Global study of family values. Princeton, NJ: The Gallup Organization.

Personal Pleasures and Problems

In Erik Erikson's scheme of life, the intimacy crisis of young adulthood is followed by the generativity crisis (Erikson, 1963). The generativity crisis begins soon after love and marriage (that is, in young adulthood) and continues throughout the middle years of life. Although generativity also has to do with work, production, and creativity, it finds its most direct expression in having children and then guiding them to maturity. In Erikson's words, "the fashionable insistence on dramatizing the dependence of children on adults often blinds us to the dependence of the older generation on the younger one. [The mature adult] needs to be needed, and maturity needs guidance as well as encouragement from what has been produced and must be taken care of" (Erikson, 1963, pp. 266–267).

There have been numerous surveys on the value of having children (Heaton and Jacobson, 1999; Hoffman, McManus, and Brackbill, 1987). The most common advantages mentioned by both younger and older parents were that children were a source of love, companionship, and family ties; both groups also mentioned children as being stimulating and fun, although this response was more common among younger than older parents. The most notable group difference was in the older parents' view of children as providing help and security in old age. In

Most young parents truly enjoy their children, and it is in having and raising children that generativity finds its most direct expression.

addition, elderly fathers reported that children "gave you a reason for being a decent person. You work hard for them and you feel good about yourself." Both groups reported fewer disadvantages than advantages to having children. The most common disadvantage reported by younger parents was a restriction of freedom and the next most common was the financial cost.

Thus, many personal satisfactions of parenthood can be listed. Humans have a need to love and a need to be loved in return. Children can satisfy these needs and, in addition, provide opportunities for touching, cuddling, and kissing in a world that provides few other outlets for the need for physical contact. Children are also young and active; they are often interesting; they often provide excitement and drama. Finally, children also fulfill certain symbolic needs. Many people see their children as a continuance of themselves, a human form of eternal life.

The Pains of Parenthood

Parents "sacrifice" great quantities of time, energy, and money to raise their children. Although such sacrifices are to some extent expected, few couples can anticipate the profound effect that children will have on their lives. One of the ironies in the effect of children on the marital relationship is that the presence of children seems to lower the likelihood of divorce, but also to lower marital satisfaction (Belsky, 1990; Kalmijn, 1999; Wilkie, Ferree and Ratcliff, 1998). The "braking effect" of children on divorce is most evident for couples with young children. The positive relationship between marital stability and children appears to be related to the barriers to divorce (Belsky, 1990). Parents report remaining married "for the sake of the children." Particularly in the early years, childrearing may be perceived as too expensive and labor intensive for one spouse alone.

Although the presence of children may increase marital stability, their influence on marital interactions and marital satisfaction is less positive (Belsky, 1990; Belsky and Rovine, 1990). This is particularly evident in the transition to parenthood. Belsky and colleagues have found that during the first year of a child's life, the couple's expressions of positive affection declined and overt conflict increased. When evaluating their marital satisfaction, young mothers report a decline within the first six months of the infant's life and this decline continues through at least the firstborn's first two years (Belsky, 1990; Belsky, Rovine, and Fish, 1989). Fathers also reported a decline in marital satisfaction, somewhat later than mothers.

Most of the research on the relationship between children and marital satisfaction has focused on the transition to parenthood with the first children. The limited longitudinal data available on the period of adolescence do not indicate a direct effect of having an adolescent child on marital satisfaction *per se* (Steinberg, 1987; Steinberg and Silverberg, 1987). However, decline in marital satisfaction during the adolescent years is associated with parent–child distancing, the adolescent's quest for autonomy and parent–child conflict (see also discussion in Chapter 3).

What are the processes by which the presence of children may lower marital satisfaction? One frequently cited explanation is that children decrease the amount of time that spouses can spend together, and they affect the nature of their interactions. Couples with children have been found to engage in less verbal communication than childless couples, and the focus of conversation was more on children and less on the couple's relationship or the individual partners (White, Booth, and Edwards, 1986). Likewise, a curvilinear relationship between companionate activities by the couple and the stage of the family life cycle was found; companionate activities decreased with the arrival of children and only increased later in the marriage during the empty nest phase (Anderson, Russell, and Schumm, 1983).

Parents' discussions about childrearing can be a source of conflict and disagreement. Couples who disagreed more on attitudes and values regarding childrearing were significantly more likely to be divorced a decade later. It may be that arguments regarding childrearing reflect broader communication problems in the couple's relationship. In this sense, children are viewed less as a cause of marital conflict and more as stimuli that promotes the manifestation of preexisting communication difficulties.

The arrival of children does not lead to a decline in marital satisfaction for *all* couples. Somewhat older and better educated couples with higher income were more likely to experience an improvement in marital relations with the birth of their first child (Rogers and White, 1998). Husbands with greater interpersonal sensitivity and wives with higher self-esteem were also more likely to have improved marital relations with the arrival of their firstborn.

The arrival of children dramatically increases the time and labor associated with child care and the household; the increased labor and how the labor is shared by husband and wives can impact marital satisfaction (Rexroat and Shehan, 1987; Wilkie et al., 1998). Currently over half of married couple families in the U.S. involve both husband and wife in the labor force, and thus, the division of household labor between the spouses has become a topic of major concern and interest. In some western European countries, particularly Scandinavia, the majority of women are also in the labor force (Kinnunen and Pulkkinen, 1998b). Of all women in the workforce in the U.S., 40 percent are mothers of children under age 18. In 1995, 83 percent of new mothers returned to the labor force within six months after childbirth (Catalyst, 1998a).

Throughout most of the family life cycle, men and women are juggling parenting, household, and work responsibilities. It is expected that the total work week, including parenting, household, and employed work responsibilities will vary across the family life cycle, with the greatest demands occurring when children are young and dependent. Figure 6-4 shows the minutes spent on household chores on work days by men and women in dual-earner couples in the Cornell Couples and Career Study (Moen, 1999). Women in the study spend more time on household chores on workdays than do men, but this varies by life stage. Women with school-aged children spend the most time on household chores, whereas men with preschool children spend more time on housework than do other men. Men's time doing chores varies little by age or life stage for this sample, but women spend more when there are children (of any age) in the home. The couples in the study

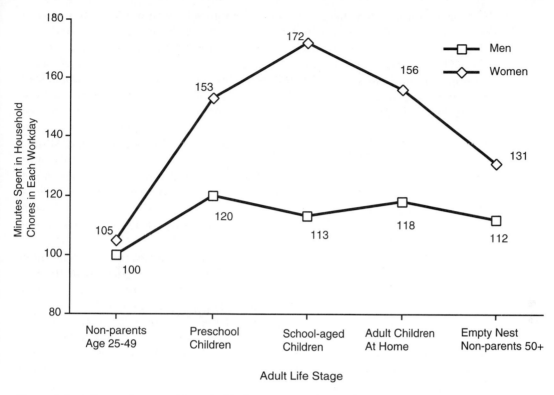

Figure 6-4   Minutes Spent on Household Chores on Work Days by Men and Women in Dual-Earner Couples. *Source:* Moen, P. (1999). The Cornell Couples and Careers study. Ithaca, NY: Cornell University.

were married or living with a partner. Men reported an average of 49 hours of paid work per week and women 42 hours. One strategy that working couples use to manage the multiple demands of their lives is to outsource whatever can be done by others at a reasonable cost (Moen, 1999). the three most popular items to hire out (besides child care) are housecleaning, yard work, and accounting/tax preparation.

Most time studies of paid work and household responsibilities have been cross-sectional in design. The question arises of whether these cross-sectional findings are similar to data from longitudinal studies of age-related changes in paid and nonpaid work. A recent report from the Baltimore Longitudinal Study of Aging (Verbrugge, Gruber-Baldini, and Fozard, 1996) compared cross-sectional, longitudinal, and period effects in hours spent in paid work and household work for men and women from young adulthood to old age. Cross-sectional and longitudinal data show different patterns across adulthood for women for both paid work and household work. Cross-sectional data show a steady decline in women's paid work across adult ages, reflecting fewer women in older cohorts being in the work-force. However, the longitudinal data show strong increases in time worked from ages 35 to 54, reflecting women's increasing employment in recent decades. Cross-sectional and longitudinal data also differ for women's time on housework but in the opposite directions from that for paid work. For women, cross-sectional data show increasing time in housework from young adulthood through midlife sug-gesting that older cohorts of women spent more time on housework. In contrast, longitudinal data show sharp decreases in housework for women in their twenties through the fifties. For men, both cross-sectional and longitudinal data show a gradual increase in the amount of time spent in housework, suggesting that older cohorts of men are engaging in more housework and also that men are doing more housework as they age. Secular or cohort trends show each cohort of women spending less time in housework and more time in paid work when at the same chronological age. For example, women aged 40 to 49 in the 1990s reported doing less housework than did women aged 40 to 49 in the 1970's.

Several studies (Wilkie et al., 1998) have found that sex roles become more traditional after the arrival of children; this is illustrated in Figure 6-4 by the dra-matic increase in total work week for women during the childrearing phase. When mothers work outside their homes, husbands do not increase their time in domes-tic labor comparably. From the perspective of the total family life cycle, the total work week is most comparable in terms of hours for husbands and wives during the early and late phases. Husbands increase their time in household labor during periods of low or no occupational involvement, that is, early in their employment careers and after retirement. Wives, on the other hand, spend less time in housework before and after childrearing.

Given the significant discrepancy between the total work week of husbands and wives over much of the family life cycle, what impact does this imbalance have on the marital relationship and on marital satisfaction? Several studies (McHale and Crouter, 1992; Wilkie et al., 1998) have found it is not the sheer amount of labor that affects marital satisfaction but rather gender-role expectations regarding work and feelings of fairness. Feeling that one is doing more than one's fair share of either paid work or household labor decreases marital satisfaction (Wilkie et al., 1998). However, husbands and wives differ in their perceptions of what is equitable in paid and household work . Husbands' marital satisfaction is increased more when there is an equitable sharing of paid work. In contrast, wives' marital satis-faction is more likely to increase when they perceive an equitable sharing of housework.

In studying the effect of children on marriage, there has been a tendency to treat all children as if they were the same. However, it seems reasonable that indi-vidual characteristics of the child may moderate their effect on the parents' relationship. Belsky (1990) noted three child characteristics of interest (gender, temperament, and disability). First, the gender of the child may influence both marital stability and marital satisfaction. In the United States, lower divorce rates were found for couples with male children; this may be related to the greater relationship between marital satisfaction and parental satisfaction for fathers than for mothers. For fathers in particular, parental satisfaction was greater with a male child (Morgan, Lye, and Condran, 1988; Rogers and White, 1998). Second, the temperament of the child affects not only parenting behaviors but also marital relationships. Children with negative temperaments (angry, easily frustrated) more frequently disrupted parents' conversations and parents reported lower marital satisfaction (Easterbrooks and Emede, 1986). Finally, a child's disability may figure into marital satisfaction; however, the disability alone may not account for lower satisfaction. Rather, it is the interaction of the disability and other family features (coping skills, economic and medical resources, social support) that account for variability in marital satisfaction (Bristol, Gallagher, and Schopler, 1988). Finally, parents of stepchildren reported significantly lower parental satisfaction than parents who have only biological children and are married to their children's biological parent (Rogers and White, 1998).

The Role of the Father

The role of the father has changed considerably in the past century. Recent trends in the composition of families indicate that the role of father is still being redefined. In agrarian societies, the father played a dominant role as the family worked together on the farm. But with industrialization, the focus on men's economic role meant that they worked away from home and spent less time with their children. Their childrearing responsibilities focused on being a good provider. In recent decades, the expectation has arisen that fathers should not only be good economic providers, but also be actively involved in child care (Pleck, 1997). As noted in the previous section, these attitudes have been fostered by the increase of mothers in the work force. Moreover, the two-parent couple with children is now less common; the number of mother-only households and step-parent families is increasing. The role of the father must also be considered in these evolving family forms.

Timing of parenthood has an important effect on fathers' participation in childrearing activities. For example, adolescent fathers are out of step with a normative life course; for them, child-care activities interfere with making educational and vocational progress appropriate to their life stage (Cooney, Pederson, Indelicato, and Palkovitz, 1993). Men who have children early in adulthood have more energy for activities typical of the father role, such as physical play. But this advantage of early fathering is offset by financial and time strains and the competing demands (equally felt by most women) of simultaneously establishing a career and a family (Rindfuss, Morgan, and Swicegood, 1988). When parenthood is postponed, a career already may have been established or career development may no longer be as important (Cooney et al., 1993). Late fathering permits greater flexibility in balancing these demands. It is possible that late fathers are more mature and have more emotional resources to use in parenting than younger fathers. In any event, late fathers have been found to spend more time with children than on-time or early fathers and to have more positive feelings toward parenthood (Cooney et al., 1993).

Although the majority of parents believe that child care should be equally shared, mothers, even when working full-time, do the majority of child care (Pleck, 1997; Wilkie et al., 1998). Pleck's (1997) summary of studies during the 1980s and 1990s indicates that, on average, fathers are engaged with their children about 40 percent of time that mothers are involved. The age of the child and day of the week also impact father's engagement. Fathers are more involved with young children than with older children, although involvement of mothers with children also declines when the children become teenagers. Fathers are more involved on weekends than on week days. Fathers tend to be more involved with their sons than their daughters, particularly with older children (Kalmijn, 1999). In much of the literature on fathers, the behavior of mothers is the benchmark for evaluation (Levine, 1993). This has lead to what feminist psychologist Vicky Phares (1996) has termed a "matricentric" approach to parenting research in which mothers are considered the standard parent and fathers are studied for how they differ from mothers.

Fathers in dual-earner families are more involved in child care than are fathers in single-earner families (Volling and Belsky, 1991) . Fathers are likely to be particularly involved when the family includes several young children and the mother works full-time or when the mother's schedule involves night work (Aldous, Mulligan, and Bjarnason, 1998). In a longitudinal study of father childrearing, it was found that fathers who were more active when the children were young were also more active with children five years later (Aldous et al.1998); in fact, fathers became more active as the physical aspects of child care diminished.

Father–child relations both inside and outside the marriage are more highly related with the quality of the spousal relationship than is true for the mother–child relationship (Doherty, Kouneski, and Erickson, 1998). Fathers appear to withdraw from their child when they are not getting along with the mother. Thus, the role of the mother has particular salience on fathering because mothers serve as partners and sometimes as gate-keepers in the father–child relationship. A father's involvement with his children especially young children is contingent on the mother's attitudes toward, expectations of, and support for the father as well as the extent of the mother's involvement in the labor force. Mother's employment characteristics are more strongly associated with fathers' involvement with children than some of the fathers' own employment characteristics. However, greater flex time and other profamily practices are associated with more father involvement (Pleck, 1997).

Recent research suggests that the fathering role is more sensitive to contextual and institutional practices than the mother role. Lack of income and poor occupational opportunities appear to have a particularly negative effect on fathering; Economic support is one aspect of responsible fathering that is nearly universally expected of fathers by their cultures. Studies have shown that it is the father's perception of his financial situation even more than his actual situation that influenced fathering behavior (LaRossa and Reitzes, 1993).

Both mothers and fathers engage in play activities with their infants and children, but fathers spend more time with their children in play than do mothers (Lamb, 1997). Fathers and mothers also differ in the style of play, providing different types of stimulation and learning opportunities. Fathers' play tends to be more physical and arousing, while mothers' play is more verbal and instructional and makes more use of toys (Power and Parke, 1982).

It is estimated that half of children today will spend part of childhood in a single-parent household, most likely a mother-only household (Bumpass 1990). Unfortunately, for many children this means a loss of contact with the father (Da-Vanzo and Rahman, 1993). Almost half of U.S.children in mother-only households had not seen their biological father in the previous 12 months; a similar finding has been reported in the Netherlands (Kalmijn, 1999). If divorced men remarry, they often assume childrearing responsibilities in their new household and have more involvement financially and emotionally with the new children or stepchildren than with the biological children from their previous marriage. The loss of contact with the father has implications also for adult child–parent relations. In studies in both the U.S. and the Netherlands, contacts between parents and their grown children are more infrequent and of lower quality when the parents divorced while their children were living at home (Booth and Amato, 1994; Cooney and Uhlenberg, 1990; Dykstra, 1997).

One positive finding regarding single-parent families is that men reared in this type of family have been found to be more willing to share household tasks when they become spouses and parents; it has been suggested that the less differentiated gender roles and tasks in a single-parent family may contribute to these egalitarian attitudes (Goldscheider and Waite, 1991). The likelihood of the non-custodial father providing child support is greater when there is more contact with the children. Better-educated and higher-income fathers and those who were married to the mothers of their children maintain more frequent contact (Furstenberg, 1989; Setzer, 1991).

Of major concern in the past decade have been shifts in the black family, particularly the increasing absence of the black father from the home. By 1998, mother-only households were as prevalent as married-couple households for blacks (Wilson, 1998; U.S. Bureau of the Census, 1998b). The number of children in mother-headed households is partially due to the great number of children born to unmarried black mothers. While the proportion of black families in which the father is present has decreased dramatically, research indicates that when he is present, black couples share childrearing and husbands are involved with their children (McAdoo, 1988; Taylor et al., 1990). Moreover, married black persons tend to be happier than unmarried blacks, and men tend to report even greater marital happiness than women (Zollar and Williams, 1987).

While most research has focused on fathers' care of young children, recent studies have begun to examine fathers' relationships with older children. As children get older, fathers tend to be more directive and instructive than mothers (Bronstein, 1988). In a series of studies, Steinberg (1981, 1987) found different patterns of interactions between adolescents and their fathers and mothers. As sons and daughters reach puberty (particularly early-maturing boys), conflicts with mothers increase and deference toward mothers decreases. Steinberg suggests that the greater conflict with mothers than with fathers may be due to the more day-to-day parenting done by mothers, which brings more opportunity for conflict; the adolescent may also feel a greater need to exert independence and a new identity in relation to the mother, the primary caregiver. In contrast, conflicts with fathers do not seem to increase with puberty for either sons or daughters; however, as the son reaches puberty, the father's assertiveness increases, as does the son's deference toward his father. Steinberg suggests that adolescent males rise above the mother's position in the hierarchy of influence in a family.

THE EMPTY NEST

One of the major events in a family is the launching of the youngest child into a family and career of his or her own. Typically, the mother is between the ages of 45 and 50; the father may be a few years older. Together, they face a new adjustment—life in the empty nest; they are, in the words of social scientists, a *postparental family.*

Like the large numbers of old people in general, the postparental family is largely a phenomenon of the twentieth century. Until 1900 or so, the average parent died about the time the nest was emptying, the cycle of life fulfilled. The number of children in an average family has also decreased considerably, so that the youngest is typically launched when the parents are still relatively young.

When the number of postparental families increased dramatically, scientists began to wonder about the psychological effect of the empty nest. They worried mostly about the mother, especially homemakers who had defined their own identity in terms of their children. For most parents, however, the emptying of the nest is not a particularly troubling experience. Indeed, many people find that their lives change for the better. Adolescent children are in some respects a burden: they are expensive; they challenge authority; they have learned how to create conflict between parents if it suits their purposes. During the *launching* phase, the parent is typically in midlife and both parent and child may be going through stressful transitions (see also the discussion in Chapter 3 on the midlife years). The child may be exploring career options or the challenges of a first job; the parent may be dealing with difficult job responsibilities and facing up to unmet dreams and expectations.

Once the children are launched, there is finally time for new projects, travel, or simply personal pleasures and now the money exists to finance them. In the typical family, the burden of children falls more heavily on the mother; and although she is supposed to suffer more from the flight of her young birds, she is also the one who benefits more from their launching. Her housework, which doubled with the first child, is cut in half as the last child leaves (see Figure 6-4).

The parents find themselves in the position of "husband and wife" again; they are no longer primarily "father and mother." Although this confrontation with their marriage can force them to admit that they no longer have much in common—leading in extreme cases to divorce—the normal pattern is the deep satisfaction of a loving relationship that is again allowed to flourish. Most parents also experience a deep contentment from the successful completion of what they see as one of "life's duties": to bear and raise children to the age at which the children can manage on their own (Ryff et al., 1994). Most women do not fear the empty nest; they look forward to it.

One of the most frequently cited findings from primarily cross-sectional research is that marital quality and satisfaction across the adult life span follows a U-shaped curve as shown in Figure 6-5 (Rollins and Feldman, 1970; Rollins, 1989). A common explanation for this U-curve is that many marriages become less satisfactory when children are born but improve when the children leave home. However, some longitudinal studies have documented a tendency for marital satisfaction to decline in the early stages of marriage even when there were no children (Bradburn, 1998). The decline in marital satisfaction early in American marriages have now been documented in numerous studies. The nature of changes in marital quality in midlife and long-term marriages is less clear (Glenn, 1998a). The

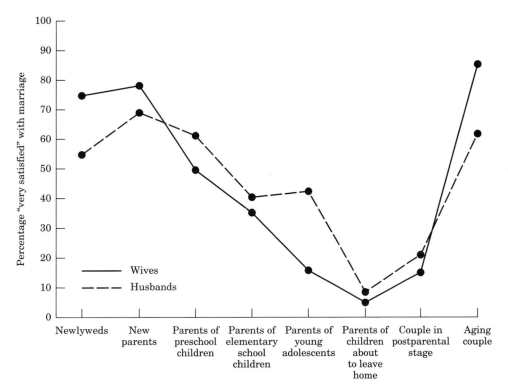

Figure 6-5 Marital Satisfaction Across the Life Span.

upturn in marital satisfaction found in cross-sectional studies of longer-term marriages could result from differences in marital quality in different marriage cohorts; older marriage cohorts may have different expectations of marriage and have reported higher levels of marital satisfaction throughout the marriage. Alternatively, reports of marital satisfaction in longer-term marriages may have resulted from removal of unsatisfactory marriages through divorce. On the other hand, there really may be an upturn in longer-term marriages. An extensive recent study by Glenn (1998a) suggests that the upturn in longer-term marriages reported in many studies is due largely to cohort differences rather than an actual increase in marital satisfaction. The better estimate of what happens to marital satisfaction during the first five decades of a marriage for both men and women is that marital satisfaction declines steeply for the first decade and then declines moderately for the next two decades; there is slightly greater decline for women than men. It is important, however, to note that reports of a decline in marital satisfaction does not mean that couples are unhappy with their marriages. Reported changes in how happy couples are in their marriage are relative and may reflect more realistic expectations of marriage rather than a change to dissatisfaction *per se* with the marriage or marital partner.

Recent studies have also examined the meaning of leaving home to the young-adult child. Leaving the nest has multiple meanings (Goldscheider and Goldscheider, 1989; Goldscheider and Lawton, 1998) including self-governance (making one's own decisions), emotional detachment (breaking family ties), financial independence, and starting one's own family. When evaluated, many young adults saw self-governance as the most important aspect of leaving home; those young adults who did seemed to navigate the separation process better, felt less lonely, and had higher self-esteem. Those young adults who rated emotional detachment (breaking family ties) higher reported being lonelier, having lower self-esteem, and having more conflicts with parents; this was particularly true for males.

Recent demographic trends suggest that the nest may be slower to empty or may be refilling with the return of young adult children (Aquilino, 1990). Prior to World War II, children normatively left the parental home at the time of marriage. Recall that age at first marriage declined in the 1950s and 1960s, but has increased in the past two decades (see Figure 6-2). Thus, the timing of leaving the nest has fluctuated with changes in age at first marriage. Because women marry at an earlier age than males, females typically have left the parental home at a somewhat earlier age. In addition, there have been societal changes in expectations regarding leaving the nest; that is, a majority of adult children now expect to live independently for a time before marrying (Goldscheider and Goldscheider, 1994). However, other societal changes, such as economic recession and divorce being most likely to occur in the early years of marriage, have resulted in some young adults needing to return to the nest, usually for relatively brief time periods.

Two questions arise then. First, what characteristics are associated with young adults leaving the nest at an earlier age than most? Second, under what circumstances are young adults likely to return to the parental home or to delay leaving the nest? With regard to the first question, two factors appear important—family structure and expectations regarding age at marriage. Children from step-families and from single-parent families leave home somewhat earlier, but perhaps for different reasons. Step-families expect children to leave the home somewhat earlier (Goldscheider and Goldscheider, 1989). It has been hypothesized that there are often less well-established parent–child roles in step-families and that this may contribute to greater conflict that is reflected in children from step-families leaving home earlier (Mitchell, Wister, and Burch, 1989). In contrast, children from single families have been found to expect to marry later and thus are likely to live independently before marriage (Goldscheider and Goldscheider, 1994). As discussed in the section on extended families, later in this chapter, black youths' home leaving is influenced by the emphasis on extended kin networks.

Who among young adults are more likely to remain at home or to return home? Approximately 37 percent of young adults aged 18 to 29 live with their parents during at least part of this age interval, with the proportion decreasing with age from 80 percent of 18 to 19-year-olds to 45 percent of 20 to 24-year-olds to 14 percent of 25 to 29-year-olds (Glick and Lin, 1986). There has been some increase in children living at home, particularly in the early and late twenties since 1970. The majority (94 percent) of 18 to 29-year-olds living at home have never been married and report schooling as their main activity. Of the small proportion of young adults living at home who have been or are married, approximately half are separated or divorced and half are living with their spouse, and often children, in their parents' home. Married returning children are more likely to be living with the wife's parents. Separated or divorced adult children appear most likely to return home during their early twenties and more men than women with disrupted marriages are likely to return home. Contrary to some stereotypes of returning children "bumming" on their parents, approximately two-thirds of returning adult children are employed. Are some parents less supportive of young adults returning home? Women who had lived separately from their parents in young adulthood were less supportive of their children returning home (Goldscheider and Lawton, 1998). Hispanics were more supportive of coresidence than other ethnic groups.

Remarriage in Old Age

An estimated half million people over the age of 65 in the U.S. remarry each year (U.S. Bureau of the Census, 1995). It is estimated that the number of older people who will remarry will increase. In addition to remarriage after the death of a spouse, increasing numbers of middle-aged and older adults are divorced and likely to remarry. Research on adults reaction to older parents remarrying has mixed findings. Some research suggests that remarriage late in life is perceived by adult children to disrupt the interdependencies of the family, threatening both the financial and emotional relationships between parents and adult children. In particular, the children may fear that their inheritance will be lost or complicated (Finch, Hayes, Mason, Masson, and Wallis, 1996), although they will rarely state this fear explicitly. Other studies suggest that adults' concerns regarding remarriage of older parents may vary with the age of the adult. Although the majority of adults thought older adults should tell children about their plans to remarry, only older respondents thought that older adults should ask the permission of children to remarry—surprisingly only one-half thought the older couple should make legal plans to protect the family estate (Ganong, Coleman, McDaniel, and Killian, 1998).

Studies suggest that older adults marriages tend to be notably successful. Of the 100 late-life marriages in one survey, only 6 were considered unsuccessful (McKain, 1972). Most of the couples had known each other for several years. Often they were previously related by marriage (for example, a woman would marry the widowed husband of her late sister) and there were a few storybook romances, where childhood sweethearts had drifted apart, only to find each other again in the twilight of their lives. The old brides and grooms also had a reasoned view of what to expect from marriage. They didn't expect radical changes in their lives or their personalities—who has such dreams at age 70? Instead they expected (and got) the satisfactions of companionship—someone to discuss things with, someone to do things with—and they felt they were useful to their new spouses. "The need to be needed does not fade in the later years" (McKain, 1972, p. 65).

THE EXTENDED FAMILY

Many of the problems young couples face with the birth of their first child would be less pressing if there were a grandparent or an aunt or uncle around—if, in other words, the couple lived in an *extended family* instead of a *nuclear family*. The nuclear family consists of a husband, a wife, and their offspring. The extended family consists of the nuclear family and other relatives (kin). Most people have both a nuclear and an extended family; the questions are: What is the role of kin in the lives of individuals? Is kinship less important than it used to be? Is the nuclear family isolated? Were the "good old days" better, when the interdependencies of family life were spread more broadly among the extended family, many of whom lived in one household?

As research evidence accumulates, it is clear that two pervasive myths, both incorrect in fact, make discussion of the role of kin in family life difficult. The first myth is that extended families "under one roof" were common in previous American eras, but have declined in recent times. The second is that the nuclear family of today is isolated and that kin support and influence have all but disappeared. The first myth has been discredited by research using diaries, sermons, novels, and other literary sources, indicating that multigenerational households were not the norm in early America (Haber and Gratton, 1994; Hareven, 1982). The early settlers of the United States brought with them the practice of a two-generation household (that is, the typical nuclear family)—a practice that was normally continued in the new country.

Recently research on multigenerational households has distinguished between upward and downward extension, that is, whether older parents come to live in the household of an adult child (upward), or whether grandchildren (with or without parents) live in the household of a grandparent (downward). Recent census data indicate a rise in downward extended households between 1970 and the early 1990s (Szinovacz, 1998; U.S. Bureau of the Census, 1994); this type of multigenerational family is more common in black families. The increase in downward extended households has been linked to increases in the divorce rate as well as in out-of-wedlock births (Beck and Beck, 1989). In contrast, older parents' living with their adult children (upward extension) has declined in the last century (Ruggles, 1994). Approximately five percent of adults over age 75 live with an adult child. It is important to note that census data record multigenerational families that are living together at one point in time—the date of the census. As we will discuss later under the heading Grandparenthood, there is the question of the length of time that family members are actually part of a multigenerational family. The greater likelihood of living in a multigenerational household with increasing age has also been observed in other societies, including Canada (Beland, 1987), Britain (Dale, Evandrou, and Arber, 1987) and Italy (Wolf and Pinelli, 1989).

The notion of the nuclear family of today as an isolated unit, more or less devoid of support from the extended family, was enunciated by several sociologists in the late 1940s (Linton, 1949; Parsons, 1949). In a general theory on the effects of industrialization, it was proposed that the isolation of the nuclear family came about because of industrial society's need for a mobile labor force, that is, for workers who were willing to leave the family farm. In the industrial society, new institutions took over the support functions of kin: banks lend money in times of need; clinical psychologists, psychiatrists, and clergy offer emotional aid; and daycare centers replace grandmothers.

Although kinship apparently plays a lesser role in industrial society than it did in predominantly agricultural economies, the degree of isolation of the modern family was probably exaggerated. The functions of the family have been redefined, but they do not appear to be diminishing.

One index of family functioning is the frequency of contact among family members. Research shows that most Americans remain in fairly close touch with their aging parents, adult children, brothers and sisters, and numerous other kin (U.S. Bureau of the Census, 1989a). Even when relatives live far apart, modern technology makes it much easier for them to remain in contact than formerly. A 1984 survey (U.S. Bureau of the Census, 1989b) of adults aged 65 or older with children living outside the household found that 40 percent of the parents reported seeing at least one of their children two or more times a week and 22 percent saw a child daily. Those proportions increased with the age of the parent: 39 percent of those aged 65 to 74 saw a child at least twice a week, while 50 percent of those over 85 saw a child that frequently. Interestingly, the frequency of seeing or talking with children did not differ for parents who lived alone or lived with others. The contact between black elderly and kin is also high (Taylor and Chatters, 1991). Over one-third of black elderly reported being in contact with family members nearly every day and 25 percent reported contact at least weekly.

The extent and nature of contact between kin vary considerably by class, race, and other characteristics. Among older people, those who come from working-class backgrounds have more contact with children than their middle-class counterparts do (Field and Minkler, 1993; Shanas et al., 1968). There are several possible explanations for this tendency. First, working-class families tend to be larger, so there are more children available to make contact. Second, middle-class children generally live at greater distances from their parents, often because their occupations require that they move to new locations. The relative infrequency of visits is balanced to some extent by the fact that the visits that they do make tend to be longer.

The black extended family (Beck and Beck, 1989; Taylor and Chatters, 1991; Taylor, et al., 1990) is particularly important in black family life. Some have even suggested that the extended rather than nuclear family is more basic to the study of black family life. The extended family has several key features: members often share living quarters or live near one another; there is a high degree of social interaction and friendship among members; considerable help and support are exchanged among members. The extended family plays a particularly important role for the one-parent family unit, with such members as grandparents, aunts, uncles, and siblings serving as surrogate parents. However, in some cases, there may also be negative effects. The marital relationship of couples may be undermined by conflicts and divided loyalties. Some members may also become overly dependent on the extended family, thus thwarting the development of independence and self-reliance. Taylor and Chatters (1991) found a negative association between proximity of the immediate family and satisfaction with family life among black elderly.

There is considerable economic interdependence among kin of all races, with parents providing at least emergency financial support for their adult children and vice versa (Goldscheider and Goldscheider, 1994). Black family members give more aid than those of other groups (Coward, Horne, and Dwyer, 1992). The flow of resources is generally from parent to child until quite late in life. However, black and Hispanic youths contribute significantly more to the family income than do whites; this reverse flow is particularly evident for youth growing up in single-parent families (Goldscheider and Goldscheider, 1991). In addition to money and valuable property, the extended family often provides valuable services, such as help with moving and, of course, babysitting. Other benefits that family members derive from each other are less tangible. Some of these benefits have occurred throughout history. For example, associating with the elderly exposes the younger generation to behavioral models of aging that provide them with anticipatory socialization for their own old age.

Other benefits are reflections of new patterns of intergenerational interaction (Bengtson and Achenbaum, 1993). One such development is that, despite disparities in chronological age, family members are entering into "social age" peerships in ways that have no historical precedent. With large numbers of middle-aged people returning to school, for instance, it's not unusual for members of two or even three generations of a family to be students at the same time. This is an example of a "renewal activity" initiated by older relatives, but social peerships may also result when younger relatives experience "accelerated activities" such as early widowhood or early retirement (Hagestad, 1986).

Family sociologists suggest that the structure of the extended family is changing because of increases in life expectancy and declines in fertility (Gatz, Bengtson, and Blum, 1990). The structure is becoming more vertical, with three to five generations, but fewer members in each generation, known as *beanpole families*. However, Szinovacz (1998) notes that although the majority of families experience four living generations at some point in time, the duration of four-generation families is typically quite short.

Burton and Dilworth-Anderson (1991) suggest that three types of intergenerational family structures are evolving for blacks. The *vertical intergenerational* family structure is similar to that described earlier, with an increasing number of generations but fewer members in any one generation. Second, there is the *age-condensed* family structure, occurring as a result of high teenage childbearing among blacks. In this family structure, the age distance between generations is greatly reduced, with 12 to 17 years between generations for teenage mothers, compared to 20 to 26 years between generations when childbearing occurs in young adulthood. A *substitutional* family structure is the third type, resulting from delayed childbearing or childlessness. In this family structure, *fictive kin*—kin related not by birth, but by friendship—become increasingly important in the social network.

There are several implications of these changes. The extended family is becoming "top heavy," with the average married couple having more living parents than children (DaVanzo and Rahman, 1993; Adams and Blieszner, 1995). Intergenerational relationships are also becoming more complex and intense. Hagestad (1986) notes that in a four-generation family, there is the potential for three sets of parent–child connections, two sets of grandparent–grandchild ties, and members of two generations holding the roles of both parents and children. Given gender differences in life expectancy, older generations of family are primarily older women and a four-generation or five-generation family may have two generations of widows. Women, therefore, are likely to have longer and more intense relationships with multiple generations of a family than are men, and there is potentially a need for younger generations to provide care to multiple generations of older women. In addition, within black families, older women are likely to continue as caregivers, particularly to grandchildren and great-grandchildren, given the increase in single parenting and teenage childbearing (Burton and Dilworth-Anderson, 1991; Wilson, 1998).

GRANDPARENTING

As parents age, their children age, too, and eventually become parents in their own right. The elders become grandparents. Thus, grandparenthood constitutes a transition determined not only by the grandparent's own characteristics and life choices but also by those of their children and grandchildren (Szinovacz, 1998). For example, age of transition to grandparenthood is contingent on the timing of births among the grandparents as well as their children. We have created an image of grandparents as "benign, gray-haired angels" (Bischof, 1976, p. 292). In fact, however, most people become grandparents in midlife (Szinovacz, 1998). There is, however, considerable variability in the age of becoming a grandparent. As we will discuss further, the majority of black women make the transition to grandparenthood either before age 40 or after age 60. What may be defined as "off-time grandparenthood among whites may be "on-time" grandparenthood for many black women. With life expectancy increasing, the experience of grandparenthood is almost universal. However, about 15 percent of black and Hispanic men report that they are not grandparents. Older Hispanic men who immigrated during midlife may have lost contact with their adult children and thus do not know whether they have grandchildren. In addition, the greater prevalence of mother-headed families in black and Hispanic households may isolate older men from their kin.

Adults, particularly women, are spending three to four decades of their lives as grandparents and know their grandchildren as infants, preschoolers, teenagers, and possibly young adults. The majority of grandmothers typically survive well into the adulthood of at least their oldest grandchild and close to two-thirds of women experience the birth of great-grandchildren. Many women will spend almost half of their lives as grandmothers (Silverstein and Long, 1998). Men, on the other hand, are unlikely to survive to their grandchildren's adulthood or to the birth of their first great-grandchild. It might be expected that both the role of the grandparents and the grandchildren's perceptions of them would evolve and change as both age.

As grandparents and grandchildren grow older, there is the question of whether there are changes in affection and contact. Silverstein and Long (1998) conducted a longitudinal study over 23 years of grandparents' report of affection and contact with their adult grandchildren. Grandparents' report of affection for their grandchildren declined somewhat during the first 14 years and then increased as grandparents aged into their seventies and eighties. Older cohorts of grandparents reported greater affection for grandchildren than younger cohorts. Contact between the generations and the proximity of their residences decreased over time. Given the rebound in affection in old age, it is suggested that the decline in contact was due to geographical mobility rather than emotional detachment. Moreover, the amount of contact-proximity increased with health problems of grandparents suggesting that adult grandchildren may be sources of support to their grandparents. Grandchildren who are in regular contact with their own parents are also more likely to have frequent contact with grandparents; grandparent–grandchild contact and closeness is also related to positive relations between the parent and grandparent generations (Kivitt, 1991; King and Elder, 1997). Some researchers go so far as to characterize the middle generation as "the lineage bridge across the generations" (Hill et al., 1970, p. 62).

As adults spend longer periods of time as grandparents, the role of grandparent overlaps with other roles. When they first become grandparents, most adults are married and employed. Thus, both retirement and widowhood typically occur after the transition to grandparenthood. There has been change in the sequence of roles during the twentieth century. Early in the century, women often became widowed before the first grandchild arrived, and men often worked until their death. Earlier retirement ages suggest that more men are available to their grandchildren.

Bengtson (1985) has suggested four symbolic roles that a grandparent may play in a family. First, a grandparent may be a stabilizer—a constant figure in times of family trouble or transition (Johnson, 1985), an expression of family continuity, and a focus for family contact and meetings. Second, a grandparent may play the role of "family national guard" or "family watchdog" to be called on to provide protection and care in an emergency and counted on as a backup if things go wrong with younger family members' finances or careers. Third, a grandparent may serve as an arbiter between second and third generations of the family, relieving tensions between generations, negotiating conflicts between parents and grandchildren, and interpreting the actions of the second generation to the third generation: "Your mom's just concerned about you." "Your dad's under pressure at work." "I remember when your mother went to her first prom—she also wanted an expensive dress." Fourth, a grandparent may be a family historian, helping the family to relate its past to the present and to understand how it has evolved: "We're a family that hangs together when times get rough—we've always supported each other." "We're a family that has always respected the environment—grandpa was concerned abut soil conservation; today we recycle."

Some researchers suggest that there are differences in the relationship of grandmothers and grandfathers to their grandchildren. Hagestad (1985) found grandmothers more likely to be concerned with interpersonal dynamics and family ties; grandfathers were more likely to give advice about or discuss education, jobs, finances, and management of life's responsibilities.

And what effect does involvement with grandchildren have on grandparents and vice versa? The influence of grandchildren is strongest, of course, when

Grandparents and grandchildren typically provide love and support for each other.

grandparents are actively involved and when they see grandparenting as a central role in their self concept (Kivett, 1991). The centrality of the grandfather role was seen as related to older men's acceptance of a more nurturing role in old age (Kivitt, 1991). Childhood experiences with grandparents influence how these adults will interact with their own grandchildren (King and Elder, 1997). Relations between grandchildren and grandparents depend on the current relationship between their parents and grandparents (King and Elder, 1995). Grandparents who believe that they can make a difference in the lives of their grandchildren (i.e., self-efficacy) and take a more active role in the lives of their grandchildren, report more frequent contact and report higher-quality relationships including providing financial support and discussing the grandchild's plans for the future (King and Elder, 1998).

There has been increasing attention to the situation of grandparents and grandchildren residing in the same household. As noted earlier, it is important to distinguish between two types of arrangements, a downward extension in which the grandchildren and sometimes the parent live with the grandparents versus an upward extension in which a grandparent lives with their adult children and their grandchildren. Grandchildren living with their grandparents is more common in black families and there has been an increase since 1970 in the number of downward extended households. The increase in grandchildren living with their grandparents is particularly large for those living with only one parent. In the 1990s the greatest increase has been in grandchildren living with their grandparents only when neither parent is present. At any one time, it is estimated that approximately 12 percent of black children live with a grandparent (with or without a parent present), compared to approximate 4 percent of white children. More importantly, approximately 30 percent of children live with a grandparent sometime during their childhood; this includes both downward and upward extended households (Szinovacz, 1996b).

How long do grandchildren reside with their grandparents? In downward extended households, grandchildren lived with their grandparents approximately six to seven years. Children raised by only one parent were likely to spend a longer time living with their grandparents. In upward extended households, the grandparent lives with adult children and grandchildren on average five or six years. Two changes in the black family have further contributed to these living arrangements, that is, the dramatic increase in unmarried black teenage mothers and the decrease in marriage rates among blacks. Black grandmothers, often still in young adulthood themselves, are called upon to assist their teenage children with parenting and family responsibilities. As described later, this "off-time" grandparenting can be stressful for all concerned.

Thus far we have focused on grandparenting when it happens at the "normal" time in an adult's life, but what happens when it begins earlier than expected? What happens when grandparenting begins in the twenties or thirties? This unexpected turn of events occurs when two successive generations are teenage parents. Burton and Bengtson (1985; Burton, 1995) studied the spillover effect of early parenting in one generation of a black family on other generations of the family and found that many young grandmothers did not experience the satisfaction that grandparenting often brings; being a grandmother did not fit their image of themselves and disrupted their lifestyles. A 27-year-old grandmother commented, "I am too young to be a grandmother. You made this baby, you take care of it." A 28-year-old remarked, "I could break my daughter's neck for having a baby. I just got a new boyfriend. Now he will think I'm too old. It was bad enough being a mother so young—now a grandmother, too."

ADULT CHILDREN AND THEIR PARENTS

Even after adult children leave the parental home and establish their own family, many parents continue to provide various types of support. However, in old age the direction of the resource flow is expected to reverse with the adult child assisting the parent. How does the flow of support change across the adult–child–parent relationship? What characteristics of the child and of the parent influence the giving and receiving of support?

In a study of a representative sample of adult children aged 20 to 64 years, Cooney and Uhlenberg (1992) studied changes in various kinds of support (advice, services, child care, and gifts) from parents to adult children. The late twenties (25 to 29 years) was found to be the peak age period for many types of support, with a sharp decrease in support by the early forties. Thus, adult children appear to be receiving the greatest support during the period of first marriage and establishment of a family. The most common form of assistance was the giving of advice, with approximately 40 percent of adult children reporting receiving counseling from their parents. Daughters were more likely than sons to receive assistance in the form of child care, services, and advice. Interestingly, characteristics of the parent rather than of the child were more strongly associated with giving assistance. In particular, parents in good health were more likely to give various types of assistance, whereas divorced or widowed parents were less likely to provide help. Of importance to the parent–child relationship was the finding that well over half of adult children reported feeling that their parents were a potential, as well as an actual source of assistance. Until their mid-forties most adult children saw their parents as someone on whom they could call for financial or emotional help.

Filial Responsibilities

As more adult children have parents living into old age, issues of filial responsibility become of increasing concern and debate (Blieszner and Hamon, 1992). *Filial responsibility* is the sense of personal obligation that adult children feel toward their aging parents' well-being. It may involve a sense of duty or willingness to protect and care for one's elderly parents. On the other hand, filial responsibility may also include a preventive dimension that promotes self-sufficiency and independence in the aged (Seelbach, 1984). A preventive perspective may take several forms, including adult children encouraging older parents to perform tasks of which they are capable, helping them seek new enriching experiences, and showing respect for their parents' autonomy and right to make decisions regarding their own lives.

Development of *filial maturity* has been described as a unique developmental challenge of midlife. Given increasing life expectancy and reduced fertility, women are likely to spend more of their life having parents over the age of 65 than having dependent children under the age of 18 (DaVanzo and Rahman, 1993). The adult child comes to accept filial responsibilities and to deal with a possible filial crisis in realizing that their parents may need assistance in facing the challenges of old age. Filial maturity, however, is not equivalent to *role reversal,* in which offspring "parent" their aging parents (Blieszner and Hamon, 1992). True role reversal is seen as a dysfunctional perception of the filial role. Filial maturity comes as the adult child sees their parents as individuals who although in need of assistance continue to be adults with their own needs, rights, and personal histories.

Although increasing numbers of adult children are faced with issues of filial responsibility, there continues to be a great deal of ambiguity concerning what this role involves. What types of attitudes and behaviors can aging parents rightfully expect of their adult children? What should adult children expect of themselves in terms of their filial roles? Is there agreement between parent and adult child generations regarding filial responsibilities?

There appears to be considerable agreement among adult children and parents that one of the most important aspects of the filial role is to provide affection and emotional support to parents (Blieszner and Hamon, 1992). In a random sample of elderly parent–child pairs Hamon and Blieszner (1990) found that both parents and children agreed on the top three items of filial responsibility, including giving emotional support, discussing matters of importance, and helping parents with understanding resources. Both parents and children agreed that expectations regarding filial responsibility did not involve living in close geographical proximity to each other. Finally, although children rated providing financial assistance to parents or taking parents into their homes as part of their perceived filial role, parents were not in agreement. A similar finding occurred in Brody's multigenerational study of filial roles, in that the oldest generation was the most receptive to formal services for the elderly (Brody, 1990). The elderly appear to have accepted the growing role of governmental agencies in providing health and housing services to the elderly. However, younger family members now take on the important role of acting as a mediating link between the elderly person and the bureaucracy (Gatz, Bengtson, and Blum, 1990). Thus, the functions of the family have been redefined, but they do not appear to be diminishing.

Caregiving

One of the more consistent findings on attitudes towards filial roles is that sons and daughters espouse very similar beliefs and attitudes toward providing care for their parents (Blieszner and Hamon, 1992). However, an even more clear-cut finding is that daughters are much more likely than sons to actually provide care. Adult daughters both provide more assistance in general than adult sons and help

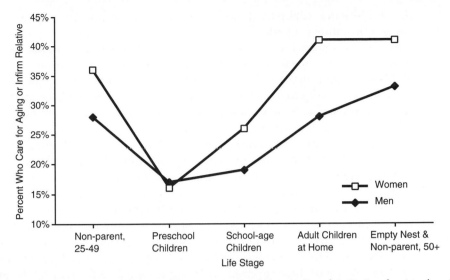

Figure 6-6 Proportion of Men and Women in Dual-Earner Couples Caring for Aged or Infirm Relative. *Source:* Moen, P. (1999). The Cornell Couples and Careers study. Ithaca, NY: Cornell University.

more with direct hands-on, intensive, instrumental, and emotional support tasks. Although more women are working, they do not appear to be reducing their caregiving (Farkas, 1992). In contrast, the help given by sons typically involves financial management advice, heavy chores, and shopping. Figure 6-6 shows the proportion of men and women caring for aging or other infirm relatives from dual-earner couples who participated in the Cornell Couples and Career Study (Moen, 1999). Older women who have adult children in the home or no children in the home are most likely to be caring for aged or infirm relatives. Across all age-cohorts and most life stages, men are less likely than women to be providing care. Dual-earner couples with preschool children are also less likely to be providing care.

This dependence may cause conflict and strain between generations. The decreasing age distance between generations and increasing life expectancy mean that many parents and children are growing old together. Children have traditionally been the chief source of support for the aged, but children who are themselves approaching retirement and suffering financial and perhaps physical constraints may have difficulty when they must care for elderly kin (Brody, 1990). The middle-aged person may face conflicts between responsibilities to aged kin and obligations to children and husband or wife.

TRANSMITTING VALUES AND TRADITIONS

The relationship of grandparents to grandchildren (that is, of the first to the third generation) is an interesting one in terms of the transmission of societal values and traditions. Parents have the major responsibility for socializing their children, and inevitable conflicts arise over the degree of conformity to the parents' standards the children are willing to accept. Grandparents can force themselves into this fracas by constantly criticizing the childrearing techniques of the parents or the behavior of the grandchildren, but they can also stand aloof from the battle. As more or less "objective bystanders," they are often in a position to influence their grandchildren in ways that the parents might find difficult. Feeling no need to rebel against the grandparents, the children often find it easier to communicate with them, to discuss with them the meaning and importance of the manners and values the parents are trying so hard to instill.

Grandparents and grandchildren tend to form unspoken agreements about areas they can discuss without violent and unproductive arguments. Both avoid the sensitive areas—creating what are called "demilitarized zones" by one researcher (Hagestad, 1985)—thus increasing their influence in other nonsensitive areas. Sensitive areas include a number of issues in which the younger generation has a vested interest because they view changes as a "contribution" of their age group and, thus, in part, an aspect of their personal identities (Bengtson, 1985).

By contrast, parents do not have the privilege of avoiding sensitive issues in the upbringing of their children. They are responsible for their children's welfare, and most parents therefore feel they must intrude if they see their children developing in what they perceive to be disadvantageous directions. Thus, parents are most subject to the conflicts spawned by generation differences.

Socialization, Intergenerational Stake, Bilateral Negotiations

Socialization is one of the major functions of a family. In its broadest definition, socialization is the attempt of a social system to ensure continuity through time. One of the classic dilemmas of human society has been the maintenance of a functioning social order despite successive invasions of neophytes: a younger generation lacking the skills and values to perform the intricate social roles of adulthood. The problem of the earlier generations, from this perspective, is to successfully transmit information that enables the young to function effectively in the increasingly complex social positions they encounter in adult life.

It is family life that provides the major portion of the solution to this problem, generation by generation. More specifically, "socialization refers to the process by which the individual acquires those behaviors, beliefs, standards, and motives that are valued by his or her family and the cultural group to which they belong" (Mussen et al., 1979, p. 328). In many instances, socialization techniques are intentional and direct, involving rewards for desired behavior and punishment for unacceptable actions. Usually, however, transmission of values and traditions proceeds by more subtle processes (Bengtson, 1975, Giaruso, Stallings, and Bengtson, 1995). In particular, observational learning occurs as the parents go about their day-to-day activities under the surveillance of their dependent children (Bandura, 1977). The parents (and grandparents and other relatives to a lesser extent) serve as models for effective and appropriate behaviors. These behaviors may be as simple as choosing the right fork at a fancy dinner or as complex as acting out the social role of a male or a female.

Observational learning plays a major role in the transmission of skills and values from one generation to the next.

In the young child, devoid of skills and lacking a well-developed sense of personal identity, the socializing function of the family may proceed without conscious intent to instruct or to learn. Later, especially in adolescence and beyond, socialization is more deliberate and becomes, as some theorists view it, a kind of bilateral negotiation (Bengtson and Black, 1973; Bengtson, 1985). The older generation champions the values it has tested and found useful, whereas the younger generation seeks a new approach, a higher purpose. It is important to recognize that socialization is a two-way (bilateral) process, with the older generation changing along with the younger. Indeed, in a technology-oriented society, the young often learn of innovations before their elders; they may have to explain to their parents or grandparents how a microcomputer operates or the meaning of TV music videos. The bilateral negotiations that constitute socialization in the family do not cease, of course, when the children grow up and move out. Aging parents continue to play a major role in "training" their adult children to become parents in their own right. Similarly, adult children and aging parents must constantly renegotiate their reciprocal exchanges, as the parents grow old and normally lose some of their independence

In his longitudinal research of multigeneration families, Bengtson (1975; Giarusso, Stallings, and Bengtson, 1995) has noted a phenomenon which he has termed the *intergenerational stake hypothesis*. The hypothesis was based on the finding that middle-aged parents consistently reported higher levels of closeness and consensus in their parent–child relationships compared to the reports of their children. They hypothesized that each generation has different developmental concerns and thus each has a different "stake" in their intergenerational relationship. Parents are more concerned with the continuity of values they have found important in life and with close relationships in the family they have spent so much of their lives founding—so they tend to minimize conflict and overstate solidarity with their offspring. Young adults, by contrast, are more motivated to establish autonomy from their parents in values and social relationships and have less commitment to the parent–child relationships and thus overstate intergenerational contrasts. In his recent longitudinal studies covering four time points in the lives of multigenerational families, Bengtson has found that the intergenerational stake hypothesis is shown at all four points and is thus manifest at different points in the development of parents and their children.

ALTERNATIVE FAMILY FORMS

"The family is in crisis," or so we've heard from people ranging from the president of the parent and teachers organization to the president of the United States. The ostensible reasons? Major changes in family values as shown in Table 6-1 the increase in women in the work force, the permissive divorce laws, heightened individualism, and abortions have been cited as causes of "crisis." Perhaps it is of some comfort to know that the same dire predictions about the demise of the family have been made throughout history. The future of the family is a discussion beyond our mandate in a textbook on adult development and aging. What does concern us is the fact that family forms are changing and that many adults now live in households quite different from the nuclear family of American mythology. As we saw earlier in this chapter (Figure 6-1), only 25 percent of households include the traditional family unit of a husband and wife with children. Due to a combination of demographic trends, including delayed age of first marriage, divorce and unmarried mothers, more households involve mother-only families and more individuals are living alone. Moreover, many children are spending at least part of their childhood with only one biological parent. In this section, we will discuss some of the alternative family forms that are becoming increasingly common.

Living Alone

The share of households with adults living alone is rapidly increasing. Single-person households in the United States are quite a mixed group, including young adults who have just begun to search for mates to divorced adults to widows. More people are delaying marriage, more people are divorcing, and more people are remaining single after divorce. In 1998, 26 percent of the total U.S. population lived alone; most young adults living alone had never married, while most middle-aged or older adults living alone were divorced or widowed.

The proportion of an age group living alone increases across the life span (U.S. Census, 1998a). Although less than 10 percent of young and middle-aged adults live alone, 30 percent of elderly 65 and older live alone. The oldest-old (48 percent) are most likely to live alone, including 57 percent of women 85+ years and over and 28 percent of men of that age. As discussed under grandparenting, white elderly are much more likely to live alone than black elderly who often are involved in multigenerational households. The increase in the proportion of elderly living alone represents a dramatic historical shift in the living arrangement of the elderly. The increase in elderly living alone is attributed to improved economic status, improved health, and the strong desire of current cohorts to remain independent.

The increasing number of single-person households raises questions about social isolation particularly for the elderly. The findings are mixed with regard to social isolation. While the elderly living alone were found in one large study to generally be in better physical health than those living with others, those living alone reported greater levels of depression, loneliness and social isolation (Mui and Burnette, 1994). Approximately 25 percent of elderly living alone have no living children. Of those who had living children, nearly half had daily contact and 86 percent had at least weekly contact with their children (Choi, 1994). Some studies suggest that the number of confidants and companions is more germane to well-being than are marital status and living arrangements *per se* (Chappell and Badger, 1989). In many ways the current generation of elderly women are pacesetters. Single women appear to be creating social environments and lifestyles to compensate for the loss or absence of a spouse.

Fortunately, increases in life expectancy mean that most young single adults will have living parents, at least into their fifties and in many cases longer. Older adults (usually widows) generally have living children. Brothers, sisters, and other blood relatives also embed the single individuals in a kinship system that supports them to some degree. When kin fail, close friends and roommates sometimes function as "substitute family" or "fictive kin."We will discuss further the large number of widowed older adults living alone (particularly women) in Chapter 7.

Single-Mother Families

Mother-only families have become increasingly common in the past three decades. In 1960, only about 9 percent of families with children were headed by nonmarried women, but by the 1990s over 16 percent were in this group (Bumpass and Sweet, 1991; U.S. Bureau of the Census, 1998a). It is hypothesized that nearly half of all children born since 1975 will live in a mother-only family sometime before the age of 18 (Bumpass, 1990). For black children, the estimate is 86 percent (Bumpass, 1984; Taylor et al., 1990). Being part of a one-parent family varies greatly by race and education. By 1998, black female headed households had already reached over 30 percent of all black households and thus were as prevalent as married couple households (Bureau of the Census, 1998b). Female-headed households include unwed, divorced, and widowed mothers. There are some ethnic differences in female-headed households, with more white mother-only families occurring as a result of divorce or widowhood and more black mother-only families involving never-married mothers, due to the decline in marriage rates among black women. The declining likelihood of marriages is strongly linked to the high levels of unemployment and low earnings of young black men (Taylor et al., 1990; McNeal, 1998).

One of the most significant differences between mother-only and married couple families is the difference in economic well-being (Teachman, Day, Paasch, Carver, and Call, 1998). Contrary to the stereotype of single mothers on public assistance, in 1997 75 percent of single mothers were in the labor force (Catalyst, 1998b). In 1993 38 percent of children living with divorced mothers, but 66 percent of those living with never-married mothers were living below the poverty line, compared with 11 percent of children living in two-parent families (U.S. Bureau of the Census, 1994). Although some women were poor prior to motherhood, the majority became poor at the time of marital disruption or the arrival of children. Single mothers have lower incomes for at least three reasons: the lower earning capacity of the mother, the lack of child support from the father, and the low benefits provided by assistance programs. Public benefits (e.g., Aid to Dependent Children) provides approximately 15 percent of the income of white single mothers and 25 percent of income for black single mothers. Because many children born to never-married parents have not had legal paternity established, the prospects of child support from the father is limited. Economic deprivation has been linked to material conditions (fewer books and games) and behavior in the home that reduces intellectual stimulation (parental conflict, inconsistent and harsh parenting practices; Teachman et al., 1998). Children in poor families are more likely to live in neighborhoods and attend schools that provide fewer incentives to achieve academically.

The question arises of whether single-mother families in other Western societies also suffer an economic disadvantage (Wong, Garfinkel, and McLanahan, 1993). In eight countries recently studied, the economic status of single-mother families was worse than that of two-parent families. However, the magnitude of the discrepancies varied by country. The Scandinavian single-mother families (Norway, Sweden) on average have net disposable incomes that are around 85 percent of two-parent family income. For other European countries studied (England, France, Germany), the ratio was between 65 and 76 percent. For the three non-European countries (Canada, Australia, the U.S.), the ratio was below 60 percent. Single mothers in the U.S. were younger than their counterparts in other countries, they had more children, and they had among the youngest children. These factors account for some of the differences between the U.S. and other countries in that mothers of young children are likely to spend fewer hours in the work force, and having more children per family increases family expenses. Single-mother families from all countries except the U.S. and France receive at least 20 percent of their gross income from public benefits; Sweden had the highest level of public benefits even though they also had the highest percentage of working single mothers (83 percent).

Low economic well-being is only one of the strains experienced by mother-only families. There are disruptions and the possible loss of social support. Changes in residence are common and result in the need to adjust to new housing, new neighborhoods, and new schools for the children. Although some studies report that the amount of contact with the family's kin does not necessarily decline with entering the single-mother status, the quality of the support provided may not always be positive. Single mothers also appear disadvantaged in terms of psychological well-being (Lorenz, Simons, Conger, and Elder, 1997). They report more worries and are less satisfied with their lives than married mothers or women without children, and they more frequently use mental-health services. These negative consequences persist for several years after a divorce.

Stereotypically, single-parent families have been considered to have a negative impact on children. However, these findings have been moderated in recent studies and reviews of literature that have controlled for such factors as socioeconomic status, gender of child, and role of family conflict (Acock, 1988; Hetherington, 1989). A number of studies suggest that boys suffer more severe adjustment problems that last for longer periods of time.

There is also some evidence that children's academic performance is negatively affected by divorce and living in a mother-only household (Teachman et al., 1998). The disadvantage is more pronounced in grades and educational level attained than in scores on intelligence tests. In addition, research consistently indicates that adolescents in mother-only families and in conflict-ridden families are more prone to commit delinquent crimes. Other studies suggest that adolescents in mother-only homes begin dating somewhat earlier and are more sexually active.

Recent research has begun to examine factors that may be related to the outcomes (positive and negative) of children from mother-only homes, parent–child relationships in particular. Some evidence suggests that not only are single mothers more liberal in their attitudes toward work and family roles, but they are also more independent and more egalitarian. Some studies have also found that single mothers hold less restrictive attitudes toward premarital sex (Thornton and Camburn, 1987). In the first year after divorce, mothers are less consistent in discipline and household routines and are clearly more likely to be stressed by financial concerns, working, parenting responsibilities, and their own social and health needs and concerns. As noted earlier in this chapter, grandparents may play a vital role in family transitions such as divorce by providing emotional support for both the mother and children.

Although remarriage may improve the happiness and well-being of the mother, evidence indicates that it may increase conflict and problem behavior in some children, particularly girls. Hetherington (1989) found that girls in step-families displayed more hostile and demanding behavior and less warmth than daughters in divorced or nondivorced families. Although these behaviors subsided somewhat during the first two years of remarriage, there appeared to be some residual effects. Why might this be? Hetherington suggests that stepfathers are viewed as intruders and competitors; because the girls had particularly close relationships with their mother and assumed more family responsibility in the mother-only household, the entrance of this new adult figure may be particularly stressful.

Much focus recently has been on the possible intergenerational and long-term consequences of growing up in a mother-only family (Lorenz et al., 1997; McLanahan and Booth, 1989). Some recent research suggests that children who grow up in mother-only families are disadvantaged not only during childhood but also as young adults. Children from mother-only families obtain fewer years of education, have lower earnings as adults, and are more likely to be poor. They are more likely to marry early and have children early, both in and out of wedlock. Those who marry are more likely to divorce. In short, children who grow up in mother-only families are at greater risk of becoming single mothers themselves. The effects of single motherhood are consistent across racial and ethnic groups including blacks, whites, Asians, and Hispanics. Low economic resources accounts for only some of these differences in outcomes between mother-only and married-couples families.

There is no universally accepted theory to explain why some children from mother-only families appear to be disadvantaged (Teachman et al., 1998). Three perspectives are often discussed: the economic disadvantage argument, the socialization argument, and the neighborhood argument. The economic perspective attributes the disadvantage to low parental income; single mothers have less time and less money to invest in their children, which affects both children's personal characteristics (e.g., educational attainment) and their view of the parental household. For example, children from single-parent homes may leave school early not solely due to poor performance but to earn money for their families or to care for younger siblings. They may have fewer economic opportunities and see marriage and parenthood as means of escaping economic problems.

The socialization argument claims that negative outcomes are due to dysfunctional parental values and parent–child relationships. Proponents of this perspective point to findings that single mothers are more accepting of premarital sex and divorce and are less involved in children's schoolwork. On the other hand, some researchers argue that these differences in values and socialization practices are not a result of the divorce, but existed prior to divorce or to the unmarried woman having a child. The neighborhood argument holds that lack of social support and community resources contribute to the negative outcomes of mother-only families. It should be noted that these perspectives are not mutually exclusive and these outcomes are likely to be a result of some combination of these factors.

Cohabitation

Although the disruption of marriages has probably had the most profound implications for changing family life, the way in which unions are being formed has also undergone revolutionary change. Cohabitation—an unmarried adult sharing the same living quarters with an unrelated adult of the opposite sex—has increased dramatically since 1960. Nearly 50 percent of Americans in their twenties and thirties have cohabited. Similar increases in cohabitation have occurred in France, Sweden, Australia, and Canada (Bumpass, Sweet, and Cherlin, 1991).

Contrary to the stereotype that cohabitation is college student behavior, education is strongly negatively related to cohabitation before first marriage. A third of college graduates have cohabited by age 30 compared to half of high school dropouts. Cohabitation is largely a phenomenon of the young, rather than the middle-aged or old.

Why the dramatic increase in cohabitation? Several factors appear to be involved. First, the revolution in sexual mores have made premarital sex less offensive. Only 20 percent of young adults disapprove of premarital sex. Second, the rising divorce rate have made couples much less sure that a marriage will last a lifetime. Many decide to "try out" a relationship by living together before a long-term commitment; this is the most common reason given for cohabiting (Brown and Booth, 1996). Over half of first cohabitations do end in marriage.

Although young adults may view cohabitation as a trial marriage, living together does not enhance marital stability. Marriages preceded by cohabitation have disruption rates 50 percent higher than marriages without premarital cohabitation. There are a number of possible reasons for this relationship. Spouses who cohabited before marriage report lower levels of commitment to marriage as an institution and have more liberal attitudes toward divorce (Axinn and Thornton, 1992; Thomson

The number of cohabiting couples has grown significantly over the past few decades.

and Colella, 1992). Circumstances that led to cohabitation (e.g., limited resources) may also reduce the likelihood of a marriage succeeding (Bumpass, Sweet, and Cherlin, 1991). Brown and Booth (1996) argue that the quality of cohabitors' relationships varies according to their plans to marry their partner. Cohabitors reporting plans to marry their partner are involved in unions whose quality of relationship is not significantly different from comparable married couples.

In what ways has the increase in cohabitation influenced our perception of the family life course? First, cohabitation has altered the meaning of being "single." Traditionally, the young adult, particularly young females, went directly from the parental home into a marital relationship. Delays in age at first marriage and further postformal education has meant a period of living apart from the parental family prior to marriage. For many young adults today, however, the time before marriage does not mean a period of unattached living. Second, cohabitation has made marriage a less clear-cut marker for other transitions, such as forming a sexual union, leaving the parental home, or becoming a parent.

It is unclear how cohabitation should be placed within the family life cycle. Cohabitation in young adulthood is most commonly viewed as a "try out" for marriage. The median duration of a cohabitation is short (1.5 years), and over half of the couples do proceed to marriage. On the other hand, 50 percent of cohabiting couples have children, usually as a result of a prior marriage. Cohabitation is becoming common following a marital disruption. In fact, cohabitation is considerably more common among separated and divorced persons than among the never-married. The divorced may be particularly reluctant to enter into another marital relationship, and cohabitation may be viewed as a long-term alternative to marriage.

Although living together, many cohabitors keep certain parts of their lives separate. In their study of traditional marriages and heterosexual cohabitations, Schwartz and Blumstein (1983) noted a sharp distinction between the two groups with regard to financial matters. Whereas husbands and wives tend to pool their incomes, such that the money's ownership gets lost, cohabitors often keep separate bank accounts. Thus, the relative contributions of each partner are much more evident.

Homosexual Relationships

Until quite recently, homosexual behavior was severely condemned in our society; it was considered morally wrong and psychiatrically unhealthy, and it was against the law. In the past few decades, however, there has been an increasing acceptance of homosexuality in some respects. In 1973, for instance, the American Psychiatric Association removed homosexuality from its list of psychiatric disorders. A recent Gallup poll (Gallup Oganization, 1999b) found that 83 percent of the American public thought gays and lesbians should have equal employment rights, compared to 56 percent in 1977. There remains less support for homosexuality as an acceptable lifestyle and even less support for legalization of gay marriages. In 1999 (Gallup Organization, 1999), 50 percent of the American public considered homosexuality an acceptable lifestyle and 62 percent did not think gay marriages should be legalized. One result of the decreasing condemnation is increasing openness. People with a predominantly or exclusively homosexual orientation have been admitting it publicly—"coming out of the closet." Several states and communities have had initiatives regarding discrimination for sexual preference and equal treatment for homosexuals under the law.

Confronted with a world that is often less than accepting, homosexuals are just as needful of the interdependencies of family life as heterosexuals. Increasingly, pairs of homosexuals who are committed to one another are forming long-term relationships that are acknowledged by their friends, if not always by their church or the legal system. Some families include children from a previous heterosexual union. Research on such committed couples shows little difference in emotional adjustment or activity patterns from similar heterosexual couples. In recent studies comparing married couples, heterosexual cohabiting couples, and male and female homosexual couples in monogamous relationships, similar factors were found to be related to relationship satisfaction (Blumstein and Schwartz, 1983; Kurdek and Schmitt, 1986). Kurdek (1998) examined predictors of maintenance and dissolution of relationships over a five-year period for married, lesbian and homosexual couples. All three types of couples showed a decrease in relationship satisfaction over the five years, but the types of couples did not differ in the rate of change in satisfaction. Five qualities of relationships was examined: intimacy, equality, constructive problem solving, barriers to leaving the relationship, and autonomy. For all three types of couples similar qualities were related to a breakup in the relationship during the five years: low intimacy, low level of equality, infrequent constructive problem solving, and weak barriers to leaving the partner. A breakup in the relationship occurred for 7 percent of heterosexual couples, 14 percent of gay couples and 16 percent of lesbian couples. Given the lack of general societal support for gay and lesbian relationships, it was considered notable that 86 percent of gay and 84 percent of lesbian couples remained together over the five years.

Kurdek (1993) also compared the division of household labor for heterosexual married couples, and for gay and lesbian couples. Three patterns of allocating household labor were studied. In the *equality* pattern, partners were equally likely to do household tasks, doing the tasks together or taking turns. In the *balanced* pattern, each partner was responsible for an equal number of tasks, but not the same tasks; each partner specialized in certain tasks. In the *segregation* pattern, one partner did the bulk of the household labor. The equality pattern was most characteristic of lesbian couples, sharing or taking turns with tasks. Homosexual couples tended to divide the household tasks, with each partner specializing in some tasks; there tended to be a balancing of the number of tasks performed by each. In contrast, the segregation pattern was most characteristic of married couples, with the wife doing much of the household labor.

The pressures of family life are magnified for homosexuals. Kinship ties to parents, siblings, and even children are threatened. Both male and female homosexual monogamous couples perceived less social support from family than did either married or cohabiting heterosexual couples (Kurdek, 1988). The most frequent social support came from, in order: friends, partners, family, and coworkers, with friends making up 43 percent of the total support network. Diminished family support is reflected in the care of AIDS patients; 59 percent of AIDS victims lived alone or with a nonrelative during the last year of life, compared with 25 percent of adults dying from other causes (Kapantais and Powell-Griner, 1989). Homosexuals have great difficulty in retaining custody of their children and find it more difficult to adopt children (Bailey, Bobrow, Wolfe, and Mikach, 1995; Falk, 1989). Outside the law of state and church, homosexuals may find that they cannot visit their partners in a hospital or nursing home (Herek and Glunt, 1988; Kelly, 1977). If the partners should die, they often are excluded from the funeral and may not be able to show their sorrow openly; they cannot file a malpractice suit as "a surviving spouse," and problems of inheritance rights occur.

The Changing Family

It seems that the family as an institution is not dying; it is simply changing. During the 1960s and 1970s, there were dramatic shifts in attitudes toward marriage and family; and in the 1980s and 1990s, we saw new forms of the family and of family relationships that were the manifestation of these shifts in attitudes (Bumpass, 1990; Thornton, 1989). One important theme to emerge is the relaxation of social prescriptions for family behavior and an expanding of the range of choice. There has been a decrease in the need to conform to a set of behavioral standards in the family and an increase in the freedom of individuals to choose. A relaxation of social prescriptions has been associated with an increase in individualism. When needs and interests conflict, as they do in any collectivity such as a family, increasing weight seems to be given to the concerns and interests of the individual.

Today, fewer individuals are living in "traditional" nuclear families that include a married couple and children. The traditional family now represents only a quarter of the households in the U.S.. Even the "traditional" family has changed as the majority of mothers are now in the work force. With over half of recent marriages likely to end in divorce, alternative family forms are becoming normative. Given the delay in age at first marriage and increasing anxiety over the stability of marriage, cohabitation is becoming a precursor to marriage for many young adults; for divorced adults, cohabitation may be viewed as an alternative to marriage. The traditional ordering of events in family life—courtship, marriage, childbearing—no longer holds in many families. The number of births to unmarried mothers is increasing. Children are increasingly likely to live in mother-only households.

What effects do these changes in family forms have on adult development? To answer this question, we have to understand many things. We need to know more about the advantages of the new forms. For example, the family of today is more mobile than before, which is probably a factor in increased income and a higher standard of living. The variety of family forms today means that people have several options when deciding on how best to satisfy their family-related needs. There is more freedom, which can be dangerous but which also presents opportunities for new forms of growth and achievement less likely in more rigidly structured societies. It is possible, for example, that some spouses are achieving degrees of intimacy unknown to couples who lived in times when marriage was based primarily on social norms and expectations.

The number of children living in single parent households is increasing.

Although the structure and the form of the family continues to be in flux, the premise of our opening statement regarding the importance of interdependencies in family relationships remains. The concept of interdependence helps us understand why men and women continue to seek meaningful relationships although family forms may vary, why parent–child relationships may be increasing in salience as greater portions of the adult life span are spent with each other, and how values and traditions are transmitted from generation to generation.

SUMMARY

1. A family can be viewed as a system of interdependent relationships in which each member depends on others for some needs and fills some needs for the others. Although interdependencies among family members remain salient, there have been major changes in family forms. The traditional family of a married couple with children under 18 years of age accounts for less than a quarter of all U.S. households. Approximately 30 percent of households involve a married couple with no children or children over age 18. Single-parent households, primarily mother-only households, represent 16 percent; and one-person households represent over 25 percent of all households.

2. A family typically begins with a union of two young people. The interdependencies on which marriages are based are sexual, emotional, and

familial (the desire to provide a context for having children). The emotional interdependency of young couples involves a constant conflict between the need to be independent and the need for emotional intimacy with another person, a conflict Erikson calls the intimacy crisis of young adulthood. Choosing a mate is a process that can be viewed as filtering out unacceptable possibilities on the basis of propinquity, attractiveness, social background, attitude similarity, complementarity, and temporal readiness for marriage.

3. Having children is part of what Erikson calls the generativity crisis, which has to do with creativity and production in careers, too, but finds direct expression in the creation of new life. Most people derive great satisfaction from their children. Children make parents feel needed and provide a link to the future.

4. In recent decades, the expectation has arisen that fathers should not only be good economic providers, but also actively involved in child care. These attitudes have been fostered by the increase of mothers in the work force. Although the majority of parents believe that child care should be equally shared, mothers, even when working full-time, do the majority of child care.

5. It is often said that the nuclear family (parents and children) is isolated from kin (the extended family) in today's world. This myth is based on the belief that extended families were common in earlier eras of American life (not true) and on the belief that nuclear families of today have little contact with kin (also not true). Family relationships remain strong, although they may take a different form than they did in earlier years.

6. As children grow up and leave home, the parents remain behind in an empty nest or a postparental family. Parents in general and mothers in particular are supposed to be distressed by this event, but research shows the opposite: satisfaction with completing a life's task (raising children) and renewed intimacy with one's spouse.

7. It is not true that most adult children and their aging parents reverse roles, with the aging parents becoming dependent on the children. In fact, an increasing number of old-old widows live alone. An older person in our society may become more dependent in limited respects, but typically relationships between adult children and aging parents simply become more mature: one adult interacting with another, with bonds of affection and duty.

8. Recent research on multigenerational households has distinguished between *upward* and *downward* extension,—whether older parents come to live in the household of an adult child (upward), or whether grandchildren (with or without parents) live in the household of a grandparent (downward). A rise in downward extended households occurred between 1970 and the early 1990s; this type of multigenerational family is more common in black families. The increase in downward extended households has been linked to increases in the divorce rate as well as in out-of-wedlock births. In contrast, older parents that live with their adult children

(upward extension) has declined in the last century

9. The structure of the extended family is changing because of increases in life expectancy and declines in fertility. The structure is becoming more vertical, with three to five generations, but fewer members in each generations. The extended family is also becoming "top heavy" with the average married couple having more living parents than children. Given gender differences in life expectancy, older generations of family are primarily older women.

10. Mother-only families have become increasingly common. It is hypothesized that nearly half of all children born since 1975 will live in a mother-only family sometime before the age of 18. Contrary to the stereotypes of single mothers on public assistance, almost three-quarters of single mothers are in the labor force. One of the most significant differences between mother-only and married-couple families is the difference in economic well-being.

SUGGESTED READINGS

Bengtson, V. L., and Giarrusso, R. (2001). The aging self in social context. In R. H. Binstrock and L. K. George (Eds). *Handbook of aging and the social sciences* (5th ed.). San Diego, CA: Academic. Examination of the interrelationship between development of the self and intergenerational relationships in a multigenerational family.

King, V., and Elder, G. H. (1997). The legacy of grandparenting: Childhood experiences with grandparents and current involvement with grandchildren. *Journal of Marriage and the Family,* 59, 848–859. Childhood experiences with grandparents are an important factor in the current involvement of men and women with their own grandchildren. The degree to which grandparents are involved in playing their role and the type of involvement they have with grandchildren are significantly influenced by having known their own grandparents.

Pleck, J. H. (1997). Paternal involvement: Levels, sources, and consequences. In M. E. Lamb (Ed.), *The role of the father in child development* (3rd ed.). New York: Wiley. The recent literature on residential father involvement has been comprehensively reviewed and analyzed.

Szinovacz, M. E. (1998). Grandparents today: A demographic profile. *Gerontologist, 38,* 37–52. Presents a demographic profile of grandparents. Due to increasing life expectancy, adults are spending a greater part of the lifespan as grandparents and are involved with grandchildren even in young adulthood. Adult life transitions are occurring in a different historical order with grandparenting occurring prior to retirement and widowhood.

Wilson, M. N. (1998). Parenting and parent–child interactions in African-American families: A synopsis. *African American Research Perspectives, 4,* 27-34. Examines the structure of African-American families and the types of interaction patterns that occur between adults and between adults and children. African-American children are more likely to live in a single-parent family or with a parent and other relatives, primarily a grandparent, than in the traditional nuclear family with two parents.

CHAPTER 7

Men and Women

Together and Apart

The relationship between men and women is an exceeding complex topic, and various aspects of the relationship have been dealt with in different chapters of this text. We discussed the couple in the context of the family in Chapter 6 and will consider dual-earner marriages in the context of careers in Chapter 8. Because finding a mate is a normative task of young adulthood, we explored intimacy and romantic love in Chapter 2. As a result of demographic changes in our society, increasing numbers of individuals can expect to spend some part of adulthood in a state (singlehood, divorced, widowed) outside the traditional married-couple relationship. Age at first marriage has been increasing and a growing number of young adults experience their early sexual encounters prior to marriage. Over 50 percent of marriages end in divorce, and the majority of elderly women experience widowhood. It is becoming increasingly important, then, to consider male and female relationships and life styles both inside and outside the marriage bond; these issues are the focus of this chapter. In the following pages, we discuss sexuality and consider life situations involving men and women outside of marriage or other forms of commitment (e.g., cohabitation, homosexual unions).

SEXUAL BEHAVIOR

The public image of sex in America as reflected in the media suggests that sexual behavior is increasingly openly discussed and acknowledged and that adults, in general, are engaging in more frequent and more varied forms of sexual activity. This increased "openness" and interest in sex, beginning in the 1960s, would suggest that sexual behavior is one of the most widely and intensively studied forms of human conduct. Paradoxically, our information on sexual behavior has been based on a small number of studies that are limited in scope and generality and often methodologically flawed.

Two volumes by Alfred Kinsey and coworkers, *Sexuality in the Human Male* (1948) and *Sexuality in the Human Female* (1953), contain perhaps the most extensive data published on sexual behavior, and much of the cited information on sexual behavior has been based on these reports, even though the data are now outdated. Alfred Kinsey, a professor of zoology, became interested in the topic when asked to teach the sexuality section of a course, and found almost no information on the topic. The challenges that he experienced and the limitations of his subsequent research reflect many of the problems still evident in the field. He first administered a questionnaire about sexual practice to his college students. Finding this method unsatisfactory, he began face-to-face interviews with members of various groups who were willing to be interviewed, including sororities and fraternities, rooming house boarders, prison inmates, and social organizations. Eventually, he and his three associates interviewed nearly 18,000 people, a remarkable accomplishment! However, Kinsey was aware of the flaws with his research methods that made questionable the representativeness and generalizability of his findings regarding sexual behavior. First, instead of studying randomly selected members of the population, he had used a sample of convenience. These were individuals who volunteered to be interviewed and who belonged to particular organizations or groups. These participants did not represent all Americans and the findings could not be generalized to describe the sexual practices of the whole population. Those who volunteer for sex surveys have been found to have wider sexual experience than those who do not.

A decade after Kinsey's study, William Masters, a gynecologist, and Virginia Johnson, his research associate, conducted a new type of sex study. Viewing sex as a natural biological process, they watched and described the sex act being performed in the laboratory by subjects whom they paid. Again, the participants were limited to volunteers willing to participate in such research. Their book, *Human Sexual Response* (Masters and Johnson, 1966) disturbed many Americans, but also became an instant best seller.

In the 1970s and 1980s, a series of popular reports on sexual practices were published, including the *Playboy* report, the *Redbook* report (Tavris and Sadd, 1975), the *Hite Report*, (Hite, 1976) and more recently the *Janus Report* (Janus and Janus, 1993). Findings from these surveys, which reported significant increases in sexual activity compared to the earlier Kinsey data, have been widely publicized. However, again, the research methodology has been flawed. First, these were mail-in surveys, so it was unclear who really completed the questionnaires. Second, these surveys were limited to volunteer participants and often reflected the characteristics of the readership of particular magazines. Also, the response rate to these surveys was very low, limiting further the representativeness of the respondents. Less than 3 percent of the readership of the *Playboy* or *Redbook* magazines returned the survey. Hite reported only a 3 percent response rate.

In the mid 1990s two large surveys with more representative samples have been reported (AARP, 1999; Michael, Gagnon, Laumann, and Kolata, 1994);

Sexual attraction is strongest in young adulthood.

findings from these surveys will provide the bases for our discussion of sexual behavior and attitudes. The two studies differ in the age range considered with the National Health and Social Life Survey (NHSLS; Michael et al.,1994) examining adults aged 18 to 59 years, and the AARP study reporting on adults aged 45 and older. The NHSLS study was conducted through the National Opinion Research Center, using well-established survey research methodology; the sample involved 3,432 adults in the United States. The AARP/Modern Maturity Sexual Survey (AARP, 1999) was a telephone and mail survey of 1,384 adults aged 45 and older completed in 1999. Both samples are comparable on demographic variables to national surveys on other topics and had high response rates of approximately 80 percent. Although the samples for these studies appear to be much more representative than prior surveys, the limited sample sizes makes it difficult to provide detailed information on certain subsamples (e.g., ethnic groups in a certain age range and educational lcvcl and homoscxuals). Thosc who wcrc homcless or living in institutions (e.g., jails, nursing homes) were excluded.

Sexual Intercourse

The NHSLS survey (Michael et al., 1994) addressed several interesting questions: How often do Americans aged 18 to 59 years have sex? Who are an individual's sexual partners? How many sex partners does the "average" American have over the life course.

Contrary to some popular stereotypes, the NHSLS survey found that the group having the most sex were married couples, not young singles. For both men and women, married and cohabiting couples are having the most sex. Three factors were strongly associated with frequency of partnered sex: how old the person was, whether people were married or cohabiting, and how long the couple had been together. Factors such as educational level, ethnicity, and religion were less salient predictors of level of sexual activity. People in their twenties had the most sex. The authors suggest that sexual activity peaks in the twenties rather than earlier because it is in the twenties that adults become increasingly likely to marry or to be living with a partner. In the thirties and forties, even though approximately 75 percent are married or living with someone, couples begin to have partnered sex less often, compared with couples in their twenties.

The AARP survey provides data on sexual activity and attitudes on adults 45 and over (Table 7-1). Table 7-1 shows the proportion of men and women at

Table 7-1 Frequency of Sexual Activity During last Six Months (About Once a Week or More Often)

Activity	Men			Women		
	45–59	*60–74*	*75+*	*45–59*	*60–74*	*75+*
Kissing/ Hugging	77.3	73.1	63.3	71.7	49.1	27.7
Sexual Touching	68.9	61.2	45.2	61.4	36.6	14.9
Sexual Intercourse	54.8	30.9	19.1	49.6	24.2	6.6
Oral Sex	20.1	6.5	8.8	19.5	2.2	0.8
Self Stimulation	33.5	14.2	5.2	4.5	2.0	0.6

Note: Question asked: During the past 6 months, how often on average, have you engaged in the following sexual activities.
Source: AARP/Modern Maturity Sexuality Study, 1999.

different ages that report engaging about once a week or more often in a sexual activity within the past six months. Men and women between the ages of 45 and 59 report similar frequencies for most types of sexual behavior. Self stimulation is the exception, as men 45 to 59 report more frequent participation in this activity than women. Men in the 60 to 74 age range report more frequent sexual behavior than women 60 to 74. Reported behavior becomes even more divergent among men and women who are 75 years old or older . Both men and women in the older age groups report less frequent sexual activity than their younger counterparts, but the amount of drop-off is greater among women than among men. Most men 75 or over report that kissing or hugging occurs weekly or more often, and almost half indicate that sexual touching or caressing occurs weekly or more often. In contrast, two-thirds of women 75 or over indicate they never engage in sexual kissing or hugging and three-quarters report an absence of sexual touching or caressing. Half of men 75 or over say that they have engaged in sexual intercourse within the last six months, while five out of six women 75 or over report no sexual intercourse during this time.

Similar findings have been reported in European research. In a Finnish study (Kivela, Pahkala, and Honkakoski, 1986), half of men above age 60 and 20 percent of women in this age group reported continuing to have sexual intercourse. Two Swedish studies also found half of men and 33 percent of women reported having intercourse at least once a month (Bergstrom-Walan and Nielsen, 1990; Skoog, 1988)

There are a number of alternative explanations of why sexual behavior decreases with age (AARP 1999; Michael et al., 1994). The biological explanation is that the sex drive, particularly the pressure to procreate, diminishes with age. Most couples complete their families by their thirties. However, it should be noted that the sex drive, as reflected in sex hormones, is not much changed until age fifty or beyond. Social factors that may influence frequency of sexual activity include the increasing demands of work, commuting, taking care of children, and managing a complicated life in the modern world. There are also the sexual stereotypes suggesting that sexual activity is the province of the young, and not appropriate for the old.

Another important change in patterns of sexual behavior becomes increasingly striking with age—that is, whether one is sexually active depends increasingly on having a partner. The AARP/Modern Maturity Sexual Survey (AARP, 1999) found that over 75 percent of men and women aged 45 to 59 years had a sexual partner. However women aged 60 and over are much less likely than men 60 and over to have a sexual partner. Whereas 75 percent of men aged 60 and over have a sexual partner only 50 percent of women of that age have a partner. The disparity is even greater for those aged 75 and over; 50 percent of men but only 20 percent of women in this age range say they have a sexual partner. Moreover, the age of the sexual partner differs for older men and women, particularly for those 75 years and over. Half of men aged 75 and over have a partner who is under age 75, while most women of that age have a partner 75 or over.

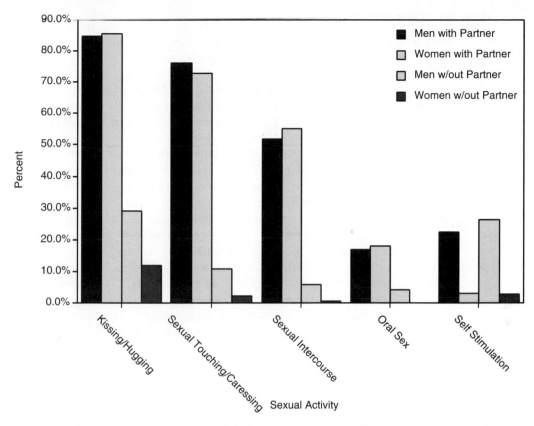

Figure 7-1 Proportion Reporting Sexual Activity About Once a Week or More: Men and Women With and Without a Partner *Source:* AARP/Modern Maturity Sexuality Study, 1999.

Figure 7-1 shows the proportion of AARP study participants with and without partners that report engaging about once a week or more often in a sexual activity within the past six months. Men and women with partners report similar frequencies for all types of sexual activity except self stimulation. Men without partners are much more likely than women without partners to report participation in various forms of sexual activity. These discrepancies in patterns of sexual activity for older men and women reflect gender differences in marital status and mortality. As discussed in Chapters 4 and 6, particularly in old age, a significantly higher proportion of men are in a couple relationship than women. In the AARP survey 68 percent of men 75 or over were married compared to 25 percent of women in that age group. As we will discuss in the next section on sexual attitudes, differences in sexual activity of older men and women may also reflect cohort differences and gender differences in opinions about sex.

Number of Sexual Partners

Another question addressed by the NHSLS survey focused on the total number of sexual partners over the lifetime. Changes in the institution of marriage have contributed to a greater total number of sexual partners for younger cohorts across the life course. While the average age of sexual intercourse has crept downward, the average age of first marriage has increased (see Chapter 6). A growing number of young adults engage in cohabitation prior to marriage. In addition, younger cohorts are more likely to experience divorce and to find new sexual partners in the period between marriages. Divorced adults as a group have more sexual partners than married individuals and as a group are more likely to have intercourse with a partner and live with a partner before they marry again. As a result of these three demographic trends (younger age at first intercourse, older age at first marriage, increasing divorce rates), younger cohorts report a larger total number of sexual partners than earlier generations. Approximately half of adults aged 30 to 50 years reported five or more partners over the life course, compared with 30 percent of adults over the age of 50. On the other hand, the vast majority of adults of all ages report having had one or no sexual partners in the past 12 months, suggesting that in any given interval most adults have a very limited number of sexual partners. Over half of men and women aged 18 to 24 had just one sex partner in the past year and another 11 percent had none. It appears that the vast majority of Americans are faithful while in a marriage or a relationship, having only a single partner.

Figure 7-2 shows cohort differences in average age at first intercourse. Men and women born in the decade 1943–1952 had first intercourse at an average age of about 18 (Michael et al., 1994). In comparison, those born two or three decades later had their first intercourse earlier. Men report having sex at younger ages than women. There are ethnic differences. Approximately half of teenagers today have begun having intercourse in the 15- to 18-year-old age range and approximately 80 percent have had intercourse by the time their teenage years are over (Besharov and Gardiner, 1993; Hofferth, Kahn and Baldwin, 1987).

Different measures are used to record frequency of sexual intercourse at various points in the life span. As illustrated in the above discussion, for adolescents, intercourse is usually discussed in terms of the percentage of boys and girls who are sexually active. After marriage, sexual intercourse is typically recorded in terms of frequency per week (see Figure 7-1).

Biological Considerations in Sexual Intercourse

A number of biological factors can affect sexual intercourse (AARP, 1999; Whitbourne, 1998). These include the sex hormones, chronic diseases, and medications prescribed for certain health problems. The sex hormones (estrogen and progesterone in females; androgens, including testosterone, in males) have a notable influence on sexual behavior at many points in the life span. In adolescence, these hormones regulate puberty which, among its other characteristics, involves a

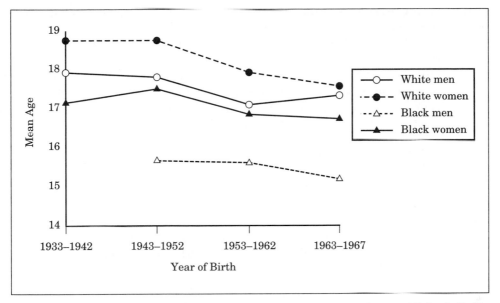

Figure 7-2 Cohort Differences in Mean Age at First Intercourse. *Source:* Michael, R. T., Gagnon, J. H., Laumann, E. O., and Kolata, G. (1994). *Sex in America.* New York: Little, Brown and Co.

dramatic increase in the sex drive. In a mature woman, the female hormones regulate the menstrual cycle and may have effects on sexual desire throughout that cycle. Sometime around the age of 50 a decline of estrogen in women accompanies the cessation of menses (Avis, 1999; Bellantoni and Blackman, 1995).

In many animals other than humans, hormones control a rigid, clearcut relationship between reproductive fertility in the female and sexual responsiveness in both male and female. In humans, this relationship is rather easily overcome by nonbiological influences. Menopause is a good example (Avis et al., 1993). In other animals a decrease in estrogen brings a decrease in sexual drive; but in humans, menopause has no direct effect on sexual capability or interest (Pedersen, 1998). After menopause, many women report an increased sex drive; their fear of pregnancy is gone, and they enjoy the "pure" tenderness and sensuality of the physical communication with their partners.

As men grow older, biological factors do affect their ability to have intercourse (AARP, 1999; Feldman et al., 1994; Segraves and Segraves, 1995; Whitbourne, 1998). By middle age, the average man takes longer than a young adult to have an erection after stimulation, ejaculates semen with half the force of youth, and has a longer refractory period, before he can have another erection. On the other hand, men in the 50- to 75-year-old age group can remain erect longer before coming to orgasm than those in the 20- to 40-year-old age group; this has been noted as a positive factor by middle-aged and older adults, because intercourse can be less hurried and there is greater opportunity for mutual satisfaction of both partners.

Impotence, the inability to have or maintain an erection, becomes a concern for men. The reports of impotence vary more widely than other sexual reports, perhaps for obvious "macho" reasons. In the AARP study, reports of complete impotence increased with age: 45 to 49 years (2.5 percent); 60 to 74 years (15.9 percent); 75 or over (37.7 percent). On the other hand, over three-quarters of men 45 to 49 years and almost half of men 75 and over report always having an orgasm when engaged in sexual activity.

The causes of impotence vary and include both biological and psychological factors. In the AARP study 40 percent of men aged 60 to 74 and 45 percent of men aged 75 and over reported having a physical condition that restricted sexual activity. High blood pressure was the most prevalent condition; diabetes and prostate problems were more common among men 60 and over and prostate cancer was the leading problem (11 percent of men) for men 75 and over. Less than twenty percent of women at any age in the AARP study reported a physical condition restricting sexual activity; the most common conditions mentioned were arthritis and rheumatism. Males (13 percent) are more likely than females (6 percent) to report seeking treatment from professionals for problems related to sexual functioning; Viagra was the most common treatment used by males seeking treatment. In the Massachusetts study (Feldman et al., 1994), a higher probability of impotence was directly correlated with heart disease, hypertension, diabetes, and associated medications, after controlling for the effect of age. Medications for cardiovascular problems can decrease potency as well as increase the likelihood of depression (Araujo, Durante, Feldman, Goldstein, and McKinlay, 1998; Feldman et al, 1994). In addition, for those men with heart disease and hypertension, cigarette smoking increased the probability of complete impotence. There has been considerable debate regarding the role of hormones, such as testosterone, in sexual potency; no association with testosterone was found in the Massachusetts study (Feldman et al., 1994).

The fear of losing potency remains either the cause or a major contributing factor in many cases of impotency (Pedersen, 1998). Sex, self-esteem, and self-image are closely related. Often one or two episodes of impotence are brought on by physical exhaustion, intemperate consumption of alcohol, physical illness (e.g., diabetes), or prescription drugs (e.g., sedatives). The individual begins to fear that he will never be able to perform adequately again. Thus, for a variety of reasons, the physical inability of the male is the most common hindrance to sexual intercourse among middle-aged and elderly couples (AARP, 1999; Michael et al., 1994).

SEXUAL ATTITUDES

A limitation of many of the surveys of sexual behavior is that they focus largely on the sexual act but leave many psychological questions unaddressed. Sex is a total human experience, not just a biological function, and it is important that we treat

Contrary to myth, many elderly people continue to express their need for tenderness, caring, and sexual intimacy.

it as such in our discussion (see also Chapters 2 and 10). Sexual attitudes play a major role in sexual behavior throughout the life span. In this chapter, we have thus far described age-related patterns of sexual behavior across the life span and considered changes in biological functioning as they influence sexual behavior. We now examine individuals' attitudes regarding the meaning and satisfaction of their sexual lives.

Age Differences in Attitudes

The recent NHSLS survey examined young and middle-aged adults' satisfaction with their sex lives (Michael et al., 1994). Interestingly, the people who reported being the most physically pleased and emotionally satisfied with their sex lives were married or cohabiting couples. Over 80 percent of couples reported themselves to be either "very" or "extremely" satisfied with their sex lives and to receive great emotional satisfaction. Lower rates of satisfaction were found among men and women who were not married or cohabiting. The least satisfied were those who were not married, not living with anyone, and who had at least two sexual partners. Only 54 percent of the unattached young and middle-aged adults reported that they were extremely or very physically pleased and only a third said that they were emotionally satisfied. Happiness with one's sex life was found also to be strongly associated with being happy in general, although it is unclear which comes first.

Are older adults as satisfied with their sex lives as young and middle-aged adults? Just as for young and middle-aged adults, how satisfied older adults were with their sex lives depended on whether or not they had a partner (AARP, 1999). The proportion of older men and women with partners reporting being extremely or somewhat satisfied with their sex lives was 64 and 67 percent respectively. In contrast, only 18 percent of older men and 27 percent of older women without partners reported being satisfied.

The common assumption of incongruity between sex and old age can in part be attributed to the overemphasis in our society on the physical aspects of sexuality and the notion that satisfying sex occurs only between youthful, attractive partners and when orgasm is achieved. One young medical student asked how exciting sex could be between two people with flabby bodies, wrinkled skin, and old faces? However, many older adults do report finding sex satisfying and pleasurable; 75 percent of the elderly in one study reported that sex now was the same or better than when they were younger (Starr and Weiner, 1981). In their interviews with 800 elderly, Starr and Weiner (1981) found that in discussing their sexual activities, the older adults emphasized the quality of the experience, rather than just its frequency. They talked about the pleasure of being unhurried and of not feeling they had to perform or reach a specific goal. One 72-year-old woman explained, "Your sex is so much more relaxed, I know my body better and we know each other better—sex is unhurried and the best in our lives" (p. 11). A 69-year-old man summed it up, "Sex is one of the pleasures of life. It is also one way in which men and women overcome loneliness and frustration. There's the added pleasure as we grow older, we can still enjoy sex and thus are still to be counted as total men and women" (p. 37).

Sex Differences in Attitudes and Behavior

Sexuality can be expressed differently in males and females, of course: anatomy differs, physiology differs, and reproductive roles differ. Therefore, questions of differences in sexuality arise. Are there differences in sexual interest, for example, so that one or the other party desires more sexual activity than the other or considers sex more important ? What has happened to the concept of the double standard?

Females generally report less interest in sex than males, although differences in attitudes and behaviors are decreasing. In the NHSLS survey, approximately 50 percent of young and middle-aged men reported thinking about sex every day or several times a day, compared to 10 percent of young and middle-aged women (Michael et al., 1994). In comparison, 30 percent of older men reported thinking about sex every day or several times a day, compared to 5 percent of older women (AARP, 1999).

Figure 7-3 shows the proportion of older adults who strongly agreed or agreed with the following two statements: "Sexual activity is important to my overall quality of life" and "Sex becomes less important to people as they age." Older men were more likely than females at older ages to state that sexual activity was important to their overall quality of life; agreement with the statement decreased for both males and females with age. Interestingly, both older men and women agreed that sex became less important with age; the gender differences in response to this statement were much less pronounced. However, agreement with this statement increased with age.

Attitudes Regarding Extramarital Sex

The secular trend toward increasing societal tolerance of premarital and marital sexual practices does not extend to extramarital sex (Michael et al., 1994). Articles and movies about mate swapping notwithstanding, both men and women, young and old, view sexual fidelity as essential to the marriage contract. Since the 1960s, attitudes toward extramarital affairs have become strongly negative, with over 80 percent of adults considering affairs as wrong all or most of the time. In the NHSLS study over 75 percent of young and middle aged adults considered extramarital sex as always wrong.

This position seems to be reflected not only in attitudes but also in the behavior of married couples in the 1990s (Michael et al, 1994). While in a steady relationship, men and women typically have a single sexual partner. In the U.S in 1990, more than 80 percent of women and 70 percent of men of every age

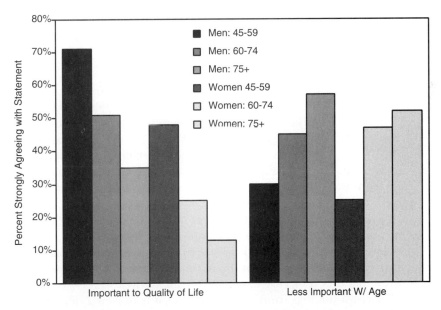

Figure 7-3   General Opinions on Sex: Gender and Age Differences. *Source:* AARP/Modern Maturity Sexuality Study, 1999.

reported no partners other than their spouse while they were married (Michael et al., 1994). Similar patterns have been reported in Europe. In a study in the United Kingdom, 73 percent of men and 79 percent of women had one partner in the past year. In France, the figures were 78 percent of men and women and in Finland, 78 percent of men and 79 percent of women.

Among the reasons given for entering into an extramarital relationship, by far the most important is resentment and dissatisfaction with the marriage itself. Next in importance seems to be premarital sexual patterns (the more sexual partners one had before marriage, the more likely one is to be extramaritally active). Men are most likely to be involved in extramarital relations during the first 5 years of marriage, while for women it is more common after 15 to 20 years (Broderick, 1982).

VIOLENT CRIME AND RAPE AGAINST WOMEN

Women are generally less likely than men to be crime victims. However, in two crime categories female victims predominate. These are violence committed against women by intimates, and rape (National Center for Victims of Crime, 1992; Rennison, 1999; see Magdol, Mofitt, Caspi, Newman, Fagan, and Silva, 1997 for an exception). Of the violent crimes by intimates reported by female victims, the vast majority were assaults, with a smaller number being robberies and rapes. A recent Gallup poll (1997b) found that a greater proportion of U.S. women (22 percent) reported physical abuse by a husband or partner than women in the three other countries surveyed, Colombia (17 percent), Canada (9 percent), and Mexico (6 percent). An intimate includes relatives (parent, child, sibling), spouses, ex-spouses, and boyfriends.

Violent Crime by Intimates

Violent crime by intimates against women most frequently involves an assault by a man with whom the woman has been previously romantically or sexually involved (Rennison, 1999; Tjaden and Thoennes, 1998). Divorced or separated women are much more likely to be victims of violent crimes than married women or widows. Although separated or divorced women compose 10 percent of all women, they reported the majority of the spousal violence. In the majority of incidences, the victim was physically attacked and over half of the victims reported being injured. Only approximately ten percent of women victimized by a violent intimate sought professional medical treatment (Greenfield, Rand, and Craven, 1998). Victims tend to be young (20 to 34 years), unemployed, and of a lower income level. The vast majority of these crimes are not reported to the police; the primary reason for not reporting was that the victim perceived it to be a personal matter or reported that they took care of the matter themselves.

Recent findings from a longitudinal study in New Zealand may provide some insight into the developmental antecedents of partner abuse (Magdol, Moffitt, Caspi, and Silva, 1998). Four domains of adolescent characteristics at age 15 were found to be predictive of males being abusive at age 21: family relation, family socioeconomic resources, educational achievement and problem behaviors. Specifically, boys at age 15 with closer parent–child attachments and with higher parental occupational status were less likely to become abusive partners. In contrast, boys at age 15 whom both the parents and the boys themselves reported to be aggressive, to have conduct problems, and to be involved in substance abuse were more likely to be aggressive partners at age 21.

Rape

Although rape is not the most common violent crime against women, it has received considerable attention and is the crime that many women fear most (Koss, 1993). The study of rape is confounded by the fact that legal definitions of rape vary from state to state. Definitions typically involve three separate elements: sexual intercourse occurs; there is force or threat of force; and the victim does not consent to the act (Koss, 1993). Estimates of the prevalence of rape or attempted rape vary widely. Approximately 16 percent of women have experienced an attempted or completed rape as a child or an adult (Tjaden and Thoennes, 1998). Rape is largely a crime both against and by the young. Women aged 16 to 24 were much more likely to be raped than older women (Hirsch, 1990). Over 40 percent of rapists were 21 to 29 years of age and approximately one-third were 30 or older (Harlow, 1991).

Acquaintance Rape

Of particular concern recently has been acquaintance rape—a rape in which the victim and the rapist are previously known to each other and have been interacting in a socially appropriate manner prior to the incident (Harlow, 1991; Rennison, 1999). How common is acquaintance rape? Ten to 20 percent of college women surveyed reported experiencing sexual intercourse against their consent and with use of force or threat of harm (Hirsch, 1990; Koss, Gidycz, and Wisniewski, 1987).

A major problem in the study of acquaintance rape is the difficulty in determining whether an incident should be labeled rape and under what conditions such a rape occurs. Individuals are less likely to perceive acquaintance rape as "real" rape, compared to rape by a stranger. Part of the ambiguity is related to societal assumptions and norms governing sexual activity among acquaintances, particularly dating couples. For example, there is some evidence that in our society it is commonly accepted that a woman will conceal her genuine interest in sexual contact and that she may be expected to resist a man's advances in the beginning stages of a sexual encounter, even though she may later consent to sexual relations. Moreover, it is commonly accepted that the male will take the dominant role in sexual activity (Burt and Albin, 1981).

Acquaintance rape is of particular concern on college campuses, given that most rapes involve young women and that over one-quarter of young adults are on college campuses (Hirsch, 1990). The vast majority of rape or sexual assault victims knew their attackers (Rennison, 1999). Many were dating or had dated him. Somewhat similar prevalence rates for college-aged women have been reported in the United Kingdom (Beattie, 1992), New Zealand (Gavey, 1991), Canada (DeKeseredy and Kelly, 1993), and Korea (Shinn, 1992).

In what context did the rape occur? Most occurred off campus, at the victim's or the offender's residence. The majority of the rape victims and offenders were using some form of intoxicants (National Center for Victims of Crime, 1992). Many of the couples had previously been involved in some level of physical intimacy. The majority of rapes were not reported to police. Women were more likely to assume some blame for the rape if it occurred with an acquaintance. It is particularly disturbing that a number of the women also reported having sex with the offender after the rape, although it was unclear whether subsequent sex was voluntary or forced.

What were the characteristics of those males (and to a lesser extent some females) involved in aggressive sexual behavior? They were more likely to have become sexually active at an early age, to report feelings of hostility toward women, to consider force and coercion to be legitimate ways to gain sexual compliance, and to be heavy users of alcohol (Koss and Dinero, 1988; Koss and Gaines, 1993). Sexually aggressive young males have been found to use several techniques to achieve sexual involvement, including reminding partners of past behaviors, pleading, lying, and ridiculing partners (Christopher, Madura, and Weaver, 1998). Aggressive males were also more likely to believe in rape myths—for instance—"a woman can escape a rape attempt if she truly wants" and certain styles of women's dress mean that she is asking to be raped.

An even more thorny issue is that of marital rape and rape by family members. Until the late 1970s most states did not consider spousal rape a crime (National Center for Victims of Crime, 2000b). Current studies suggest that marital rape is most likely to occur in marriages that are violent in other ways as well. Compared with victims of other types of acquaintance rape, women who were raped by their husband or other family member reported more severe anger and depression; they were also the least likely of all victims to report the rape (Koss, Dinero, Seibel, and Cox,1988). In addition, victims of spousal rape often have to overcome additional legal hurdles to prosecution not present for other victims of rape, including time limits for reporting the offense, a requirement that force or threat of force be used, and the fact that some sexual assault offenses still preclude spousal victims (National Center for Victims of Crime, 2000b).

Stranger Rape

Although female victims rated stranger rape as more violent than acquaintance rape, involving threats of bodily harm and use of weapons, there was little difference in reports of injury or receipt of medical care between the two groups (Harlow, 1991; National Center for Victims of Crime, 2000a). Rape by a stranger was more likely to be reported to the authorities, in contrast to acquaintance rape, in which victims considered the rape a personal or private matter. Victims of stranger rape were also more likely to be using drugs, including alcohol, at the time of the rape (Koss, et al., 1988). In the types of avoidance strategies used, there were no differences between the victims, although women raped by strangers were more likely to have screamed for help. Finally, while acquaintance rape was rated by both males and females as somewhat less serious, the psychological effects on the victims of both types of rape were quite similar and included feelings of depression and anxiety (Koss, et al., 1988).

MARITAL INSTABILITY

Most couples enter marriage with dreams of sharing years of happiness and intimacy together. But increasingly these days, intimacy does not grow with the years; instead it withers. Eventually the couple looks at what seems to be an empty relationship and calls it quits. Divorce follows.

What happened? What went wrong? In this section, we will look at some of the factors that can impede or disrupt marriage, the growing incidence of divorce, and the "ripple" effect to adjacent generations in the family.

Divorce: Incidence and Attitudes

The divorce rate in the United States has been increasing for more than 100 years (Bumpass, 1990). Figure 7-4 shows the number of divorces from 1940 to 1998. Also shown are the number of children involved in divorces; data on children are only currently available from 1950 to 1990. Except for a sharp spike during the 1940s associated with World War II, the increase in the divorce rate was gradual until a sharp rise occurred in the 1960s. Between 1960 and 1980, the divorce rate more than doubled. Now, over half of marriages end in divorce. The number of children involved in divorce increased as the number of divorces increased (National Center for Health Statistics, 1995, 1999).

Why this steep increase in divorce rate? Several factors may have contributed (DaVanzo and Rahman, 1993). First, the entry of the large baby boomer cohorts into young adulthood resulted in an increase in the proportion of new marriages. Then, because divorce is most likely to occur in the first few years of marriage, divorce as well as marriage rates increased. However, the increase in divorce rate cannot be attributed solely to the baby boomers since succeeding cohorts also had higher rates of marital dissolution. The increased labor force participation of women at all stages in the family life cycle have given them greater financial independence and possibly less incentive to remain in an unsatisfying marriage. In addition, changes in gender roles and an increase in the primacy of individual needs over the needs or mores of society have been cited as factors.

There is much debate on whether the slight decrease in the divorce rate beginning in the 1980s reflects a plateauing of the divorce rate or a change in the timing of divorce (Bumpass, 1990; DaVanzo and Rahman, 1993). The majority of divorces have occurred for individuals in their teens or twenties. However, increasing age at first marriage may result in divorces for recent cohorts occurring at later

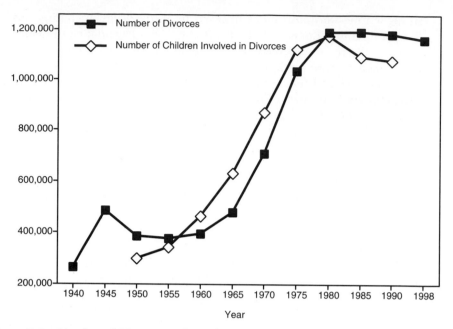

Figure 7-4 Number of Divorces and Number of Children Involved in Divorce: 1940–1998
Source: National Center for Health Statistics, 1995,1999.

ages, in their forties and fifties (Bumpass and Sweet, 1991). Delays in timing of first marriage also result in a decline in the proportion of a cohort ever getting married. As fewer people are getting married, the marriages that are taking place may be those that are more stable. Cohabitation may be screening out some potential marriages that would not succeed. The slight decline in number of children involved in divorce may reflect that at least the earlier baby boomer cohorts have completed child bearing.

Several major risk factors for divorce have been identified. Divorce is more likely to occur for young people and early in a marriage (National Center for Health Statistics, 1995; DaVanzo and Rahman, 1993). Divorce is much more frequent for men and women under the age of 40. However, as noted above, the median age for divorce is increasing, with the modal age for men now being in the early thirties and women in the late twenties. Likewise, most divorces occur within the first 10 years of marriage; the median duration in 1990 was 7 years for first marriages (National Center for Health Statistics, 1995). Divorce occurs earlier in the duration of remarriages. Individuals with lower levels of education tend to have higher divorce rates. The relationship between education and divorce rate may actually be U-shaped, because women with graduate levels of education have been found to be more likely to divorce than those with college degrees.

Money can reduce one prominent source of stress in a marriage—financial worries—and thus promote stability. In fact, longitudinal research suggests that instability of the husband's employment and income may be a critical factor in the increased incidence of divorce in low-income families (Da Vanzo and Rahman, 1993; Heckert, Nowak and Snyder, 1998). An independent income for the wife, however, makes it possible for her to survive on her own and thus lessens the financial obstacles to her divorce. Recent research suggest that it is not the wife becoming economically independent *per se* but a *relative* imbalance in earnings of husband and wife that may precipitate divorce; wives who earned 50 to 75 percent more than their husbands were more likely to divorce than marriages in which the husband had higher earnings or even marriages in which the wife earned 75 to 100 percent of the family income (Heckert et al., 1998).

Marital disruption patterns for blacks are particularly complex. Marital dissolution is higher for black males and females. Some research suggest that black men and women do not perceive divorce to be as damaging to other areas of their lives as do whites (Rank and Davis, 1996). Blacks marry later on average and hence divorce at a later age than for whites. In addition, the proportion of black women who are marrying is declining. There are ethnic differences, also, in separation versus divorce patterns. Black couples separate sooner than white couples but take more than twice as long to end their separations in divorce (National Center for Health Statistics, 1995).

As divorce rates have soared during the past two decades, attitudes about divorce have changed, too, each partly a cause and partly an effect of the other (Thornton, 1989). For centuries, divorce was permitted only in the most extreme cases of flagrant adultery or cruelty (and divorced people were not allowed to remarry). One of the major reasons for low divorce rates in the past was the unequal status of men and women. The wife was considered the "property" of the husband. Uneducated and almost totally dependent on their husbands for financial support, most women could not survive by themselves. Thus a man's divorcing his wife was viewed as roughly akin to deserting his children.

In nineteenth-century Europe, the wife's status improved somewhat. A new element was added: emotional intimacy . A husband was expected to *love* his wife, to be affectionate and friendly, and to be a good companion. Attitudes about divorce slowly began to change, until "the withholding of affection" was added to adultery and cruelty as reasons that one might seek a divorce. More recently, largely since 1960, a new attitude toward marriage has further reduced inhibitions about divorce. Many people today believe that marriage should be a positive experience for each of the partners. If either spouse finds the marriage unsatisfying, they have the "right" to end the marriage. The interests of the individual outweigh the concerns and mores of the larger social community (Bumpass, 1990). This attitude that argues that incompatibility is reason enough for divorce is represented in the no-fault divorce laws of many states today.

A long-lasting marriage, nevertheless, remains the ideal for most adults. Three-quarters of adults in a U.S. national survey believe that ideally a couple should remain together for a lifetime (Bumpass, 1990). At the same time, the realities of demographic trends are reflected in beliefs and attitudes. Only a third actually disapproved of divorce, and 80 percent say that a couple should not stay together for the sake of the children.

Personal Effects of Divorce

Much of the problem of divorce comes down to the balance between intimacy and independence. Divorce is the disruption of intimacy, a splitting apart of two interdependent people into two independent agents. The attractions of intimacy are pitted against the attractions of independence, which include sexual enjoyment with other people, unencumbered self-actualization, and the opportunity to make important decisions by oneself (Bumpass, 1990). As intimacy breaks down from the pressures on the relationship, independence becomes more attractive.

The deterioration of a marriage is rarely a sudden development (Amato and Rogers, 1997; Heaton and Blake, 1999). In many cases, divorce is the culmination of a long process of emotional separation and growing independence. The final months of a marriage are usually remembered as unhappy. Research evidence confirms that a mutually shared decision to divorce is uncommon. One partner typically wants to terminate the relationship more than the other. When a divorce or separation is suggested, it is usually the wife who raises the issue first (Amato and Rogers, 1997; Heaton and Blake, 1999). This is probably because women tend to become dissatisfied with a marriage that is not working sooner than men do. It also usually falls to the mother to inform children of the impending divorce. Mothers maintain closer ties with and receive more support from children before, during, and after divorce (Cooney and Uhlenberg, 1990).

The breakup of the intimate relationship between a man and a woman is a stressful event. Most people perceive divorce as a kind of failure. Even an unhappy marriage has some benefits, and the idea of living alone elicits considerable anxiety for many people. One woman said, "When the idea occurred to me that I could live without Dave and be happier, my immediate next feeling was just gut fear. It's really hard to explain. It was just terror" (Weiss, 1979, p. 203). These feelings of anxiety appear in men and women whether the marriage has been happy or not, whether the divorce has been sought or not.

The spouse's role in terminating the marriage has been found to be significantly related to certain behaviors, feelings, and overall adjustment in the immediate postseparation period (Heaton and Blake, 1999). Because many separations are not mutual, the separation is an extremely stressful experience, particularly for the rejected spouse. Feelings of humiliation and powerlessness are common. Many rejected spouses appear to have been completely unprepared for their partner's decision to divorce. While they may have felt as ungratified by the marriage as their partner, they themselves were not actively contemplating divorce and were shocked by the decision. Marital discord of even extreme intensity does not equally prepare each spouse for divorce. For the men and women who did not participate in the spouse's divorce decision, the period of greatest stress occurs more often immediately after learning there is to be a divorce. For the spouses who decided to divorce, the period of greatest stress is prior to the decision, during those months and years of agonizing over whether to divorce. Spouses who initiate the divorce often do so with sadness, guilt, and anger, but a clear differentiating feature is their sense of control and the absence of feelings of humiliation and rejection.

They often had rehearsed and prepared mentally for their separation status (Melichar and Chiriboga, 1985).

Divorce in Midlife

Most divorces occur in the early years of marriage, when people are relatively young. It has been hypothesized that longer marriages may be more immune from divorce because they have survived the periods of highest risk and benefit from the marital partners' growing investments in children, property, and each other over time. However, there has been much less research on factors leading to divorce in marriages that have lasted over a decade.

The effect of the empty nest on long-term marriages has been debated. Some research has shown that marital satisfaction increases as the children leave home, pressures of childrearing subside and the couple has more time for themselves. Alternatively, some have suggested that if the couple has stayed together because of the children and their investment in the marriage has been in terms of rearing and educating the children, then the empty nest may signal the opportune time to divorce. Heidemann, Suhomlinova and Rand (1998) did find that risk of marital disruption increased at the beginning of the empty nest phase, particularly if the couples reached this phase relatively early in their marriage, and perceived that there was time for a "new beginning" in their lives. In addition, wives economic independence measured in terms of income also increased the risk of divorce in midlife couples. However, midlife women with a college education were less likely to divorce. College-educated women are hypothesized to be more likely to marry later, to have had wider marriage options, to marry husbands with more education and to have brought higher earning potential to the marriage from the beginning.

Another study (Chiriboga, 1989) showed that adults over the age of 50 reported greater psychological stress after a separation than did younger people. The older group reported greater disruption of their social lives, experiencing difficulty going alone to such places as restaurants and the theater. Their personal lives were disrupted more as well; they felt that their lives were more disorganized and out of control. In general, they were more unhappy and less optimistic about the future. These findings may be a result of the deeper entrenchment of middle-aged and older adults in a certain social order and of the difficulties in adjusting to unmarried life. They may also perceive themselves as having fewer options for the future than younger groups do. In contrast, Marks and Lambert (1998) found that midlife adults evidenced more psychological resilience than did younger adults when faced with a marital transition.

Physical and Mental Health Effects of Divorce

The stress of divorce is apparently too much for some people, who succumb to serious mental or physical disorders (McLanahan and Casper, 1995; Simon and Marcussen, 1999). Physical illness of almost every variety is more common among divorced and separated people than among the married or never married. Presumably this is due to stress, which can affect the body's resistance to disease. Similarly, stress can affect mental health; divorced people are disproportionately represented in psychiatric facilities, and their alcoholism and suicide rates are higher. In some cases, of course, the physical or mental problem may have existed before the divorce—in fact, may have precipitated the divorce—but there is no question that divorce itself is a traumatic event for most people. Beliefs about marriage may also affect the severity of marital disruption. Negative effects of marital loss were greater for people who believed in the permanence of marriage (Simon and Marcussen, 1999).

Children, Divorce, and the "Ripple Effect"

When divorce occurs, it has a "ripple effect." It affects not only the couple themselves, but the two adjacent generations: the couple's children and the couple's parents (Gohm, Oishi, Darlington, and Diener, 1998; Hetherington, Bridges and Insabella, 1998; Shapiro and Lambert, 1999; Thompson and Amato, 1999). About half of today's young children in the United States will spend some time in a single-parent family (Castro-Martin and Bumpass, 1989). A prospective study of divorce suggests that spillover from marital difficulties to parent–child relationships may occur several years prior to the actual divorce (Amato and Booth, 1996). Parents who reported increased problems with their children were more likely to be divorced several years later. These problems included one of the spouses being abusive with the children and being dissatisfied with the other spouse's relationship with the children. Sadly, marital discord also led to divorced fathers reporting lower levels of affection for their children at age 18.

A second prospective study suggests that the residence of the child after the divorce may moderate the father–child relationship after the divorce (Shapiro and Lambert, 1999). The level of parent–child relationship of divorced fathers who lived with their child did not differ from that of continuously married fathers who lived with their child. Thus, it was fathers who no longer live with their child who report the largest decrease in the quality of the relationship over time. There are several reasons why divorced fathers co-residing with their children may have a better relationship. Fathers with custody may value their relationship with their children more due to their struggle for custody. Alternatively the presence of the child in the home permits the father a greater sense of control over the lives of his children. However, there are psychological tradeoffs. Fathers who reside with their children are less happy than divorced nonresident fathers and continuously married fathers. Single parenthood may be more taxing for fathers than for mothers in terms of household chores and child care responsibilities.

A number of studies have reported that divorce may have long-term effects in that young adult offspring report lower general psychological well-being than individuals whose parents remain married (Amato and Keith, 1991) The size of the differences in well-being between the two groups are small and suggest that some offspring may not be adversely affected by divorce. In an international study, Gohn et al (1998) examined factors related to the marital relationship and divorce that may affect whether young adult offspring report lower well-being. Marital conflict, rather than divorce *per se,* was found to be a particularly salient factor in lower well-being (see also Heatherington, 1999; Hetherington and Stanley-Hagen, 1999). Low life satisfaction was reported even for offspring of never-divorced couples having high marital conflict. In addition, a cultural factor that was associated with level of well-being in young adult offspring was whether the culture was characterized as collectivist versus individualist. Collectivist cultures encouraged interdependence, the importance of obligations to others rather than self-interest and encourage harmony with others; it was hypothesized that such a culture would offer greater social support to children of divorce and mitigate the long-term effects of the divorce on psychological well-being. There was some support for this hypothesis.

In Chapter 6, we discussed the effects of single-parent families on young children and adolescents. There has been much less research on the effects of divorce that occurs when the children are young-adults (Cooney, Smyer, Hagestad, and Klock, 1986; Cooney and Uhlenberg, 1990). However, since 19 percent of divorces end marriages of over 15 years, the children involved in these divorces are likely to be young adults. Similar to reports by younger children, young-adult children (especially daughters) report stress related to their parents' divorce, particularly in the early phase of the process; many report feeling angry. The stress is also likely to compound the difficulties of making other transitions (such as entering college) that these young-adult children are experiencing.

When parent–adult child relations do deteriorate following a divorce, it is most likely to occur with the father (Cooney and Uhlenberg, 1990; DaVanzo and Rahman, 1993). A drop in contact with a father following divorce is also of interest because it no longer can be associated with the custody rights often at issue with younger children; young-adult children would be legally free to continue contact with both parents. Yet children often report feeling loyalty conflicts and pressure to take sides with one parent. Holidays are troublesome in deciding which parent to visit. Young-adult children also report being worried and concerned about their parents and feeling more responsible for them (especially their mother) following a divorce.

ALTERNATIVE LIFE-STYLES

Changes in attitudes toward men–women relationships, the increasing entry of women into full-time employment and professional roles, and the growing number of divorces have contributed to new alternative life styles. These new forms include singlehood, in which there is no intimate commitment to one other person. Also included as singles are widows. As the gender difference in life expectancy has increased in the last century, more women are experiencing widowhood. The life styles considered in this section do not involve a long-term "couple relationship" or family unit. Alternative life styles that do involve a couple relationship, such as a homosexual couple, or involving a family unit, such as a single-parent household, were discussed in Chapter 6.

Singlehood

Singlehood traditionally has been thought of as a stage of young adulthood prior to entering into a marital relationship. A small segment of the population remains in singlehood throughout adulthood, choosing not to marry. Moreover, recent cohorts are marrying later. Among 25 to 34 year-olds, 35 percent have never married. For blacks in this age group, 54 percent had never been married.

Singlehood is becoming a state that an individual may enter and exit many times during adult life. For example, given that 40 to 50 percent of all marriages today end in divorce, a significant proportion of the adult population returns, at least temporarily, to singlehood following the dissolution of marriage. Moreover, many elderly are single, due to the death of a spouse. Nearly half of women 65 years and older are widowed; of elderly widows 70 percent live alone. The average widow can expect to spend 10 to 12 years in singlehood. Clearly, the experience of singlehood is different depending on one's life stage and one's prior experiences. We have discussed various aspects of being single in different places in the text. Earlier in this chapter, we mentioned some feelings that those recently divorced may encounter as they reenter singlehood. Later in this chapter, we discuss issues related to widowhood. Issues related to singlehood from the perspective of a never-married young adult were considered in Chapter 2.

Widowhood

Most old men are still married, but most old women are widowed or divorced. Between the ages of 65 and 74 about 35 percent of women are widowed, compared with 9 percent of men. Among those 75 to 84 years, 60 percent of women are widowed, compared with 19 percent of men (U.S. Bureau of the Census, 1993b). For elders 85 years and older almost 80 percent of women are widowed compared to 39 percent of men. At age 75 and older, black women are more likely to be widowed than white or Hispanic women; a similar pattern exists for black men. The reasons for this disparity between the sexes in the last years of life are clear: Women generally marry older men and, in addition, have a longer life expectancy than men. According to population projections, by 2050 the proportion of widows will have declined as men improve their chances of survival beyond age 65. However, the proportion of divorced elderly will increase as the baby boomer cohorts become old. As a result of the increasing proportion of divorced elderly, it is predicted that the proportion of married elderly females will change little by the middle of the next century (U.S. Bureau of the Census, 1998a).

The widow's chances of remarrying are slim and they have been getting slimmer throughout the past century. Eligible males over 65, if they do marry, often marry women under 65. Given the greater opportunity to find a mate, widowed men over 65 are eight times as likely as widowed women to remarry. Fortunately, perhaps, many older widows do not consider getting married. Seventy-five percent of a sample of older urban widows said they did not wish to marry, citing as reasons loss of independence, not wanting to care for another sick spouse, and fear of fortune hunters (Lopata, 1980).

Elderly women whose husbands have died experience a host of economic, social, and psychological difficulties (Bengston, Rosenthal, and Burton, 1990). Although the income of the elderly in general has improved since the 1970s, the economic well-being of the oldest-old and widows in particular has improved much less (U. S. Bureau of the Census, 1993a). Almost 20 percent of elderly women aged 75 and older are in poverty. Over half of those over 75 years and living alone had very modest incomes. The problem is complicated by the fact that most elderly widows live alone in older homes that are considerably more expensive than new homes to operate and maintain.

This trend toward living alone has been growing in recent decades. The sharpest increase in elderly living alone has been among the oldest-old, those 85 years and older. Thirty-two percent of women aged 65 to 74 live alone; and 51 percent of women over 75 live alone and 57 percent of women 85 years and older live alone. (U.S. Bureau of the Census, 1993b). As noted in Chapter 6, black elderly are more likely to live with other family members and thus fewer black older women live alone. Although elderly widows have received the least increase in income, the improved economic status of the elderly in general has contributed to more older women living alone. In addition, women report that they prefer to live alone because they want to remain independent and manage their own homes and work. They also wish to avoid the disadvantages of living with their children.

Other effects of widowhood can be equally severe. Losing a spouse can cause social loneliness and emotional loneliness (Lichtenstein, Gatz, Pedersen, Berg, and McClearn, 1996; Lopata, 1993). The death of a spouse immediately removes the source of many of an individual's social interactions. In addition, many of a person's relationships with other people and with social organizations are organized in terms of a husband–wife unit. Friends, especially couples, may find interactions with an unattached individual difficult. The widow (or widower) may find that going out to a movie theater, a restaurant, or even church is less pleasant and satisfying by oneself. Some people, embarrassed by signs of grief, may avoid the widow and may even justify their avoidance by assuming that the individual wants or needs to be alone. Emotionally, the surviving spouse is deprived of his or her most intimate relationship and of the person to whom he or she was most important. They cease to be loved by a person, and they lose the person they loved most; the sense of loss is often and quite understandably severe. The widow or widower misses the companionship of his or her spouse and the spouse's partnership in the division of labor (Lopata, 1993).

Unlike many cultures, the United States does not have a well-defined social role for widows to play and even looks with some disapproval on those men and women who continue grieving too long. Since widowhood is more likely in old age, social support for widowhood is somewhat greater then. As a result, young widows often experience a more difficult adjustment than older women in the same circumstances (Lopata, 1993). Not only are the young widows more likely to lack friends and relatives in the same circumstances, but they may feel the unfairness of the situation more strongly. The older widow's role is more acceptable, and she is also more likely to have friends in a similar position.

The psychological effects of widowhood may be extremely painful. Two stages of grief are often experienced. During the stage of acute grief (mourning), the widow or widower attempts to adjust to the loss of the most significant person in her or his life. This stage usually takes somewhat less than a year. The health of the widow or widower suffers. Some researchers claim that the death rate rises sharply (DeSpelder and Strickland, 1992; Lichtenstein, Gatz, and Berg, 1998) with the highest risk in the first weeks or months closest to the loss. Loneliness, anxiety, and depression are commonplace. In the first month of bereavement, crying and sleep disturbances are frequent. A sizable percentage of widows and widowers, about one in five, report terrible feelings of guilt, believing that they should have been able to do something to prolong the life of their spouse (Clayton, Halikes, and Maurice, 1971).

During the second stage of grief, the bereaved person gradually reconstructs an identity as a partnerless person. If the individual's health is good and finances are adequate, chances of leading a happy and satisfying life are fairly good (Lichtenstein et al., 1996; Umberson, Wortman and Kessler, 1992). Some widows, however, find it quite difficult to "move on" with their lives. They understand, at least vaguely, that society allows them a brief period of extreme mourning and that then they are expected to pull themselves together. These widows find that they cannot, and this alarms them more. Still grieving for their departed spouses, frightened, with a profound sense of hopelessness, they may withdraw from life and become true social isolates. Lack of community sympathy for the widows' plight, combined with their lack of social skills tends to produce passive, helpless old women. These

Many elderly men and women maintain a strong sense of self-identity even after losing a spouse.

widows have difficulty with adaptive activities, such as joining a club or a church, moving to a new neighborhood, finding a job, or turning a stranger into a friend.

One of the changes that may result from widowhood is a change in self-perception (Lopata, 1993). Older, more traditional, and particularly less-educated women report no change in themselves as a result of becoming a widow. However, many more educated and socially adept widows report greater feelings of competence and independence (Pearlin and Skaff, 1995; Umberson, Wortman, and Kessler, 1992). This does not mean that they look back at their marriages negatively, but that they experience a positive change in themselves after the acute grief period is over.

A woman's reaction to widowhood depends not only on her personal resources, but also on the nature of her relationship with her husband before his death. This, in turn, has been shown to be related to the couple's socioeconomic status. Well-educated, middle-class couples tend to be more communicative with each other, sharing their lives and spending their leisure time together much more than working-class couples (Lopata, 1993). As a result, middle-class couples may be quite mutually dependent, and widows from such couples may experience severe disruption of their lives when their husbands die (Lopata, 1993).

The activities of working-class couples, on the other hand, tend to be much more segregated along gender lines. Men's contacts are with coworkers and with other men at sports and other leisure events. Women's contacts are with other female family members and with women at church and volunteer activities. As widows, working-class women's identities and life styles may undergo less change. Middle-class women may encounter more disruption of their social worlds following the deaths of their husbands than do working-class women, whose social lives were more independent and segregated to begin with.

Variations are also found in how widows speak about and remember their deceased husbands (Lopata, 1986). Some widows tend to idealize or even "sanctify" their former husbands, remembering them as being far more perfect than they actually were. In a group of women who tended to sanctify their husbands, one in four strongly agreed with such statements as "my husband had no irritating habits," and half thought that their husbands had been unusually good men. Sanctification of this sort may have some useful functions for the survivor. The process of grieving involves preserving the deceased in the memories of survivors. At the same time, mental health demands that the process of grieving be completed. Sanctification may permit both: The husband is remembered in such favorable terms that he becomes distant, unreal, and otherworldly, and this distance helps the widow end her grieving (Lopata, 1986).

Although there are far more widows than widowers in the United States, widowers face some special problems (Lee, Willetts, and Seccombe, 1998). The risk of mental illness and death appears to be greater among widowers (Lee et al., 1998; Lichtenstein, Gatz, and Berg, 1998; Lopata, 1996a). Widowed men were found to have higher rates of depression than widowed women or married men (Lee et al., 1998). Because men usually depend on their wives as their major social support and as their means of keeping in contact with others, they are more likely to suffer from isolation when their spouses die. Women, on the other hand, often have social support systems of family members and female friends. The more severe problems of widowers may be related to the need to have a confidant to maintain psychological health. Extreme social isolation has been identified as a factor that precipitates psychiatric illnesses, and marriage and social relationships are important in maintaining the well-being of older adults (Lopata, 1993). It is also possible that widowhood is a more difficult experience for men than women in psychological terms because widowhood is more unexpected for men. Men expect to predecease their wives and have fewer models of successful adaptation to widowhood. On a more practical level, older widowers may face additional problems because they often lack experience in dealing with routine household chores.

RELATIONSHIPS: CHANGE AND CONTINUITY

The nature of the intimate relationship between men and women is constantly changing, constantly aligning itself to the changing society in which it is embedded. Medical discoveries such as effective contraceptives, and diseases such as AIDS have changed the nature of sexual interactions. Technological advances have created occupations in which strength and speed count less and intellect more; women compete successfully with men for these jobs, and this is bound to affect the male–female relationship. Some changes seem to have negative or at least dubious value, for example, the rising divorce rate and mother-only families suffering from poverty.

Nevertheless, throughout the uncertainty, conflict, excitement, and wonder that change can bring to a relationship, "the fundamental things apply, as time goes by." The fundamental things about a relationship between a man and a woman are intimacy and sharing, and no social change is likely to affect the priority of these qualities. An intimate relationship was and is a vulnerable position, an opening up of oneself to another person, a sharing not only of life's tasks but also of life's conflicts and fears.

SUMMARY

1. As a result of demographic changes in our society, increasing numbers of individuals can expect to spend some part of adulthood in a state outside the traditional married couple relationship (singlehood, divorced, widowed). Over 50 percent of marriages end in divorce and the majority of elderly women experience widowhood. It is becoming increasingly important, then, to consider male and female relationships and life styles outside the marriage bond.

2. Contrary to some popular stereotypes, the NHSLS survey found that the group having the most sex were married couples, not young singles. Three factors were strongly associated with frequency of partnered sex: how old the person was, whether people were married or

cohabiting, and how long the couple had been together.

3. An important change in sexual behavior becomes increasingly striking with age—that is, the difference in the amount of partnered sex for men versus women. Although men continue to have sex into old age, women experience a significant decrease in sexual activity over the adult life course. These discrepancies in patterns of sexual activity for middle-aged and older men and women reflect gender differences in marital status and mortality. Beginning in middle-age and particularly in old age, a significantly higher proportion of men are in a couple relationship than women.

4. Sex is a total human experience, not just a biological function. Sexual attitudes play a major role in sexual behavior throughout the life span. The people who report being the most physically pleased and emotionally satisfied with their sex lives are married or cohabiting couples. Lower rates of satisfaction were found among men and women who were not married or cohabiting. Males across the adult life course report thinking about sex more frequently than women and considering sex more important to quality of life.

5. The divorce rate in the United States has been increasing for more than 100 years. Except for a sharp spike during the 1940s due to World War II, the increase in the divorce rate was gradual until a sharp rise occurred in the 1960s. Between 1960 and 1980, the divorce rate more than doubled. Over half of marriages now end in divorce. The number of children experiencing the divorce of their parents has increased as the divorce rate has increased.

6. Several major risk factors for divorce have been identified. Divorce is more likely early in a marriage and divorce rates are higher for those marrying at young ages. Individuals with lower levels of education tend to have higher divorce rates. The relative difference in salaries of husbands and wives is a factor in marital instability. An independent income for the wife makes it possible for her to survive on her own and thus lessens the financial obstacles to divorce.

7. Most old men are still married, but most old women are widowed or divorced. Between the ages of 65 and 74 about 35 percent of women are widowed, compared with 9 percent of men. Among those 75 to 84 years, 60 percent of women are widowed, compared with 19 percent of men. For elders 85 years and older almost 80 percent of women are widowed compared to 39 percent of men. The reasons for this disparity between the sexes in the last years of life are clear: Women generally marry older men and, in addition, have a longer life expectancy than men.

8. According to population projections, by 2050 the proportion of widows will have declined as men improve their chances of survival beyond age 65. However, the proportion of divorced elderly will increase as the baby boomer cohorts become old. As a result of the increasing proportion of divorced elderly, it is pre-

dicted that the proportion of married elderly females will change little by the middle of the next century

9. Women are generally less likely than men to be crime victims. However, in two crime categories female victims predominate. These are violence committed against women by intimates, and rape. Violent crime by intimates against women most frequently involves an assault by a man with whom the woman has been previously romantically or sexually involved. Divorced or separated women are much more likely to be victims of violent crimes than married women or widows. Victims tend to be young, unemployed, and of a lower-income level. The vast majority of these crimes are not reported to the police and no professional medical treatment is sought.

SUGGESTED READINGS

AARP (August, 1999). *AARP/Modern Maturity Sexuality Study.* Washington, D.C.: AARP Research Group (available at www.aarp.org). The objective of the survey was to understand the role that sexuality plays in the quality of life of older adults and the satisfaction of older adults with their sex lives. The study involved a representative sample of adults aged 45 and older.

Hetherington, E. M, Bridges, M., and Insabella, G. M. (1998). What matters? What does not? Five perspectives on the association between marital transitions and children's adjustment. *American Psychologist, 53,* 167–184. This article presents an analysis of five views of factors that contribute to the adjustment of children in divorced families or stepfamilies, including individual vulnerability, family composition, SES, and stress.

Lopata, H. (1996a). *Current widowhood: Myths and realities.* Thousand Oaks, CA: Sage. Review of literature on widowhood, including the impact of changes in intergenerational relations and cohort differences.

Michael, R. T., Gagnon, J. H., Laumann, E. O., and Kolata, G. (1994). *Sex in America: A definitive survey.* New York: Little, Brown and Co. A very readable report of findings from the most recent survey of sexual behavior and attitudes of a representative sample of young and middle-aged adults in the United States.

Moen, P. (2001). Gender, age and the life course. In R. H. Binstrock and L. K. George (Eds). *Handbook of aging and the social sciences* (5th ed.) San Diego, CA: Academic. Reviews current research on gender differences and age/cohort trends from a life course perspective.

8

Careers

Earning a Living

For most people, the primary purpose of work is to earn a living. Some are lucky enough to earn their living in activities that they would pursue whether or not they were paid for them. And money is rarely the sole reward in a job; there are opportunities for friendship, wielding power, solving interesting problems, and creating valuable goods and services. Some workers (homemakers, for example) do not receive money for their efforts (relying on spouses to provide their living in a marital barter system). Others have no need for money, and work for them is like a hobby, an activity pursued for its own sake. Nevertheless, for most people, a job is first and foremost a way of earning money, which the worker can exchange for the necessities of life and perhaps a few luxuries.

A career is a lifelong pattern of work. The word *career* derives from the French word for racetrack or racecourse; it aptly implies the course of jobs, occupations, and vocations through which we race in a lifetime. There was a time when career and job were more or less synonymous, when a young-adult chose an occupation (e.g., carpenter, teacher, salesperson) and stayed with it. Today, however, people are likely to have several quite different occupations and certainly many different jobs during their lives. Indeed, many young-adults deliberately plan for a series of jobs. Realizing that the first job that they choose is not likely to be their last, they think in terms of "what this job might lead to" or the valuable experience they will gain that might support their application for a different job.

People's jobs are a major element in their sense of who they are, their sense of personal identity. Many people introduce themselves with their occupations: "I'm Mary Watts. I'm a real estate broker." One's job affects one's life in so many ways.

CHOOSING AN OCCUPATION

In many respects, choosing an occupation is similar to choosing a spouse. There are family pressures to take this job and not that one. Social factors to some extent determine the choice and satisfaction with the choice once made. Similarity of interests between job applicant and satisfied members of a profession predict happiness on the job as similarity of attitudes and values plays a role in predicting marital success. When people are ready to choose a job, they select from among those available at the time, just as the readiness factor influences their choice of mate. Job selection is also a reciprocal process, like mate selection. As the individual checks out the employer, the employer checks out the potential employee; one or the other might terminate an unsatisfactory relationship in a kind of industrial "divorce." Vocational development, like marriage, is a process that continues throughout life (Mortimer and Finch, 1996; Super, 1992; Vondracek, 1998). It begins before adolescence and does not end when one takes a first job.

EARLY INFLUENCES ON VOCATIONAL ASPIRATIONS

Like many other areas of development, choice of a career is strongly influenced by the family. Of major concern are the processes by which the family influences children's vocational aspirations, expectations, and eventual occupational achievement (Mortimer and Johnson, 1998; Vondracek, Lerner, and Schulenberg, 1986).

The family influences vocational development in two major ways. First, the family can provide *opportunities* for children. These may range from providing a computer and internet access for school work to paying college tuition to using business and social connections to access job opportunities. Second, the family influences vocational development through *socialization* and parent–child relations. Adolescents who have close relationships with their parents are likely to be affected by their parents' hopes for their future. Most children learn values that resemble those of their parents. The pressures exerted by families may be either direct or indirect. One set of parents may insist that their child take college preparatory classes in high school. Another may try to direct a child's vocational interests by arranging for summer or part-time jobs in a particular field.

The family's influence on career choices is reflected by a strong association between family socioeconomic status (family income, occupational and educational status of parents) and children's vocational aspirations, expectations, and eventual occupational attainment (Mortimer and Finch, 1996; Penick and Jepsen, 1992). The parents' occupational status is related directly to children's educational attainment, which is in turn an important influence on children's occupational attainment.

The exact nature and causes of this link between parents' occupational status and a child's educational and occupational achievements are unclear, but several factors seem to be influential. Parents tend to hold values for themselves and their children that are consistent with the demands of their jobs. Working-class parents, whose jobs require compliance with authority, tend to value obedience and

The world of work has been changing dramatically for women. Today there are more job opportunities open to women, who compose almost half of the work force.

conformity in their children, whereas middle-class parents, whose jobs depend more on self-direction, tend to value initiative and independence in their children (Kohn, 1977; Kohn and Schooler, 1983; Kohn and Slomczynski, 1990). Thus, parents may teach their children values that are appropriate for occupations resembling their own, which would tend to increase the children's chances of entering such occupations (Mortimer and Borman, 1988). Male senior college students from business families were more concerned with extrinsic values such as high income and advancement, whereas sons from professional families were more concerned about the intrinsic people-oriented aspects of their occupations. The extent of "occupational transmission" from parent to child was greatest when children reported a close relationship with the parent and when the parent had high occupational status.

Family influences on children's vocational aspirations can, however, be dysfunctional if there is undue pressure for children to think and act according to a set of family norms and values (Penick and Jepsen, 1992). Children from "enmeshed" families, which strongly emphasized parental goals and expectations, had difficulty identifying their own unique vocational interests and aspirations.

Family influences on career aspirations of young women is of particular interest, given the change in gender roles and that the majority of women are now in the workforce (Hackett, 1997). Young women's career orientations, expectations, and achievements are affected both by whether or not the mother works during the daughter's childhood and adolescence and by the relationship between the mother and daughter (Moen, Erikson, and Dempster-McClain, 1997; Rainey and Borders, 1997). Having a mother who works outside the home increases the chances that the daughter will work outside the home. Indeed, the mother's employment status is one of the most consistent predictors of the daughter's aspirations in a nontraditional career (London and Greller, 1991). Furthermore, the father's attitude toward working women is important (Leadbeater and Way, 1996). The father's attitude may influence the daughter's choice of a career by encouraging nontraditional socialization practices and by exposing the daughter to career options, including the father's own. This type of father is more likely to be supportive of his wife's working and thus the daughter can observe the satisfactions as well as stresses of a dual-earner family.

The majority of teenagers work sometime during adolescence and these early work experiences may influence career aspirations and expectations (Perron, Vondracek, Skorikov, Tremblay, and Corbierre, 1998; Skorikov and Vondracek, 1997). Some recent research suggest that work experiences during adolescence may affect attitudes toward general job characteristics (e.g., coworkers, hours) rather than choice of career; most jobs held by teenagers are entry level, part-time and may not be substantively related to career goals or interest. One striking observation is that the earliest work experiences of adolescents are typically sex-segregated and tend to reinforce traditional gender roles. That is, the earliest work experiences of girls are likely to be as babysitters or in providing domestic assistance to their mother or neighbors. In contrast, boys are likely to be first employed in manual labor. Boys typically earn more and are more likely to have experienced a formal employer–employee relationship; in contrast, girls frequently are employed by friends or family in informal work arrangements.

College experiences may influence subsequent career development and achievement. Indeed, it is common practice for businesses and other organizations to recruit on college campuses with recruiters looking at such things as level of education, grades, major, and extracurricular activities in order to identify those most likely to achieve job success.

Howard (1986, 1995; Howard and Bray, 1990) in a longitudinal study of AT&T managers examined the relationship of various college experiences (level of education, grades, major, extracurricular activities) to critical behaviors related to job success, such as administrative skills and interpersonal skills. Her study, unique in that it enabled her to relate college experience to job success in management 20 years later, provided some interesting findings. First, grades were significant predictors not only of intellectual ability, but also of the manager's career commitment and motivation to do good work. Second, those managers who had been humanities or social science majors were found to have the best overall performance as managers. Managers with these majors were rated as having particularly good interpersonal and verbal skills. Third, the number of extracurricular activities in which a person was involved in college was related to having better interpersonal skills and to having leadership skills. Alternate explanations of this relationship may suggest that either people who seek leadership roles have an aptitude for them and elect to participate in extracurricular activities or that involvement in extracurricular activities may help to develop managerial and leadership skills.

Matching Vocational Interests to the Work Environment

Making a wise choice regarding a vocation involves not only knowing one's own interests and abilities but also understanding the characteristics and demands of the work context (Tett, Jackson, and Rothstein, 1991; Ackerman and Heggestad, 1997). The work environments of engineers, ministers, and artists vary considerably on dimensions, such as how frequently one interacts with other people, what types of work equipment or tools one uses, and whether one works indoors or outdoors. One of the major vocational theories focuses on the "fit" or match between an individual's interests and personality and the environmental demands or characteristics of a particular vocation (Betz and Hackett, 1997; Holland, 1985, 1996; Osipow, 1990). Holland has developed his person–environment fit model based on extensive study of the personality characteristics and interests of individuals successful in a given vocation and the contextual characteristics of the vocation.

Six personality types were identified: investigative, social, realistic, artistic, conventional, and enterprising (Holland, 1966, 1985, 1996). Theoretical descriptions of the six types are given in Table 8.1. Briefly, the investigative person likes to work with ideas and is therefore likely to choose a scientific occupation. The social person likes to work with people and might therefore be found in human services or religious work. The realistic person likes to work with objects and is therefore likely to be found in mechanical occupations. The artistic person likes to work with emotions and might therefore be found in the arts or other creative occupations. The conventional person is a conformist; he or she is practical, conservative, neat, and correct, but lacks spontaneity, originality, and flexibility. Occupations in finance (bank teller) or business (accountant or office manager) suit this pattern of interests. Finally, the enterprising person is adventurous and persuasive and likes to dominate. The enterprising individual enjoys work in business, particularly in sales and supervisory positions.

The relationship of personality type to career choice is generally moderate but significant. In other words, personality doesn't explain all aspects of career choice, but it has an influence. Careers in the ministry appear to draw people who score, on the average, highest on the social scale. Both males and females in car sales average highest on the enterprising scale (Benninger and Walsh, 1980). But these averages include some individuals whose personalities do not fit the characteristics of the job: a minister with strong intellectual interests, a salesperson with artistic interests. These "misfits" usually adapt in one of three ways: they quit their job and try to find one more to their liking; their interests change to become more in line with their job; or they reconstruct their work to satisfy their interests. For example, our intellectual minister might shy away from social duties, preferring to dig through books for religious insights. Or the artistic salesperson might begin to create websites for businesses.

TABLE 8-1   Holland's Six Basic Personality Types and their Relationship to Vocational Preferences

Investigative

The model type is task-oriented, intraceptive, asocial; prefers to think through rather than act out problems; needs to understand; enjoys ambiguous work tasks; has unconventional values and attitudes; is anal as opposed to oral. Vocational preferences include aeronautical design engineer, anthropologist, astronomer, biologist, botanist, chemist, editor of a scientific journal, geologist, independent research scientist, meteorologist, physicist, scientific research worker, writer of scientific or technical articles, and zoologist.

Social

The model type is sociable, responsible, feminine, humanistic, religious; needs attention; has verbal and interpersonal skills; avoids intellectual problem solving, physical activity, and highly ordered activities; prefers to solve problems through feelings and interpersonal manipulations of others; is orally dependent. Vocational preferences include assistant city school superintendent, clinical psychologist, director of welfare agency, foreign missionary, high school teacher, juvenile delinquency expert, marriage counselor, personal counselor, physical education teacher, playground director, psychiatric case worker, social science teacher, speech therapist, vocational counselor.

Realistic

The model type is masculine, physically strong, unsociable, aggressive; has good motor coordination and skill; lacks verbal and interpersonal skills; prefers concrete to abstract problems; conceives of self as being aggressive and masculine and as having conventional political and economic values.

Vocational preferences include airplane mechanic, construction inspector, electrician, filling station attendant, fish and wildlife specialist, locomotive engineer, master plumber, photoengraver, power shovel operator, power station operator, radio operator, surveyor, tree surgeon, and tool designer.

Artistic

The model type is asocial; avoids problems that are highly structured or require gross physical skills; resembles the investigative type in being intraceptive and asocial, but differs in that he or she has a need for individualistic expression, has less ego strength, is more feminine, and suffers more frequently from emotional disturbances; prefers dealing with environmental problems through self-expression in artistic media.

Vocational preferences include art dealer, author, cartoonist, commercial artist, composer, concert singer, dramatic coach, freelance writer, musical arranger, musician, playwright, poet, stage director, symphony conductor.

Conventional

The model type prefers structured verbal and numerical activities and subordinate roles; is conforming (extraceptive); avoids ambiguous situations and problems involving, interpersonal relationships and physical skills; is effective at well-structured tasks; identifies with power; values material possessions and status.

Vocational preferences include bank examiner, bank teller, bookkeeper, budget reviewer, cost estimator, court stenographer, financial analyst, business machine operator, inventory controller, payroll clerk, quality control expert, statistician, tax expert, and traffic manager.

TABLE 8-1 **Holland's Six Basic Personality Types and their Relationship to Vocational Preferences**

Enterprising

The model type has verbal skills for selling, dominating, leading; conceives of himself or herself as a strong leader; avoids well-defined language or work situations requiring long periods of intellectual effort; is extraceptive; differs from the conventional type in that he or she prefers ambiguous social tasks and has a greater concern with power, status, and leadership; is orally aggressive. Vocational preferences include business executive, buyer, hotel manager, industrial relations consultant, manufacturer's representative, master of ceremonies, political campaign manager, real estate salesperson, restaurant worker, speculator, sports promoter, stock and bond salesperson, television producer, and traveling salesperson.

Source: Adapted from J. L. Holland. (1966). The psychology of vocational choice (p. 16) Waltham, MA: Blaisdell. Reprinted by permission of the author. See Holland, J. L. (1985). Making vocational choices: A theory of vocational personalities and work environments. Englewood Cliffs, NJ: Prentice-Hall.

Personality types such as those described by Holland tend to remain stable over time, as do vocational interests. Longitudinal data collected over 20 years indicate that vocational interests remain about the same from late adolescence onward (Johannson and Campbell, 1971; Strong, 1955).

The relationship between Holland's vocational interest typology and a three-dimensional model of personality has been examined (Costa, McCrae, and Holland, 1984; see Chapter 9). Personality traits in the Costa model are divided into three broad categories: neuroticism (N), extraversion (E), and openness to experience (O). Neuroticism includes such traits as anxiety, hostility, depression, and vulnerability. Extraversion includes traits such as warmth, assertiveness, gregariousness, and positive emotion. Openness to experience covers areas such as aesthetics, feelings, actions, ideas, and values. The Holland types and the NEO model tend to support each other. For example, the personality category openness to experience includes the same people as Holland's investigative and artistic types, as you would expect. The social and enterprising types fell into the NEO category of extraversion. These relationships were found for both men and women. Furthermore, the NEO categories tend to confirm the occupational preferences suggested in the Holland types. Openness to experience was related to occupational preferences for professions such as author, journalist, research scientist, and anthropologist. Extraversion was related to occupational preferences such as advertising executive, sales manager, marriage counselor, and manufacturer's representative. Thus, comparisons with the NEO model tend to confirm the accuracy of the Holland types.

On all six Holland types, significant sex differences have been found (Costa, McCrae, and Holland, 1984). Women fall more often into the artistic, social, and conventional categories. This tendency was found in all age groups. The preference for work in these areas is in accord with the roles and values traditionally associated with women in the United States.

Career theories based on vocational interests and work context are not without limitations, of course. Such perspectives are static and do not take into account the total lifespace of the individual. Career decisions are not made by personalities acting in a social vacuum. It is also important that interactions between the work-related and non-work-related aspects of a person's development be taken into account insofar as they affect career aspirations and achievement. For example, career choices may be moderated by the individual's marital and family commitments. Likewise, economic booms or recessions can impact an individuals's ability to find a position in a chosen occupation.

Much of the research linking personality factors and work has been focused on men. In a longitudinal study in Finland, the long-term effects of personality factors on career orientation for women and men have been examined (Pulkkinen, Ohranen, and Tolvanen, 1998). The relationship of personality factors measured at ages 8,14, and 27 were examined for two career variables at age 36—career orientation and stability of career over the past nine years. Career orientation involved occupational status, education, and current position. Career stability focused on whether the person had worked continuously over the past nine years. Personality factors were more predictive of women's career orientation and stability than for men. The authors hypothesized that women have to make more conscious decisions regarding the priority of work and family and that personality may enter into the decision process. Personality factors were particularly salient in predicting whether a woman worked continuously over the past nine years that would typically also involve childbearing. Women who as children and teenagers were constructively active and agreeable were more likely to work continuously. Being an extravert at age 27 was related to both high career orientation and working continuously. High parental socioeconomic status was also a predictor of women having a high career orientation.

Establishing a Career

Once an occupation is chosen (sometimes with great care and sometimes without much deliberate thought), the individual next faces the problems of what psychologists call "early professional socialization." Workers must learn exactly what it is that they are supposed to do. They must learn how to get along with coworkers, even with those who are unfriendly and competitive; how to respond to authority, including when to conform and when to complain; and how to defend themselves, to protect their own interests. They have to learn who can do what for them; that is, they must decipher the true power and service relationships, which do not always correspond to official titles. The knowledge acquired in such early professional socialization has recently been studied as tacit knowledge (Sternberg and Horvath, 1999).

The Dream

In Daniel Levinson's theory of adult development (Levinson, 1990; Levinson, Darow, Klein, Levinson, and McKee, 1978), the "novice phase" of early adulthood is characterized by four major tasks. One is getting married and starting a family. The other three have to do with the individual's career: choosing an occupation, forming a "Dream," and finding a mentor. The Dream is an individual's general expectation of what he or she would like to become. The Dream is more structured than pure fantasy, less articulated than a plan; it is "a vague sense of self-in-adult-world." As a vision of the kind of life a person wants to lead as an adult, the Dream includes images of a certain kind of family life and community environment, but for most people occupational images are central.

What aspects of a job are most important to workers today? Three major work domains have been found to be important to the worker (Mortimer and Lorence, 1994): Physical work environment and pay; human relations at work, including supervisory relations; and third, the nature of the work itself, whether it is of interest and challenging. The first two factors are considered *extrinsic* in that they focus on aspects of the occupation (physical and social environment) other than the work itself; the third factor is *intrinsic* because the focus is on the qualities of the work task *per se*.

Two recent surveys have examined various aspects of work and the balancing of work and family roles. The two surveys are The National Study of the Changing Workforce (Galinsky, Bond, and Friedman, 1993) and the Cornell Couples and Careers Study (Moen, 1999; Moen and Shin-Kap, in press; Moen and Yan , 1999). The Cornell Couples and Careers Study focuses on dual-earner couples in different industries. The National Study of the Changing Workforce is a recent large-scale study of a representative sample of 3,400 U.S. workers. This study found that salary was not the most salient issue in selecting a job (Galinsky, Bond, and Friedman, 1993). The primary reason most workers report taking or leaving a particular job is the quality of their work life. In the Galinsky et al study the main reasons for taking a new position were: open communications at the workplace, the effect of the job on personal and family life, the nature of the work, quality of the management, and characteristics of the supervisor.

Similarly, in the Cornell study, the main reasons for staying with the present job were: workload, control over scheduling one's work, working a standard schedule, and flextime. Thus, both intrinsic (e.g.,workload, control of scheduling) and extrinsic (e.g., management and supervisor) factors were of importance to workers. Workload involves a job that requires working hard, fast, and excessive amounts of work. Having a demanding job has both positive and negative effects. Those with a higher workload had higher ratings of personal growth and development but also more negative spillover from work to family and higher rates of depressive mood.

Particularly important for workers with children are aspects of the position that facilitate balancing work and family responsibilities (Moen, 1999; Moen and Yan, 1999). Parents were particularly concerned about control over work hours and scheduling—ability to determine when one starts and ends work, where one works, the amount of work one takes home, and the ability to receive personal calls and e-mail. Having control over one's work hours and scheduling is associated with higher feelings of personal growth and mastery and more positive spillover from work to family. Finally, supervisor support seems particularly important for women in professional roles. Unfortunately, the work conditions desired by workers do not tend to occur together in the same job. There was a inverse relation between workload and control over work hours. Those with the highest workloads reported relatively little control over when they work.

Only 35 percent of workers in the Galinsky et al (1993) study rated salary or wages as a very important reason for joining their current employer. One reason that salary may be less salient is that many workers may not be offered a wide range of salary options when taking new jobs—thus, aspects of the job other than salary become more important in choosing among job alternatives.

Even for people who embark on the career of their Dream, the first experiences with their jobs can be shocking. The Dream, especially when newly formed, contains many fantasy elements, so there is inevitably some degree of "reality shock", as new assistant professors discover how much time is spent in committee meetings, as new carpenters discover that supervisors play favorites, as new factory workers discover how little the union can do for them, even when safety is the matter in dispute.

The Mentor

The new worker may not face the trials of reality shock alone. Typically, guidance is provided through the early years (the early professional socialization) by other persons. Advice and assistance is most frequently given by coworkers somewhat older, and more professionally advanced than the entering worker. However, for some young workers, there are one or more *mentors*—supervisors with expertise and at an advanced level in the organizational or professional hierarchy (Ragins, 1999; see Poole and Bornhold, 1998, and Stiver and O'Leary, 1990, for discussions of mentoring in higher education).

The functions of the mentor are many, and all are quite important to the career development of the young worker—coaching, protection, providing information to interpret or anticipate actions, and sponsorships or support (Ragins and Scandura, 1999; Whitely and Coetsier, 1993). As coaches, mentors seek to develop the intellectual and interpersonal skills of their protege. As protectors, mentors ensure that their proteges are not exposed to political forces before they are ready or before they are well-briefed on the situation and how to deal with difficult people. As sponsors mentors actively contrive to get their proteges exposure and visibility through assignments that involve working with other influential professionals and by endorsing the protege for promotion or special challenging projects. As mastering a given vocation or profession becomes increasing complex, these mentoring functions may be carried out by more than one mentor.

Research on mentoring has traditionally focused on two major questions. What are the characteristics of young workers who receive mentoring? What are the outcomes of mentoring for the young worker? In a study by Whitely, Dougherty, and Dreher (1992), characteristics were examined of early career managers and professionals from a wide variety of organizations and industries who had a mentor. Younger individuals and those from a higher socioeconomic background were more likely to report having a mentor. Because higher-level supervisors tend to come from higher social class origins, similarity in social origins may

Finding an appropriate mentor is an important step in developing a successful career.

have influenced the protege selection process. Those having a mentor were more involved in their work as indicated by the number of hours per week worked. There may actually be a reciprocal relationship between work involvement and being mentored. Those more invested in their work may be seen by mentors as more committed and more likely to succeed. Likewise, working longer hours may increase the likelihood of contact with potential mentors. At the same time, being rewarded for work by a mentor may lead to a "success syndrome" that leads to even greater work involvement.

In another study young managers and professionals that initiated the mentoring relationship received greater amounts of mentoring; young managers with higher internal locus of control and self-monitoring were more likely to initiate contact with a potential mentor (Turban and Dougherty, 1994). Although males were predicted to be more likely to receive mentoring, no gender differences were found. The authors suggest that lack of gender differences may be due to their focus on career aspects of mentoring as contrasted to psychosocial mentoring, which has been the emphasis in some cross-gender studies of mentoring. Although previous research on mentoring has noted the limitations or potential problems with cross-gender mentoring with the likelihood of the mentor being a male, several recent large scale studies found no gender differences in selection for mentoring or outcomes (Dreher and Ash, 1990; Gaskill, 1991; Turban and Dougherty, 1994).

Does mentoring make a difference in the career development of the young worker? A study of formal mentoring at a Fortune 100 company found that engineers with mentors reported greater job satisfaction and somewhat greater organizational commitment (Seibert, 1999). Mentoring was related to salary level and promotions for a random sample of managers in manufacturing in the United States (Scandura, 1992; Turban and Dougherty, 1994). Interestingly, a study of mentors found that one of the predictors of becoming a committed mentor is having been mentored oneself; thus, there may be an intergenerational connection in mentoring (Ragins and Scandura, 1999)

CAREER DEVELOPMENT

Young adults spin their Dreams from their values. A young businessperson in e-commerce may think autonomy and flexibility are most important in creating a new company. A scientist who thinks recognition is important might picture winning a Nobel Prize. A young attorney concerned with the environment might envision a "landmark case" victory over a major industrial polluter.

A different type of worker is emerging, according to findings from several studies including: The National Study of the Changing Workforce (Galinsky, Bond, and Friedman, 1993) and Two Careers and One Marriage (Catalyst, 1998c). The Two Careers study is of dual-career couples. The worker's commitment is less to the employer or to career advancement in the traditional sense, and more to the quality of the work that they themselves produce. When asked "What does being successful in your work life mean to you?" the most frequent response was the personal satisfaction from doing a good job (Galinsky et al., 1993). These findings support the value placed on the *intrinsic* features of work as discussed in a previous section. While the vast majority of workers agreed with the statement "I always try to do my job well," working hard was for personal satisfaction of a job well done rather than for career advancement *per se*.

Several characteristics of a work task have been found to be associated with high involvement in the work and commitment to the work (Catalyst, 1998c; Mortimer and Lorence, 1994). Characteristics include challenging assignments, involving previously acquired skills; variety in work; autonomy over direction of the work; and being able to produce a complete product, rather than an isolated part. Dual-earner couples (Catalyst, 1998c) mentioned similar desirable characteristics of the work environment: supportive management, ability to work independently, control over working hours and planning work. Dual career couples viewed supportive management as a prerequisite to the other work environment characteristics desired. Without supportive management, employees could not gain the ability to work independently and have control over their work and hours and be evaluated on their productivity rather than time spent at the office. As might be expected from the worker attitudes described above, few employees felt extremely loyal or committed to their employers. This was particularly true of dual-career couples who reported that having two incomes gave them the ability to take risks professionally and to seek new employment opportunities; the majority of dual career couples expected to move to other job opportunities.

This focus on the self has been described as the "self-ethic" (as opposed to the work ethic). Contrary to the way the label sounds, the focus of workers is on doing their best in their own jobs. It has been suggested that this new ethic may be good news to those who think that our future economic competitiveness rests on the quality of the work produced as a nation. Unclear, however, are the implications for workers' relationships and loyalty to companies and organizations.

What forces may be influencing this shift in worker commitment? It is speculated that when adults begin to lose control over their external environment, they focus internally (Galinsky, Bond, and Friedman, 1993). The 1980s and 1990s witnessed much turmoil and change in the workplace. Many workers at all occupational levels experienced corporate downsizing and cutbacks in management. Corporate mergers and sell-offs of sections of a company sometimes resulted in radical changes in the nature of the organization. The rapidity of these changes in many sectors of the economy may have had the effect of turning workers inward to something they could *control*—the quality of their own work. Worker commitment and loyalty to a given company or organization was reduced by the insecurity of the market place. Also, many young professionals were attracted by opportunities in the expanding economy of the late 1990s to start their own businesses in technology, a venture that was not viewed as possible in traditional companies.

Settling Down and Career Success

Sometime in midcareer, many people begin to analyze their Dream: Has it changed? How close have they come to fulfilling it? Do they seem to be headed toward eventual fulfillment? Is the job meeting their expectations? Have their values and interests changed to such an extent that the job is no longer in line with them? With increasing life experiences, most individuals become more mature. Their sense of personal identity has stabilized, and there has been a deepening of interests.

One of the intrinsic features of work that becomes increasingly important in midlife is autonomy (Lorence and Mortimer, 1985). Work autonomy is characterized by work that involves innovative thinking and that permits wide decision-making latitude. Having autonomy in one's work was the most salient predictor of workers level of involvement with their jobs. Work involvement is defined as having high personal standards for performance and giving high priority to work-related activities—attributes of concern to employers and related to job productivity. Notably, having autonomy in one's work was a better predictor than income or occupational prestige in determining how involved a worker was in his/her work.

One aspect of work autonomy that is gaining increasing attention is what is known as "customized career paths" (Catalyst, 1998c). Customized career paths involve features such as the option to specialize in an area of the organization rather than to work one's way through each department in an organization—to move laterally. In addition, customized career paths involved the ability to stay in a position for a longer period of time or to turn down advancement and be offered the option again in the future. In a study of dual-career couples, workers who were most successful and most valued by employers had in the past engaged in customizing their career and were seeking this option in future work positions.

For example, under their previous system the company of Price Waterhouse classified people as staff, senior, manager, senior manager, or partner. The partnership tract generally meant an individual's spending three years at each level, working full-time and being measured against same-year hires. People moved along according to the firm's plan and went elsewhere if they didn't make partner or were not perceived as partner material. This "up-or-out" model has been revised to focus more on competencies and create paths which allow individuals to progress at their own pace. Individuals are allowed to develop deep levels of expertise rather than to move vertically through all parts of the organization and to slow down their advancement time in order to balance work and personal responsibilities.

"Spillover" Effects

Most men and women in the work force are engaged in multiple roles. Most workers are parents and many are members of dual-earner families. There is considerable debate currently whether being involved in multiple roles (e.g. parent, employee, spouse, adult–child) is more likely to be beneficial or stressful to one's mental health. The *role enhancement* hypothesis is based on work indicating that the more roles a person (male or female) occupies, the better their mental health (Thoits, 1982). The role enhancement model focuses on role-related rewards and assumes that the rewards associated with one role would mitigate the stress from other roles, thus enhancing overall mental health (Barnett and Marshall, 1992a,b).

In contrast, the *role stress* hypothesis argues that being involved in multiple roles will increase psychological distress and lower mental health. The assumption is that multiple roles create multiple sources of stress. The stress associated with one role would compound the stress from other roles, thus having a particularly negative effect on mental health. Although originally, the *quantity* of roles was the focus in both stress and enhancement models, it is now recognized that the *quality* of the experiences in the roles, rather than the sheer number of roles, is the critical factor.

Spillover effects are assumed in both models. Experiences (rewards, stress) in one role or aspect of one's life (e.g., family) spills over and affects one's experience in another domain (e.g., work). The role stress model predicts *negative* spillover effects. The stress in one aspect of life has a negative effect on other aspects of life. For example, stress in one's role as a parent would spillover and negatively impact one's role as a worker; this negative spillover effect would result in increased psychological distress. In contrast, the role enhancement model predicts *positive* spillover from one role to another, thus enhancing overall mental health.

Spillover can occur in either direction—from home to work, or from work to home (Moen and Shin-Kap, in press; Mortimer and Lorence, 1994). Given the traditional gender roles for men and women, greater spillover from home to work has been hypothesized for women. Men are expected to manifest greater spillover from work to home. However, findings from clinical studies of men's psychological development suggest that men are more likely to compartmentalize their affective experiences in different domains of their lives; they have more "rigid boundaries" between, for example, work and family, such that less spillover between roles would be expected to occur (Barnett and Marshall, 1992b).

Current research findings indicate there is some support for both role enhancement and role stress models and for positive and negative spillover (Barnett and Marshall, 1992a,b; Moen, 1999). Negative and positive spillover effects from home to work and vice versa were examined in the Cornell Couples and Careers Study (Moen, 1999). The effects of age cohort, family life stage, and occupational status on negative and positive spillover were considered.

Work to family spillover. Negative spillover from work to family was measured by dual-earner couples' assessment of how often "your job makes you feel too tired to do the things that need attention at home" and "job worries or problems distract you when you are at home." Occupational status and age cohort are related to negative spillover from work to family. Managers, particularly couples in which both were managers, reported higher negative spillover. In addition, younger age cohorts reported higher negative spillover, suggesting that work stresses may be most difficult to manage at the beginning of one's career. The lowest negative spillover was reported by older age cohorts and empty nesters. In a study of Finnish couples, negative spillover from work to childrearing was also found (Kinnunen and Pulkkinen, 1998b). Jobs with high time demand and low control at work resulted in negative affect and job exhaustion. The negative affect and exhaustion spilled over into stress in childrearing activities and reduction in supervision of children's activities.

Positive spillover from work to family was measured by couples assessment of how often "the things you do at work help you deal with personal and practical issues at home" and "make you a more interesting person at home." Age cohort was also found to be related to positive work-family spillover with older age cohorts reporting more positive spill-over from work to family. In addition, women in every age cohort reported more positive spillover. A similar gender finding was reported in a study of mothers employed as nurses and social workers (Barnett and Marshall, 1992a). Having a rewarding job mitigated the effect of troubled relationships with one's children and reduced psychological distress. A second study examined more specifically the rewarding aspects of the job and problems in the parenting relationship (Barnett, Marshall, and Sayer, 1992). Women who derived a sense of accomplishment and feelings of competence from their jobs experienced less psychological distress associated with conflicts and disaffection with their children. Thus, the aspects of the job that mitigated distress and the types of parenting problems relieved were quite specific.

Family to work spillover. Negative spillover from family to work was measured by responses to how often "personal or family worries and problems distract you when you are at work" and "activities and chores at home prevent you from getting the amount of sleep you need to do your job well." As gender roles would predict, women report more negative family to work spillover, particularly those with preschool and school-age children. Likewise, older age cohorts who also were most likely to be empty nesters reported the least negative spillover. Positive family to work spillover was measured by responses to how often "talking to someone at home helps you deal with problems at work" and "the love and respect that you get at home makes you feel confident about yourself at work." Again, women reported more positive family-to-work spillover at all life stages. In addition, young couples without children reported greater support for positive family to work spillover. In summary, the findings from the Cornell study do suggest that women are more affected than men by both positive and negative spillover, particularly family-to-work spillover. Women, however, who had a rewarding job also reported more positive work to family spillover.

Spillover effects from work to other areas of life have been of particular concern to those studying the sociology and psychology of work (Mortimer and Lorence, 1994; Kohn and Schooler, 1983). The spillover hypothesis has received perhaps the greatest support with regard to affect. That is, job satisfaction has been found to affect life satisfaction (Rain, Lane, and Steiner, 1991). Research has also indicated that work factors such as job loss or insecurity, work overload, and work conflict have a negative affect on self-esteem, sense of control, and family relationships (Menaghan, 1991).

While the preceding discussion has focused on spillover effects involving mental health and psychological distress, one of the most extensive studies

Work-related stress can cause feelings of disaffection and burnout.

spanning 30 years has examined the effects of the cognitive demands of work on maintenance of intellectual functioning and on the qualities of activities in other domains of life (Kohn and Schooler, 1983; Schooler, 1984; Schooler, Mulatu, and Oates, 1999). Kohn and Schooler studied cognitively complex work that requires dealing with ideas and people. Such work involves the use of initiative, thought, and independent judgment. In contrast, a job that is less intellectually challenging such as work on an assembly line is generally simple and repetitive; the worker may spend the entire workday doing the same task over and over again.

In their most recent findings, the researchers found that people who had jobs that required independent decision-making and that involved working with a complex set of environmental circumstances tended to become more intellectually flexible. The work one does affects how one thinks. This finding was maintained when prior levels of intellectual flexibility were controlled for. Recently Schooler (Schooler et al., 1999) extended his prior work by examining how substantively complex work affected the intellectual function of adults during the later parts of their work careers. Does dealing with cognitively demanding environments continue to lead to relatively high levels of intellectual functioning as we age? Yes! Schooler found that doing cognitively complex work had an even greater effect for older than for middle-aged employees. Similar findings of complex work on maintenance of intellectual flexibility were found for both men and women.

One of the most interesting developments is the use of information technology to stay in touch with family while at work and to use this technology for work while at home (Moen, 1999). Parents with children at home are more apt to use a pager or cellular phone to remain connected to their families while at work, compared to young non-parents and those whose children are grown (see Figure 8-1). In contrast, both young non-parents and older empty nesters are more likely to use e-mail to remain in contact with family, suggesting that family members may be more dispersed geographically. Use of pagers and cell phones were more common in younger-age cohorts and those early in their careers. Moreover, there may be some spillover from use of information technologies for work purposes to use of them to stay connected with family. Workers in the utility industry were more likely than those in other industries to use pagers or cellular phones both for work and for family—above 70 percent of utility workers in both cases.

Work-Related Stresses

Career changes in midlife are becoming more and more common. In fact, the days of a single career in life are virtually gone. There are many reasons for such changes. Technological innovation, for example, results in career shifts, as workers move from jobs rendered obsolete by automation or new techniques, or into more attractive jobs created by the new technology. Look at the "help wanted" section of a newspaper and ask yourself how many of the listings would have been there 25 years ago, or 50 years ago. Technological change is creating and drastically transforming jobs at an increasingly rapid rate.

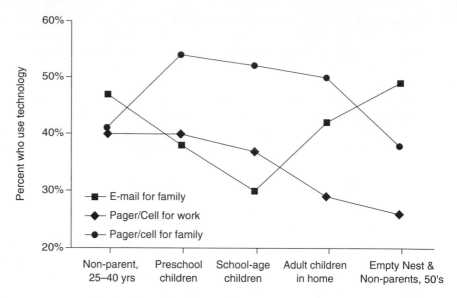

Figure 8-1 Use of technology at Home and Work. *Source:* Moen, P. (1999). The Cornell Couples and Careers Study. Ithaca, NY: Cornell University.

People are spending longer periods than ever before in the labor market. In 1900, when the average worker spent only 21 years in the labor force, career changes were much less common. By 1980, the average working life had grown to 37 years. A person could begin a new career as late as age 45 and still put in the 20 years required to earn a retirement pension. The longer period of work also increases the chances that a person's job will change significantly enough that he or she may be motivated to try or will be forced to try something new. We can expect that fewer and fewer people will keep the same job throughout their lifetimes.

We have moved rapidly from an industrial to an information society, and this is affecting the types of jobs available and the types of skills required. More jobs are concerned with providing and using information (e.g., teachers, lawyers, technicians, webmasters, e-commerce) than with directly producing goods. Two factors affecting an information society are the rate at which the volume of information is increasing and the rapidity with which information can be accessed. In such an information society, the knowledge and skills that one uses in his or her profession change at a rapid rate.

People's responses to rapid change vary. For those who don't keep up with changes in their profession, there is the threat of obsolescence. Knowledge obsolescence has been defined as the use of theories, concepts, or techniques that are less effective in solving problems than others currently available in the field of specialization (Willis and Dubin, 1990). It does not reflect an age-related loss of ability; rather, it reflects the failure to continue to learn and update as new knowledge and techniques become available. Levels of obsolescence are higher in fields that change rapidly. Both industry and the employee must bear responsibility for the retraining and updating required in a rapidly changing work world.

There may also be a growing concern with values and ethics as a result of being confronted with choices that did not exist before certain technological advances made the options possible. For example, the arbitrariness of the meaning of death with life-sustaining technology available has resulted in some medical schools adding professors of philosophy and ethics to their faculties in order to offer students the chance to gain a broader perspective of life–death decision making.

A work-related problem of increasing concern is known as job strain and stress (Karasek and Theorell, 1990; Williams et al., 1997). Current research suggests that work-related stress should be conceptualized and studied as a multifaceted problem involving personal characteristics of the individual, situational factors, and the organizational and cultural context in which such stress occurs. The most stressful jobs are those characterized by the combination of high psychological workload demands and low decision latitude. A job with high workload demands is one that requires workers to work fast and hard to accomplish an excessive amount of work in too short a time. A job with low decision latitude is one that does not allow workers to make decisions on their own, does not involve learning new skills or developing special abilities, and may involve a lot of repetitive work. Increased job strain has been related to increased risk of cardiovascular disease and mortality from all causes.

There is some evidence that psychosocial factors such as social support can moderate the effects of job strain on health risks. In a recent study of job strain in working women (Williams et al., 1997), workers who reported higher job strain were more depressed, anxious, angry, neurotic, and hostile than women reporting lower job strain. High strain workers felt they had less social support and reported more negative interactions with coworkers and supervisors. It appears that workers perception of the level of job strain may be more important than objective measures of job strain as strain relates to health factors. Individual characteristics of the individual may influence their perception of job strain.

Various pathways by which perceived job strain leads to health problems have been proposed. From a biological perspective, negative affect and social isolation may be associated with biological characteristics that contribute to pathology such as decreased immune function. Alternatively, from a behavioral perspective, risk behaviors such as smoking, increased alcohol consumption, and failure to adhere to prescribed medical regimens have been found to be associated with the types of negative affect and social isolation correlated with job strain. Of particular interest is the possible role of job supervisors in providing social support and mitigating job strain. A supportive supervisor may buffer or compensate for negative work conditions. According to Repetti (1987), workers in a stressful work situation were less likely to report negative mental health indicators (depression, anxiety) if they perceived themselves to have a supportive supervisor. In the Cornell Couples and Careers Study, dual-earner wives found a supportive supervisor to be particularly salient in meeting job demands (Moen, 1999).

WOMEN, MINORITIES, AND CAREERS

The world of work has been changing dramatically for women. For one thing, women represent a much larger proportion of the workforce today than they did formerly. Sixty percent of women are in the workforce, and 74 percent of the women who work, work full time. (Catalyst, 1998c). Women have not achieved equality in the workplace, however. There is a substantial difference between the sexes in the kinds of jobs they take and the pay that they receive. As you can see in Figure 8-2, although women are represented in all occupational groups, they are disproportionately represented in certain kinds of occupations. They remain concentrated in technical, clerical, and service jobs. Almost two-thirds work in either technical-clerical or service occupations. Occupational segregation results in domination of certain sectors of the labor force by men and others by women, that is out of proportion to their overall participation in the work force. Many women hold "pink-collar" jobs, which are low-paying white-collar jobs held predominately by women.

As the number of women in the work force has increased, questions arise regarding gender similarities and differences in work commitment and values, and factors that influence job satisfaction (Catalyst, 1998c; Moen, 1999; Tolbert and

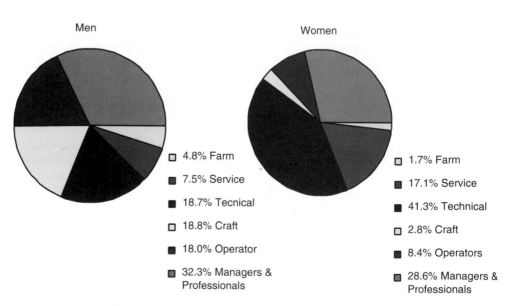

Men

- 4.8% Farm
- 7.5% Service
- 18.7% Tecnical
- 18.8% Craft
- 18.0% Operator
- 32.3% Managers & Professionals

Women

- 1.7% Farm
- 17.1% Service
- 41.3% Technical
- 2.8% Craft
- 8.4% Operators
- 28.6% Managers & Professionals

Figure 8-2 Occupational Distribution of Employed Men and Women in Each Job Category. *Source:* U.S. Bureau of the Census (1998b). Current population Reports Series P20-515. Washington, DC: U.S. Government Printing Office.

Minorities may suffer from many career disadvantages.

Moen, 1998). Hypotheses based on traditional gender roles suggest that men, as the primary breadwinner, would value extrinsic aspects of work, such as finances and job security, while women would emphasize intrinsic features of jobs that make work more enjoyable. However, for many women their jobs are not discretionary, and recent surveys find that men and women value work for many of the same reasons.

In a study of dual-career couples, there was high consistency in what men and women say they need from the workplace to balance their work and personal lives (Catalyst, 1998c). No gender differences were found in valuation of financial dimensions of work, such as income or promotion opportunities (Bokemeier and Lacy, 1987; Lincoln and Kalleberg, 1990). Women report slightly higher work involvement and being somewhat more satisfied with their jobs than men, even when controlling for social background and job characteristics (Moen, 1999). The types of work factors that men and women consider important to their jobs are similar and differ only in degree to which these features are important (Catalyst, 1998c). Both men (50 percent) and women (72 percent) want more flexible work schedules. Both men (65 percent) and women (72 percent) want the option to have more control over their career advancement.

Despite the fact that most women work primarily because they or their families need the income, women continue to receive low pay in comparison to men. Although there are far more women in the workplace, their relative earnings have changed little over the last 30 years. In 1955, women earned 63.9 percent of what men earned; in 1997, the figure was only 76 percent (Catalyst, 1998c). At the managerial level, white women earned 74 percent, African-American women 58 percent, Hispanic women 48 percent, and Asian/other women 67 percent of what white male managers did (Catalyst, 1998c). Level of education does not seem to reduce the inequity of earnings, although there is greater comparability in pay within the professions than in the sales and service jobs. Some have argued that gender differences in pay are due to men and women being employed in different types of jobs (e.g., technical versus crafts). However, most of the sex difference in earnings occurs *within* occupations; men and women in the same occupation hold different job titles and pay varies by job title.

Dual-Earner Marriages

The traditional family, where husband worked and wife stayed at home is changing into a family in which both parents are employed. Dual-earner couples have increased from 45 percent of married couples in 1976 to 56 percent in 1998. Sixty-eight percent of married couples with children under 18 years involve both the husband and wife in the workforce (U.S. Bureau of the Census, 1998b).

In studying couples with both spouses in the workforce, it is important to distinguish between *dual-earner* and *dual-career* couples. In dual-career couples both spouses are often in managerial or professional positions (Catalyst, 1998c). In dual-earner couples, both spouses typically work close to 40 hours a week but usually only one or neither of the spouses are in managerial or professional roles (Moen, 1999). One distinct difference between dual-earner and dual-career couples is their perception of whose job has priority. In fact, dual-earner couples often distinguish one spouse as having a "job" rather than a "career" (Becker and Moen, 1999). In a study of dual-earner couples, men were much more likely to say that their career had priority over their wives, regardless of life stage. The proportion of men indicating their job as primary increased significantly for couples with young children. Older-age cohorts of dual-earner couples also were more likely to define the husband's job as primary.

In contrast, dual-career couples, particularly younger dual-career couples, are much more likely to view their careers as equal (Catalyst, 1998c). Fifty-eight percent of men and 49 percent of women classified the two careers as equal. When dual-career couples defined one spouse's career as primary it was for traditional reasons, a higher salary or children in the family. Husband and wives in dual-career marriages were similar in the priority of work in their lives and in their perceptions of the benefits and challenges of their jobs. Over two-third (men 69 percent, women, 67 percent) reported that they would continue working with or without financial need.

In dual earner couples, men at all life stages and in all age cohorts tend to have continuous work lives since age 30. There appears, however, to be age cohort differences for women, with young age cohorts of women more likely to have worked continuously since age 30 even while having young children, as compared to older cohorts of women (Moen, 1999). Thus, the work lives of recent cohorts of women in dual-earner marriages may be more similar to that of men than in prior cohorts.

As discussed in Chapter 6, although most women are in the workforce, they continue to spend more time in household chores than men. Although the time men spend in household chores varies little by age cohort or life stage, women spend more time when there are children (of any age) in the home (Moen, 1999; see Figure 6.4). In spite of the demands of children and household chores, women report being more involved in their work and feeling higher work demands than do men. Work load involves beliefs that the job requires working very fast, working very hard, and being asked to do excessive amounts of work. Women in all industries studied and at all life stages reported a higher perception of work load. Women also report less control over work hours, including when and where they work and whether they can tend to personal matters while at work. Women with higher work loads rated their general health lower. At the same time women report higher commitment and investment in their jobs and assess themselves as demonstrating higher quality and accuracy in work then dual-earner males.

Women in dual-earner marriages rate themselves higher in personal growth than dual-earner men, but women also report lower levels of personal mastery, at least during childrearing. Personal growth was assessed by responses to statements such as "for me, life has been a continuous process of learning, changing and growth." Women perceived themselves to experience higher levels of personal growth at all life stages but particularly before and after children leave home. Being high in personal mastery involves beliefs about being able to do anything one sets one's mind to and believing that the future depends on the individual. Men report higher personal mastery for all age cohorts but particularly for younger, more recent age cohorts. Women of older age cohorts and past the childrearing stage report higher personal mastery than women with young children.

Child care is a particularly important issue for the 40 percent of the workforce with children at home. Finding high quality child care is the problem reported most frequently. One way that their family affects workers on the job is through absenteeism. When children are too ill to be cared for by their usual child-care providers, when child-care arrangements break down or when children are too upset to go off to school on their own, family demands may interfere with work. Workers report that flexibility in their work schedules is most critical in their ability to manage responsibilities at home and at work. Only about half of workers have flexible schedules, in which they could take an extended lunch break or work fewer hours one day and make it up later.

In the United States, employers, rather than government, are mainly responsible for deciding what fringe benefits workers receive and what policies govern work schedules, leaves of absences, and vacations. In our voluntary, employer-based system, there is no assurance of equal access or coverage for those workers with the greatest needs. Only recently has the United States addressed on a national basis the need for family and medical leaves. The 1993 Family and Medical Leave Act guarantees unpaid job-protected leaves of 12 weeks in a year-long period for workers; workers in companies with less than 50 employees were not covered by this act.

Many western countries have much more generous family leave policies than the United States (Hyde, Essex, and Horton, 1993). Particularly notable is Sweden's family-leave policy (Haas, 1991, 1992). Swedish couples have 15 months of job-guaranteed paid leave. For the first 12 months, the pay is approximately 90 percent of salary; for the last 3 months it is reduced. The typical pattern, as shown in Haas' research is for mothers to take the first five to six months; the father then takes the next month and a half and the mother returns to work. The mother may return to the home for the remaining leave.

If these are some of the costs of the dual-earner and dual-career marriage, what are the gains? The Catalyst study of dual-career couples provides findings on this issue. As noted earlier, dual-career couples are much more likely to view their careers as having equal importance with fewer couples giving a priority to one spouse's career over that of the other. Couples see the top advantage of a dual-career marriage as increased income. About one-third name more psychological benefits including personal fulfillment and emotional support. The major difficulty in dual-careers for both spouses was lack of time. One of the new emerging trends in dual-career couples is that two incomes increase a sense of freedom to take risks, particularly career risks. Dual-career couples report that the financial safety net of a second income gives these individuals the opportunity to change jobs and professions, step off and on the fast track and start their own business. The majority of men (56 percent) and even higher proportion of women (65 percent) indicate that having a spouse with a career had a positive impact on their careers. Husbands, with few exceptions, take great pride in their wives' accomplishments, and they see other benefits for themselves as well. Their wives, they perceive, are more vital, more interesting, and have more self-esteem, with greater competence as a helpmate in life.

Minorities and Careers

Sixty-three percent of African-American women and 66 percent of African-American men are in the civilian labor force. Twenty-four percent of African-American women and 17 percent of men work in managerial and professional positions. For Hispanics, 12 percent of men and 19 percent of women work in managerial and professional roles. In addition to concerns specific to ethnic differences, minorities appear to suffer many of the career disadvantages documented for women in the previous section.

Minorities are seriously underrepresented in the managerial-professional sector. A recent report by Catalyst (1998d) documented some of the concerns of women of color in management positions. The percentage of women managers or administrators in the private sector who are a minority include: African American (7 percent), Hispanic (5 percent) and Asian/Other (3 percent). Minority female managers are underpaid compared to white male managers, earning approximately 60 percent of what white male managers earn. Women of color in management positions reported the factors that limit their advancement: lack of an influential mentor, lack of access to networking opportunities with influential colleagues, and lack of company role models from ethnic groups. African-American women managers (22 percent) are more likely to be single parents with children under 18 than white (8 percent) or Asian women managers (5 percent).

There have been numerous theories regarding the disadvantaged position of African Americans in the labor market (Herring, 1995). The cultural deficiency theory postulates that minority groups often live in cultural contexts that devalue work. As a result of this culture minority groups fail to internalize proper work values, concern themselves only with short-range pleasures and lack acceptable work habits. An alternative theory favored by economists is based on human capital theory. Inequality in the market place exists because some workers are more productive; workers are more productive because they have invested more in themselves in schooling, job training, health care, and activities that increase future income. This theory has lead to job training schemes to deal with labor disadvantages of minority groups. Herring (1995) suggests another theory called *structural discrimination*. Minority groups are hypothesized to be denied access to good jobs by policies that are not inherently racially discriminatory but have negative effects on access to jobs. These include seniority rules, location of plants, public transit decisions, and trade policies. For example a company decides to locate a plant away from urban areas that have high concentrations of black residents. Public transit lines do not provide convenient access to job sites. Trade agreements lead to a reduction in the number of jobs in industries that often employ African Americans.

Considerable debate exists regarding racial differences in work commitment and values and job satisfaction. However, representative surveys report no racial differences in whites and blacks in level of work commitment or to psychological involvement in jobs when variations in job quality and characteristics are controlled (Lorence, 1987). While blacks are shown to have lower job satisfaction than whites, these differences generally disappear when job rewards and job characteristics are controlled (Tuch and Martin, 1991).

According to Gibson (1987), middle age may be a particularly difficult period for the black worker. Low work morale, declining physical abilities, and decreased labor participation can make this an exceptionally tumultuous time of life, during which many black workers enter a new category that has been labeled the "unretired-retired" group. This issue is discussed more extensively in the next section on the older worker.

THE OLDER WORKER AND RETIREMENT

Although our focus in this section will be on the older worker, we must begin by considering historical changes in retirement since changes in when and how one exits the workplace have impacted the definition of who is an older worker (Schaie and Schooler, 1998). The concept of retirement is fairly new in human history. Until the 1800s, the majority of workers did not live to old age, so the concept had little meaning. Individuals who did live into old age continued to work, as landowners or as businessmen. As the average life expectancy increased and as society and the nature of work changed from agrarian to industrial, the concept of retirement grew in acceptance—there should be a time in the life span when the individual ceased being employed in a formal job.

Retirement: Mandatory Age and Benefits

As retirement became a normative life event, two major public policy issues have emerged. The first issue deals with retirement *entitlement*—the older worker being entitled to benefits after retiring. The second and more recent issue deals with whether there should be a *mandatory age* for retiring.

The issue of retirement entitlement was first addressed in the late nineteenth century when Chancellor Otto von Bismarck of Germany established a state pension for people over 65, the first institutional support for retirement. In the United States, the Social Security Act of 1935 established the age of 65 as the "time to retire." Before Social Security, most men over 65 continued to work. Recent shifts in the age structure of the U.S. population (see Chapter 1) have resulted in significant changes planned for the timing of retirement. The proportion of people over 65 is increasing, as the baby boomers reach old age. Currently, 6 workers support 1 retiree, but by the end of the twentieth century, this ratio will have dropped to 4 workers per 1 retiree; by 2030, the ratio will be 3 to 1. Social Security and other pension systems could become a significant burden on younger workers. In anticipation of these shifts in the ratio of workers to retirees, changes in Social Security will soon be phased in. The Social Security Amendments of 1983 provide for raising the age of eligibility for normal retirement benefits to 66 in 2009 and to age 67 by 2027. These amendments will delay the age at which the worker is entitled to full benefits, but it is currently unclear what impact the raising of the age of eligibility for benefits will have on age of retirement.

The second public policy issue regarding retirement is whether there should be a *mandatory retirement age*. Over the past two decades, public policy in the U.S. has moved toward the elimination of a mandatory age for retirement. The 1978 Age Discrimination in Employment Act limited mandatory retirement to age 70 for most workers; some states (Maine, California) prohibited mandatory retirement altogether. The Age Discrimination in Employment Amendments of 1986 abolished mandatory retirement at any age and required employers to extend benefits to older workers regardless of age. The only exceptions are pilots and aircraft controllers, who are still required to retire at an earlier age.

As the number of elderly people in Western societies increases, mandatory retirement is an issue of considerable concern in many countries. Government policies and attitudes on compulsory retirement vary widely. Representative samples in four countries were asked the same question "Do you think that all employees should be required to retire at any age set by law?" As shown in Figure 8-3, attitudes in the two European countries were in favor of mandatory retirement, while attitudes in the U.S. were opposed (Hayes and VandenHeuvel, 1994). A

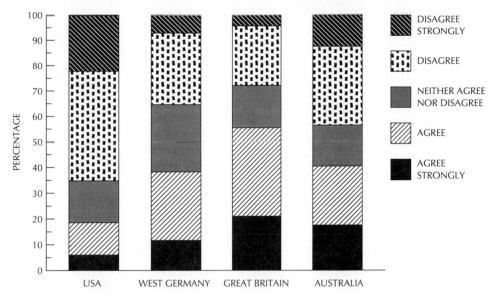

Figure 8-3 Attitudes toward Mandatory Retirement: U.S.A., West Germany, Great Britain, and Australia. Source: Hayes, B.C., and VandenHeuvel, A. (1994). Attitudes toward mandatory retirement: An international comparison. *Aging and Human Development,* 39, 209–231.

number of factors, psychological, social, economic, and political contribute to these differences in attitudes. Several factors are of interest from the perspective of the psychology of aging. Those in support of mandatory retirement view it as a mechanism for providing employment and promotion opportunities for younger workers, women, and minorities. The elderly are viewed as a reserve labor force that can and should be displaced when necessary. Other arguments suggest that it is a humane way to retire older workers who might otherwise be forced to retire on the basis of inadequate job performance; mandatory retirement is said to provide employers with a means to avoid both the difficult and controversial task of making case-by-case decisions.

A major argument against mandatory retirement is that the practice exemplifies age discrimination and violates the rights of the individual (Inkeles and Usui, 1989; Warr, 1998). Forced retirement ignores the diversity of abilities of older workers and may adversely affect the elderly economically, physically, and mentally. Further, it is argued that as western societies continue to age and birth rates decline, greater numbers of older workers will be needed; their continued participation in the labor force could help ease the anticipated demand on social security schemes and would allow employers to retain the skills and expertise of older workers.

Cultural differences in attitudes toward the period of old age and the role of government may also contribute to attitude differences toward mandatory retirement (Inkeles and Usui 1989). Some have suggested that Europeans generally believe that it is the right of the aged to have a number of years of leisure and to be supported by the government during their later years. In the U.S., on the other hand, there has been increasing emphasis placed on productive aging and the use of the abilities and capabilities of the old. Likewise, there may be cultural differences in perspective on the role of employment and the meaning of work. Inkeles and Usui suggest that for Americans work is fairly central to one's identity and is closely associated with strong sentiments toward autonomy and independence. Whereas mandatory retirement has been seen as at least part of the cure for unemployment in some European countries (Kinsella and Gist, 1995; Kohli and Von Kondratowitz, 1987), Americans have been far less willing to allow government to solve labor market problems by promoting early retirement. Finally, different perceptions of the role of government in various countries may contribute to differences toward mandatory retirement (Haller, Hollinger, and Raubal, 1987). While in some European countries the government may be viewed as the ultimate protector of the rights and well-being of its citizens, there is much greater support in the United States for individualized responsibility and greater opposition to government intervention. Support for government intervention into price and wage controls was positively associated with support for mandatory retirement in Britain and Germany, but not in the U.S. (Hayes and VanderHeuvel, 1994).

Most experts expected the number of workers remaining in the labor force past age 65 to increase when the mandatory retirement age was raised to 70 in 1978. However, as shown in Figure 8-4, there has been a long-term trend among men in their mid-fifties and early sixties to retire early, before the age when they can receive full retirement benefits (U.S. Bureau of the Census, 1998b; U.S. Bureau of Labor Statistics, 1994). A similar trend has occurred for white and black males although labor force participation has been somewhat lower for black males partly because of health and educational differences. In contrast, there are no meaningful differences between rates for older white and black women except for those aged 55 to 59.

The labor force participation pattern for older women has differed from that of older men (Pienta, Burr, and Mutchler, 1994). Women in their late fifties have been increasingly likely to be labor force participants. Today's older women grew up in an age when society did not encourage or expect married women to work outside the home. In the 1950s only approximately 40 percent of women in their thirties were in the labor force while in 1990 approximately 75 percent of women aged 30 are in the labor force. Younger cohorts of women today will spend much more of their adult life in the labor force compared to their mothers and grandmothers. In contrast, current cohorts of men are spending somewhat less of their adult life in the labor force, compared to earlier cohorts; this is due in part to entering the labor force at a later age due to increasing years of education and also the trend toward earlier retirement.

The increasing life expectancy plus the trend toward earlier retirement means that men and women will spend greater proportion of their lives in retirement than earlier cohorts. In 1990 men aged 55 years would, on average, live about 22 additional years and women an additional 27 years. Thus, future retirees could spend 15 to 25 percent of their life span in retirement (Kinsella and Gist, 1995). As

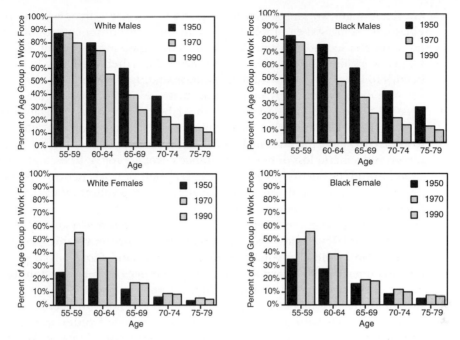

Figure 8-4   Change in Proportion of Whites and Blacks in Labor Force in Middle and Later Adulthood: 1950, 1970, 1990. *Source:* U.S. Bureau of the Census (1998b). *Current Population Reports,* Series P20-515. Washington, DC: U.S. Government Printing Office.

a result of early retirement and increased life expectancy, pension savings, and Social Security may need to be spread over a longer period than in the past for many retirees. It appears that we can expect the burden on the younger generation to continue.

The trend toward retirement at earlier ages is also evident for most western European countries (Kinsella and Gist, 1995). The average retirement age in 1990 in the following European countries was: Austria 60; France 62.4; Germany 61.4; Portugal 64.9; Spain 63.9; United Kingdom 62.9. The average retirement age in Canada and Japan were respectively 65 and 61.5.

The Older Worker

Figure 8.4 does show that approximately 30 percent of men in their sixties and even 10 percent of men in their late 70s remain in the labor force. What do we know about these older workers? First, most workers remain in the same occupations during their later work lives and men in certain occupations are more likely to work in the later years than in other occupations (Parnes and Sommers, 1994). Laborers and operatives were more likely to leave the labor force at age 55 than were professionals, managers, and men in sales (Hayward and Grady, 1990). Self-employed workers had the longest working life, compared to other classes of workers. The longer working life of the self-employed may reflect two different forces. For some, being self-employed means that they have more control over their work life; they can set their own work schedule and phase in retirement. For others, the longer work life of the self-employed may reflect their difficulty in accumulating savings to finance retirement, thereby necessitating a longer work life.

Since the mid-1980s there appears to be an increase in the "working retirees"—those who have reentered the labor force after their first retirement (Herz, 1995). A number of factors play a role in early retirees returning to the workplace. These include improved health, longer life expectancies, unplanned forced retirement, loss of health insurance coverage for retirees, and erosion of retirees' annuities due to inflation. More than half of workers over age 65 are working only part time and for the vast majority it is a voluntary choice, not due to inability to find full-time employment.

Older workers are often victims of stereotyping; they may suffer discrimination based solely on their age even when their competence and qualifications are comparable to those of younger workers (Geller and Simpson, in press; Lincoln and Kalleberg, 1990; Warr, 1998). Age differences in job functioning are influenced by the type of measures used (McEvoy and Cascio, 1989; Warr, 1998). Objective measures of job performance (productivity) showed no decreases or relatively minor decreases with age. However, supervisors rated older workers somewhat lower than younger workers. Supervisory ratings were particularly likely to be lower for older workers in nonprofessional jobs.

Stereotypes are often inaccurate. Several major reviews of the work literature (Geller and Simpson, in press; Lincoln and Kalleberg, 1990; Warr, 1998) have come to the following conclusions:

1. The attitudes and work behavior of older workers (age 55 and older) are generally consistent with effective organizational functioning.
2. Job satisfaction is higher among older workers than in other age groups.
3. Older workers are more loyal and less likely to leave their current employer.
4. Healthy older workers have lower rates of absenteeism than younger workers. Unhealthy older workers, however, may have higher rates of absenteeism.
5. Older workers are less likely to be injured on the job. Those who are injured, however, take longer to recover and are more likely to be disabled than younger workers.
6. Older workers do continue to learn and can profit from retraining.

Several hypotheses for why older workers have more positive work attitudes (e.g., job satisfaction, loyalty) have been suggested (Mortimer and Lorence, 1994). There may be cohort differences in work ethics and the valuing of work between depression-era older workers and recent cohorts. Alternatively, work-related commitment and responsibility may increase with age. A third explanation is that older workers have explored more jobs across the work life and are likely to have settled into jobs that match their needs and interests and/or jobs that they have been able to "mold" to their situation. Mortimer and Lorence (1994) argue that the literature is supportive of the third hypothesis—age differences in work attitudes are largely attributable to differences in job conditions. Contrary to popular opinion, there is little evidence for a historic decline in the work ethic; across several decades, workers have indicated that they would continue to work even if they were rich. In fact, women have shown a greater commitment to work roles outside the home. Moreover, behavioral indicators of work commitment (absentee rates, quit rates, over-time hours, etc.) show no systematic trends indicating a decline in work behaviors in the U.S., although changes have been noted in other industrialized nations (Lipset, 1990).

Several studies indicate little or no age-related declines in job performance for older workers in a number of job categories (McEvoy and Cascio, 1989; Salthouse and Maurer, 1996; Warr, 1998). In jobs in which experience is important, older workers may remain as productive as younger workers (Avolio, Waldman, and McDaniel, 1990; Salthouse and Maurer, 1996; Warr, 1998). Older workers maintain high levels of job performance because they have acquired greater amounts of job-relevant knowledge and skills. Salthouse (1984) examined younger and older typists and found that although the older typists were somewhat lower in speed of response, they were able to process at each glance larger chunks of the information to be typed and thus were able to compensate for any behavioral slowing. In a review of the literature Warr (1998) found that age was not significantly related to performance, however level of experience was directly related to performance. Age-related declines in job performance are most likely to occur in jobs that are physically strenuous or demand quick responses (Czaya, 2001; Panek, 1997). However, recent research in ergonomics suggests that in many cases the job can be redesigned to the individual so that as workers age, their productivity need not be compromised (Gang, 1991; Winn, 1991). For example, the Volvo automotive assembly plant in Uddevalla, Sweden, was constructed with the intent to have 25 percent of the employees over 45 years of age (Ekelof, 1988).

Discussion of the competence of the older worker in the previous paragraph focused on employees who had worked in a given job for a number of years. However, a major question, given rapid technological change, is the capability of older workers in jobs requiring new skills (Czaya, 2001; Morrell and Echt, 1997). Older workers may be particularly disadvantaged in periods of profound and paradigm-shifting technological innovation (Bartel and Sicherman, 1993). The Commonwealth Fund (1991) reported case studies at two major American corporations and one major British firm showing that older workers can be trained in new technologies, are flexible about work assignments and schedules, and are often better sales people. For example, Days Inns of American began hiring older workers (defined as those 50 and over) as reservations agents. Older workers were trained to operate sophisticated computer software in the same time as younger workers. Because job turnover was significantly less for older workers, training and recruitment costs were half that of younger employees. Finally, older workers were judged to be better sales people than younger workers. They booked more reservations than younger workers, although they took longer to handle each call. Similar findings on the success of employing older workers have been reported by McNaught and Barth (1992) and Hogarth and Barth (1991).

Quality of work appears to be a strong suit of the older worker. In a simulated data entry task, three groups of workers; ages 20 to 30, 40 to 59, and 60 to 75) worked for three days (Czaja and Sharit, 1998a). The oldest did the least amount of work, yet when production was controlled for quality there were no significant differences in performance. Moving out of the laboratory, a field study of workers from 20 to 59 in a variety of work environments found that workers from 30 to 39 produced the highest quantity but older workers produced higher quality as measured by supervisor ratings (Rao and Rao, 1997). To the extent jobs in late carer often include supervisory responsibilities, it would be important to know whether older managers can stimulate higher levels of performance among the people who report to them. In a study of sales organizations, Liden, Stilwell and Ferris (1996) found that the sales people reporting to older managers performed better than those reporting to younger managers.

Despite findings such as these, which indicate that older workers function well in their jobs, mature workers, although relatively unlikely to lose their jobs, have more trouble finding work if they are unemployed (Coberly, 1991; Gardner, 1995; U.S. Bureau of the Census, 1998b). Older workers, especially women, tend to be concentrated in declining industries such as manufacturing and textiles which put them at higher risk of losing their jobs. More over, older unemployed persons often suffer a decline in earnings compared with their previous employment if they find new employment. Among displaced full-time wage and salary workers aged 55 to 64 years only 20 percent were reemployed in full-time jobs where their earnings in their new job were the same as or higher than in their previous job (Gardner, 1995). The Age Discrimination in Employment Act of 1978 notwithstanding, unemployed mature workers still face age discrimination. Many workers are unaware of the protection offered by the law or are reluctant to become involved in legal tangles. In the 1990s, greater unemployment among older workers aged 55 to 59 years has also been reported in Western European countries (Kinsella and Gist, 1995)

The Decision to Retire

The meaning of retirement has gradually changed over the last few decades (Atchley, 2000; Ekerdt and DeViney, 1990). In the 1950s, retirement was considered justified only if a person was physically unable to work (Ash, 1966). Today, retirement has come to embody the notion that, by virtue of their long-term contribution to the growth and prosperity of society, people earn the right to a share of the nation's prosperity in their later years without having to hold a job.

The American ideal has been a long and stable career rewarded by retirement (Hayward, Friedman, and Chen, 1998). There is the assumption that retirement is a discrete event and that most workers make a "crisp exit" from the labor force (Mutchler, Burr, Pienta, and Massagli, 1997). However, research suggests that retirement for many workers is a "blurred transition" that may span months or even years and may include repeated moves in and out of the workforce. The crisp exit pattern of retirement has been found to be most common among men who re-

With the existence of more working women, retirement decisions increasingly involve both husband and wife.

tire before age 65. A blurred transition to retirement was somewhat more common in later retirement between the ages of 60 and 67. Blurred transition to retirement were more common for men with less economic resources who lacked pensions and had low levels of nonwage income. Moreover, the retirement process is not solely a product of the work and life situation *immediately* prior to retirement. Rather, when and under what conditions one retires is also influenced by one's work in midlife (Hayward et al., 1998). For example, persons whose longest work positions in midlife involved personal communication and dealing with people (e.g., teachers, insurance agents, managers, sales workers) had later rates of retirement. Two alternative hypotheses have been proposed for why workers involved in dealing with people may retire later. These types of occupations may have fewer barriers to working later in life and the type of experience acquired in this type of work may be particularly beneficial to the older worker. Alternative, these types of occupations may foster strong work-based social networks that increases workers' long-term ties to the workplace.

The meaning of retirement becomes more complicated if subjective as well as objective measures of retirement are considered. Atchley (2000) proposed a three-part definition of retirement that incorporates receiving retirement benefits, decreased time in paid work, and labeling oneself as retired.

What factors predict the decision to retire? Historically, the two major factors predicting retirement for all men have been health status and adequacy of income in retirement (George, Fillenbaum, and Palmore, 1984; Henretta, Chan, and O'Rand, 1992). However, the reasons for retirement are changing and becoming more complex; most decisions to retire involve multiple reasons. Both "push" and "pull" forces may be operating in the decision to retire (Schultz, Morton, and Weckerle, 1998). "Pull" forces include the attractions of retirement and the opportunity to do what one wants. Adequate retirement income would be a "pull" factor. The "push" factors include the problems or pressure in the workplace that impel one toward retirement. Health problems or disability would be a "push" factor. The nature of the job has been shown to be an important "push" factor, including factors such as lack of job challenge, and reorganization and downsizing. Positive retirement decisions are associated with adequate pension resources, pre-retirement planning, and a feeling of having accomplished one's career goals (Mutran, Reitzes, and Fernandex, 1997; Hansson, DeKoekkoek, Neece, and Patterson, 1997). The way in which the decision to retirement is made has considerable impact on satisfaction during retirement. Particularly important is whether the retirement decision was voluntary or under the worker's control (Gall, Evans, and Howard, 1997).

Retirement may occur for health reasons or be either employee initiated or employer initiated, for such reasons as job loss or compulsory retirement. Note that there has been a significant increase in employee-initiated reasons for retirement and a significant decrease in the portion citing health as a reason for retirement (Social Security Administration, 1985; Henretta, Chan, and O'Rand, 1992).

The most common reason for employee-initiated retirement was because the male worker wanted to retire. Henretta and colleagues (1992; 2001) examined factors that were significantly associated with men who reported retiring because they wanted to retire. The wanted-to-retire reason is unique in that it is the only reason (compared with health or employer-initiated retirement) affected by family variables. Being currently married and having the youngest child over age 21 speeded the retirement decision for these men. Among this group of men, having a younger wife slowed the husband's retirement, while having an older wife speeded the process.

Several work-related factors influence retirement. Among men retiring for health, or employer-initiated reasons, blue-collar workers were more likely to retire earlier than white-collar workers. Higher income was associated with later retirement. Among men citing retirement for voluntary or compulsory reasons, having a pension or Social Security was associated with earlier retirement.

Quite a different set of factors was associated with those reporting health concerns as the major reason for retiring. Having a lower occupational status and lower wages was associated with retiring for health reasons. The health limitations of older workers are due in part to premature aging, but job-related injuries are also a problem. You will recall that older workers, although less likely to be injured than the young, are more likely to be disabled when they are injured. Overall, it is difficult to assess the significance of health problems as they relate to retirement. Some people may cite health as the reason for retirement because they see it as more socially acceptable than the simple desire to retire.

Given the changing age structure in our society and the aging of the huge baby boom cohorts, there has been considerable recent interest in those taking early retirement. There appear to be two distinct classes of early retirees (Stanford, et al., 1991). The first group are in poor health, have low income, and possibly are unemployed; the second group are in good health, have above-average incomes, and, more important, have private pension plans. As you might expect, the second group tend to be in high-status jobs and it is their access to private pension plans that is the strongest predictor of retirement.

Employers may exert pressure on employees to retire in several different ways. Sometimes an employer will simply state outright that it's time for a worker to leave. Unattractive job transfers or job reclassification that significantly change the working conditions may be used. There is no way to estimate what proportion of older workers experience such pressures. Relatively few complaints about age discrimination concern retirement. Asking retirees directly if they retired against their will probably yields underestimates of the number who would like to have continued working, because people do not enjoy describing major career decisions as being out of their control. In a national survey of adults 55 years and over who were not in the labor force, 28 percent reported that they had little or no choice about stopping work (Herzog, House, and Morgan, 1991).

There have been a number of instances in which workers were offered incentives to retire as early as age 55 (Ruhm, 1989). The worker may be offered a financial bonus if he or she decides to retire early or is allowed to retire early without a reduction in benefits. These workers are typically in good health. So what factors determine who accepts incentives to retire early and who remains on the job? One study of faculty at a major university found that dissatisfaction with the work setting and expectations of adequate income in retirement were related to accepting early retirement options. The amount of time spent considering the retirement option was also positively related to early retirement.

The minimum age of retirement has a much more direct effect on the retired proportion of the population than do mandatory retirement policies. This is illustrated by the fact that the typical age of retirement under Social Security quickly went from 65 to 63 as soon as benefits became available to men at age 62 rather than 65, even though early retirement means a reduction in benefits. Early retirement may also be promoted by employer policies that allow employees to generate entitlement of early retirement. Under such plans, supplemental pension payments are provided to keep pensions at an adequate level until the retired person becomes eligible to collect Social Security. Employers may encourage early retirement to make room for the promotion of younger workers, deal with technological change, or make reductions in the labor force necessitated by plant closings and production cuts.

Minorities and Retirement

Blacks and Mexican Americans are more than twice as likely to have retired at an earlier age than whites (Stanford et al., 1991). Occupational differences across ethnicity were quite apparent between retirement groups. Early retired whites tended to have been in white-collar positions as opposed to blacks and Mexican Americans, the majority of whom were blue-collar and service workers.

Blue-collar jobs have been associated with factors such as increased job injuries, low job satisfaction, and lower income, which may contribute to early retirement decisions. Among early retirees, Mexican Americans reported themselves to be in the poorest health and most disabled in terms of functional health. As long as minority groups are concentrated in the blue-collar work force, the incidence of early retirement may well be elevated.

Jackson and Gibson (Gibson 1987; Gibson, 1991; see also Gardner, 1995; Gendell and Siegel, 1996) argue that the subjective meaning of retirement for the black elderly is particularly complicated by the fact that many blacks may be receiving no retirement benefits and that decreases in time spent in work may not be that clear-cut, in view of their discontinuous work patterns and need to work in old age. Over one-quarter of a national sample of black elderly defined themselves as "not retired," although not working or working less than 20 hours per week. Nearly 40 percent of nonworking blacks, aged 55 or over, appear to behave as if they are retired, but do not call themselves retired. This is the group that researchers have labeled the "unretired-retired," because they do not meet formal definitions of being retired such as being over 65, deriving income from retirement sources, or defining themselves as being retired.

Just who are these unretired-retired? They are middle-aged blacks who are leaving the work force mainly because of physical disability. They do not define themselves as retired for several reasons. First, because these people have often worked sporadically all their lives, the distinction between work and retirement is ambiguous. Secondly, Gibson hypothesizes that the disability role may have greater benefits than the retirement role. The Social Security financial assistance received is more likely to come from disability payments than from retirement payments. Likewise for disadvantaged workers, the sick role may have a better psychological fit than the retirement role.

The unretired-retired group is of great public concern. Having had a sporadic work life and no regular income, these are among the neediest of middle-aged blacks. Moreover, although they are a large group, because they are not defined as retired, the group is screened out of major retirement research and thus are deprived of the retirement-benefit planning and policy that stems from the research.

Women and Retirement

The vast majority of research on retirement has focused on men. Now, however, over half of women are in the workforce and most workers are married. As a result of these demographic changes, many more dual-earner couples will be in the workforce in the future and retirement will become a process of joint decision making and adjustment (Henretta, O'Rand, and Chan, 1993; Smith and Moen, 1998). Some research on couples' retirement decisions have been based on a life course perspective. Two key tenets of that perspective are that early experiences affect later life choices and transitions such as retirement. Secondly lives, such as husband and wife, are interdependent. Does the earlier work histories of husbands and wives influence the timing of retirement for both spouses? Do their beliefs about gender roles established earlier in the marriage affect retirement decisions? The synchronization of the timing of retirement by husbands and wives does seem to be influenced by the wife's prior work history. Women who were employed during the childbearing years were more likely to retire in tandem with their husband's retirement than did wives who had not worked for pay earlier in life. Constraints such as pension eligibility for women who enter the workforce late may act to delink a wife's timing of retirement from that of her husband.

Although the wife's continuing to work after the husband retires is currently less common, its frequency may increase for current cohorts of women who entered or reentered the labor force in midlife or after childbearing. What effects does a working wife with a retired husband have on marital quality and the couple relationship? Recent research by Szinovacz (1996a) suggests that the couples' employment-retirement status *per se* does not affect marital quality. Rather, couples with traditional gender roles in which the wife is working and the husband retired can experience negative marital quality. A decrease in marital quality may occur because the husband's provider role status is threatened or because there is conflict over the husband's participation in housework with the wife working. Employed wives of retired husbands reported similar levels of housework to wives in dual-earner marriages (Szinovacz and Harpster, 1994).

Life events are more likely to influence a woman's retirement decision than the husband's retirement decision (Szinovacz and Washo, 1992). Caregiving, for example, is disproportionately done by women and is typically done in late midlife, the time when for current cohorts of women labor force participation peaks. Being employed does not affect whether or not women start caregiving but women who do start caregiving are more likely to reduce employment hours or to stop work (Pavalko and Artis, 1997). National data on caregivers suggest that 27 percent of employed caregivers reduce their work hours and 19 percent take some time off work without pay (Pavalko and Artis, 1997). Moreover, women's adaptation to retirement is more affected by life events; adjustment to retirement is often negative when a number of life events occur during the retirement process. The differential impact of concurrent life events on adjustment to retirement for men and women may be due to women across the life course being more vulnerable to chronic life stresses.

Given these factors, some have argued that retirement is a qualitatively different process for women than men, and generalization to women of findings from previous research on men is to be questioned. Women's retirement decision appears to be more influenced by considerations (e.g., husband's health, surrounding life events) outside of the woman's own personal needs and desires. In addition, given gender differences in income and occupational status, women are likely to have less financial resources in retirement.

Reactions to Retirement

Although most of us think of retirement as an event—one abruptly stops going to work—studies suggest that it is actually a *process* extending over a period of time (Ekerdt and DeViney, 1993; Hayward, Friedman, and Chen, 1998). Atchley

(1976; 2000) has suggested that the process of retirement may be viewed as a series of adjustments, perhaps representing five phases. These phases are not a sequence of events that everyone goes through, nor are they necessarily associated with any particular chronological age or length of time. The *honeymoon period* begins immediately after retirement. It is a euphoric time during which the person tries to do all the things that he or she never had time to do before. The honeymoon is based in part on preretirement fantasies concerning what retirement should be like. It may involve extensive traveling. A honeymoon period is more common among those who retire voluntarily and have plenty of money.

Following the active honeymoon period, there may be a *rest and relaxation period* during which the retired person decides to take it easy. Atchley found that activity levels dropped after retirement but rose to preretirement levels again three years after retirement. There may also be a *disenchantment period* if retirement expectations do not work out as planned or if plans are disrupted by the illness or death of a spouse. In some cases, this period may involve serious depression. Although the proportion of persons who experience disenchantment is not known, it is thought to be relatively small.

During a *reorientation period,* the person takes stock of the situation and explores new avenues of involvement. The goal is to develop a realistic set of choices for providing structure and routine to retirement. The final period is the development of a stable and satisfying *routine* in retirement.

Atchley's periods of retirement have been widely accepted in the literature, and there has been some support in recent studies (Bossé, Aldwin, Levenson, and Workman-Daniels, 1991; Theriault, 1994). Gall, Evans and Howard (1997) assessed a group of male retirees a few months prior to retirement and then one year after retirement and six to seven years after retirement. In support of Atchley's honeymoon phase, retirees in the first year of retirement showed an increase in psychological health, energy level, financial and interpersonal satisfaction. Of particular interest was an increase in internal locus of control one year after retirement and also an increase in internal control from one year to seven years postretirement (see Chapter 10 regarding locus of control). It is suggested that as retirees become more self-directed during retirement, they experience an increase in perceived control over events. This may be particularly the case for retirees who perceived work to be externally controlled. In addition, retirees higher in locus of control prior to retirement were more satisfied with their health seven years after retirement. It may be that retirees who believe they have control over different life situations may demonstrate more initiative and persistence in problem solving when faced with life changes, such as health issues. Alternatively those who take greater responsibility for their daily life may report being more satisfied with their lives.

Given increasing life expectancy and the pattern of earlier retirement, it is becoming increasingly important to study husband–wife relationships after retirement. Vinick and Ekerdt (1991) looked at how the transition to retirement—the first year of retirement—affected the male retiree and his spouse. One of the most widely anticipated results of retirement was an increase in leisure activities as a couple. This increase occurred for approximately half of the subjects. Dining out was the most popular activity. Companionship appears to be particularly important to wives; wives who reported an increase in leisure activities with their husbands rated themselves significantly more satisfied with retirement than those who did not. When asked about personal leisure activities without the spouse such as hobbies, half of the husbands reported an increase. The pattern however was different for wives, in that 40 percent of wives reported a decrease in personal activities when the husband retired. Satisfaction in retirement for husbands focused on the personal level—freedom to pursue individual desires and to leave behind deadlines and work schedules. For wives, satisfaction focused on the interpersonal level. Thirty-nine percent of women reported that the best thing about their husband's retirement was the increased amount of time together. It should be noted that in this cohort of retirees, many of the women had not worked or worked only part-time. Whether similar findings regarding adjustment to retirement will be reported by dual-earner couples is in need of investigation.

Although most workers do not assess their self-worth in terms of their jobs, a few do. Most are high-salaried executives and professionals with high-status jobs that are intrinsically interesting and involving. When these workers approach the age of 65, they are often reluctant to retire and, in fact, are less likely to do so. This is true even though these people typically have less economic need to keep working and have the education and the money to enjoy their leisure. It is a bit paradoxical that wealthy candidates for a "leisure class" are instead the "unexpected candidates for a 'working' class characterized by conspicuous occupational involvement."

There is an ongoing debate whether work or retirement in later life is beneficial or harmful. Herzog and colleagues (1991) have argued that the degree to which work or retirement is associated with well-being depends on personal preferences regarding labor force participation or not. They hypothesized that persons whose work or retirement reflected their personal preferences would report higher levels of physical and psychological well-being. Indeed, voluntary retirement was found to be related to higher life satisfaction than involuntary retirement. Moreover, mental health was associated with individuals' having control and being able to make their own decisions regarding work and retirement.

A related myth about retirement is that the worker, deprived of the activity that gives meaning to life, is likely to go into physiological decline (Ekerdt, Bossé, and LoCastro, 1983). A number of studies have found no negative effects of retirement on health and no increase in the risk of death as a result of retirement (Ekerdt, 1987; Henretta, 2001). Why then does the myth that retirement leads to poorer health prevail, despite data to the contrary? People over 65, working or not, have a higher death rate than younger adults. Individuals also neglect to take into account health prior to retirement and attribute decline in health after retirement solely to the fact of retirement. Although 20 to 30 percent of workers retire due to illness or disability, in more than a few cases the cause of death after retirement is an illness that began during the work years and forced an early retirement.

During the past 30 to 35 years, the economic status of older adults has increased significantly—both in absolute levels of financial resources and in relation to young and middle-aged adults (George, 1993; Harris, 1986). There are several reasons for this fact. Cost of living increases in Social Security payments were implemented in the mid-1970s. More people have private pension plans. Particularly important is that current cohorts of elderly had higher levels of education, higher lifetime earnings and assets such as a home. On the other hand, old age remains a time of income loss. On average, retirement results in a 50 percent decrease in income. This average is somewhat misleading in that under Social Security low-income workers often replace much of their pre-retirement incomes whereas high-income workers may replace only a quarter of their pre-retirement earnings. High-income workers, on the other hand, often have pensions.

What is interesting is subjective impressions of financial well-being. One might expected that subjective feelings regarding financial well-being are strongly related to objective levels of financial resources. The rich elderly should feel more financially secure than the poor. However, actual economic resources are less strongly associated with subjective feelings of financial security in old age than for younger age groups. Some older people who have low levels of income nevertheless report being satisfied with their income. In fact, although income is dramatically reduced in retirement, 85 percent of older adults reported being satisfied or very satisfied with their financial resources (George, 1993). Why the limited association between objective financial worth and subjective well-being regarding finances? One explanation lies in aspiration theory, which states that perceptions of satisfaction are largely dependent on individuals' comparisons of their achievements to their aspirations. Research suggests that many people lower their aspirations with age. Income levels that once seemed inadequate are viewed as sufficient for one's needs. Another example is older people's satisfaction with housing that is familiar and their own. Even older adults who live in substandard housing report high levels of satisfaction with their homes and do not want to move.

One feature of age-related reductions in aspirations involves the reference groups to whom we compare ourselves. While a large majority of young adults base their aspirations on the most successful members of society, many older adults report that they compare their own situations to those of other older adults. Social surveys indicate that the vast majority of older adults view themselves as better off than most other older adults. Older adults may also be susceptible to aging stereotypes and believe that most older adults are poor, sick, and demented, and thus perceive themselves to be in an advantaged status. Hence, lower aspirations with age and biased views regarding their own advantaged status may contribute to the elderly's satisfaction with their level of financial well-being.

TRENDS IN THE WORKPLACE

Changes presently occurring in the workforce and in the nature of jobs will pose challenges for the worker and for society in general.

Demographic Changes in the WorkForce

The American workforce is aging and growing at a slower rate, as the baby boom cohorts move into mid- and late-career stages in the next few decades. In the 1970s, there was a large entry-level labor force (i.e., baby boomers); employers could be quite selective and set high standards for hiring. In contrast, the current entry-level labor force is much smaller. The two largest groups of potential workers continue to be the baby boomers, who are now in mid-career, and recent immigrants. There has been a trend over the past few decades toward earlier retirement. It is unclear whether this trend will continue as the baby boomers approach retirement age; some surveys of baby boomers report that they plan to work longer than prior cohorts.

The proportion of the work force that is female will continue to grow. Female workers are almost half of the working population in 2000. Women in the workforce are typically mothers, involved in dual-earner or mother-only families. Middle-aged women from the baby boomer cohorts are a major portion of females in the workforce. There are spillover effects to the families of these women in the workforce; over half of working women have at least one older living parent (Catalyst, 1998c).

The racial and ethnic composition of today and tomorrow's workforce will be different due to shifts in population distribution and immigration patterns. Of particular relevance is the dramatic increase in Hispanics and Asian Americans. Racial inequalities in the workplace and under- and unemployment of minorities, particularly blacks, will continue to be important issues.

As baby boomers make up the bulk of the workforce, we will have, in general, a better educated work force than previously. The increase in educational attainment is encouraging because the new jobs in technology and "information" will require higher levels of training. At the same time, the high school drop-out rate stands at 25 percent nationally. Thus, youths attempting to enter the labor force with limited educational training will be increasingly seriously disadvantaged.

Finally, there will be increasing job mobility, due to several factors. As businesses try to compete in more volatile and competitive markets, organizations are changing directions and strategies. This has led to "downsizing" and midcareer displacement in many companies, even in those that employees once viewed as secure. In addition, there has been a shift to a contingent work force. The number of part-time, temporary and contract employees is increasing (Howard, 1998). Retirees are increasingly seeking part-time employment. Such a workforce, with little job security, increases job mobility.

Several implications of demographic changes in the labor force can be projected. First, as the rate of growth in the workforce decreases due to smaller baby-bust cohorts, there will be fewer entry-level workers. We are already seeing labor shortages in lower paying jobs. Second, the increasing participation of women in the labor force will mean greater concern for pay equity, flexibility in work scheduling, and care of dependents (both children and elderly). Job flexibility is also of interest to the midcareer and older worker. Third, the increase in the minority workforce will also bring different cultural values about work and work expectations.

Changes in the Nature of Work and the Workplace

There has been a shift away from goods-producing industries and, hence, a decrease in the portion of the workforce employed in manufacturing. In contrast, there has been growth in the service and trade industries, especially in the information or knowledge industries. Jobs in these industries tend to be nonunionized jobs in small businesses with fewer hierarchical levels of management.

The nature of work and thus of careers is changing. There is a decline in long-term careers in one organization and the emerging need for workers to develop a portable portfolio for an open market. Movement across jobs and organizations is likely to accelerate. Workers will ad value through the knowledge and experience they bring to their jobs, but they must continually refresh their skills to stay competitive.

Many organizations now encourage people to take charge of their own self-development and careers. Given the unpredictable nature of work, firms are no longer planning employees' long-term careers within a given organization. Rather the emerging employment contract calls for organizations to provide systems, tools, and work assignments for training and development, but for employees to assume primary responsibility for acquiring the skills and competencies they need.

There is a growing understanding that careers can no longer be studied and managed without taking into consideration the context of the family. The male breadwinner with wife homemaker is no longer the dominant family form. Women are entering and remaining in the workforce in large numbers, meaning that both working men and working women are typically married to other workers. Family considerations including need for flexible work hours, customized career paths, and caregiving responsibilities influence the career paths of both men and women. The increasing number of dual-career couples suggest that both husbands and wives careers will be given priority, and due to the safety net of two incomes, spouses will feel free to take risks in exploring new job opportunities.

Finally, technology is affecting the location of the workplace. High-tech industries tend to locate on the east or west coasts. There has also been an increase in telecommuting—working from home or neighborhood satellite offices.

SUMMARY

1. A career is a lifelong pattern of work. Social backgrounds influence career choices. Holland distinguishes six personality types associated with certain types of professions: investigative, social, realistic, artistic, conventional, and enterprising. The family has a powerful influence on its members' career aspirations. Sometimes influence is expressed directly, as when a child is pressured to pursue a particular career; more often it is indirect, a reflection of family socialization practices, values, and interests.

2. One of the most important tasks in adult life is establishing a Dream of what one would like to become. Most young workers begin with high expectations, but lower their sights once they come into contact with the realities of the workplace. Some workers are socialized into their profession by a mentor, a more experienced person working in the same field.

3. A different type of worker is emerging. The worker's commitment is less to the employer or to career advancement in the traditional

sense, and more to the quality of the work that they themselves produce. When asked "What does being successful in your work life mean to you?" a frequent response is the personal satisfaction from doing a good job. These findings support the value placed on the *intrinsic* features of work. While the vast majority of workers agreed with the statement "I always try to do my job well," working hard was for personal satisfaction of a job well done rather than for career advancement *per se.*

4. Midcareer is a period of reassessment, of establishing a niche in society, and striving for advancement. One of the intrinsic features of work that becomes increasingly important in midlife is autonomy. Work autonomy is characterized by work that involves innovative thinking and that permits wide decision-making latitude. Having autonomy in one's work was the most salient predictor of workers level of involvement with their jobs. Dealing with a complex, demanding environment tends to keep people intellectually flexible. Those who work in static, repetitive environments often learn conformist values. There are spillover effects from work to family and family to work; spillover effects are somewhat more evident for women than men.

5. The number of women in the workforce has increased dramatically over the last several decades. The majority working have childrearing and sometimes caregiving responsibilities as well. Recent research shows the growing interface between work and family. Desired job characteristics include flexibility in work hours, control over one's work, challenging work, and the opportunity to customize one's career advancement—characteristics that reflect the need to balance work and family responsibilities.

6. Minorities seem to suffer many of the same career disadvantages documented for women. Blacks are particularly underrepresented in the managerial-professional sector. Women of color in management positions reported the factors that limit their advancement: lack of an influential mentor, lack of access to networking opportunities with influential colleagues, and lack of company role models from ethnic groups.

7. The status of retirement in the United States is changing. The mandatory retirement age has been abolished for most workers. In spite of the abolishment of mandatory retirement, the number of people retiring before 65 has increased in recent decades; many older adults in recent cohorts have retired as soon as it was financially feasible. It is unclear whether the trend of early retirement will continue as baby boomers approach retirement. Recently the number of retirees involved in part-time work has increased. The older worker is faced with the need to acquire proficiency in new technologies to remain competitive in the workplace; research suggests that older adults can acquire new technology-based skills. They may be somewhat slower than younger workers, but compensate in accuracy and in commitment to the job. It appears

that the majority of people are satisfied with retirement. There is no evidence of physical decline associated with retirement age *per se.*

8. Changes in the work force and in the nature of jobs will pose a challenge for workers and society in the future. The work force is aging and growing more slowly. The number of women in the work force will continue to grow. There has been a shift away from producing goods to service and trade industries. The organization of the workplace is changing with fewer hierarchical levels and more focus on teamwork. Workers are less likely to spend their entire career at a single organization or to proceed through traditional careers stages within an organization. Workers are assuming more responsibility for shaping their own career development and acquiring the necessary skills through work assignments that lead to new positions at other firms. Technology is also affecting the nature of work and also the site of the work place through the increase in telecommuting.

SUGGESTED READINGS

Czaya, S. (2001). Technological change and the older worker. In J. E. Birren and K. W. Schaie (Eds.). *Handbook of the psychology of aging* (5th ed.). San Diego, CA: Academic Press. Examines older workers ability to learn new technologies and the strengths and limitations of older workers in technology-intensive job settings.

Farr, J. L., Tesluk P. E., and Klein, S. R. (1998). Organizational structure of the workplace and the older worker (pp.143-185). In K. W. Schaie and C. Schooler (Eds.), *Impact of work on older adults.* New York: Springer Publishing Co. Workers 55 and older are the fastest growing segment of the work force. Farr and colleagues examine the demographic and economic workplace trends as the workforce ages.

Henretta, J. (2001). Work and retirement. In R. H. Binstock and L. K. George (Eds.). *Handbook of aging and the social sciences* (5th ed.). San Diego, CA: Academic Press. Scholarly review of research on older worker and retirement issues.

Howard, A. (1998). New careers and older workers. In K. W. Schaie and C. Schooler (Eds.), *Impact of work on older adults* (pp. 235–244). New York: Springer Publishing Co. Discusses some of the changes in the organization of the workplace and how this affects the older worker.

Becker, P. E. and Moen, P. (1999). Scaling back: Dual-earner couples' work-family strategies. *Journal of Marriage and Family,* 61, pp. 995–1007. Summary of findings from the Cornell Couples and Careers Study. Examines the interface of work and family as increasing numbers of women are in the workforce throughout the adult lifespan.

Warr, P. (1998). Age, work, and mental health. In K. W. Schaie and C. Schooler (Eds.), *Impact of work on older adults.* New York: Springer. Examines dimensions of mental health related to work and outlines characteristics of work that support mental health and well-being.

CHAPTER 9

Personality Development

Continuity and Change

One of the most difficult topics that faces behavioral scientists is the organization of those unique aspects of individuals that we study under the heading of "personality." The primary concern in the study of adult personality development is the interplay of *change versus continuity*. This paradox is central to much of the study of adult development (see Chapter 1). We usually think of personality in general, and adult personalities in particular, as being stable and enduring. But we also like to think that there is a potential for change in one's personality. We all know of instances that appear to illustrate the possibility of radical personality change: someone who in youth was hard and persistent, but who in later life is peaceful and philanthropic; someone who in youth was weak and vacillating, but in later life is assertive and self-assured; someone who was altered by a great event—an alcoholic who dries out after a serious automobile accident, or a person who experiences a religious conversion as the basis for a new life.

Early experiences often set a powerful course for further development, and personality characteristics once established are strongly reinforced for most of us as long as we remain in a relatively constant environment. Nevertheless, many early experiences (good or bad) may not have long-lasting effects because they are related primarily to the needs of a particular life stage, for example, the survival of the young infant through that period when the infant is completely dependent on caregivers or when adults in advanced old age may again require external supports to sustain a high quality life (Caspi and Bem, 1990; Field and Milsap, 1991; Kagan, 1980).

This discontinuity makes it possible for the individual to be responsive to meaningful events that occur later on in life and can lead to substantial change within individuals. Rarely, however, will an individual's changes lead to total reversals of early personality patterns. Rather, they will involve relatively limited positive or negative adjustments in response to the event or events that caused the change. This is why average patterns of personality development do show remarkable continuity despite the many individual personality changes that occur throughout life.

APPROACHES TO PERSONALITY

Personality theorists have struggled with defining personality since the beginnings of psychology. Early theorists often resorted to metaphorical(or circular) statements such as "an entity of the sort you are referring to when you use the first person pronoun 'I'" (Adams, 1954) or "what a person really *is* " (Allport, 1937). The classic definition of personality, given by Gordon Allport in 1937, suggests that personality is the dynamic organization within the individual of those biosocial systems that determine his or her unique adjustment to the world. The biosocial systems include personality traits, habits, motives, and values that are partly biologically based (genetically transmitted, for example) and partly the result of learning and experience (induced by social influences). These biosocial systems are interrelated (organized) in a complex manner. In active (dynamic) interaction with the environment; they determine an individual's unique adaptation to life.

A distinction is also made between the concepts of state and trait in personality. A *state* reflects a response to a transient situation, while a *trait* represents the enduring response patterns that are exhibited by a person in many different contexts. The two are not totally unrelated, of course, and systematic responses to many transient situations may well crystallize into trait patterns over time (Kim, Nesselroade, and Featherman, 1996; Nesselroade, 1988b).

Theories of personality differ in their choice and definition of the biosocial systems that they view as most useful in explaining human behavior. The *psychoanalytic approach* initiated by Sigmund Freud, for example, divides the human personality into *id, ego,* and *superego,* which represent impulsive, realistic, and moralistic tendencies in the individual. The *individual differences approach* emerged from early attempts to develop psychological tests for measuring human characteristics; personality traits or, more globally, personality types are the units usually described. A *learning approach* to personality emphasizes behavior elicited, controlled, and maintained by stimuli and reinforcements. The *humanistic approach* seeks to move away from explanations of human behavior to those that would be equally appropriate to an explanation of behaviors that can be found in lower animals; it is marked by discussions of higher human motives such as self-actualization. The *cognitive approach* holds that the way people perceive their world is the most direct determinant of their behavior. The biosocial systems in the cognitive approach are social perceptions, beliefs, attributions, and the like. Finally, a *contextual approach* recognizes the impact of social roles and historical contexts as they interact with personality patterns (Schaie and Hendricks, 2000).

Every one of these approaches has been used to describe the course of personality development in the adult years. Each theory has its advantages and disadvantages, and each may have a place in the overall attempt to understand what happens to human personality as it ages. But not all theories fit all aspects of adult development equally well, and the choice of a theoretical model to be used for explanatory purposes will often depend on the specific topic to be considered. The psychoanalytic approach, for example, focuses on ego development through the life span; we will discuss theory and research in this area in the following section. This will be followed by an example of the cognitive approach. The individual differences approach focuses on age differences and age changes in personality test scores; therefore some research on personality assessment will be covered in the latter part of the chapter (see also Aldwin and Levenson, 1994, or Wiggins and Pincus, 1992). The remaining approaches to personality development will be discussed in Chapter 10 on motivation, because most of the topics influenced by these approaches fall into areas traditionally considered to be based on motivational theories.

EGO DEVELOPMENT

The psychoanalytic theory of personality was formulated by Sigmund Freud over many years, beginning in 1900 with the publication of *The Interpretation of Dreams*. Freud and his associates, including Carl Jung, revised and extended psychoanalytic theory until Freud's death in 1939. Since Freud's death, further modifications and extensions were made by a number of important theorists, including Erik Erikson, Anna Freud (Sigmund's daughter), David Rappaport, and many others. The resulting theory provides a rather complex approach to personality and psychotherapy that cannot be described here in detail. We will limit our discussion here to the three aspects of psychoanalytic theory that have proved to be most influential in the study of personality development in adulthood.

First of all there is the concept of *unconscious mental processes* that is important for understanding personality. By definition, the unconscious can only be described indirectly. The concept of the unconscious therefore led to the development of projective tests that contain ambiguous stimuli. It is assumed that individuals who describe these stimuli reveal (without being aware of doing so) their deepest desires and values (see Schaie and Stone, 1982). Second, we will consider the concept of *defense mechanisms,* or the cognitive tricks people play on themselves to reduce anxiety and personal embarrassment. And third, we will discuss the notion of *ego development,* which is based on the idea that we are constantly refining our personal identities as we live our everyday lives.

Defining personality in terms of *id, ego,* and *superego* came late in Freud's theory. Earlier on he thought of maladjustment and mental disorders as arising from conflict between unconscious ideas that were in conflict with conscious intentions. But as Freud encountered a greater variety of mental disorders, he realized that some of these disorders actually involved conflict between unconscious ideas and equally unconscious intentions. To improve his theory's ability to represent this kind of conflict, Freud introduced the constructs of id, ego, and superego, and portrayed conflict as a discrepancy between the aims of any two of these constructs.

The *id* is the power system of the personality, providing energy (sexual and aggressive) for the actions of the individual. It is said to operate on the *pleasure principle,* which holds that what is immediately pleasurable is good and that what is unpleasant should be avoided, regardless of later consequences. The id does not tolerate delay of gratification.

The *ego* is the strategist of the personality. It operates on the so-called *reality principle,* which focuses on the distinction between what can be accomplished and what cannot. The ego moves to satisfy the desires of the id in a realistic manner, by assessing the situation and planning actions in a logical sequence to achieve a certain purpose. The ego is Machiavellian; it has no moral principles. Unless arrest and imprisonment made theft impractical, the ego would steal to satisfy the id. It still would steal, that is, except for the pressure that comes from the superego.

The *superego* is the moralist part of the personality, that part that fills individuals with pride when they do "good" (ego-ideal) and with shame when they do "bad"; it could be referred to as our conscience. According to Freud, the superego develops from interactions with parents, as the parents interpret for the child the moral principles of the society in which they live, or of the subculture to which they feel allegiance.

The desires, plans, and demands of the id, ego, and superego are often in conflict. If you can imagine a sex-starved hedonist, a humorless computer scientist, and a frock-coated Puritan minister being chained together and turned loose in the world, then you have a reasonable approximation of what Freud was trying to say about personality. The id, ego, and superego cannot break their chains and go their separate ways. They have no alternative but to adjust to one another. The result, in the psychoanalytic view of life, is the adult human personality (Quintar, Lane, and Goeltz, 1998).

Defense Mechanisms

As the individual matures, the role of the ego becomes more important. To control the impulsive id and the moralistic superego, the ego often relies on cognitive tricks called defense mechanisms (Freud, 1946). Defense mechanisms are adaptive techniques designed to provide psychological stability in the midst of conflicting needs and stresses that are part of human existence; they are characteristic ways in which people deal with anxiety, aggressive impulses, and frustrations (Butler, Lewis, and Sunderland, 1991). As the person develops from adolescence to early midlife, such development entails the relinquishment of immature defenses and the adoption of more mature defenses (Vaillant, Bond, and Vaillant, 1986; Vaillant and McCullough, 1998; see Costa, Zonderman, and McCrae, 1991 for a critique of defense mechanisms from the point of view of trait psychology).

A defense mechanism often used by middle-aged and older people is *denial,* a form of *repression*—driving an idea out of consciousness. Indeed, denial of aging itself is a way some people handle the anxieties and uncertainties of advancing age

(Butler, Lewis, and Sunderland, 1991; Thompson, Itzin, and Abendstern, 1990). Denial of one's own imminent death is also not uncommon, as is denial of the death of a loved one, as we shall see in Chapter 15. Also often denied are some of the sensory and energy losses that accompany growing old for many persons.

Another form of repression is *selective memory,* in which one recalls the pleasant moments of one's past but banishes the unpleasant. As Nietzsche once said of distasteful actions in his past, "My memory says that I did it, my pride says that I could not have done it, and in the end, my memory yields." Sigmund Freud himself, who formulated the concept of repression, made frequent errors in dates and facts when trying to recall his experiences with cocaine in young adulthood (Quintar, Lane, and Goeltz, 1998).

The common defense mechanism of *regression* represents a return to less mature behaviors. Some people react to growing old by acting "babyish," that is, by assuming a passive and dependent role. In one study, about 10 percent of a sample between the ages of 70 and 79 were classified as "succorance seekers," that is, they wanted others to take care of all their physical and emotional needs. Often these seekers move in with an adult child who is then expected to play the role of parent.

There are other defensive behavior patterns identified by psychoanalytic theorists that are often used by adults, although perhaps no more often than by children. *Projection* is the denial of an anxiety-arousing impulse in oneself and its attribution instead to another person. Persons anxious about their own sexual urges may complain that "everyone" has been making sexual advances to them; others, harboring unconscious aggressive impulses, may assert that adult children, physicians, and politicians dislike them and are out to do them harm. *Displacement* is the repression of the true object of a sexual or aggressive impulse and the substitution of a new, less threatening object. Angry at her "deteriorating" body, an aging woman may complain that the world is going to ruin. *Reaction formation* is the replacement of an objectionable idea by its opposite. Unconscious hate may be covered over by conscious love, or desperate sexual desires may result in living a prim life and indulging in antipornography tirades.

Isolation involves separating an idea from its emotional significance. In one form of isolation, issues that might provoke too much anxiety if discussed in personal terms can be dealt with more easily if the discussion remains "abstract" and "objective." For example, a woman who is anxious about sexual desires for people other than her spouse may start a discussion on the nature of marital fidelity. This form of isolation, called *intellectualization,* is in some situations a valued ability in our culture; scientists and judges, for example, are expected to consider the evidence of a matter without letting emotions "distort" their judgment. A good sense of humor is another form of isolation. Isolation is more frequently used by people as they grow older, whereas other defenses, notably reaction formation, are observed less often (Vaillant, 1995b).

Sublimation is the ingenious defense in which one satisfies base impulses while acting in a way highly valued by society. For example, an artist may be driven at some deep psychoanalytic level by the desire to smear feces. But instead the artist smears paints—and earns, not scorn, but universal acclaim. Of course, the motives

Wearing fanciful clothing on festive occasions allows adults to act out their fantasies in a socially acceptable way, the defense mechanism called sublimation.

in any activity are many, and not all artists are driven, even unconsciously, to smear feces or otherwise express vulgar desires. Similarly, a musician with conflict about putting things in his or her mouth (part of an old desire to suckle at the mother's breast) may relieve it by playing the oboe. Novelists may have the best of all possible worlds; they can write about the most direct and vulgar expression of the basest motives and be praised for their efforts. Successful human development in the adult years requires the successful sublimation of many potentially evil instincts into socially acceptable behaviors that benefit rather than harm other people.

Activity and Cautiousness

Psychoanalytic theory describes defense mechanisms that people of all ages are presumed to use, but there are similar processes that have been described as being characteristic of older persons. Older people use certain defenses against anxiety and uncertainty that are particularly appropriate to their life circumstances. Notable among these are activity and cautiousness.

Activity is a common enough defense at younger ages as well. Following some unexpected tragedy, such as the loss of a spouse or a job, a person might be heard to say, "Well, I'll just bury myself in my work." In the later years of life, such tragedies become more frequent, although the anxiety caused by them does not necessarily decrease. Activity—"working off the blues" (Butler, Lewis, and Sunderland, 1991)—is still one of the most common and effective defenses. Some of the most successful retirement programs are based on activity: building things, getting involved in church activities, and so on. Activity keeps your mind too busy to think about your problems. As noted in Chapter 4, however, such activities have to be meaningful; activities that merely have the appearance of productivity do not suffice, and the beneficial effects of programmed activity interventions soon dissipate (Okun, Olding, and Cohn, 1990; see also the discussion of disengagement versus activity theory in Chapter 10). Continuity theory suggests that middle-aged and older adults try to preserve existing psychological and social patterns by applying the skills and knowledge that they have acquired earlier in order to maintain a stable pattern of activities (Atchley 1989a, 1993).

Cautiousness is another way some older people defend themselves against the anxieties of old age. They tend to become more careful, trading off speed of response in order to increase accuracy (Salthouse, 1994). They often appear to be motivated by the desire to avoid mistakes more than to succeed at a task. For example, some older people, more often than younger subjects, will make no response at all to a question on an intelligence test.

By late midlife, many people perceive some decline in their ability to compete with younger adults in tasks that require quick response. To compensate (in defense), they may reorder their priorities; they may begin to place greater value on accuracy, quality, and other "timeless" characteristics (cf. Baltes, 1997; Schaie and Willis, 2000a). An aging psychologist may strive to complete one or two "superior theoretical papers" and wonder about the young psychologists who produce a dozen research papers a year that are only slight variations of one another. An aging quarterback values his knowledge, his ability to stand in one place as 280-pound linemen struggle to reach him, his cautious approach, his ability to withhold a response until the defensive pattern becomes clear and he knows when and where a receiver will break into the open. He may not be able to move around as quickly as a younger quarterback or to throw a football as far, but are these abilities the important ones? Not in his mind.

Cautiousness is often a virtue, for many aging quarterbacks and for many aging psychologists. Sometimes, however, it results in inferior performance, as shown by slowness and poor quality. On many ability tests, for example, older people earn lower scores on average than do younger people. Some of these age differences may represent a decline in the ability being tested, but often some of the difference could be due to the increased cautiousness of older people. They are less willing to guess on a questionnaire item, or they slow down on a manual task, perhaps believing that to do two things out of two successfully is better than to do four things out of six—even though the test is scored for the number of tasks completed, not for the percentage of tasks tried and accomplished successfully (Birkhill and Schaie, 1975; Schwarz and Knäuper, 1999).

Older persons' cautiousness may well exaggerate the apparent decline in such abilities as intelligence, learning and memory, and perception. Perhaps one of the clearest examples of the effect of cautiousness on an interpretation of psychological research is in sensory psychology. Consider the typical hearing test. The examiner presents tones at varying degrees of loudness and asks when the individual hears them. Subjects who are very cautious will not say that they have heard the tone until it is quite loud. Hence, traditional hearing tests are likely to overestimate the degree of hearing loss in older people, confusing actual loss with cautiousness of report (Fozard and Gordon-Salant, 2001).

Stages of Ego Development

Psychoanalytic theorists view personality development over the life span as being largely a matter of ego development. In other words, the processes and abilities that we use to cope with reality emerge, are strengthened, become more complex, and become more integrated. Our defense mechanisms become more mature, utilizing gross adaptations such as denial and projection less and refined adaptations such as intellectualization and sublimation more (Marcus, 1999; Vaillant, 1995b).

The description of ego development often involves the notion of developmental stages. Stage theories break the life span (or some part of it) into chronological age periods, each of which is characterized by a set of developmental issues. As we have seen in the three chronologically oriented chapters at the beginning of this volume, the issues in each stage may be quite different, in degree if not in kind, from those in other stages.

Perhaps the most important extension of the psychoanalytic approach into the adult years was Erik Erikson's (1963) stage theory. This theory marked a sharp departure from previous theories of ego development, which tended to see the personality as relatively fixed by the age of 5 or 6. Although Erikson's most famous concept, the identity crisis, is placed in adolescence, the turmoil of deciding "who you are" continues in adulthood, and identity crises often recur throughout life, even in old age (Erikson, 1979). Moreover, Erikson (1982) emphasized that "human development is dominated by dramatic shifts in emphasis." But in his latest writing, Erikson redistributed the emphasis on the various life stages more equitably. He argued that the question of greatest priority in the study of ego development is "how, on the basis of a unique life cycle and a unique complex of psychosocial dynamics, each individual struggles to reconcile earlier themes in order to bring into balance a lifelong sense of trustworthy wholeness and an opposing sense of bleak fragmentation" (Erikson, Erikson, and Kivnik, 1986; Goleman, 1988).

The *intimacy crisis* (discussed in some detail in Chapter 2) is the primary psychosocial issue in the young adult's thoughts and feelings about marriage and family. However, recent writers suggest that this crisis must be preceded by identity consolidation whch is also thought to occur in young adulthood (cf. Pals, 1999). The primary issue of middle age, according to Erikson, is *generativity versus stagnation* (see McAdams and de St. Aubin, 1992; Snarey et al., 1987). Broadly conceived, generativity includes the education of one's children, productivity and creativity in one's work, and a continuing revitalization of one's spirit that allows for fresh and active participation in all facets of life. Manifestations of the generativity crisis in midlife are career problems, marital difficulties, and widely scattered attempts at "self-improvement" through sometimes outlandish therapies, mystical religions, and even "physical meditation" (or jogging). Successful resolution of the generativity crisis involves the human virtues of caring, giving, and teaching, in the home, on the job, and in life in general.

In Erikson's view of ego development, the final years of life mark the time of the *integrity versus despair crisis,* when individuals look back over their lives (Haight, Coleman, and Lord, 1994) and decide that they were well-ordered and meaningful (integrated) or unproductive and meaningless (resulting in despair). Those who despair approach the end of life with the feeling that death will be one more frustration in a series of failures. In contrast, the people with integrity accept their lives (including their deaths) as important and on the whole satisfying. In a sense, ego integrity is the end result of the life-long search for ego identity, a recognition that one has coped reasonably successfully with the demands of both the id and society (Erikson, 1979, 1982; Whitbourne, 1996). Once old age is reached it may be most advantageous for the person to rigidly maintain this identity (Tucker and Desmond, 1998).

The final stage of life includes an exploration of personal grounds for faith. Erikson points out that the aged share with infants what he calls the "numinous" or the experience of the "ultimate other." This experience was provided for the infant by its mother. By contrast, the experience of ultimate confidence is provided for the older person by the confirmation of the distinctiveness of their integrated life and by its impending transcendence (Erikson, 1984).

A formal investigation of the progression through the Eriksonian stages from young adulthood into midlife has been conducted by administering an inventory of psychosocial development to three cohorts of college students, followed up after 11 and 22 years (Whitbourne et al., 1992). This study showed not only inner psychological changes as postulated by Erikson, but also showed effects of exposure to particular historical, cultural, and social realities of the environment. As higher stages were attained there also seemed further resolution of the earlier stages of development, suggesting a process of continuous reorganization, beyond the stage-specific issues confronted by the individual. In addition, this study raises the possibility that the sequencing of stages may not be unidirectional, and it further suggests cohort differences that implied less favorable resolution of ego integrity versus despair over the decade of the 1980s (Whitbourne and Connolly, 1999).

Ego functioning has been described as a two-dimensional process. The first dimension, *ego resiliency,* is the person's ability to meet new demands. Those who have high ego resiliency are resourceful and flexible and able to adapt themselves to novel circumstances. Those who have low ego resiliency tend to be hypersensitive, moody, and uncomfortable with themselves and their environment. The second dimension, *ego control,* is the ability to master impulses. People who are overcontrolled tend to be strongly conformist, narrow in interest, and poor in the ability to interact with other persons. Undercontrolled persons tend to be spontaneous, inclined toward immediate gratification of impulses, and willing to attempt new relationships and ways of doing things. Recently, the importance of developing and maintaining flexible personality styles has been further supported by showing that persons with flexible attitudes and behaviors in midlife showed greater maintenance of intellectual abilities into old age (Schaie, 1984b, 1996b; Schaie, Dutta, and Willis, 1991).

Gender Differences in Personality with Age

Another phenomenon of ego development concerns the masculine and feminine parts of personalities (Gutmann, 1987). The early psychoanalytic theorist Carl Gustav Jung (1960) first suggested that young adults tend to express only one sexual aspect, often taking considerable pains to inhibit the other. The particular behaviors expressed are usually defined by sex-role stereotypes, which may differ from culture to culture and from generation to generation. Such gender-differentiated personality styles may develop quit early and remain stable over substantial periods of time, although they may be life-stage specific (Pulkkinen, 1996). In most Western cultures, the male role is active and aggressive and the female role is passive and nurturant. As people age, however, the suppressed part of their personalities emerges; men as they grow older may express more behaviors that earlier in life would be considered feminine, and women may show more traits that in their youth would have been viewed as masculine. What Gutmann (1992b) calls postparental transition, is said to make men discover feelings of nurturance and aesthetic sensibility, while women unveil assertive and competitive qualities. This does not necessarily mean that there is a reversal of sex roles. What this trend accomplishes is to provide a greater sense of balance (androgeny) that permits both men and women as they age to express personality styles that fit their individual needs and circumstances rather than being governed by the societally imposed sex-role stereotypes.

In a cross-sectional study, using the Bem Sex Role Inventory (Bem, 1978), sex-role attributions of 426 women and 378 men were examined at 8 stages in the family life cycle from adolescence through grandparenthood (Feldman, Biringen, and Nash, 1981). Characteristics studied included leadership, autonomy, acquiescence, nonassertiveness, compassion, tenderness, social inhibitions, and self-ascribed masculinity and femininity. Most of the life-stage differences found were associated with the particular life stage of the family rather than with chronological age. Both femininity and masculinity varied only within gender, and at that quite modestly.

Women showed greater tenderness than men at all life stages, except during the married-childless and grandparenthood stages. Men were more autonomous and less acquiescent than women during the stage of expecting a child and during young parenthood, but not at other stages. Other changes occur in complex ways and reveal both diverging and parallel developmental differences occurring for men and women with role shifts related to the stage of family life.

However, in a related study conducted in Australia involving a sample of dating, cohabiting, and married couples and divorced partners (Cunningham and

Antil, 1984), it was found, that masculinity and femininity scores were more related to the individual's involvement in work or education than to the stage of family development. In this study, employed women were found to have lower femininity scores and their male partners lower masculinity scores than did nonemployed women and their partners. Women who were engaged in graduate education had lower femininity scores than those who were not. The latter study, however, did not extend beyond the period of working life and therefore does not challenge previous findings on the convergence of sex-role related behaviors in old age.

Still another longitudinal study of college graduates and their partners followed at ages 37, 43, and 52 (Wink and Helson, 1997), showed that goals and values of men and women converged in less gender-traditional ways from young adulthood into midlife (Harker and Solomon, 1996). An important mechanism, suggested from this study, which women may use to deal with stressful midlife changes, is "ego resiliency" (Klohnen, Vandewater, and Young, 1996).

As primary breadwinners, men must suppress emotional sensitivity and dependency needs to succeed as economic providers. Later in life, the demands of parenthood subside, and men can afford to express tenderness. Women, on the other hand, are traditionally the primary caregivers, so they must suppress their aggressiveness to avoid breaking up the family or damaging a child's developing personality. When they grow older and have adult children, they reap a number of rewards: receiving a good deal of affection and having a certain amount of power over their kin. Freed from their earlier restrictions, they find outlets that give them more recognition; that is, they become more aggressive. Women generally adjust better to the role losses of old age because they are socialized to expect less consistency in their roles.

These different age changes for men and women have been noted in many cultures around the world (Gutmann, 1987, 1997). Finding them in several cultures with economies ranging from agricultural to highly technological adds weight to the conclusion that a basic developmental process is involved and not simply one dictated by specific events in a particular society (Fry, 1985; Gutmann, 1997; Huyck and Gutmann, 1999).

COGNITIVE APPROACH TO DEVELOPMENT

In contrast to stage models derived from psychoanalytic theory, cognitive approaches to the study of personality are concerned with the individual's own conception of how his or her life should proceed. An interesting example of such an approach is Whitbourne's (1985b, 1986, 1996, 1998) formulation of an individual *life-span construct* that relies on distinguishing how a person's life course differs from age norms and expectations that exist for society as a whole.

Whitbourne (1985b, 1989, 1998) proposes that the translation from a person's core identity into what she calls superficial (or observable) manifestations of identity are accomplished by means of the individual's ideas about his or her life span as a totality (Figure 9-1). The life span construct has two basic structural

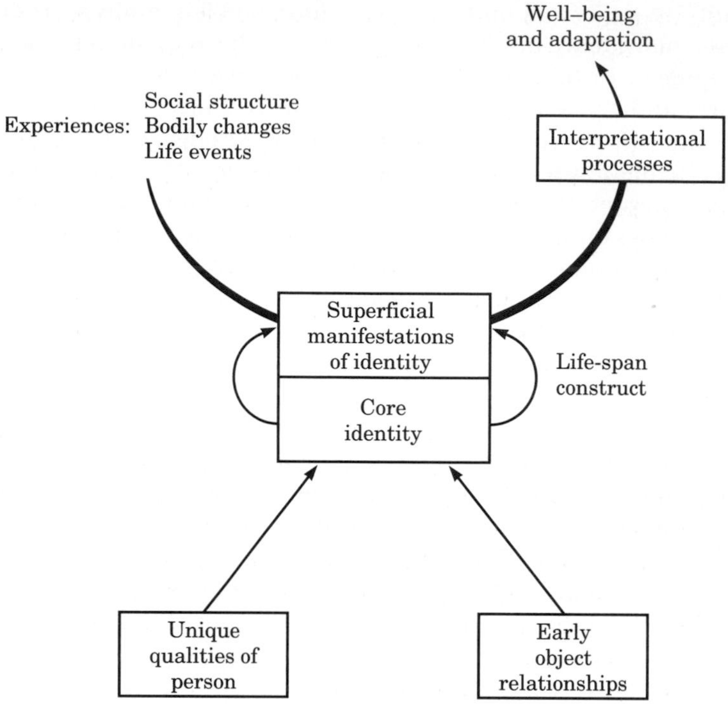

Well–being
and adaptation

Experiences: Social structure
Bodily changes
Life events

Interpretational
processes

Superficial
manifestations
of identity

Core
identity

Life-span
construct

Unique
qualities of
person

Early
object
relationships

Figure 9-1 Components of Whitbourne's Life-Span Model of Identity Formation. *Source: Whitbourne, S. K. (1989). Comments on Lachman's "personality and aging at the crossroads." In K. W. Schaie and C. Schooler (Eds.), Social structure and aging: Psychological processes (p. 196). Hillsdale, NJ: Erlbaum.*

components, the *scenario* and the *life story*. The scenario consists of a person's expectations about the future. As soon as a sense of identity develops in adolescence, one begins to acquire some notion of what one wants to do with one's life and to imagine what one will be doing at various points in the years to come. Suppositions about how life will progress are strongly influenced by culturally determined age norms.

Throughout life, one continually compares actual performance to the scenario, using it as a basis for self-evaluation and adjusting it as circumstances dictate. These expectations represent schemata that are learned as members of a social group and that eventually develop as personality prototypes (Mayer and Bower, 1986). Distinctive developmental trajectories also have been related to the crystallization of specific choice behaviors (Mumford, Wesley, and Shaffer, 1987). As the past widens with aging, new combinations and scenarios become available from the earlier life span (Ogilvie, 1987). In turn, emotionally intense experience can affect cognitive development by facilitating the development of the abstract thinking that is required to make sense out of one's life story (see Haviland and Kramer, 1991; Maciel, Heckhausen, and Baltes, 1993). Even changes in physical functioning to which the individual is sensitive will require identity assimilation to maintain self-esteem (Whitbourne and Collins, 1999).

As an example, consider the case of a high school senior who has decided that she wants to be a scientist. Her scenario might well include events and circumstances such as these: She expects to graduate with the class and then go to a four-year college, where she will major in biology. She expects that she will have many women friends and perhaps a boyfriend. After college, she knows that she will have to go to graduate school, but she isn't sure whether a doctorate will be necessary. She imagines herself doing research in a laboratory of some sort. She expects to marry at some point and vaguely assumes that she will have children, but these are matters about which she is unsure at present. She expects to remain in contact with her friends and make new friends among her colleagues at work. She has an image of herself addressing a large audience at a convention of some sort and being loudly applauded when her speech is finished. In short, she expects herself ultimately to be successful.

She will use this scenario as a guide for planning and as a means of assessing her progress toward her goals. Every time she passes an important transition in her life—graduating from school, getting her first job, publishing her first paper, getting married—she will compare her actual performance to the way that she imagined life would be at that point; her progress will influence how she feels about herself. If she gets a doctorate by the time she is 26, she may feel very proud of herself. If she is not married by 35, she may begin to fear that she will miss out on having children. As a result, she may begin to denigrate herself in some ways. Inevitably, the scenario that she originally imagined for herself will change; she might marry and have children immediately after college and put off continuing her education for a few years.

As the person moves into the scenario that she has imagined, she begins to build a life story. This is the second component of the life span construct. The life story is the narrative of personal history into which one organizes the events of one's life to give them personal meaning and a sense of continuity. It is called a "story" because the person alters it as it is retold, distorting the actual events to make them acceptable. If the woman in our example didn't graduate from college until she was 28, she might tell herself that she graduated "in her twenties, like most people who go to college"; this permits her to think of herself as "on time" according to the development schedule that she has set for herself. She might make other distortions as well, simplifying the circumstances surrounding complex decisions or exaggerating the importance of events of which she feels proud.

Together with the scenario, the life story encompasses the individual's sense of the future and the past; it is the central principle around which people organize and assess their progress through their own lives. Many women "rewrite" their life stories after the early years of childrearing, as they discover new abilities at midlife that permit them to break through emotional stereotypes and permit them to connect their thoughts with practical realities. Thus, new directions may be given to their life stories (Helson, 1992; Labouvie-Vief and Hakim-Larson, 1989; Whitbourne, 1998).

CONTEXTUAL MODELS OF PERSONALITY DEVELOPMENT

The cognitive personality model of Whitbourne introduced some environmental factors that influence personal identity development. The importance of sociocultural and historical factors becomes even more prominent in what Kogan (1990) refers to as *contextual models of personality development*. Social transitions may carry different meaning for different individuals with different life histories or resources and socioeconomic status may be a persistent selection factor that has important developmental implications (Caspi, 1995; Elder and Caspi, 1990; Elder and O'Rand, 1994; Schaie and Hendricks, 2000).

Contextualist approaches trace developmental paths over extended periods of time and pay attention to the impact on personality of life events such as occupational status, divorce, or retirement. Often this is done by using national survey data bases or doing secondary analyses of longitudinal data sets that originally may have been collected for other purposes (Brooks-Gunn, Phelps, and Elder, 1991). For example, Helson and colleagues (Helson, Mitchell, and Moane, 1984) talk about social clocks that determine personality pattern. They examined three such social clock patterns for women (starting a family by age 28, advancing into a high status job by age 28, or attaining neither by that age). When personality profiles were examined for the three groups of women, those who either started a family or reached a high status by the specified age showed normative positive personality development, and those who lagged failed to conform to the positive pattern (Helson and Moane, 1987). Women who had traditional roles were found to be higher on scales of well-being and effective functioning when they were 21, but traditional roles were associated with adverse changes in psychological and physical health by age 43. However, traditional women who were in the labor force seemed to be role-juggling with success (Helson and Picano, 1990). Increases in individualism and self-focus were found to help women respond to radical changes in female roles beginning with the late 1960s (Roberts and Helson, 1997).

Another contextualist approach is to examine effects of role transitions on personality development. This has been done in the context of the Berkeley Guidance Study (Eichorn et al., 1981; Hightower, 1990) by examining the interactions of personality characteristics such as temper tantrums, despondency, and shyness that were observed in childhood with successfulness in adult role transitions such as work, marriage, and parenthood. Unfavorable personality traits in childhood were shown to correspond to unfavorable adult role transitions (Caspi, 1987, 1995; Caspi, Bem, and Elder, 1989). The context of social structures has also been related to changes in the direction of social control (see discussion below; Kohn, 1989; Lachman, 1989).

CHANGE AND CONTINUITY OF THE SELF-CONCEPT

The self-concept is one of the basic elements of the personality. Tendencies toward stability or change in self-conceptions might therefore be expected to be representative of the personality as a whole. The self-concept consists of a collection of knowledge structures that helps individuals to lend coherence to their life experiences. These knowledge structures are called self-schemas that vary in content and that reflect what persons thinks about, what they care about, and what they spend their time on. Self-schemas usually represent one's present behavior, but they also relate to what happened to individuals in the past as well as what may be possible in the future (Herzog and Markus, 1999; Markus and Herzog, 1992; Markus and Nurius, 1986; Whitbourne, 1985b, 1998).

Studies of various aspects of the self-concept indicate that, in most respects, it is quite stable over long periods. Some changes do occur, however. One study investigated the stability of self-concepts among several hundred people undergoing one of four major adult transitions: leaving home after finishing high school, having one's first child, having one's youngest child leave home, and retiring from work. In all four groups, the structure and interrelationships among different dimensions of the self-concept remained stable over a 5-year period. The level of self-assessment did change for some of the dimensions, but not for others. What remained stable over time included the concept of personal security, amiability, and assertion. Changes were noted in other dimensions, however, including social poise, self-control, and hostility (Pierce and Chiriboga, 1979). Other studies yield similar results. One showed substantial stability over the 14 years of early adulthood (Mortimer, Finch, and Kumka, 1982).

The presence of possible selves in the self-report of middle-aged and older persons is seen as one of the salient predictors of successful aging (Baltes, M. M. and Carstensen, 1992, 1996). However, it has been shown that a focus in middle age on possible selves that involve the acquisition of new roles and material possessions shifts in old age to a focus on preventing possible selves such as illness and dependency from becoming reality. Nevertheless, themes that involve purpose in life or expected leisure roles do remain important. Older adults report fewer possible selves than do younger adults and most of these possible selves are related to hope for good physical health (Bearon, 1989; Cross and Markus, 1991; Hooker, 1992; Hooker and Kaus, 1992; Ryff, Kwan, and Singer, 2001).

Sex-role identification is another significant realm of the self-concept. In this area, there do seem to be some changes as people age, but they are relatively modest. Fitzgerald (1978) investigated sex-role-related self-concepts, using a measure that assessed variations along two major dimensions: nurturance and dominance. His findings were that college males described themselves as more aggressive than older males considered themselves to be. The older males, however, scored higher in areas such as cooperation and nurturance. Younger women scored higher than younger men on scales related to cooperativeness, docility, and dependence. But older males had dominance scores only slightly higher than those of older women. Other studies also suggest that traditional sex differences in self-concept are less evident in older men and women compared with younger individuals (Gutmann, 1997; Hyde and Phyllis, 1979; Ryff and Baltes, 1976).

The assumption that the self-concept should become more positive with age is compatible with formulations of adult development such as Erikson's (1982) contention that the positive resolution of the final psychosocial crisis results in ego integrity, implying a sense of positive self (also see George, 2000). But others, such as Buehler (1968) and Rosow (1974), who emphasize the restriction of socialization and role loss in old age, argue that there ought to be negative changes in self-concept. The arguments of the latter authors have been rebutted by Brim (1988), who suggests that older people adjust their methods and goals so that they can continue seeing themselves as successful in their daily pursuits. This may involve the lowering of aspirations, changes in timing and methods, or change in the goals.

A sequence of assimilative and accommodative strategies that prevent depression and promote well-being in older persons has been described by Brandtstädter and Renner (1990). The assimilative strategy involves engaging in activities that aim to prevent further losses or substituting alternative activities when encountering undesired life changes. The accommodative strategy involves adjustment of goals, and expectancies (possible selves) are adjusted to match changes in personal resources and functional capacities (Brandtstädter and Greve, 1994; Brandtstädter and Wentura, 1995; Brandtstädter, Wentura, and Greve, 1993). When frailty ensues, these strategies may still be applied to the maintenance of self-esteem by turning one's psychological energy to a vital inner life that may be totally unseen by others (see Atchley, 1991). A similar approach using the terminology of personal meaning systems has been applied to a study of accommodation to social change and different political systems following the reunification of Germany (Westerhof and Dittman-Kohli, 2000).

An interesting empirical question is whether individuals at different ages have age-specific vocabularies that they can use to express their perceptions of past, present, and future selves. Heckhausen and Krueger (1993; Krueger and Heckhausen, 1993) asked groups of young adults (21 to 35 years), middle-aged (40 to 55 years), and old adults (60 to 80 years) to rate a list of 100 adjectives as to their desirability, their expected change in adulthood, the perceived controllability of each attribute, how characteristic the attribute was for each rater, up to 10 attributes on which raters thought they would change positively or negatively, and the normative age at which people would typically attain the developmental goal for that attribute. Subjective conceptions of self-descriptions indicated growth during early and middle adulthood and decline in old age. But these conceptions were quite optimistic. They involved more growth than decline. Older subjects tended to be more optimistic about late-life development than were younger adults. There was strong agreement between normative ratings for each age group and the self-assessment of those in that age group. There were also more favorable expectations for the self to be attained in old age, and aspirations for self-improvement to attain positive self-attributes ascribed to older age groups. Other studies have also shown that the self-concept of older persons is perhaps more complicated or richer than that of young adults, suggesting the retention of past selves even though they may no longer be realistic as future selves (Mueller et al., 1992; Ryff, Kwan, and Singer 2001).

INDIVIDUAL DIFFERENCES APPROACH TO PERSONALITY

Differences among the individual members of a species became an important area of study as soon as Charles Darwin formulated his theory of evolution based on "the survival of the fittest." Francis Galton, an English biologist, became interested in human evolution and began to ask the question of which persons are more fit than others. To identify the more intelligent individuals, of course, Galton needed some means of assessing intelligence, and he pioneered the development of intelligence tests. By doing so, he simultaneously pioneered the individual differences approach in psychology, which, since Galton's time, has always relied heavily on psychological tests and questionnaires.

The individual differences approach to personality is sometimes described as *trait psychology* (Costa and McCrae, 1992d; Starratt and Peterson, 1997). It focuses upon discovering the structure of personality, by means of self-report or by objective ratings by others. For this purpose (as in the measurement of intelligence), it often derives latent (unobserved) personality constructs represented by scores on inventories that contain many individual items, the response to which is not of particular interest, except as they contribute to our definition of the latent constructs. One of the major contributions of longitudinal studies in the context of trait psychology has been to demonstrate substantial stability of personality traits across adulthood. Although not universally conceded, these findings provide a major challenge to stage theory. As will be seen, most empirical studies following groups of the same individuals have demonstrated this stability, even though there may be change in some individuals under certain circumstances, and that there may be considerable differences in average trait scores over different generations and in different cultures (see Costa and McCrae, 1992b, 1993d).

Self-Report Inventories

The first fomal personality test was called the *Personal Data Sheet,* which was developed to screen recruits for the U.S. armed services during World War I (Woodworth, 1920). The Personal Data Sheet was simple in theory and in practice. The author, psychologist Robert Woodworth, first made a list of symptoms generally considered to indicate emotional maladjustment. From that list, Woodworth constructed 116 questions (e.g., "Do you usually feel well and strong?") that could be answered yes or no. The total number of questions answered in a way that Woodworth thought of as maladjusted constituted the "psychoneuroticism" score; if the soldier scored high enough, he was seen by a psychiatrist.

The Personal Data Sheet is a type of personality test called a *self-report inventory,* because the individual is asked to report on his or her own feelings and activities. Unfortunately self-reports represent a fallible source of data. Minor changes in wording, the way questions are formattted, or the order in which questions are posed can seriously influence the answers questionniare repondents provide (Schwarz and Käuper, 1999).

The most famous of the self-report inventories used to detect abnormal personality characteristics is the *Minnesota Multiphasic Personality Inventory* (MMPI). The MMPI consists of items, such as, "I am frightened to read of prowlers in my neighborhood," to which the individual responds true, false, or cannot say. From the pattern of responses, the individual receives scores on the scales originally designed to discriminate between normal and psychiatric populations. One scale, for example, is the mania scale, on which a high score was presumed to indicate manic tendencies (tendencies to become extremely excited).

In addition to its uses for psychiatric screening and clinical counseling, the MMPI also has been used extensively for personality research with normal subjects. Researchers may want to know, for example, if old people check more items that reflect depression or paranoia than do young people. The investigators would not be particularly interested in extreme scores that might indicate severe depression or debilitating paranoia, but would rather look for differences between the averages for young and old subjects (e.g., Aaronson, Dent, Webb, and Kline, 1996).

For example, studies using the MMPI have asked whether or not there is an increase in introversion with age. The answer is usually yes. Consider, for example, data on 50,000 patients at the Mayo Clinic in Rochester, Minnesota (Swenson, Pearson, and Osborne, 1973). Both males and females show a general increase with age on the MMPI introversion scale, although women are somewhat more introverted than men throughout the life span. These are age differences from a cross-sectional study, and we cannot be sure that they reflect true age changes (see the following).

What of Gutmann's (1977) hypothesis, that men become more feminine and women become more masculine as they age? The Mayo Clinic data support only the female portion of this hypothesis. Older women have more masculine interests than younger women, but older men also show an increase in masculinity (see also Feldman, Biringen, and Nash, 1981). Other MMPI scales also show similar patterns for men and women. Psychopathy (unemotional disregard for laws and social norms), paranoia, psychasthenia (excessive worry, lack of confidence, compulsive behavior), schizophrenic tendencies, and mania all decrease systematically over the life span. Depression, which does not decrease, is relatively higher in older people; this fact may account for its apparent increase. In the Mayo Clinic patients, two scales increase to middle age and then decrease: hypochondriasis (excessive concern with physical health) and hysteria (physical symptoms caused by excessive anxiety, such as "writer's cramp"). These two scales may present some support for the idea of a midlife crisis in neurotic concern for what's happening to one's body.

Other cross-sectional investigations of MMPI trends with age corroborate the Mayo Clinic data, for the most part. In particular, young adults tend to score higher than older people on the scales measuring psychopathy, schizophrenic tendencies, and mania. These scores paint a picture of the average youth as someone with an energetic approach to life and attitudes that sometimes run to the unusual and untraditional. Around middle age, there is a transition from concern with impulse control to concern with physical and mental health. Older adults are more introspective and introverted than young people and possibly more susceptible to depression.

Age differences in average MMPI scores are rarely sizable and some studies show no statistically significant differences at all. The MMPI also has been criticized because many of the scales are scored for the same items, building in correlation between scales, and because scores are affected by the tendency to deny socially undesirable items. Because of cohort differences in socially desirable attitudes (Schaie, 1996b; Schaie and Parham, 1976), it may therefore follow that the MMPI does not discriminate equally well among the young and the old. The apparent decrease with age for some MMPI scales could simply reflect a greater desire by the older cohorts to appear socially respectable.

The MMPI has gone through a process of revision and renorming. In a study by Colligan and colleagues (1983, 1992) of healthy adults ranging in age from 18 to 99, numerous significant relationships were found between age and various MMPI scales. This study once again found age differences involving higher scores on the neurotic traits measured by the MMPI as well as several other scales. However, a later study of community-dwelling healthy men and women between the ages of 39 and 89 conducted in another part of the country could not replicate the earlier age difference findings (Koeppi, Bolla-Wilson, and Bleeker, 1989). The latter authors conclude that many of the previously reported MMPI age differences should be attributed primarily to geographical differences and to changes in social and population factors. Similar findings occurred in a study of male veterans (Butcher, Aldwin, Levenson, and Ben-Porath, 1992).

One pervasive criticism of the MMPI for the study of normal personality development has addressed the fact that this questionnaire was first developed and continues to be used to screen for the presence of psychopathology. As a consequence there have been a number of derivatives that were specifically designed to measure traits thought to be important for the assessment of individual differences in normal population. One such measure that was specifically developed for purposes of counseling adolescents and young adults is the *California Personality Inventory* (CPI; Gough, 1987). This test was constructed by asking high school principals and counselors to nominate individuals that were at opposite poles of traits such as socialbility, social responsibility, masculinity–femininity, flexibility and other normal personality traits. Although some mean level age changes have been reported for this inventory, on the whole substantial stability over time was also shown to hold in the Oakland Growth and Guidance studies extending over 50 years (Haan, Milsap, and Hattka, 1986). The limited evidence for change seems to occur largely in young adulthood, during the shift from student to employed status and not during middle or old age (see Helson, 1993; Helson and Moane, 1987;

Kogan, 1990). However, there is also evidence that societal events such as the women's movement may result in cohort-specific changes in personality at those life stages particularly affected by the events (Agronick and Duncan, 1998; Duncan and Agronick, 1995).

Adapted versions of the social responsibility scale (Schaie and Parham, 1974) have also been used in the Seattle Longitudinal Study, with findings reported over as long as 35 years. Social responsibility tends to increase with age in women, and attitudinal flexibility tends to decline, with negative cohort differences occurring for social responsibility and positive cohort differences found for flexibility (Schaie, 1996b).

Another MMPI derivative that is unique in identifying primary personality dimensions in terms of affective experience is the *Multidimensional Personality Questionnaire* (MPQ; Tellegen, 1985). This instrument includes the personality factors: traditionalism, harm avoidance, control aggression, alienation, stress reaction, achievement, social potency, well-being, and social closeness. Although developed on a normal poulation, this test has been used to identify patterns diagnostic of affective disorders anxiety, substance dependence, and conduct disorders in young adults (Krueger, Caspi, Mofffitt, Silva, and McGee, 1996). The instrument also identifies higher-order personality factors such as positive emotionality, negative emotionality, and constraint. These constructs have also been measured by an adjective checklist constructed by Gough, Bradley, and Bedeian (1996). In a study of college graduates from young adulthood to midlife it was found that negative emotionality declined in both men and women, while women increased in positive emotionality and constraint (Helson and Klohnen, 1998).

Another self-report inventory that has been used to investigate age changes in personality is the *Sixteen Personality Factor Questionnaire* (16 PF) constructed by Raymond B. Cattell as part of his monumental work to chart human personality through factor-analytic investigations. The 16 PF was designed for normal adults and provides scores on 16 general personality traits (factors) that are usually described by two ends of a personality dimension. Examples are reserved—outgoing, humble–assertive, and shy–venturesome. Even more general dimensions (called second-order factors) can also be assessed, notably extraversion and anxiety.

There have not been many longitudinal studies of personality development. In one of the few, a brief test that estimates 8 of the 16 traits measured in the 16 PF was given to people aged 25 to 88 (Schaie, 1996b). The test was administered 5 times, in 1963, 1970, 1977, 1984, and in 1991. The results were quite revealing. Changes within subjects are quite modest and reach statistical significance for only 4 of the 8 traits. Most noteworthy are modest within-subject decreases with age in Superego Strength and Threctia (threat reactivity). Affectothymia (extraversion) also decreases from young adulthood to middle age but increases again into old age. And for Untroubled Adequacy, there is a slight downtrend until midlife, followed by slight increment until age 84, and then a sharp decline.

Is this young man likely to become more reserved as he grows older (an age change), or do earlier generations have different standards of social behavior (a cohort difference)?

However, many of the traits showed age differences that on statistical analysis were found to be actually cohort differences (Figure 9-2). Four traits are characterized by negative cohort differences until the turn of the century. Thereafter, the cohort gradient for Low Self-Sentiment remains virtually flat. Affectothymia, Untroubled Adequacy, and Premsia continue to decline, but they rise again for the baby-boomers.

The other four traits show systematic increment for the older cohorts until at least 1924. Threctia (threat reactivity) continues to rise throughout the entire period, except for a dip for the 1924 cohort. Conservatism of Temperament peaks for the 1924 cohort, but shows a sharper downturn for the baby boomers. Downturns for the latter group are also seen for Group Dependency and Superego Strength. What does all this mean? Although traits remain rather stable within individuals over their lifetime, successive generations differ in level on these traits. For example, people born in earlier years were "more reserved, less outgoing" than people born in later years.

This age difference makes one think of the hypothesis that introversion increases with age, and indeed reserved–outgoing is one of the traits that make up the second-order introversion factor. But the age difference turns out to be attributable to differences in generations. People born in later years (the younger subjects) were less reserved than people born in earlier years (older); they did not become more reserved as they got older. Apparently, people born in different generations have been taught different things about the proper amount of reserve to show in social situations; once learned, this lesson is carried throughout life (see also Schaie and Willis, 1995).

Other cohort differences in personality found in this study indicated that across time there have been generational shifts that first increased and more recently has lowered levels of impulse control (superego strength) and increased levels of threat reactivity (see Figure 9-2). Strong positive cohort differences also have been found in various measures of behavioral and attitudinal flexibility, while negative cohort differences were observed on a measure of socially responsible attitudes (Schaie, 1996b; Schaie and Willis, 1991; Schaie, Dutta, and Willis, 1991).

In another study, in which subjects were followed for 21 years, those subjects who experienced cardiovascular disease described themselves as more conscientious, moralistic, and honest, but they were also less concerned with political issues or community involvement (Maitland, Willis, and Schaie, 1993; see also discussion of other personality characteristics related to survival from cardiovascular disease in Chapter 13).

Another longitudinal study used the complete 16 PF. Testing 331 men and women who were 54 to 70 years old at the time of first measurement (between 1968 and 1970), the researchers found practically no age changes over an 8-year interval (Siegler, George, and Okun, 1979). In addition, the correlations between testings were high. Similar findings occur for data coming from the Boston Normative Aging Study of veterans. A comparison of data for 139 persons who took the 16 PF in 1965–1967 and again in 1975 showed that there was no significant change for 14 of the scales. For the two scales in which change was observed (intelligence and social independence) movement was in a positive direction (Costa and McCrae, 1978; McCrae and Costa, 1984). In a 15-year follow-up, it was found that those individuals who had high scores on the suspiciousness scale of the 16 PF had higher risks of mortality (Barefoot et al., 1987).

A recent cross-sectional study with the 16 PF compared centenarians, octogenarians, and sexagenarians in order to predict the impact of personality dimensions on morale in advanced old age, In this study, low tension and high extraversion predicted high morale in the centenarians. Guilt proneness was the most important personality trait predicting morale for the 60-year-olds (Adkins, Martin, and Poon, 1996).

These studies indicate high stability of personality characteristics. There was no change in average scores as people grew older, and the ranking of people also did not change much. The sizable differences between generations suggest that early childhood experiences are crucial in the formation of personality (for an example see, Franz, McClelland, and Weinberger, 1991); the absence of age changes and the high correlations in the adult years suggest that, once formed, personality does not change a lot.

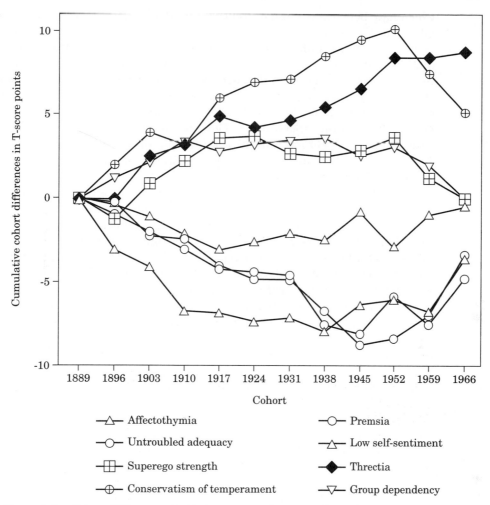

Figure 9-2 Cohort Differences in Various Personality Traits for Cohorts Born from 1889 to 1966. *Source:* Adapted from Schaie, K.W. (1996b.) Intellectual development in adulthood: The Seattle Longitudinal Study. New York: Cambridge University Press

Extensive factor analyses of personality descriptors using the English language typically have shown five core dimensions at most life stages (Costa and Mc-Crae, 1992a; Digman, 1990; Goldberg, 1993; Hofer, Horn, and Eber, 1997; Robins, John and Caspi, 1994). These core dimensions have most explicitly been measured by the *NEO Personality Inventory* (NEO; Costa and McCrae, 1985b, 1988, 1992c; Mc-Crae and Costa, 1985; McCrae and John, 1992). The NEO is a 240-item questionnaire that offers measures of the traits of neuroticism, extraversion, openness to experience, agreeableness, and conscientiousness (the so-called "big 5"), all of which have been shown to have remarkable stability throughout adulthood in longitudinal studies. These dimensions have also been studied cross-sectionally with fairly comparable adult age differences (e.g., Costa, McCrae, Martin et al., 1999; McCrae and Costa, 1997; Yang, McCrae, and Costa, 1998), including the finding that there are parallel age differences between college age and middle adulthood (Costa, McCrae, de Lima, et al., 1999). As is to be expected, despite the structural similarity, correlations with culture-related outcome variables differ in cross-cultural comparions (Staudinger, Fleeson, and Baltes, 1999). The same factor structure of the NEO has a been confirmed in a psychiatric sample (Bagby et al, 1999). And the five dimensions have been shown to have substantial heritability (Loehlin, McCrae, Costa, and John, 1998).

The factors identified in this inventory also have been shown to emerge from the analysis of quite independent lines of personality research: the *California Q-Sort* (Block, 1978; McCrae, Costa, and Busch, 1986). The Q-Sort involves the study of the relative importance of personality traits within individuals. Partial congruence of the NEO with factors derived from the MMPI has also been reported (Costa and McCrae, 1992d; Trull, Useda, Costa, and McCrae, 1995).

A relationship has further been demonstrated between the NEO factors and various dimensions of well-being. For example, the well-being dimensions of self-acceptance, environmental mastery, and purpose in life were linked with neuroticism, extraversion, and conscientiousness, while personal growth was linked to openness to experience, and extroversion; positive relations with others were linked with agreeableness and extraversion, and autonomy was linked to neuroticism (Schmutte and Ryff, 1997). What is most important for our purposes, however, is that these studies demonstrate the equivalence of constructs across both intraindividual and interindividual methods of analyses and therefore increase confidence in these findings (McCrae, Costa, and Busch, 1986).

Costa and McCrae (1992d, 1993) have shown impressive stability for the NEO factors. The factor structure remains the same over the life course from adolescence on. As far as score level is concerned, they report modest declines in neuroticism and extraversion and an increase in agreeableness between college age and later adulthood. In fact, individual differences show only modest stability in young adulthood, but after age 30 both average levels and individual differences in personality traits remain extremely stable, suggesting that full maturity of the adult personality is reached by that age. The earlier changes have been interpreted as important antecedents of establishing the dynamics of social support in midlife (Von Dras and Siegler, 1997). The long-term stability of personality has also been shown in a study which transformed trait ratings of college graduates over a 45-year period to the NEO dimensions (Soldz and Vaillant, 1999).

Personality traits, while quite stable across age, are, of course, also related to contextual variables. Thus, openness of experience correlates positively with education and income, while neuroticism is negatively related to education, social support, extent of group membership, income, and health (Hooker et al., 1992; Peterson and Maiden, 1992–93; Soldz and Vaillant, 1999).

Several studies show that men feel emotions more deeply and express them more openly as they grow older.

Combining what we know of the results from the MMPI, the 16 PF, the CPI, and the NEO Personality Inventory, a fairly consistent picture emerges of personality development in the adult years. It is a picture, first and foremost, of stability and continuity, and not of frequent and extensive change. Psychologists have long considered personality to be an enduring organization of traits, and the test results support this view for most people.

Perhaps, if we want to learn more about changes occurring in some individuals under specific circumstances we need research methods that are designed for the collection and analysis of extensive data over time in such selected individuals or in diads of individuals that affect each other, such as mother–child pairs or spouse pairs. What has become known as the *P-Technique* method is becoming more popular for such analyses (for examples, see Garfein and Smyer, 1991; Kleban, Lawton, Nesselroade, and Parmalee, 1992; Shifren, Hooker, Wood, and Nesselroade, 1997).

A second major conclusion from the test studies is that many of the age differences that we once thought of as personality development are in fact generational differences. A number of cross-sectional studies, for example, show that older people are more reserved or restrained than younger people. Here is a personality trait that we might expect to change with age. Aren't younger people more happy-go-lucky, becoming more serious-minded and more reserved with age?

Apparently not. The evidence from several longitudinal studies shows that restraint differs between generations but does not increase with age within a given generation.

Three personality dimensions give evidence of change with age. One is masculinity, for which the evidence applies only to men. As men age, they become less comfortable with masculine activities such as hunting, and they report that they feel emotions more deeply and express them more openly. The other personality traits that show age changes are two that we would expect to be positively related: excitability and general activity. But excitability goes up with age, and general activity goes down. Interestingly enough, it is the triad of emotionality, activity level, and sociability for which individual differences have been shown to be substantially accounted for by genetic factors in twin studies conducted in childhood as well as old age (Baker et al., 1992; Plomin, Pedersen, Nesselroade, and Bergeman, 1988; Pedersen and Reynolds, 1998). Another contradiction in the research literature? Perhaps. Another possibility, however, is that both findings are valid, that the "activation" described by general activity is different from the "activation" described by the excitability factor.

Excitability, on the other hand, refers to a quality of instability in arousal level, an inability to keep one's emotions on an even keel, as reflected in a tendency to become perplexed and befuddled by relatively trivial incidents. This quality seems to increase with age. In fact, these two self-reported personality traits may be related to two characteristics of the human nervous system that also appear to change in different ways with age. To put it rather glibly, older people seem to be harder to "turn on" than younger people, but also harder to "turn off". The older nervous system is less active generally, but it is also less stable (Finch and Seeman, 1999).

Projective Tests

A projective test is one in which the stimuli, which may be pictures or abstract images and which are comparable to questions in other tests, are deliberately vague and ambiguous. For example, the best-known projective test, the Rorschach inkblot test, uses inkblots that were originally created by dropping ink on papers and folding them in half. The individual is shown each blot in turn and asked what it makes him or her think of. In another popular projective test, the *Thematic Apperception Test* (TAT), pictures rather than inkblots are the stimuli. The theory behind projective tests is that persons "project" their own personalities onto the ambiguous stimulus to construct a coherent response; thus, in describing the stimulus, individuals are telling us about their basic needs and values. There is considerable doubt, however, that this assumption is correct and that the Rorschach, the TAT, and other projective tests actually measure what they purport to measure (see Anastasi, 1976).

In studies of adult personality development using the Rorschach, one of the more common findings is that older people are more likely than younger people to make responses considered indicative of introversion. Similar results have been obtained with the TAT. Asked to tell brief stories that might account for the scenes in the TAT pictures, older subjects tend to describe introspective, shy, conforming characters to whom things happen beyond their control, while younger subjects relate stories of active, outgoing, assertive people who make things happen. It is primarily these results that led one reviewer to conclude that studies of personality change "add up to the generalization that introversion increases with age in the second half of life" (Neugarten, 1977, p. 636).

Projective tests must be interpreted with care for subjects of all ages, but it is worth mentioning that older subjects present unique problems. Many older people may give unusual responses because they don't see the stimuli clearly or because they can't hear the examiner's questions. Also, consider a picture of an old person interacting with a young person presented to an old and a young subject. People are likely to identify with the character in the picture closer to their own age and to form the story around that character. In essence, they are telling stories about two different pictures, one with the older person as hero and the other with the young person as the center of attention. Comparing their stories may tell us something about their age, but little about their personality.

Some researchers have proposed that it would be better to use stimuli specifically designed for use with older persons. Examples of such tests are the *Senior Apperception Technique* (SAT) developed by Bellak (1975) and the *Gerontological Apperception Test* (GAT) by Wolk and Wolk (1971). However, these special tests have questionable value. The elderly figures on the test cards are depicted to be physically decrepit, they are in socially submissive situations, and they wear old-fashioned clothes. Older persons asked to respond to these cards may either have great difficulty identifying with the elderly figures, if they are still in good health and live an active life in the community, or may give responses that the professional interviewer might interpret as evidence of pathology, but that are no more than accurate descriptions of the characteristics built into the stimulus material. Projective tests are nowadays used primarily as aids in eliciting free associations from clients in clinical practice. Their role as research tools is now largely of historical interest.

CONTINUITY AND CHANGE IN THE ADULT PERSONALITY

What is the nature of personality change with age? Is one's personality relatively stable throughout life, or does it change significantly? Are there general trends reflecting universal or nearly universal changes in personality that occur as one grows older?

Although we do not have complete answers to these important questions, the research evidence does suggest, however, that there are few general trends. Few personality traits systematically increase or decrease with age. Perhaps excitability increases or general activity level decreases. Perhaps people become more introverted as they grow older. Perhaps men become a little less masculine and women a little more so. Beyond these few characteristics, there is little evidence for general change.

People often report that they have changed more than they really have in fact. In an intriguing study, personality test scores of people first tested in 1944, when they were about 20 years of age, were compared with their scores in 1969, when they averaged 45 years of age (Woodruff, 1983; Woodruff and Birren, 1972). The test measured personal and social adjustment, with a higher score indicating better adjustment. There were no significant differences over the 25-year period, supporting the conclusion that personality changes in few general ways. At the time of the second testing, however, the participants were asked to take the test again; this time they were to answer each question as they thought they probably had answered it back in 1944. These "remembered" scores were quite a bit lower than the real scores. People imagined themselves as less well-adjusted 25 years previously than they actually were. They believed that they had improved considerably over the years, even though the true test scores showed no evidence of change at all.

In a more recent study using the NEO 398 adults aged 26 to 64 were asked to describe their own personality in the present, when they were 20 to 25 years old, and when they will be 65 to 70 years old and what they thought their ideal personality to be like. Using this format these subjects showed more anticipated change across adulthood than is shown in the longitudinal studies. Their perceptions were characterized by early adulthood exploration, midlife productivity, and late-life comfortableness. They anticipated late adulthood to contain more losses than gains but expected gains at each life stage (Fleeson and Baltes, 1998; Fleeson and Heckhausen, (1997).

Continuity can be viewed as a grand adaptive strategy that is promoted both by individual preference and by social approval (Atchley, 1989, 1993, 2000). Continuity theory holds that middle-aged and older adults make adaptive choices that attempt to preserve and maintain internal and external structures. They prefer to accomplish this objective by the use of strategies that are closely related to their past experience. Inevitable change is somehow linked to a person's perceived past, thus providing continuity in individuals' inner psychological characteristics and their social behaviors.

To say that there are few general trends in personality development in the adult years does not mean that personality change is impossible or even infrequent. In fact, personality changes are common, even in the final years of life. The absence of general trends simply indicates that change, when it does occur, is in different directions for different people and that age by itself is not the major factor.

Life experiences have an influence on one's personality. Losing one's job after 30 years can be disillusioning; the individual may become anxious and depressed, less confident. A satisfying marriage may provide a solid base in life, turning an anxious personality into a vital, optimistic, and self-assured personality. The death of a loved one, an increase in responsibility for others, a religious conversion, drug addiction, medical problems, psychotherapy—all these can change an individual's personality in significant ways. It is characteristic of such life experiences, however, that they are not experienced by everyone or at the same age or life stage. Psychologists sometimes call them "nonnormative events" (see Baltes P. B., Cornelius, and Nesselroade, 1979; Schaie, 1984a, 1986). The death of one's child, for example, is not "normal" in the sense that it does not happen regularly to everyone at the same time; in contrast, a normal or normative event like retirement usually occurs around the same time in the life of every worker. Normative events, to the extent that they have a general influence on personality, should result in clear age changes on personality measures. Nonnormative events also result in change, but for the individuals experiencing them and not for others the same age.

Normative and nonnormative events may not only influence one's personality as a whole, but they may also have an effect on specific aspects of the personality. The self-concept is one such aspect. Many researchers have noted that the stability or variability of the self-concept may be a function not purely of intrapsychic forces or "distant" circumstances, such as childhood experiences, but of environmental events occurring in one's current life (Duncan and Agronic, 1995; Giarusso, Feng, Silverstein, and Bengtson, 2000; Herzog and Markus, 1999; McCrae and Costa, 1984; Mortimer, Finch, and Kumka, 1982; Schmitz-Scherzer and Thomae, 1983; Ryff, Kwan, and Singer, 2001).

As the social environment becomes more stable in adulthood, some attitudes and values also become more stable. This is not to say that "distant" life experiences are uninfluential. It has been shown that life experiences throughout the decade after college have significant effects on feelings of competence at the 10-year point (Roberts and Helson, 1997). Specifically, employment insecurity has a negative effect on feelings of competence, whereas income, work autonomy, and close relationships with one's father have a positive effect (Mortimer and Lorence, 1979; Mortimer, Finch, and Kumka, 1982). On the other hand, declining intellectual competence may make it more difficult to maintain a stable self-image (Field, Schaie, and Leino, 1991).

This relationship between environmental events and self-concept is a reciprocal one. Just as events may influence self-concept, self-concept may influence the kind of life stresses that one experiences. For example, those whose self-concepts reflect neurotic tendencies tend to have more marital troubles, lower job satisfaction, and other problems (Costa and McCrae, 1980a,b; Petersen and Maiden, 1992–1993). People who have better adjusted self-concepts may achieve objectively and subjectively better life situations, which in turn enhance their self-concepts. It also appears that certain types of self-concepts are predisposed toward well-being, independent of life events (Mortimer, Finch, and Kumka, 1982). Earlier self-concepts may influence later objective and subjective events, and these events contribute to the further stability or variability in self-concept.

As we have seen, the correlations of self-report inventories administered two or more times as the individuals grow older are generally high (Costa and McCrae, 1992d; McCrae and Costa, 1984). This is another indication of the basic stability of the adult personality, but the high correlations by no means preclude the potential

Physical appearance changes markedly across adulthood, but personality characteristics remain remarkably stable, unless external forces require marked change in one's ways of dealing with others.

for change. For one thing, descriptions of oneself by oneself tend to be more stable and consistent than other measures of personality, for example, descriptions by others and actual behavior patterns. Even so, correlations that run as high as .70 still leave 50 percent of the variability of test scores unexplained. Some of this variability is unexplained because of imperfections in the test itself, but a good deal must be attributed to true shifts in the ranking of people on the personality characteristic in question. In personal terms, some people who were among the highest in, for example, dominance at age 25 may fall to the middle ranks by age 40 or 50; others who were low may move up.

The average score for a given trait is likely to remain the same, which means that the people whose scores on the trait increase are balanced by people whose scores decrease. As they grow older, people experience a variety of nonnormative events, changing them in different ways. There is little general change, but quite a bit of individual change.

THE NATURE OF THE ADULT PERSONALITY

Research on personality change in the adult years is beset with many difficulties of measurement, experimental design, and interpretation. Nevertheless, it is possible to draw some conclusions on the nature of adult personality. First, one is impressed with the number of age differences in personality that turn out to be due primarily to differences between generations. Indeed, one could conclude that the most important fact about an individual's personality is the historical period when that person was born rather than the chronological age. Someone born in 1920 grew up in different circumstances from someone born in 1980. Methods of child training were different; interactions between children and parents, between brothers and sisters, and between friends were different; values and attitudes were different; education was different; historical events were different. In short, life was profoundly different for people growing up in the early 1900s compared to people growing up in the 1980s and 1990s, and these differences make for sizable differences in certain personality characteristics.

Second, the adult personality appears to be remarkably stable. There are a number of reasons to expect a significant degree of stability, of course. For one, many personality traits may in part be genetically determined and recent work is even beginning to localize the relevant DNA loci for various personality traits (Plomin and Caspi, 1998). But the adult personality is a highly complex organization . Traits, habits, ways of thinking, ways of interacting, ways of coping all are patterned in a unique fashion for each individual. Like any organized system, the adult personality resists change, for change in one part requires change or realignment in the other interrelated parts (Pulkkinen, 1998).

Once formed, the adult personality will not change radically, even in such pressing circumstances as retirement and impending death. In fact, personality is one of the prime determinants of how someone will react to such pressures. We have discussed different reactions to retirement, for example. People with well-integrated personalities may have little difficulty "mellowing out" in what they perceive to be the final stage of a successful life cycle. They are able to accommodate changing circumstances and can "roll with the punches." People with poorly integrated personalities, on the other hand, may encounter the same event with despair and hostility, turning "sour" in the last years of their lives (cf. Staudinger and Fleeson, 1996). This ability of some older persons to stay well, recover and experience improvement is sometimes referred to as the phenomenon of "resilience" (Ryff, Singer, Love, and Essex, 1998).

Findings from a number of studies spanning several decades of life and using different measurement instruments indicate that self-esteem of middle-aged or older individuals equals or surpasses that of younger subjects (Atchley, 1982; Cross and Markus, 1992; Heckhausen and Krueger, 1993). This may simply be a result of cohort differences; older respondents may have had higher levels of self-esteem throughout their lives than younger cohorts do now. A more plausible explanation is that the findings reflect changes resulting from maturation. Despite the losses and difficulties that often accompany old age, it appears that people can maintain or even increase their level of self-esteem as they age.

A third source of stability in adult personality is the tendency to choose environments that suit the individual's personality and to avoid those that might demand change. As people with acrophobia avoid tall buildings, people in general avoid situations in which their personality puts them at a disadvantage; shy people avoid public speaking, for example. Kind, gentle people who like a slow pace choose to live in small towns, thereby creating a match between personality and social environment that promotes stability in both. Also people tend to choose mates with similar interests and values and careers that fit with their personal identities (Caspi and Herbener, 1990; Caspi, Herbener, and Ozer, 1992; Gruber-Baldini, Schaie, and Willis, 1995).

Although adults' personalities are generally stable, certain critical events may disrupt patterns for whole groups as well as individuals. For examples, the Great Depression had an important influence on the generation then in its adolescence. The exact nature of this influence, however, depended on the individual's earlier socialization (Elder, 1979). In a major German longitudinal study of personality, people's stability seemed to depend on a complex interaction among age, sex, social condition, health, and a variety of psychological predispositions (Schmitz-Scherzer and Thomae, 1983). And cultural differences may generate differences in personality pattern that may change over time as a society moves from a predominantly traditional to a largely modern pattern (e.g., Liang, Bennett, Akiyama, and Maeda, 1992; Pearson, 1992).

The potential for individual change in personality should thus not be denied, the evidence of the stability of traits for groups of individuals not withstanding. The human being is characterized by the ability to adapt, to adjust to changing conditions. The human being can learn. Thus, when the environment presents situations that require readjustment, people do change, sometimes radically.

Many researchers are concluding that the search for unchanging and unidirectional developmental functions in adulthood is not very useful (Baltes, 1987). Chronological age may simply not be the best organizing principle to explain personality change within individuals. The psychoanalytic and Eriksonian models have provided much stimulation for research, but it is clear that there is no strong empirical support for universal stages of personality development (Costa and McCrae, 1992d; Datan, Rodeheaver, and Hughes, 1987; Hoyer and Hooker, 1989). Instead we are probably better off examining the sources of stability and change in the continuous interaction of individual and environment (Bengtson, Reedy, and Gordon, 1985; Kogan, 1990; Ruth and Coleman, 1996; Ryff, Kwan, and Singer, 2001).

SUMMARY

1. Personality is a dynamic organization within individuals of those biosocial systems (traits, habits, values) that determine their unique adjustment to the world.

2. Psychoanalytic theory divides the personality into id, ego, and super-ego, which represent impulsive, reality-oriented, and moralistic tendencies in the individual. The ego uses defense mechanisms such as denial, regression, projection, intellectualization, and sublimation to defend itself against anxiety and guilt resulting from unacceptable or unrealistic id or superego demands. Elderly people also use activity and cautiousness as defense mechanisms.

3. Erik Erikson extended the psychoanalytic theory of ego development into the adult years, describing three stages in which intimacy, generativity, and integrity are major concerns. Gutmann hypothesized that men and women become similar, men becoming more feminine, women becoming more masculine. Studies indicate that traditional sex differences among men and women diminish with age; it may be one's stage in the family life cycle rather than aging *per se* that actually influences traditional sex-role identification.

4. The cognitive life span approach to personality development (Whitbourne) has two basic components, the scenario and the life story. The scenario consists of one's expectations about the future. One continually compares one's actual experiences with the scenario one had imagined. The life story is the narrative of personal history into which one organizes the events of one's past life to give them personal meaning and a sense of continuity.

5. Whitbourne's cognitive model emphasizes ways in which environmental factors influence personality. Various contextual models of personality development examine the effects of sociocultural and historical factors and of role transitions on personality development.

6. The self-concept tends to remain stable over long periods of adult life. It contains both current conceptions of self, as well as conceptions of future possible selves. Events in the environment also influence locus of control and self-concept, which will in turn influence what kind of experiences one has.

7. The individual differences approach to personality development

compares test scores at different ages to determine stability or change. Stability is indicated by no difference in average trait scores, which suggests no general trend with age, and by high correlations between scores at different ages, which suggests little shifting in the ranking of individuals. Correlations can be computed only if the same individuals are involved at different ages, that is, if the study is longitudinal.

8. On the self-report inventory known as the MMPI, cross-sectional studies show older people as more introverted and both older men and older women more masculine than younger adults. Younger people appear as more energetic, with attitudes that are more unusual and more amoral. One of the few longitudinal studies of 16 PF scores found only excitability increasing as subjects grew older.

9. Projective tests such as the Rorschach inkblot test and the Thematic Apperception Test assume that subjects will "project" their needs and values into a story about an ambiguous stimulus (inkblot, picture). Projective tests are used currently as interview aides in clinical practice; as research tools they are primarily of historical interest.

10. The psychoanalytic and individual differences approaches, both of which rely heavily on psychological tests for empirical results, show that the adult personality, once formed, remains remarkably stable. Since personality is a highly organized system of traits, habits, and values, a fairly high degree of stability seems reasonable. Even levels of self-esteem appear to persist into later adult life. In addition, there is a pronounced tendency of individuals to place themselves in environments, including marriages and careers, that promote the stability of their personalities. Nevertheless, the human being is characterized by exceptional adaptability, and the potential for change is significant, especially if unexpected changes in the environment (nonnormative events) demand it. This adaptability to changing circumstances is amply demonstrated by the widely diverging "average personalities" formed by cohorts growing up in different historical eras.

SUGGESTED READINGS

Ryff, C. D., Kwan, C.M.L., and Singer, B.H. (2001). Personality and aging: Flourishing agendas and future challenges. In J. E. Birren and K. W. Schaie (Eds.), *Handbook of the psychology of aging* (5th ed.). San Diego, CA: Academic Press. A consideration of adult personality with particular emphasis on stability and change in the self system.

Schwarz, N., and Knäuper, B. (1999). Cognition, aging, and self-reports. In D. C. Park and N. Schwarz (Eds.), *Cognitive aging: A primer* (pp. 233–252). Philadelphia, PA: Psychology Press. This chapters reviews how respondents interpret self-report instruments, and how these interpretations may affect their interpretation of data on age differences and age changes in personality.

Whitbourne, S. K. (1996). Psychosocial perspectives on emotion: The role of identity in the aging procdess. In C. Magai and S. H. McFadden (Eds), *Handbook of emotion, adult development, and aging* (pp. 83–98). San Diego, CA: Academic Press. An expanded exposition of Whitbourne's identity model relating how health and well-being in older adults are thought to be affected by their identity development.

Chapter 10

Motivation

Beliefs, Goals, and Affect

Much of psychology is concerned with various aspects of behavior. Motivation is said to be concerned with three issues related to behavior (Deci, 1992). What initiates or energizes behavior? What influences the direction of behavior? Finally, what affects the termination of behavior? A major problem in studying motivation is that there is no commonly accepted definition and no one all-encompassing theory of motivation (Filipp, 1996; Schaie and Lawton, 1998). Rather, various approaches to the study of motivation have focused on one of the three above questions. Early in the study of motivation, there was considerable focus on the first question—what initiates or energizes an action? Motivation was conceptualized in terms of drives or needs from within a person (Hull, 1943; Murray, 1938). These drives or needs could be biological or psychological in origin. These biological or psychological needs were believed to create a state of arousal and the state of arousal resulted in action or behavior to satisfy the need. For example, food deprivation resulted in a biological need that produced a hunger drive; the hunger drive created a state of arousal that led to behavior (e.g., eating) to satisfy the hunger. Spence (1958) is the author of one of the best-known drive conceptions of motivation, and it is in the context of this conception that much of the research on primary biological needs such as hunger and thirst has been conducted. (Much research on primary biological needs has been conducted with animals because it would be unethical to deprive humans of such basic needs.)

While physiological drives may be sufficient to explain the actions of some animals, the behavior of humans is much more complex. It is now recognized that our actions to satisfy even quite basic physical needs, such as hunger and thirst, represent a complex interaction of physiological mechanisms and psychological processes. As adults, our behaviors related to basic physical needs, such as eating, drinking, and toileting, reflect cultural expectations, socialization experiences, and learned behaviors, as well as physiological factors. Thus, study of even the more biologically based needs must take into account psychological processes and cognition.

More recently, research on motivation has focused on the second question above—what directs or regulates behavior? What influences the intensity and duration of our actions, and the particular direction of our behaviors? For example, what determines how long or how intensely you study for a test? What influences whether an individual strives to reach a certain level in a career? Recent theories of motivation have focused on goal-directed activity (Dweck, 1992; Heckhausen and Dweck, 1998). Behavior is directed toward achieving or maintaining certain goals or outcomes. How attractive or desirable a certain goal is for an individual will determine how motivated he or she is to strive to reach the goal. Also important is the individual's expectations and beliefs about how likely it is that they can achieve a certain goal.

Many goals are learned or acquired through socialization; they are not primary biological drives. In animals, for example, sexual activity is considered a biological drive. Although hormones play a role in human sexual functioning, the specific forms of human sexuality have been learned through socialization. Motives that are acquired through socialization and that are therefore uniquely human are called complex or *higher-order motives* (Dweck, 1992; Grant and Dweck, 1999). Examples include the need for achievement, moral and religious attitudes and beliefs, and the need for self-actualization. Later in this chapter, we discuss Carstensen's work on how certain goals or needs influence the types of social interactions that older adults either seek or avoid.

In the study of human motivation, we deal primarily with people's beliefs, expectations, and cognitions. We cannot directly observe higher-order goals, drives, and motives. Rather, we infer people's goals, needs, and motives from their behavior and what they tell us about their needs and desires in questionnaires and self-report inventories. Accordingly, some investigators see themselves as studying "motivated behavior" rather than motivation *per se*. A researcher, then, might study eating behavior rather than the hunger drive and mating behavior rather than the sex drive.

The study of the needs, goals, and beliefs that motivate people is a complex field in itself. The question of development across the adult years adds to the complexity: How do motives change as adults develop and age? Several areas of change have been suggested (Wigdor, 1980). First, the *intensity* or *strength* of certain needs, such as hunger, may change. These changes in intensity may be related to physiological changes. Second, the *temporal nature* of certain goals may change. The aged may be more concerned with short-term or present goals than with long-term or future goals. Third, the *substance* of the motives may change. The elderly might be more motivated to read meaningful or personally relevant materials than highly novel or speculative materials.

As we noted earlier, there is no one global theory or approach to the study of motivation. We consider in this chapter a variety of *domain-specific* models of motivation. We progress from more biologically based needs to the higher-order motives. In the discussion of higher-order motives, we consider the influence of cognitive factors on motivation and how beliefs regarding control and efficacy can affect behavior. Next, we describe the factors that influence achievement motivation during adulthood and the value of social interactions in later life. Finally, we discuss moral and religious values and the process of self-actualization.

PHYSIOLOGICAL-BASED NEEDS

Biological or physiological needs produce a heightened state of arousal. Arousal results in activity designed to satisfy the biological need. Thus, arousal is central to the process of meeting physiological needs. It rarely occurs by itself, but it can be considered by itself, as we do later in this chapter. Here we examine the role of arousal in several physiological-based needs.

Hunger and Thirst

There is growing agreement that eating behavior in humans involves an interaction between physiological (internal) needs and situational (external) factors (Blandford, 1998; Hetherington and Rolls, 1996). Exactly how internal and external factors interact in regulating eating is still being debated.

Several age-related physiological changes affect hunger and thirst drives in the elderly. First, recent research suggests that there are small but measurable declines in some of the senses as people age. Small declines in the ability to detect sweet and salty tastes and to identify or label odors have been found (Blandford, 1998; see also Chapter 13). Enjoyment of food involves the senses of smell, taste, and touch, and decrements in the senses can reduce the appeal of eating. Second, there is evidence that the functioning of the central nervous system slows with aging and that the basal metabolic rate drops as a result (Blandford, 1998). A decrease in the basal metabolic rate often results in a reduction in physical activity. As one becomes less physically active, one's need for food also decreases. Third, age-related changes in the hypothalamus reduce the reliability of homeostatic control in the aged, that is, the hypothalamus may become less sensitive in reading blood sugar levels and less efficient in making adjustments in levels. Thus, changes in eating patterns may be needed to compensate for this inefficiency. For example, some older adults may need to eat smaller quantities but more frequently to maintain appropriate blood glucose levels.

Aging may also result in a decrease in *sensory-specific satiety*. The pleasantness and desire to eat a particular food normally decreases as that food is eaten to satiety, regardless of the nutrient content of the food. As satiety is reached the rate of eating the food and the pleasantness of the food decreases; one is less likely to eat that particular food for several hours. Research suggests, however, that sensory-specific satiety is decreased in older adults (Hetherington and Rolls, 1996). This decrease in satiety for a specific food may result in older adults having less varied diets and in eating the same limited foods at successive meals. Reduced satiety may be due to elderly becoming less responsive to changes in internal cues. Reduced responsiveness to internal cues has also been associated with dehydration in the elderly.

Lunch programs for senior citizens provide nourishing meals and a chance to socialize.

Eating and drinking are not completely controlled by physiological needs or drives, of course. Eating and drinking habits are learned across a lifetime (Hendy, Nelson, Greco, 1998; Wigdor, 1980). In our culture, eating is often a social affair—a time to converse with others, to celebrate a happy event—or a way to console ourselves in stressful or unhappy situations. In old age the motivation to eat may be more a function of life-long eating habits and the immediate social situation than of the need to satisfy basic drives. The social incentives to eat may be reduced if, for example, one's spouse has died. There is less motivation to prepare a meal for only one person, and eating alone can be depressing. Some elderly people suffer from malnutrition even when they have money for food because they lack the social incentive to prepare meals or to eat alone.

Arousal

Arousal has been studied with regard to the autonomic nervous system (ANS) and also the central nervous system. We will first review findings with regard to arousal and the ANS. Recall that the ANS comprises the sympathetic and parasympathetic systems. The sympathetic system expends energy (e.g., accelerates heart rate; secretes adrenaline) and the parasympathetic system conserves energy (e.g., slows heart rate, constricts bronchi).

For the past twenty years, there has been a continuing debate regarding the nature of changes in the ANS with age and how these changes relate to behavior

(Elias and Elias, 1977; Marsh and Thompson, 1977; Woodruff-Pak, 1997). Some contend that behavioral changes in the elderly are a function of *underarousal*; others argue that the problem is *overarousal*.

The major research supporting the overarousal hypothesis was conducted by Eisdorfer and colleagues (Eisdorfer, 1968; Eisdorfer, Nowlin, and Wilkie, 1970). These researchers noted that older persons do less well in learning experiments. They make more errors of omission than commission (that is, they fail to make a response more often than they make a wrong response), and they make an especially large number of errors when the pace of the task is speeded up. This leads to the hypothesis that errors of omission were a result of increased situational anxiety, or overarousal. The hypothesis was supported by research that showed that omission errors decreased and the elderly's performance improved when the pace of the task was slowed. To examine the hypothesis further, a measure of arousal that was independent of learning performance was needed. Eisdorfer assessed arousal by measuring levels of free fatty acid (FFA) in the blood, because FFA level reflects a metabolic response to stress.

The research showed that older adults in a learning experiment did have higher levels of FFA than younger adults. Furthermore, the FFA levels of the older adults returned to normal after the experiment much more slowly than those of younger adults. The older people were in a physiological state defined as overaroused and they remained in that state longer than young adults. A final experiment was undertaken to determine whether lowering arousal levels experimentally (that is, reducing FFA levels) would improve performance in learning tasks. Subjects were given the drug propranolol, which blocks autonomic nervous system arousal but has little influence on central nervous system functioning. The learning performance of the treatment group was compared with that of a control group who received a placebo. The results showed that the experimental group with lower FFA levels had fewer total errors during the learning experiment. Unfortunately, the most direct measure of overarousal, a decrease in the number of omission errors compared with commission errors, did not show a significant drop. Nevertheless, this research has been interpreted as evidence that decrements in the learning performance of the elderly may be associated with overarousal and not solely with cognitive factors. It should also be noted that findings from the Eisdorfer research have never been fully replicated (Froehling, 1974).

The studies indicating that underarousal is the problem have used different physiological measures of arousal and different behavioral measures than the studies indicating overarousal as the problem (Woodruff-Pak, 1997). Instead of biochemical measures such as FFA level related to the autonomic nervous system and cognitively stressful behavioral measures such as learning tasks, the underarousal approach has assessed arousal with bioelectric measures such as galvanic skin response and heart rate (Marsh and Thompson, 1977) and behavioral measures that focus on conditioning and vigilance tasks. These types of tasks tend to be repetitive and boring, so the elderly may not have been motivated to perform at their best.

Why the conflict in these overarousal versus underarousal findings? Part of the problem, of course, is the use of different measures. Another aspect, however, is related to the growing consensus that autonomic arousal is not a unitary concept. Various forms of arousal may differ functionally and anatomically (Lacey, 1967). This creates problems in the useful study of physiological arousal as it relates to age changes in meaningful behavior (Woodruff-Pak, 1997).

Research on age-related changes in arousal within the *central nervous system* supports the *underarousal* hypothesis. The electroencephalogram (EEG) is often used in this research (Woodruff-Pak, 1997). Various EEG frequencies have been associated with stages of arousal, ranging from deep sleep to alert problem solving. Very slow EEG frequencies, called delta waves, are associated with deep sleep; theta waves are associated with light sleep and the transition to wakefulness; alpha frequencies occur during alert wakefulness; and the faster beta frequencies are associated with thinking and problem solving. Studies have found that there is a tendency for EEG frequencies to slow with age. For both the delta and alpha stages smaller amplitudes of waves and slower frequencies occur in older subjects. The question is whether this slowing of EEG frequencies, especially alpha frequencies, is related to age changes in behavior and thinking. Reliable relationships have been found between the slowing of alpha frequencies and cognitive impairment among institutionalized groups of elderly (Woodruff, 1985). Such a relationship, however, has not been found among elderly people dwelling in the community. Thus, the nature of the relationship between EEG frequency and behavioral competency in community-dwelling elderly remains unclear.

Emotions

Terms such as *emotion, affect,* and *mood* are often used interchangeably in everyday discussions. *Affect* is considered a general term referring to the continuum of states comprised of emotions, moods and feeling states (Magai, 2001; Schulz, O'Brien, and Tompkins, 1994). The term *emotion* describes a heightened state of arousal, usually associated with an environmental stimulus. Emotions often interrupt ongoing behavior and redirect it toward something in the environment. Emotions tend to be transient and intense experiences, in contrast to moods that are more pervasive states.

Affect and emotions involve behavioral, cognitive, physiological and subjective components (Schulz et al., 1994). When we have a near accident in a car or on a bike, our behavior may slow down, we have cognitions of being injured, and experience sweaty palms and a racing heart, along with subjective feelings of fear. Emotions are measured quantitatively in terms of *intensity, frequency,* and *duration.* Extreme or intense emotions such as rage elicit significant ANS arousal, while less intense emotions such as sadness elicit less ANS arousal. Affect can vary in duration from a *state* involving an isolated instance of an emotion to a *trait* representing a common disposition of a person. In a later section we will refer to state versus trait anxiety as one example of differences in duration of emotions.

There is considerable debate regarding the extent to which there are specific, qualitatively different types of emotions, such as fear, sadness, or anger (Cacioppo, Berntson, Klein, and Poehlmann, 1998; Zautra, Potter, and Reich, 1998).

The *dimensional approach* claims that emotions do not exist as discrete phenomenon but rather are best described in terms of a few broad dimensions. For example, emotions can be organized along a continuum of pleasure/displeasure, positive/negative affect, and high/low activation. Thus anger is a nonpleasant, negative, high activation emotion.

In contrast, the *specific affects approach* maintains that there are 6 to 12 independent emotional factors. The argument is that each affect can be measured uniquely and exhibits specific psychophysiological responses. For example, universal facial expressions that reflect the basic emotions of anger, disgust, enjoyment, fear, sadness, and surprise have been identified in both Western and non-Western cultures.

Levenson (1999; Levenson, Carstensen, Friesen & Ekman, 1991) has been studying emotion from a specific affects approach. In an interesting recent study, three facets of emotion were examined in the elderly and compared to similar emotional responses in younger adults (Levenson et al., 1991). The three facets included physiological (autonomic nervous system, [ANS]), expressive (facial expressions), and subjective (self-reports of emotions) responses. Older adults were asked to recall a situation in their lives associated with each of six emotions (sadness, fear, disgust, happiness, surprise, anger). In addition to their subjective reports of these emotions, the facial expressions of the older adults were assessed, as was ANS activity. Prior research with young adults had shown that when subjects were asked to recall a particular type of emotional situation, they produced facial expressions related to the emotion and also exhibited specific ANS responses. That is, recalling a angry situation, also resulted in production of a facial expression of anger and resulted in increased heart rate. Moreover, there were distinct physiological responses to different emotions—heart rate increases with emotions such as anger and sadness, but not with disgust.

The elderly were found to exhibit the same pattern of physiological and facial expressions when recalling an event associated with a particular emotion. Thus, even in old age, ANS responsivity was intact and differentiated among emotions. However, the magnitude of ANS activity (e.g., magnitude of increase in heart rate) was much smaller in the old. These findings are of particular interest in work with the elderly, given the popularity of reminiscence as an activity of the old. The study findings indicate that when older adults relive emotional memories, these memories are experienced subjectively, produce emotional facial expressions, and involve specific ANS activity as when young people engage in these activities.

There has been little research on whether there are age differences in ability to perceive emotion in others. Sensory changes in hearing and vision may make it more difficult for older adults to detect subtle changes in the communication of emotion. Likewise, elderly without their glasses or dentures (often the case in nursing homes) may lead one to perceive negative affect (squinting, slack jaw) more frequently.

Anxiety

In the preceding section, emotion or affect as a broad domain was discussed. However, we do not typically describe ourselves as simply being emotional, but rather provide a cognitive label for the arousal—anxiety, elation, fear, and so on.

Anxiety has been defined as an aroused condition characterized by vague fears. Anxiety can be thought to involve cognitive (worry, concentration difficulties), somative (fatigability, muscle tension, sleep disturbances), and emotional (restlessness, irritability) components (Scogin, 1998). Personality psychologists have focused on self-reports of anxiety or on behaviors said to manifest anxiety, rather than on physiological indices of arousal.

Spielberger (1972) makes a distinction between trait and state anxiety. *Trait anxiety* is a relatively stable characteristic of a person; an adult high in trait anxiety becomes anxious in many different contexts. *State anxiety*, on the other hand, involves tension and heightened autonomic system arousal caused by a particular situation; the anxiety is specific to a certain situation, rather than being a characteristic of the individual. This type of anxiety may affect cognitive performance, especially in stressful situations such as test taking. There is some evidence that state anxiety, such as that experienced while taking a test, may decrease with age.

Age-related changes in trait anxiety have been examined longitudinally as part of the Normative Aging Study (McCrae and Costa, 1984; see also Chapter 9). This study examines longitudinal changes in three dimensions of personality: neuroticism, extraversion, and openness. Trait anxiety is considered a component of neuroticism, the other components being depression, hostility, and vulnerability. Although one might expect anxiety to increase with age because of the increasing stresses and losses that people face as they grow old, the data indicate that this does not occur. Trait anxiety tends to remain quite stable with age. This has been demonstrated in longitudinal studies involving both self-reports (Costa and McCrae, 1978; Douglas and Arenberg, 1978) and ratings by professionals (McCrae and Costa, 1982). Epidemiological studies have reported anxiety disorders were lowest in the 65 years and older cohort (Scogin, 1998). There do appear to be age differences in what people worry about, with older adults more prone to worry about health problems and younger adults worrying most about family and finances.

COGNITION AND MOTIVATION

In many cases, what we think about a situation—our cognitions, as psychologists call them—determines how we respond to the situation. If we believe that our behavior will affect the outcome, that we have control over the outcome, then we will respond differently than if we believe that the outcome is due to chance or other people's behavior (Bandura, 1997; Langer, 1975). In this section, we discuss the relationship between individuals' perception of control and their behavior in various situations and the influence of emotion on control processes.

Control

Schulz and Hechausen (1998) have proposed that control is a central theme in studying and understanding human development across the life span. The underlying assumption is that individuals try to exert primary control over their environment so that what they experience is largely a result of or due to their own behaviors. Two types of control, *primary* and *secondary* are postulated; both primary and secondary control involve cognition. Primary control focuses on the cognition or perception of the extent to which one's actions affect what happens in one's *external* world. Secondary control focuses on the cognition or perception of internalized control mechanisms. Secondary control strategies often develop and come into play in response to failure or inability to exert primary control; secondary strategies include changing one's aspiration levels, denial, egoistic attributions, and reinterpretation of goals (Heckhausen and Dweck, 1998). Secondary control is concerned not with the individual's ability to influence the external world, but rather the individual's ability to adapt or accommodate one's goals, desires, and beliefs to fit the existing situation. Secondary control has been described as a form of adaptive accommodation.

It is hypothesized that primary and secondary control strategies show different trajectories across the life span Figure 10-1. Primary control strategies develop very early in life. In fact, perceptions of control may be highly exaggerated early in life, showing little correspondence to actual control; the child and teenager think they have more control than they actually have. In early adulthood both primary and secondary control strategies increase. The domains of life (e.g., work, relationships, childrearing) in which control strategies are focused become increasingly selective with age. Secondary control strategies are hypothesized to predominate in the later years.

Our perceptions of primary control influence our behavior; they help determine where we will direct our efforts, how long we will persist, and how effectively we will work (Rodin, Schooler, and Schaie, 1990; Schulz and Heckhausen, 1998). For example, how long and hard we study for an exam depends in part on whether we believe that the grade that we receive will be largely determined by our efforts. If we fail to make the "A" that we strove for, secondary control strategies may lead us to adjust our aspirations and revise our goals. Likewise, if the physical or intellectual abilities of the older adult decline, the adult adjusts their goals and efficacy beliefs to fit their existing capabilities.

How are emotions related to primary and secondary control? Schulz and Heckhausen (1998) propose that emotions are the fuel that energize and regulates the individual's striving for primary control. As the individual interacts with the environment, both positive and negative emotions are generated that supposedly fuel the individual's further striving for primary control. Emotions may stimulate secondary control strategies to help the individual to compensate and accommodate internally to challenges from the external world.

How does one make an accurate judgment about the controllability of an outcome? Weisz (1983) suggests that in order to make accurate judgments about one's primary control over an external outcome, one must be able to assess two factors: (1) control of the outcome—the degree to which the outcome of an event can be determined by the individual; (2) self-efficacy—the degree to which an individual believes he or she has the knowledge and skills necessary to achieve a certain outcome.

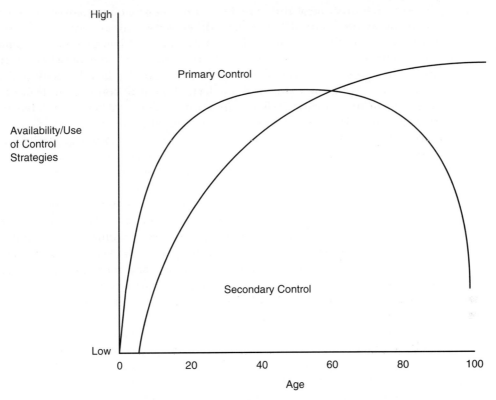

Figure 10-1   Availability and Use of Primary and Secondary Control Strategies Across the Life Course. *Source:* Schulz, R. and Heckhausen, J. (1998). Emotion and control: A life-span perspective. In K. W. Schaie and M. P. Lawton (Eds). *Annual Review of Gerontology and Geriatrics: Emotion and Adult development,* Vol 17. New York: Springer.

In addition to primary and secondary control, two additional terms are frequently used in the control literature. Individuals are said to have an *internal locus of control* when they believe their behavior influences the outcome of an event and an *external locus of control* when they believe the outcome of an event is beyond their control. Levenson (1975) suggests two types of external locus of control—*chance* and *powerful others.* Individuals may believe that the outcome of events is determined by chance or fate and thus cannot be controlled. Alternatively, individuals may believe that although they themselves are not competent or in control, the outcome of events is controllable by powerful others. For example, older adults may defer to the judgments of powerful others, such as their doctor, lawyer, or even an adult child, whom the older adult sees as more competent and capable of effecting an outcome.

Research on control and self-efficacy now focuses on domain-specific systems of control beliefs. Control beliefs may differ across diverse areas of life such as health, work, intellectual functioning, and memory (Clark-Plaskie and Lachman, 1999; Lachman and Weaver, 1998a). Thus, measures of control beliefs related to specific domains have been developed—for example, health locus of control (Wallston and Wallston, 1981) and intellectual locus of control. Study of domain-specific locus of control beliefs is important because greater age-related change has been found to occur in some domains, compared to others. For example, in a sample 25 to 75 years of age, increases in internal control by age were found for control over work, finances, and marriage, whereas decreases were found for control over relationships with children and sex life (Lachman and Weaver, 1998b).

Why are beliefs about locus of control and self-efficacy important? Those with a more internal sense of control have been found to be in better health, have better memories and intellectual functioning, and to have higher education and socioeconomic status (Lachman and Weaver, 1998b; Lachman, Ziff, and Spiro, 1994). Control is also related to mental health; those who say they feel in control of their lives are less depressed, more open-minded, and more assertive. Moreover, epidemiological studies indicate that a sense of control is an important predictor of mortality and psychological well-being (Kahn, 1994). In a prospective study, self efficacy was found to buffer decline in functional activities (self care tasks) for older adults who declined in physical capacity; that is, older adults who experienced physical declines but who had high self efficacy showed less decline on functional activities compared to older adults with low self efficacy and physical decline (Mendes de Leon, Seeman, Baker, Richardson, and Tinetti, 1996).

A number of studies have shown that people with an internal locus of control and high estimation of their self-efficacy invest more effort in a difficult task, are more persistent, more likely to seek challenges, and set higher goals for themselves. Young people who have an internal locus of control and perceive themselves as highly competent consider more career options and are more likely to enroll in difficult educational courses to achieve their career goals (Bandura, 1988).

Do internal and external locus of control and self-efficacy change with age? Cross-sectional and longitudinal studies indicate that internal control beliefs remain relatively stable or decrease slightly with age. In contrast, external control beliefs increase markedly (Lachman and Leff, 1989; Willis et al., 1992). The magnitude of age-related changes varied by the domain of control beliefs studied. Control beliefs about health or cognitive functioning showed greater age-related change than beliefs regarding political or interpersonal control. Specifically, beliefs in the importance of powerful others increase for health and intellectual control domains. Older adults increasingly believe that other people are better able to do things and therefore they become more dependent on others to solve problems. External control beliefs are also more likely to be adopted by those who have a greater number of medical problems and have lower fluid intelligence.

Is this increasing belief in the control of powerful others adaptive in old age? Giving up or at least sharing responsibility for some tasks may be an effective coping strategy, especially for older adults with health problems or lower intellectual functioning. On the other hand, delegating responsibility could also lead to further loss of competence as well as declines in perceived competence and increased dependency.

Learned Dependency

There is the common perception that older adults become dependent primarily due to physical and/or mental limitations. M. Baltes and colleagues (M. Baltes and Carstensen, 1999; M. Baltes, 1996), however, have maintained that the older adult learns to be dependent and that dependency is the product of particular types of exchanges between the older adult and others in their social environment. In our society, there is the stereotype that older adults are incompetent and thus dependency in old age is expected and viewed as acceptable. As a result, those who work with and care for the elderly are sometimes overly protective and create environments that are overly protective. M. Baltes (1996) has demonstrated this learned dependency in her observational work in nursing homes. Baltes found that staff in nursing homes reinforced older adults for dependent behavior ("Wait and let me help you," "Don't try to go to the bathroom by yourself, you will fall."); and ignored or punished independent behavior ("See what a mess you made trying to feed yourself; you should have waited for me to help you"). Elderly were rewarded for being dependent since waiting and being dependent on the staff led to greater

Elderly people who are given responsibility for something other than themselves, such as a pet, generally are more mentally alert, active, and content.

social contact and interaction. In a socially deprived environment, such social contract can be a powerful reinforcer for dependency. M. Baltes notes, however, that learned dependency is not totally without benefits. Dependent behaviors are learned and adaptive given an environment such as a nursing home, and the reward for being dependent can be social contact. The elderly trade independence in some domains (e.g. self-care) and possible increasing loss of their remaining skills (through no longer exercising these skills) in exchange for social contact and reinforcement of being a "good patient."

People's beliefs in their efficacy/independence may be enhanced in several ways (Bandura, 1997). One way is through mastery experiences. Not only does the successful accomplishment of challenging tasks build a sense of competence, but some setbacks and difficulties are also useful in teaching people to persevere in the face of adversity. Beliefs about one's competence also can be strengthened by observing models, seeing other people who are similar to oneself succeed by sustained effort. Finally, social support and reinforcement are useful in enhancing efficacy. If individuals are reinforced for acting independently and taking responsibility for their needs, their sense of self-efficacy is increased (Baltes, 1996).

Achievement Motivation

As commonly conceptualized, achievement motivation is the desire to succeed in behaviors that will be evaluated by others or by oneself in terms of some standard of excellence (Atkinson and Birch, 1978; Raynor and Entin, 1982). Many people, including many psychologists, believe that achievement motivation decreases in the second half of life. Cross-sectional studies (Mellinger and Erdwins, 1989) have found that need for achievement was lower at older ages, with one exception. Need for achievement did not drop with age for single career-women, suggesting that factors other than age affect achievement motivation.

Study of developmental changes in achievement motivation are limited due to lack of longitudinal data and the fact that various measures of achievement motivation have been employed in different studies. Achievement strivings may take many forms in adulthood. Research from the AT&T study of managers (Howard and Bray, 1988) provides some data on longitudinal changes through adulthood in two types of achievement strivings: need for advancement and inner work standards. *Need for advancement* is defined as motivation to advance in one's career faster and further than one's peers. This type of achievement striving was assessed with interview ratings, personality and motivation questionnaires, and projective tests. *Inner work standards* is defined as motivation to perform to the best of one's ability regardless of one's place in the hierarchy and having one's own high standards of work performance, even though a lesser level would satisfy one's superiors. This form of achievement motivation was assessed with interview ratings, projective tests, and, most importantly, with performance on simulated work exercises.

The study found that people who were motivated by need for advancement were oriented toward upward mobility and financial rewards. They had a desire to lead and were self-confident and outgoing. Those who were motivated primarily by inner work standards were less outgoing and had a strong sense of responsibility and a strong desire to be accepted and do the proper thing. They were likely to be persistent.

How did these two types of motivation change over the years? Were they related to job success as measured by the level of management that the person eventually reached? These motives were assessed three times, at year 0, year 8, and year 20.

On average, managers declined in need for advancement over time, regardless of the level of management that they reached. Howard and Bray (1988) suggest that this decline may reflect the realization that in a pyramid organizational structure, they had reached a plateau and would not advance further. Inner work standards shows a different longitudinal pattern. Although the average rating for this motive remained steady over the 20 years for the total group, those at the higher management levels had increasing work standards, whereas those at the lower levels had lowered their standards. In other words, levels of inner work standards seemed to have been progressively shaped by career success; it appears that career success is a good motivator of inner work standards. Nevertheless, it is interesting to note that inner work standards remained relatively constant from year 8 to year 20 even for the majority of managers who did not reach the higher levels. This suggests that adults in midlife continue to be motivated to perform competently and to meet their own inner standards even in the absence of external reinforcements such as vertical career advancement.

DISENGAGEMENT VERSUS ACTIVITY

Toward the end of the life span, people interact with others less frequently. There is little argument among gerontologists that this occurs, but there is considerable disagreement about the psychological reasons for and ramifications of this reduction in social activity (Carstensen, 1992a; Carstensen, Gross and Fung, 1997). For several decades, two theories have been central to discussions regarding whether a decrease in social contact among the old is desirable and "normal." In the original statement of *disengagement theory*, these reductions in social contact were seen as natural and in some sense ideal (Cumming and Henry, 1961). In contrast, *activity theory* has argued that decreases in social contact are imposed upon the elderly by society and are detrimental to the well-being of the old (Lemon, Bengston, and Peterson, 1972). More recently, Carstensen has proposed a new perspective, *socioemotional selectivity theory* to account for why older adults maintain or increase social contact in some spheres while disengaging in others.

Disengagement

Disengagement theory maintains that social withdrawal is an internally motivated (intrapsychic) process in which older adults by choice lessen their psychological investment in social relationships and reduce their social activity. According to disengagement theory, social withdrawal "is accompanied by, or preceded by, increased preoccupation with the self and decreased emotional investment in persons and objects in the environment; . . . in this sense, disengagement is a natural rather than an imposed process" (Havighurst, Neugarten, and Tobin, 1968, p. 161).

The research on which disengagement theory was initially based was a cross-sectional study of a small number of elderly residents in Kansas City. Cumming and Henry (1961) derived several basic tenets regarding disengagement theory from this study. First, they argued that the process of disengagement is inevitable and universal. The disengagement process, they said, could be initiated by the older person or by society. The aging person could withdraw rather markedly from some groups of people (e.g., former business associates) while remaining close to others (e.g., family). But in some cases, the timing and needs of society and the individual will differ. Society, for example, may force a person to retire before he or she is ready because it needs to open up jobs for younger people and maintain the equilibrium of the social system.

Disengagement theory had the happy result of stimulating a great deal of research on the relationship between activity and life satisfaction in old age. Unhappily for the theory, however, most of the research was critical and supported alternative positions. Much criticism of the theory has focused on the assumed universality of the disengagement process and the lack of attention to individual differences.

Disengagement can be a consequence of several factors. One of the most prominent of these is role loss as the individual's position in society changes. A woman was an office manager; now she is retired. She was in charge of dependent children; now they are out on their own. She was chairperson of the city airport commission; now she is consulted only infrequently. She was a wife; now she is a widow (Tobin and Neugarten, 1961).

A second factor is more psychological: "With an increasing awareness that his future is limited and that death is not only inevitable but no longer far distant, the older person may be more likely to attend to himself and to whatever is extremely important to him, simultaneously pushing away what is not extremely important" (Kalish, 1975, p. 64).

A third factor in disengagement is biological. Most old people experience some biological loss: some loss in sensory capacity (seeing, hearing), some memory loss, or a reduced energy level. These conditions may require some curtailment of social activities.

Activity Theory and Life Satisfaction

It has been argued that to cope with the problems of old age and to grow old gracefully, one must keep active, continually finding new interests to replace work and new friends to replace those who have moved or died (Havighurst and Albrecht, 1953). This perspective came to be known as the activity theory of aging (Lemon, Bengston, and Peterson, 1972). Activity theory is concerned with the

An active life is more satisfying than an inactive one, and school volunteer work is one of many opportunities for involvement.

relationship between social activity and life satisfaction in old age. Activity theorists assert that the decrease in social interaction is not initiated by the older adult, but is imposed by society and external circumstances. The value of activity is seen as providing roles for an individual, which are necessary in maintaining a healthy self-concept. As a person ages, he or she is often deprived of many of the major roles that have sustained him or her throughout adulthood. There is a need for optional roles to take their place.

Lemon, Bengtson, and Peterson (1972) were among the first to articulate activity theory. The central assumption in this early articulation was that "the greater activity, the greater one's life satisfaction" (p. 515). They described three types of activities. The most intimate was informal activity, socializing with friends, neighbors, and relatives. Less intimate but still social was *formal activity,* participating in voluntary groups that have established agendas. The third type was *solitary activity,* activity undertaken independently, such as maintaining one's household and pursuing leisure activities on one's own. The intimate activities were hypothesized to be more reinforcing and to contribute more to life satisfaction than solitary activities because they provided opportunities to reaffirm one's important roles and one's perceptions of self with significant others in one's life. The early research of Lemon, Bengtson, and Peterson provided only partial support for their hypotheses. A replication of the study, however, provided more substantial support. Longino and Kart (1982) found that informal, intimate activity was in fact the form of activity most highly associated with life satisfaction.

Recent research has, however, brought into question a basic assumption of activity theory—the greater the social activity, the greater the life satisfaction. A critical issue appears to be the health of the individual; healthy people at any age tend to be more active than unhealthy people, and healthy people also have higher life satisfaction. When health status is taken into account, activity levels no longer predict well-being (Lee and Markides, 1990).

Socioemotional Selectivity Theory

Recently Carstensen (1992a; Baltes and Carstensen, 1999) has proposed *socioemotional selectivity theory* to account for changes in social contact that accompany aging. The theory focuses on the purpose of social interactions and the quality of social contacts, rather than on the sheer frequency of social activities. Longitudinal research has shown that while some forms of social contacts (e.g., acquaintances) do decrease with age, beginning in middle age, other forms of social contact are maintained with no decline into old age (Carstensen, 1992a; Field and Minkler, 1988; Lang, Staudinger, and Carstensen, 1998). Emotional closeness increased throughout adulthood in relationships with relatives and close friends. Thus, from a life-span perspective, individuals begin narrowing their range of social partners long before old age. There appears to be selectivity with regard to social contacts, rather than total social withdrawal.

Disengagement and selectivity theories disagree regarding why reduction in social interactions occurs. An essential premise of disengagement theory is that reduced social interaction is precipitated by the older person's need to emotionally distance themselves from others. In contrast, Carstensen's work suggests that older people report the emotional aspect of social contact to be the most important; an integral part of social interactions are the emotions evoked. Selectivity theory argues that a major function of social interaction in old age is to help regulate affect and emotion. Social interactions involve emotions and as the individual ages, they increasingly select those types of social contacts that are most likely to lead to positive emotional experiences. Social contacts that could involve negative affect or that sap one's energies with little positive emotional payoff are increasingly likely to be avoided. Therefore, selectivity in social interactions is viewed as an adaptive strategy in old age to optimize the likelihood of happy, enriching encounters (Baltes and Carstensen, 1999).

An important implication of the theory is that not all activities are equally helpful in adjusting to old age (Carstensen, 1992a). The advice commonly given to "become more active, do something, get involved" is insufficient in itself. Sheer frequency of activity is not as important as the quality of the activity. Choice of activities must be based on the needs and personality of the individual.

MORAL VALUES AND SPIRITUALITY

As we move through the range of human motivations from biological-based needs to the higher-order motives, we encounter moral and religious values. These values develop from one's own experience, from the teachings of organized religions,

and from socially accepted ethical principles. An until recently little-studied feature of adult life, moral and religious values have wide-ranging effects on behavior.
But as the number of studies of adult development has increased, the information
on spirituality also has begun to increase because it is impossible to ignore the
strong ethical emphases that most adults place on changes in their lives (Thomas
and Eisenhandler, 1999).

Moral Values

Lawrence Kohlberg (1973, 1981; Levin, Kohlberg, and Hewer, 1985) developed a theory of moral reasoning, which focuses on the individual's conception of
justice. For Kohlberg, moral reasoning involves judging the rightness or wrongness
of an action in terms of its impact on the legal rights and well-being of the various
people involved. To assess moral reasoning, Kohlberg analyzed people's responses
to moral problems, presented in story form. For example, a person must decide if
it is morally "right" for a man to steal in order to obtain lifesaving medicine
needed by his critically ill wife. In such moral problems, universal principles of
conscience (saving a life) are juxtaposed with societal-legal regulations (breaking
the law). Kohlberg proposes that people pass through several stages of moral development. In stage 1, early childhood, children judge the rightness or wrongness of
behavior solely by whether or not it is rewarded or punished. The parent is the primary authority figure who rewards or punishes the child's behavior. In stage 2,
children judge the rightness or wrongness of behavior not only by whether it is rewarded or punished but also by whether it satisfies a personal need. In stage 3, individuals begin to internalize these moral standards, developing notions of what a
"good girl" or a "good boy" is, regardless of whether or not the behaviors are punished or rewarded. In stage 4, usually beginning in adolescence, individuals recognize the need for obedience to rules, even if the rules are less than optimal; the
world is viewed as a giant baseball game, where one may complain about an um-
pire's decision but still recognize that without umpires the game would be chaos.
Many people never progress beyond this law-and-order morality, even in
adulthood.

Kohlberg describes additional stages of moral development, all of which supposedly occur in the adult years (Levin, Kohlberg, and Hewer, 1985). The social-
contract, legalistic orientation (stage 5) has been described as the official morality
of the United States government. What is right is that which the majority of citizens
agree on and set into law. Any citizen who disputes any part of this legal code can
bring it up for further discussion; the social contract can be revised; laws can be
changed. This sort of reasoning has been shown to increase dramatically in young
adulthood (Kohlberg and Kramer, 1969; Tapp and Levine, 1972).

In Kohlberg's stage 6, which he claims very few people reach, morality is
based on universal ethical principles. Legitimate legal authorities are rejected
as the source of moral authority. Some universal principle of justice is chosen as
the arbiter of right and wrong. An example of a universal ethical principle is
the Golden Rule: "Do unto others as you would have them do unto you." Such

principles are philosophical abstractions; they do not involve the particular people or the particular events in question. Very few adults ever reach this stage of moral development and reason this way about moral issues. Most recently, Kohlberg has acknowledged that stage 6 has not yet been empirically validated (Levin, Kohlberg, and Hewer, 1985). Furthermore, stage 6 is not viewed as being logically derived from the preceding five stages. Its development is not based solely on logic or cognitive reasoning ability. This final stage reflects societal values and norms regarding what is considered to be the "highest" level of moral thought.

There has been a good deal of debate about whether level of moral reasoning changes with age. Some cross-sectional research (Bielby and Papalia, 1975) suggests that people over age 50 have lower stage levels of moral judgment than those in the 30 to 50 age range; however, this may be due to cohort differences in factors such as education. Kohlberg (1973), on the other hand, has suggested that old age may be associated with new forms and levels of ethical and moral thinking, for some elderly at least.

Another form of advancement would involve not progression to a higher stage but greater consistency in the application of a moral perspective in different tasks and contexts. Research by Pratt, Golding, and Hoyer (1983) found no differences in average stage of moral reasoning for young, middle-aged, and older adults when level of education was controlled. There was evidence, however, that the elderly were more consistent in applying their level of moral reasoning. Old age may then be characterized by an increasing coherence in level of moral reasoning.

In a democracy, all citizens are party to the "social contract," under which the government operates, and therefore all citizens have a right to be heard.

Why do some people rise to higher levels of moral reasoning than others? Based on limited evidence, Kohlberg has suggested that reaching higher levels of moral reasoning is associated with prerequisite levels of cognitive development and exposure to certain types of life experiences. Early formal operational reasoning has been found to be associated with stage 4 and above (Walker, 1986). Educational level, too, has been found to be a predictor of moral reasoning. Level of education may reflect not only cognitive ability, but also the likelihood of exposure to certain experiences, like exploring alternate value systems and one's personal identity, that foster advanced reasoning. The kinds of life experiences that one has when making important family decisions or supervising others on the job—those that require sustained responsibility for the welfare of others—are associated with level of moral reasoning as well (Walker, 1986).

There have been a number of criticisms of Kohlberg's theory. In his own research, Kohlberg (1973) had difficulty demonstrating that the higher stages (4 and 5) always occur in an invariant sequence; he found instances in which there appeared to be regression to a lower stage after an individual reached one of the higher stages. The universality of Kohlberg's stages has also been questioned (Reid, 1984). The higher stages have not been demonstrated cross-culturally. Kohlberg has emphasized that higher stages (for example, stage 6) are indeed value-laden and may reflect the norms and values of particular cultures, most notably Western cultures.

The question has also arisen of whether the same stages of moral reasoning occur for men and women (Gilligan, 1982; Gilligan and Attanucci, 1988). Kohlberg originally developed his theory of moral development on an all-male sample, and much of his research has indicated a gender difference, with many women at stage 3 and many men at stage 4 or 5. No gender differences were found in some recent research (Walker, 1984, 1986). Gilligan (1982) argues that women's moral development follows a different course than men's and that Kohlberg's stages and scoring procedures reflect a male orientation toward morality. Piaget's and Kohlberg's theories define morality in terms of justice, where as Gilligan extends the moral domain to include care. Gilligan suggests that an alternative form of morality places more value on ensuring that human relationships are maintained and seeing that the needs of the vulnerable are met through caring. Gilligan believes that many women view morality in terms of protecting the integrity of relationships and minimizing the hurt, whereas men see morality as a system of rules for adjudicating rights. In response to these arguments, Kohlberg has recently redefined stage 5 to include the aspect of caring. At the same time, only limited empirical support has been found for Gilligan's assertion that men and women follow different paths of moral development (Ford and Lowery, 1986). The significance of Gilligan's contribution may lie less in the suggestion that men and women differ in their orientations to moral conflict than in broadening our definition of what constitutes an adequate description of the moral reasoning process.

Marcia and colleagues have explored the relationship between a care-based morality modeled after Gilligan's theory and ego identity (Marcia, 1993; Skoe and

Marcia, 1991). Three levels of care-based morality were identified and assessed. The highest level involves caring for both self and others. The individual is able to deal with conflicts between selfishness and responsibility by new understanding of the interconnection between others and self. Higher levels of reasoning with regard to care-based morality were strongly associated with higher identity status. Marcia (1993) has suggested that identity development is not solely about individual development, but also about self in relation to others, and hence a strong association between ego identity and care-based morality would be expected.

As noted previously, Kohlberg's theory is primarily concerned with moral reasoning in childhood and young adulthood. What types of moral problems do older adults experience? In a recent study, a sample of older adults reported that the most common moral problems involved the relationship between the older adults and members of their families (Rybash, Roodin, and Hoyer, 1983). The elderly reported being concerned about whether advice should be "given to" or "taken from" a family member of another generation. For example, should one push one's morals on an adult daughter? A second type of family relationship problem involved decisions about caregiving and living arrangements—whether to live with an adult child, whether or not to place a spouse in a nursing home. Moral dilemmas involving legal and societal expectations represented less than a fourth of the total number of problems described. The majority of problems that older adults faced primarily involved family relationships and their rights and responsibilities in relation to these family members, rather than conflict with a legal authority.

Religious Values

Religious motivation has until recently received little attention from researchers in adult development. This is especially surprising when we consider that many adults in the United States report religious beliefs and activities to be central to their lives, particularly older adults. In a recent Gallup poll, 60 percent of adults reported religion to be very important in their life (Newport, December 24, 1999). As shown in Figure 10-2 the proportion of adults attending churches or synagogues in the United States has remain remarkably stable over the past 60 years (Gallup, 1999). The high point of church attendance came in the mid-1950s to mid-1960s which coincided with the huge number of baby boom children coming of age across the country. This percentage fell back to roughly the same percentage found in 1939 and has stayed at almost precisely that point ever since.

With respect to religion, the United States is somewhat of an anomaly in that religious participation and affiliation remain much higher than in other Western industrialized nations. In Canada, Australia, Belgium, and the Netherlands, church attendance levels are 20 to 25 percent (Bibby, 1993; Kaldor, 1987; Lechner, 1989). Lower church attendance is reported in England (10 percent) and in Scandinavia (4 percent) (Hatch, 1989).

Much of the literature on religiosity has focused on a single measure—participation in formal, organized religion, which was generally assessed in terms of attendance at church services (Strawbridge, Cohen, Shema and Kaplan, 1997).

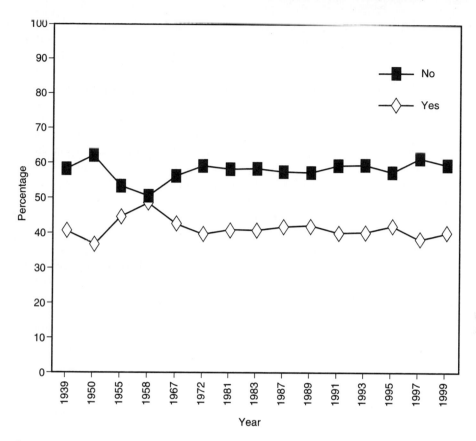

Figure 10-2 Church or Synagogue Attendance in the Last Seven Days. *Source:* Gallup Organization (1999). Long-term Gallup Poll Trends: A Portrait of American Public Opinion Through the 20th Century. Response to Question "Did you, yourself, happen to attend church or synagogue in the last seven days or not?"

There is growing awareness, however, that religiosity is a multidimensional construct and, more importantly, that the various dimensions are not necessarily highly related (Ainlay and Smith, 1984; Levin, Taylor, and Chatters 1994). Studies that examine only one aspect of religiosity, then, may yield distorted results. When church attendance is used as the primary measure of religiosity, for example, it may be concluded that religious participation declines in later adulthood due to a decline in attendance (Markides, Levin, and Ray, 1987). This is not necessarily true, however, as we shall see. The elderly may attend church less frequently due to health problems, but remain active in other dimensions of religion.

Recent studies have focused on three dimensions of religiosity(Ainlay and Smith, 1984; Krause, 1998; Levin, Taylor, and Chatters 1994). The first is participation in organized religious activities—being a member of a formal religious organization, attending church services, or serving as a Sunday school teacher. A second dimension involves *nonorganizational religious activities* including private religious behaviors that do not necessarily take place within a formal institution. These include prayer, Bible reading, watching religious programs on television. A third dimension, *subjective religiosity,* reflects perceived level of religious commitment and the importance of religion in people's lives. One component of subjective religiosity is religious coping (whether respondents turn to God during difficult times and whether they feel it important to seek God's guidance in major decisions).

A number of cross-sectional studies found that participation in organized religious activities peaked in the late fifties or early sixties and then showed a slight decrease in old age (Koenig, 1995; Levin, Taylor and Chatters, 1994). Longitudinal studies suggest that church attendance may peak at a later age, sixties and early seventies, than suggested in cross-sectional data (Atchley, 1995, 2000). However, participation in nonorganized aspects of religion has been found to remain constant or even increase with age (Levin, Taylor and Chatters, 1994; Koenig, 1995). Interestingly, in a cross-sectional study of age-differences in prayer, Peacock and Paloma (1991) found older respondents were more likely than younger respondents to engage in meditative prayer and less likely to engage in petitionary or ritual prayers. One's perception of oneself as a religious person can encompass more than participating in religious organizations; it also includes private religious behavior. Among aged people, there may be shifts in the form of religiosity. Mindel and Vaughan (1978) conclude:

> "These data again seem to be saying that we must separate religiosity as a community activity from religiosity as a personal subjective experience. Our data indicate that the elderly in this sample might have disengaged from religion in the community activity sense but they have continued to maintain or perhaps transformed the way in which they experience religion" (p. 107).

The role of religiosity in old age is of particular interest because various dimensions of religiosity have been associated with physical and mental-health concerns, such as well being, self-esteem, depression, and even mortality (Levin, 1996; Strawbridge et al., 1997). It has been suggested that some aspects of religion may be particularly important for the elderly in buffering the effects of stressors. Krause (1998) examined the role of religious coping (an aspect of subjective religiosity) in buffering the effects of stress on mortality. That is, he examined the impact of religious coping on mortality as assessed approximately three years later. Religious coping was particularly effective for older adults with less education that experienced stress associated with meaningful roles (being a wife, parent, etc). Krause hypothesized that roles that are highly valued by older adults are a major source of meaning in later life. Stressors that impact these roles are particularly damaging because they undermine the older adult's sense of meaning. By promoting a sense of meaning in the face of adversity, religion may be an important asset for helping older adults cope successfully with stressful events that arise in roles they value highly.

The salience of the church and religion among African-American elderly is well documented (Chatters and Taylor, 1998; Ellison, 1998). Both public and private aspects of religious involvement are higher among African Americans in general, and the highest rates are for older people and women (Taylor, Chatters, Jayakody, and Levin, 1996). It has been suggested that among institutions in the black community, the church is second in importance only to the family. The black church historically has been closely involved with a variety of health and social welfare, educational, political, and civic and community activities as well as addressing spiritual needs. As a result, the church may be perceived as more integrated into the everyday lives of blacks, rather than as an institution to visit once a week. The church has often been one of the few institutions totally owned and controlled by the black community.

In large national surveys life satisfaction has been found to be related to both organizational and subjective religiosity among African Americans, even controlling for health (Levin, Taylor, Chatters, 1995). Researchers have begun to formulate hypotheses regarding the mechanisms by which religious involvement may reduce psychological distress and mortality and may increase health status and psychological well being (Ellison, 1998; Levin et al, 1994). Four mechanisms have been proposed. First, religious involvement may generate high levels of social resources, including formal and informal social support. Study of the black church has found church members to be important providers of information and social support, especially for black elderly. Second, religious involvement may enhance the elderly's self-esteem and personal mastery. High religious involvement has been found to be associated with a greater sense of intrinsic moral self-worth and sense of control over one's affairs. Third, religious involvement may foster lifestyles that reduce health problems or family conflict. African-American males who attended church infrequently were more likely to smoke and consume more alcohol than their churchgoing counterparts. Fourth, religious involvement may enhance coping mechanisms that involve emotional regulation. Several studies report the importance of prayer in coping with personal difficulties.

SELF-ACTUALIZATION

How are all the needs and drives and goals and values that motivate humans related? Is it possible to organize the vast variety of human motivations into one coherent framework? One psychologist who tried was Abraham Maslow (1970).

In Maslow's view, human needs arrange themselves in a hierarchy, as depicted in Figure 10-3. The defining characteristic of the hierarchy is that lower needs must be satisfied before higher needs; in Maslow's term, the lower needs are *prepotent*. The lowest and most compelling are *physiological* needs; they are needs that lead to behaviors necessary for the survival of the individual (as hunger leads to eating) or the species (as the sex drive leads to childbearing). If unsatisfied, these needs can dominate a person's thoughts and actions; a starving person has no interest in philosophy.

Next in the hierarchy are the *safety and security* needs. These include the need for protection from danger, and the needs for stability, law and order, and freedom from fear. If we are reasonably safe, we may begin to express the need for *love*

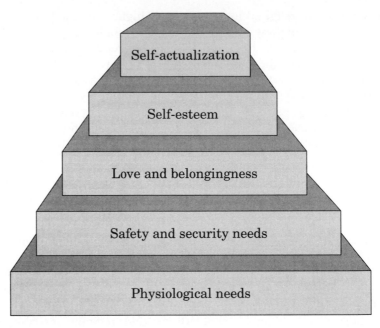

Figure 10-3 Maslow's Hierarchy of Needs. *Source:* From Gerwitz, J. (1980). *Psychology: Looking at ourselves* (2nd ed.). Boston: Little, Brown.

and belongingness. We desire friends, lovers, and children. If we do not get them, we become lonely, just as we become hungry without food, frightened if safety needs go unsatisfied.

If love and belongingness needs are satisfied, needs for *esteem* emerge. We need to respect ourselves, and we need the respect of others. At the top of Maslow's hierarchy is the need for *self-actualization.* Self-actualization is defined as the desire to become everything that one is capable of becoming.

Limited Capacity, Unlimited Dreams

It may come as a surprise that Maslow first based his concept of self-actualization on studies of brain-injured soldiers (Goldstein, 1939). The behavioral effects of brain injuries are many. Some can be traced directly to the injury; the soldier might be blind or partially paralyzed or have difficulty interpreting or producing speech. Other effects are secondary symptoms that reflect attempts to adjust to a new life with reduced sensory or cognitive abilities. For example, brain-injured patients are typically neat and orderly; they are the favorites of the nursing staff. This symptom can be observed in a wide variety of patients with injuries in widely varying parts of the brain. All of them have lost some of their ability to cope with novel situations and thus, defensively, they try to organize their lives to avoid surprises.

Other secondary symptoms are *compensatory,* attempts to regain a previous level of competence in another way. Therapists often note that patients who have lost a function completely (for example, the totally blind) adjust more quickly than those who have severe but incomplete losses. The partially blind keep trying to improve their vision, which may be impossible, while the totally blind develop their other senses and adjust more successfully.

A third class of secondary symptoms has been labeled *self-actualizing.* Maslow observed clear attempts by the brain-injured soldiers not to simply defend or compensate, but to become better than they were before the injury. Many took up a musical instrument and became quite skilled. Others developed unusual cognitive abilities such as computing numbers mentally. With brain injuries, the avenues of expression were limited, but the desire was clearly apparent. The desire was to grow, to be the best one can possibly be: self-actualization.

Maslow's Heroes and Their Values

Maslow studied normal, healthy people to understand self-actualization more clearly. In fact, he studied what he considered to be above-normal, super-healthy people, in an attempt to describe self-actualization at its best. His study sample included subjects both living and dead, subjects defined primarily by a consensus that they were exceptionally healthy in a psychiatric sense. Living subjects were interviewed. Subjects who were dead (including historical figures such as Lincoln and Einstein) were examined through biographies and other writings. From these observations, Maslow constructed a list of characteristics of the average self-actualizing person, shown in Table 10-1. It's an interesting list, with few surprises; it depicts what most of us would consider to be an "ideal" person.

An individual who has had a taste of self-actualization and of the "peak experiences" that one can have in this pursuit may become "addicted." If you experience in a profound way what "justice" means, for example, it can take over your life completely, as you devote yourself to the pursuit of "perfect justice." An artist may begin pursuit of perfect beauty; a philosopher may start tracking truth. Once experienced, the highest needs may become prepotent over the lower needs, according to Maslow. The need for food becomes a need for skill in preparing and appreciating food: The individual becomes a gourmet. The need for sex becomes a need for a sensual, loving experience, part of a contract between two self-actualizing persons.

Goals in general become indistinguishable from what we consider the great virtues in life. According to Maslow, we strive for truth, honesty, beauty, justice, order, and playfulness. Playfulness? Yes! We strive for joy, not pleasure; for satisfaction, not gratification. And the happy, altruistic attitude of play is a basic attitude of the self-actualizing individual.

SUMMARY

1. Motivation is said to be concerned with three issues related to behavior. What initiates or energizes behavior? What influences the direction of behavior? Finally, what affects the termination of behavior?

TABLE 10-1   Characteristics of Self-Actualizing Types

Characteristic	Comment
1. Self-actualizing people perceive reality accurately,	Self-actualizing people detect absurdities and dishonesties quickly, even their own; they do not live in a dream world.
2. even in regard to themselves, and	
3. are not afraid of it.	They are unorthodox, especially in their thoughts
4. They are spontaneous and natural.	They do not act rebelliously simply because they disagree with the opinions of others. They do not act for effect unless the principle involved is highly valued. They have ideals, in other words, but they also understand reality.
5. They focus on problems, not on themselves.	They are not focused on their own personal problems to the exclusion of the problems of society; they think in terms of contributions they can make.
6. They like privacy and detachment;	They are relatively independent of both the physical and the social environment; they enjoy but do not *need* friends.
7. they can be called autonomous.	
8. They have a continued freshness of appreciation.	Life does not become old and stale for them.
9. They have peak experiences.	They have out-of-the-ordinary (mystical) experiences.
10. They have a feeling of relationship with all people and	They are realistic reformers, attempting to improve the lot of all people, and their personal friendships and love-relationships are also more intense.
11. more profound interpersonal relations.	
12. They have a democratic character structure and	They are not prejudiced and they have a strong sense of ethics.
13. discriminate between means and ends.	
14. They are creative.	This follows from the other characteristics, does it not?
15. They have a philosophical sense of humor.	They laugh at absurdities, not at other people's failings.
16. They resist enculturation.	Each is his or her own person.

Source: From Geiwitz, J. (1980). *Psychology: Looking at ourselves* (2nd ed.). Copyright © 1980 by James Gerwitz. Copyright © 1976 by Little, Brown and Company. Reprinted by permission. The characteristics adapted for use in this table were described by Abraham Maslow (1970). Motivation and personality (2nd ed.). New York: Harper & Row.

Early in the study of motivation, there was considerable focus on the first question—what initiates or energizes an action? Motivation was conceptualized in terms of drives or needs from within a person. These drives or needs could be biological or psychological in origin. These biological or psychological needs were believed to create a state of arousal and the state of arousal resulted in action or behavior to satisfy the need. More recently, research on motivation has focused on the second question above—what directs or regulates behavior? Recent theories of motivation have focused on goal-directed activity. Behavior is directed toward achieving or maintaining certain goals or outcomes.

2. Many goals are learned or acquired through socialization; they are not primary biological drives. Motives that are acquired through socialization and that are therefore uniquely human are called complex or *higher-order motives.*

3. There is growing agreement that eating behavior in humans involves an interaction between physiological (internal) needs and situational (external) factors. Enjoyment of food involves the senses of smell, taste, and touch, and decrements in the senses can reduce the appeal of eating. Second, there is evidence that the functioning of the central nervous system slows with aging and that the basal metabolic rate drops as a result. Eating and drinking are not completely controlled by physiological needs or drives. Eating and drinking habits are learned across a lifetime. In our culture, eating is often a social affair—a time to converse with others, to celebrate a happy event—or a way to console ourselves in stressful or unhappy situations. In old age the motivation to eat may be more a function of life-long eating habits and the immediate social situation than of the need to satisfy basic drives.

4. The term *emotion* describes a heightened state of arousal, usually associated with an environmental stimulus. Emotions tend to be transient and intense experiences, in contrast to moods that are more pervasive states. Affect and emotions involve behavioral, cognitive, physiological, and subjective components. Emotions are measured quantitatively in terms of *intensity, frequency,* and *duration.* There is considerable debate regarding the extent to which there are specific, qualitatively different types of emotions, such as fear, sadness, or anger. The *dimensional approach* claims that emotions do not exist as discrete phenomenon but rather are best described in terms of a few broad dimensions. In contrast, the *specific affects approach* maintains that each emotion can be measured uniquely and exhibits specific psychophysiological responses.

5. Schulz and Hechausen have proposed that control is a central theme in studying and understanding human development across the life span. The underlying assumption is that individuals try to exert primary control over their environment so that what they experience is largely a result of or due to their own behaviors. Two types of control, *primary* and *secondary* are postulated; both primary and secondary control involve cognition. Primary control focuses on the cognition or perception of the extent to which one's actions affect what happens in one's *external* world. Secondary control focuses on the cognition or perception of internalized control mechanisms.

6. In addition to primary and secondary control, two additional terms are frequently used in the control literature. Individuals are

said to have an *internal locus of control* when they believe their behavior influences the outcome of an event and an *external locus of control* when they believe the outcome of an event is beyond their control. Levenson (1975) suggests two types of external locus of control—*chance* and *powerful others.*

7. Two theories have been central to discussions regarding whether a decrease in social contact among the old is desirable and "normal." *Disengagement theory,* holds that reductions in social contact are seen as natural and in some sense ideal. In contrast, *activity theory* has argued that decreases in social contact are imposed upon the elderly by society and are detrimental to the well-being of the old. Recently, a new perspective, *socioemotional selectivity theory* seeks to account for why older adults maintain or increase social contact in some spheres while disengaging in others.

8. Kohlberg's theory of moral development suggests that people pass through a number of stages as they age. Relatively few people reach the higher stages. Gilligan suggests that the moral development of women may emphasize different values than the moral development of men.

9. There is growing evidence that religiosity is a multidimensional construct and that the various dimensions are not necessarily highly related. Recent studies have focused on three dimensions of religiosity. The first is participation in *organized religious activities*—being a member of a formal religious organization, attending church services, or serving as a Sunday school teacher. A second dimension involves *nonorganizational religious activities* including private religious behaviors that do not necessarily take place within a formal institution. These include prayer, Bible reading, watching religious programs on television. A third dimension, *subjective religiosity,* reflects perceived level of religious commitment and the importance of religion in people's lives. One component of subjective religiosity is religious coping.

10. Maslow's hierarchical theory of motivation describes physiological needs as most basic, followed by safety and security, love and belongingness, and esteem needs. At the top of Maslow's hierarchy are growth or self-actualization needs.

SUGGESTED READINGS

Baltes, M. M. and Carstensen, L. L. (1999). Social-psychological theories and their applications to aging: From individual to collective. (pp. 209–226). In V. L. Bengtson and K. W. Schaie (Eds.), *Handbook of theories of aging.* New York: Springer.

Ellison, C. G. (1998). Religion, health, and well being among African Americans. *African American Research Perspectives, 4,* 94–103.

Krause, N. (2001). Social supports. In R. H. Binstock and L. K. George (Eds.), *Handbook of aging and the social sciences.* (5th ed.). San Diego, CA: Academic.

Labouvie-Vief, G. (1999). Emotions in adulthood. In V. L. Bengtson and K. W. Schaie (Eds.), *Handbook of theories of aging.* (pp. 253–270). New York: Springer.

Magai, C. (2001). Emotion over the life span. In J. E. Birren and K. W. Schaie

(Eds.), *Handbook of the psychology of aging.* (5th ed.). San Diego, CA: Academic.

Scogin, F. (1998). Anxiety in old age. In I. H. Nordhus, G. R. VandenBos, S.

Berg, and P. Fromholt (Eds.), *Clinical geropsychology.* (pp. 205–210). Washington, DC: American Psychological Association.

CHAPTER 11

Learning and Memory

Acquiring and Retaining Information

Learning and memory are obviously closely related concepts (Howard and Howard, 1997). People must learn before they can remember, and learning without memory has limited utility. Learning is often assessed by memory tasks. "How much have you learned?" is translated into "How much can you remember?" Memory is often assessed by learning tasks (e.g., memorizing a list of words). How can we distinguish between learning and memory?

Learning is typically defined as the acquisition or encoding of new information through practice or experience. *Remembering* is typically defined as the retrieval of information that has been stored in memory. *Memory* is discussed in terms of information, that is, how you put information into "the system," how you store it, and how you retrieve it. This is the approach of information processing theories. In this view, learning is the acquisition or encoding phase of memory.

How do learning abilities change with age? How does memory change with age? Does it fade gradually? Do old people tend to forget new things, remembering better the events from the more distant past? There are other questions as well. How does society affect the demands placed on learning and memory? For example, we live in a culture marked by rapid technological change, so that much of what we learn is soon outdated. We must learn new techniques, and new facts. In our society, old and young alike must continually learn new skills as new technology alters basic systems of communication, transportation, finance, and recreation.

HUMAN MEMORY

At different times, various approaches to the study of learning and memory have been dominant. Until the early 1960s, the associative (S-R) view dominated the work on adult learning and memory (Hultsch and Deutsch, 1981). In the 1970s

316

and 1980s, stage theories of learning and memory, focusing on encoding, storage, and retrieval, were emphasized (Smith, 1996). More recently, two approaches to memory have become dominant. One approach conceptualizes memory as being composed of several different but interrelated *memory systems* (Bäckman, 2001; Hultsch, Hertzog, Dixon, and Small, 1998; Nyberg and Tulving, 1996; Tulving, 1993). These memory systems include short-term memory and a number of different long-term memory systems including procedural, semantic, and episodic memory. These memory systems can be represented and studied at both the neural level and in terms of behavior. An important question in memory systems research is which memory systems are impaired with increasing age and which are spared. Episodic memory appears to show significant age-related losses, while semantic memory and some aspects of short-term memory (i.e., primary memory) show little or no impairment in healthy elders.

A second approach focuses on several processes involved in memory rather than different memory systems. In this view, memory is determined by the processing operations carried out on to-be-remembered information (Craik and Salthouse, 1999; Li, 2000). These processes include working memory and speed of processing. Process-oriented researchers take the position that memory problems can occur in any memory system; it is the *type of processing* required in a particular memory task, rather than a particular memory system, that is important. The same processes can be studied across different memory tasks. Again, a major concern is how age-related deficits or limitations in these processes impair memory functioning. There also has been interest in a contextual approach, individual differences, and metamemory (Hess and Pullen, 1996; Hultsch and Dixon, 1990).

In this chapter, we review research on learning and memory from these various approaches and try to provide an integrated view. We begin with discussing various memory systems and the processes that are believed to affect memory functioning, particularly with regard to aging. We will focus primarily on episodic memory, since this memory system has been most extensively studied and shows some of the largest age-related changes. Next, we look at memory in everyday life and adults' beliefs about memory (metamemory). Finally, we turn to training studies on adult learning and memory and some of the factors that facilitate memory in old age.

A STAGE MODEL OF MEMORY

Figure 11-1 presents a stage model approach to the study of memory. Encoding is the learning or acquisition phase. The manner in which information is processed during encoding is very important. Many older adults may not process new information effectively, leading to later memory problems (Craik and Jennings, 1992).

Sensory Memory

Information can be encoded along three stages or systems. *Sensory Memory* is conceptualized as a brief way station for information from the environment. In order for information to be recalled, it must be processed and transferred to the

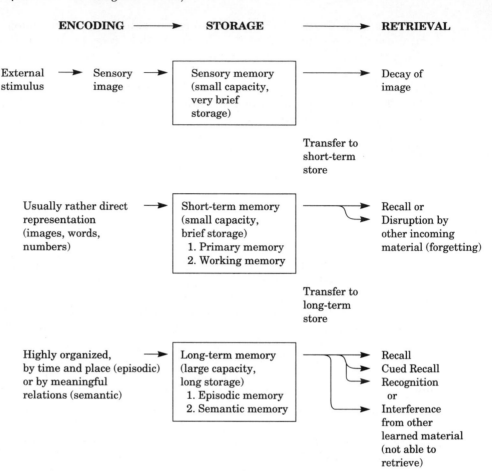

Figure 11-1   Three Stage Model of Memory: Three Stages of Memory (Encoding, Storage, and Retrieval) and Three Systems (Sensory, Short-Term, Long-Term) *Source:* Based on Atkinson, J.W. and Shreffrin, R.M. (1968). *Human Memory: A proposed system and its control processes.* K.W. Spence and J.T. Spence (Eds.), *The psychology of learning and motivation* (Vol. 2). New York: Academic Press.

later stages. This memory is sense-specific, that is, the information is stored according to the sensory modality that receives it (Poon, 1985). Visual information is stored as a fleeting memory called the icon, and the visual memory store is called iconic memory. Facsimiles of auditory stimuli, called *echoes,* are also produced, and the auditory memory store is called *echoic memory.* Many psychologists consider these brief facsimiles to be an initial stage of information processing, holding information in a straightforward way for a short time so that patterns can be recognized for later processing. In the perception of speech, for example, one must remember the first sound of a word long enough to join it to the other sounds and determine the word's meaning.

There is very limited information available on the effects of aging on echoic memory (Crowder, 1980); as a result, we must focus on the iconic memory in discussing the sensory store. Iconic memory is often studied by briefly presenting a stimulus (e.g., a letter or letters) to a subject and then presenting a second stimulus that eliminates or "masks" the first. Iconic memory is assessed as the extent to which the initial stimulus is recalled after the mask. The age differences in iconic memory are small (Walsh, Till, and Williams, 1978; Cerella, Poon, and Fozard, 1982). The minor deficits in sensory store that do occur probably don't contribute significantly to the more severe memory problems in short-term memory experienced by the elderly (Mitchell, 1989; Craik and Jennings, 1992).

Short-term Memory

Short-term memory is presumed to hold relatively small amounts of information; the to-be-remembered items are being held in consciousness. It is in short-term memory that information is prepared for long-term memory. Short-term memory can be divided into *Primary Memory* and *Working Memory*. The two types of short-term memory differ in whether the information is held passively in consciousness (primary memory) or whether the information is manipulated in some fashion (working memory). Primary memory, or memory span, involves holding in mind a small amount of information, such as a telephone number. When you dial directory assistance for a telephone number, the sound of the operator's voice was first encoded in sensory memory. The number is then held in primary memory until you can dial the number or write it down. Primary memory has a very small capacity and is quite brief. If you need to remember the number for later use, then the number may be encoded into working memory. Information in working memory is processed in the form of concepts that can be recalled. For example, you might organize a phone number (237–3076) schematically, by remembering that 237 is the local prefix and 3076 are the last four digits of your Social Security number. Information in the short-term store may be in either visual or verbal form. Most research has focused on verbal material; however, recent research by Park and colleagues has examined spatial (visual) memory (Park et al., 1990).

With regard to primary memory, there do not appear to be large age differences in *storage*, or the amount of information retained (Craik and Jennings, 1992; Poon, 1985). Studies of *memory span*—the longest string of items (numbers, letters, words) that can be repeated perfectly after a single brief presentation—show few age differences (Wingfield et al., 1988). Memory-span tasks are something like hearing a phone number from directory assistance with no pen at hand; you have to recall it perfectly to dial your party. The average memory span for digits is about seven or eight and for words about five letters.

Findings from the Gothenburg longitudinal study indicate some modest declines in memory span in the late seventies and eighties (Johansson and Berg, 1989); evidence for terminal drop was also found in that survivors had higher scores at earlier occasions of testing than did the deceased. Age-related change in memory-span performance is of interest from a clinical as well as a developmental perspective. Memory-span tests are used in screening for dementia. While there appears to be limited age-related decline in memory span until advanced old age in healthy, nondemented elderly, deficits in memory span are one of the early signs of pathology. As older and older patients are seen by professionals, clinicians will need to take into account findings from longitudinal studies of age-related change in normal elderly. It may be quite difficult in some cases to determine whether lower memory-span performance in the very old is due to normal age-related loss or due to early pathology.

A second line of evidence on the lack of age differences in storage in primary memory comes from what psychologists call the *recency effect* (Poon and Fozard, 1980; Craik and Jennings, 1992). Given a list of words to recall, subjects typically do best on the last, or most recent words given. Older as well as younger subjects show this effect, and the older subjects remember the last few words from the list as well as younger subjects do, albeit somewhat more slowly. Because the recency effect has been attributed to primary memory (the most recent items are placed in short-term store, whereas the others must be retrieved from the long-term store), the conclusion again is that old and young people do not differ significantly in the amount of information in short-term store.

Working Memory

A different picture with regard to age differences and age changes occurs in research on working memory (Salthouse, 1990; Salthouse and Babcock, 1991). Working memory involves holding information in mind and at the same time "working on" or manipulating the information. Information is worked on so that it is in proper form for storing in the permanent long-term memory, involving processes of organization, mnemonics, and depth of processing (Hultsch and Dixon, 1990). Working memory is also involved when information must be manipulated or "worked on" in solving a problem or making a decision. For example, you are in the grocery store and want to compare the prices of several brands of cereal. You must hold in mind the price of three or four brands, but must also manipulate the information in order to determine which cereal is less expensive (per unit weight).

Both cross-sectional studies and longitudinal studies indicate that there are age differences and age changes in working memory (Salthouse and Babcock, 1991; Hultsch et al., 1992). However, there is considerable debate on the source(s) of age-related deficits in working memory. Deficits could occur in storage (capacity); it may be that in later adulthood less information (capacity) can be "worked on" at one time. Deficits may occur in the processing or working on the information. As tasks become more complex, the elderly may have difficulties in using efficient processing strategies. Alternatively, it may be that there is a slowdown in the speed at which working memory carries out these activities. Salthouse and Babcock, (1991) suggests that deficits in processing may be the most important determinant of working memory problems. It may also be that the older adult gives higher priority to processing at the expense of other encoding operations and thereby capacity is reduced.

Most of the studies on working memory have been cross-sectional. However, Hultsch and colleagues (Hultsch et al., 1992) have published longitudinal change in verbal working memory over a 3-year interval see Figure 11-2. Two cohorts (birth years 1900–1915; 1916–1931) were studied. The earlier-born cohort was in the old-old age range, 75 at Time 1 and 78 at Time 2; the later-born cohort (young-old) was 65 and 68 at Time 1 and 2, respectively. There was greater decline across the 3-year interval for the old-old. Also there were differences between the two cohorts in level of performance at both occasions; these differences probably reflect both cohort differences (differences in level of performance when at the same chronological age) and previous age-related change for the old-old.

Long-term Memory

This is seen as having a large capacity for storing information, which can be retained over long periods of time. There are various systems of long-term memory including *Episodic Memory, Semantic Memory, Procedural Memory* and *Prospective Memory* (Hultsch et al., 1998). Episodic and semantic memory have been studied more extensively. *Episodic memory* is concerned with remembering things associated with a particular time or place—remembering what you did on a particular day or remembering when to take a medication. *Semantic memory* involves memory for knowledge—remembering division facts or the capital city of Sweden. *Procedural memory* is the form

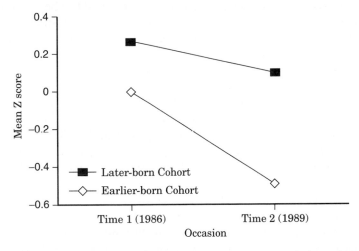

Figure 11–2 Three-Year Longitudinal Change in Verbal Working Memory Performance for Two Cohorts. *Source:* Hultsch, D.F., Hertzog, C., Small, B.J., McDonald-Miszlak, L., and Dixon, R.A. (1992). Short-term longitudinal change in cognitive performance in later life. *Psychology and Aging, 7,* pp. 571–584.

of memory underlying the learning of skills and actions; it is often studied via rou-tinized behaviors (walking, skating, driving, typing). *Prospective memory* involves mem-ory for actions to be carried out in the future, for example remembering to send a birthday card on a certain date or to call to make a dinner reservation.

Forgetting can occur at various stages or systems in the memory process. For example, just after the operator repeated the phone number, there may have been a loud noise that distracted you and the information in sensory memory decayed before it could be transferred into short-term memory. Alternatively, the informa-tion may have been transferred into short-term memory, but just as you were hang-ing up the phone, someone told you a date that you also needed to remember. Because the capacity of short-term memory is small, the phone number was re-placed by the date in short-term memory before it could be processed.

The major age differences in memory performance are most commonly asso-ciated with tasks that have high processing demands with regard to working mem-ory and to long-term memory (Poon, 1985; Smith, 1996). Thus, much of our discussion will focus on age differences and age changes in working memory and in long-term memory, particularly episodic memory.

INFLUENCES ON LONG-TERM MEMORY

The focus in memory research on processing suggests that memory should be viewed as an *activity*, rather than as a static receptacle or storage container. There are a number of factors that can influence the processing of information, that is, how well information is learned and remembered. Four major categories of factors that influence processing have been identified: (1) characteristics of the person; (2) factors related to encoding or learning the information, (3) the characteristics of the material to be learned, and (4) factors related to retrieval (Bäckman, Mantyla and Herlitz, 1990; Craik and Jennings, 1992). Figure 11-3 presents a cube representing these four types of factors and the possible interactions among these factors.

Encoding factors influence the learning or acquisition phase. Retrieval fac-tors influence the context or conditions under which information is remembered. Person-related factors include characteristics and abilities of the individual that in-fluence the learning and memory process at all phases. Material factors include characteristics of the material-to-be-remembered that facilitate or handicap encod-ing and retrieval.

Several person-related factors have been identified that affect memory in-cluding verbal ability, health, and sensory functioning (Bäckman, Small, and Lar-son, in press; Zelinski, Crimmins, Reynolds, and Seeman, 1998). Verbal ability and general knowledge have been related to better recall (Hultsch et al., 1993; Kemper, 2001). Poorer memory performance in old age has been associated with physical health limitations and cardiovascular functioning in particular (Elias, Elias, and Elias, 1990; Madden and Blumenthal, 1998). Poorer sensory functioning has also been associated with memory limitations (Lindenberger and Baltes, 1994).

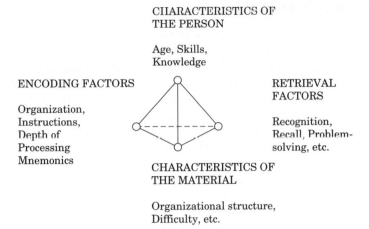

CHARACTERISTICS OF
THE PERSON

Age, Skills,
Knowledge

ENCODING FACTORS

Organization,
Instructions,
Depth of
Processing
Mnemonics

RETRIEVAL
FACTORS

Recognition,
Recall, Problem-
solving, etc.

CHARACTERISTICS OF
THE MATERIAL

Organizational structure,
Difficulty, etc.

Figure 11-3 Conceptual Framework for Four Types of Influences on Long-Term Memory Performance. *Source:* Adapted from Jenkins, J.J. (1979). Four points to remember: A tetrahedral model of memory experiments. In L.S. Cermak and F.I.M. Craik (Eds.). *Levels of processing in human memory.* Hillsdale, NJ: Erlbaum.

Women have been found to perform better on episodic memory tasks than men (Herlitz, Nilsson, and Bäckman, 1997).

The four influences may be seen as representing the conditions or context in which learning and remembering occurs. Certain conditions facilitate or optimize the likelihood of learning and remembering. For example, using an organizational strategy at encoding and requiring only recognition of the correct answer at retrieval increases the likelihood of both encoding and remembering the information. Identifying the conditions that support or facilitate encoding and retrieval are particularly important in helping older adults to remember information. We will refer to facets of this cube in discussing factors that optimize (facilitate) or handicap memory in older adults.

ENCODING AND LONG-TERM MEMORY

Encoding is the learning or acquisition phase of memory. Memory research indicates that many older adults do not spontaneously engage in the types of processing that aid encoding (Bäckman, Mantyla, and Herlitz, 1990; Challis, Bradford, Velichovsky, Boris, and Craik, 1996; Craik and Salthouse, 1999). When older adults are given instructions to use certain types of encoding strategies, age differences between the memory performances of young and older adults are reduced or eliminated. Much research has examined the effects of organizational instructions and of levels of processing on encoding and remembering information.

Organizational Instructions

One of the best ways to encode information for later retrieval is to organize it (Craik, and Jennings 1992). Here we may think of filing systems as an analogy. If material is filed neatly and systematically in reasonable categories, our chances of finding it when we need it are greatly enhanced. If material is stuffed without rhyme or reason into folders as it comes in, we will surely have difficulty later.

Much research evidence suggests that many older subjects do not spontaneously organize information for later recall (Bäckman, 2001; Challis, et al., 1996). A common type of study involves randomly assigning young and old adults to two types of instructional conditions and asking them to learn lists of words. Each list had several "clusters" of words based on similarity in meaning (e.g., *ocean* and *sea*) or on relatedness (e.g., *piano* and *music*); subjects were not told explicitly of the clusterings. In one instructional condition, subjects are told to learn the words as best as they can. In another instructional condition, subjects are told to organize the words into categories and to use these categories in learning the list. Older adults perform better when told explicitly to use the organizational strategy.

Younger adults tend to use an organizational strategy spontaneously, whether they are instructed to do so or not by the experimenter. Because the number of words recalled in such a task is highly correlated with the degree to which the subject organizes the list, age differences in memory performance are reduced in the organizational instruction condition. Being instructed to use organizational strategies is particularly helpful for older adults with low verbal memory. Thus, we have identified two conditions in Figure 11-3 associated with older adults' memory performance. Under the *encoding factor,* organizational instructions enhance memory performance of the old. Under *person characteristics,* adults with low verbal ability are particularly disadvantaged in some types of memory tasks and profit from organizational instructions.

Depth of Processing

Information can be encoded or processed at different levels, from shallow to deep. Deeper levels of encoding produce more enduring memory traces, more resistant to forgetting. In typical laboratory tasks used to define depth of processing, subjects are presented with lists of words and asked to make certain judgments. They might be asked to decide whether or not the word is in capital letters; this is considered a shallow level of processing. A somewhat deeper level is obtained by asking the subjects about the sound of the word, for example, if the word rhymes with *pain.* The deepest level of processing is obtained by asking subjects something that requires them to think about the meaning of the word. For example, does the word fit in the sentence: "The girl placed _____ on the table?" In general, the deeper levels of processing involve the word at a semantic level; that is, they involve examining the meaning of the word rather than superficial characteristics such as with what letter the word starts. Typically, depth of processing defined in these ways is highly related to later recall of the words; the deeper the level, the more remembered (Cherry and Smith, 1998; Whiting and Smith, 1997).

Mnemonics

Another effective way to encode information for later retrieval is to use mnemonic techniques. Mnemonic techniques use verbal or visual associations to link pieces of information that might not by themselves have clear relationships (Bäckman, 2001; Cherry, Park, Frieske, and Smith, 1996). A common verbal mnemonic is the rhyme that we use to remember an otherwise forgettable rule of spelling: "I" before "e," except after "c." Visual mnemonics involve picturing the material to be remembered in some sort of imaginary scene. To remember a shopping list of milk, mushrooms, and an ear of corn, for example, one might visualize a cow eating an ear of corn while sitting on a toadstool. Such sometimes bizarre images have been shown to improve memory. They are especially useful in the encoding process. Older adults may have trouble forming images, but they can be trained to form them and use them in memory tasks (Yesavage, Lapp, and Sheikh, 1989).

In a series of studies (Kliegl, Smith, and Baltes, 1989; Baltes and Kliegl, 1992), people in their sixties and seventies were taught a mnemonic called the *method of*

Elderly people are less likely to have difficulty performing familiar tasks than tasks that require concentration and place demands on memory.

loci. The method of loci involves imagining items to be remembered in various familiar locations, such as places in your home. In this study, the subjects were asked to pair 30 imaginary objects (corresponding to the 30 to-be-remembered words) with 30 locations in their city. The old people who learned this trick, remembered significantly more of the words on the list than did a control group of old people who weren't taught the method of loci. Age differences in training effects were found when older adults were required to recall words under speeded-up conditions.

Age differences in encoding and in the use of organizational strategies are most evident in *effortful tasks* (Hasher and Zacks, 1979; Zacks, Hasher, and Li, 2000). These are tasks that require sustained attention, may be novel or unfamiliar, or require a different combination of strategies than that which is typically used: following a new recipe, driving an unfamiliar car, or walking to a familiar place by a different route. *Automatized tasks,* on the other hand, are thoroughly familiar and require little attention or conscious awareness: performing a routine household chore, playing a familiar tune on the piano from memory. Effortful tasks require more concentration than automatized tasks and make greater demands on memory (Park, 1999). Thus, they are an especially appropriate area for the use of encoding strategies that facilitate memory storage. Tasks that have become automatized probably required the use of encoding strategies when they were first learned, but with automatization the need to use these strategies decreases.

In summary, several lines of evidence suggest that part of the age difference typically observed in studies of memory lies in the encoding phase of memory. Older subjects do not spontaneously organize information as quickly or as effectively as younger subjects. In general, older people do not seem to process information as deeply as young adults (Shaw and Craik, 1989). Research, however, also suggests that older adults' processing of information can be facilitated when taking into account encoding and person-related factors (see Figure 11-3). Older adults' recall is improved when they are given instructions to use organizational strategies. Organizational instructions are particularly useful for those with low verbal ability (person characteristic). In addition, older adults' recall can be enhanced, often to the performance level of young adults, when they are given instructions to use deeper levels of processing. Alternatively, recent research suggests that older adults may encode information at a deeper level, but maintaining the semantic representation in memory so that it is available at retrieval may be more difficult for older adults (Burke and Harold, 1988; Light, 1990). They therefore store less information and obviously can retrieve less.

We still do not know why older adults often do not spontaneously use organizational strategies, but can do so if instructed (Craik, Anderson, Kerr, and Li, 1995; West, 1995). Motivation seems to play a role; older subjects might not be interested in processing deeply the silly lists presented in experiments, or they might be so anxious that they can't explore meaning in depth (Bäckman, 1989b). The older adults' attentional resources may have declined; they have more difficulty giving sustained effort and attention to encoding (learning) and retrieving certain information (Zacks, Hasher, and Li, 2000; Camp and McKitrick, 1989). Their information processing systems may be slowing down, making it more difficult for them to make the associations necessary for organization and mediation. Or the average older subject may simply be suffering from less education; perhaps he or she was never taught how to process information effectively in the schools of the early 1900s that emphasized rote learning. All these possibilities may contribute to a lack of use of spontaneous organizational strategies.

Transferring information into long-term storage, thus, requires different memory strategies than merely maintaining information in short-term storage. If the person wishes simply to hold information temporarily in primary memory, rehearsing, or repeating the words or letters, is a useful strategy. However, if the goal is to encode the information for long-term storage, the encoding strategies discussed earlier are needed.

RETRIEVAL AND LONG-TERM MEMORY

We have considered evidence that older adults have more difficulty than young adults in encoding information. We now consider evidence that older adults also have more difficulty retrieving the information that they have stored (Zacks, Hasher, and Li, 2000). We are, in effect, suggesting that old people have trouble getting the information into their long-term stores and that they also have trouble getting it out. Difficulties in encoding and retrieval account for most of the overall age differences observed in memory experiments.

Recall Versus Recognition

One way to demonstrate retrieval difficulties is to show that people can recognize words that they cannot recall. *Recall* is the ability to retrieve a particular piece of information. What was the name of your third-grade teacher? What were the words on the 30-item list that we just showed you? *Recognition* is the ability to identify a given piece of information. What was the name of your third-grade teacher, Johnson or McNally? Or, here are 60 words; pick out the 30 that we just showed you. As you know from taking multiple-choice and essay tests, recognition is generally easier (Craik and McDowd, 1998). Often you can recognize an answer that you cannot recall; you can't dredge up "McNally" when asked about your third-grade teacher, but once it is presented you say, "Well, of course! Mrs. McNally! How could I forget?"

Recognition tests provide the item itself as a retrieval cue; simple recall tests provide no more than instructions to retrieve what has been previously presented. Between these two extremes are a series of tasks that vary in the effectiveness of retrieval cues. These tasks are called *cued recall* (Craik, Byrd, and Swanson, 1987). For example, you might fail to recall the name of your third-grade teacher until you are given a hint, a retrieval cue: "Her name starts with 'M.'" "Oh, yes, Mrs. McNally!" You retrieve successfully.

Older subjects benefit relative to young adults in cued recall compared to simple, free recall (Craik and Jennings, 1992; Poon, 1985; Hultsch, 1985). Consider a list that contains four words in each of four categories: animals, names, professions, and vegetables. During recall these categories are effective as retrieval cues, even if the subject is unaware of the categories at the time of learning. Older subjects may even equal the performance of young adults when category words are given as cues. Thus, again we are drawn to the conclusion that old people have more difficulty retrieving information from memory and receive more aid than young people from hints about the to-be-remembered material.

A number of studies also show that older subjects benefit more than younger subjects when recognition tests are used instead of recall tests (Craik and Jennings, 1992; Whiting and Smith, 1997). Cross-sectional studies show that age differences on recognition tests are small or nonexistent, whereas the age differences on recall of factual information are significant. Longitudinal research also shows that there are differences in age-related decline for recall versus recognition. Zelinski and colleagues (Zelinski and Burnight, 1997) studied changes in recall and recognition memory over a 16-year period. There were significant declines in list and text recall but not in recognition after age 55.

Retrieval of Ancient Memories

It is a common belief that old people cannot remember recent events but can recall with great clarity events in the distant past (Camp and McKitrick, 1989; Bahrick, 1984). An old woman, for example, may claim to remember her first day in school "as if it were yesterday," even though the real yesterday seems to have passed from her memory. Is the old woman telling the truth? Is there anything to the notion of the persistence of ancient memories?

Rubin has proposed a "reminiscence bump" in ancient memories (Rubin, Rahhal, and Poon, 1998). That is, elevated levels of recall have been shown by older adults for memories occurring from their tenth to thirtieth years relative to other times in their lives. Older adults recalled more autobiographical events which occurred from the ages of 10 to 30 than events that occurred earlier in childhood or in middle age (Rubin, 1999). Similarly, older adults recalled more correctly events such as World Series, Academy Awards, and current events that occurred when they were 11 to 30 years old, compared to events that happened at other periods in their lives.

What explanations can be offered for such a phenomenon? Rubin has suggested that affect may be involved; older adults also rated their favorite films, music, and books as coming from these same decades (Schulkind, Hennis, and Rubin, 1999). Positive affect may enhance long-term recall. Alternatively, personal experiences and events may be more unique during this period (e.g, completing school, getting married) and hence the distinctiveness of the events insulates the memories and helps to preserve them.

In a series of studies, Bahrick examined retention of a second language that respondents had learned in school (Bahrick, 1984; Bahrick and Phelphs, 1987).

The general finding was that memory for these types of well-learned knowledge declined exponentially for 3 to 6 years but then showed very little further change over the next 6 to 25 years. Bahrick introduced the term "permastore," an analogy to permafrost, the suggestion being that the durability of these memories is analogous to the unchanging permanently frozen ground in the Arctic.

What is probably happening when people feel that ancient events are clearer in their mind than recent events is that a particularly sharp memory from the past is being compared with some vaguely encoded more recent event. Recent events may be poorly encoded because of distraction, lack of interest, decreasing abilities, or a number of other reasons. Remote events may be in sharper focus also for a number of reasons. A remote event may have been of such personal significance that it was thought about (rehearsed) many times after the actual event, leading to an exceptionally strong memory called a "flashbulb" memory (Brown and Kulick, 1977). People who were adults in 1963, for example, often remember with great clarity what they were doing at the moment when they heard of John F. Kennedy's assassination.

In summary, memory of an event is greatest immediately following the event and then declines. The amount of forgetting does not occur in a linear fashion. A greater amount of forgetting appears to occur in the first few years after an event. Recognition memory declines less rapidly than recall. Positive affect and the

Reminiscence strengthens memories of earlier events.

uniqueness or personal significance of the event may enhance recall many years later. Even though remote memory holds up well in older adults, it is not superior to the recall of very recent events

MEMORY IN EVERYDAY CONTEXT

In 1978, Ulric Neisser commented that if something is an interesting or socially significant aspect of memory, then psychologists have hardly ever studied it. Two decades later Neisser (1991) marveled at the dramatic change in the direction of memory research—"Nowadays, if X is an ecologically common or socially significant domain of memory, somebody is probably studying it intensively" (p. 34).

One of the most notable shifts in research on memory has been the virtual explosion in studies on everyday memory. This shift has occurred in the general study of memory (Loftus, 2000), as well as in cognitive aging (Hess and Pullen, 1996; Meyer, Talbot, Stubblefield, and Poon, 1998; Park, Morrell, and Shifren, 1999). The definition of everyday memory remains vague. However, several characteristics of everyday memory studies have been identified (Hess and Pullen, 1996). First, everyday memory research focuses on phenomena that are relevant to daily living (e.g., recalling faces and names, remembering phone numbers and grocery lists). Second, the stimuli or test materials have some *a priori* meaning to the subjects and are ecologically representative. Face-name recall studies involve videos of individuals introducing themselves (Crook and West, 1990), television news programs are used to assess text recall (Crook, Youngjohn, and Larrabee, 1990). Third, the research ideally is conducted in naturalistic settings or contexts familiar to the subjects. Fourth, subject characteristics and particularly individual differences among persons is a focus of study. Two types of subject characteristics that have not been part of traditional memory research are a focus of inquiry in everyday memory studies. First, the beliefs of adults about their memory are considered to be an important aspect of everyday memory (see following discussion of metamemory; Hertzog, Dixon, and Hultsch, 1990; Cavanaugh, 1996) Second, there is recognition that noncognitive personality or affective factors contribute to the understanding of memory in everyday contexts (Park and Mayhorn, 1994; Schulkind et al., 1999).

A major focus of everyday memory research, as in traditional memory studies, has been on age differences in performance. Age differences in performance have been found for a number of everyday memory tasks, including face-name recall, recall of the spatial location of everyday objects, and reaction time in a driving simulation task (West, Crook, and Barron, 1992). While age was a salient correlate of everyday memory performance, the amount of variability in performance accounted for was generally less than 10 percent. Of particular note was that age differences were often reduced or eliminated when task conditions were closest to those likely to be encountered in the daily lives of older adults. For example, no performance differences in recalling a 7-digit number was found between old and young adults when the number was presented in chunks analogous to a local phone number; in contrast, age differences did occur in an unchunked condition

(West and Cook, 1990). Older adults had more difficulty with a 10-digit number, simulating a long-distance phone number.

Another type of memory task common in everyday experience is the recall of text (prose) material. For example, we obtain general information from written sources such as newspapers and magazines. Text research has yielded two major findings (Hultsch and Dixon, 1990; Meyer et al., 1998). First, age differences are not as common in text memory performance as they are in recall of lists. Second, the presence or absence of age differences is a function of the contextual factors that mediate the subject's processing of text materials. Age differences have been found to be smaller when the text material is well organized, when the subject has prior knowledge of the topic, and when the subject has above-average verbal ability (Hultsch and Dixon, 1984; Zelinski and Steward,1998). Why are adults with higher verbal abilities often better at remembering text information? Recall our earlier discussion of factors that facilitate encoding of information; high verbal ability may be related to more elaborate encoding of information and also deeper levels of processing. In addition, high-verbal people may engage more frequently in verbal activities, such as reading, that require use of memory.

Several studies indicate that older adults recall the "gist" of a well-organized text passage as well as young adults (Hultsch and Dixon, 1990; Meyer et al., 1998). If, however, the central meaning of the text is difficult to extract from the prose passage and the subject has lower verbal ability, the elderly may have more difficulty identifying a passage's main idea. The elderly's recall of specific details may be more limited than recall of a central idea. This may be because old and young employ qualitatively different processing styles (Blanchard-Fields, 1996; Zacks, Hasher, and Li, 2000). The old may focus on the main idea, whereas the young may be more observant of detail and minor points. Thus, what appear to be inefficient processing behaviors on the part of the elderly may actually reflect adaptive changes. As a result of life experiences or lower levels of mental energy, the old may focus on higher levels of meaning, devoting less attention to details.

Contributions of Everyday Memory Research

Both in the general study of memory (Loftus, 2000) and in cognitive aging, there has been some debate regarding the contributions and merits of taking research on memory outside of the laboratory and the focus on everyday tasks (Hess and Pullen, 1996; Park, 1992). Some have questioned the loss of scientific control when conducting research in naturalistic settings. Others question what new insights everyday memory research has contributed to the study of memory. Examining several questions may help to clarify the contributions and role of everyday memory research.

One issue is whether older adults deal with everyday memory problems in the everyday world in a manner similar to that demonstrated in the laboratory (Blanchard-Fields, 1996). Laboratory studies of memory have focused on the individual's use of internal memory aids (organization, mnemonics, depth of processing).

One of the most common external memory aids is the familiar shopping list.

However, in real-life memory tasks, people often use external memory aids (lists, appointment schedules, timers). In terms of the types of information for which they use memory aids and the types of aids used, younger and older adults are quite similar. Older adults use aids more frequently than younger adults (Lovelace and Twohig, 1990). All age groups use external aids more often than internal aids. Thus, although the internal aids most often studied by psychologists are useful and important, they are not the aids used most often by either young or older adults in their daily lives (Poon and Schaffer, 1982; West, 1989). Internal and external memory aids are probably most useful in different types of situations. Internal memory aids may be most useful, for example, when being introduced to a stranger and trying to remember the person's name; external aids may be particularly useful in prospective memory tasks (tomorrow's schedule) or when recalling a list of grocery items.

Everyday memory research has provided linkages between memory constructs (primacy and recency effects, verbal learning, recognition versus recall) as studied in the laboratory and memory as used in everyday life. Park and colleagues have examined the association of various systems of memory to medication adherence in old age (Park, Morrell, and Shifren, 1999; Park, Hertzog, Kidder, and Morrell, 1997.) Whereas traditional laboratory memory research focuses on one or two constructs, everyday memory activities are complex and usually involve multiple operations studied in the laboratory. For example, name recall in young adults was found to be associated with paired associates, reaction time, and vocabulary. Everyday memory tasks also have been found to be associated with clinical and neuropsychological measures used in screening for dementia. Such findings should aid clinicians in interpreting clinical findings as they apply to the everyday functioning of normal and demented elderly.

Finally, discussion on contributions of everyday memory should not be taken as a criticism of traditional approaches to the study of memory. Both approaches are needed and can contribute to our understanding of memory in old age. As Tulving (1991) said, "There is no reason to believe that there is only one correct way of studying memory. . . the study of memory from different vantage points is not a zero-sum game in which only one side can win" (p. 41).

Metamemory

Metamemory is concerned with people's knowledge and beliefs about their own memory and about memory processes in general (Cavanaugh, 1996; Hertzog, Dixon, and Hultsch, 1990; Gilewski and Zelinski, 1988). Metamemory is a multidimensional phenomenon involving at least four major dimensions: factual knowledge about how memory functions and the use of memory strategies; memory monitoring; memory self-efficacy; and memory-related affect (depression, anxiety).

Two questions regarding metamemory have been studied recently. Are there age differences in various dimensions of metamemory? Are the dimensions of metamemory related to actual memory performance, either on laboratory memory tasks or in real-life memory functioning?

With regard to the first question, the largest age differences are found in the memory self-efficacy dimension (Cavanaugh, 1996; Hertzog, Dixon, and Hultsch, 1990). *Memory self-efficacy* is concerned with the individual's beliefs about their own memory ability (Welch and West, 1995). In addition to self-assessment of memory ability, memory self-efficacy includes beliefs regarding locus of perceived control over memory, perceived change in memory ability, and anxiety about memory (see also Chapter 10, "Motivation"). Older adults, as might be expected, reported greater perceived change in their memory ability than did young adults (Hertzog, Dixon, and Hultsch, 1990). In addition, older adults assessed their memory capacity to be lower than did young adults, and reported more complaints about their memory.

There were, however, few age differences in young, middle-aged, and older adults' knowledge of memory functions and the utility of memory strategies. This finding appears ironic because young adults' memory performance is higher than that of older adults on average, and one might assume that higher performance reflects greater understanding of memory functioning and strategies. These findings are actually related to the results of the Shaw and Craik study (1989) in which young and older adults did not differ in their predictions of memory performance as a function of different encoding strategies.

This leads us to the second question regarding the relationship between metamemory knowledge and beliefs, and actual memory performance (Cavanaugh, 1996; Lachman, Weaver, Bandura, Elliott, and Lewkowicz, 1992; Hertzog and Hultsch, 2000). Somewhat surprisingly, there are only modest relationships between adults' performance on memory tasks and their knowledge of memory functioning and strategy use (Hertzog and Hultsch, 2000). Adults' self-reports of the use of memory strategies in their daily lives is only weakly related to their performance on recall tasks. Furthermore, there are only modest relationships between memory self-efficacy beliefs and memory performance. Of particular note is that memory complaints are only weakly related to actual memory performance. Memory complaints appear to be more a reflection of negative affect, poor health, and depression than actual memory deficits (Hess and Pullen, 1996).

Distortion of Long-term Memory

It is widely believed by psychologists and laypeople alike that information is permanently stored once it has been placed in long-term memory (Tulving, 1972). The information is not lost even when it cannot be retrieved. Recent research, however, suggests that information in long-term memory can be distorted by the introduction of misleading information after the event occurred (Bahrick, 1998; Loftus, 2000). A paradigm for studying memory distortions involves participants first witnessing a complex event, such as a simulated violent crime or automobile accident. Subsequently, half the participants receive new misleading information about the event in a written report. A stop sign, for instance was referred to as a yield sign. The other half do not get any misinformation. Finally all participants attempt to recall the original event. When asked whether they originally saw a stop or a yield sign, participants given the phony information tended to adopt it as their memory; they said they saw a yield sign. People who had not received the phony information had much more accurate memories. In some experiments, the deficits in memory following receipt of misinformation have been dramatic with performance differences as large as 30 percent or 40 percent.

Several variables were found to influence the likelihood that a memory would be distorted by a postevent suggestion. First, distortions in memory are more likely when the interval between the event and the presentation of the misinformation is long rather than short. Second, memories of violent events are more likely to be distorted than memories of nonviolent events. Those who see events that they find stressful have poorer retention, probably because the encoding of information into long-term storage is disrupted. In addition, the duration of more stressful events is likely to be overestimated, particularly by women (Loftus et al., 1987). Third, postevent misinformation is more likely to be accepted if it is presented in a subtle manner. For example, including the misinformation in an auxiliary clause. "Did the intruder with the mustache say anything to the woman?"—subtly suggesting the man had a mustache. That is, misinformation is more likely to be assimilated if it is presented casually and assimilated unintentionally. Fourth, memory distortion is minimized if subjects are warned that the postevent message that they are about to receive might contain misinformation. To be effective, the warning must be given just before the presentation of the misleading information.

In a recent study including subjects between the ages of 5 and 75, accuracy of recall and susceptibility to misinformation was examined. Young children and older adults both recalled less information accurately and gave more misinformation. Several interpretations of these findings are possible. It may be that older adults with poorer memories never encoded the original information and used the misinformation when asked to recall events. Alternatively, it may be that the elderly are more susceptible to misinformation effects (Loftus, Levidow, and Duensing, 1992). Once the participant is given misinformation, it is difficult to induce the witness to retrieve the original memory. Even when warned that a written report following the original event should not be used, subjects given misinformation claimed to have seen the misinformation in the original episode (Lindsay, 1990).

The possibility of distortions of long-term memory is of significance in a number of real-life situations. For example, the credibility of an eyewitness in a court case is based on the assumption of accurate recall of long-term memories (Loftus, 2000). Likewise, national surveys on topics such as voting behavior, health, or crime victimization are based on the assumption that the respondents accurately remember and report events and decisions occurring sometime in the past (Schwarz and Park, 1999). Research on the conditions under which memory distortions occur can be useful in judging the accuracy of recall of long-term events in daily life.

MEMORY COMPLAINTS, DEPRESSION, AND DRUG USE

Although adults may not be aware of incidents of memory distortion and resulting faulty recall in everyday life, they are certainly aware of times when they are unable to retrieve items from memory. Studies show that, when questioned about their memory in everyday living, older adults report more memory failures than younger adults report, and they are more likely to be upset when a memory failure occurs (Bieman-Copland and Ryan, 1998; Erber, Szuchwan, and Prager, 1997; Hess and Pullen, 1996). Older adults also report that they forget names, routines, and objects more often than young adults do. Memory failures are more common in situations outside the older adults' normal routine and when they are required to recall information that they have not used recently. Several studies found that forgetting names is the most commonly reported failure of memory (Lovelace and Twohig, 1990). The extent of memory problems in healthy older persons probably has been exaggerated by the elderly themselves and by the relatives and professionals who associate with them. This is reflected in the finding that complaints about memory problems, which are quite common, do not always correlate with scores on objective tests of memory performance (Hess and Pullen, 1996; Johansson, Allen-Burge and Zarit, 1997).

Significant correlations are found among depression, memory performance, and complaints of poor memory for both normal and demented adults (Bäckman and Forsell, 1994). The effects of depression on memory performance seem to be greater when memory tasks require effortful processing of information, such as in recall; the effects of depression on memory performance appears to be less when less processing is required as in recognition tasks. Memory complaints among the depressed, and perhaps other self-perceptions of cognitive performance, may be influenced by stereotypical age expectations and also by the tendency for depressed persons to underestimate their abilities.

Alcohol and other drugs may also affect cognitive functioning in general and memory in particular (Perlmutter et al., 1987). Drugs such as tranquilizers, antidepressants, sedatives, and hypnotics are widely prescribed for and used by older populations. Although older adults comprise approximately 12 percent of the U.S. population, they consume 35 percent of all prescription drugs (Health Care Financing Administration, 1990). Unfortunately, these drugs can reinforce some of the slowing tendencies observed in older people and aggravate any existing sense of aging and depression. In some cases inappropriate dosages can result in mental confusion and memory loss. These potential side-effects are especially serious in older people because they often have inefficiencies in metabolism. Older people absorb drugs more slowly, distribute them through their bodies differently, and break them down and excrete them from their systems more slowly than the young. As a result, high levels of medication can build up in their systems over a relatively brief period.

There is also potential for drugs to improve cognitive functioning and memory. Pharmacological research is currently focusing on the use of drugs to improve neurotransmitter and neuroendocrine functioning in the elderly. The results of research in this area are in the early stages but are hopeful (Woodruff-Pak, 1997).

LEARNING, MEMORY, AND EDUCATION

Learning and memory have always been important topics in psychology because of their profound implications for human behavior. Unlike other animals, who have a vast stock of instinctive behaviors that guide functioning in their environments, humans learn to function and learn to make adaptations in their behavior. Life, for us, is an educational process, some of it formal (in schools) but most of it informal (through everyday experience). We hear now and then that education for middle-aged and older adults is senseless. The truth is, however, that adults of all ages can profit from education. Moreover, in a rapidly changing society, adults in particular are in great need of formal educational experiences to permit them to maintain responsible citizenship and to prepare them for career changes, retirement, and life at different age stages (Willis and Margrett, in press). Adult education can also be useful in compensating for the deficits that often do occur with aging.

Memory Training Studies

Although the research that we have reviewed in this chapter suggests that nondemented older adults may have more difficulties than young adults in the acquisition or encoding of information and in retrieving stored information, these age differences are generally modest. The clear conclusion is that most adults of all ages, barring illness or neural pathologies, may benefit from formal training and educational opportunities. One area of growing interest is memory training with the elderly (Camp, 1999; Leibowitz and Rudorfer, 1998).

Most research on memory training often focuses on training older adults in encoding strategies. Many older adults do not spontaneously employ encoding strategies, although they can do so when they are instructed in their use (Kotler-Cope and Camp, 1990; Yesavage, Lapp, and Sheikh, 1989). One of the most common memory problems is face-name recall, remembering people's names when you meet them. In a series of studies examining the effectiveness of mediational procedures involving imagery, Yesavage taught subjects to form associations using visual imagery (Sheikh, Hill, and Yesavage, 1986; Yesavage, Lapp, and Sheikh, 1989). Those who learned this imagery mnemonic had significantly improved face-name recall. Learning of the mnemonic was improved when subjects were given pretraining in forming images or in anxiety reduction.

In a series of training studies, Bäckman and colleagues (Stigsdotter and Bäckman, 1989a, 1989b; Stigsdotter and Bäckman, 1993) have compared multifactorial memory training to the effects of unifactorial training. Multifactorial training was based on findings that there are several origins of memory deficits and that a multifactorial approach is needed to remediate these complex deficits. The multifactorial training program involved intervention on three components: encoding operations, attentional functions, and relaxation. A relaxation component was included based on prior research that memory functioning may be associated with anxiety and level of arousal. The unifactorial training focused on encoding operations, but not on attention or relaxation. Results showed that the multifactorial group improved performance following training in free recall of concrete words and maintained this improvement six months later. The unifactorial group showed less improvement following training but also maintained improvement six months later. None of the groups showed training transfer to digit span or the Benton visual retention test. The findings indicate that multifactorial training may result in larger gains immediately after training, compared with unifactorial training, but that both programs lead to maintenance of improvement.

In another series of studies, the relationship between memory training, memory complaints, and depression was examined (Zarit, 1980; Zarit, Cole, and Guider, 1981). You will recall that memory complaints have been found to be associated with depression, but that there is often no relationship between memory complaints and actual memory performance. In these studies, older adults were randomly assigned to one of two groups, a memory-training group that focused on encoding strategies and a current-events discussion group. The current-events group was included to provide group interaction and to allow for the possibility that people's abilities would improve even without actual instruction in procedures likely to enhance memory. Four 90-minute sessions were held with each group. There were several important findings. First, the group that received memory training did better on several memory tasks. No similar improvement was found for the current-events group. Second, the level of subjective complaints about memory, which was the same in both groups prior to training, declined for those who received memory training and for those who discussed current events. Third, because memory complaints decreased in both groups, it could be concluded that the reductions in memory complaints were not related to actual improvements in memory resulting from training.

Training older adults to use external aides for prospective memory tasks has also been found to be effective (Rebok, Rasmusson, and Brandt, 1997; Sczomak, 1989; Sharps and Price-Sharps, 1996). In one study, older adults were asked to call the investigator at a specific time each day for three weeks and report on their sleep patterns in the preceding night. One group was given a printed "reminder" sticker that could be placed in a prominent place to serve as a memory aide. A second group received a nightly "reminder" phone call. A control group received no memory aides or assistance. Over 70 percent of the groups given either a printed sticker or a phone call remembered to phone the investigator at the time requested. Only 50 percent of the control group remembered to call.

The memory performance of healthy elderly people can be improved through memory training, but there are conflicting findings regarding whether older adults continue to use the learned memory strategies after completion of study (Camp, 1999). Training improvement was maintained for six months for subjects who learned to use imagery strategies to recall names and faces (Sheikh et al., 1986) and for subjects trained in encoding strategies (Stigsdotter, Neely, and Bäckman, 1993). However, a follow-up study of subjects trained to use the method of loci indicated that although subjects could recall the strategy, they did not use the strategy in learning new word lists (Anschutz et al., 1987).

The training studies just described used as subjects normal elderly people living in the community. Can similar procedures in memory training be used to improve the functioning of those who suffer from dementia? The evidence so far is mixed (Camp, 1999; Stigsdotter-Neely, 1994; Woods, 1996). In a study of the effectiveness of visual-imagery training among those with senile dementia, it was found that subjects improved somewhat in tests given immediately after the training, but that the improvements were not maintained in later tests (Zarit, Zarit, and Reever, 1982). Research by Yesavage and colleagues (Yesavage, 1982; Yesavage, Westphal and Rush, 1981) indicate that improvement can be accomplished by training only in very mild cases of dementia and has minimal practical impact.

Recently Camp has successfully used a technique known as spaced retrieval with demented patients. The person is given practice in successfully recalling information over successively longer time intervals. The technique seems to require little expenditure of cognitive effort on the part of persons with dementia and has been used to train memory for face-name associations, names of objects, location of objects and even a strategy (remembering to use an external aid, i.e., a calendar, in order to complete tasks and appointments (Camp, Foss, O'Hanlon, and Stevens, 1996; Camp, Bird, and Cherry in press). In addition, caregivers have been trained to implement the intervention in the homes of the elderly. (McKitrick and Camp, 1993).

In summary, it appears that future studies should give greater attention to procedures that encourage older adults to use the training strategies in everyday situations after the study is completed. It seems, however, that participation in a treatment group can lead to a decrease in memory complaints whether or not actual memory performance has improved. Finally, memory training for people with clinical problems requires more intensive procedures and the effects are more modest.

The Older Adult Learner

An ultimate goal of most psychological research is to help people function better in their everyday lives. Much of the memory research that we have been discussing has practical implications for adults' learning and functioning in their daily life (see Figure 11-3 for framework for the factors discussed below).

As you will recall, research shows that the elderly often do not spontaneously use encoding strategies, but that they can use them when instructed or reminded to do so. Whether older adults never acquired these strategies in their youth or whether their use of these strategies declined with age is still being debated, but it is clear that they benefit greatly when these strategies are used. Thus, it may be beneficial for educational programs for the elderly to take into account their need for "instruction in learning" as well as instruction in the substantive material of the course itself (Willis and Margrett, in press).

Use of encoding strategies can be fostered in a number of different ways. The instructor can provide mnemonics to aid the adult in remembering steps in a procedure or in recalling technical terms. Some research indicates that it is particularly effective for students to generate their own mnemonics or imagery mediators, rather than relying on others' mnemonics. It is also useful to discuss with students which types of memory strategies are appropriate for various memory tasks (Camp, 1999; Wilson, 1997). For example, rehearsal may be an effective strategy when the goal is to keep information in short-term memory; it is probably not the most effective strategy for storing information in long-term memory. For encoding information into long-term memory, organizational strategies, mnemonics, and imagery mediators are more useful. Time-monitoring strategies and timing devices have been shown to be particularly effective in prospective memory tasks.

Older people remember best when appropriate encoding strategies are used and when a supportive retrieval context is provided (Craik and Jennings, 1992; Smith, 1996). Thus, concern for retrieval cues, as well as encoding strategies, is needed. The elderly, you will recall, often do just as well as younger people on recognition tasks, but have more trouble when it comes to recall. Older adults are also adept at retaining the gist of a text, but have trouble remembering details. These findings have implications for the selection of procedures for assessing the learning of older adult students. Multiple-choice and true-false items may be more effective procedures because both involve recognition memory. Adults might also do well on essay questions that require discussion of the main points or essence of a topic. Short-answer or fill-in-the-blank questions, on the other hand, would be difficult because they require recall of specific information. In addition, providing sufficient time for recall is important. Research suggests that older adults particularly benefit from additional time during the retrieval phase.

It is especially important that reading materials for older adults be well organized. Research on prose learning and text recall shows that older adults can remember the gist of a well-organized text as well as younger people, but that age differences increase when the key points in text material are difficult to identify (Hultsch and Dixon, 1990, Meyer and Talbot et al., 1998). The use of good examples in instructional materials is also helpful. The meaningfulness of the material facilitates deep processing, thereby increasing retention in long-term memory.

Older learners may be anxious about undertaking new learning, in part because stereotypes suggest that the elderly have poor memories and are poor learners. Training in anxiety reduction accelerated learning of memory strategies (Stigsdotter, Neely, and Bäckman, 1993; Yesavage et al., 1989). Thus, it is especially important that the educator and the learning environment be supportive when disseminating information to the elderly. Finally, older learners may have some loss of vision or hearing, and compensation for this loss can facilitate their processing of information. Use of reading materials with larger print is a well-recognized aid. It is also helpful if instructors do not speak too quickly, not only to make things easier for those who have hearing problems, but to allow for slightly slower rates of information processing. Normal speech presents little problem in most cases. Seating the hearing-impaired near the speaker where they can see lip movements is helpful, too. Repeating the main points several times during a presentation may also be useful. Some research suggests that capacity to pay attention may decline with age (Craik and Jennings, 1992), and repetition ensures that the student may grasp a point even if he or she was inattentive when it was first presented.

Adult Education

A surprisingly large number of adults are involved in formal educational pursuits. Some take classes for credit, but most take noncredit classes given by continuing education or extension programs, industry, community agencies, and other organizations.

Those involved in adult education are more likely to be in young or middle adulthood and to be above average in education level and family income. Those who work outside the home or who are looking for work outside the home are more likely to be involved than those who do not work. College graduates are more than twice as likely to be involved as high school graduates, and high school graduates are more than twice as likely to be involved as high school dropouts. Fewer adults over age 54 participate. The best single predictor of whether an adult is involved in adult education is level of education, so the lower levels of participation among current cohorts of elderly may be partially a function of these cohorts' lower level of education. High school graduation appears to be a significant benchmark in determining who participates in adult education, and while the median level of education for the adult population as a whole is 13 years, roughly the

Like these computer pro-
grammers, workers in
many occupations must
return to school now and
then to update their
knowledge.

equivalent of a high school education, the median level for current elderly cohorts
is below 12 years. The median years of schooling vary considerably by race.

The low participation rate of the elderly may be in part a cohort effect. As the
education level of future elder cohorts rises, their participation in adult education
may also. Only 60 percent of noninstutitionalized elderly have at least a high
school education compared to 85 percent of persons aged 25 to 34. Only one-third
of elderly blacks and a quarter of elderly Hispanics had completed at least high
school. Approximately one- quarter of elderly have only an eighth grade education. The future educational profile of the elderly will be quite different It is estimated that by 2030 approximately 80 percent of elderly will have completed high
school or more (U. S. Bureau of the Census, 1990).

Another important consideration with regard to the adult learner is the proportion of adults and elderly who are foreign-born and speak a foreign language at
home. Of the total elderly population about 9 percent are foreign-born. Hispanics
have been an increasing proportion of the elderly foreign-born. About one of
every 8 elderly (12 percent) speaks a language other than English at home, and
Spanish is the most common language among elderly who speak another language
at home (U. S. Bureau of the Census, 1990). It is estimated that Spanish speakers
will become an increasing share of the future elderly population that speaks a language other than English at home. Adult education typically involves goals that are
different from those of early education. These goals are often closely related to the

types of transitions experienced in young and middle adulthood. Two broad categories account for over half the formal educational coursework undertaken by adults. These are courses related to career, and courses related to personal development, hobbies, and recreation.

Career-related education can take numerous forms. The adult may return to school to upgrade his or her occupational status or to combat the threat of obsolescence. A number of professions (e.g., medicine, teaching, accounting) now require continuing education for continued certification (Willis and Dubin, 1990). A growing number of middle-aged women are returning to school. Women now account for two-thirds of all adult students. In the early 1970s, women cited personal growth as the major reason for returning to school; today, they are returning to upgrade their skills in anticipation of entering or reentering the workforce.

Personal development, hobbies, and recreation are of greatest interest to the adult learner, except for professionals, involved in continuing education. The professional's major objective is job advancement. For the rest of the adult learner population the primary reason for engaging in adult education is to become better informed and for personal enjoyment and enrichment. This broad category can represent a variety of concerns that adults may have. Adults may feel the need to understand the rapid societal and technological changes that are occurring. For example, computer literacy is a popular topic. Likewise, adults may seek information about their own well-being (e.g., nutrition, exercise) or about the aging process being experienced by their elderly parents.

The United States considers itself to be a literate society, and so it comes as a shock to many that there is a need for adult education in basic skills such as reading, spelling, and basic math. The problem of illiteracy is increasing, because a greater degree of literacy is required to cope effectively in today's high-tech job market. While illiteracy is more prevalent among the poor, it is not limited to minorities or immigrants. Many functional illiterates have completed high school.

Unfortunately, few people participate in programs of retirement preparation (Atchley, 1994). Again, level of education is an important predictor of the need for preparation for retirement. The less education that a person has, the more likely he or she is to need retirement preparation. Level of education and occupation go hand in hand, however, and those who have good jobs offering pension plans may be in relatively good shape for retirement. Those who most need preparation for retirement, on the other hand, are at income and occupational levels at which they are least likely to get it. Probably the most important part of any retirement preparation program deals with financial planning, which suggests that the most beneficial programs should begin long before retirement.

One of the most notable and well-received educational programs for the elderly has been Elderhostel. The term "Elderhostel" was borrowed from "youth hostel." In Elderhostel, the college campus is the hostel and the elders are the hostelers. Elderhostel involves a international network of colleges and universities engaged in providing short-term, on-campus, college-level courses to the elderly at a low cost. The elderly hostelers live in college dormitories that are vacant during the summer and take from one- to three-week college courses taught by regular faculty members.

There are no examinations, homework, grades, or credits. The growth of the Elderhostel movement has been spectacular. Begun in 1975 by a small number of colleges in New Hampshire, the program now has extended to all 50 states.

SUMMARY

1. Human memory is commonly viewed as a three-stage process, involving the encoding, storage, and retrieval of information. Human learning can be considered as the acquisition or encoding phase.

2. Information can be encoded into three memory systems. Sensory memory is conceptualized as a brief way station for information from the environment. In order for information to be recalled, it must be processed and transferred to the later systems. Short-term memory is presumed to hold relatively small amounts of information for a slightly longer time than sensory memory. Short-term memory can be divided into primary memory and working memory. Primary memory involves passive holding of a small amount of information and recalling it immediately. Working memory involves simultaneously holding information in mind and using that information to solve a problem or make a decision. Age changes in primary memory are relatively modest, while significant age changes are shown in working memory

3. Encoding is the learning or acquisition phase of memory. Memory research indicates that many older adults do not spontaneously engage in the types of processing that aid encoding. When older adults are given instructions to use certain types of encoding strategies, age differences between young and older adults' memory performance are reduced or eliminated.

4. Recall is the ability to retrieve a particular piece of information. Recognition is the ability to identify a given piece of information. Older people have fewer difficulties with recognition than with recall.

5. One of the most notable shifts in research on memory has been the increase in studies on everyday memory. Everyday memory research focuses on phenomena that are relevant to daily living. The stimuli or test materials have some *a priori* meaning to the subjects and are ecologically representative. Research ideally is conducted in naturalistic settings or contexts familiar to the subjects.

6. Metamemory is concerned with people's knowledge and beliefs about their own memory. Metamemory involves at least four major dimensions: factual knowledge about how memory functions and the use of memory strategies; memory monitoring; memory self-efficacy; and memory-related affect (depression, anxiety). Older adults report lower efficacy and more memory complaints.

7. The memory performance of healthy older people can be improved through memory training. There have been recent successful memory interventions with demented elders.

SUGGESTED READINGS

Bäckman, L. (2001). Learning and memory. In J. E. Birren and K. W. Schaie (Eds.), *Handbook of the psychology of aging,* (5th ed.) San Diego, CA: Academic. Comprehensive review of literature on memory and aging.

Camp, C. (1999). Memory interventions for normal and pathological older adults. In R. Schulz, G. Maddox, and M. P. Lawton (Eds), *Annual Review of Gerontology and Geriatrics: Interventions research with older adults.* Vol. 18, (pp. 155–189). New York: Springer. Excellent overview of various approaches to memory interventions for both normal and demented elderly, and comprehensive review of the literature.

Hertzog, C., Dixon, R. A. and Hultsch, D. F. (1990). Metamemory in adulthood: Differentiating knowledge, belief, and behavior. In T. M. Hess (Ed.), *Aging and cognition: Knowledge organization and utilization.* Amsterdam, Holland: Elsevier. Review of the literature on metamemory. Examines interrelationship among various dimensions of metamemory. Considers association between metamemory and memory performance.

Hess, T. M. and Pullen, S. M. (1996). Memory in context. In F. Blanchard-Fields and T. M. Hess (Eds.), *Perspectives on cognitive change in adulthood and aging.* (pp.387–428).New York: McGraw-Hill. Overview of issues and literature related to what is known as everyday memory.

Hultsch, D. F., Hertzog, C., Dixon, R. A., and Small, B. J. (1998). Chapters 3 and 11. *Memory change in the aged.* Cambridge: Cambridge University Press. Extensive report on findings of Victoria Longitudinal Study of memory.

Zacks, R. T., Hasher, L., and Li, K. Z. H. (2000). Human memory. In F.I.M. Craik and T. A. Salthouse (Eds.), *Handbook of aging and cognition.* Overview of research on memory and aging.

12

Intellectual Development

The Display of Competence

Mental abilities have long been esteemed in Western culture as the basis for learning, problem solving, and adjustment. Thus, intelligence quite understandably was one of the major concerns of the earliest psychologists. Great efforts were made to define intelligence, to measure it, and even to try increase it. The study of intelligence has had a long and often stormy history. Indeed, the controversies are no less stormy today, as perhaps we should expect when dealing with an ability so highly valued.

Some of the controversy has to do with the role of intelligence in everyday activities. Are intelligent people better in school than less intelligent people? Are they more successful in life? Can they repair a car more efficiently? Can they run a business more effectively? What other factors besides intelligence are involved in competence? What is the relationship between "academic" and "practical" intelligence? Is competence in the elderly the same as competence in young adults? These questions, which will help us distinguish intelligence from other psychological processes, are the focus of the first section of this chapter.

In the following sections, we discuss theories of intelligence and research on adult intellectual development. The questions that we seek to answer are fairly simple, such as "Does intelligence increase or decline with age?" The answers, however, are more complicated; they vary with age, the specific intellectual function we are talking about, and even the year in which the individual was born. This last influence, which comprises a number of "generational" factors, is analyzed in some detail. And finally we look at the last few years of life, when illness and social isolation frequently have an increasingly adverse effect on intellectual performance. We encounter here a recurring problem in gerontology, that is, how to disentangle the effects of disease from those of aging *per se.*

ADULT STAGES OF INTELLECTUAL DEVELOPMENT

What is the nature of intelligence in adults? How is it similar to the intelligence of young persons and how does it change? If we are going to construct IQ tests that are fair to older people, we must know more about wisdom; we need to know in what sense people might increase their competence as they grow older.

The famous Swiss psychologist Jean Piaget described the ways in which children's intelligence increases as they grow older (Flavell, 1963). Infants are said to be at a relatively primitive, sensory-motor stage of intellectual development. They learn simple but basic ways of perceiving and reacting to the world. With the onset of speech, children enter a stage in which they grow primarily in the "conceptual-symbolic rather than purely sensory-motor arena" (Flavell, 1963, p. 121). This stage, called *preoperational,* is succeeded around the age of 6 by the stage of *concrete operations.* In Piaget's theory, operations are the mental routines that transform information in some way, for example, adding two numbers to get a third or categorizing, as in placing all red objects together. The stage of *formal operations* is entered around the age of 12 and is defined by the ability to use mental operations on abstract material. For example, an adolescent can solve a problem such as "If a suitcase can eat four rocks in one day, how many can it eat in two days?" Younger children cannot imagine a suitcase that eats rocks, so they will refuse to solve the problem; they cannot disregard the content of the problems (its concrete aspects)

Does the ability to learn decline with age?

and reason in a purely hypothetical way (using the form, or formal aspects, of the problem).

Intellectual development, of course, is not complete at the age of 12 when the average child enters the stage of formal operations, but Piaget does not provide us with much detail on later development. Although we can assume that there are advances in the use of formal operations, as people progress from "rock-eating suitcases" to elegant mathematical theories of the physical universe, no new Piagetian stages were specified for adulthood (Flavell, 1970; Piaget, 1972). Psychologists who focus on adult development find this child-centered approach restrictive and wish to expand it so as to delineate those changes in the quality of intellectual function that they observe in adult subjects. As Erik Erikson and Daniel Levinson expanded the psychoanalytic stages of ego development to the adult years, these psychologists have done the same for Piaget's stages of intellectual development (see Commons, Sinnott, Richards, and Armon, 1989; Sinnott 1984, 1993, 1996). We will return to these efforts in the section on Piagetian intelligence later in the chapter.

A Stage Model of Adult Cognitive Development

K. Warner Schaie (1977–1978; Schaie and Willis, 2000a) has used findings from research on adult intellectual development to formulate six adult stages (Figure 12-1). He begins with the observation that Piaget's childhood stages describe increasing efficiency in the *acquisition* of new information. It is doubtful that adults progress beyond the powerful methods of science (formal operations) in their quest for knowledge. Therefore, if one is to propose adult stages, they should

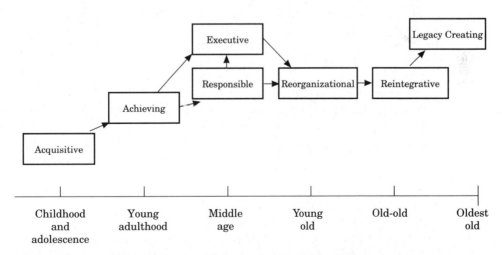

Figure 12-1   Schaie's Stages of Adult Cognitive Development. *Source:* Schaie, K.W., and Willis, S. L. (2000a). A stage theory model of adult cognitive development revisited. In R. Rubinstein, M. Moss, and M. Kleban (Eds.), *The many dimensions of aging: Essays in honor of M. Powell Lawton,* (pp. 175–193). New York: Springer Publishing Co.

not be further stages of acquisition; instead they should reflect different uses of intellect.

In young adulthood, for example, people typically switch their focus from the acquisition to the application of knowledge, as they use what they know to pursue careers and develop their families. This is called the *achieving* stage. It represents most prominently the application of intelligence in situations that have profound consequences for achieving long-term goals. These situations are not the hypothetical ones posed on IQ tests or encountered in classroom studies, nor are they the problems of childhood, whose solutions are closely monitored by parents and society. Instead, they are problems that the adult must solve for him- or herself, and the solutions must be integrated into a life plan that extends far into the future. The kind of intelligence exhibited in such situations is similar to that manifested in scholastic tasks, except that it requires more careful attention to the possible consequences of the problem-solving process. Attending to the context of problem solving as well as to the problem to be solved may be thought of as being a quality-control process like that used in industry when the consequences of a mistake are severe.

Young adults who have mastered the cognitive skills required for monitoring their own behavior and, as a consequence, have attained a certain degree of personal independence will next move into a stage that requires the application of cognitive skills in situations involving social responsibility. Typically, the *responsible* stage occurs when a family is established and the needs of spouse and offspring must be met. Similar extensions of adult cognitive skills are required as responsibilities for others are acquired on the job and in the community (Hagestad and Neugarten, 1985).

Some individuals' responsibilities become exceedingly complex. Such individuals—presidents of business firms, deans of academic institutions, officials of churches, and a number of other positions—need to understand the structure and the dynamic forces of organizations. They must monitor organizational activities not only on a temporal dimension (past, present, and future), but also up and down the hierarchy that defines the organization. They need to know not only the future plans of the organization, but also whether policy decisions are being adequately translated into action at lower levels of responsibility. Attainment of the *executive* stage, as a variation on the responsibility stage, depends on exposure to opportunities that allow the development and practice of the relevant skills (Avolio, 1991; Avolio and Waldman, 1990; Smith, Staudinger, and Baltes, 1994).

In the later years of life, beyond the age of 60 or 65, the need to acquire knowledge declines even more and executive monitoring is less important because frequently the individual has retired from the position that required such an application of intelligence. What, then, is the nature of competence in an elderly adult? As Schaie (1977–1978) puts it, there is a transition from the childhood question "What should I know?" through the adult question "How should I use what I know?" to the question of later life "Why should I know?" This stage, *reintegration,* corresponds in its position in the life course to Erikson's stage of ego integrity. The information that elderly people acquire and the knowledge they apply is, to a

An executive must monitor the past, present, and future and also the activities up and down the hierarchy that define the organization.

greater extent than earlier in life, a function of their interests, attitudes, and values. It requires, in fact, the reintegration of all of these. The elderly are less likely to "waste time" on tasks that are meaningless to them. They are unlikely to expend much effort to solve a problem unless that problem is one that they face frequently in their lives (see also Berg, Klaczynski, Calderone, and Strough,1994; Berg and Klaczynski, 1996). This stage also frequently includes a selective reduction of interpersonal networks in the interest of reintegrating one's concern in a more self-directed and supportive manner (cf. Carstensen, 1993; Fredrickson and Carstensen, 1990). Such efforts are likely to involve a reduction in information-seeking activities while increasing the importance of emotional regulation involved (Carstensen, Gross, and Fung, 1997).

The original stages were formulated some twenty years ago. Since that time we have learned a lot about the differentiation of our older population into distinct life stages. In the research literature distinctions are now commonly made between the young-old, the old-old and the oldest-old (or very-old; see Chapter 1). This differentiation is informed by the fact that today's young old are distinguished from the middle-aged primarily by the fact that the vast majority in this life period is no longer engaged in the world of work. A major effort is now required to reorganize one's life in order to replace the earlier engagement with family-raising and job responsibilities with meaningful pursuits for the last part of life.

In addition, efforts must be directed towards planning how one's resources will last for the remaining 15 to 30 years of post-retirement life that are now characteristic for most individuals in industrialized societies. These efforts include active planning for that time when dependence upon others may be required to maintain a high quality of life in the face of increasing frailty. Such efforts may involve changes in one's housing arrangements, or even one's place of residence, as well as making certain of the eventual availability of both familial and extra-familial support systems. The activities involved in this context include making or changing one's will, drawing up advanced medical directives and durable powers of attorney, as well as creating trusts or other financial arrangements that will protect resources for use during the final years of life or for the needs of other family members.

Although some of these activities involve the same cognitive characteristics of the responsible stage, we think that the objectives involved are generally far more centered to current and future needs of the individual rather than the needs of their family or of an organizational entity. Efforts must now be initiated to reorganize one's time and resources to substitute a meaningful environment, often found in leisure activities, volunteerism, and involvement with a larger kinship network. Eventually, however, these are activities are also engaged in with the finitude of life in clear view, for the purpose of maximizing the quality of life during the final years and often with the objective of not becoming a burden for the next generation. The unique objective of these demands upon the individual represent an almost universal process occurring at least in the industrialized societies, and designation of a separate *reorganizational* stage is therefore warranted.

The skills required for the reorganizational stage require the maintenance of high levels of cognitive competence which is increasingly exercised within the parsimonious principles of selection, optimization and compensation (cf. Baltes, M. M., and Carstensen, 1996; Baltes, P. B.,1997; Baltes P. B. and Baltes, M. M., 1990; Baltes, P. B., Staudinger, and Lindenberger, 1999; Dittman-Kohli and Baltes, 1990; Freund and Baltes, 1998). In addition, maintenance of flexible cognitive styles are needed to be able to restructure the context and content of life after retirement, to relinquish control of resources to others and to accept the partial surrender of one's independence (Schaie, 1984b; 1996b).

More and more older persons reach advanced old age in relative comfort and often with a clear mind albeit a frail body. Once the reintegrative efforts described above have been successfully completed, and perhaps temporally overlapping with them, there is yet one other stage that is frequently observed. This last stage is concerned with cognitive activities by many of the very old that occur in anticipation of the end of their life. We call this a *legacy-leaving* stage which is part of the cognitive development of many, if not all, older persons. This stage often begins by the self- or therapist-induced effort to conduct a life review (Butler, Lewis, and Sunderland, 1991; also see Chapter 14). For the highly literate and those successful in public or professional life this will often include writing or revising an autobiography (Birren, Kenyon, Ruth, Schroots, and Swensson, 1995).

There are also other more mundane legacies to be left. Women, in particular, often wish to put their remaining effects in order, and often distribute many of their prized possessions to friends and relatives, or create elaborate instructions for distributing them. It is not uncommon for many very old people to make a renewed effort at providing an oral history or to explain family pictures and heirloom to the next generation. Last but not least, directions may be given for funeral arrangements, occasionally including donation of one's body for scientific research, and there may be a final revision of one's will.

Athough an approximate time line for this stage model is provided in Figure 12-1, it should be stressed that the precise chronological age at which these stages occur may be quite variable in different societies as well as for individuals at different levels of intellectual competence and personal engagement. What is important is the sequential process of these developmental stages.

Research on adult competencies requires adaptive approaches to the assessment of intelligence. More information is needed, for example, about the situations in adult life in which intelligence is expressed. In one study, the investigators simply interviewed older individuals whom they encountered in parks, senior citizen centers, and the like (Scheidt and Schaie, 1978). These persons were asked to identify situations occurring in their life in which they had to apply their intelligence. "Look for a new place to live" was one common response; "figure out how to pay a debt" was another. Over 300 such situations were collected. These situations could be classifed into four major dimensions: social–nonsocial, active–passive, common–uncommon, and supportive–depriving. Examples of specific situations that contain each of the 16 possible combinations of attributes are given in Table 12-1.

The dimensions identified in the Scheidt and Schaie study were then used to study age differences in perceived competence in a group of 234 persons, ranging in age from the thirties to the eighties (Schaie, Gonda, and Quayhagen, 1981; Willis and Schaie, 1986a). The study revealed that older people described themselves as being more competent in situations of common occurrence and those that involved social interactions. Perceived competence declined for situations that involved an active response or had depriving consequences. As a corollary, we may infer that older people feel less competent in nonsocial and uncommon situations and more competent in those that have supportive attributes.

ASSESSMENT OF INTELLECTUAL FUNCTIONS

As we mentioned in the section on personality assessment (Chapter 9), psychological tests were originally developed to identify intelligent people. Francis Galton (a half-cousin of Charles Darwin) believed that human intelligence is mostly inherited and, as a result, he urged his country (England) to begin a program of selective breeding. By allowing the most intelligent people to have the most babies, the English population would get smarter and smarter, claimed Galton; it would evolve to even greater heights in Darwin's phylogenetic tree.

A Test of Intelligence

But how could the most intelligent people be identified? A test of intelligence would have to be created. Galton took on the job and in 1883 published the first intelligence test (Galton, 1883). Influenced by British philosophers who considered intelligence to be based on the ability to process sensory information, Galton devised a series of tasks designed to measure how well a person could see, hear, smell, taste, and feel. For example, in one task, the person was asked to lift two weights and say which was the heavier.

Galton's "mental test" (as he called it) was not very successful; it showed only trivial correlations with measures of intellectual competence in the real world, such as scholastic performance (Wissler, 1901). Recent investigators, however,

TABLE 12-1   Attributes and Illustrative Content of 16 Classes of Situations

Situational Attributes	Social	Nonsocial
High-activity		
Common-supportive	Arguing with person about important point	Gardening in yard, planting seeds, weeding
	Being visited by son or daughter and their children	Doing weekly shopping in crowded supermarket
Common-depriving	Pressured by salesperson to buy merchandise	Climbing several steps to building entrance
	Quarreling with relative	Cleaning apartment or household
Uncommon-supportive	Having sexual intercourse	Preparing large meal for friends
	Traveling around city looking for new residence	Exercising for a few moments each day
Uncommon-depriving	Waiting at end of long line for tickets to entertainment	Moving into new and unfamiliar residence
	Returning faulty or defective merchandise to store	Driving auto during rush hour traffic
Low-activity		
Common-supportive	Seeking aid or advice from friend or family member	Browsing through family photo album
	Offering money to son or daughter who needs it	Making plans for future
Common-depriving	Hearing from friend that he or she is considering suicide	Eating meal alone in own home
	Hearing that close friend has recently died	Worrying about ability to pay a debt
Uncommon-supportive	Entering darkened night-club to dine	Recording day's events in diary
	Attending art exhibit	Wading in waist-high water in ocean
Uncommon-depriving	Opening door to stranger selling product or soliciting opinion	Slipping on slick part of floor and falling
	While talking with someone, you feel you have unintentionally hurt his or her feelings	Discovering you locked keys in car while shopping

Source: Scheidt, R. J., and Schaie, K. W. (1978). A situational taxonomy for the elderly: Generating situational criteria. *Journal of Gerontology, 33,* 848–857. Reproduced by permission.

have revisited the relation between sensory functions and intelligence showing that Galton's intuitive choice of measures was not as off-the-wall as some contemporaries thought (cf. Li., Jordanova, and Lindenberger, 1999).

Almost 20 years later, a French psychologist by the name of Alfred Binet tried again to construct a test of intelligence. Binet did not intend to better the French genetic stock. He had been given a much more practical problem to solve by the French Ministry of Public Instruction. They needed a test to distinguish students of low ability (mentally retarded) from those of adequate ability but low motivation.

Binet held a more traditional view of intelligence than Galton, believing, for example, that playing chess was a better indicator of it than smelling vinegar. He decided to assess "reasoning, judgment, and imagination" by a series of cognitive problems rather than sensory tasks. Instead of lifting weights, for example, the child was asked to tell the difference between "yesterday" and "tomorrow." Because Binet's miniature tasks were quite similar to those that children faced in school, scores on his test were highly correlated with scholastic performance. First published in 1905, Binet's test (Binet and Simon, 1905) was quickly translated into other languages, including English. In the United States, his test was translated and revised by Stanford psychologist Lewis Terman in 1916 and became known as the widely used Stanford-Binet Intelligence Scale.

Terman's first revision of the Stanford-Binet introduced the concept of the intelligence quotient, or IQ. Binet had arranged his test in age scales, each consisting of 4 to 8 items, that children of a certain age should be able to pass. A 6-year-old child who passed all the items for 7-year-olds (but no more) was said to have a "mental age" of 7, even though his or her chronological age was 6. Terman divided the mental age obtained from the test by the chronological age to get the child's IQ. In our example the child with a mental age of 7 and a chronological age of 6 has an IQ of 7/6 = 1.17, multiplied by 100 to clear the decimal, or 117. An average IQ by these standards is obviously 100, and 117 indicates a somewhat brighter than average youngster.

The background information on intelligence testing is relevant for our discussion of adult intelligence for two reasons. The first is to show that the testing movement in psychology began in practical circumstances—there was a need to predict potential scholastic success. The first widely used intelligence test (Binet's), on which all later tests are at least partially modeled, was designed to forecast the school performance of young children and not the everyday performance of old people. The second is to show that IQ tests are age graded, that is, the average score for each age level is given the score of 100. A question such as "Who has the higher IQ, an average 10-year-old or an average 70-year-old?" is meaningless. They both have IQs of 100, the average for any age group. However, as we will see other kinds of comparisons can be made that inform us as to how intelligence changes from childhood into advanced old age.

The Nature of Intelligence

From the very beginning, there has been a great deal of debate about the nature of intelligence and whether there may be different kinds of intelligence. Is intelligence a single, general ability or are there several different intellectual abilities? Binet favored the idea of a "general ability" (sometimes called the "g" factor), but later researchers have favored the notion of several factors in intelligence.

Some intelligence tests have a number of subtests covering different content. The Wechsler Adult Intelligence Scale (WAIS) is the test most frequently used by clinical psychologists for the individual assessment of adult intelligence. It has 11 subtests (Table 12-2). Six of these subtests make up the verbal scale, so named because the tests rely heavily on language. Examples are the vocabulary subtest, in

TABLE 12-2   Subtests of the Wechsler Adult Intelligence Scale

Verbal Scale

1. *Information:* 29 questions covering a wide variety of information that adults have presumably had an opportunity to acquire in our culture. An effort was made to avoid specialized or academic knowledge.
2. *Comprehensive:* 14 items, in each of which the examinee explains what should be done under certain circumstances, why certain practices are followed, the meaning of proverbs, etc. Designed to measure practical judgment and common sense.
3. *Arithmetic:* 14 problems similar to those encountered in elementary school arithmetic. Each problem is orally presented and is to be solved without the use of paper and pencil.
4. *Similarities:*   13 items requiring the subject to say in what way two things are alike.
5. *Digit span:* Orally presented lists of 3 to 9 digits to be orally reproduced. In the second part, the examinee must reproduce lists of 2 to 8 digits backwards.
6. *Vocabulary:* 40 words of increasing difficulty presented both orally and visually. The examinee is asked what each word means.

Performance Scale

7. *Digit symbol:* A version of the familiar code-substitution test that has often been included in nonlanguage intelligence scales. The key contains 9 symbols paired with the 9 digits. With this key before him, the examinee has 1 and 1/2 minutes to fill in as many symbols as he or she can under the numbers on the answer sheet.
8. *Picture completion:* 21 cards, each containing a picture from which some part is missing. Examinee must tell what is missing from each picture.
9. *Block design:* A set of cards containing designs in red and white and a set of identical 1-inch blocks whose sides are painted red, white, and red-and-white. The examinee is shown one design at a time, which he or she must reproduce by choosing and assembling the proper blocks.
10. *Picture arrangement:* Each item consists of a set of cards containing pictures to be rearranged in the proper sequence so as to tell a story.
11. *Object assembly:* In each of the four parts of this subtest, cutouts are to be assembled to make a flat picture of a familiar object.

Source: Anastasi, A. (1988). *Psychological testing* (6th ed.). New York: Macmillan. Reprinted with permission.

which the subject is asked the meanings of various words, and the comprehension subtest, in which the subject is asked to explain items such as proverbs (designed to measure practical judgment and common sense). Five of the subtests make up the performance scale, so named because the subject can solve the problems without recourse to language. In the block design subtest, for example, the subject tries to reproduce a design with colored blocks. Performance tests were first used in World War I to test illiterate draftees and those whose native language is not English. As we shall see, old people generally do not do as well on the performance subtests.

The fact that there are slightly different subtests on an intelligence test is of course no guarantee that these subtests actually measure different intellectual abilities; they may simply be different ways of measuring a single ability: "general intelligence." Further exploration has therefore taken the form of factor analysis, a statistical procedure that identifies the number of basic dimensions or factors in a set of data.

For example, if we knew nothing but the distances between a dozen pairs of cities, applying factor analysis would provide us with two dimensions. We could call these dimensions "north–south" and "east–west;" dimensions that would enable us to describe the location of any of the cities. In a similar fashion, we can use degrees of relatedness (correlations) between each pair of a set of intellectual tasks (such as the subtests of the WAIS), and factor analysis will tell us if intelligence is one dimensional or whether it is many faceted.

The answer to this question is both. In a factor analysis of the WAIS subtests, for example, the major dimension was found to be that of general intelligence, a large factor that accounted for about half of the information contained in the test (Cohen, 1957). Three much weaker factors were also identified and labeled "verbal comprehension," "perceptual organization," and "memory." The labels are not important for our purposes. What the analysis means is that the WAIS can be described fairly well with a single factor. Three other factors appear to be important for some purposes. For example, an individual high in perceptual-organizational abilities might do better on the block design subtest than we would expect from his or her general intelligence alone. One finding of interest in this study is that the memory factor, a relatively weak factor among young subjects, became a major factor among subjects over the age of 60. This means that specific memory abilities vary more among older people and affect scores on more of the subtests.

With the advent of major survey studies of virtually every issue that might be public policy relevant, there has been an attempt to include short tests of intelligence in major population surveys (Herzog and Rodgers, 1999). These simple scales do not have the reliability and validity of the standard intelligence tests used in laboratory work. They are particularly problematic when used with older persons who may tend to respond "don't know" more frequently and may have difficulty in properly understanding questions (Knäuper, Belli, Hill, and Herzog, 1997). We will therefore limit our discussion to data obtained from direct administration of individual or group tests.

Intelligence as Multiple Abilities

If one's goal is to map the broad scope of intelligence and not simply tthat of the WAIS, many different intellectual tasks must be administered to a large number of people. Factor analysis of a wide variety of intellectual tasks has regularly turned up between 6 and 12 primary mental abilities, the most prominent of which are listed in Table 12-3. These abilities have sometimes been described as the "building blocks" or basic elements of intelligence (Thurstone and Thurstone, 1941). The "purest" tests of these factors are sometimes administered as tests of the "primary mental abilities." The most recent adult version of these tests is called the Schaie-Thurstone Adult Mental Abilities Test (STAMAT; Schaie, 1985, 1996b).

But what is the nature of the relationship between such elementary building blocks of intelligence and the tasks that people face in real life? To find out, performance on the different primary mental abilities was supplemented in a sample of over a 1,000 persons by administering real-life tasks such as interpreting medicine bottle labels, reading street maps, filling out forms, and comprehending newspaper and yellow page advertisements (Educational Testing Service, 1977). The researchers found a substantial correlation between abilities and performance on tasks; correlations varied, however, depending on the task. Furthermore, it was found that composite performance on the real-life tasks could be predicted by several abilities, particularly reasoning, but also by verbal knowledge to a lesser extent (Schaie, 1996b; Schaie and Willis, 1986).

Another study examined the relationship of the primary abilities to the situational dimensions involved in competent behavior described earlier in this chapter (Willis and Schaie, 1986a). It was found that perceived competence in social situations was predicted by spatial ability, competence in active situations was predicted by both spatial ability and inductive reasoning, and competence in passive situations was predicted by verbal ability. This also suggests a strong relationship between "building blocks" of intelligence and perceived real-life competence.

We have come, then, from the view of intelligence as primarily a single trait to the view of intelligence as a number distinct abilities. One group of psycholo-

---

TABLE 12-3   Primary Mental Abilities Discovered Through Studies Using Factor Analysis

V   *Verbal comprehension:* The principal factor in such tests as reading comprehension, verbal analogies, disarranged sentences, verbal reasoning, and proverb matching. It is most adequately measured by vocabulary tests.

W   *Word fluency:* Found in such tests as anagrams, rhyming, or naming words in a given category (e.g., boys' names, words beginning with the letter T).

N   *Number:* Most closely identified with speed and accuracy of simple arithmetic computation.

S   *Space (or spatial orientation):* May represent two distinct factors, one covering perception of fixed spatial or geometric relations, the other manipulatory visualizations, in which changed positions or transformations must be visualized.

M   *Associative memory:* Found principally in tests demanding rote memory for paired associates. There is some evidence to suggest that this factor may reflect the extent to which memory crutches are utilized. The evidence is against the presence of a broader factor through all memory tests. Other restricted memory factors, such as memory for temporal sequences and for spatial position, have been suggested by some investigations.

P   *Perceptual speed:* Quick and accurate grasping of visual details, similarities, and differences.

I (or R)   *Induction (or general reasoning):* Early researchers proposed an inductive and deductive factor. The latter was best measured by tests of syllogistic reasoning and the former by tests requiring the subject to find a rule, as in a number series completion test. Evidence for the deductive factor, however, was much weaker than for the inductive. Moreover, other investigators suggested a general reasoning factor, best mesaured by arithmetic reasoning tests.

Source: Anastasi, A. (1988). *Psychological testing* (6th ed.). New York: Macmillan. Reprinted by permission.

gists has gone even further, combining logical and statistical analyses to come up with as many as 120 factors in intelligence (Guilford, 1967; Guilford and Hoepfner, 1971). As we shall see, the distinctions of several different abilities are vital for the study of intellectual development in adults (for a recent comprehensive survey of the factor analytic literature on human abilities, see Carroll, 1993). Nevertheless, it should be noted that there have also been recent cross-sectional studies that have revived interest in the concept of a single central-nervous system driven aging process (e.g. Salthouse, 1998).

A comprehensive model of intelligence has been proposed that explains the basic components of intelligence, the processes by which they are established and maintained, and their relationship to everyday competence. This theory, developed by Sternberg (1984; Berg and Sternberg, 1985), contains three subtheories: one that relates intelligence to the individual's inner world, one that relates intelligence to the outer world, and a third that relates intelligence to both the internal and external facets.

The subtheory concerning the inner world specifies the mechanisms responsible for the learning, planning, execution, and evaluation of intellectual behavior, including the manner in which new information is acquired and selectively compared to old information. The subtheory concerning the outer world follows from Sternberg's suggestion that the normal course of intelligent functioning in the everyday world involves adaptation to the environment. If an environment fails to fit a person's values, skills, or concerns, the person may attempt to alter the environment to meet his or her needs or to find a new environment that meets them better. The second subtheory considers intelligent behavior in terms of the selection of real-world environments relevant to a person's life and how the person shapes and adapts to these environments.

The third subtheory, which relates the inner and outer world to each other, states that intelligent behaviors involve adaptation to novelty, automatization of information processing activities (i.e., performing information processing without conscious awareness of it) or both. A person who automatizes processing efficiently can allocate resources to cope with novel situations; conversely, efficient adaptation to novelty will allow automatization to occur earlier in one's experience of new tasks and situations.

The notion of allocation of intellectual resources is particularly relevant to the study of intellectual aging. As we shall see, recent data and thinking suggest that the response of older persons to tests is far more selective than that of youngsters, and such allocation is often directed to optimize functions that meet the individual's needs and goals (Baltes, 1997; Baltes and Baltes, 1990; Raykov, 1989; Staudinger, Marsiske, and Baltes, 1995). Baltes (1993) further distinguishes between the mechanics (or basic processes) of intelligences, the efficiency of which decreases with increasing age, as contrasted to the pragmatics (or substantive content) of intelligence, which in many circumstances can increase until very old age.

The history of studies of adult intelligence, according to Woodruff-Pak (1989), has also had discernable secular trends in relative emphases on different aspects of adult intelligence that cut across theoretical positions. She identifies four stages: In the first, lasting until the mid-1950s, concerns were predominantly with identifying steep and apparently inevitable age-related decline. The second stage, in the late 1950s to mid-1960s, involved the discovery that there was stability as well as decline. External social and experiential effects influencing cohort differences in ability levels identified during this period led to a third stage, beginning with the mid-1970s, in which the field was dominated by attempts to alter experience and manipulate age differences. In the latest stage, the impact of successful demonstrations of the modifiability of intellectual performance has led investigators to expand definitions of intelligence and explore new methods of measurement.

Relevance of Test Instruments to Stages of Intellectual Development

The simple tasks in the traditional IQ tests are well-suited to measure progress in the performance of many basic skills through the stages of knowledge acquisition described by Piaget (Humphreys and Parsons, 1979). But they are decidedly less adequate for the assessment of adult competence. Even a test that was constructed explicitly for adults, the WAIS, is deficient in several respects. First, the test was designed with the intent of measuring cognitive dysfunctions in clinically suspect individuals, and second, it was originally normed on young adult samples, those who in our conceptual scheme would be classified as being in the achieving stage.

What we need, therefore, is to construct adult tests of intelligence relevant to competence at different points in the life span, just as the traditional test is relevant to the competencies of children in school settings. In the achieving stage, for example, we should expect an increase in the ability to solve relevant problems, an ability that should remain high throughout the adult years. In the executive stage, when integration of information from several sources becomes more important, we should expect gains in tasks involving pattern recognition, inductive thinking, and complex problem solving—fundamental strategies of information processing that might be assessed in ways suggested by cognitive psychologists (e.g., Pellegrino and Glaser, 1979; Sternberg and Berg, 1987). In the reintegrative stage, we can expect relevancy to become even more important and, thus, a sharp decrease in scores on tests that assess simple information-processing capabilities. Indeed studying how older persons define their problems is essential in understanding their capability for solving problems (Berg, Strough, Calderone, Sansome, and Weir, 1998).

Practical Intelligence

Some would argue that intelligence in adults should be studied by asking well-functioning people how they go about solving their everyday problems (Berg, 1990; Berg and Sternberg, 1985, 1992). This is what is known as a "naive" theory of intelligence; that is, it is not derived from objective analyses of experts, but rather from the collective perceptions of laypersons. Perhaps it is indeed the conceptions of adults about their own competence that ought to be the basis for defining intelligence. But there is the distinct danger that in this process we would confuse intelligence with socially desirable behavior. Moreover, the attributes of intelligence obtained in this manner may be characteristic only of the specific group of persons interviewed or may be governed by time-specific and place-specific conceptions. We would be remiss, then, if we were to discard the objective knowledge of mental functioning that is now in hand and is directly applicable to adult intelligence (Schaie and Willis, 1999). Instead, we may wish to consider how the basic intellectual processes that are important at all life stages relate to everyday tasks (also see Diehl, 1998; Park and Gutchess, 1999).

There have been a number of efforts to develop objective measures of people's abilities to engage in effective problem solving and perform on tasks required for daily living (see Denney, 1982; Marsiske and Willis, 1995; Willis, 1996, 1997; Willis and Schaie, 1993, 1994a). For example, the Educational Testing Service (1975) developed a test to assess whether high school graduates had acquired the necessary information and skills to handle everyday problems. This test includes tasks such as interpreting bus schedules, tax forms, labels on medicine bottles, advertisements in the yellow pages, and understanding instructions for the use of appliances, and the meaning of newspaper editorials. This test has been given to large samples of adults ranging in age from the twenties to the eighties (Schaie, 1996b; Willis and Schaie, 1986a). The test correlates with a number of the primary mental abilities; in fact, most of the individual dif-fer-ences on the test can be predicted from a knowledge of scores on the basic abilities test.

Another effort to measure everyday problem solving was a test constructed to assess the skills that old people are thought to need to function independently in the community. These skills, called the instrumental activities of daily living (Lawton and Brody, 1969), include the ability to engage independently in food preparation, housekeeping, medication use, shopping, telephone use, transportation, and financial management activities. Obviously, each of these activities requires the exercise of practical intelligence. Willis (1993, 1997) collected written materials (e.g., medication labels, bus schedules, telephone instructions, mail order forms, appliance instructions, etc.) that are actually used for each of the seven types of activities. She had these items rated as to their relevance by professionals working with older people, and then constructed a test that measured proficiency with the information to carry out each activity of daily living independently. The validity of these measures was validated further by observing individuals in their homes actually using these materials to engage in activities such as measuring out medications, using a microwave oven, and so forth. (Diehl, Willis, and Schaie, 1995). Again, individual differences on this everyday problems test could be explained in large part by the performance of individuals on the basic ability tests (Marsiske and Willis, 1995; Willis et al., 1992).

INTELLIGENCE AND AGE

What happens to intelligence with age? This is the key question in this chapter, although our previous discussions should alert you to the fact that the answers are many and complex. It is argued by some that intelligence enters a process of irreversible decline in the adult years, because the brain becomes less and less efficient, just like the heart and lungs and other physical organs. Others contend that intelligence is relatively stable through the adult years, with the brain providing more than enough capacity for anything that we would want to contemplate until serious disease and declines in sensory functions sets in late in life.

Another view is that intelligence declines in some respects (in mental quickness, for example) and increases in others (in knowledge about life, or wisdom, for example). Some argue that individual differences can be explained by compensatory experiences for those who age well, while others place more stock in the above-average maintenance of physiological and psychological resources for these favored individuals (cf. Salthouse, 1999).

Early Cross-Sectional Studies

If we were to administer a typical IQ test such as the WAIS to various groups representative of people their age, we would find that each group has an average IQ of 100. By definition, because the average IQ for any age group has been set to 100. This automatic adjustment disguises the fact that a 20-year-old must earn a higher raw (unadjusted) score to be assigned an IQ of 100 than does a 50-year-old. On one test, a raw score of 80 places a 50-year-old slightly above average for his age group, with an IQ of 101; but a 20-year-old with the same score would be decidedly below average with an IQ of 87. If we compare raw scores across age groups, we would find that average scores are highest in young adulthood and early middle age and systematically decline with advancing age. Figure 12-2 depicts an early study of this sort.

The interpretation of early cross-sectional studies that made such findings was straightforward: An individual's intellectual abilities gradually but inexorably decline over the adult years. David Wechsler, creator of the WAIS, believed that the "decline of mental ability with age is part of the general senescent process of the organism as a whole" (Wechsler, 1972, p. 30). Wechsler believed that mental ability deteriorated in ways similar to the decline of lung capacity, reproductive function, and other physical abilities.

It was soon apparent, however, even from cross-sectional studies, that intellectual decline was not as pronounced on some tasks as on others.

Researchers have noted that certain subtests on the WAIS showed less decline than others (Busse, 1993; Field, Schaie, and Leino, 1988; Siegler, 1983). Wechsler (1972) proposed to use the term "hold subtests" for those subtests on which older adults do about as well as younger adults in contrast to "don't hold" subtests that showed a greater decline. In general, the verbal subtests "hold" and the performance subtests "don't hold" (Figure 12-3). It has been shown that there is improvement on the WAIS from 40 to 61 years on the information, comprehension, and vocabulary subtests; mixed change on picture completion (improvement on easy items and decline on difficult items); but decline on the digit symbol and block design subtests (Sands, Terry, and Meredith, 1989). The hold-don't-hold

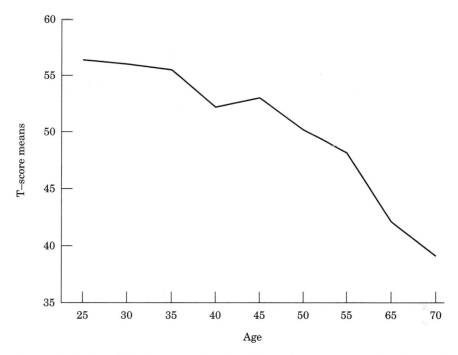

Figure 12-2 Plot of IQ Scores Against Age. This early cross-sectional study would lead us to believe that intelligence test scores decline with age, but read on. *Source:* Adapted from Schaie, K.W. (1958). Rigidity-flexibility and intelligence: A cross-sectional study of the adult life span from twenty to seventy. *Psychological Monographs, 72,* No. 462 (Whole No.9)

pattern has also been observed in a study with a Chinese sample (Dai, Xie, and Zheng, 1993).

Why should some tasks show almost no decline, and others show the older subjects doing much more poorly than the younger subjects? One possible explanation is that the subtests in which older people do poorly are all speeded tests; the scores reflect the time that it takes for the person to solve the problem, or it reflects the number of responses in a given time interval. One might conclude older people are just slower, but not necessarily less able. This hypothesis, however, has been partially discredited by research in which the participants were given unlimited time to solve problems and only the number correct was counted. Older people still did less well on "don't hold" tasks, relative to younger subjects.

This type of research, of course, changes the "problem" considerably, from "How long does it take you to solve it?" to "Can you solve it at all?" It is perhaps instructive to see that the slower average speed of solution among older persons is contributed to in large part by those who fail to solve the problem at all. We will return to the effects of speed in interpreting studies of intelligence later on.

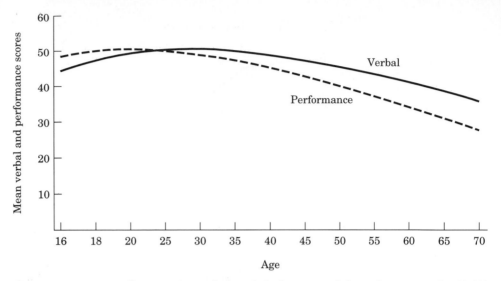

Figure 12-3   Age Differences in Verbal and Performance Subtest Scores on the WAIS. *Source:* Adapted from Wechsler, D. (1958). *The measurement and appraisal of adult intelligence* (4th ed., p. 28). Baltimore: Williams & Wilkins, Co. Copyright © 1958 Dr. David Wechsler.

Crystallized and Fluid Intelligence

One of the most prominent theories of hold and don't hold tests was formulated by Raymond Cattell and elaborated by John Horn. In factor analyses of cross-sectional studies of several intellectual tasks (not from the WAIS), Cattell and Horn repeatedly discovered that the tests on which older adults do well compared to younger adults show up as a factor that they call *crystallized intelligence* (G_c). As represented by tests of general information and vocabulary, crystallized intelligence is said to reflect the mental abilities that depend on experience with the world—on education in the broad sense, including both formal schooling and informal learning experiences in everyday life. The don't hold tests show up as another factor, termed *fluid intelligence* (G_f). Fluid intelligence is more akin to what Wechsler called "native mental ability," reflecting presumably the quality of one's brain: how quickly a signal can get in and out, how well organized are the neurons involved in associations, pattern recognition, and memory (Horn, 1982; Horn and Hofer, 1992).

Adult intellectual development, viewed in terms of the G_c—G_f theory, implies progressive deterioration in the neural structures underlying intelligence and, thus, systematic decline in fluid intelligence. Crystallized intelligence, as long as we do not require speedy responses, should not be affected as much; it may even increase as a result of adult educational experiences (Figure 12-4). The theory is a

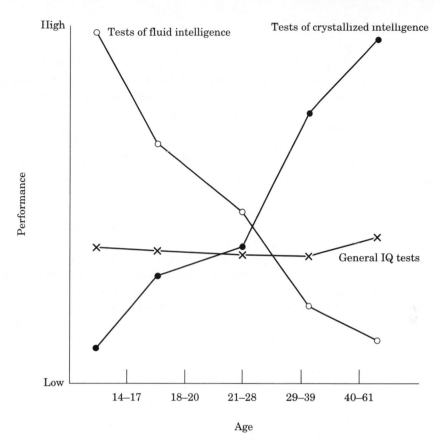

Figure 12-4   Performance of Various Age Groups on Tests Used to Define Fluid, Crystalized, and General Intelligence. *Source:* From Horn, J. L. (1970). Organization of data on life-span development of human abilities. In L.R. Goulet and P.B. Baltes (Eds.), *Life-span developmental psychology: Research and theory.* New York: Academic Press, p.63.

popular one, for it more clearly specifies the intellectual tasks that can be used to represent each type of intelligence. Indeed, it is a sophisticated form of the general notion that in some respects older adults are not as sharp as they once were, but in other respects they are as knowledgeable as ever, perhaps even wiser.

Differential decline of intelligence that supports the G_c—G_f theory also comes from a variety of longitudinal studies in various Western countries that show greater decline for measures of fluid abilities (e.g., Rott, 1993 [Germany]; Rabbitt, 1993 [England]). However, as will be shown below, in the detailed discussion of a major American longitudinal study (Schaie, 1994a,1996b), this pattern may not hold for all abilities, and in addition may be attenuated in advanced old age, when crystallized abilities also show substantial decline (Bosworth, Schaie, and Willis, 1999).

Longitudinal Studies

Widespread use of intelligence tests among college freshmen began in the United States about 1920. By 1950, therefore, it was possible to find a sizable group of 50-year-olds who had taken an IQ test some 30 years earlier. Several psychologists, seeing their chance to run a relatively inexpensive longitudinal study, seized the opportunity by retesting these middle-aged individuals. No one expected results different from those found in cross-sectional studies, which suggested a marked decrease in IQ scores after the age of 25 or 30. Thus it came as somewhat of a surprise to find that not only did the longitudinal studies show virtually no decline in IQ by middle age; instead they showed an increase! The average person seemed to have gotten smarter with age, at least up to age 50 (Owens, 1966). Later follow-ups showed that the participants in the Owens study actually maintained their intellectual abilities into their sixties (Cunningham and Owens, 1983).

Most of the early longitudinal studies tested highly educated people (college graduates), whose professional careers required continuing use of academic skills—mathematics, extensive reading, and formal reasoning. Later studies of people at all levels of intelligence and education in all walks of life showed the increase in IQ scores to late midlife and beyond to be characteristic primarily for the highly educated part of the population. But the absence of significant declines, except for slowing of response time, during midlife and into early old age were replicated again and again.

One large-scale study combined features of both cross-sectional and longitudinal designs (Schaie, 1979, 1983b, 1988c, 1993b, 1994a,1996b; Schaie and Hertzog, 1986; Schaie and Zuo, 2001; Willis and Schaie, 1999). In 1956, people ranging in age from 22 to 70 were tested in a cross-sectional study. In 1963, as many of these same people as could be found and convinced to participate were retested. This was repeated a third time in 1970, a fourth in 1977, a fifth in 1984, a sixth in 1991, and a seventh time in 1998. Thus, the researchers had 7 cross-sectional studies in addition to longitudinal data covering a period of 42 years.

The cross-sectional studies showed the typical pattern of intellectual decline in the adult years; the longitudinal data, however, told a quite different story. Consider, for example, "verbal meaning" (the ability to understand ideas expressed in words), one of the "primary mental abilities" assessed by the investigators. Figure 12-5 is the most dramatic way to represent the difference between cross-sectional data and an estimate of what the longitudinal data would look like if the youngest group of subjects were followed for the rest of their lives (Schaie, 1996b). The cross-sectional data show a peak at age 39, followed by a relatively sharp decline. In striking contrast, the longitudinal data suggest increases in this ability until 53 or 60, with a small decline thereafter; even at age 74 the estimated performance is better than at 25 (Schaie and Strother, 1968; Schaie and Willis, 1993). Similar comparisons were made with tests of reasoning ability, numerical ability, word fluency, and spatial visualization.

The data just described came from a single longitudinal study over the period from 1956 to 1963. More recently, longitudinal data for 5 mental abilities have

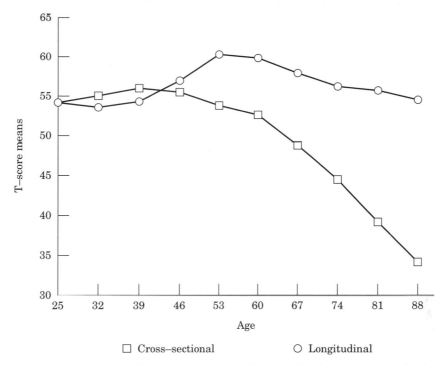

Figure 12-5 Comparable Cross-Sectional and Longitudinal Age Gradients for the Verbal Meaning Test. *Source:* Adapted from Schaie, K.W. (1988c). Variability in cognitive functioning in the elderly: Implications for societal participation. In A. Woodhead, M. Bender, and R. Leonard (Eds.), *Phenotypic variation in populations: Relevance to risk management.* New York: Plenum.

been reported from the expanded investigation covering 1956 to 1991, a period of 35 years (Schaie, 1996b). Representative findings, shown in Figure 12-6, suggest little if any decline in these abilities until the age of 60; in several instances, increases occur during the adult years. Even after age 60, decline is slight until age 74 or 81. (The mental abilities investigated in this study are described in Table 12-3).

Other investigators also have observed the fact that even in fairly advanced age, change in abilities proceeds quite slowly, and in fact is difficult to document in studies that extend only over two or three years (Hultsch et al., 1992, 1998; Zelinski, Gilewski, and Schaie, 1993). Once the high eighties and nineties are reached, however, declines become more rapid and extend across most abilities because of the increasing failures of sensory capacities and other physiological infrastructures (Baltes and Lindenberger, 1997; Baltes, Staudinger, and Lindenberger, 1999; Li, Jordanova, and Lindenberger, 1999, Salthouse, Hambrick, and McGuthrie, 1998; Salthouse, Hancock, Meinz, and Hambrick, 1996; see also Chapter 14).

The data in Figure 12-6 are actually quite conservative because they were adjusted for the various sources that typically confound longitudinal studies (discussed in Chapter 5). These adjustments take into account experimental mortality

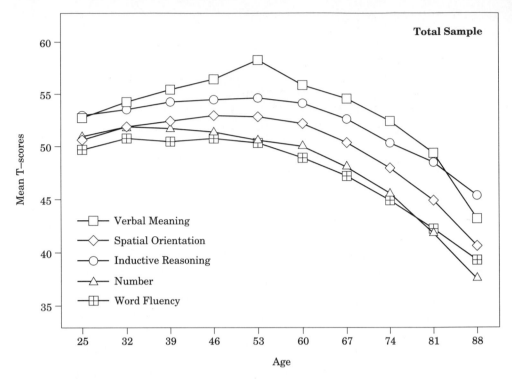

Figure 12-6 Effect of Age on Five Mental Abilities in Longitudinal Studies. *Source:* Schaie, K. W. (1996). *Intellectual development in adulthood: The Seattle Longitudinal Study,* New York: Cambridge University Press, 1996b.

(attrition) and reactivity (practice effects), which tend to make unadjusted longitudinal findings often look unduly optimistic. However, no adjustments were made for the well-documented decline in perceptual speed that puts older people at successively greater disadvantage (Salthouse, 1993, 1996). Nor were any of the participants removed who were later known to have been in the early stages of dementia, thus perhaps underestimating mean levels for the normal elderly (cf. Sliwinski, Lipton, Buschke, and Stewart, 1996). In a study by Schaie (1989c), the contribution of perceptual speed was removed statistically from the scores of 838 adults ranging in age from their twenties to their eighties. This adjustment removed most of the observed age decrement for highly practiced tasks and markedly reduced aging effects for novel tasks. Recent work in a Swedish twin study suggests that much of the correlation between cognitive measures and speed may be genetically mediated (Finkel and Pedersen, 2000).

Cohort Differences

What accounts for the difference between the cross-sectional and longitudinal results, with the latter not only showing no decline through midlife and early old age, but also, in some cases, clear increases in intellectual abilities? Why do the longitudinal studies give us such a different picture from the earlier, cross-sectional investigations?

The answer is "cohort" differences—differences among generations. The reason longitudinal studies give different results from cross-sectional studies is that cross-sectional studies compare people of different ages and of different cohorts. Many of the differences that have been attributed to age must, for the most part, be relegated to differences among groups of people differing in year of birth. Cross-sectional studies make it appear that intelligence declines steeply over the years, but much of this apparent decline is an illusion. Longitudinal studies suggest generally that each generation is smarter than the previous one on many abilities.

Why is one cohort more advantaged in intelligence than another? Why is it that people born more recently earn higher averages on IQ tests than their parents or grandparents? Various answers may be suggested. Over the last several generations in most countries, education has improved and the average person gets more of it. In the United States, among the members of the oldest cohorts now living, the majority may not have achieved a high school diploma and relatively few have had college experience. Nutrition has vastly improved in the last 70 or 80 years, and so has medical care; the physical condition of the brains of the more recent cohorts may therefore be superior. The use of tests like those for IQ has burgeoned, and thus later generations may be better than earlier generations at performing well on such instruments because of the added experience.

Because experiences that may be relevant to differential performance across different cohorts is due to many different influences we still are unsure of the psychological mechanisms involved. Laboratory studies have employed popular recreational activities such as crossword puzzles or jigsaw puzzles to determine whether regular performance on these activities is related to age differences on related abilities. Crossword puzzles have been related to verbal (crystallized) ability and jigsaw puzzles to spatial (fluid) ability (Tosti-Vasey, Person, Maisr, and Willis, 1992). However, another analysis did not show that practice on crossword puzzles either reduced age difference on fluid abilities or enhanced age-related increases on crystallized abilities (Hambrick, Salthouse, and Meinz, 1998; also see Salthouse and Maurer, 1996).

Cohort differences in intelligence are not uniform across different abilities. Figure 12-7 shows the change in cohort level in percent of the performance of the earliest cohort for 11 cohorts born from 1889 to 1966. Continuous gain occurred for each successive cohort for the primary mental abilities of verbal meaning and reasoning. However, gain peaked in 1938 for spatial orientation (although there was another most recent gain for the 1966 birth cohort). Number ability peaked in 1924 and then went down below the level of the oldest cohort. Word fluency declined for successive earlier cohorts, but has been gaining since 1938. These differential data suggest that older cohorts are at a particular disadvantage on the fluid abilities, but may have an advantage with respect to number skills (Schaie, 1996a, 1996b; Willis, 1989a). Interestingly enough a cross-cultural study of cohort differences in number skills comparing young and old chinese with Americans has shown that the advantage generally shown by current Chinese over American students may be due to positive cohort change in numeric ability in China co-occurring with negative differences in the United States (Geary et al., 1997).

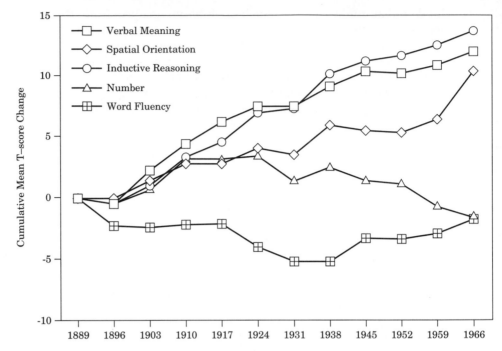

Figure 12-7 Cumulative Cohort Differences from Oldest to Youngest Cohort for Five Mental Abilities. *Source:* Schaie, K. W. (1996). *Intellectual development in adulthood: The Seattle Longitudinal Study.* New York: Cambridge University Press.

The cohort differences data described above come from the study of unrelated individuals, but generational differences of very similar magnitude have been observed also in studies comparing parents and their adult children when compared at the same ages. This kind of data can, of course, be collected only in studies carried on for long periods of time (Schaie, 1996b; Schaie et al., 1992).

There is some evidence that the differences between generations have begun to turn in favor of the earlier-born cohorts. Average test scores on the Scholastic Aptitude Test have been declining since 1962; before 1962, averages were stable or increasing. The decline has been blamed on many factors, but chief among them are poorer educational standards in our schools and "the passive pleasure, the thief of time"—television. For whatever reason, the youth of today are doing somewhat less well on IQ tests than their elders did at the same age, and this fact will eventually show on cross-sectional studies of intelligence. It will then appear that people get smarter as they grow older, a conclusion that will be no more justified than the one based on present cross-sectional studies that people decline in intelligence (cf. Willis, 1989a).

Gender Differences in Adult Intelligence

Throughout the history of intelligence testing, evidence has been accumulated on systematic gender differences in cognitive performance. Most researchers have suggested that these gender differences are the consequence of differential socialization patterns for boys and girls. The gender differences tend to persist throughout adulthood and old age (Feingold, 1993; Schaie, 1996b). On the WAIS, males are at a significant advantage on the arithmetic, information, block design, and digit symbol subtests, with only the digit symbol subtest favoring females (Kaufman et al., 1991). On the primary mental abilities, males do better on spatial orientation and number, but women excel on inductive reasoning, verbal memory, and perceptual speed (Schaie, 1996b). Similar differences were found in a meta-analysis of 25 studies, which also found lesser age-related declines for females on measures of speed and reasoning (Meinz and Salthouse, 1998). It should be noted, however, that there is considerable overlap, such that many women, for example, exceed the average for males on the spatial orientation test.

The cultural specificity of these gender differences is illustrated by the fact that the gender difference favoring males on spatial orientation was not found in a Chinese sample (Schaie, Nguyen, Willis, Dutta, and Yue, 2000). And, gender differences on this ability were eliminated in a sample of persons over age 65 by means of cognitive training (Willis and Schaie, 1988, 1994b). Gender differences may often be test-specific and get attenuated when abilities are measured by a broader variety of tests (Maitland, Intrieri, Schaie, and Willis, 2000).

Dropouts and Death

One of the difficulties of longitudinal studies, especially with older people over a long period, is that it is often difficult to find the participants for retesting. Some have moved and cannot be traced; some are sick; others are tired of psychologists and their tests; and still others have died. One cannot retest all subjects; one can only hope to find a decent percentage still alive, still available, and still willing. In the better studies, where good records are kept and systematic efforts to contact subjects are made, "a decent percentage" may be in the neighborhood of 50 to 60 percent (Schaie, 1996b). This loss of subjects haunts researchers who are trying to interpret their data in ways that are relevant to people in general. Who are these people who disappear or decide not to participate? Are they different from the subjects who can be found and retested? How about the people who die? Are they different from the survivors?

Subjects who eventually drop out or die share one important characteristic. Compared to subjects who continue in a longitudinal study, they generally perform at a lower level (Botwinick, 1977; Schaie, 1988b, 1998; Siegler and Botwinick, 1979; Siegler, McCarthy, and Logue, 1982). If researchers begin their study with a group of people representative of the population as a whole, they are likely to end up with a sample biased in favor of those who do well on IQ tests. The investigators then cannot generalize their findings to people in general, but only to those people who are more able than the average. If the more intelligent people show a different pattern of age change in intelligence, then the conclusions made from longitudinal studies would be quite different from those one could make for "people in general." For example, smarter people might show an increase in some mental ability, whereas the average person might decline. College students (presumably of superior intellect) are more likely to enter careers in which they continue to use academic skills, such as abstract reasoning. They might thus maintain or increase their level of functioning on tests of this ability.

One way to determine the effects of dropouts is to compare the people that were retested with a more representative sample of the original population. In the large-scale longitudinal investigation that we have been discussing, at each time of retesting a new sample of subjects was also tested. Data from these new samples can be viewed as an estimate of what the retested longitudinal group would have done, had they not lost several members due to geographical mobility, uncooperative attitudes, and the other reasons for dropping out. For example, one cohort had an average age of 25 in 1977, 32 in 1984, and 39 in 1991. These people were compared with a new sample of 32-year-olds in 1984 and a new sample of 39-year-olds in 1991.

The results from the new samples led to a not-unexpected conclusion. The average scores on tests of intellectual abilities begin a decline somewhat earlier than shown in the longitudinal studies. Figure 12-8 shows comparative results for verbal meaning, or vocabulary scores. In the longitudinal data, average scores increase until age 60 and then decrease slightly, such that even at age 81 the average score is not meaningfully lower than at age 25. In the independent-sample data,

Cross-sectional studies compare different generations, who differ in many ways beyond those changes wrought by aging.

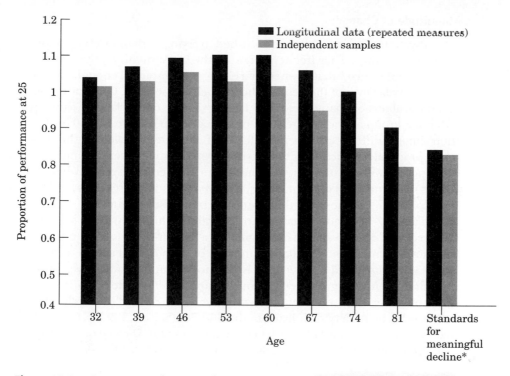

Figure 12-8 Comparison of Repeated Measures and Independent Samples to Assess the Influence of Subject Dropouts. *Source:* Adapted from Schaie and Parr (1981), and from Schaie, 1996b.

average scores decrease rather consistently throughout the adult years, although they do not decline to a "meaningfully lower level" until the age of 81. Similar analyses have been conducted for each successive stage of this study (Baltes, Schaie, and Nardi, 1971; Schaie, Labouvie, and Barrett, 1973; Gribbin and Schaie, 1979; Cooney, Schaie, and Willis, 1988; Schaie, 1996b).

There are, of course, several ways to interpret these data. One is to say that the longitudinal studies are of little value because they end up with such a special sample that is unrepresentative of people in general. Another is to say that the longitudinal data are quite valuable, in showing the developmental trends in intelligence among "special" people—the more gifted and more stable—the people who form the foundation of most societies. Still a third point of view suggests that the decline among people in general, however slight, is particularly misleading because the people added originally to the special people in the longitudinal samples are precisely those for whom the tests make least sense. In any event there are good reasons to believe that the rate of aging is fairly constant for different socioeconomic groups even though their level might differ markedly. Hence, estimates from samples that have differed significant dropout are still valuable in informing us about the shape of the aging pattern (Baltes and Mayer, 1999; Caskie, Schaie, and Willis, 1999).

Magnitude of Change

Psychologists often become absorbed in trying to demonstrate the presence or absence of change. They frequently ignore the question of whether or not a change "makes a difference," that is, whether a change is substantial enough to be important in the everyday lives of the people who are being discussed. One way to estimate the meaningfulness of change is to look for the degree of overlap between a particular older age group and a younger group if the overlap is large (say 80 or 90 percent), then the age difference does not affect a great many people and should not be of much practical significance. Even an overlap of only 50 percent still means that many older people will perform as well as many younger people. It is only when the overlap begins to shrink to 20 percent or less, that we can indeed argue that most older persons do significantly less well than younger comparison groups.

Table 12-4 provides data that are relevant to this analysis. This table shows the proportion of overlap at each older age with a 25-year-old reference group. Note that for number ability, there is almost complete overlap even at age 88, and that for verbal meaning and word fluency there is still more than 50 percent overlap for the oldest with the youngest group. On the other hand, most people perform outside of the range of young adults on inductive reasoning by age 81, and there is less than 50 percent overlap on tasks of daily living by the mid-70s (Schaie, 1996b). Certainly the idea that people steadily lose their intellectual abilities after the age of 25, dropping into near incompetence by the age of 60 or so, deserves to be called a myth.

Frequency of Decline

In addition to knowing the age at which the average person declines, it is also important to know what proportion of people are likely to decline at a given age. Such knowledge is useful in at least two ways. First, it alerts us to the fact that there

TABLE 12-4   Proportion of Overlap at Successive Ages with Score Distribution at Age 25

Ability	Age								
	32	39	46	53	60	67	74	81	88
Verbal Meaning	99.7	99.9	99.9	99.7	99.7	97.3	93.0	75.2	53.4
Spatial Orientation	99.6	99.6	99.7	99.3	98.7	96.9	90.2	70.8	38.7
Inductive Reasoning	99.6	99.5	99.1	98.2	95.9	87.0	70.1	12.6	0.0
Number	99.9	99.9	99.9	98.9	99.9	99.9	99.7	98.7	96.6
Word Fluency	99.7	99.7	99.7	99.4	98.8	98.0	94.7	93.2	81.9
Immediate Recall	99.2	99.3	98.9	96.2	94.4	91.9	76.9	51.7	49.0
Everyday Tasks	99.7	99.7	99.3	97.8	97.2	91.3	42.1	43.7	24.9

Source: Adapted from Schaie, K. W. (1988). Variability in cognitive function in the elderly: Implications for societal participation. In A. D. Woodhead, M. A. Bender, and R. C. Leonard (Eds.), Phenotypic variation in populations: Relevance to risk assessment (pp 191–212). New York: Plenum.

may be more stability than change in intellectual aging and that some persons may still grow even at an advanced age. Second, just as longevity tables permit life insurance companies to forecast the odds of someone's dying, a knowledge of the proportion of those declining at a given age permits us to determine the probability that intellectual changes will have important consequences. For example, such knowledge would permit us to determine the odds that an elderly president might show mental decline before completing his term in office.

Frequency distributions were prepared for several hundred participants in the Seattle Longitudinal Study to determine how many of them had declined significantly over the 7-year age ranges from 53 to 60, 60 to 67, 67 to 74, and 74 to 81 (Schaie, 1989c). Although data were available also for persons under age 53, they were not examined because very few people of this age show a reliable decline. The researchers examined frequencies for the five primary mental abilities: verbal meaning, inductive reasoning, word fluency, numerical ability, and spatial orientation. The proportion of persons who maintained their level of functioning over the 7-year period are shown in Figure 12-9. Note that, although ability varied greatly in

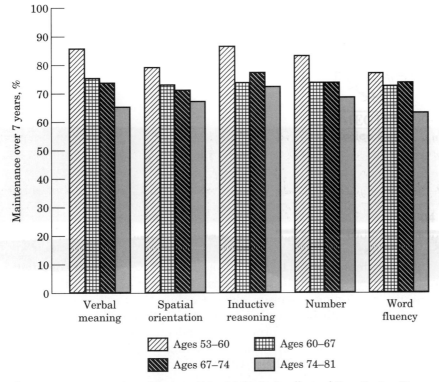

Figure 12-9   Proportion of Persons Who Maintain Intellectual Functioning Over a 7-Year Period. *Source:* Adapted from Schaie, K.W. (1989c). The optimization of cognitive functioning in old age: Predictions based on cohort-sequential and longitudinal data. In P.B. Baltes and M.M. Baltes (Eds.), *Successful aging: Perspectives from the behavioral sciences.* Cambridge: Cambridge University Press.

the various areas tested, at least 75 percent of those studied maintained their previous ability level to age 60. By age 74, there were still 70 percent who showed no change over the previous 7 years, and even by age 81, at least 60 percent of the study participants remained at a stable level of performance.

Terminal Drop

We know that people who are no longer alive at the time of a longitudinal retesting generally scored lower on their first tests than did survivors. There are many possible explanations for this fact. The subjects who die before retesting may have been poorer, unable to afford adequate medical care or nutrition, or ill (sometimes without knowing it) at the time of the first testing; all these and similar factors would predict lower than average scores. But there is another issue involved: does a dramatic drop in intelligence foretell impending death?

The issue of terminal drop was first studied by Kleemeier (1962), who tested elderly men on 4 occasions over 12 years. Kleemeier compared the rate of decline for those who died soon after the testing to that for subjects who were still living and found a more rapid decline for those who died. In another study, identical twins, who generally are remarkably similar in IQ scores, were tested in old age (Jarvik and Bank, 1983). When one twin had a noticeably lower score, it was always that twin who died first. Data from the Duke Longitudinal Study have also been examined for evidence of the occurrence of terminal drop. Of those subjects in this study who had died, 76 percent showed decline prior to death. However, most of this decline was relatively gradual; only 20 percent of the decliners showed an abrupt drop (Siegler, 1983).

In the Seattle longitudinal study, evidence for terminal drop has been found primarily in the very old. Among the young-old it is actually those who dropped out of the study for reasons of ill health and disability that showed excess drop in ability scores; those who died in this age group (mostly due to heart attack or other acute disease) had no evidence of predeath decline (Cooney, Schaie, and Willis, 1988). More recent analyses of longitudinal data from this study has implicated decline in the crystallized abilities as particularly useful predictors of impending death (Bosworth and Schaie, 1999; Bosworth, Schaie, and Willis, 1999; Bosworth, Schaie, Willis, and Siegler, 1999).

If you think about it, terminal drop makes sense in the very old. In the period preceding death, various bodily systems often begin to malfunction. Chief among these malfunctioning systems in older people is the cardiovascular system, which delivers blood to the body, including the brain. With its food supply diminished, it is no wonder the brain performs at a less adequate level. The terminal drop may simply reflect the physical decline preceding death (also see Bäckman, Small, Wahlin, and Larsson, 1999; Berg, 1996).

PIAGETIAN INTELLIGENCE

The growth of intellect as described by Jean Piaget proceeds through several stages, culminating in the stage of formal operations, which many children reach in adolescence (Piaget, 1967). There has been some speculation that Piaget's stages may also be repeated in old age—in reverse! The ability to perform mental routines (operations) on information is said to decline gradually with age, until many old people return to the preoperational stage.

Consider Piaget's famous conservation problems, which children in the operational stages can solve with relative ease. In the conservation of quantity problem, children are shown two identical glasses filled with an identical quantity of liquid. Before the child's eyes, the contents of one glass are poured into a third glass, which is taller and thinner than the others. Young children, under the age of 7 or so, respond to the superficial features of their perceptual experience and are likely to say that the taller, thinner glass has more liquid, because the liquid rises to a higher level. They cannot mentally adjust the two dimensions (adults would say, "The increase in height is compensated for by the decrease in width"); they cannot perform the proper mental operation.

A number of studies have shown that old people also do poorly on these simple conservation problems (Papalia and Bielby, 1974). It is as if the basic cognitive abilities that are gained in youth are lost in old age. On the other hand, there is evidence that the mental abilities are not lost, but instead are for some reason not used. To illustrate, consider a study of women aged 65 to 75 who were tested on a "conservation of surface" task (Hornblum and Overton, 1976). The women were shown two identical green cardboard rectangles, which were meant to represent grass fields. Each had a little plastic cow in the center of the field and two small red barns along the top edge. The women were asked if each of the two cows had the same amount of grass to eat. After they answered, the two barns on one of the fields were moved to other parts of the field, and the question was repeated. Then the whole task was repeated with 6 and 10 barns. "Conservation" was defined as answers, on at least two of the three trials, that indicated that the women knew that moving the barns had no effect on the exposed surface. Although this may seem to you a supremely simple task, only 26 of the 60 women were successful.

Then, however, the women who failed were divided into two groups. Each woman was given 20 trials with a task similar to the one that she had failed. Half the women were told if they were right or wrong on each trial, whereas the other half were given no feedback. The women with feedback improved rapidly and, on later tests of conservation of surface, performed nearly perfectly. The women in the comparison group, without feedback, improved only slightly. The ease of training these women suggests that they had the basic capacity for solving these conservation problems, but for some reason performed poorly. Among the possible reasons are lack of familiarity with the testing situation, lack of motivation (who cares about plastic cows and cardboard fields?), problems with vision or memory, and a misguided desire to please the experimenters by giving silly answers to what they perceived as silly questions.

In a similar study, older adults were presented with a green surface supposed to represent a meadow and a number of miniature houses that could be arranged in different ways. They were asked whether the spatial arrangement of the houses affected the amount of grass left to mow. The older subjects did not give the correct solution, which is that the spatial arrangement of the houses is insignificant. Instead, they noted that mowing would be harder and take more time if the houses were arranged such that there were many small spaces between them rather than a single large, open space. Time, energy, and the spatial arrangement of the surface were thus seen to be important variables, and these practical concerns influenced how the task was solved. Within these pragmatic parameters, however, the older subjects' thinking was perfectly coherent and logical (Newman-Hornblum, Attig, and Kramer, 1980).

Kuhn, Pennington, and Leadbeater (1983), in a study of the reasoning strategies of jurors age 21 to 73, assessed reasoning in terms of the ability to evaluate various accounts of a crime. Jurors varied widely in their ability to base their inferences on more comprehensive data, coordinate information, and avoid basing their conclusions on isolated instances. Although this study did not report any correlations with age, Lougee and Packard (1981) have reported that older adults commonly are judged to be more competent evaluators of such social information.

Despite evidence that the elderly have superior effectiveness in some situations, the research also suggests that performance on certain intellectual functions, as measured by Piaget's tests, does decrease in old age. This has been attributed variously to inevitable neurological deterioration (Hooper, Fitzgerald, and Papalia, 1971), social isolation (Looft, 1972), and superficial performance factors (Hornblum and Overton, 1976). These studies, however, are all cross-sectional; it seems likely, given the high correlation of Piagetian tasks with general tests of intelligence (Humphreys and Parsons, 1979), that longitudinal studies would show that much of this so-called cognitive regression can be attributed to generational differences, not age change. Those age changes that remain after controlling for the generational effects may still be caused by factors other than inevitable neurological deterioration with age. The ease of training old people in these tasks suggests that the neurological structures necessary for the appropriate behavior still exist.

It may also be that a Piagetian conception of intelligence, however helpful it may be in understanding the development of thinking in children and adolescents, is simply inappropriate when applied to older adults. Older people have different concerns than younger people, and, as a result, they may use their intellectual skills differently. If this is the case, then it would be improper to use the early Piagetian tasks in assessing adult intelligence.

A number of authors have speculated about the characteristics of what they term to be an adult stage of *postformal operations*. This stage is characterized by awareness of the relativistic nature of knowledge, the acceptance of contradiction, as well as the ability to integrate the contradictions into a dialectical whole (Alexander and Langer, 1990; Kramer, 1983; Labouvie-Vief, 1992; Sinnott, 1984, 1993, 1996). In a study of 60 young, middle-aged, and older men, Kramer and Woodruff (1986) gave life dilemmas and tasks that required the coordination of frames of reference and the separation of variables in complex task. The older men were superior to both young and middle-aged men in performing on these ambiguous tasks and the life dilemmas. In another study expert research administrators were found to show post-formal thinking on standard problems as well as job-related tests. This study confirmed that a high degree of interaction with people and complex problems is associated with adults' postformal thinking (Sinnott, and Johnson, 1997).

One of the difficulties with appraising the conflicting results of studies inspired by Piagetian theory has been the lack of standardized tasks that would permit meaningful comparison across different studies. Some progress has been made in the past decade in creating standardized Piagetian assessment instruments (e.g., Humphreys, Rich, and Davey, 1985). The opportunity therefore now exists to revisit some of the issues raised earlier, based on improved methods of assessment (see also Hooper, Hooper, and Colbert, 1984).

HEALTH, LIFESTYLES, AND "NATURAL" DEVELOPMENT

One of the thorniest problems in the study of old age is the separation of the "natural" aging process from the effects of disease (see Busse, 1993; Solomon, 1999). On the one hand, we would like to know what happens to the intellect in a body that lives its full life free from disease and then expires, like the "one-hoss shay," at its appointed time. On the other hand, such a desire may be unrealistic, because part of the "natural" aging process seems to involve an increasing susceptibility to disease, so that a completely healthy 90-year-old is just as unusual as a 10-year-old invalid. Nevertheless, disease is a hit-and-miss affair, affecting some old people primarily in their physical functions (e.g., arthritis) and others primarily in their mental functions (e.g., the ailments that are commonly grouped as dementia or "senility"). Recognizing then that disease becomes more and more likely as one grows older, we want to know the effects of specific diseases on the intellectual functioning of older people.

Some diseases affect intellectual behavior directly by damaging the brain. Others affect intelligence indirectly by making it more difficult to perform in an intelligent manner. The distractions of pain and economic worries that accompany illness in the later years, for example, often lead to poorer performance on tests of intellectual capacity.

Perhaps the most important diseases affecting intelligence in old age are those classified as cardiovascular (having to do with the heart and blood vessels). When the blood flow to the brain is affected (cerebrovascular diseases), mental abilities usually decline to some degree, although the decline may be temporary. A stroke (a blocking of blood vessels in the brain) may result in permanent impairment, depending on the areas of the brain affected, but even mild cardiovascular disease has been shown to be related to deficits in memory and lower scores on the WAIS (Elias, Elias, and Elias, 1990; Elias et al., 1998). Apparently, the lowered blood flow decreases the oxygen supply to brain cells, resulting in temporary "malnutrition" or permanent "starvation" and death of the affected tissue.

Other types of disease may also cause problems in intellectual behavior. Among institutionalized patients who have various types of brain disorders, for example, there is generally a positive correlation between degree of brain impairment and intellectual malfunctioning. Such a relationship may not occur among elderly persons who are living in the community in relatively good health, however, which suggests that changes normally thought to be age-related may actually be a function of disease. Studies that show intellectual declines among the elderly may do so because the elderly population generally includes a considerably higher percentage of people with health problems. When studies systematically exclude patients with even minimal dementia or other physiological problems, it may be found that cerebral oxygen consumption levels among older adults resemble those of younger adults.

Several studies suggest that intellectual declines among the elderly are associated with disease. There is evidence that a relationship exists between intellectual decline and high blood pressure, for example; but the relationship was consistent only when the blood pressure was elevated above a certain critical level (Elias, D'Agostino, Elias, and Wolf, 1995; Elias, Robbins, Elias, and Streeten, 1998; Manton, Siegler, and Woodbury, 1986). Medically controlled mild hypertension does not seem to affect intellectual functioning (Schultz et al., 1989), and there are some data that suggest that psychological effects of hypertension may actually be greater in midlife than in old age (Madden and Blumenthal, 1998). Subjective reports of good health status are also positively correlated with good intellectual functioning in older persons (Hultsch, Hammer, and Small, 1993; Perlmutter and Nyquist, 1990).

In several longitudinal studies, it has been possible to examine retroactively performance changes related to dying and death (Cooney, Schaie, and Willis, 1988; Riegel and Riegel, 1972). Once subjects had died, the researchers were able to relate performance changes to the onset of the illness that proved to be terminal. This research convincingly shows that intellectual declines related to chronological age were a statistical artifact. Throughout most of their adult lives, people maintained a more or less stable level of performance, with dramatic changes occurring primarily in the five years immediately preceding death. These data support the claim made by some that there may be a brief and precipitous decline as death approaches (Fries and Crapo, 1981).

If declines among the elderly are frequently a function of diseases, it becomes increasingly important to define precisely what we mean by "disease." This is frequently more complicated than one might expect. Some authors, for example, consider senile dementia (Alzheimer's disease) to be merely the extreme end of the spectrum of normal aging changes (Terry, 1978). Others contend that normal aging and disease involve qualitatively different sorts of changes; there is some research support for this view (Anstey, Stankov, and Lord, 1993; Birren and Schroots, 1996).

Even when it is possible to discover physiological changes in the brain, it may not be clear how they affect intellectual functioning. It may be tempting, for example, to speculate that minor atrophy of the cortex plays a profound role in intellectual deficits. It appears, however, that even moderate atrophy may be compatible with normal intellectual functioning (Roberts and Caird, 1976; Kaszniak et al., 1979; also see Chapter 14). Another instance of how confusing it can be to relate brain pathology to patterns of intellectual performance is the finding that performance patterns among the elderly may parallel those of young adults with various degrees of brain damage. Such patterns are often found among elderly subjects who have excellent health and levels of social adaptation.

Further data on this matter come from Schaie's longitudinal study, in which the subjects were members of a health maintenance organization; thus, fairly complete medical records were available. Only minor relationships were discovered between poor health and mental ability scores, and then only when the most severe illnesses were considered; and only verbal meaning and word fluency were affected. Cardiovascular disease was related to generally lowered mental function. But this finding was due primarily to the fact that cardiovascular disease was more common among older people and people in the lower social classes. When people of the same age and class were compared, those with cardiovascular diseases scored significantly lower on only two measures: number and a composite measure of intellectual ability (Gruber-Baldini, 1991; Hertzog, Schaie, and Gribbin, 1978; Schaie, 1990, 1996b). This suggests that one must be cautious in interpreting studies that simply compare people with and without cardiovascular disease. It may not be the presence of disease that is crucial; other factors such as age or social class may be more important.

The participants in the Schaie longitudinal study also provide evidence that changes in style of life affect IQ scores (Gribbin, Schaie, and Parham, 1980; Schaie, 1984b, 1996b). On the basis of intensive interviews, four types of participants were identified. What might be called the "average persons" (average social status, intact family, average involvement with their environment) do quite well intellectually as they age, maintaining most of their abilities over the 14 years of testing. The "advantaged persons" (high social status, with lives that require or allow them to keep learning new things) do even better, often increasing their test scores over the years. The "spectators" (average social status, intact family, passive participation in social activities, declining interest in new learning situations) generally show a decline in abilities. Finally, the "isolated older women" (poor, unhappy, likely to be divorced or widowed, isolated either by choice or circumstances) show the greatest decline of all. Favorable consequences for cognitive functioning of higher education and favorable environments also have been found in a study of Canadian World War II veterans over periods as long as 45 years (Arbuckle Gold, Andres, and Schwartzman, 1992; Arbuckle, Maag, Pushkar, and Chaikelson, 1998). In short, it seems that those who live by their wits, die with their wits.

Equally interesting is the finding that favorable lifestyles seem to enhance the development of flexible attitudes (see Chapter 9). Such attitudes at midlife appear to be highly predictive of the maintenance of intellectual functioning into advanced old age. But do flexible attitudes maintain intellectual functioning, or do high levels of intellectual functioning encourage flexible attitudes? The evidence indicates that flexible attitudes affect intelligence. Correlational information on the relationship between intelligence and flexibility has been gathered from longitudinal studies over as long as 35 years. The data clearly show that correlations between midlife flexibility and intelligence in old age are much greater than those between intelligence at midlife and flexibility in old age (Dutta, 1992; Schaie, 1983b, 1984b, 1996b; Schaie, Dutta, and Willis, 1991; Schaie and Willis, 1991).

Similar evidence indicates that lack of environmental stimulation leads to cognitive loss. For example, we know that the greatest risk of cognitive decline occurs among widowed women who have not pursued a career and whose environmental stimulation has been reduced by the death of their spouse (Gribbin, Schaie, and Parham, 1980; Schaie, 1984b). By contrast, those who chose marital partners with high intellectual levels, seem to benefit throughout their marriage (Gruber-Baldini, Schaie, and Willis, 1995). And there have been several studies that show demanding job environments tend to enhance intellectual function in adults (Miller, Slomczynski, and Kohn, 1987; Schooler, 1987; Schooler, Caplan, and Oates, 1998).

PERCEPTIONS OF INTELLECTUAL CHANGE

Whatever the objective evidence on intellectual change with age may be, many individuals may base their actions, at least in part, on their perceptions of how they compare with their contemporaries, people at other ages, as well as their retrospective view of their own earlier performance. Several investigators have argued that these perceptions may be influenced largely by persons' control beliefs (see Chapter 10). That is, persons who think that they are in control of their lives are more likely to report high levels of cognitive performance than those who feel that they are losing their independence and have to rely on others for the exercise of cognitively challenging decisions (Lachman and Leff, 1989). Some researchers have found little correspondence between their prediction of current performance and their actual performance (Rabbitt and Abson, 1991). They argue that subjects with high self-regard may report higher performance, because they describe themselves relative to their currently more lenient existential demands. Other researchers who have studied changes in control beliefs and cognitive function over time conclude that it is more likely that changes in control beliefs follow actual loss in cognitive abilities (Dittmann-Kohli et al., 1991; Grover and Hertzog, 1991; Willis, Jay, Diehl, and Marsiske, 1992).

In a study of 837 subjects who had been followed for 7 years on 5 primary mental abilities, the subjects were asked immediately after the tests were given, whether they thought they had improved, remained stable, or declined over the 7-year period. Their report was compared to the objective change and they were classified as optimists if their self-report was better than the actual change, as realists if their self-report was accurate, and as pessimists if they reported stability or decline even though they had actually improved or remained stable. The majority of study participants reported quite accurately whether they had changed or remained stable over the 7-year period. However, the accuracy of subjects' report varied across abilities. Women were more likely to be pessimists on spatial orientation than men. Older individuals were more likely to be pessimists on the verbal meaning and inductive reasoning abilities and more likely to be realists on number ability as compared with younger study participants (Schaie, Willis, and O'Hanlon, 1994).

CAN INTELLECTUAL DECLINE BE REVERSED?

Summarizing the research that we have discussed so far, we might say that few intellectual abilities show substantial decline in adulthood until the mid-sixties or so. Evidence for decline after that age is open to several interpretations: biological, environmental, and various combinations. If one takes the view that much of the decline not due to specific diseases may be the result of a restricted social environment (particularly following retirement) and a culture that provides few incentives for further acquisition of knowledge or even the maintenance of knowledge. Then one must accept the hypothesis that, by providing incentives and instruction in later life, it should be possible to stabilize declining trends and perhaps even reverse them. We should indeed be able to teach old dogs new tricks (see Chapter 11).

The research evidence suggests that older adults can indeed continue to learn and that could be said to represent an "untapped resource," if we care to put it in such materialistic terms. They are capable of learning and performing at very high levels (Baltes and Labouvie, 1973; Willis and Schaie, 1994b). Not only can they learn a new job, but, given proper incentives, they can markedly improve their performance on tests of "fluid intelligence," highly abstract skills that often include a measure of response speed (Schaie and Willis, 1986; Willis, Blieszner, and Baltes, 1981).

The evidence of the effectiveness of training has been reviewed by many authors (Baltes and Lindenberger, 1988; Baltes and Willis, 1982; Denney, 1981; Salthouse, 1997; Willis, 1985, 1987, 1989b, 1990; see also Chapter 11 on memory training). In general, this evidence indicates overwhelmingly that significant gains in performance can be brought about, often with minor interventions. A number of different treatments have been tried. Some studies have assessed the effects of physical exercise (Blumenthal and Gullette, 2001) and of approaches designed to highlight certain dimensions of tasks (Denney, 1974; Denney and Heidrich, 1990; Sanders and Sanders, 1978). Others have focused on providing training in the component strategies involved in completing tasks (Baltes P. B., Kliegl, and Dittmann-Kohli, 1988; Blackburn et al., 1988; Schaie and Willis, 1986; Willis and Schaie, 1986b, 1994b) or on performance factors that may not be related directly to a particular task, but that do influence cognitive performance, such as a reluctance to guess (Birkhill and Schaie, 1975), or stress (Hayslip, 1989). Most of this work has involved the use of trained instructors, but improvement has also been shown when older adults were provided materials for self instruction (Baltes, Sowarka, and Kliegl, 1989).

An objection sometimes raised to such research is that training may not actually modify intellectual functioning *per se;* rather, it may simply provide more "extraneous" support for improved performance by increasing motivation, social reinforcement, or other influential factors. In other words, there may be different kinds of training effects—those that are ability-specific (that actually improve intellectual functioning) and those that are ability-extraneous (that improve performance in ways not related to intellectual functioning).

This matter was the object of a study involving 5 training sessions and 2 delayed posttests, one after 25 days and the other after 23 weeks (Willis, Blieszner, and Baltes, 1981). The study demonstrated that training actually does improve skills and not just motivation and other extraneous factors. The researchers found that the results of training fell into a hierarchical transfer pattern. Training was most helpful in improving performance on tasks directly related to the training task. Poorer performance was found on tasks related less directly to the task used in training. Similar effects have since been established in further studies using different target abilities (Baltes and Willis, 1982; Blackburn et al., 1988; Blieszner, Willis, and Baltes, 1981; Willis and Schaie, 1986b). These studies clearly support the contention that the cognitive behavior of the elderly can be modified.

A second objection to research concerning the trainability of the elderly has to do with the failure to use young control groups. The argument is that if deficits among the elderly result from a lack of environmental stimulation, one should not find similarly large training effects among "nondeprived" younger controls. But to function as an adequate control group, younger subjects would have to resemble the older ones in all respects other than ability, and as we have pointed out they do not. Today's elderly have had substantially different life histories than today's young people, and differences discovered between the two groups could easily be a result of these differences (Baltes and Willis, 1982; Schaie, 1996b).

A major defect in most of the cognitive training studies is that they did not determine whether the elderly trainees had experienced declines before training began. Did the studies remediate declines, or did they simply teach the elderly new skills? Schaie and Willis (1986) gave 5 hours of individual training to 229 older persons ranging in age from 64 to 94. The training was on one of two abilities, spatial orientation or inductive reasoning. All the subjects had been assessed over at least 14 years before the study; about half had shown declines. When the training results of those who had declined was examined, it was found that more than half gained significantly, and about 40 percent were returned to their pre-decline level of performance; about a third of those who had not shown declines improved their performance above the previous level; and cognitive training on spatial orientation was more effective for women than for men (Willis, 1989b; Willis and Schaie, 1988). Seven years later, 141 of these subjects were retested and given booster training. All subjects were now seven years older and, thus, on average showed some decline. However, the trained subjects were still at an advantage compared to their controls. Recent studies even show residual advantage for the trained study participants after 14 years. Their cognitive aging has been slowed by the training intervention (Schaie, 1996b; Willis and Schaie, 1994b). Similar long-range training effects in fluid abilities were also found in a sample of rural elderly persons (Willis and Nesselroade, 1990). It seems then that much of the decline seen in many older people may be due to disuse of skills, but that a person's prior level must be known before we can be sure whether the improvement occurring with training represents remediation of a loss or the attainment of new learning.

The results of the training study do not deny biological interpretations of intellectual decline in the last years of life (although training can provide some help even to a brain-injured patient, for example), but the research is most compatible with an interpretation of intellectual decline (as measured by IQ tests) at least until very old age, that implicates disease and lack of environmental stimulation as major causal factors.

THE ELUSIVE CONCEPT OF WISDOM

Although behavioral slowing and the accumulation of insults to the physiological infrastructure may reduce the efficiency of the mechanics of intelligence, many would argue that experience should provide some compensation, and beyond such compensation should result in some unique late-life capabilities, that are most often called "wisdom." The research literature is divided on the question of whether experience does indeed provide compensation. For example, Salthouse and Mitchell (1990) only found small benefit of prior occupational experience in a spatial orientation task. On the other hand, it has consistently been found that while the basic mechanisms of intelligence decline with age, that there is no correlation between age and industrial productivity (Avolio and Waldman, 1990; Salthouse and Maurer, 1996).

But what about the development of wisdom as the positive event in the otherwise somewhat negative account of old age? There have been many theoretical accounts of what wisdom might mean and how it might be acquired over a long life (see Baltes P. B., Smith, and Staudinger, 1992; Sternberg, 1998; Sternberg and Lubart, 2001). Nevertheless, in the past there were few *empirical* psychological studies of this concept. It is only relatively recently that questions have been asked on how one might measure attributes of wisdom, such as wisdom-related skills and knowledge. Similarly, we want to know in what areas of behavior one might find examples of wisdom, and among which groups of individuals high levels of wisdom-related behaviors might be found.

Early work on wisdom was not concerned with objecctive analyses of what the construct of wisdom might imply, but rather with determining what people thought wisdom ought to be. For example, Clayton (1982) asked samples of younger, middle-aged, and older adults to judge pairs of words related to wisdom. These judgments could be represented as two dimensions (affective and reflective). With respect to age Clayton also found that the mental representation of wisdom seemed to become more differentiated with increasing age. Studies investigating implicit dimensions of wisdom have also been conducted by Sternberg (1990) who asked 200 professors in each of the fields of art, business, philosophy, and physics to rate characteristics of ideally wise persons in their occupation.

A major effort to answer these questions has been conducted over the past decade by researchers at the Max Planck Institute in Berlin, Germany (Baltes P. B. and Smith, 1990; Dittman-Kohli and Baltes, 1990; Staudinger, Maciel, Smith, and Baltes, 1998). They define wisdom as an expert knowledge system in what they call the fundamental pragmatics of life. This knowledge system, if present, permits individuals to exercise insight and judgment, and to dispense advice involving complex and uncertain matters of the human condition. Central to the exercise of wisdom are questions concerning conduct, interpretation and the meaning of life. To exercise wisdom, these authors suggest that one must have knowledge of one's own strengths and weaknesses, as well as management strategies that can be applied to optimize the ratio between the gains and losses involved in any consequential decision or advice. The skills involved seem quite similar to those postulated for the "executive stage" in the Schaie (1977–1978; Schaie and Willis, 2000a) stage model described earlier in the chapter.

Wisdom is measured by asking study participants to respond to a set of life dilemmas. These answers are then scored to give an approximation of the quantity and quality of wisdom-related knowledge of a particular subject (Smith and Baltes, 1990). One of the examples given is the problem of a girl who wants to get married at 14 years of age. What should be considered in giving advice in this situation? Baltes and his associates argue that five areas of information and skill are involved. First, there is *factual knowledge,* of the particular circumstances and the multiple options available. Second, there is *procedural knowledge.* This includes strategies of obtaining information, advice giving, timing of advice, and analyzing the impact of the decision on immediate and future consequences. Third, there is *life-span contextualism;* that is, appropriateness of the decision to the person's life stage, the current cultural norms, unusual context (e.g., the person has a terminal illness), and priorities of life domains. Fourth is *relativism,* involving an assessment of religious preferences, current and future values, as well as the cultural context of the particular circumstance. Finally, there is *uncertainty,* the realization that there is rarely a perfect solution, that the future is not fully predictable, that the best one can do is try to optimize gains and minimize losses, and that part of the process should be consideration of alternative back-up solutions. A wise person would consider all of these aspects in their analysis of the dilemma, while an unwise person would come up with a simple response, probably guided by cultural stereotypes (for another view of the relation of gains and losses with aging, see Dixon, 1999).

Living a long life is not a sufficient condition for acquiring wisdom, but exposure and openness to experience over a long time is certainly a necessary condition (cf. Wink and Helson, 1997). When Baltes and colleagues compared young adults (men age 32 years) and older adults (men age 71 years) they found little overall differences. But the older adults showed higher levels of wisdom-related knowledge and skills specific to problems of their own age group; many of the top performers on tests of wisdom were older adults, and in a study of clinical psychologists (who performed generally better than samples of the general population), there were as many older as younger persons in the top quarter (Smith, Staudinger, and Baltes, 1994; Staudinger, Smith, and Baltes, 1992). In addition, up to the age of 80 older adults nominated as wise persons performed as well as younger adults (Baltes, Staudinger, Maercker, and Smith, 1995).

The personality trait of openness to experience, and mid-range position on the trait of introversion–extroversion have also been implicated as predictors of wisdom-related performance (Staudinger, Maciel, Smith, and Baltes, 1998). It seems to be the interaction of favorable personality traits and high levels of intelligence that are particularly appropriate for the expression of wisdom (Staudinger, Lopez, and Baltes, 1997). Wise behavior is not restricted to individuals acting on their own. In a study of interactive wisdom-related performance, dyads performed better in performance settings that were judged to be ecologically relevant (Staudinger and Baltes, 1996).

In sum, while there are average declines in the basic intellectual processes, these researchers provide evidence that wisdom-related knowledge in many circumstances can indeed be retained and enhanced into old age, a most encouraging finding (see also Staudinger, 1999).

THE NATURAL HISTORY OF INTELLECT

What happens to one's intellectual powers as one grows older? This is the primary question in this chapter, and we have a tentative answer. It is, in fact, not a bad answer, as answers go in the field of adult development and aging. It is an answer based on considerable research.

Average IQ scores were at first thought to indicate a gradual decline after the age of 25. Later studies showed this interpretation to be wrong, to be an artifact of increasing abilities with successive generations. We now believe that the pure numbers decline only later in life, largely after the age of 60. Although, decline occurs for persons at all ability levels (Christensen and Henderson, 1991), advantaged groups, such as college graduates, often decline very late and may remain well above the average level of young adults until their eighties and nineties (Schaie, 1989a).

Performance levels for certain tests, those variously called "speeded" or "fluid" or "performance" or whatever, drop somewhat more rapidly, but the reasons for this remain the most controversial. These may be the basic biological aspects of intellect, as some theories assert (Birren, 1974; Birren and Fisher, 1992; Horn, 1978). Or these may be the abilities most subject to variations in training, motivation, and historical circumstances (Abeles and Riley, 1987; Baltes P. B., 1987; Baltes and Labouvie, 1973; Labouvie-Vief and Chandler, 1978).

The decline in IQ test scores over the age of 60 is similarly subject to several interpretations. In addition to notions of inevitable biological decrement, we could attribute intellectual decline to social isolation, decreasing motivation to perform irrelevant intellectual tasks, disease (including disease related to impending death and terminal drop), or some combination of such factors. Some people decline in intellectual ability; others increase. The patterns of change for different abilities and even different measures of the same ability differ remarkably (Schaie and Willis, 1993). Some abilities seem to be increasing with each new generation; others seem to be decreasing. An environmental event (e.g., the development of television) can change trends for some people and have little effect on others. Thus, the search goes on, but it is a search now for the determinants of change or stability and much less for inevitable and irreversible decrements.

If you keep your health and engage your mind with the problems and activities of the world around you, chances are good that you will experience little if any decline in intellectual performance in your lifetime. That's the promise of research in the area of adult intelligence.

SUMMARY

1. Intelligence is usually defined as the ability to learn or manipulate symbols. Intelligence is an inference from competence demonstrated in several situations, but competence involves more than simply intelligence—motivation, for example. The particular abilities and motivations necessary to do well on IQ tests, which were designed to predict scholastic performance, may bias these tests in favor of young people.

2. Adult stages of intellectual development include the achieving stage, which involves planning and periodic assessment of programs designed to achieve major goals in career, family, and life in general. In the responsible stage, abilities are applied to both short- and long-term concerns for family units, coworkers, and community groups. In the executive stage, planning and assessment abilities are applied to the organizations for which one is at least partly responsible. In later life, the reorganizational stage requires making choices mandated by the transition from work to retirement and planning the economic bases for the rest of life, the reintegrative stage requires a reintegration of abilities, interests, and values, and the legacy-leaving stage involves disposing of ones assets and creating legacies for the next generation.

3. IQ tests were developed in the early 1900s by Alfred Binet. Factor analyses of such tests typically show a major factor called "general intelligence" or "g." Slightly different analyses have turned up two major factors called crystallized and fluid intelligence, about 6 to 12 factors called primary mental abilities, and 120 factors in the most complex model of intelligence. Sternberg's comprehensive model of intelligence consists of 3 subtheories: one that relates intelligence to the individual's inner world, one that relates intelligence to the outer world, and one that relates intelligence to both the internal and outer facets.

4. Intelligence tests provide information on the basic mechanics of

intellectual functioning. For the appraisal of performance of adults on everyday problems these tests may need to be supplemented by measures of practical intelligence. However, performance on such measures is highly correlated with the basic ability measures. Practical intelligence represents a combination of basic skills applied to specific problems of everyday experience.

5. Early cross-sectional studies of the relationship between age and intelligence showed decline after the age of 20 or 30. Some tests, usually of simple information processing abilities that make up fluid intelligence, showed sharper decline than others; tests of general information, vocabulary, and the like (crystallized intelligence) sometimes even increased.

6. Longitudinal studies, the first of which were published around 1950, showed that the cross-sectional studies had been seriously misinterpreted. Many individuals typically show little or no decline in IQ scores with age, and some brighter individuals, in intellectual professions, may actually increase. The cross-sectional studies had reflected not age changes in intelligence but cohort or generational differences in average IQ scores.

7. Interpretations of longitudinal studies have their own difficulties, not the least of which is the problem of dropouts and deaths, subjects who usually score somewhat lower than average on IQ tests. Nevertheless, a "sizable" intellec-

tual decline that reduces the average of an older group to the level surpassed by 75 percent of the younger group was found for only 3 of 7 measures in a major longitudinal study and 2 of the 3 only at age 81. In a comparable study using "independent samples" to avoid the problem of dropouts, two measures show a sizable decline (as defined above) at 53, 2 at 67, 2 at 74, and 1 not at all. The abilities of the majority of people remain stable throughout adulthood and old age, and some older people even increase their performance.

8. Cross-sectional findings that elderly subjects perform poorly on simple Piagetian tasks, such as conservation, probably reflect generational differences. Training studies suggest that even these differences may represent differences in motivation, familiarity with the testing situations, or similar factors. Some researchers have suggested that adult thinking differs qualitatively from that of younger persons. Studies of the occurrence of a "postformal operations" stage in adulthood indicate that older adults may actually be better than younger persons on tasks involving uncertainty and ambiguity. Cognitive training on the primary mental abilities resulted in bringing 40 percent of subjects who had declined back to the performance level held 14 years previously. The advantage of those trained persisted over the 7-year period.

9. Current levels of intellectual ability are often overestimated by persons

who feel in good control of their lives. Self-report for intellectual change over seven years was quite accurate but differed across abilities. Women were pessimistic about their performance on spatial orientation, older persons tended to be more pessimistic on all abilities except number skill, where they were more realistic than younger subjects.

10. Although the average older person declines in the "mechanics" of intelligence, they are likely to hold their own when it comes to the application of experience or what is commonly called "wisdom." Wisdom-related skills that are retained into old age include the dimensions of factual knowledge, procedural knowledge, life-span contextualism, relativism, and the appreciation of uncertainty.

11. Why do some people decline in IQ scores over the age of 60? One possible answer is normal biological deterioration (of the brain and nervous system, presumably). However, diseases, especially cardiovascular diseases, are a significant factor for some individuals; life-threatening diseases are known to produce a "terminal drop" in IQ scores. Social isolation induced by retirement, deaths among family and friends, and disabling diseases can also reduce one's IQ score. A number of researchers have shown that appropriate training can often remediate declines. It's possible that healthy individuals who maintain an active intellectual life will show little or no loss of intellectual abilities even into their eighties and beyond.

SUGGESTED READINGS

Baltes, P. B., Staudinger, U. M., and Lindenberger, U. (1999). Lifespan psychology: Theory and application to intellectual functioning. *Annual Review of Psychology, 50,* pp. 471–507. A review of recent research on adult intelligence featuring the work of the selection-optimization-compensation view of intellectual development.

Horn, J. L., and Hofer, S. M. (1992). Major abilities and development in the adult period. In R. J. Sternberg and C. A. Berg (Eds.), *Intellectual development* (pp. 44–99). Cambridge: Cambridge University Press. An exposition of the Horn-Cattell theory of fluid and crystallized intelligence and a re-

view of primarily cross-sectional data on age differences in the light of that theory.

Schaie, K. W. (1996). *Intellectual development in adulthood: The Seattle Longitudinal Study.* New York: Cambridge University Press. A full account of the history and results of one of the major longitudinal studies of intellectual development in adulthood.

Sternberg. R. J., and Lubart. T. I. (2001). Wisdom and creativity. In J. E. Birren and K. W. Schaie (Eds.), *Handbook of the psychology of aging* (5th ed.). San Diego, CA: Academic Press. A comprehensive discussion of the literature on wisdom and adult creativity.

Willis, S. L. (1996). Everyday problem solving. In J. E. Birren and K. W. Schaie (Eds.), *Handbook of the psychology of aging* (4th ed., pp. 287–307). San Diego, CA: Acadmic Press.

Reviews the literature on practical everyday intelligence and relates this literature to traditional psychometric intelligence.

13

Biological Development

The Aging Body

Biological aging is commonly equated with biological decline: sagging skin, greying hair, flabby muscles, failing eyesight. Considered across the entire life span, however, the early years are years of biological growth and development. Muscles become stronger and coordination improves; the information from eyes becomes better integrated with information from other senses and from the brain's repository of accumulating experience. Most bodily functions reach maximum capacity and efficiency early in life, in late childhood or in young adulthood, but decline is typically slow through the adult years. In many instances an increase in experience may more than compensate for the slight decrease in the efficiency of biological functions, so that even in athletically demanding tasks, a middle-aged adult may excel. A slight decline in finger dexterity in a concert pianist, for example, is often more than balanced by a growing intellectual ability to grasp the poetic insights in a musical composition. Then, too, decline in some functions is not necessarily negative. Decreasing hormone levels, for example, may result in lessened hostility and anxiety, reduce the chances of a heart attack in males, and eliminate the fear of pregnancy in women.

Our understanding of biological aging is derived in large part on the basis of data that come from cross-sectional studies, although recently there has been a flurry of longitudinal inquiries. As with intellectual abilities, younger cohorts compare favorably to older ones in terms of biological factors. Better health care and nutrition have rendered the younger groups more physically fit. Thus cross-sectional data on today's elderly probably present a somewhat pessimistic picture of the early declines associated with increasing age that can be expected by those now in young adulthood or middle age. The longitudinal data suggest that physiological deficits are fairly minor until the sixties are reached and it is once again important to note that individual patterns of physiological change over the adult life span also vary greatly (Shock, 1985; Solomon, 1999).

This chapter first discusses general theories of biological aging: What exactly is biological aging? What causes it? Then we consider the effect of age on sensory capacities, most notably vision and hearing, and normal age changes that occur inside the body (in the brain, in hormone levels). Finally, we turn to the relationship between age and disease, a complex and tangled web of theory and research that is basic not only to our understanding of "normal" aging but also to an appreciation of our own individual lives.

BIOLOGICAL AGING

We know them well, the signs of encroaching age. The thinning hair turns gray, if it remains at all. The skin is less elastic and more wrinkled, and where it has been exposed to the sun, it is often leathery and sprinkled with dark spots. The body moves more slowly and with less agility, the result of muscle atrophy, bone degeneration, and possibly arthritis; posture may be stooped. Often teeth are missing, a few or even all of them, sometimes replaced by dentures. The voice is slightly higher in pitch, weaker, and softer. Eventually the person dies. Death may have a specific cause—heart disease, perhaps, or cancer—but if the person is very old, the disease seems less relevant than the declining ability of the aging body to fend off environmental insults.

Why do people grow old? Why do they die? The answers to these questions do not come easily. For centuries, scientists have pondered these questions, but we have come a long way from the early gerontological debates conducted in the absence of much relevant data. New molecular genetic techniques permits testing of many of the theories of biological aging, some of which are discussed in more detail in the following section.

Life Expectancy

Before we discuss the data on human longevity, it is necessary to distinguish between two related concepts: life expectancy and potential life span. *Life expectancy*, as used in vital statistics, is the age by which half the population cohort born in the year that statistic is published is expected to have died. For example, the life expectancy at birth of a child born in the United States in 1997 was approximately 76 years (Figure 13-1; see also Chapter 1). This means that half the children born in that year could expect to reach or exceed their 76th birthday. As we shall see, life expectancy has been going up rapidly because of medical and technological advances that have kept more and more people from dying before their time. By contrast, *potential life span* is the maximum age that could be attained if an individual were able to avoid or be successfully treated for all illnesses and accidents. Potential life span, then, represents the absolute limits of human life; it is

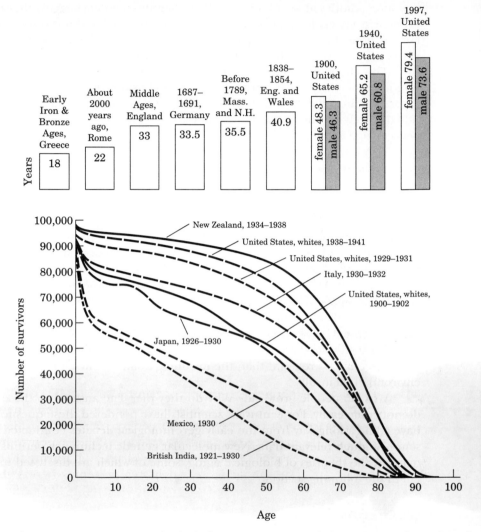

Figure 13-1 Average Length of Life for Various Times and Places (Top) and Number of People, of Each 100,000 Born, Still Living at Each Age (Bottom). *Source:* Top, National Center for Health Statistics (1983) and Kramarow et al. (1999). Bottom, Comfort, A. (1965). *Aging: The biology of senescene.* Copyright © 1964, 1965 by Alex Comfort. Reprinted by permission of A.M. Heath & Company Ltd.

genetically determined in part, but may also be set by the limits of our knowledge about compensating for the detrimental effects of aging.

The average female infant can look forward to approximately six years more in life than her male counterpart. This gender difference has at various times been attributed to many different sources, including the supposedly "easier life" of the typical female and the "sinful life" of the typical male (smoking and drinking and drugs being the obvious life-threatening vices). Nicotine and alcohol probably do play a role, but the "easy life" of the female is an implausible hypothesis for a number of reasons. Gender differences in life expectancy are found in virtually all cultures around the world, including those in which the typical woman does physical work which is as hard as or harder than that of the typical man even though she receives less than her share of food protein. The old saying, "hard work never killed anybody," may not be far from the truth: the wear-and-tear theory of aging is one of the least tenable, as we shall see, and the worry and anxiety of work, which may be its chief life-shortening ingredient, does not seem to have been allotted in disproportionate shares to one sex or the other.

As the number of women in the workforce in industrialized countries increased, one would expect the average life span of women to decline. If anything, however, gender differences in life span have increased over the last three decades, even as more women have taken jobs outside the home (Myers and Manton, 1984). Gender differences in life expectancy do vary in different population segments within the same country as well as among different countries. For example, the difference in life expectancy between nonwhite men and women in the United States is slightly higher than between white men and women (Hoyert, Kochanek, and Murphy, 1999).

The female advantage in life span is not limited to the human species. It is characteristic also for a number of animal species, including rats, mice, flies, and dogs (Hakeem et al., 1996). This finding suggests a genetic basis for the sex difference, probably in the second X chromosome that females have but males don't; this chromosome also protects the female against a large number of genetic diseases, including hemophilia (uncontrolled bleeding) and color blindness.

Life expectancies for both sexes have been increasing in the United States at a fairly rapid rate. A child born in 1900, for example, could expect to live only 47 years, compared to well over 70 years today (see Chapter 1). During the 1970s, the life expectancy of a 45-year-old increased by 6.6 percent, whereas the life expectancy of a newborn increased by 4 percent (McGinnis, 1982). During the 1980s, life expectancy in the United States increased by another 2.2 years (National Center for Health Statistics, 1993). And from 1990 to 1997 there was another gain of 1 year (Kramarow et al., 1999). Improved safety, nutrition, and hygiene along with new medical discoveries account for most of these increases, primarily by reducing the likelihood of illnesses and injuries that bring a person to an "untimely" end.

Cardiovascular diseases are the leading cause of death in the United States (Pamuk, Makuc, Heck, Reuben, and Lochner, 1998). If all mortality caused by cardiovascular disease was eliminated, the gain in life expectancy would be 11 years at age 65 and 12 years at birth. The gain among the elderly is so great because this is a disease that most often strikes the elderly. Even so, mortality from this cause has decreased by more than 30 percent in the past 30 years, with much of the gain occurring between the early 1970s and the mid-1980s (Davis, Dinse, and Hoel, 1994). If all deaths from cancer were eliminated, on the other hand, the gain in life expectancy would be 1.5 years at age 65 and 2.5 years at birth. The gain at age 65 would be smaller for cancer than for cardiovascular disease because cancer has a lower incidence than cardiovascular disease. Over the past 15 years, cancer mortality among those under age 55 has decreased between 20 and 43 percent. Studies in the United States and in Sweden have shown that mortality from cancer has increased in those over 55, however, primarily as a result of cancers related to smoking, but also due to an increase in environmental carcinogenic sources (Adami, Bergstrom, and Sparen, 1993; Davis, Dinse, and Hoel, 1994). If medical science were able to eliminate heart disease and cancer, the major causes of death in old people, it would simply reduce the number of possible ways in which death now occurs, and would probably allow accidents and infections due to failure of the immune system to become the leading causes of death.

There must be some sort of genetic program that sets an upper limit to life span in humans. Those persons whose parents lived long lives may themselves have greater life expectancies than those with parents who died at a relatively early age. However, recent studies in Australia have shown that health status and self-rated life expectancy may be more important than the age attained by one's parents (Van Doorn and Kasl, 1998). Social mobility, whether upwards or downwards, also seems to increase life expectancy (Samuelsson and Dehlin, 1989). A long life, then, is probably due to the combined effect of many different genes, not just one or a few. Animal experiments designed to obtain long-lived specimens by selective inbreeding usually have failed; in fact, the inbred strains almost always have shorter-than-average life spans (Hakeem et al., 1996). The inbreeding has the effect of reducing the variety of genes in the offspring, increasing the probability of gene combinations that lead to the occurrence of normally rare defects that may actually shorten life. It seems then that variety may indeed be the spice of a *long* life.

The acceleration of mortality that occurs in all populations from midlife to at least the eighties would suggest that there has to be a maximum life span. However, the evidence that this acceleration slows at ages beyond the current average life span (see Chapter 1), also suggests that survival at later years than is now the case may be possible (Finch, 1996). In a study of mortality among the oldest-old from 1950 to 1990 in 11 western European countries, Kannisto (1994) found a 20 percent decline of mortality in men over 80. For woman the decline in mortality for the oldest-old was approximately 30 percent in the eighties and 20 percent in the nineties.

Longevity

The maximum potential life span of a member of the human species has often been described to vary between 70 and 110, with 90 or so probably average. However, in 1997 the French woman, Jeanne Calment achieved a record life span of 122.4 years. But the lifespans of sexually reproducing organisms vary over a million-fold range, with humans being in the middle. Organisms that have an extensive childhood are often characterized by very gradual senescence. In fact some plants, such as bristle cone pines have virtually negligible senescence. Thus the final word on maximum lifespan is still out, and much expanded life spans might be ahead for future generations (Finch, 1998; Finch and Tanzi, 1997).

We have mentioned that factors such as one's sex and the longevity of one's ancestors affect maximum span. Environmental factors also predict individual differences in life span. Heavy cigarette smoking lowers life expectancy by about 12 years, on the average, and obesity lowers it by about a year and a half for every 10 percent overweight. Pollution of our air and our water, dangerous food additives, overuse of pesticides and weed killers, and other side effects of an industrial economy have negative effects on longevity. On the other hand, being married can add up to 5 years to life.

People who live to be very old have certain characteristic personality traits (Poon, Sweaney, Clayton, and Merriam, 1992). Although individual differences among people aged 90 to 100 are almost as great as in younger groups, one trait they seem to have in common is a moderate and flexible attitude toward life. Very old people are rarely extreme in their habits. They are neither health-food fanatics nor junk-food gluttons; they are likely to enjoy drinking in moderation, and they usually exercise a bit each day. Their lives are quite varied—some relatively placid, others full of storm and stress. It is not so much the presence or absence of pressure in their lives that marks these unusually old people, but their adaptability, their ability to handle whatever comes their way.

The increase in longevity and the accompanying greater numbers of older people has shifted interest to some extent from the projection of life expectancy in terms of mortality to the study of *active life expectancy* (Katz et al., 1983). The latter concept is concerned with the number of years at a given age that one can expect to remain an active participant in our society. Improved health care and other services to the aged have resulted in the relative improvement of health for most of the elderly including those residing in rural areas. (Dansky, Brannon, Shea, Vasey, and Dirani, 1998; Palmore, 1986). Active life expectancy is a rather complicated matter because there is little agreement on how it should be measured (Crimmins and Hayward, 1996). It is further complicated by the fact that older people not only get worse, but sometimes also get better. For example, a study of a large representative sample of 5,151 adults over 70 years found that over a 2-year period, disabilities caused by disease led to some loss in functioning in 45 percent of those who were surveyed, however, 20 percent reported regaining previously lost functions (Crimmins and Saito, 1993). Despite these complications, the concept of active life expectancy is likely to become increasingly important because we want to know not only whether we will live longer, but also whether the additional years will be worth living!

Theories of Biological Aging

It seems clear that some sort of genetic program allows us a certain maximum span of life, but no more. As we grow older, biological changes occur that affect our ability to survive, that is, to avoid accidents and fight off disease. In very old persons, death is a result not so much of the particular disease or accident that happens to kill them, but of age-related biological decrements that made the disease or accidents more likely. For this reason, aging is sometimes defined as "that period in the lifespan that begins at some indeterminate period following maturity and, after a progressive decline in functional competence and increase in disease susceptibility, terminates in death" (Timiras, 1985, p. 105).

But what exactly is the nature of the decline? There is a large number of theories of biological aging, most of them at least plausible (Cristofalo, Tresini, Francis, and Volker, 1999; Schneider, 1993; Solomon, 1999). In science, one often finds a large number of theories in an early stage of scientific development; eventually all but one or two are eliminated after relevant scientific research has been conducted. That the field of aging still offers several is thus a sign of relative scientific infancy. Various theories are stated quite speculatively and permit no experimental tests. Others could be tested in principle, but the techniques to do so are only now emerging. Some theories, for example, specify certain functions of human DNA, the large molecule that contains each individual's genetic code. We have discovered the structure of DNA and now have some knowledge of how it works in simple organisms, such as bacteria. Thus, a gene has been identified that regulates life span in nematodes, primitive small worms. But human DNA is much more complex—a molecular strand 6 feet long and a 250-millionth of an inch wide, repeated in every body cell (Hayflick, 1987). Much progress is being currently made in describing the human genome. Nevertheless, we are probably still many years from completely understanding its function, and thus we are not yet quite ready to test many genetically based theories of biological aging.

In many theories of aging, genetic mechanisms are presumed to operate at the *cellular level* to bring about the symptoms of aging. One theory proposes "aging genes" that program biological changes such as menopause, gray hair, and, at a more basic level, partial or complete loss of function of body cells (Hayflick, 1987; Monti et al., 1992). Another theory suggests that our genetic mechanisms are designed to promote growth and, eventually, reproduction. Once duty is done for the preservation of the species, the organism has no more useful genetic information and "runs down," like a clock that one no longer winds. Advocates of this theory point out that "old age" is an "unnatural" phenomenon, rarely found among animals in the wild. Wild animals have roughly half the average life span of zoo animals; they are killed off by disease or predators when loss of their speed and strength makes them vulnerable. No genetic code for "later life" is needed, because for most animals there is no such thing (Finch,1998).

Probably the most widely accepted theory of aging maintains that the genetic mechanisms begin to use inaccurate, distorted information, a view that is sometimes called the *stochastic theory* of aging (Schneider, 1993). The genes or the DNA molecules may be damaged by radiation (including heat) or chemicals (such as alcohol), or inevitable mutations may occur in the process of repairing DNA or producing other molecules. "Self-poisons" manufactured (deliberately or by accident) in other parts of the body are another possibility (Hayflick, 1985). In any case, damage to DNA or other molecules in the genetic system would result in less efficient replacement and repair of body cells or the manufacture of abnormal (cancerous) cells (Campisi, 1997). One version of this theory, the *error catastrophe theory* suggests that cumulative errors in the pathway from DNA to the formation of proteins result in the production of so many defective proteins that cell and tissue death and dysfunction eventually results. It recently has been argued that some of these age-associated dysfunctions can be identified and possibly interrupted (Martin, Dammer, and Holbrook, 1993).

Another theory, the *cross-linking theory* of aging, begins with the observation that many tissues in the body become less elastic with age. Skin is the most directly observable of these tissues, taking on a leathery look as the individual grows old. The reason for this change is known. Proteins called collagen and elastin, which compose the connective tissue in skin and also in various other parts of the body (such as the muscles of the heart and lungs and the blood vessels throughout the body) form bonds, or cross-linkages, either within the protein molecule or between molecules. Cross-linking itself has many deleterious effects, decreasing the efficiency of heart and lungs and raising blood pressure (Kohn, 1985). In addition, it has been proposed that the same sort of cross-linking occurs within the body's cells, in the intracellular proteins such as the enzymes and DNA itself. If this were true, the efficiency of the intracellular proteins would be significantly reduced, with the same unfortunate results that we described for damaged DNA.

Cross-linking occurs much more rapidly in the presence of a class of chemicals called aldehydes. These substances are produced in abundance in the body as a by-product of cell metabolism, a fact that makes the cross-linking theory of aging at least plausible. Aldehyde production also varies as a function of diet, which may offer some hope to those who wish to avoid the ravages of time; low-fat and low-calorie diets with plenty of vitamins are best, and vitamin E may help, too.

Perhaps the oldest theory of aging, one that still has a few attractive aspects, is the *wear-and-tear theory*. The theory holds that people are like machines: the longer in use, the more worn the parts. Unfortunately for the theory, however, people are not very much like machines. Unlike machines, worn-out parts of the body usually are replaced or repaired. Also, there is no relationship between hard work and early death. In fact, vigorous exercise in the form of hard work is a factor predicting longer, not shorter life.

Nevertheless, some aspects of the wear-and-tear theory must be considered in a general theory of aging (Finch, 1988; Finch and Seeman, 1999). For example, prolonged exposure to sunlight damages the skin, and weaknesses or ruptures in blood vessels are most likely in areas of turbulent blood flow (for example, near branchings). Agents such as radiation and alcohol destroy irreplaceable cells, including neurons. But wear and tear cannot explain much of the aging process.

In contrast to the cellular theories, which depict age changes in structures and functions within the cell, *physiological theories* see the primary cause of aging in something outside the individual cell. The thymus gland, for example, controls many important immune reactions; if it functions poorly, the body may lose its ability to fight off disease or to destroy cancerous cells. Or, for some reason, the immune system may lose its selectivity and begin to attack normal body cells as if they were foreign intruders (Finch and Seeman, 1999; Johnson, 1985).

The most widely accepted theory of aging at the physiological level is based on assumptions of a general decline of the body's endocrine system, which

The goal in later years is to enjoy a life as satisfying and as free from disease and unnecessary decline as possible.

controls many bodily activities through hormones (Finch and Rose, 1995). Decline in the function of the ovaries in adult women is a prime example; menopause around the age of 50 is the most obvious result. Menopause is clearly not a disease; it is a normal facet of the aging process in women.

Other important glands in the endocrine system include the thyroid gland, which controls metabolism. In general, the endocrine system controls many vital balances in the body, such as the level of sugar in the blood, acting to increase it when it is low and to lower it when it is elevated. Other "homeostatic" (balancing) mechanisms keep the body temperature from becoming too high or too low and keep water, salt, and acid levels in the normal range. To the extent that the efficiency of mechanisms is impaired by age, the body loses its ability to react to stress. In many old people, death is due to a relatively mild stress (e.g., a change in the fluid balance caused by diarrhea) to which the aging body can no longer adapt (also see Finch, 1990).

One of the best arguments for a *metabolic theory* of aging comes from experiments such as those of Roy Walford and Edward Masoro (e.g., Masoro and McCarter, 1991), who found that if the caloric intake of rodents is reduced by about 40 percent, while maintaining necessary nutrient and vitamin levels, one can lengthen their life by approximately 35 percent. Caloric restriction even seems to work when started in the animals' midlife. Caloric restriction also delayed the onset of many age-dependent diseases. Obviously no such experiments would be ethical with human samples.

Natural experiments of starving populations were always accompanied by deficits in nutrients and vitamins, so the fact that there is no reported increase in longevity following episodes of starvation is not surprising. Some pertinent evidence comes from studies of obesity in humans. It appears, though, that the shortest life span occurs at both underweight and overweight extremes. In addition, there has been a recent tendency for increase in overweight in the United States, with 33 4 percent of the population estimated to be overweight (Kuczmarski et al., 1994). However, a very large number of elderly men and women are currently known to be habitually undernourished (Kendall, Wisocki, and Pers, 1991). Hence, there is at present no evidence that caloric restrictions at acceptable levels of comfort would extend the average person's life!

Physiological theories of aging, of course, are not incompatible with cellular theories. If a theorist views aging primarily as a function of declining endocrine activity or a decline in the nervous system, he or she must still answer the cellular question: What is it about the cells of the endocrine or nervous system that accounts for the decline? Aging genes? Damaged cells? An adequate biological theory of aging will have to specify the age changes at both the cellular and the physiological level. And it is going to be difficult to advocate inexorable biological processes that are directly attributable to intrinsic causes, unless they can be demonstrated to occur in virtually all members of the species (Solomon, 1999; Williams, 1993).

The interactions between different levels of bodily functions are intricate. Damaged cells can cause a decline in physiological function, which in turn can damage more cells. A decline in one part of the body causes decline elsewhere, which in turn affects the part that started the decline, and the cycle begins anew. For most of the adult years, the decline in physiological functioning is slight, but it accelerates with age. At the end of life there is a neuroendocrine cascade, a catastrophe of errors and malfunctions that results inevitably in death (Finch, 1990; Finch and Seeman, 1999; Schneider, 1993).

It is not inconceivable that future advances in basic biology could lead to substantial extensions of the potential life span. While it may be possible to extend life considerably beyond the years currently allotted to us, there are many ethical questions whether that would indeed be good for humankind. The greater hope is that we will learn to deal with the aging mechanisms so that life in the later years is more satisfying and as free as possible from debilitating disease and unnecessary biological decline.

SENSORY CAPACITIES

Psychologists are particularly interested in that part of the biological equipment which is used for processing information from the environment. In the following section, we consider the effects of aging on the central nervous system: the brain and the spinal cord. We begin our discussion where information processing begins—at the periphery, with the sense organs.

Vision

Several biological changes occur in the visual system during the adult years, especially toward the end of life (Fozard and Gordon-Salant, 2001; Kline and Scialfa, 1996). These changes sometimes create problems in coping with life, but usually we can compensate for significant losses of visual ability through external devices such as eyeglasses. Thus, about half the population needs some visual correction by the mid-forties and virtually everyone does so by the late fifties. On the other hand, more serious visual impairments, including cataracts and glaucoma, do not reach a high incidence until the late sixties are reached, but do become a major problem in the very old (Figure 13-2).

Two major classes of biological events occur at somewhat different times in life. Changes in some external parts of the eye (cornea, lens, muscles, and other parts), affecting the transmission of light waves and visual abilities, begin to assume importance between the ages of 35 and 45 (Corso, 1987; Kline and Scialfa, 1996). Changes in the retina and the nervous system begin to become noticeable between 55 and 65 (Fozard, 2000: Keunen, Van Norren, and Van Meel, 1987).

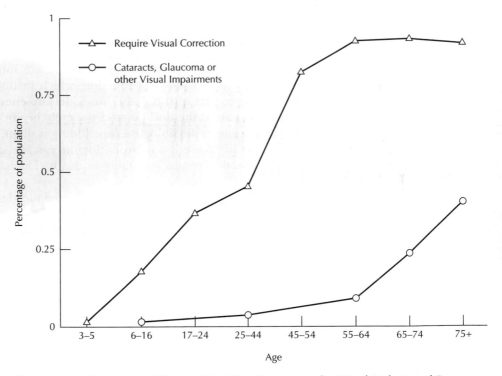

Figure 13-2 Percentage of Persons Requiring Corrections for Visual Defects and Percentage of those who Suffer from Cataracts, Glaucoma and other Visual Impairments. *Source:* National Center for Health Statistics (1983, 1994c).

A population-based survey of older adults (West et al.,1997) identified those aspects of vision that are likely to be affected by age in ways that may cause problems for older persons. These included declines in visual acuity, contrast sensitivity, glare, and reduction of visual field. Reduced acuity was associated with adaptation to changing light conditions and activities requiring good visual resolution. Serious visual impairment in advanced age can lead to unfavorable emotional and behavioral consequences and invariably lead to a shrinkage of the person's spatial environment (Wahl, 1998).

As the average individual ages, the lens of the eye becomes harder and less flexible. The lens is made up of epithelial tissue, like the skin, hair, and nails. Like all other body parts of this sort, the lens continues to grow throughout life. Unlike the skin, hair, and nails, however, the lens cannot shed excess cells; instead it becomes more compact and hence less flexible (if it did not become more compact, it would grow too large for the eyeball). The result of this loss of lens flexibility is a decrease in the ability to accommodate the shape of the lens for viewing objects that are close to the eye. Thus, many adults around the age of 40 or 45 begin experiencing difficulty in reading and doing "close work"; but eyeglasses can compensate for most of this difficulty. Likewise, added attention to typographical design is helpful, but this does not necessarily mean that "bigger type is better," but rather that more attention needs to be paid to typographical features that aid the aging eye (for example the use of serifs for easier following of lines; see also Adams and Hoffman, 1994).

The lens also becomes yellower with age, although the cause of this change is not well understood. The result is a reduction in the amount of light that reaches the retina and also a change in the quality of light, because yellow absorbs wavelengths from the blue-green end of the spectrum (Weale, 1988). Older people thus require more illumination than young adults to read. On the other hand, a 10-year longitudinal study of color vision in 577 males, ranging in age from 20 to 95, showed little change in accuracy until the eighties were reached (Gittings, Fozard, and Shock, 1987). Upon more detailed analysis, it appears that age differences in color vision occur as the consequence of selective absorption of the lens in the shorter wavelengths with age, and increasing difficulty with color discrimination associated with loss of photoreceptors, other retinal accentricities, and possibly age-related changes in the central nervous system (Fozard and Gordon-Salant, 2001). Color constancy seems to be maintained by compensatory mechanisms except when illumination is low (Kraft and Werner, 1999).

Increasingly with age, especially in the seventies and beyond, the lens may become clouded so as to block or scatter the entering light; vision is of course severely impaired. Cataracts (extreme conditions of lens opacity) are found in 20 to 25 percent of those over 75 (National Center for Health Statistics, 1994c). The appearance of a cataract in one eye is often followed by the appearance of a cataract in the other eye, albeit several years later (Corso, 1987). Cataracts have been associated with a substantial risk of automobile accidents (Owsley, Stalvey, Wells, and Sloane, 1999). Cataracts are fairly easy to cure. A relatively simple operation can remove the faulty lens and with eyeglasses, a contact lens, or a plastic replacement lens nearly normal vision can be restored.

Another consequence of an increasingly opaque lens is glare, the scattering of light waves as they enter the eye. Glare puts older adults in a bind, because they need greater illumination to see well, but more light also increases problems with glare. Night driving may be particularly difficult, because most of the viewing must be done in dim light and shadows and, in addition, the lights of oncoming automobiles are exceptionally effective in producing glare, even in younger people (Carter, 1982). Age changes have also been observed in contrast senitivity which becomes particularly severe under dim lighting conditions, making it difficult to detect objects from background thus further complicating night driving (Owsley and Burton, 1991).

In addition to the lens, the pupil also changes with age (Kline and Schieber, 1985). Older pupils are smaller than young pupils in the same light, and responses to changes in illumination are slower (Koretz, Cook, and Kaufman, 1997). These changes affect the eye's ability to adapt to changing light conditions, making night driving difficult for still another reason. Also some eye muscles become so much less effective with age that, to cite one example, adults at the age of 40 have significantly more difficulty looking up without raising their heads. It's a minor difficulty, perhaps, but it could be a problem when trying to read overhead street signs or see overhead traffic-control signals.

Once again we need to be reminded that there are great individual differences in rate of change in visual functions. These findings suggest that some older persons should avoid driving at night, but for most people, the findings simply mean that greater care and attention are required to compensate for the slight physiological changes. Persons with only minor visual changes find that corrective glasses are particularly helpful in night driving, even though they might be safely dispensed with during the day.

Changes in the lens, the pupil, eye muscles, and other parts of the eye account for a good part of the age differences usually found in common visual abilities such as visual acuity and depth perception. Visual acuity is the ability to see clearly in the sense of being able to read an eye chart in a doctor's office. The decrease in the illumination that reaches the retina through a yellowing lens and a pupil gradually decreasing in size affects acuity. Glare, which is the visual equivalent of static on a radio, also cuts down on the ability to see clearly. The result is a decline in visual acuity that begins around the age of 40 or 50. By the age of 75, poor vision is common, although most problems can be corrected with eyeglasses (Gittings and Fozard, 1986; Kline and Scialfa, 1996).

Depth perception is the ability to estimate the distance of objects. It depends on several cues, many of which are affected by the changes that we have been discussing. For example, texture is a cue to depth, because the "grain" of something is clearer and less dense up close. Decreases in visual acuity and increases in glare would make it more difficult to discriminate small details in the distance, reducing the perception of texture. Similarly, less flexibility in the lens makes accommodation less effective as a cue to estimates of distance. The result is a general decrease in the accuracy of depth perception after the age of 50 or so (Owsley and Sloan, 1987; Schieber, 1992). In most real-life situations, however, the many redundant cues to distance make it unlikely that this deficit will cause any major problems, at least not until quite late in life. In other words, if one cue to distance becomes unreliable, the person can turn to other cues (for example, is one object in front of another?) without much loss in the accuracy of depth estimates.

The field of vision is the total area that the individual can see adequately when looking straight ahead at a fixed point. The extent of the field of vision has important consequences in daily life. A person with a broad visual field is aware of cars pulling out of side streets when he or she is driving; a person with a narrow field of vision sees only the road that he or she is driving down.

Field of vision is generally measured with a technique called kinetic perimetry, in which an object is slowly moved from a position outside the person's field of vision to a position where the person can detect it. Kinetic perimetry shows that the visual field constricts with advancing age. In a study of the peripheral vision of 17,000 persons between the ages of 16 and 92, Burg (1968) found that the total horizontal (left and right) visual field remained constant up to age 35, declined slightly between the ages of 40 and 50, and declined more quickly thereafter. A study using a different technique found that the visual field remained stable through age 55 and then began to shrink. The total size of the field of vision was found to diminish most markedly in those over 70 (Ball and Owsley, 1992, 2000; Scialfa, Kline, and Lyman, 1987).

Visual decline in advanced age has been associated with many unmet needs of the elderly, such as housekeeping, grocery shopping, and food preparation, as well as with physical and emotional disabilities (Branch, Horowitz, and Carr, 1989; Marsiske, Klumb, and Baltes, 1997). Some of these difficulties could be alleviated by greater effort to adapt the visual environment of older people so as to compensate at least in part for age-related decrement in visual performance (Schieber, Fozard, and Gordon-Salant, 1991; Wahl, 1994; Wahl and Oswald, 2000). Major work is in progress that specifies more directly those age changes in vision that reduce mobility by forcing many older persons to give up driving (Ball and Owsley, 2000; Schieber et al., 1992). This work requires the specification of accidents peculiar to older drivers, as well as the particular characteristics of displays that are used as aides for safe driving (Kline, 1994).

In addition to the effects of changes in the eye as a whole, a second major class of age changes involves the basic receptor cells for light in the retina. Decreased blood circulation starves retinal cells, resulting in their destruction or malfunction. Such damage may be caused by disease in addition to normal aging, but the changes are normal in the statistical sense. Retinal cell damage can be detected in most people by the age of 55 to 65 (Fozard, 2000; Kline and Scialfa 1996).

One retinal ailment that afflicts the elderly is senile macular degeneration (SMD). The macula, the area of the retina where vision is most acute, begins to deteriorate. Some macular deterioration has been observed in as many as 60 percent of individuals over age 70 (Jackson, Owsley, Cordle, and Finley, 1998). The ailment begins slowly, typically progressing until the visual acuity declines to between 20/50 and 20/100. Within this range, reading becomes extremely difficult, although it remains possible with a strong handheld magnifying glass. A television

Most people can compensate for slight losses in sensory capacities with devices such as glasses and hearing aids.

screen is visible only as a blur. Peripheral vision is usually not seriously affected, so the person can still function in familiar environments. The disease usually affects both eyes, and although treatment has been found to be beneficial, it does not prevent reoccurrence (Marmor, 1992). A devastating variant of SMD, disciform macular degeneration, is accompanied by leakage of blood vessels, which will destroy the nervous tissue of the macula (and central visual acuity) if not halted by laser photocoagulation.

Damage to the retina in old age can also be caused by a group of disorders called glaucoma. Increasing intraocular pressure is accompanied by atrophy of the optic nerve and abnormalities in the visual field. The primary cause of the increasing pressure is resistance to the outflow of liquid in the front of the eye. The increase in pressure leads to subsequent changes in the optic disc (the blind spot at the end of the optic nerve) and the retina. Longitudinal and cross-sectional studies show marked increases in glaucoma among older people in the age range from 60 to 85 (National Center for Health Statistics, 1994c). Age-related changes in the prevalence of glaucoma may be related to normative changes in the volume of the lens and the rigidity of the iris and surrounding tissue. It has also been demonstrated that intraocular pressure is correlated with systolic blood pressure (the higher number in the blood pressure reading).

An important aspect of open-angle glaucoma, the most prevalent type among the elderly, is that no symptoms become apparent in many cases until the retina has been irreparably damaged. Advanced cases reveal themselves by a characteristic cupping of the optic disc as seen through the ophthalmoscope. However, the pressure increases that cause glaucoma can be detected well before significant damage has occurred through the use of tonometry, a method of estimating the pressure in the eye by measuring the force needed to depress the surface of the eye. Because early detection is crucial, people over age 50 should have regular glaucoma screenings.

Any retinal loss, of course, affects vision directly. Visual acuity is reduced and sensitivity to low levels of illumination decreases, making night driving even more hazardous than before. Color vision is also affected, so much so that persons near the age of 90 fail to identify the color of over 50 percent of objects presented (Weale, 1988). Most people do not experience serious problems with vision until the age of 80 or later, but in a few cases, the retinal damage is so severe as to leave the individual legally blind. According to a survey by the National Society for the Prevention of Blindness, the incidence of blindness increases from a rate of 2.5 per 1,000 individuals between the ages of 40 and 64 to 5.0 per 1,000 between 65 and 69 and to 14.5 per 1,000 over 70.

Hearing

Hearing difficulties show approximately the same progression with age as problems with vision (see Figure 13-2). With both senses, the number of people with objectively diagnosed impairments begins to increase around the age of 40 and shows sharp increases after 60. In the 45 to 54 age group, about 19 percent experience some difficulties with hearing; between 75 and 79, about 75 percent (Fozard, 2000). Reported hearing loss is greater for males than females and greater for whites than African Americans (National Academy on an Aging Society, 1999). Of a sample of 2,506 persons aged 55 to 74 who participated in the National Health and Nutrition Survey, 35.1 percent showed significant pure tone hearing loss (Reuben, Walsh, Moore, Damasyn, and Greendale, 1998). However, in a comparable Italian study only half this number of people are ready to report that they have hearing difficulties (Maggi et al., 1998).

Some hearing impairment can be attributed to external factors (excessive accumulation of ear wax; arthritis in the bones of the middle ear), but most of the loss is due to degenerative changes in the cochlea, the primary neural receptor for hearing . The cochlea is to hearing what the retina is to vision. Cochlear problems generally involve the loss of hair cells (the end organs transmitting sound to the brain) or disturbances of the inner-ear metabolism (Fozard and Gordon-Salant, 2001) The reduced flexibility of inner-ear membranes and restrictive adhesions may also be implicated. Although particular patterns of hearing loss are associated with the degeneration of specific structures in the ear, a person often suffers from several types of structural degeneration at the same time (Olsho, Hawkins, and Lenhardt, 1985).

Hearing loss is generally greater for sounds of high frequency (Brant and Fozard, 1990; Stevens, Cruz, Marks, and Lakatos, 1998). Thus, the average old person will have more difficulty hearing sopranos than basses, more difficulty hearing women than men, more difficulty with tweeters than woofers. Men, who at all ages hear less of high-pitched sounds than women, also show more loss with age, so that by the later years of life, the difference in the abilities of a husband and wife to hear high-frequency sounds can be considerable. However, after age 70, there is a faster decline for males in the speech range, because they already have lost much capacity at higher frequencies (Brant and Fozard, 1990; Morrell and Brant, 1991). Hearing is a case where cross-sectional data actually underestimates age-related decline; particularly in advanced old age, recent longitudinal findings suggests that hearing loss in the eighties and beyond is an even more serious problem than earlier cross-sectional findings suggest (Brant and Pearson, 1993).

Hearing loss is one of the prime sources of the difficulty that old people sometimes have understanding speech. By a standard test of speech understanding, there is not much change between the ages of 20 and 50, but by age 80 the average loss is about 25 percent. Rapid speech is particularly hard for old people with hearing loss (Brant and Fozard, 1990; Vaughan and Letowski, 1997; Wingfield, 1996). Hearing difficulties increase when there is competing speech noise as in cocktail parties, traffic noise or continuous discourse (Prosser, Turrini, and Arslan, 1990; see Figure 13-3). Memory constraints also have a significant effect on elderly listeners' ability to use linguistic context for retrospective analysis of what had been heard (Wingfield, 1996, 1999).

Reductions in the amount that a person can hear with clarity and comprehension often create a sense of increasing social isolation, as the familiar sounds of life become dimmer and dimmer; depression and other emotional disorders are a common result. People with a hearing deficit who also have paranoid tendencies will often misinterpret poorly heard conversation as hostile toward them (Fozard, 1990). Mental competence may decline also, if the individual begins to avoid interpersonal interactions (Carabellese et al., 1993).

Fortunately, much of the hearing loss can be compensated for through modifying the acoustic signal that arrives at the ear by redesigning the acoustic environment. One of the common devices used by people with hearing loss is the hearing aid. The ordinary hearing aid increases the intensity of sounds at the eardrums, and by blocking the ear canal, it also reduces the transmission of low frequencies, thereby limiting the hearing of some sounds even as it improves the hearing of others. Furthermore, conventional hearing aids amplify background noise just as much as the desired signal. Binaural hearing aids (for both ears) often present problems because transmitted sounds may not stimulate both ears at the proper time, which may introduce distortions. Some of these difficulties can be resolved by a proper prescription for hearing aids based on the results of an examination. Hearing aids should not be purchased directly from hearing-aid salespeople without prior examination by a qualified audiologist. But even when the hearing aid is chosen with the assistance of professionals, it tends to be less useful as people age.

While most adults readily compensate moderate visual problems by means of prescription glasses, the use of hearing aids is far less frequent. A recent survey of 1,629 adults aged 48 to 92 years found that only 14.6 percent of persons with a

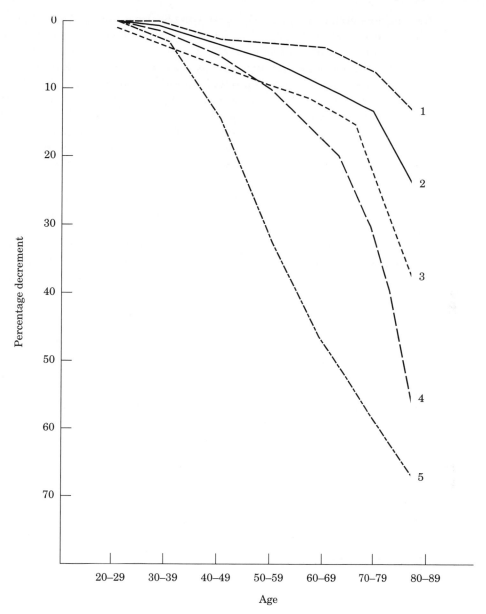

Figure 13-3 Cross-Sectional Study of Speech Intelligibility, Shown as Percentage Decrement from the Scores of Subjects Aged 20 to 29. Conditions: (1) Normal Speech (2) Speeded Speech; 2H Times the Normal Rate; (3) Selective Listening, That is, Tracking One Speaker Among Many, as at a Cocktail Party; (4) Reverberated or Echoed Speech, as in a Hall with Unfavorable Acoustics; (5) Interrupted Speech, as on a Poor Telephone Connection. *Source:* Bergman et al. (1976). Age-related decrement in hearing for speech: Sampling and longitudinal studies. *Journal of Gerontology, 31,* 533-538. Reproduced by permission.

hearing loss greater than 2.5 decibels wore hearing aids, and even among those who were severely impaired only 55 percent wore hearing aids (Popelka et al., 1998). A study of the psychological effect of hearing aid use in older adults showed that while the use of the hearing aids has a positive effect on self-perceived hearing handicap, there was no effect on improvement in domains such as social activities, satisfaction with social relations and report of well-being (Tesch-Römer, 1997).

Traditional hearing aids are analog devices; that is, the voltage created by the microphone transducer, which is an exact analog of the input signal is filtered and amplified to enable the user to hear speech sounds at a comfortable level. The conflicting requirements of the individual's hearing loss makes such devices difficult to calibrate optimally. Perhaps the most promising recent development has been the introduction of digital hearing aids that allow greater precision, particularly in achieving appropriate noise reduction, which often bothers hearing-aid users (Schieber, Fozard, and Gordon-Salant, 1991).

A much neglected technique that holds particular promise for those who are not helped much by hearing aids involves changing the person's acoustic environment. Modifications of this kind often cost little or nothing. Furniture can be arranged to provide better face-to-face contact, and obstructions can be removed. Noisy appliances can be located where they won't interfere with the intelligibility of speech. Mechanical devices such as telephone amplifiers may be helpful because intelligibility of consonant sound is improved by amplification. In some cases, modest structural alterations might be considered. Designers and builders of housing for the elderly might take specific design features into account. Studies show, for example, that the increased reverberation that occurs in narrow rooms helps the hearing-impaired and that the suitable placement of soft and rough surfaces can improve speech discrimination (Fozard and Gordon-Salant 2001; Regnier, 1996; Schieber, Fozard, and Gordon-Salant, 1991).

The approaches discussed above, of course, are of little value to the totally deaf, but there are some promising advances here also. The FDA has recently approved electronic cochlear implants that allow deaf people to hear such sounds as automobile horns and doorbells and to detect rises and falls in inflection, which is helpful in lipreading.

Other Senses

Taste and smell appear to decrease in sensitivity slightly with age (Murphy, 1983), and older persons seem less aware of their decline in smell sensitivity (Nordin, Monsch, and Murphy, 1995). Anecdotal evidence and a few research studies suggest that sensitivity to bitter tastes (unfortunately) lasts longer than sensitivity to sweet or salty tastes; sour tastes, too, may be more easily detected by the elderly (Stevens et al.,1998; Weiffenbach, Tylenda, and Baum, 1990). Older persons also have greater difficulty in remembering specific odors (Larsson and Bäckman, 1998).

In advanced old age people are robbed of many of life's pleasures when the senses of taste and smell do become less sensitive: the smell of flowers, the taste of a good meal (which is partly smell as well) are no longer quite as appealing. Those who can no longer appreciate subtle flavors may also be less inclined to meet friends for meals, so they may be deprived of an important social outlet. Fortunately, one can compensate somewhat for the loss of sensitivity to taste through the use of various flavor enhancers. In fact, increasing older adults' enjoyment of food by using healthful food additives may be an effective way to ensure their eating proper amounts and variety of food (Schiffman and Warwick, 1988).

Equally important as the loss of pleasure in eating is the fact that older persons lose some of their ability to avoid poisons, which are often identified by taste. An older person might be less likely to notice that a potato salad "doesn't taste right," a clue that deadly bacteria are forming. Also lost is some of the ability to detect life-threatening events such as leaking gas or fire, which often are identified by the smell of smoke. An electronic smoke detector is a good idea for people of all ages, but for an elderly person living alone, it represents a particularly wise enhancement of human sensory capacity.

If there were justice in this world, we would hope to find age-related decreases in sensitivity to pain to compensate the elderly for decreases in the other, more pleasant senses. The research evidence is not completely consistent, but the bulk of it suggests that old people do indeed suffer less pain with the same obnoxious stimulus than young people. Because old people experience more obnoxious stimuli (injuries, diseases, surgery), this is a blessing of sorts. On the other hand, decreasing sensitivity to pain can be dangerous if reduced to the point that injuries, such as burns, are ignored (Harkins, Price, and Martelli, 1986). The perception and recognition of pain in older persons also differs from the young across many conditions. For example, diseases that are associated with severe pain in younger persons, such as heart attacks or appendicitis, often produce minimal discomfort in the old. On the other hand, older persons may complain about pain from simple procedures primarily because they create anxiety (Sturgis, Dolce, and Dickerson, 1988).

A major problem in research on pain is that pain tolerance is only partly a function of the painful stimulus; it also depends on the individual's attitude (e.g., a young male may submit to considerable pain to validate his macho self-concept), the situation (whether the pain is expected or perceived as part of a healing process), and the culture (e.g., British patients have more of the "stiff upper lip" and are willing to accept more pain than Americans). Assessment of pain and its management therefore becomes a rather individualized process (Dolce and Dickerson, 1991; Wisocki and Powers, 1997).

Sensitivity to temperature also declines in old age (Stevens et al., 1998). This is a particular problem because temperature regulation also becomes less efficient (Fox et al., 1983). From about 65 to 85, differences between the temperature of the skin and the body core decline. This probably means that temperatures in the body core cannot be maintained adequately when the outside temperature (and hence the skin temperature) is low (Macey, 1989). The combination of lowered awareness and poor temperature regulation means that older people face a greater risk of frostbite and even death from exposure to cold. As would be expected, social isolation increases the risk of sudden temperature drop, or hypothermia (Rango, 1985).

Degeneration of the structures related to balance lead to instabilities of posture and gait among the elderly, and in the very old there is an increased chance of falls (Buchner et al., 1993; Duncan and Studensky, 1994). Visual stability in old age has also been found to be impaired under increased cognitive demands (Maylor and Wing, 1996).

Surveys of older persons show that about 30 percent of those over 65 fell at least once during the preceding year (Campbell, Borrie, and Spears, 1989). Falls are of particular concern in advanced old age, because one of the consequences may be a hip fracture. Hip fractures, however, seem to be more common when a fall occurs while turning (Cumming and Klineberg, 1994; Simoneau and Leibowitz, 1996).

Among those who have poor balance, fear of falling can lead to restrictions in physical activities and social contacts. Those who do fall and injure themselves may not be able to care for themselves. They may have to depend on family members for assistance, and some eventually have to be institutionalized (Lachman et al., 1998).

THE BRAIN AND THE NERVOUS SYSTEM

The central nervous system consists of the brain and the spinal cord. The brain is the primary biological basis for intelligence and personality; and, thus, we are concerned with what happens to it and the central nervous system with age. Research on the human brain is difficult and fraught with the possibility of serious error. For example, much of the research has been done on old people who for some reason required an autopsy after death; a high percentage of these subjects may, of course, have suffered from diseases affecting the brain (Cohen, 1992). Thus, the fact that these subjects' brains weigh less, on average, than those of people who died young may not be very meaningful.

Nevertheless, it is clear that even healthy people experience some loss of brain neurons over the years. It has also been suggested that the neurons that remain lose some of their branches, or dendrites (Scheibel, 1996). A variety of explanations of neuron loss have been offered. Possible causes include accumulation of the pigment lipofuscin, which may impair the neuron's protein metabolism (Ordy, 1981); reduction of the rate of blood circulation through the brain (Drachman, 1993); a progressive increase in errors in protein synthesis of the nuclei of the neurons (Lynch and Gerling, 1981); and degeneration of the dendrites due to insufficient environmental stimulation (Greenough and Green, 1981). On the other hand, recent work suggests that enviromental stimulation can create new dendrites, even in old age (Cohen 1992; Scheibel, 1996).

The efficiency of the aging brain may also be affected by the availability of appropriate amounts of neurotransmitters, which are the chemicals that mediate synaptic communication between neurons. Neurotransmitters control the flow of information in the brain by regulating inhibitory and excitatory patterns. If the

Athletic people who remain active as they age may have faster reaction times than young nonathletic people.

supply of neurotransmitters is inadequate, nerve impulses are conducted more slowly. Levels of a neurotransmitter known to affect memory, acetylcholine, have been shown to decrease with age (Tatemichi, Sacktor, and Mayeux, 1994).

Much less is known about brain changes that take place at the subcortical level. Age does not seem to affect the neurons in the basal ganglia that are responsible for gross motor movement. The cerebellar cells, on the other hand, appear to decline more rapidly after the age of 60. This change may result in impaired balance, loss of muscle tone that results in premature muscle fatigue, and increased difficulty in coordinating fine motor movement (Cohen, 1992).

Estimates of neuron loss in the cortex range from zero to almost 50 percent, another indication of the difficulty of research in this area. Perhaps 5 to 10 percent is a reasonable figure for people at the age of 75, with loss at an accelerating rate after that. Several researchers have proposed that any loss of neurons may be made up by the plasticity of the remaining neurons, which may develop new synaptic connections by elaborating their dendritic branches (Curcio, Buell, and Coleman, 1982). This sort of proliferation of branches may occur in response to environmental stimulation (Diamond et al., 1985; Greenough and Green, 1981); it has even been suggested that it may result in a net gain in the density of synapses with increasing age (Scheibel, 1996). All in all, however, it appears that the physical loss in the central nervous system is remarkably low, considering losses in other systems; kidney filtration, for example, may decline by 50 percent. Because nerve fibers are not replaced in the body, the maintenance of neurons is testimony of the protection and repair mechanisms of the brain.

Reaction Time

One of the most consistent findings in the study of aging is an increase in reaction time. Typical reaction time tasks range from the simple (e.g., How long does it take to press a button after a light goes on?) to the more complex (e.g., How fast can one write or type?). The decrease in speed with which older adults perform such tasks is sizable; it is around 20 percent for simple tasks and can be 50 percent or more for complex tasks (Cerella, 1990). In the view of some psychologists, this increasing slowness in response with age reflects a basic change in the speed with which the central nervous system processes information. The cause for this slowing has been attributed to disruptions of connections within the neural network. Each disruption increases the time required to process information, with cumulatively increasing effect as people age (Cerella, 1990).

Reaction time has three major components: sensory transmission time; motor execution time; and central processing time, which involves interpretation, decision, and association. Through various means, it has been possible to show that sensory input and motor output are usually small compared to the central processing component. For example, the time between the onset of a stimulus, like a light, and the arrival of an impulse in the brain, which can be measured electronically, is short. The first signal to the muscle (of the forearm that controls the finger that is to be lifted, for example) can be detected, so we know how much is motor time and how much is premotor (Salthouse, 1985). Unless the stimulus or response is unusually complex, the central processing time accounts for up to 80 percent of the total reaction time.

The notion that the central nervous system gets sluggish with age, thus increasing reaction time, is an appealing hypothesis. The decreasing speed of processing information could account for many of the observed age differences in learning, memory, perception, and intelligence (Birren and Fisher, 1992; Salthouse 1994). The advantage to older subjects of a slower pace of learning, for example, would be explained directly. The hypothesis is difficult to test experimentally, especially because we don't really know what "central processing" means in terms of brain function. In addition, reaction time does not correlate highly with unspeeded measures of intellectual ability. The correlations are higher for old people than for young, but this can be interpreted in several ways. It may be that, for older adults, speed of response is a more important component of intellectual performance. Or it may be that intelligence tests, for older adults, often measure reaction time instead of intellectual ability (see Schaie, 1989c). Speed of processing as a central explanatory factor has received much recent attention, because new statistical methods have made it possible to identify the contribution of processing speed to performance (see Chapter 12).

What is the nature of the "neural sluggishness" underlying increasing reaction times with age? Several possibilities have been suggested—irreversible neural deterioration, decreasing blood flow to the brain (which may be reversible), faltering arousal processes, the effects of disease—and, indeed, there are probably a multiplicity of factors at work (Birren and Fisher, 1992; Earles and Salthouse, 1995). One relevant consideration is that reaction times can be significantly improved by physical (Emery, Burker, and Blumenthal, 1992). Among active old people, such as those who run or play racquetball, average reaction times are faster than among nonathletic young people; in one study these differences were sizable, even though the oldsters were 60 to 70 years old and were being compared to 20-year-olds (Spirduso and MacRae, 1990). Because exercise increases blood flow to the brain, increases the amount of oxygen in the blood, and may even affect the character of neural tissue, these factors are implicated in the more typical age differences in reaction time. The likelihood of engaging in exercise in adulthood, however, is mediated by personality factors (also see Chapter 9) such that the probability of exercising past midlife can be predicted by the presence of positive personality characteristics (Siegler et al., 1997).

Another possibility is that inefficient coordination of the body's arousal processes with the brain's activity patterns is at fault (Prinz, Dustman, and Emerson, 1990). Reaction time tasks, especially the more complex tasks, require alertness and penalize both underarousal and overarousal. If the average old person is less easily aroused and, once aroused, is more easily rattled (as we concluded in Chapter 10 on motivation), we would expect reaction-time performance to suffer.

Difficulties in achieving and maintaining the proper degree of alertness may be directly responsible for the problems that old people have in reaction-time tasks that require efficient preparation. Unlike nerves that have deteriorated, however, inefficient arousal processes apparently can be improved somewhat by practice or expertise with reaction-time tasks, which significantly enhance performance (Salthouse, 1993).

Sleep Disturbances

The total time of actual sleep remains fairly constant throughout adulthood. After age 60, people spend an increasing amount of time awake in bed trying to fall asleep initially, during wakeful periods throughout the night, and lying awake before rising in the morning. Periods of wakefulness during the night begin in the thirties and increase thereafter; for people over age 50, an unbroken night's sleep is extremely rare. When it does occur, the sleep of older persons is less restful, with less time spent in deep, dreamless sleep. Older persons also awaken more readily than do young people. The major causes of sleep disturbances in old age are sleep apnea (a halting of respiration in sleep), periodic leg movements, and heartburn. Depression and anxiety also have been observed in elderly insomniacs (Middelkoop, Smide-van den Doe, Neven, Kamphuisen, and Springer, 1996). In addition, quality of sleep is reduced by many conditions that affect brain function, including cardiovascular disease, dementias, and various drug states. These sleep-impairing conditions become more frequent with advancing age (Jensen, Dehlin, Hagberg, Samuelsson, and Svensson, 1998).

There are two possible reasons that older people spend more time in bed even though they sleep no more than other adults. It may be simply that it takes longer for older people to accumulate a sufficient amount of deep sleep to meet their physiological needs. On the other hand, older people may spend more time in bed because they have more time to spend there; often as many as 10 or 12 hours.

Many old persons complain primarily about sleeping less soundly; it has been found that the most damaging aspect of sleep disturbances is the frequent interruption of sleep. This sleep fragmentation has been related to sleepiness and reduced daytime well-being in the aged. Inadequate nighttime sleep is frequently compensated for by daytime naps, and the elderly often make extensive use of drugs to promote sleep. However, the most commonly prescribed sleep medications may increase the incidence of apnea and cardiac arrhythmia (Murtagh and Greenwood, 1995). Evidence from sleep deprivation studies suggests that sleep loss may actually improve the quality of sleep (that is, increasing the proportion of time in deep sleep) the following night. Consequently, it appears that older persons could improve the quality of their sleep if they avoided sleeping pills and stayed in bed for shorter rather than longer intervals. Likewise, participation in stimulating activities may be helpful, because the sleep–wake cycle may be unnecessarily interrupted by intermittent daytime naps that take the place of meaningful activities and interests (Gatz, et al., 1998).

AGING AND DISEASE

It has been remarkably difficult to document significant age changes in the functioning of the central nervous system in the disease-free older person. Several diseases that affect the central nervous system, produce a range of mental disorders that, in old people, are often lumped under the catch-all term of senility. These diseases are examined in more detail in the following chapter on mental illness. Here, we will consider ill health in general and its relationship to aging. It is a thorny issue, as we have already indicated more than once.

The probability of disease increases dramatically after the age of 65. People over 65, who constitute about 12.5 percent of the population, account for 30 percent of the nation's health-care expenditures. They consume 25 percent of all drugs, fill a third of the nation's hospital beds, and account for 40 percent of visits to physicians' offices. They are also the major users of facilities for long-term care and home-care facilities (Hing, 1994; National Center for Health Statistics, 1994b).

The medical picture of the elderly, though hardly a bright one, is often painted in colors too gray for the facts. At any one time, only about 5 percent of the population over 65 are found in nursing homes and other long-term facilities; these are predominantly white (94 percent), widowed (64 percent), females (70 percent), and those who are over the age of 75 (74 percent). In a given year, around 83 percent of the elderly do not require short-term hospital care, only slightly less than the 89 percent of those under the age of 65. Nevertheless, 86

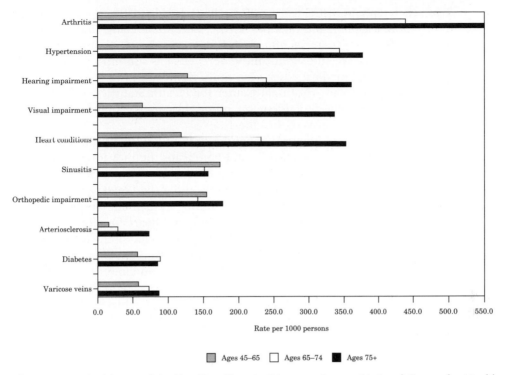

Figure 13-4   Incidence of the Top Ten Chronic Diseases. *Source:* National Center for Health Statistics (1994c).

percent of the elderly do have some sort of chronic condition; arthritis is the most common (45 percent), with hypertension and hearing impairments next frequent (National Center for Health Statistics, 1994c,). Figure 13.4 shows the incidence of the 10 most common chronic conditions, comparing persons from 65 to 74 and those 75 or older with those from 45 to 64. Illness incidence varies by ethnic groups. Higher rates of decline in functional health over a 6 year period have been reported in young-old Afro-Americans, while in the oldest-old, the black survivors show less decline (Clark, Maddox, and Steinhauser, 1993).

The perception of illness and actions taken to ameliorate disease by older persons is frequently a function of the elder's perception of bodily changes that seem to go beyond what is perceived in one's peers (Haug, Musil, Warner and Morris, 1998). Whether individuals report themselves to be in good health as well as objective assesments of functional health status also seem to depend substantially on their economic well-being and levels of attained education (Maddox, Clark, and Steinhauser, 1994).

Effects of Disease

As psychologists, we are interested in the effects of disease on the individual's life and mood and his or her ability to adjust to the illness. Disease has many effects. For example, there is often pain with arthritis. Chronic pain steals pleasure from each day and distracts the sufferer from more satisfying pursuits; it may affect motivation, learning, and memory (Crose, Leventhal, Haug, and Burns, 1997; Parmalee, 1994). The financial effects of disease, despite Medicare and other government programs, are still significant; elderly citizens still must pay over 25 percent of their personal medical costs; even more significant, they pay 44 percent of the cost of long-term care (National Center for Health Statistics, 1994c). The fear of becoming financially dependent on others because of lingering illness remains one of the chief concerns of the elderly.

To the threat of financial dependence is added the possibility of physical dependence if the disease is chronic and handicaps the individual. Some 11 million persons, almost 40 percent of people over 65, experience some limitation in carrying out major activities, such as work or housekeeping (National Center for Health Statistics, 1994c). The diseases most often resulting in such limitations are heart conditions, diabetes, asthma, and arthritis. Arthritis and heart conditions are also among the prime villains in limiting mobility, keeping 5 percent of the noninstitutionalized elderly confined to their homes and another 12 percent from getting around by themselves. These forced dependencies may isolate and lower the self-esteem of the older person; it certainly makes "old age with integrity" more difficult. On the positive side, it should be noted that the proportion of the elderly population suffering disability has been steadily declining, and that disability is negatively correlated with factors such as education and income (Manton, Stallard, and Corder, 1995).

Heart Disease

Heart disease presents an illuminating topic for review, as it affects people of different ages. However, of those over age 65, almost 55 percent of their visits to medical specialists are to cardiologists as compared to about 20 percent for those under 65 (Schappert, 1993a). The heart is the most important muscle in the body; when it is diseased, severe limitations on activity and mobility are likely. Among people over 65, heart disease accounts for about half of all deaths; that is why this disease presents a major model for the study of the relationship between disease and aging (National Center for Health Statistics, 1993).

Normal age-related changes in the cardiovascular system are difficult to distinguish from pathological changes such as hardening of the arteries and those resulting from high blood pressure. The problem is complicated by the fact that one cannot, of course, perform autopsies during the progress of longitudinal studies. It is difficult also to relate the structural changes that are discovered to alterations in cardiovascular functioning. There are wide individual variations, which reflect such factors as the rate of physiological aging, the amount of environmental stress, diet, smoking patterns, and amount of exercise. Nevertheless, several types of changes in the cardiovascular system appear to be age-related. First, the heart muscle needs more time to relax between contractions. Second, blood ejected from the left ventricle (heart chamber) into the aorta (the main artery leading from the heart) during contraction meets more resistance from the less flexible wall of the aorta. Third, the heart muscle is less responsive to the stimulation of the pacemaker cells. Fourth, the amounts of elastin, collagen, and fat in the walls of the heart increase, while the amount of muscle decreases. The heart valves show abnormal thickenings and ridges as well as deposits of fatty substances.

The personality trait of hostility as measured by questionnaires has been found to predict higher rates of mortality in general, but also specifically of the occurrence of cardiovascular disease. In a study of 4,710 men and women, hostility level had been measured while in college. It was found some 21 to 23 years later that those who had had high hostility scores were significantly more likely to consume caffeine, have a larger body-mass index (weight in kilograms squared by height in centimeters), and to have higher lipid levels (all cardiovascular risk factors) than those with lower hostility (Siegler et al., 1992).

Heart disease is by no means restricted to the elderly. The dreaded phrase "heart attack" is most often heard in reference to middle-aged men, among whom it is actually more common than among older men and among women in general. About 80 percent of heart-attack victims are male; about 1 in 5 men will experience a heart attack before the age of 60. Although the reasons why middle-aged men are particularly prone to heart attacks are not entirely clear, it seems that some combination of stress, bad habits (e.g., smoking), and the male hormone testosterone is involved; when the level of testosterone drops in later life, so does the probability of a heart attack. On the other hand, women's risk increases after menopause; but estrogen replacement therapy as protection from heart disease remains somewhat controversial (see Chapter 7). Survival from a heart attack is actually quite likely, provided early action is taken to combat heart failure (Brody, 1993).

Some might say that a heart attack is to middle-aged men what menopause is to middle-aged women; it is often perceived as a definitive sign of the approach of "old age," an end to the "good life" that was full of activity and fun. It is not surprising therefore to find that reactions to heart attacks vary with the man's age. Men under the age of 40 seem to need to demonstrate that their virility and vigor are intact. Nurses describe them as cheerful, jovial, even manic, and also flirtatious. They tend to minimize the dangers of heart disease and, more than older patients, deliberately disobey doctors' orders. The elderly heart-attack victims, those over 60, are also cheerful, but unlike the younger patients, they follow instructions to the letter. They seem to accept the heart attack, not as inevitable or fortunate, of course, but as an event that "old men" like themselves must consider a distinct possibility.

Hypertension (elevated blood pressure) is considered to be one of the most significant risk factors for both heart attacks and stroke. Treatment is considered necessary when the systolic blood pressure regularly exceeds 160 and the diastolic pressure exceeds 90. Until recently, physicians were reluctant to treat a condition known as "isolated systolic hypertension," in which only the systolic pressure is elevated. However, a clinical trial involving 4,736 participants over a 5-year period found a 36 percent reduction in stroke and a 32 percent reduction in cardiovascular disease for those treated with antihypertensive medications (Petrovich, Vogt, and Berge, 1992).

Hypertension and heart disease are of particular interest to psychologists because these conditions tend to be associated with lower levels of cognitive performance (Elias, d'Agostino, Elias, and Wolf, 1995). For example, it has been shown that older individuals who experienced cognitive decline over a 14-year period showed twice as many cardiovascular symptoms and related physician visits than those who did not experience a decline (Gruber-Baldini, 1991; Schaie, 1989b). However, the relationship between cardiovascular disease and behavior may depend upon the age of onset and the severity of the disease. Hypertension has also been associate withy accelerated memory decline (Sacktor et al., 1999). And there is evidence of a negative relationship between emotional stability and hypertension (Spiro, Aldwin, Ward, and Mroczek, 1995).

The increased risk for adverse behavioral changes is only modestly greater in individuals with hypertension but no other evidence of heart disease. Recently, however, it has been shown that untreated blood pressure is inversely related to cognitive functioning; that is, those with high untreated blood pressure scored lower on tests (Elias et al., 1993). Untreated hypertension has also been associated with sleep disorders and with generally lover levels of well-being (Robbins, Elias, Croog, and Clayton, 1994).

Heart disease illustrates the reciprocal relationship between health and behavior (cf. Deeg, Kardaun, and Fozard, 1996). Many of the lifestyle variables that contribute to cardiovascular disease are found with much higher incidence in smokers. The great variety of measures one can take to avoid heart disease involve changes in lifestyle, such as the avoidance of stress and weight control through a regular exercise regimen and a healthful diet. But note that excessive preoccupation with one's health may in itself induce stress, and so-called yoyo diets, which lead to substantial variations in weight that may be stressful for the heart (Keuthen and Wisocki, 1991).

Cancer

Cancer is another disease whose incidence increases markedly with age. Over half of all cancers occur in people over 65, and 60 percent of all cancer deaths occur in the older population (National Center for Health Statistics, 1993). In recent years there has been a decrease in cancer mortality in persons under 55 (due to advances in the treatment of leukemias, Hodgkin's disease, lymphomas, and testicular cancers), but cancer mortality increased for those over 55 (Davis, Dinse, and Hoel, 1994; Ershler, 1993).

Figure 13.5 gives age- and gender-specific data on cancer mortality for the population of the United States. Total cancer mortality peaks in advanced old age, but this statistic is a function of the numbers of older people remaining in the population; so the actual number of people available to get cancer will of course become smaller in advanced old age even though mortality rates continue to increase (Kramarow, Lentzner, Rooks, Weeks, and Saydah, 1999; Miller, 1994; Sondik, 1994). Nevertheless, since mortality from cancer reaches the highest rates in the eighties, cancer turns out to be the second leading cause of death (after heart disease) among those over 65 (Pamuk, Makuc, Heck, Reuben, and Lochner, 1998). Not everyone will get cancer as he or she ages, of course, but cancer is much more

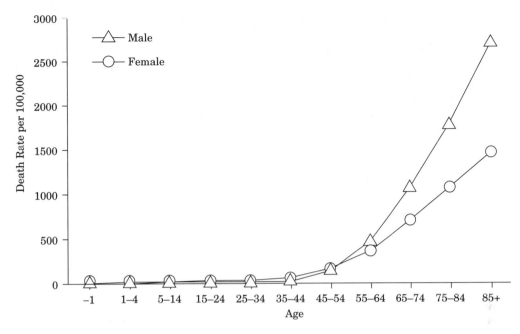

Figure 13-5 Age- and Gender-Specific Cancer Mortality *Source:* Kramarow et al, (1999).

common in older groups than in younger ones. Note that the death rate from cancer in old age is higher in men than in women, even though the actual number of
men dying from cancer is smaller because of lower male longevity, (also see Miller,
2001).

Similar to many other diseases among the elderly, cancer often escapes early
detection because of the prevailing assumption that "feeling bad" is a normal part
of aging and does not necessarily warrant medical attention. But changes in self-report of increase in restricted activity days or having to stay in bed, and negative
changes on questionnaires on self-rated health, and in positive affect, all seem to
be accurate predictors of declining health (Wagner et al., 1993). Such changes
therefore deserve serious attention. On the other hand, elderly people who do pay
regular visits to their doctors often undergo lab tests that reveal spurious abnormalities, which can lead to fruitless but expensive and hazardous exploratory
surgery.

Breast cancer is the most common type of cancer in women over 65 and the
incidence of this cancer has risen sharply in recent years. A number of primary
prevention programs have been attempted, particularly the drug Tamoxifen,
which also has been shown to have some estrogen-like effects on bones and which
may be beneficial for postmenopausal women (Balducci et al., 1991). Greatest consensus, however, is with respect to secondary prevention by means of mammography screening. However, there has been a tendency for older women to have lower

rates of mammography, either because physicians underrefer or because these older women are not certain of the value of the procedure and thus forego it. In a survey of women aged 65 to 74 who were members of a health maintenance organization (therefore cost of the mammograms would have been fully covered), it was found that women in this age group who had never had a mammogram were less likely to accept the test. Their comments reflected the attitude that the procedure meant "looking for trouble" or made them nervous (King et al., 1993).

For older men, prostate cancer is one of the most common types of cancer. In 1997, the estimated number of new cases of prostate cancer was 210,000, and close to 42,000 American men died of the disease.(National Institute on Aging, 1998). Enlargement of the prostate occurs in almost half of all men by their sixties, resulting in discomfort, loss of sleep, and occasional incontinence. However, only a relatively small proportion of enlarged prostates are cancerous. An important secondary prevention measure is an annual PSA (prostate specific antigen) test. While there is no long-range prediction of cancer from the PSA level, rate of change in PSA level has been found to be one of the best early clinical markers for the development of prostate cancer (Carter et al., 1992).

AIDS

Although HIV infection and AIDS are often thought to be conditions that affect primarily young adult (and homosexual) males, these conditions have spread more widely. In the United States, approximately 20 percent of the case incidence is female, a proportion much exceeded in several African countries (Pamuk et al., 1998). AIDS is now the ninth-leading cause of death in the United States (National Center for Health Statistics, 1993). Because of the long dormancy of the HIV virus, as well as the possibility of infection from tainted blood supplies, needles shared among drug abusers, or infected health-care providers, the incidence of AIDS in middle-aged and older persons is increasing (National Commission on Aids, 1993). Because drug abuse is so prevalent among blacks and Hispanics in New York City and other large urban cities, these groups are at particular risk (Peterson and Bakeman, 1988). As will be seen in Chapter 14, AIDS in its later stages has become another major potential cause for dementia (American Academy of Neurology AIDS Task Force, 1991)

One of the major preventative activities to contain the AIDS epidemic have been extensive health-education programs. A national survey of the impact of these programs suggests that they have been least effective with persons of low education and those over the age of 50 (Aguilar and Hardy, 1993). On the other hand, by ethnicity, blacks were slightly more likely than whites to have correct AIDS-relevant information (Dawson and Hardy, 1989).

Other Diseases

A number of other diseases affect behavioral competence in old age. For example, approximately 53 percent of all office visits for diabetes occur for persons above the age of 65 (Schappert, 1992). Chronic diabetes has been shown to affect verbal fluency and memory (Geringer et al., 1988, Gruber-Baldini, 1991), although memory changes may well be mediated by the depressive effect often associated with diabetes. Diabetes also has been implicated as a risk factor for motor vehicle collisions in older adults, although it is not clear whether the transient metabolic imbalance due to hypoglycemia or the long-term complications of the disease explain the behavioral effects (Koepsell et al., 1994).

Osteoporosis, which involves physiological changes in mineral metabolism, results in decreases in bone mass, which in turn lead to an increase in risk of fractures (Cumming and Klineberg, 1994). Such fractures may lead to lengthy hospitalizations and disabilities, and fear of their occurrence also reduces the mobility and social interaction of many older persons. Increased risk of osteoporis recently has been shown in women who drink two or more cups of coffee per day, and who do not drink milk on a daily basis (Barrett-Connor, Chang, and Edelstein, 1994). Family histories of osteoprosis have also been implicated as risk factors. Hip fractures occur more frequently among whites and Asians and less frequently in African-American and Hispanic populations (Turner, Taylor, and Hunt, 1998).

Urinary incontinence occurs at all ages, but is most prevalent among those 65 and older. Studies of community populations report that 6 to 15 percent of elderly men and 11 to 50 percent of elderly women experience incontinence. It is even more common in nursing homes, where 38 to 56 percent of residents have uncontrolled urine loss. Incontinence may also be a major factor in reducing social participation and in leading to early institutionalization. Mild incontinence may be addressed by minor life-style changes, but severe incontinence predisposes to other health problems, as well as depression and anxiety (Burgio and Burgio, 1991). Because incontinence is so common in old age, it is often attributed to aging and is left untreated, even though effective treatments, particularly those involving behavior therapy, are readily available (Burgio, et al., 1994; McDowell et al., 1999). Behavioral treatments have been found to be more effective than drug treatments (Burgio et al., 1998). For a discussion of behavior therapy, see chapter 14.

Stress and Illness

Whether or not a person will have a heart attack may be predicted to some extent by his "life style." Medical researchers have labeled as "Type A" a behavior pattern characterized by competitiveness, striving for achievement, a constant feeling that time is too short, and the general hostility born of the inevitable frustrations that an extremely competitive and impatient person will experience (Chesney and Rosenman, 1985). Research on stress and illness has largely been conducted on men. Type A men have more than twice the number of heart attacks experienced by Type B men, who are relatively easygoing and patient. Why this is so is not entirely clear, but several aspects of the different attitudes probably play a role. Type A men are more likely to smoke cigarettes in large quantities, for example. In addition, stress itself results in increases in blood cholesterol, and cholesterol, in turn, has been associated with heart disease.

Although it may be said that Type A individuals create stress for themselves, stress may also be induced externally. Occurrences, such as a change in sleeping habits, can also have their effect. Negative life events, for example, have been demonstrated to cause long-term patterns of depression (Cui and Vaillant, 1996).

An approach to the study of the relationship between stress and illness begins with an attempt to estimate the degree of stress associated with various life events; the Social Readjustment Rating Scale assigns a "stress value" to each event experienced by a person. The most stressful event is the death of a spouse. Divorce, landing in jail, and getting fired all rank high, but even minimal changes, even if they are pleasurable, are presumed to be stressful; marriage, for instance, ranks seventh on the scale. The scale is used typically by tabulating all the events an individual has experienced in a certain period of time (within the last six months or so) and then predicting near-future illness in the people with the higher scores (Rahe, 1972).

An unusual number of life changes has been found to be related to an unusual number of illnesses of various kinds (Rahe and Arthur, 1978). The role of stress in the occurrence of disease is indicated by studies showing that those subjects reporting high stress levels tend to have more infections and other minor disease episodes (Solano et al., 1993). Significant changes in one's life lead to bodily stress. One study, for example, found that the experience of wartime combat led to early physical decline and premature death (Elder, Shanahan, and Clipp, 1997)

The Type A person is competitive, impatient, and hostile—and likely to have an early heart attack.

The individual's response to stress, including the perception of ill health itself, turns out to be an important influence on the maintenance of physical health (Aldwin and Brustrom, 1997). For example, stress has been related to the development of cancer and to decreased immune system functioning. However, we still do not know the precise physiological or psychological mechanisms involved in this linkage (Elias, Elias, and Elias, 1990). Individuals who are highly stressed, who feel little control over their lives, and who have limited social support systems also make excess use of health services (Krause, 1988; Valiant, Meyer, Mukamal, and Soldz, 1998).

Environmental and psychosocial stresses may have a different effect on the elderly than they have on younger people. It has been observed that older persons often turn to others to cope with difficult situations. However, the recognition that individuals have lost control, or that they have lost significant others upon whom they relied for support may be a particularly stressful experience, resulting in social isolation from others (Krause, 1991; Pearlin and Mullan, 1992). In addition, financial strain has been found to be a major stress and threat to psychological well-being in older persons in both the United States and Japan (Krause, Jay, and Liang, 1991). Late life stress may also exacerbate the effect of life-long cumulative stressful experiences (Kahana and Kahana, 1998).

The biological evidence suggests that older persons have less resilient reactions to stress; they may be more vulnerable because their "reserve" capacities are lower; or stress may be more likely to affect endocrine control mechanisms (Finch and Seeman, 1999; Leventhal, H., Patrick-Miller, Leventhal, E. A., and Burns, 1998; Sapolsky, 1993). One study even found that there was a decrease in immune system efficiency in persons who expressed pessimistic control beliefs (Kamen-Siegel et al., 1991). Stress management in the elderly as it affects health might be greatly improved by training in self-regulation skills, because it has been shown that some of the biological factors involved in stress are related to the person's feelings of loss of control (Rodin, 1983; Rodin, Schooler, and Schaie, 1990; Schulz and Heckhausen, 1998). Also see the earlier discussion in Chapter 10 in relation to the phenomenon of "learned helplessness."

Perceptions of Health

People's subjective appraisal of their health influences how they react to their symptoms, how vulnerable they consider themselves, and when they decide to obtain treatment. Often a person's self-appraisal of his or her health is a good predictor of physicians' evaluation, but such assessments may also differ in many ways. In old age, perceptions of one's health may be determined in large part by one's level of psychological well-being, one's economic status, and whether or not one continues in rewarding roles and activities (Wagner et al., 1993).

One interesting study showed that even when age, sex, and health status (as evaluated by physicians) were controlled for, perceived health and mortality from heart disease were strongly related. A Canadian longitudinal study followed persons from 45 to 65 (Hirdes and Forbes, 1992). Over three years, the mortality of those who described their health as poor at the beginning of the study was about three times the mortality of those who initially described their health as good. But maintenance of good health ratings was highly related to socioeconomic status (Hides and Forbes, 1993). In fact, the excess health decline obseved in African Americans has been shown to be a consequence of economic and educational disadvantages (Peek, Coward, Henretta, Duncan, and Dougherty, 1997).

Global health ratings have been found to be most likely to predict objectively measured health status; however, a measure of activity as compared to peers may provide added information (Mangiano et al., 1993; Rakowski et al., 1993). Negative perceptions of health have also been found to lead to increased health problems in both black and white adults; the former declining at a faster rate (Ferraro, Farmer, and Wybraniec, 1997). Persons who are "optimists" about their health status have also been found to be less likely to die over a 3 year period than those who described their health in pessimistic terms (Borawski, Kinney, and Kahana, 1996).

Despite the apparent awareness among older people of their actual state of health, it is also true that older persons fail to report serious symptoms and illnesses and wait longer than younger persons to seek medical help. But if older persons underreport actual symptoms, do they instead report symptoms that they do not have? The popular view that older persons are somewhat hypochondriacal turns out to be wrong. In their review of the literature, Costa and McCrae (1985b) found that there is an increase in real physical diseases in those areas representing most of the complaints of older persons and that enduring individual differences in neuroticism turn out to be much better predictors of hypochondriasis than age. Interestingly, there is not a high correlation between neuroticism and disease, perhaps because neurotic individuals are more likely to seek out health care (Costa and McCrae, 1987). The conclusion to be made is that most elderly persons certainly deserve serious attention when they bring complaints of ill health to their physician.

Disease-free Aging

What is the effect of age on the heart and circulatory system in the absence of disease? This is an important question, but one not easily answered. Some loss of elasticity in the major arteries is probably normal, for example, because the cross-linking of molecules is a general phenomenon of aging, as we have mentioned. This slight "hardening of the arteries" is probably a major cause of increasing blood pressure with age in otherwise healthy individuals. In addition, aerobic capacity declines with age, although at a slower rate for active than sedentary individuals (Buskirk and Hodgson, 1987). Disease can amplify these processes, laying down deposits of fatty tissue in the arteries, producing a further increase in blood pressure. The heart may have to work too hard. Or blood flow may be restricted, starving body tissue of necessary oxygen, killing cells, and damaging organs. A blocked artery in the brain may lead to stroke and death of brain tissue. The heart, itself a muscle fed by blood, may be damaged, too. A cycle ensues in which a weakened heart provides less oxygen and nutrients to itself, which leads to further weakening and so on to heart attack. The normal processes of aging, slightly exaggerated, may become deadly disease (Williams, 1993).

More generally, one major fact of aging is that the probability of disease increases with age. The greater the age, the less likely it is that an individual will be free of disease (Siegler, 1989). Beyond the age of 80, a disease-free person is unusual—one could say "abnormal." So what does it mean to ask what is aging free of disease? Whatever it is, there's precious little of it (cf. Solomon, 1999).

As in the case of the heart, the biological changes that are generally considered "normal" aging are associated with disease or at least make disease or injury more likely. Slowing of nerve impulses in the central nervous system, decreased elasticity of body tissue, increased time needed for damaged tissue to regenerate or repair itself, increased brittleness of bones: all these "normal" changes reduce the body's capacity to fend off disease, avoid accidents, and recover from these events when they occur. However, a major difference between disease and the normal processes of aging is that changes due to disease are often reversible or at least can be arrested (Williams, 1993). This fact is too often overlooked in the case of an old person who is faltering, either physically or mentally: "They are just getting old." We hear it said, and it seems to follow that "they will die soon anyway."

It is true that the nature of the diseases that people suffer from changes with age. Among younger people, the most common diseases are acute, that is, they reach a crisis quickly. Among the elderly, chronic diseases are more prevalent (Gruber-Baldini, 1991). In fact, most premature deaths today are a result of chronic diseases; 80 percent of the years of life lost to acute diseases have been eliminated.

Most chronic disorders begin to develop long before their presence is diagnosed by a physician. The longer one lives, the more likely it is that such a disease will develop. It is possible that some chronic diseases are preventable and that the most effective approach is to postpone them rather than attempt to cure them. If a disease can be postponed throughout the person's natural life span, the disease will have been eliminated for all practical purposes. It may be possible to postpone diseases through changes in life style in such areas as nutrition, exercise, stress management, social support systems, interests, and meaningful activities (Bosworth and Schaie, 1997; Schmidt, 1994). Also different coping strategies may become relevant with advancing age to assure positive health outcomes (Arbuckle, Pushkar, Chaikelson, and Andres, 1999).

Table 13-1 lists some of the many relationships between disease conditions and life style that have been reliably demonstrated. To summarize, the importance of life style in the prevention of disease suggests that our emphasis ought to shift from concern with treatment to life style interventions that foster positive human health (cf. Ryff and Singer, 1998).

A program of moderate exercise, a sensible diet, and the elimination of unhealthy habits like smoking can produce a turn for the better in the health of even a very old person. And healthy habits tend to go together (Evans, 2000; Leigh and Fries, 1993; Maier, 1995). The concern among young and middle-aged people today about diet and exercise, a relatively new phenomenon, may produce

TABLE 13–1   Disease Conditions and Lifestyle Factors

Disorder of Disease	Lifestyle Factors
Arteriosclerosis, atherosclerosis, coronary disease, hypertension	High fat, high refined carbohydrate, high salt diet; obesity; sedentary lifestyle; cigarette smoking; heavy drinking, alcoholism; unresolved, continual stress; personality type,
Cerebrovascular accidents	Sedentary lifestyle; low fiber, high fat, high salt diet; heavy drinking, alcoholism (which contribute to atherosclerosis, arteriosclerosis, hypertension, risk factors for cerebrovascular accidents)
Osteoporosis and periodontitis	Malnutrition—inadequate calcium, protein, vitamin K, fluoride, magnesium, vitamin D metabolite; lack of exercise; immobility; for women, sex steroid starvation
Chronic pulmonary disease	Cigarette smoking; air pollution; stress; sedentary habits
Obesity	Low caloric output (sedentary) and high caloric intake; high stress levels; heavy drinking, alcoholism; low self-esteem
Cancer	Possible correlation with personality type; stress; environmental carcinogens; nutritional deficiencies and excesses; radiation; sex steroid hormones; food additives; cigarette smoking; occupational carcinogens (for example, asbestos); occult viruses; diminution of immune response (immune surveillance)
Dementia, pseudodementia	Malnutrition; long illness and bed rest; drug abuse (polypharmacy, iatrogenesis); anemia; other organ system disease; bereavement; social isolation
Sexual dysfunction	Ignorance and stereotypical attitudes (the older individual and society at large); early socialization; inappropriate or no partner; drug effects (for example, antihypertensive drugs); psychogenic origin; long periods of abstinence; serious systemic disease

Source: Adapted from R. Weg (1983). *Changing physiology of aging: Normal and pathological.* In D. W. Woodruff and J. E. Birren (Eds.), *Aging: Scientific perspectives and social issues* (p. 274). Monterey, CA: Brooks/Cole. Reproduced by permission.

generations of old people who will be quite different from those of today. This concern is being reinforced by thoughtful attention given by both broadcast and news media to information relevant for the development of healthier lifestyles. The trend towards health maintenance organizations and preferred provider systems for the delivery of health care also has included preventive programs as possible devices to reduce health-care costs (Walker, 1994). If younger people act on their concerns, they may be healthier both physically and mentally and may even show us that some of the biological changes that we consider to be normal aging are not inevitable at all (Schmidt, 1994). However, it has been shown, that even after experienceing a heart attack, adoption of healthier lifestyles such as smoking cessation, is highly related to educational status (Wray, Herzog, Willis, and Wallace, 1998).

One's physical and mental capacities need to be exercised not to reduce the risk of disease, but also to prevent the effects of disuse. "Use it or lose it" is one of the primary messages that can be derived from the study of biological aging, and we have to be careful to distinguish the effects of disease from disease-induced (or socially induced) disuse of some function. Even a young adult, who is immobilized by an accident will notice a decline in certain physical functions. Even a young adult who is socially isolated may find his or her memory failing. Old people often suffer more from lack of physical and mental exercise because of society's expectations that it is thought to be "customary" for the elderly to be less active and to disengage themselves from social intercourse.

In earlier chapters, we discussed the relationship between lifestyle and the maintenance of mental abilities (Schaie, 1984b, 1996b) as well as the possibility that certain mental functions can be improved by training (Willis and Schaie, 1994b). In the same way, it is possible to prevent the loss of physical vigor and help prevent disease by physical conditioning (Emery, Burker, and Blumenthal, 1992). It has been shown, for example, that exercise training has been effective in increasing bone density and body mass in men over 60 (Blumenthal et al., 1991; Blumenthal and Gullette, 2001; Evans, 2000), to improve gait and balance in persons in their seventies and eighties (Buchner et al., 1993), and to improve memory performance (Hassmén, Ceci, and Bäckman, 1992).

Both middle-aged and older healthy people can participate in physical conditioning programs; their improvement will be proportionally as great as that of young people, although they may start from a lower level. For example, low-intensity walking for three months was shown to increase exercise capacity markedly (Hassmén, Ceci, and Bäckman, 1992). Exercise programs for middle-aged and old persons have been related to important health benefits such as lowered body fat and blood pressure and improved ability to achieve neuromuscular relaxation. Such programs should emphasize the rhythmic activity of large muscle groups. Natural activities such as walking, jogging, running, and swimming seem best suited for this purpose (Blumenthal and Gullette, 2001; Buskirk, 1985; Spirduso and MacRae, 1990).

We are not yet able to extend the normal life span by any significant amount, nor is it very likely that we can do so within the lifetime of our readers. But what we can do is try to maintain a fully functioning system as long as possible, to decrease the period of dependency at the end of life. By keeping oneself physically and mentally active and also by compensating for minor deficits in eyesight and hearing with eyeglasses, hearing aids, and the like, it is already almost possible to achieve this ideal.

SUMMARY

1. Life expectancies have increased dramatically in the United States, from age 47 in 1900 to nearly 76 today. Women live an average of 7 to 8 years longer than men, probably because they have a second *X* chromosome or some other source of biological superiority. The increase in life expectancy for both sexes is due to improved nutrition, sanitation, and medical cures for diseases that formerly interrupted the life span; there is no evidence of an increase in the maximum potential span of life. A longer-than-average life is predicted for people whose ancestors were long-lived, who avoid cigarettes, who keep their weight under control, and who face life with a moderate and flexible attitude.

2. Theories about the genetic causes of biological aging include the notions of aging genes, the absence of genetic control in an organism that is "winding down," and more or less inevitable damage to genetic molecules, possibly caused by crosslinking, which impairs the body's ability to replace and repair body cells. Physiological theories of aging implicate the body's endocrine system and, specifically, the thymus gland, which controls immune reactions; if these reactions are deficient or abnormal, cancerous growths and other diseases are more likely. "Wear and tear" does not appear to be a major factor in aging.

3. The lens of the eye becomes less flexible and yellower with age, the response of the pupil becomes slower, and some retinal receptor cells are lost. As a result, visual acuity and depth perception decline. Eyeglasses may compensate for some visual losses. Night driving typically becomes more difficult because the old driver needs more light than a young driver, suffers more from the glare of oncoming headlights, and adjusts less rapidly to changes in illumination. The retina may be damaged by senile macular degeneration (SMD) or by glaucoma. The visual field diminishes with age as well. Hearing loss, especially in the higher frequencies and under "masking" conditions, also becomes more probable in late life. Wearing a hearing aid prescribed by an audiologist and making changes in the acoustic environment can help many older people compensate for their hearing losses. Sensitivity to taste and smells also decreases with age. A reduction in sensitivity to pain may be welcome, but it can be dangerous if injuries are ignored. Declining sensitivity to temperature and degeneration of the structures related to balance may cause additional problems among the elderly. Many old people find that loss of

sensory abilities increases their sense of social isolation, which may lead to emotional problems or intellectual decline.

4. A reasonable estimate is that on the average people lose only 5 to 10 percent of their cortical neurons by the age of 75, providing that they remain free of diseases that can destroy brain tissue in larger quantities (e.g., cardiovascular diseases, alcoholism). Some psychologists have used reaction-time tasks to study what they consider to be age-related increases in the "sluggishness" of the central nervous system (brain plus spinal cord). Reaction times typically increase with age, especially in complex tasks that require "preparation" for the impending stimulus. Hypotheses that posit irreversible neural deterioration are troubled by studies showing (1) no age differences in simple reaction time tasks; (2) improved reactions after practice or experience with the task; (3) shortened reaction times in subjects, young and old, who exercise. Reversible deficiencies in blood–oxygen supplies to the brain and in the ability to prepare for an impending stimulus (possibly because of faulty arousal processes) are alternative hypotheses to explain the general slowing of reactions with age. Older people sleep less soundly but spend more time in bed than younger people

5. The probability of disease increases dramatically after the age of 65, to the point that researchers often find it hard to separate the effects of aging from those of illness. Only 5 percent of those over 65 are institutionalized, however, and only 9 percent rate their personal health as poor. Disease has many effects on the elderly: straining financial resources, limiting activity and mobility, and in general threatening to place them in the much-feared position of being dependent on others.

6. Heart disease accounts for 40 percent of the deaths of people over 65, but it is a problem for younger adults, too. It is difficult to distinguish normal age-related changes in the cardiovascular system from those resulting from pathology. Cancer is the second leading cause of death among those over 65. Stress is a factor in many ailments, especially among the competitive and impatient Type A personalities. A stressful environment makes illnesses of various kinds more likely. Studies show that, contrary to popular belief, the elderly are good judges of their own health and generally deserve serious attention when they bring a problem to a physician

7. What is disease-free aging? It appears that even "normal" aging produces changes in the body that make disease more likely, so that a disease-free person of age 80 is rare. However, disease is at least an exaggeration of normal aging. The elderly are much more likely than younger people to suffer from chronic diseases. Such diseases can sometimes be prevented or their impact reduced (through exercise, for example) or they can be reversed (through medical treatment).

SUGGESTED READINGS

Fozard, J., and Gordon-Salant, S. (2001). Sensory and perceptual changes with aging. In J. E. Birren and K. W. Schaie (Eds.), *Handbook of the psychology of aging* (5th ed.). San Diego, CA: Academic Press. A review of recent research developments on visual and auditory processes in older persons.

Leventhal, H., Rabin, C., Leventhal, E. A., and Burns, E. A. (2001). Health risk behavior and aging. In J. E. Birren and K. W. Schaie (Eds.), *Handbook of the psychology of aging* (5th ed.). San Diego, CA: Academic Press. Covers the recent research literature on the effects of lifestyle choices and health behavior on the maintenance of health in old age.

McClearn, G. E., and Vogler, G. P. (2001). Gerontological behavior genetics. In J. E. Birren and K. W. Schaie (Eds.), *Handbook of the psychology of aging* (5th ed.). San Diego, CA: Academic Press. A discussion of the methods and findings on the genetics that affect human behavior.

Solomon, D. H. (1999). Major issues in geriatrics. In V. L. Bengtson and K. W. Schaie (Eds.), *Handbook of theories of aging,* (pp. 133–150). New York: Springer Publishing Co. A brief overview of recent advances in the biology of aging and the health care of older persons from the point of view of an eminent geriatric physician.

CHAPTER 14

Mental Disorders

Failing to Cope

Mental illness is usually diagnosed from some form of abnormal behavior. A woman is asked the time of day, and she begins to rub her arms and recites the Apostles' Creed. A man is so convinced that someone is "out to get him" that he refuses to leave his apartment. Unusual behaviors such as these are often taken as evidence that the person's mental apparatus is not working quite right, and the presence of mental illness is inferred.

There are many problems with the diagnosis of mental illness. The term itself is a matter of some controversy. Prior to the nineteenth century, people who exhibited bizarre behaviors were considered to be "morally inferior" if their actions were only slightly neurotic, or were thought to be "possessed by a demon" if their behaviors were extreme. In the early 1800s, the French physician Philippe Pinel proposed a different view, suggesting that people who behave in strange ways are really "sick people whose miserable state deserves all the consideration that is due suffering humanity" (Zilboorg and Henry, 1941, pp. 323–324). Labeling mentally disordered people as "ill," rather than as "inferior" or "lazy" or "possessed," had a profound effect on their treatment by society. As a consequence they were put in "hospitals," and they were called "patients."

Compared to the beatings and inhumane confinements previously administered, "medical care" was a distinct improvement. But problems arose with the label "mentally ill." People began to think of those who behaved in unusual ways in the same way that they thought of people with a broken arm or a touch of pneumonia: "Put them in a hospital until they recover." Unusual behaviors, such as bed wetting, were seen as "symptoms" of underlying "disease," and children as "patients" were asked why they wanted to soil the bed sheets of their parents—instead of being given training in bladder control, which for many of them was all the treatment necessary.

Mental hospitals were once thought to be safe havens ("asylums") for people who were badly abused outside. But, unlike hospitals for the physically ill, mental hospitals do not always promote recovery. Even with the best intentions, overworked hospital staff often find themselves rewarding passivity and punishing "patients" who make demands on their time. For these and other reasons, many people who would have been in hospitals are now treated in the community; they are trying to adjust. On the other hand, many of those who formerly found shelter within the walls of mental hospitals from a world with which they could not cope, have now joined the ranks of homeless street people. Some of these changes have been genuine efforts to improve the care of the mentally ill, but many changes in the mental-health system are driven by efforts to contain health-care costs (Gatz and Smyer, 1992, 2001).

In this chapter, we consider "mental health" to be adequate adjustment and adaptation to the "real" world. "Mental disorders" are considered to imply inadequate adjustment and maladaptive behaviors. The emphasis is on people's ability to cope with their environment and handle the developmental tasks required of them at their stage of life. Of course, biological factors are sometimes involved in mental illness: there may be metabolic deficiencies, genetic defects, or brain damage. In other cases, however, social stress is paramount—social isolation, economic hardship, a major life crisis, or perhaps the loss of a spouse. Especially in the case of older people, biological and social causes often combine in intricate patterns. A hearing loss, for example, makes the comprehension of speech more difficult; individuals might respond to this sensory loss with a paranoid belief that people are deliberately mumbling or speaking about them behind their backs. Simply growing old can be a terrible blow to the self-concept of some people, who may have a great need to think of themselves as always young and vital.

Many of the criteria for mental health for young adults also apply to the aged. These include freedom from symptoms of psychological pathology; adequate life satisfaction; self acceptance; mastery of the environment; and the ability to work, love, and play. What changes with age, however, is the way that these criteria can be met. The current, often youth-oriented approach to mental health must be balanced by additional criteria that emerge in middle adulthood and that become more important as people get older. Birren (1993; see also Butler, Lewis, and Sunderland, 1991; Hagberg, 1995; Young, Beck, and Weinberger, 1993a) suggests that these include the increasing importance of self-evaluation, life review, and reconciliation. These criteria are thought to be important for older individuals because meeting them reflects whether they have exerted good stewardship of their lives and been faithful in their responsibilities to younger generations. Sense of coherence from life review has also been identified as being related to well-being and health in advanced old age (Rennemark and Hagberg, 1997).

In response to this position, it has been argued that the very vagueness of such mental-health criteria is likely to encourage stereotypes of normal aging that

Growing old can be a blow to the self-concept of some people, who like to think of themselves as independent.

set arbitrarily high standards that would be hard to meet by most people. Such standards are said to disregard group norms, cultural factors, personal histories, and situational pressures (see Danielson, Moffitt, Caspi, and Silva, 1998; Gutmann, 1992a; Steen 1992). Indeed, current thinking about developmental psychopathology tends to favor an interactionist point of view that would examine the problems faced by a person as a function of his/her history within that person's societal context (Bergman and Magnusson, 1997). Thus some would argue it might be preferable for professionals to limit themselves to diagnosing psychopathology and leave aside what are primarily existential issues, instead of making dogmatic assumptions about mental health.

We begin this chapter with a description of the various mental disorders that show relationships with advancing age. Some disorders are more common in late life, including those arbitrarily grouped under the lay label "senility." Others are more common among young adults. Following this review of what is sometimes called the epidemiology of mental disorders, we consider (once again) the notion of "life crisis," this time as it applies to stress and mental breakdown.

We discuss depression, a common problem among younger adults, but a major problem among the elderly. Depression could perhaps be considered a quite understandable reaction to frustration and failure (inability to cope), but it is also influenced by body chemistry and drugs. We also consider suicide, which is sometimes the extreme consequence of depression. In addition, we use the case of depression to discuss drug therapies and psychotherapies that have been found to be relatively effective treatments of mental disorders.

We then review the mental disorders known to be associated with brain malfunction or brain damage. Often, an overdose of drugs produces a state of confusion that can easily be misdiagnosed as reflecting brain damage; in a section on drug use among the elderly, we look at some of the benefits and dangers derived from these chemical comforts. Finally, we return to psychotherapy, discussing the general issues of goals and obstacles to treatment, including the negative attitudes held by some psychotherapists toward treating elderly clients.

AGE AND GENDER DIFFERENCES IN PSYCHOPATHOLOGY

Age Differences

Like physical illnesses, mental disorders are often found in different proportions in different age groups. Schizophrenia, a mental disorder marked by loss of contact with reality, is most likely to appear in young adulthood, before the age of 30 (Bernheim and Lewine, 1979). Schizophrenia, in fact, was once called "dementia praecox," which means disturbed thought processes (*dementia*) that show up early in life (*praecox,* a word related to "precocious"). Elderly schizophrenics are not uncommon, however, because many forms of schizophrenia resist treatment. Hence, substantial numbers of aged schizophrenics can be found in mental institutions and nursing homes, as well as occasionally among the homeless. Many of these persons were diagnosed early in life and have lived their entire lives in institutions of one sort or another. Others were stabilized and returned to the community, but may in old age be again at risk, because they typically have lived a rather marginal existence throughout their adult lives (Clausen, 1984; Lavretsky, Matsuyame, Gerson, and Jarvik, 1996).

One of the problems of determining the true relationship of mental disorders to age is that the diagnostician's knowledge of the patient's age is likely to affect the diagnosis. Thus, an old person with no history of schizophrenia who exhibits mental confusion, disorientation, and childish emotions is quite likely to be diagnosed as suffering from dementia although the same symptoms in a young person would almost certainly be called schizophrenia. The primary distinction between dementia and schizophrenia, besides age of onset, is evidence of brain cell deterioration in dementia. However, such brain damage is not easy to diagnose, at least until after the patient dies and an autopsy is performed. There is a diagnostic category called "late-life schizophrenia," but some psychiatrists refuse to use it, claiming that no such disease exists (Cohen, 1990).

Mental disorders in which anxiety is a chief component appear to be more common in young adults than in middle-aged or elderly people (Gurland and Meyers, 1988). But there may be substantial group differences, as indicated by a national survey of black elderly, in which 51 percent of the sample reported that they had a serious personal problem and 26 percent reported that they were close to the breakdown level (Chatters and Jackson, 1982; Jackson, Chatters, and

Neighbors, 1982; Jackson, 1996a). It should also be noted that the more severely impacted often have multiple disorders (Newman, Moffitt, Caspi, and Silva, 1998).

Mental retardation, like schizophrenia, is usually diagnosed early in life and if it was correctly diagnosed continues throughout life (Lavin and Doka, 1999). Manic disorders also begin early, as do antisocial, and borderline disorders; all are uncommon among the elderly (Straker, 1982). Personality disorders have been reported to decrease in old age (Vaillant and Perry, 1980), but this finding may reflect patterns of service utilization rather than rates of these disorders *per se.*

Middle age is not a period characterized by peaks in many disorders (except acute alcoholism, which is one disorder that does peak in early midlife). During this period, rates of mental disorders generally decrease. But, as can be seen in Figure 14-1, the proportion of discharges from acute inpatient treatment facilities by age, proportions for brain syndromes (chronic and acute) increase dramatically at about age 65. Although alcoholism and schizophrenia are the most common disorders among the young and middle-aged, they are less common after age 65, where they account for only 17 percent of discharges in that age group (National Center for Health Statistics, 1994a). Dependency is particularly painful for many older people. On the one hand, becoming dependent appears to be a prominent fear in old age; on the other hand, learning to do without the help to which one has become accustomed can also present problems.

Many of the serious disorders that led to the hospital admissions noted in Figure 14-1 involve not only brain disease or alcoholism, but may also occur because of severe depression. The type of depression experienced by elderly mental patients is different from the depression of young patients. The young patients often experience mood swings, with depression giving way to extreme elation (mania); this disorder is called manic-depressive psychosis or bipolar depression. The older patients more commonly experience only depression; this is called unipolar depression (Gaylord and Zung, 1987; Newman, 1989), with a most common age on onset between 45 and 55 years (Lewinsohn et al., 1986).

Three points need to be made concerning statistics on mental illness among the elderly. First, older people perform differently than young or middle-aged adults on virtually all psychodiagnostic instruments, including personality and mood scales as well as tests of cognitive function (Kaszniak, 1990, 1996a; LaRue, 1992; Zarit, Eiler, and Hassinger, 1985). For example, older persons will typically get a higher (more pathological) score on the depression and hypochondriasis scales of the Minnesota Multiphasic Personality Inventory (MMPI) because it would be normal for them to affirm the presence of minor physical complaints and feelings of loss in interpersonal relationships (Costa and McCrae, 1985a; also see the discussion of personality assessment in Chapter 9). As a result, certain disorders may be over- or underdiagnosed in the aged.

The possibility that the assessment instruments used to diagnose the elderly are inaccurate has led to a wave of studies that attempt to "recalibrate" existing instruments for use with older people. In addition, special assessment devices have been constructed. For example, the mental-health scale from the OARS (Older Americans Resources and Services; Duke University Center for the Study of Aging

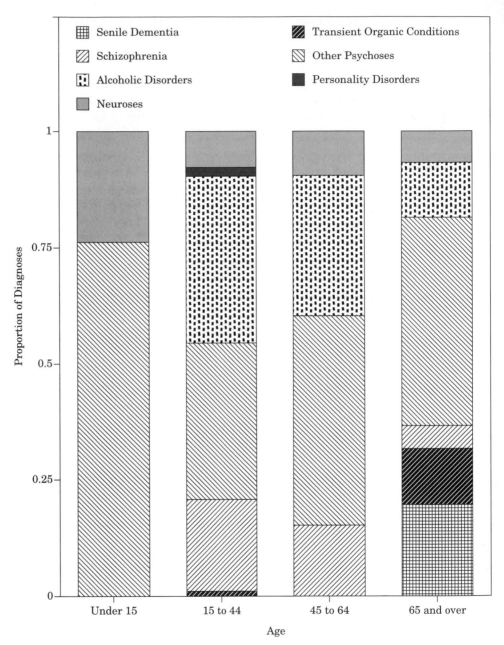

Figure 14-1 Proportion of Discharges from Initial Hospitalization for Mental Disorder. *Source:* National Center for Health Statistics (1994a).

and Human Development, 1978) when administered to a Swedish sample, did not show age differences in alienation or depression scores, but somatic items even here were frequently endorsed by older respondents (Gatz, Pedersen, and Harris, 1987).

The issue of inadequate age norms is probably most significant for diagnosing mild disorders. It may account, at least in part, for our current difficulty in distinguishing between early forms of dementia and the mental changes normally expected in old age. These assessment problems clearly contribute to the current confusion about the presence or absence of age differences in mental disorders.

The second point concerns age differences in the risk factors associated with mental illness. Sensory deficits, physical illness, poverty, bereavement, and social or geographical isolation are all more common among the old than the young. The prevalence of certain conditions such as adjustment disorders and mild depression may be inflated among the elderly because of high rates of physical or psychosocial disability (e.g., Blazer, Hughes, and George, 1987). How these risk factors contribute to more serious disorders, such as major depression and various forms of dementia, is unclear. Some researchers claim that there is a particularly close association between physical and psychiatric disorders among the aged. In a study of 191 people aged 84 to 98 years, stresses such as vision loss, concerns about falling, lowered physical ability, and declining strength were indeed associated with difficulty in coping (Dunkle et al., 1992).

A third point relates to the matter of individual differences. Although on average mental-health symptoms seem to decline from young adulthood into midlife and then show a marked increase, this pattern is certainly not true for all individuals (Aldwin, Spiro, Levenson, and Bossé, 1989). For example, quite different coping strategies have been found for depressed and nondepressed older persons (Foster and Gallagher, 1986), and those in poorer mental health and under greater stress tend to use less adaptive coping strategies such as escapism.

Gender Differences

In addition to age differences in psychopathology, there are also gender differences. These differences emerge quite early in life. For example, in a 10-year longitudinal study of the emergence of depression in adolescents and young adults, greater incidence of depression in females was found as early as age 15 (Hankin et al., 1998). However, gender differences may also occur as a function of diagnostic practice. Women are substantially more likely to be diagnosed as mentally ill in certain diagnostic categories, including schizophrenia, depression (bipolar and unipolar), and the neuroses (Lavretsky et al, 1996). Men are more common in categories based on alcoholism, drug addiction, and violent criminal behavior.

In some cases, diagnostic categories are defined with women in mind. For example, the diagnosis of late-life depression (originally called "involutional melancholia" was first used exclusively for postmenopausal women. Similarly, women who suffer an emotional letdown after giving birth to a child are said to be in the throes of "postpartum depression." Hysteria, a form of neurosis designed to ward off extreme anxiety, was named by Hippocrates, a Greek physician of the fourth century, B.C., who thought the disorder was due to a malfunctioning or "wandering" womb; hysteria has the same root as the word *hysterectomy*. For 2000 years after Hippocrates, the label was used only for women.

As people grow older, the sex difference in rates of mental disorder decreases and may even reverse. After the age of 65, men may be more likely than women to suffer serious mental disability (Boyd and Weissman, 1982). Another factor is cumulative brain damage caused by excessive alcohol consumption, industrial pollution, and the like, which, at least in today's elderly, is likely to be more frequent among men than women. A third possibility is the genetically based difference in life span between men and women; a man at age 65 is closer to the end of life than a woman is at the same age. Probably some combination of these factors is necessary to account for the sharper rises in late-life disorders among men than among women.

Marital Status

The higher rate of mental disorders among women is contributed almost entirely by married women. Married women have a much greater incidence of mental disorder than married men, but in other categories of marital status—single, divorced, or widowed—men have a higher rate than women. Considering this and other evidence, one is led to the conclusion that there is something about the institution of marriage that makes mental disorder more likely for women who enter it and less likely for men (Tavris and Offir, 1977).

The findings that married women are the ones particularly at risk in regard to mental disorder argues against biological interpretations of sex differences. If women in general were biologically more susceptible to mental disorder, one would expect them to exceed men in illness rates in all categories of marital status, not just in the "married" category. Most current interpretations of the sex difference, therefore, place the blame on the social role of "housewife" (Unger, 1979). "Housewife" is a position of low prestige, one that does not require a great deal of skill (or so most people believe). Modern society has isolated the nuclear family to some extent, leaving many housewives who have young children with television as their chief source of entertainment; they may often be bored and lonely. Many married working women tend to have low-paying, low-status, low-interest jobs. If the job is more interesting and high-status, it may lead to conflict between family and career goals (see Chapter 7).

Cultural Variations

Symptoms of mental disorders, and particularly of the affective disorders such as depression, may also vary across different cultures (Henderson and Hasegawa, 1992). For example, several studies have found that the prevalence for depressive symptoms in the United States is higher for older blacks than for whites, although part of the difference may be attributable to social-class differences as well (Gallo, Cooper-Patrick, and Lesikar, 1998). On the other hand, a survey of Japanese studies of depression concluded that symptoms on the whole were less than those found in Western countries (Hasegawa, 1985). It is claimed that the better integration of Japanese elderly into the typical family structure provides greater support for the elderly. Similar findings have been reported for Taiwan by Cheng (1989). In a three-nation study of depressive symptoms of large samples from the United States, Taiwan, and Japan, using alternate forms of the same symptom inventory, Krause, Jay and Liang (1991) confirmed that Japanese had indeed the lowest symptom prevalence, while American blacks had the highest.

PSYCHOPATHOLOGY, STRESS, AND HELPLESSNESS

Although many mental disorders can be traced to genetic bases or to physical illnesses (cf. Lavretsky, Matsuyama, Gerson, and Jarvik, 1996), environmental stress is the primary agent in most others. The relatively powerless position of many women in our society is one such source of stress. The lack of power of people in the lower social classes is another and may help to explain why the rate of mental disorders is ten times as high in the lower classes as it is in the upper classes, and that functional impairment progresses at faster rates for the poor and less well-educated segments of the population (Maddox and Clark, 1992). Some of this difference can be accounted for by the "social drift hypothesis," which proposes that mentally disordered people are found in the lower classes because they cannot hold a job that would give them the status and income necessary to enter the upper classes; "they're poor because they're disordered," not "they're disordered because they're poor." But the constant stress of poverty, poor housing, and deteriorating neighborhoods plays a role, too (also see Rodin, Schooler, and Schaie, 1990).

In addition to groups that are defined by their lack of power in a society dominated by white, upper-class males, groups defined by the common experience of a particularly stressful life event are also prone to mental disorders. Divorced people form one such group, widowed people another; in both, rates of mental disorder tend to rise, especially in the year or so following the event that defines entry into the group. Retirement or being fired from a job can also trigger mental or psychological vulnerability; removal of the stress in a high-powered job with great responsibilities might be thought to bring relief, but the stress of having no job at all appears to be greater, on the average.

Stress in today's world often means that problems with no obvious solutions result in profound feelings of helplessness. In Chapter 10, we discussed research on learned helplessness, which is broadly defined as the perception, born of a series of failures, that nothing works. In laboratory experiments, humans or other animals exposed to an aversive event (loud noise, electric shock) over which they had no control eventually gave up trying to do something about it. Even when an effective response was later made available, the subjects who had learned to be helpless did not avail themselves of it; they simply sat and whined or moped.

The feeling that one is helpless to do anything about one's problems is related to several negative emotions, such as anxiety and depression, which in extreme form constitute mental disorder. Psychoanalysts sometimes refer to anxiety as "psychic helplessness," which reflects the fact that nothing is quite so terrifying as the feeling that one is threatened by something and there is no way to combat the threat. Anxiety is probably more common as a response to perceived helplessness among young adults, who are in a life stage in which much is expected of them. They must build a career and choose a mate, both complicated tasks fraught with the dangers of failure and rejection. Not all the determinants of success are controlled by the individual; bosses and prospective mates make many of the important decisions. Thus, many times the situation seems to render the individual helpless, even when something should certainly be done. Anxiety seems to be the rather ineffective but common response in this situation (Seligman, 1981; Lawton, DeVoe, and Parmelee, 1995).

Depression is another response to perceived helplessness. Although young adults are also subject to the debilitating effects of deep depressions, depression is a particularly common problem among older people (Blazer, George, and Landerman, 1986). Anxiety is an emotion one feels when things look almost hopeless, when there is still a chance that things might work out. Depression abandons hope; it gives up striving. When an older adult loses a job, he or she has little chance of getting another. When a spouse dies, there is often no hope left; it's not like losing a dating partner in one's youth.

Helplessness theory has been revised to take into account how people's causal explanations of events may influence their feelings of helplessness (Abramson, Seligman, and Teasdale, 1978). When people face uncontrollable bad events, they ask why; their answers influence how they react. Three explanations are offered. First, does the person attribute the events to something in him- or herself (internal explanation) or to something outside (external explanation)? Those who believe the cause of the event is internal are more likely to suffer loss of self-esteem than those who believe the cause is external and hence beyond their control. Second, does the person believe the cause is a factor that will persist (stable explanation) or a factor that can change (unstable explanation)? Those who believe the cause to be a stable factor are more prone to chronic helplessness and depression than those who believe in an unstable explanation. Third, does the person think the cause is the result of a factor that affects a variety of outcomes (global explanation) or just a few (specific explanation)? Those who choose global causes tend to have pervasive deficits; they may feel helplessness in many areas of their lives. Those who accept more specific explanations may feel helpless only in the areas that the explanation affects.

The relationship among the variables in this theory is diagrammed in Figure 14-2. On the extreme right are the effects, the symptoms of helplessness, such as increased rate of disease and lowered appetite. These symptoms are the result, helplessness theory says, of the expectation that no action that one takes can control outcomes in the future. The question becomes, then, how do processes and events bring about this expectation? The expectation is usually triggered by the perception that bad events are uncontrollable. This perception, in turn, is strongly influenced by the causal explanations to which a person is prone. People have a tendency to choose certain kinds of explanations for events; that is, they have different explanatory styles.

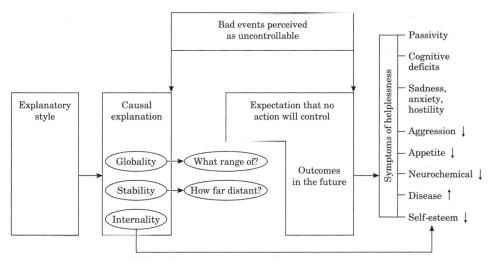

Figure 14-2 The Process of Learned Helplessness. *Source:* From Peterson, C., and Seligman, M.E.P. (1984). Casual explanations as a risk factor for depression: Theory and evidence. *Psychological Review, 91,* 347–374. Copyright 1984 by the American Psychological Association. Reprinted by permission of the publisher and author.

One person may attribute poor marks in school to biased teachers and meaningless work and his or her resulting lack of interest. Another person may feel that he or she just isn't smart enough and can't manage to do well despite intense efforts. What is most important, however, is whether or not the person attributes the bad events to causes beyond his or her control. Those who tend to give stable, global explanations for bad events are most likely to experience helplessness. A person's explanatory style and the particular explanation that he or she gives for an event are not sufficient to cause symptoms of helplessness, however. These variables influence expectations, and it is expectations that are a sufficient cause.

Who are the people who are most likely to perceive themselves as helpless and who believe that control over significant events lies in the hands of fate or other people? Women are more likely to experience feelings of helplessness than men. People in the lower social classes, more so than those in the upper classes. Minority groups feel more helpless than do members of the majority. Old people (over the age of 60 or so), feel more helpless relative to young people. These are the comparatively powerless groups in our society, whose perceptions of helplessness are often quite realistic. But whether they are realistic or not, these perceptions can lead to emotional disorders that compound the trials and tribulations of the members of these groups (Blazer, 1992; Blazer, Hughes, and George, 1987).

DEPRESSION AND SUICIDE

It is difficult to imagine someone who has not experienced depression to some degree, so we need not dwell at length on the symptoms of depression. Briefly, however, we can note a few of depression's more prominent characteristics (Blazer,

George, and Landerman, 1986; Pachana, Gallagher-Thompson, and Thompson, 1994): painful sadness; generalized lack of interest in life; general inactivity; pervasive pessimism that manifests itself as low self-esteem and a gloomy evaluation of one's present and future situation; difficulty in making even minor decisions; dreams of being lost and lonely in isolated, frightening, desolate places and crying out for help with no one responding. According to the diagnostic manual of the American Psychiatric Association, these symptoms must last at least two weeks to help distinguish clinical depression from an ordinary case of the "blues." Depression has physical symptoms as well: loss of appetite, severe fatigue, sleep disturbances, and changes in bowel habits (constipation or diarrhea).

Considerable argument remains over whether or not depression increases with advancing age. Studies that use screening scales to determine the presence of depressive symptoms do report an increase in symptoms, particularly over age 70. However, the age effects appear to be due primarily to physical health problems and disability (Roberts, Kaplan, Shema, and Strawbridge, 1997). Chronic illness has also been implicated as a major source of depression in urban African-Americans (Bazargan and Hamm-Baugh, 1995). Hence, studies that rely upon clinical diagnostic interviews do not seem to find marked increases in depression with increasing age(e.g., Blazer, Hughes, and George, 1987; Teri 1991).

Depression often masks itself in physical symptoms for which there is no discernible cause. Such symptoms may be a mental disorder in and of itself called *hypochondriasis*, but more often than not, hypochondriasis tends to be closely related to depression. The individual (usually elderly) complains of severe and constant pain, most commonly a headache or backache; a medical examination, however, discovers no physical problem. The person often manifests some symptoms of depression—frowning expression, low activity level—but denies feeling sad.

Causes of Depression

A number of different theories concerning the causes of depression among the elderly have been proposed. Some emphasize purely physiological factors associated with the aging processes. Others place more importance on the social circumstances that may attend aging. It is likely that factors of both types are influential, at least in some cases.

Several theories propose that depressive symptoms result from insufficient supplies of specific neurotransmitter substances or from more general neurotransmitter imbalances in the brain. It appears that age does influence a number of neurotransmitter systems The fact that depressive symptoms in the elderly often respond to drug treatment also suggests that the problem may be biochemical (Gerner and Jarvik, 1984; Smyer and Downs, 1995).

Depression among the elderly is also strongly correlated with physical illness (Bazargan and Hamm, 1995; Jarvik and Perl, 1981). In a study of 900 people aged 65 and older, it was found that 44 percent of the subjects who were depressed were also physically ill. Because illness is more common among the elderly than among younger adults, a comparatively high proportion of older people with depression is

Although few elderly people are seriously depressed, many aging individuals experience some level of depression as a normal reaction to loss and change.

not surprising. Physical illness and depression may occur together for several reasons (see Jackson, 1996a; Jarvik and Perl, 1981). Feelings of sadness, anxiety, or fatigue are to be expected when someone is ill, in reaction to pain or disability or awareness of the illness. In some cases, these feelings are severe and protracted enough to constitute a depression. Symptoms of depression may also be either a direct consequence of illness or a side-effect of medication. Longitudinal and retrospective studies indicate that people who are depressed may be predisposed to develop physical illnesses, so a cycle of physical and emotional illnesses may become established. With our current state of knowledge in this area, it is difficult to disentangle cause and effect when a person has both a psychiatric and a physical illness.

Depressed people often complain of loneliness and social or emotional isolation, and it may be that having strong social supports decreases the chances that one will have a depressive reaction following a loss. Nevertheless, isolation is not strongly associated with severe depression among the elderly. In most cases, it seems to be close personal relationships that are important rather than social contact *per se*. Although low morale or low levels of life satisfaction cannot be equated with depression, research suggests that they are related. It seems reasonable to assume that isolation may contribute to the high rates of mild depression observed among older people.

Relocation to a new residential setting is widely assumed to contribute to depression among the elderly. Several studies of involuntary relocation have, in fact, found that life satisfaction decreases after the move. The relationship between moving and levels of adjustment is complex, however. A number of variables are influential, including the desirability of the move, the nature and quality of the new home, how much the move disrupts the person's social network, and other factors. Admission to a nursing home often is accompanied by an increase in depressive symptoms. A study of 454 consecutive new admissions to a nursing home found that 12.6 percent of those admitted had depressive disorders and 18 percent had depressive symptoms, most of which were not recognized by nursing home staff and were left untreated (Rovner et al., 1991). The same study found an increase of 59 percent in the likelihood of death in the year following admission for those suffering from depression.

In sum, it appears that depression may develop among the elderly in reaction to age-related stresses and losses (Lewinsohn et al., 1985; Teri 1991). One report concluded that "much of what is called 'depression' in the elderly may actually represent decreased life satisfaction and periodic episodes of grief secondary to the physical, social, and economic difficulties encountered by aging individuals" (Blazer and Williams, 1980, p. 442). Lehmann (1982) makes the same observation in stronger terms: "Aging may be regarded as an ongoing process of increasing entropy or a continuous chain of losses. Since depression is the normal reaction to any significant loss, the aging individual seems to be prone, in a tragic existential scenario, to become easy prey to depression" (p. 29). Nevertheless, few elderly people are seriously depressed and most adapt successfully to developments such as bereavement and retirement.

Further research is needed to resolve several unanswered questions related to depression. For example, it is not clear whether mild and severe depression are variants of the same illness; they may have different causes and respond to different treatments. Similarly, people who become depressed for the first time in old age may differ in important ways from those who have recurrent depressive illnesses. Until questions such as these have been answered, we cannot assume that we have arrived at a definitive understanding of depression.

Treatment of Depression

Depression is an ailment that comes in all shapes and sizes. We all feel depressed at times, and sometimes our depressions are deep. Psychologists generally distinguish three levels of depression. "Normal" depressions are fairly realistic responses to life. The death of a close friend, a child, a parent, or other loved one will trigger in most people a depressive reaction that may last for a long time, perhaps even a year or so. The minor insults of life, such as a poor grade on an examination in which one expected to do well, can also elicit depression, in lesser degree for a shorter time. Neurotic depressions are usually more severe and invariably less realistic; psychotic depressions usually involve a serious loss of contact with reality.

All forms of depression can benefit from therapy (Thompson and Gallagher, 1985; Teri, 1991). Slight depressions that occur in realistic reaction to unfortunate events in life often can be kept from becoming deeper and more debilitating with a little insightful advice from an experienced psychotherapist, counselor, or friend. This kind of therapy is called "supportive"; its purpose is something like a cast put on a broken bone, keeping it from more serious injury during a healing process that requires a certain amount of time. For the more severe cases of depression, something stronger than supportive therapy is used. Various drugs and several forms of psychotherapy have been found useful in combating depression; in particularly stubborn cases, electroconvulsive therapy may be used.

Drug Therapy. The drugs most often used to control severe depression are called the tricyclic antidepressants. ("Tricyclic" refers to the fact that all these drugs have three benzene rings in their molecular structure.) These drugs have been shown to be effective in most cases, and side-effects are generally mild; dryness of the mouth is the most common complaint. How they relieve depression is not well known, but apparently they increase the ease with which electrochemical signals are passed along the central nervous system (Vollhardt, Bergener, and Hesse, 1992).

Another group of drugs used for depression, MAO inhibitors, apparently have a similar effect in the nervous system (they presumably inhibit MAO, a substance that makes signal transmission more difficult). The MAO inhibitors are generally less effective than the tricyclic antidepressants and may have severe side-effects. The MAO inhibitors probably would not be used at all if not for the fact that they work for some patients who are unresponsive to the tricyclics. Obviously, a physician has to monitor the patient closely (Smyer, 1995).

The danger of side-effects is also prominent with lithium salts, which are most commonly used for the treatment of manic states or manic-depressive illness (bipolar depression). Although they are quite effective when used properly, there is a fine line between a therapeutic dose and a toxic dose, so that lithium levels in the bloodstream must be constantly monitored. Because they, like all other salts, raise blood pressure, they are dangerous for people with heart or kidney disease. Lithium salts seem to work in smaller doses in elderly people, but many doctors do not know this, which occasionally leads to overdoses (Vollhardt, Bergener, and Hess, 1992). Elderly patients are also more likely to require low-salt diets, in which case lithium salts should not be prescribed.

Psychotherapy. Psychotherapy is a form of treatment that involves discussion and education but not drugs, although it is often combined with the latter. All major types of psychotherapy have been applied to depression. These include Freudian psychoanalysis; the humanistic therapies of Rogers, Maslow, and the Gestalt school; and the behavioral therapies of Skinner and Bandura (Knight, 1986).

Two of the most effective therapies are behavior modification and cognitive therapy. The major assumption of behavioristic therapy is that the depressed person is not receiving enough reinforcements in life (Ferster, 1973). According to this view, all animals (not just humans) react with "behavior patterns characteristic of depression" when their responses do not earn the rewards they seek. Such behavior patterns include a generally low level of activity combined with behavioral indications that the animal considers this state unpleasant—moping, whining, irritability.

It is worth pointing out that such behaviors are similar to those that define learned helplessness. Learned helplessness is usually defined in the context of responses that do not eliminate an aversive stimulus, or punishment; the behavioral analysis of depression focuses on responses that do not produce a desired state of affairs, or reward.

Behavior modification therapy for depressed humans seeks to increase the number and availability of reinforcements in the individual's environment (Zeiss and Lewinsohn, 1986). One way to do this is simply to increase the individual's level of activity, especially in pleasant activities. A problem arises, however, in that people who are easily depressed are less likely than nondepressed people to enjoy any given activity. Talking with friends, catching a big fish, seeing a good movie—all these activities are less rewarding, on the average, to depression-prone individuals.

In behavioral therapy, the first step therefore is to encourage the depressed person to think of their depression as a skill deficit that can be overcome by new more effective skills. Efforts are then made to teach these skills, which include relaxation training, increasing pleasant activities, combating negative cognitions, and increasing social skills (Teri, 1991). Part of the therapy for most patients includes programs designed to teach them how to get pleasure from reinforcements—how to increase their enjoyment of life! There are a number of ways to do this, and treatment programs are always individualized, because each person's problems are unique. There may be training in "fishing appreciation" or "how to enjoy a talk with a friend." There may be "assertiveness training" to encourage the depressed person to engage more fully in the activity that he or she is trying to enjoy.

Psychoeducational programs are designed to teach persons to cope with their depression (Lewinsohn et al., 1985). Training is offered, for example, on how to get along with a spouse, because a good marriage makes depression less likely. Positive behaviors such as smiling and statements of self-praise are quickly rewarded with attention, approval, and sometimes even money or other objects of value. Patients who suffer from anxiety as well as depression are taught how to relax (desensitization therapy).

In addition to "accentuating the positive," the therapy works to "eliminate the negative." Tendencies to think gloomy thoughts, dwell on self-deprecation, feel guilty, and focus on real or imagined physical ailments are handled by nonreinforcement: Instead of offering sympathy for such "woe-is-me" behaviors or reacting to them in any way, family and friends are instructed to ignore them. Usually the frequency of the behaviors decreases quickly. In sum, behavior therapy for depression is a multifaceted

Learning a new and interesting hobby is a good way to increase the frequency of reinforcements in one's life.

attack on the many problems of the depressed patient, each problem carefully specified in behavioral terms (Gallagher-Thompson and Thompson, 1996).

Cognitive therapy for depression is based on the assumption that depression results from maladaptive cognitions (thoughts, beliefs, attitudes, expectations). The depressed person may consider him- or herself to be inadequate and unworthy, the world as insensitive and ungratifying, and the future as bleak and unpromising. He or she questions the meaning and purpose of life with consequent reduction in feelings of well-being (Reker, Peacock, and Wong, 1987). The depressed patient is taught to identify these thought patterns, which in many cases have become so automatic that the patient is unaware of other possibilities. Then he or she is taught how to evaluate self, the world, and the future more realistically. Therapeutic tasks might be to chart the relationship among various activities, thoughts, and moods and to try to experience the power of positive thinking (Gallagher-Thompson and Thompson, 1996; Thompson et al., 1986; Yost et al., 1986).

Both behavioral, psychodynamic, and cognitive therapies have been shown to be quite effective with anxiety and depression (Gatz et al., 1998; Teri, Curtis, Gallagher-Thompson, and Thompson, 1994; Wisocki, 1998), with a combined behavioral-cognitive approach even better than either alone (Thompson et al, 1991). A study that followed depressed patients for a year after treatment found that a combination of cognitive and behavior therapy showed better results than the use of insight therapy (Gallagher and Thompson, 1983). Another study compared cognitive theory to drug therapy Cognitive therapy was found to be roughly equal to the effects of anti-depressant medications as well as equally effective to results obtained with younger patients (Scogin and McElreath, 1994).

Most severely depressed patients today are treated with a combination of all the therapies that we have discussed. The drugs have their strongest effect on current mood (they keep the individual from feeling so bad), while psychotherapy permits adjustments in the individual's environment that allow him or her to live a more satisfying life.

Suicide

Although one need not be depressed to take one's own life, depression is by far the most common cause of suicide (Blazer, Bachar, and Manton, 1986). Suicide for the depressed person is the ultimate reaction to hopelessness, an acting out of the sincere belief that the future holds no promise, that things are not going to get any better. Most researchers believe official figures of about 12 suicides in 100,000 each year (McIntosh, 1992; Kramarow, Lentzner, Rooks, Weeks, and Saydah, 1999) to be an extreme understatement, mostly because suicide is not given as an official cause of death unless the evidence is overwhelming. If an overdose of sleeping pills can reasonably be ruled an accident, for example, most officials will so rule; many single-car accidents are believed to be suicides as well, though proof must usually be indirect. The family thus avoids the stigma of a family member who "must have been out of his mind" and is able to receive life insurance payments that would not be allowed for self-induced deaths.

Suicide is related to age, sex, race, and a number of other demographic variables in some informative ways (Kramarow et al,, 1999). Males have the highest rate; and both white and nonwhite men are more likely to commit suicide than women (Figure 14-3). For white males, suicide rates have an early peak in late adolescence and young adulthood. The rate then drops slightly until the fifties, when it begins a rise that continues until very old age (above 80). Nonwhite males also show an early peak, but for them there is no rise after midlife, except for those of Asian origin. Theorists commonly attribute this difference to social power. White males have more social power than nonwhite males, which makes them more frustrated and depressed in late life when they lose it through retirement or illness. However, Native Americans, who turn out to have the highest overall suicide rate of any U.S. subpopulation in young adulthood, have suicide rates in old age that are below those for the general population.

Suicide rates among people over 65 have dropped by about half over the past 50 years. The latest available data, for 1997, indicate that suicide among those over age 65 is 20.9 per 100,000 people as compared to an overall suicide rate of 10.8 (Kramarow et al., 1999). Suicide rates for men in general are four times those for

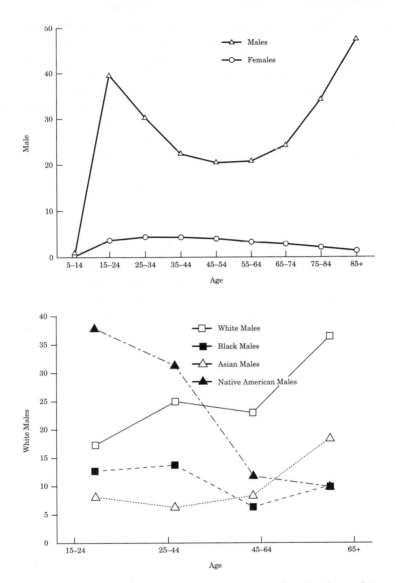

Figure 14-3 Suicide Rate per 100,000 (1997), by Gender and Race. *Source:* Kramarow, Lentzner, Rooks, Weeks, and Saydah (1999).

women (and seven times those for women over 65) although this statistic may reflect no more than the fact that the men are generally more successful in their suicide attempts (McIntosh and Jewell, 1986). Women outnumber men in unsuccessful attempts by about three or four to one. Some theorists believe many women do not really intend to succeed and are putting out dramatic "cries for help" in the form of apparent suicide attempts. Another possible explanation is that men use more lethal methods (guns, jumping from high places) that women find repulsive; even at death's door, women prefer sleeping pills and poisons, which are clearly less efficient and effective. Nonwhite women, who have the lowest rate of any group defined jointly by sex and race, show an age pattern similar to that of nonwhite men: an early peak followed by stability or gradual decline.

Suicide rates vary widely among different countries. Statistics provided by the World Health Organization (1991) show that overall suicide rates were highest in Hungary, Sri Lanka, Denmark, and Finland, but lowest in Colombia, Ecuador, Greece, and Venezuela. The United States rate falls well within the middle range. Virtually everywhere, suicide rates are higher for people over 65 years of age, by a multiple of from two to three times that of the national average range. There are international differences also in gender differences of suicide incidence. For example, in both Hong Kong and Japan, suicide rates for elderly women have been rising steadily over the past three decades, a trend that might be attributed to the progressive loss of the traditional importance of older women in these societies (Shimizu, 1992).

Considering age by itself, we find that more young adults attempt suicide than actually succeed. The ratio of attempts to deaths is around 7 to 1. Around the age of 50, the ratio swings in favor of actual suicides, so that older adults usually manage to take their own lives when they set out to do so. Theorists believe that suicide attempts among young people are often cries for help or expressions of hostility, even though they may not be consciously aware of these motives. In this view, the young person is making a statement: "Hey, look! I'm really hurting! It's serious!" Or "If you won't be nice to me, I'll kill myself! Then you'll feel guilty!" Parents and lovers are the usual targets for such communications.

The older suicidal person is not necessarily more sincere than the younger. Younger persons who contemplate suicide typically have more extensive personal networks and are likely to be monitored more often by friends and family. The probability is greater that the suicide attempts by young persons will be foiled. There may be no one likely to interrupt the suicidal act of older persons living by themselves. Feeling helpless and viewing the present and future as hopeless, elderly candidates for suicide typically telegraph their intentions, if anyone cares enough to pick up their signals. They are likely to state their intentions explicitly, or they may become unusually quiet and withdrawn. One clue is the giving away of valuable personal possessions.

Suicide threats must be taken seriously at any age. Needless to say, anyone who suspects that a friend is contemplating suicide should enlist professional help immediately. Many cities have suicide prevention centers or suicide hotlines, which can be of great service in such an emergency.

BRAIN DISORDERS

Together with the various mental disorders involving severe depression, organic brain disorders constitute the majority of the mental-health problems that develop late in life. The term *organic* is used in psychology and psychiatry to identify those mental disorders that are known to be at least partly caused by a malfunction of or damage to the brain.

Acute Brain Disorders

Certain mental disorders resulting from brain malfunctions often can be treated successfully, restoring normal mental processes. These are called *acute brain disorders*. "Acute" should be contrasted with "chronic." Chronic disorders continue for a long time and are usually irreversible.

Acute brain disorders are characterized by a sudden onset. Their causes are many and varied. A stroke, which cuts off the blood supply to parts of the brain, is one common cause (Ostermann and Sprung-Ostermann, 1988). A heart attack is another, because heart damage affects the ability of the heart to pump blood to the brain; indeed, 13 percent of heart attacks come to the attention of doctors primarily because the individual suddenly begins to "act crazy" (Butler, Lewis, and Sunderland, 1991). Malnutrition is another surprisingly frequent cause of acute disorders, especially among the elderly, who may suffer from low income, decreased mobility, illness, loss of appetite, or loss of teeth. Vitamin deficiencies and other metabolic disturbances can result in severe depression, irritability, confusion, and memory deficits—the kinds of symptoms that many physicians diagnose as senility (Tatemichi, Sacktor, and Mayeux, 1994). It is not clear yet whether neurologic manifestations in the late stages of AIDS (HIV-1) represent acute or irreversible changes in brain tissues (American Academy of Neurology AIDS Task Force, 1991). Head injuries, brain tumors, infections, diabetes, thyroid malfunctions, and liver disease are common causes of acute disorders. Drug overdoses, whether from alcohol abuse, from intentional or nonintentional use of other drugs, or from improper prescription of dangerous psychoactive drugs by doctors, are often mistaken for irreversible brain damage. All in all, there are nearly a hundred reversible conditions that can mimic the symptoms of the few irreversible conditions (DeAlberto, McAvay, Seeman, and Berkman, 1997; Levy, Derogatis, Gallagher, and Gatz, 1980).

Acute brain disorders usually can be treated and the patient can usually be returned to a state of physical and mental health, but many cases go untreated through misdiagnosis and inadequate medical care, especially in the elderly. In the words of the former director of the National Institute on Aging, Robert Butler, "The failure to diagnose and treat reversible brain syndromes is so unnecessary and yet so widespread that I would caution families of older persons to question doctors involved in care about this" (1975, pp. 175–176).

Chronic Brain Disorders

Chronic brain disorders more closely correspond to what lay people often call senility. Typically (but not always) these disorders develop gradually, beginning with mild symptoms of depression or anxiety with occasional confusion and memory difficulties, then becoming progressively more severe with a general loss of intellectual abilities, or dementia (Kaszniak, 1996b; Nussbaum, Kaszniak, Allender, and Rapczak, 1995; Thal, Grundman, and Klauber, 1988). Sometimes early signs may be the deterioration of driving behavior (Carr, LaBarge, Dunnigan, and Storandt, 1998). The progressive loss of victims' ability to function independently places enormous stress and existential conerns on their families and other caregivers (Farran, 1997).

Persons suffering from these disorders have trouble recalling common facts that most of us can remember with ease. Simple mental status questions such as those in the commonly used Mini-Mental Status Examination (MMSE; Folstein, Folstein, and McHugh, 1975; Morris et al., 1989) may be useful in identifying those who may have these disorders (see Table 14-1). In fact, carefully calibrated short questionnaires of everyday functioning have been found to be the most useful methods for the initial screening of suspected dementia (see Albert, 1994; Kaszniak, 1990, 1996a).

In dementia, there are identifiable changes in cognitive functioning because of the destruction of selective areas of brain tissue. Neuropsychological testing is therefore helpful in differentiating dementia from depression (Benton, 1994; Kaszniak, 1996b; LaRue, 1992; Teri, Logsdon, and Yesavage, 1997). Assessment of differential patterns of memory loss is helpful in distinguishing dementia from the effects of the alcoholic Korsakoff syndrome and from Huntington's disease (Moss et al., 1986), as well as from depression (Reifler, 1992; Safford, 1993).

Careful appraisal of memory functions are particularly important because of the observation of certain forms of age-related memory impairment (see Crook, Larrabee, and Youngjohn, 1989; Larrabee et al., 1992; Youngjohn, Larrabee, and Crook, 1992) that may simply represent modest normative chages in performance on certain memory tests that must not be interpreted as evidence of early stages of dementia. One of the best differential criteria may be the much greater difficulty in delayed recall experienced by patients in early stages of dementia (Welsh et al., 1991). Also of importance is the finding that Alzheimer's patients are largly unaware of their memory deficits (Feher et al., 1991), and that in some cultures, such as China, memory loss in the elderly is not interpreted as a sign of dementia (cf. Ikels, 1998b).

TABLE 14-1   Examples of mental status questions for detecting brain disorders

Type of Question	Question or Task
Time orientation	Give year, season, month, date, and day
Place orientation	Give state, county, city, building, and floor
Immediate memory	Repeat three words (e.g., ball, flag, tree)
Attention	Subtract 7 from 100 serially
Recall	Repeat the three words given earlier
Naming	Identify pencil and watch
Repetition	Repeat "No ifs, ands, or buts"
Follow command	"Take a piece of paper in the right hand, fold it in half, and place it on the floor"
Visual Construction	Copy two intertwined pentagons

Source: Adapted from Folstein, Folstein, and McHugh (1975).

Detailed studies of differences in memory functions between the alterations accompanying normal aging (see Chapter 11) have also been conducted in the laboratory of Lars Bäckman at the Stockholm Gerontology Center in Sweden (Herlitz et al., 1997; Small, Herlitz, Fratiglioni, Almquist, and Bäckman, 1997). For example, recall of object names and the colors of objects was found to be much below normal in older persons who were diagnosed as suffering from Alzheimer's disease (Herlitz and Bäckman, 1990). Both normal and demented subjects were better at recognizing the names of dated than of contemporary public figures—they were better in recognizing Greta Garbo than Stefan Edberg! This study points out the supportive effect of prior knowledge; nevertheless, the demented subjects did more poorly on both tasks (Bäckman and Herlitz, 1992). It appears then that the major difference may be the lessened ability of the demented to use cognitive support mechanisms (Herlitz, Lipinska, and Bäckman, 1992; Lipinska, Bäckman, and Herlitz, 1992).

Emotions are also disturbed in dementia, so that unexpected outbursts of anger or laughter may become frequent. Anxiety symptoms are also common (Teri, Logsdon, and Yesavage,1997; Teri et al., in press). In advanced cases, motor control is impaired and patients cannot feed or toilet themselves. Wandering and disorientation are also characteristic of the more advanced stages of dementia (Hussain, 1987). Although the cognitive impairment may be the basic problem, it is the disruptive behavior and loss of social functioning that place particular burdens on caregivers (Kettle, 1999; Teri, Logsdon, and Truax 1997). The last stage is one in which patients no longer respond to their own names; coma and death follow. Multiple psychiatric symptoms in Alzheimer's diesease are more common in women than in men, but both sexes experience equal degrees of agitation (Cohen et al., 1993).

Forms of Dementia. Among elderly patients, there are two major forms of chronic brain disorder: senile dementia (officially, "diseases of the Alzheimer's type [DAT] and multi-infarct dementia, also called cerebrovascular disease (Tatemichi, Sacktor, and Mayeux, 1994). The average age of onset of Alzheimer's disease is 75, and more women are affected than men, but this fact may simply reflect the greater average life span of women (Butler, Lewis, and Sunderland, 1991). Between age 65 and 85 years, the prevalence of all dementias doubles approximately every 5 years (Katzman and Kawas, 1994). In a Swedish longitudinal study of the oldest-old (ages 84 to 90) the frequency of dementia increased from 31 percent base to 42 percent four years later (Johansson and Zarit, 1995). Autopsies show considerable brain damage, as well as two characteristic changes in brain structure called senile plaques and neurofibrillary tangles. In more familiar terms, the brains of people who exhibited Alzheimer's disease while alive are shrunken, covered with patches (plaques) that look something like rust or mildew, and filled with tiny twisted tubes (Banner, 1993).

Multi-infarct dementia was called "cerebral arteriosclerosis" until 1980 because the disorder is an indirect result of a hardening or a narrowing of the arteries supplying blood to the brain. In what is essentially a series of small strokes, several small areas of the brain are destroyed, or "infarcted." These multiple infarcts (many small areas of tissue death) are the direct cause of the dementia, hence the name change (American Psychiatric Association, 1987). Symptoms are generally similar to those of senile dementia, although they are more variable, with "spotty" rather than complete losses of intellectual abilities, especially with respect to language functions (Hassing and Bäckman, 1997; Tatemichi, Sacktor, and Mayeux, 1994). Another diagnostic criterion is a localized disturbance of cerebral blood flow (Drachman, 1993).

Multi-infarct dementia, like all heart and arterial diseases, has been attributed to various factors, including poor diet (too much fat), lack of exercise, smoking, and genetic predisposition. Hence, much of its incidence could be reduced by the lifestyle changes and medical treatments advocated for vascular disease in general (Hachinsky, 1992). Like most heart ailments, men are more likely to suffer from it than women, with 66 the average age of onset (Katzmann and Kawas, 1994). Multi-infarct dementia is less common than senile dementia, accounting for only approximately 20 percent of the cases of dementia in the elderly (Tatemichi, Sacktor, and Mayeux, 1994). Many patients with dementia due to cerebral arteriosclerosis do not show evidence of extensive brain lesions when studied by computer tomography.

The major therapeutic approach to the prevention of multi-infarct dimentia is, of course, the prevention of strokes by means such as the management of high blood pressure and the use of anticoagulants, aspirin, and, if needed, coronary bypass surgery. In those already affected, again the emphasis is on the prevention of further stroke occurrences.

Alzheimer's Disease. The symptoms of dementia—intellectual deterioration and emotional and behavioral abnormalities—are also observed among some middle-aged adults. Several types of early-onset dementia have been identified. The most common is Alzheimer's disease (Alzheimer, 1987). Brain atrophy, plaques, and neurofibrillary tangles are found on autopsy, although such deposits are also found in older people who are presymptomatic (Morris et al., 1995). It can attack people as early as their forties and fifties with a deadly virulence. However, other individuals may remain cognitively stable until the onset of dementing symptoms in advanced old age at which time sharp declines in performance are observed (Rubin et al., 1998). However, younger victims of the disease may follow a downhill course for 10 or 20 years. Alzheimer patients tend to be prone to accidents, strokes, and certain cancers. About one-fifth of those with Alzheimer's disease also suffer from infarcts.

There are conflicting opinions on the actual incidence of senile dementia of the Alzheimer's type. It is estimated to affect more than 100,000 persons a year. Epidemiological studies suggest that the incidence may be approximately 5 percent above age 65 and as high as 20 percent above age 85 and 40 percent after age 90 (Lavretsky and Jarvik, 1994). However, findings emerging from prospective longitudinal studies suggest lower rates of incidence, averaging perhaps between 2 percent and 4 percent for all persons over age 65. Recent studies of centenarians in Sweden also yielded a lower estimate of 27 percent for these oldest-old persons (Samuelsson et al., 1997). The newer findings may imply better diagnostic procedures that rule out other causes of dementia, as well as possible changes in the population.

Lack of education is considered a risk factor for both Alzheimer's and multi-infarct dementia. It has been suggested that increased education and occupational attainment may reduce the risk of Alzheimer's by providing a reserve capacity that delays the onset of clinical manifestation of the disease (Stern et al., 1994), but the effect of education may simply reflect greater cerebral capacities (Pedersen, Reynolds, and Gatz, 1996). Other risk factors include history of Alzheimer's in a first-degree relative, head injury, and maternal age. Individuals with a family history of the disease appear to deteriorate at a faster pace (Luchins et al., 1992).

Much of what we know about factors associated with Alzheimer's and the natural history of the disease once again come from a series of longitudinal studies. The first of these studies was the Lundby Study in Sweden, begun in 1947 (see Hagnell et al., 1993). More recent longitudinal studies are in progress in the United States, Sweden, and China (Arenberg, 1990; Brun and Gustafson, 1993; Katzman, Aronson, and Fuld, 1989; Small, Herlitz, Fratiglioni, Almquist, and Bäckman, 1997; Yu, Liu, and Levy, 1989).

Several possible causes of Alzheimer's disease have been investigated in recent years. There are at least six alternative models being given serious consideration, all of which may have some value in understanding the changes occurring in various subtypes of the disease. They involve genetic defects, abnormal protein mechanisms, infectious disease, toxic substances, abnormal blood flow, and impaired acetylcholine supply (Lavretsky and Jarvik, 1994; Wurtman, 1985).

The *genetic defect* model is based on the observation that there are families in which the incidence of Alzheimer's disease is unusually high, raising the suspicion that one or more faulty genes render persons vulnerable to some environmental factor that triggers the disease (Gatz et al., 1997). It is argued that aging might further impair an inborn abnormality in the genetic (DNA) material that leads to the failure to manufacture enzymes essential for proper brain function. Genes for familial Alzheimer's disease, the precursor gene whose turning on leads to the amyloid protein changes observed in the disease, and a gene for late-onset cases have been located on chromosomes 14, 19, and 21 (Lavretsky and Jarvik, 1994; Lavretsky et al., 1996). The mechanism for the gene action is not yet completely known (Katzman and Kawas, 1994). Most recently much attention has been given to Apolipoprotein E4 as the major genetic susceptibility factor for Alzheimer's disease (Banner, 1993; Gatz et al., 1997). The importance of this factor lies in the fact that the brain of persons having this particular mutation of the gene produces more of the substance that leads to the plaques found at post mortem. They also decline at a faster rate (Craft et al., in press). Recent data also suggest that persons with the E4 allele may show greater decline than those with other alleles even if they do not become demented (Kennett and Schaie, 1999; Small, Basun, and Bäckman, 1998). Persons having the E3 form of the gene show less decline, while the E2 form is thought to have some protective property (Katzman, 1994). Another allele HLA-A2, which appears to have additive effects with the APO-E4 alele, has been associated with early onset of the disease (Payami et al., 1997).

Another explanatory model is based on the observation of *abnormal protein* in the brains of Alzheimer patients. It has been found that the activity of the enzyme choline acetyltransferase (ChAT) progressively decreases in the brain tissue of Alzheimer's disease patients (McEntee and Crook, 1992; Lavretsky and Jarvik, 1994; Plotkin and Jarvik, 1986). The decrease appears to be caused by the loss of certain nerve cells in the part of the brain that controls this enzyme. Such cell loss is not a normal result of the aging process; recently, it has been suggested that it may be associated with hormonal effects triggered by stress (Henry, 1985). Abnormal biochemical processes may also be implicated in the process that leads to the formation of the plaques and tangles in the cortex that are so typical of Alzheimer's disease (Selko, Ihara, and Salazar, 1982). The presence of a protein, called beta-amyloid, in the brain of Alzheimer patients seems to be correlated with the severity of the disease.

Studies of some rare neurological diseases that can be transmitted under unusual circumstances have led some investigators to consider an infectious disease model for Alzheimer's disease also. This idea has been reinforced by the finding that a protein particle, called a prion, that occurs in these diseases has structural qualities similar to those found in the brains of Alzheimer patients. Experimental attempts to transmit Alzheimer's disease in animals have been unsuccessful thus far. The possibility still exists that, if there is an infectious agent, it may require some prior genetic predisposition, a concurrently occurring immune disease, or exposure to some toxic substance in the environment before an infection can occur (Wurtman, 1985).

The *hazardous environment* model is based on some evidence that individuals might be exposed to toxic metals or toxic radiation that might have destructive effects on brain tissue. One Swedish study found that occupational exposure to magnetic fields led to excess occurrence of dementia (Feychting, Pedersen, Svedberg, Floderus, and Gatz, 1998).

Also being investigated is the *impaired acetylcholine supply* model. The abnormality may be due to inadequate production, below normal levels of activity, or too rapid breakdown of this neurotransmitter. Ideally, treatments for a disease result from an understanding of cause. In some cases, however, helpful treatments may be discovered before a disease is fully understood. Quinine was used to treat malaria before the parasite that causes it was discovered, and Parkinson's disease can be treated with the drug l-dopa, which helps relieve deficits in the important neurotransmitter dopamine. Some proposed treatments for Alzheimer's disease and other dementias are based on the hope that such efficacious compounds may be discovered.

Several of the proposed theories on the causes of Alzheimer's disease have resulted in suggestions for treatment. The finding that the activity of acetylcholine decreases in Alzheimer patients, for example, has prompted diet therapy in which the patient is given foods rich in the raw materials that make up the neurotransmitter. Another approach involves the drug physostigmine, which prevents the rapid breakdown of acetylcholine after it is released from nerve cells. However, effective methods of replenishing the cholinergic deficit remain to be found, and effective treatment of Alzheimer symptoms may require correction of multiple neurotransmitter deficits not yet completely understood (Khachaturian, Phelps, and Buckholtz, 1994).

In general, other drug treatments have also been quite disappointing. The most promising approaches in recent years have been those involving cholinomimetic agents, either alone or in combination with other drugs. Although drugs such as physostigmine, tacrine, or aricept may produce mild improvements in learning and memory performance for short periods, particularly in normal or mildly impaired individuals, longer-term treatments based on the acetylcholine precursors choline and lechithin have usually not had positive outcomes (e.g., Rogers, S. L., Friedhoof, L. T. et al., 1996; Kettle, 1997). We must conclude that at this time there is no known cure for Alzheimer's disease. Memory enhancers have been used in humans in conjunction with behavioral treatment such as supportive counseling and cognitive training. There is as yet no conclusive evidence that cognitive training in combination with drug treatment is a useful approach and further work in this direction is needed.

Some positive results in slowing the progress of the psychological symptoms associated with the disease have been reported from using a variety of behavioral approaches (Camp and Mattern, 1999). In a technique known as *spaced retrieval,* cognitively impaired individuals in an adult day care center were presented with pictures and given the name of individuals pictured. After a brief interval, they were then asked for the name of the individual in the picture. If the name could not be retrieved, it was provided by the trainer. The memory interval was successively increased, and improvement in retention of names was reported (Brush and Camp, 1998). On the other hand, maintenance or generalization of imagery-based menemonic training in dementia has not been demonstrated (Bäckman et al., 1991). Another approach of providing special care units that either supplied stimulation or provided relief from excess stimulation also provided only temporary relief, but did not succeed in reducing long-term worsening of negative behaviors (Lawton et al., 1998)

Group-therapy techniques have also been applied to cognitively impaired elderly, and the impaired person's spouse has been employed as a primary agent for behavior modification. Group interventions also include a variety of reality orientation procedures (Camp and Mattern, 1999). Of course, all of these interventions are designed to maximize the remaining functional capacity of the impaired older person; they obviously cannot reverse the neurological deficits that have alreadey occurred.

The great hope for the future, of course, is that pharmaceuticals might be developed that would inhibit the genetic expression of proteins that lead to the formation of amyloid plaques. Such pharmaceuticals could then be given prophylactically to those at high familial risk. While the regeneration of neurons has been demonstrated in some lower species, we still do not know if techniques for that purpose might have potential promise in the treatment of Alzheimer's disease (cf. Gould, Reeves, Graziano, and Gross, 1999).

Other Disorders. Alzheimer's disease is a leading cause of dementia, but it is not the only one. Although the other disorders that lead to dementia are less common and each affects a relatively small group of people, they account together for over a million people with progressive and dementing brain disease in America today.

One of the better known neurological disorders is *multiple sclerosis,* which is characterized by the destruction of the insulating material that covers nerve fibers. The disease usually progresses through a series of acute episodes followed by partial recoveries. In time, both physical and mental deterioration can occur. *Huntington's chorea* (or Huntington's disease) is another type of presenile dementia. The disease is sometimes called Woody Guthrie's disease, after the American folksinger who died from it. The ailment is caused by a dominant gene; children of victims have a 50–50 chance of inheriting it. The symptoms usually appear in early middle age. They include personality change, mental decline, psychotic symptoms, and movement disturbance. Restlessness and facial tics may progress to severe uncontrollable flailing of head, limbs, and trunk. At the same time, mental capacity may deteriorate to dementia (Tatemichi, Sacktor, and Mayeux, 1994).

Dementia also develops sometimes (but not always) in disorders of the central nervous system defined by physical symptoms such as paralysis or "the shakes." *Parkinson's disease* (and the related Lewy-body disease), a disorder that strikes 80 to 200 out of 100,000 older adults, is one such ailment. The symptoms of Parkinson's disease are tremors and difficulty in originating voluntary movements. Rapid mood changes have also been found (Shifren, Hooker, Wood, and Nesselroade, 1997). Drugs can relieve symptoms but do not halt the progression of the disease. Symptoms of dementia may appear in severe or advanced cases, particularly those with late onset (Tatemichi, Sacktor, and Mayeux, 1994).

Some individuals not functioning well cognitively in old age are actually developmentally retarded individuals whose old age is complicated by cognitive decline from a previous low level. Dementia-like symptoms have been observed particularly in individuals who early in life were diagnosed as suffering from Down syndrome (Lavin and Doka, 1999).

There are a number of conditions known as *fronto–temporal dementia* that seem to have certain common features. This condition has been described primarily in Britain and Scandinavia (Lund and Manchester Groups, 1994). The disorder is thought to be limited to nerve cell loss and spongiform change in the frontal and temporal lobes (in contrast to the parietotemporal tissue disruption in Alzheimer's disease) and characteristically results in behavioral disorders that include emotional unconcern and loss of affect and inhibition (see also Wallin, Brun, and Gustafson, 1994).

Other quite rare conditions include *Creutzfeldt-Jakob disease,* and *Pick's disease,* both with an onset usually between 55 and 75 years of age (Lavretsky et al., 1996). Creutzfeldt-Jakob disease, which has recently been in the news as "mad cow disease," is caused by an unusual virus (a prion) that may lie dormant in the body for years (therefore, called a slow virus). This disease is contagious. When the virus is activated, it produces a rapidly progressing dementia along with muscle spasms and changes in gait. However, only one new case per million persons is discovered each year (Prusiner, 1995). Pick's disease has symptoms similar to those of Alzheimer's, but is associated with somewhat different changes in the brain tissue; it is confined to atrophy of the frontal and temporal lobes, with normal levels of neocortical acetyltransferase despite severe neuron loss (Hansen, 1994).

We have described many different forms of dementia, and many different causes. For most of the dementias, however, the causes and cures remain much of a mystery. The mystery is particularly frustrating in cases of presenile or senile dementia of the Alzheimer type, which afflicts the greatest number of adults in the latter half of life.

Because of the chronic nature of senile dementia, it has consequences beyond the plight of those directly affected. The cost of long-term care imposes great burdens upon the families of the patients as well as upon society, which must finance the cost for those who have exhausted their own resources (Huang, Cartwright, and Hu, 1988; Teri, Logsdon, and Truax, 1997). The hidden victims of these disease conditions are often the spouses and adult children who share the primary burden of care for their relatives. For example, a study of spousal caregivers showed that caregivers of Alzheimer's patients had poorer mental health than those caring for spouses with Parkinson's disease (Hooker, Monahan, Bowman, Frazier, and Shifren, 1998). Care and treatment programs for senile dementia must therefore also include support groups and respite programs for the caregivers (Hooker et al., 1998; Quayhagen and Quayhagen, 1989).

ALCOHOLISM AND DRUG MISUSE

Most Western societies are drug cultures in which only very few people are not involved, to one degree or another. Drugs are prescribed for physical illnesses, and drug therapy is common for mental disorders. Nonprescription drugs such as aspirin are consumed by the cartload, and "recreational" drugs such as alcohol and marijuana are used by millions. From our drugs, we derive many benefits: the cure of many diseases and relief from pain, anxiety, depression. But drugs invariably involve risks as well, short-term and long-term "side-effects" that range from an upset stomach or hangover to death.

Alcoholism

Harmful effects may result from use of the drug alcohol over a long period although there is still a continuing debate over whether alcoholics differ from others before the onset of their alcoholism (Vaillant, 1995a). Alcohol abuse and dependence are usually reported to be less common among the elderly than among younger people. The proportion of heavy drinkers in both sexes decreases after age 50 and drops still further at about age 65 (McAneny, 1992). Of those aged 66 or older, about 5 percent of the men and 1 percent of the women are heavy drinkers. On the other hand, 60 percent of the women and 35 to 40 percent of the men in this age group do not drink at all. Some of these age differences are a result of the fact that problem drinkers are less likely to survive to old age, but it has been reported that half the elderly nondrinkers were former drinkers and that most older people who continue to drink imbibe less than they did formerly. It is important to recognize, however, that the apparent age decline in alcoholism may actually reflect cohort differences. Interestingly negative correlations have been found between drinking and depression in older adults (Schutte, Moos, and Brennan, 1998).

Today's young and middle-aged adults are less likely to have grown up in environments where drinking was discouraged; as these people age, rates of later-life alcoholism may increase. Indeed, as the popular press reports on research that suggests possible benefits of moderate drinking, so do we see a rise in the proportion of the population that reports consuming alcohol (Levenson, Aldwin, and Spiro, 1998). A second peak of incidence of alcoholism has been found among the 65- to 74 -year age range, and the appalling rate among elderly widowers is 105 per thousand as compared to 19 per thousand for the general population (Zimberg, 1987). While alcohol use tends to decrease with age in white Americans it increases with age in African Americans (Jackson, Williams, and Gomberg, 1998). Also, late life onset problem drinkers tend to increase alcohol consumption in response to stressor and negative affect (Schutte, Brennan, and Moos, 1998).

There are at least two distinct subtypes of aging alcoholics. They can be differentiated in age of onset, which typically either appears early or late in life. Of the elderly people who have drinking problems, at least two-thirds have had the problem for many years; they typically began drinking before or during their early twenties. There is some evidence that many late-onset problem drinkers are women; among younger age groups, male alcoholics are more common. Early-onset alcoholics seem to have a lifelong personality pattern of addiction, while the late-onset alcoholic is thought to drink in response to external stresses associated with aging (Horton and Fogelman, 1992). There is also some evidence that alcoholism is frequently preceded by some other psychiatric disorder (Kessler, Crum, Warner, Nelson, Schulenberg, and Anthony, 1997; Vaillant and Hiller-Stumhoefel, 1996).

It is clear, then, that heavy drinking over a long period can impair an older person's functioning. But the pros and cons of moderate social drinking are still open to debate. On the positive side, older people who drink moderately tend to be more active and sociable and perceive themselves as being in better health than elderly persons who abstain completely. Providing opportunities for limited social drinking in nursing homes has been reported to have beneficial effects on mood and social interaction. On the negative side, small deficits in the cognitive performance of social drinkers compared to abstainers have been observed, and programs providing for the "medicinal" use of alcohol are regarded by some as a sign of excessive reliance on pharmacological approaches to managing problems of the aged (Glantz, 1981).

Drug Effects

Psychoactive drugs (drugs that affect the brain) are particularly dangerous, because their side-effects also can affect the brain in less beneficial ways. Each year close to 300 million prescriptions for psychoactive drugs are written in the United

States (Salzman, 1992). Over 90 percent of the patients under the age of 65 in mental hospitals and over 55 percent of patients over 65 receive psychoactive medication of some sort; the lower figure among the elderly reflects the greater incidence of chronic brain disorder, for which fewer drugs are effective. Most of the psychoactive drugs can be classified as antipsychotic (used most commonly for schizophrenia), antidepressant, or antianxiety. Many of these are prescribed over a relatively long period of time, making them especially dangerous.

For most old people, iatrogenic illnesses (illnesses caused by doctors or the medication that they prescribe) are a much more serious problem than alcoholism. The elderly have a higher overall rate of drug intake than any other age group (Smyer and Downs, 1995). They also have a higher rate of use for a number of different prescription medications, including psychoactive drugs such as tranquilizers, sedatives, and hypnotics (Diehl et al., 1992).

Adverse drug interactions are an added risk, but there is only limited consensus on what medications are most likely to produce adverse interactions in the elderly. Particularly dangerous are combinations of drugs that have anticholinergic properties. Such drugs include several commonly prescribed tranquilizers, antidepressants, anti-Parkinsonian drugs, sedatives, and antihistamines (Diehl et al., 1992). In a survey of 5,902 nursing-home residents over age 65 and a comparable sample of persons living at home, it was found that 60 percent of the nursing home residents and 23 percent of those living at home received prescriptions of drugs with such anticholinergic properties. Based on the recommended dosages, it was concluded that 10 percent of the nursing-home patients and 7 percent of those living at home received a combination of three or more prescriptions that might result in toxic side effects (Blazer et al., 1983). Often physicians have little or no information on potential drug interactions, which may produce severe reactions, including death. Prescription drugs may also interact with nonprescription drugs; patients on tranquilizers, for example, are generally warned to avoid the consumption of alcohol.

There are few adequate investigations of the extent of drug misuse among older adults, but some interesting preliminary statistics are available. First, it appears that misuse of medications in the aged generally occurs in the context of medical treatment. Only a small number of the patients seen in acute-care medical settings for drug-related emergencies are elderly; overdoses are most common with psychotropic drugs such as Valium, Tuinal, Luminal, and Darvon. Among younger patients, drug-related emergencies usually involve illicit drugs such as heroin and cocaine.

Data suggest, however, that emergency-room statistics severely underestimate the extent of total drug misuse among the elderly. Studies indicate that the elderly are more likely than other age groups to fail to comply with doctors' orders in taking medications. For example, people in their seventies are twice as likely as people in their forties to fail to follow doctors' instructions about medication. Of the medication mistakes made by the elderly, 47 percent involve omitting the medication; 20 percent, inaccurate information; 17 percent, self-medication; 10 percent, incorrect dosage; and 4 percent, incorrect sequence or timing. Several factors contribute to such mistakes, including incomplete communication between physician and patient, decreased mental competence on the part of the patient, and inadequate supervision of the drug regimen by either professionals or family members.

Even when patients adhere strictly to doctors' orders, they may encounter problems with drug side-effects (Callahan, 1993). These side-effects include general signs of toxic dosages (diarrhea, vomiting, tremor, drowsiness, slurred speech, confusion) as well as specific dangers in specific drugs. Even in the correct dosage, medications taken by the elderly may have such side-effects as lethargy, fatigue, depression, and anxiety (Grossberg et al., 1992). One danger of the major antipsychotic drugs is tardive dyskinesia, which occurs in 10 to 20 percent of the cases in general and in up to 40 percent of the cases involving elderly patients (Butler, Lewis, and Sunderland, 1991). The ailment is characterized by slow, rhythmic, involuntary movements of the face and extremities; the "fly-catcher" tongue is a common symptom, and so are a number of other spastic motions. It is a rather sad state of affairs that the psychotic patient faces the alternatives of dementia, which makes adaptation to the real world impossible, and dyskinesia, which means living without complete motor control.

Potential benefits and potential risks of drug therapy must always be weighed. When the decision is that the benefit-to-risk ratio is high enough, a program of medication can be undertaken. However, even when the approach to drug treatment is cautious, a certain number of patients will find such programs to their disadvantage; they will experience more of the risks than the benefits.

Nursing homes have been criticized for the frequent use and occasional misuse of psychotropic drugs. Educational efforts directed to reduce the use of antipsychotic drugs in favor of other methods of behavior control generally have been fairly unsuccessful (Ray et al., 1987). However, a study of 419 nursing-home residents found that only 23 percent of the residents received antipsychotic drugs on a routine or as-needed basis; the users were typically more irritable, disoriented, and withdrawn than the non-users (Spore et al., 1992).

Many physicians prescribe the wrong drug or too much of a drug and thereby induce iatrogenic mental disorders. One is reminded of the comment of the eighteenth-century French writer Voltaire, who said, "Doctors pour drugs of which they know little, to cure diseases of which they know less, into human beings of whom they know nothing" (Butler, 1975, p. 200). Physician-induced disorders may account for a significant proportion of the mental disorders in the elderly. Perhaps 10 percent are unnecessarily induced (that is, the mental disorder results from medication that was incorrectly prescribed), and perhaps another 10 percent result from medication that was prudently advised but had unavoidable side-effects, such as tardive dyskinesia.

Many of the most commonly prescribed drugs for people over 65 have a sedating effect (Salzman, 1992). Older people who are already experiencing some slowness in response and a decrease in coordination will find these trends exaggerated by sedative drugs. In addition to the problems that slower reactions might cause, many elderly patients become frightened or depressed, feeling that their slow behaviors are signs of failing health and approaching death. In high dosages, these drugs can produce severe depression or mental confusion that is sometimes misdiagnosed as chronic brain disorder.

These side-effects are more likely in elderly patients than in young adults, because drug metabolism is generally less efficient in the elderly. A given dosage has a more pronounced effect in an older patient, on the average, and the drug stays in the body for a longer time before the liver can break it down or the kidneys excrete it (Vollhardt, Bergener, and Hesse, 1992). Furthermore, it is quite possible for an elderly person to develop a drug dependency, particularly if he or she is anxious, depressed, or hypochondriacal. Still, medications remain the preferred treatment and guidelines for managing medications in the aged which may help reduce the risk of medication-related problems are gradually becoming available (Bressler, 1987; Keuthen, 1991; Smyer and Downs, 1995).

PSYCHOTHERAPY ACROSS THE LIFE SPAN

Too often, drugs are the only form of treatment of mental disorders, especially among elderly patients. Although we should not discount the potential benefits of psychoactive drugs, drug therapy alone is rarely the most effective treatment. Psychotherapy attempts to deal with the environmental pressures and problems that the individual faces in relationships with family, friends, business associates, and social acquaintances. The cognitive and behavioral therapies that we discussed in the case of depression are examples of psychotherapies that can help the mentally disordered patient cope with difficulties in life. In general, psychotherapy can help even those patients suffering from irreversible, progressive brain disease. An informed, supportive therapeutic program can encourage them to be "the best they can be" within the context of their physical limitations. More importantly there has now been substantial research that empircally validates the the utility of psychological treatment for many mental-health problems facing older adults (Gatz et al., 1998).

Goals of Psychotherapy

The developmental tasks that one faces in youth—choosing a career, choosing a mate—are different from the tasks that one faces in middle age—adjusting career aspirations, adjusting to growing children and aging parents. In old age, the tasks are still different—adapting to retirement, losses of loved ones, and declining physical abilities. Because the tasks change with age, the goals of psychotherapy change, too.

Young adults, more than middle-aged and elderly adults, are in a position to develop their character or to reconstruct their personality. They are in the final stages of Erikson's identity crisis and, at the age of 25 or 30, they may be still uncertain about their most basic attitudes and values. They are still learning social skills, including the interpersonal techniques necessary for a long and satisfying marital relationship. In contrast, middle-aged adults are more likely to be suffering from the failure (or perceived failure) of the adaptations made in young adulthood.

Their careers may not be going the way that they think they should; their marriages may be disintegrating. Psychotherapy for middle-aged adults, therefore, may focus on transitions, providing emotional support during a change in job or spouse and information about how the transition can be made efficiently and with a minimum of stress.

Psychotherapy for the elderly presents a number of special problems. Indeed, some have argued that growth-oriented therapies are not appropriate for the aged. Freud offered three reasons why older persons may not benefit from psychotherapy: they have decreased mental "elasticity" and presumably less ability to change; they have accumulated a vast amount of experience, which the therapist might find difficult to work with; and they attach less importance to mental health than younger persons do. Many modern therapists question these assumptions, but many still assume that older persons would derive few benefits from therapy.

Nevertheless, therapy has been undertaken with elderly people, and certain assumptions about how such therapy should proceed have evolved. Modifications of traditional approaches include a contextual, cohort-based, maturity-specfic challenge model that applies gerontological theory and data to psychotherapy (Knight, 1996; Knight and McCallum, 1998). Because late-life presenting problems are often biopsychosocial in nature, group therapy seems to be the treatment of choice for problems of social isolation, feelings of inadequacy, and the sense of anonymity arising from older adults' low status in a youth-oriented society (Tross and Blum, 1988).

It is argued that treatment programs should reflect the goals of both client and therapist and that such goals should be both explicit and realistic (Knight, 1996). Of course, one's opinion about whether a specific therapy is "realistic" will be influenced by one's views about the elderly and the probable outcome of various disorders. There also seems to be some agreement that the goal of therapy should be equilibration, that is, restoring adequate daily functioning, rather than exploring symptoms as a means of attaining personal growth or development, as might be attempted with younger clients (Mahoney, 1982).

Another problem that therapists working with the elderly must face is that compensation for the psychological losses that the older person faces are relatively difficult. For example, there is no way that therapy can compensate for the death of a spouse. Given that the client may live for only a few more years anyway, the therapist may be tempted to use therapeutic sessions to discuss such issues as time and death. But therapy ought not to be devoted to such issues exclusively; the whole purpose is to help people live better. Indeed, the basic model for psychotherapy should be to induce psychological well-being and positive functioning (Ryff, 1996).

Therapy for the elderly may also serve educational functions. Explicit cognitive training approaches can remediate moderate deficits that may occur in the early phases of dementia. More traditional therapies may also be offered in the form of psychoeducational programs, if only to avoid clients' fears of seeing a mental-health professional (Gatz et al., 1998; Thompson and Gallagher, 1985). Educational approaches of this sort tend to focus on discussions of the normal aging process, physiological changes, and cultural stereotypes of the aged.

Regardless of the nature of the therapy, many authorities believe that the treatment should be of short duration (Gallagher and Thompson, 1996). An average treatment may involve as few as six sessions or take as long as a year. The usual recommendation is to begin with more frequent sessions, perhaps two or more times a week, and then gradually taper off toward the end of the program. The client should be permitted to return as needed for a "booster shot" after the therapy has ended. Clients who have transportation or physical mobility problems may benefit from telephone sessions in between face-to-face appointments. Midweek calls to encourage clients to complete self-monitoring assignments may also be helpful (Gallagher and Thompson, 1981).

The prospect of the end of life triggers in many people a kind of *life review* (Birren, 1993; Butler, 1975; Svensson, 1996). Life reviews can be used in therapy in many ways (Haight and Webster, 1995). Generally, the therapist asks clients to construct autobiographies. They might use family albums, old letters, and even interviews with other family members to gain information about their behavior and emotions at crucial points in their lives. By elaborating and formalizing the life review, the therapist can explore suppressed guilts, long-standing fears, and unspoken ambitions still unfulfilled. In some cases, simply having someone who is willing to listen to one's life story can allow the elderly client to integrate the disparate features of his or her life. In other cases, by allowing unresolved conflicts to surface, client and therapist can deal with them more directly. Life review, however, can raise anxiety and feelings of depression over what may be perceived as a wasted life. Such responses can best be handled by a trained professional. That is why, like any other method of psychotherapy, use of life review by nonprofessionals may be dangerous.

Obstacles to Treatment of the Elderly

Older people have as much need for psychotherapy as younger adults, perhaps more. Yet they receive less. In mental hospitals, the elderly patients are too often given only custodial care; if there is therapy, most likely it is drug therapy and nothing else. In outpatient mental-health clinics, community mental-health centers, and the offices of psychotherapists in private practice, elderly clients are seen in far fewer numbers than we would expect on the basis of the proportion of old people in the general population. For example, a survey of clinical psychologists in private practice in Los Angeles county showed that only 4.4 percent of these professionals specialized in serving older adults and their families (Gatz, Karel, and Wolkenstein, 1991). Why aren't old people getting the psychotherapy they need?

There are a number of reasons. The expense of psychotherapy plays an important role in an age group hampered by dwindling income and rampant inflation. In addition, the generation that is elderly today belongs to a cohort that may be less psychologically minded. They were born and raised in an era that stigmatized mental illness as an inherited condition that could not be cured. They may believe that people don't see mental-health professionals unless they are really crazy, that those who do have problems are likely to be institutionalized, or that seeing a psychiatrist means lying on a couch and revealing all of your emotional and sexual secrets, which will not help and is immoral to boot.

It has been suggested that older people may also have a different understanding of just what constitutes a mental illness, but little research on this matter has been conducted. It may be that older adults tend to deny the existence of problems, stating that they don't want to bother a professional unless the problem is really serious, but actually fearing that they will be institutionalized. People may also be afraid that they will learn that they have a terminal illness or be told that they should no longer live alone (Kovar, 1980). In the future, older adults will have grown up with psychotherapy as a routine part of life and will perhaps be more inclined to take advantage of professional mental-health services.

It may be that skepticism about the benefits of psychotherapy that keeps people from using it. Older people may tend to assume that their problems are an inevitable result of aging, even though some may be remediable. They may also believe their mental problems have a physical basis and require physical remedies. Many older people assume that physicians are not trained for or interested in working with older adults. They expect physicians to regard their problems as trivial. Indeed, they not only expect to receive no help, they sometimes expect medical intervention to have harmful effects. And, some of these fears and complaints have some basis in fact (Gatz et al., 1998).

Older persons represent a larger proportion of patients in the offices of most general practitioners and specialists than their proportion of the general population, but they are vastly under-represented in psychiatrists' practices (Schappert, 1993b). They may believe that young therapists have little to offer them. But the research findings on this point are inconclusive. Although the influence on therapy effectiveness of degree of demographic "match" between therapist and client has been studied, little research has focused on the age variable. On variables other than age, it appears that experience with a population is more important than demographic similarity. A young therapist may have different values and a different historical perspective than an older client, but the life experiences of therapist and client are rarely identical. It may be safe to assume that differences in age, although perhaps not an asset, do not preclude a constructive relationship between therapist and client. As far as personal preferences are concerned, one study indicated that people generally do prefer helpers of about the same age as themselves (Furchtgott and Busemeyer, 1981). The study found two exceptions to this trend: age preference for clergy was unrelated to the age of the respondent; and, among more highly educated respondents, older people preferred a slightly younger physician.

Interpretations of studies dealing with age preferences should be made with caution, however. Subjects might prefer physicians of a certain age (and presumably therapists as well) for reasons other than their age *per se*. An older therapist might be perceived as having more experience or a younger therapist as being more familiar with the most recent developments (Mintz, Steuer, and Jarvik, 1981).

Probably the most common reason for the lack of elderly clients in psychotherapy is the lack of interest among therapists. Psychiatrists, clinical psychologists, and psychoanalysts are generally more interested in treating young, attractive, verbal, intelligent, and successful clients. They often justify such discrimination by suggesting that older clients are usually senile and do not benefit from psychotherapy (Stenmark and Dunn, 1982; Haug and Ory, 1987). The negative attitudes of psychotherapists toward treating the elderly have been attributed to prejudice and psychological conflicts in the psychotherapist (Gatz, VandenBos, Pino, and Popkin, 1985).

In short, the negative attitude expressed by people in general toward old age is, not surprisingly, held by many psychotherapists as well. Therapists feel that treatment of elderly patients is "depressing" and if they have a choice, they will generally choose to stick with young adult, white clients. We can only hope that these negative attitudes will change in the future. There is some basis for this hope because many of the attitudes are founded in incorrect beliefs (the elderly cannot benefit from therapy, for example), perhaps the attitudes will change as better information spreads. In addition, the coming generations of old people will have different views of therapy; they may not consider it embarrassing, for example, at least not to the degree that old people do today. The elderly population in the future will be better educated than it is today and probably in better physical condition, making elderly clients more palatable to psychotherapists. Finally, we will know

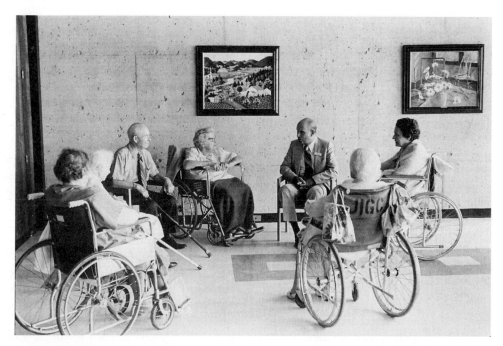

Older persons with psychological problems can benefit from psychotherapy even if they are physically disabled.

more about chronic brain disorders, which will lessen the psychotherapists' fear of treatment failure (Gatz, 1989).

SUMMARY

1. Schizophrenia and anxiety disorders are more likely to be diagnosed among young adults than among older people. Alcoholism is a problem that occurs in disproportionate numbers in early middle age. Depression and organic brain disorders are common among elderly mental patients. Age and sex biases exist in certain diagnostic categories such as involutional melancholia, which until recently was used only for postmenopausal women. Women, especially housewives, are more likely than men to be diagnosed as mentally disordered; after the age of 65, however, the ratio reverses. Statistics on mental illness among the elderly must be interpreted with caution.

2. Groups of people with less power in society have higher rates of mental disorder: women in general, lower social classes, minority groups, old people. Feelings of helplessness and an external locus of control, often somewhat realistic in these powerless groups, appear to be related to anxiety and depression. A recent revision of helplessness theory relates helplessness to factors associated with a person's explanatory style.

3. Depression is sometimes masked by physical complaints and sometimes mistaken for irreversible brain disorder, especially among elderly patients. The incidence of new cases of hypochondriasis peaks between the ages of 60 and 65. Other age-related stresses and losses may also contribute to depression among the aged. Types of therapies available for mental disorders in general and used for severe depression include drugs, and psychotherapy. Behavior modification tries to increase reinforcements in the patient's environment, and cognitive therapy tries to eliminate the patient's maladaptive cognitions. Both of these psychotherapies have been shown to be effective.

4. Suicide, which often results from severe depression, may claim as many as 50,000 or 100,000 victims a year. The ratio of unsuccessful to successful suicide attempts is higher among women than men, and higher among young adults than old people, which may reflect a greater tendency of women and young adults to use suicide attempts as a "cry for help." In the United States, white males have the highest suicide rate, especially in late life; white females peak in midlife, whereas blacks (male and female) peak in young adulthood. Suicide rates vary greatly across different countries, but they are uniformly higher in the elderly than in the general population. Suicide rates for older Asian women have been increasing as the importance of their role in the family has been declining.

5. Acute brain disorders, which are often reversible, may result from strokes, heart attacks, malnutrition,

vitamin deficiencies, head injuries, tumors, infections, diabetes, liver disease, drug overdoses, and many other causes, including AIDS. The two major forms of chronic brain disorder are diseases of the Alzheimer's type (senile dementia, by far the most common) and multi-infarct dementia. The latter is due to multiple little strokes, which in turn are related to cerebral arteriosclerosis (hardening or narrowing of the blood arteries feeding the brain). One of the early-onset dementias is Alzheimer's disease. Other types of dementia are multiple sclerosis, frontotemporal dementia, Huntington's chorea, Parkinson's disease, Creutzfeldt-Jakob disease, and Pick's disease.

6. Psychoactive drugs have many uses in the control of psychotic symptoms, anxiety, and depression, but they often have dangerous side-effects, such as tardive dyskinesia (involuntary body movements). Alcoholism and heavy drinking generally decline in old age. Drug misuse among the aged usually occurs in the context of medical treatment. The elderly may self-medicate or not follow doctors' orders. Doctors often overprescribe and incorrectly prescribe drugs, with little consideration of drug interactions, sometimes producing iatrogenic disorders. Sedatives, for example, can produce depression and mental confusion.

7. The goals of psychotherapy shift with the age of the patient. Young adults have identity and intimacy crises and middle-aged clients have midlife crises. The elderly present special problems for therapists. Older people do not always get the psychotherapy that they need because of expense, beliefs that psychotherapy marks an individual as "mentally ill," and the unwillingness of many therapists to treat elderly clients.

SUGGESTED READINGS

Cohen, G. D. (1992). *The brain in human aging.* New York: Springer. An excellent text quite accessible to the lay person, which provides information on the structure of the brain and developmental brain changes with age, relating structural changes to changes in function.

Gatz, M., and Smyer, M. A. (2001). Mental health and aging at the outset of the twenty-first century. In J. E. Birren and K. W. Schaie (Eds.), *Handbook of the psychology of aging* (5th ed.). San Diego, CA: Academic Press. A comprehensive review of recent research on diagnosis and interventions to enhance the mental health of the elderly.

Kaszniak, A. W. (1996). Techniques and instruments for assessment of the elderly. In S. H. Zarit, and B. G. Knight (Eds.). *A guide to psychtherapy and aging: Effective clinical interventions in a life-stage context* (pp. 163–218). Washington, DC: American Psychological Association. A thorough review of the difficult problems in identifying clinical depression and its differentiation from early stages of dementia, as well as the measurement of disease progression.

CHAPTER 15

The End of Life

Death and Bereavement

Although death can occur at any age, it is only in old age that we think of it as the natural biological end of life. Not only is death the cessation of a person's life, it is also a social event that affects family, friends, and usually other persons as well. The death of an important public figure—for example, Winston Churchill or Mao Tse-Tung—is sometimes taken to mark the end of a historical era; the death of Jesus marked the beginning of an era. We are concerned here with the role of death as a psychological event, one with which each individual must come to grips, whether it is with regard to the death of loved ones or to one's own death.

Eastern philosophies accept disease and death as part of the natural rhythm of life (Kastenbaum, 1998; Kothari and Mehta, 1986), but most Western cultures tend to regard death as the final assault upon our personhood, one that we would postpone as long as possible. Given a choice, most people would prefer to die a sudden death in old age of a cause that is associated with no prior hospitalization or warning signs (Kalish, 1985). When death becomes inevitable, some modicum of personal control is still desired, and in cases of prolonged terminal disease there may be substantial conflict between dying persons and their caretakers on where and how dying is to occur (Hays, Gold, Flint, and Winer, 1999). In this last chapter of our book, we deal with what is involved in facing death. We then consider contemporary issues related to death—the hospice movement and concerns about "the right to die." Finally, we deal with the aftermath of death, the manner in which the survivors experience bereavement and grief.

FACING DEATH

Anxiety About Death

Most people experience some conscious or unconscious anxiety about death (Lonetto and Templer, 1986; Tomer, 1992). They dislike the thought of death, whether it is the ending of their own life or the death of someone else. Specific fears of death vary from person to person. Some fear death because it is an unknown and unknowable experience: Is it painful? Is there "life" after death? Anxiety about death reflects existential concerns and a philosophical wonderment about the nature of the human soul, but it may akso reflect depression (Triplett et al., 1995). It may even reflect childhood conflicts that, deep in the unconscious, may remain unresolved. There may be a fear of separation from the protection of loved ones or feelings of guilt for having failed to discharge one's responsibilities to one's self, the family, and the community.

A complete understanding of the concept of death requires at least three components. Irreversibility involves the understanding that once a living organism dies, its physical body cannot be restored to life. *Nonfunctionality* requires the realization that living functions cease at death. Finally, *universality* implies an understanding that death occurs to all living organisms (Brent, Speece, Lin, Dong, and Yang 1996; Seale, 1998).

Children go through distinct stages in their beliefs about death (Bertman, 1991; Brent et al., 1996). Preschoolers fail to appreciate the finality of death; they often think of it as "going away," a separation that might be reversible (Wass, 1991). Between the ages of 6 and 11, children usually gain an understanding of all three components of the death concept. However, death often becomes personified, often expressed in children's fairy tales such as the notion that the "death man" comes to take away those of whom it is later said, they have died (Bertman, 1991; Lammers, 1995). But after the age of 12, death is perceived more or less accurately by most children as the end of life.

Cultural differences may affect death imagery. In a study of Swedish healthcare professionals death was most often described as an old man in dark clothing, a gentle though distant comforter. About one-fourth of the women, but virtually no men, saw death as a female figure (Tamm, 1996).

Death anxiety, when studied empirically, turns out to be a complex phenomenon characterized by at least four distinct components: (1) concern about physical change, (2) awareness of the passage of time, (3) concern about the pain and stress that accompany dying, and (4) concern about intellectual and emotional reactions to death (Kastenbaum, 2000; Lonetto and Templer, 1986). Death anxiety therefore involves the fear not only of separation from a loved one, but the fear of change and the consequences of change.

One of the major problems is that information on death and dying is relatively infrequent in educational curricula (Brown and Kayashima, 1999; Wass, 1991). Hence, it is not surprising that anxiety about death reaches its peak during adolescence. Most people in our society reach adolescence with little help from society in conceptualizing and coping with death. This situation is changing now with the advent of "death education" in schools and colleges. Instructors have found that many students keep emotion-laden concerns about death to themselves for lack of opportunity to discuss them. Often these concerns focus on specific people and events in their lives, not on the abstract idea of death. In fact, death educators suggest that the freedom to deal with mortality on a conceptual level is often hindered by unresolved personal problems, such as guilt feelings about relationships with persons thought to be close to death.

Death for most people is frightening primarily because it involves loss (Kastenbaum, 2000; Rando, 1991; Weenolsen, 1988). Death means the end of personal identity, the loss of self. No more will the individual smell jasmine or taste honey, solve a problem, or have an orgasm; no joy, no hope, not even sweet sorrow. The dead can no longer love or hate, be loved or be hated. Death marks the end of relationships—"till death do us part." The prospect of never again seeing a spouse, a friend, or even a beloved pet is saddening. Many people think about what their death will mean to others, the loss that the living will experience, and the possible hardships that their death will impose on their families (Tamm, 1996).

Anxiety about death is related in complex ways to factors such as age, religious beliefs, and the degree to which the individual has lived a full and satisfying life. Some people are concerned about death from an early age (Blueband-Langner, 1996); others, of a less reflective nature, may move into advanced old age, continuing their habitual one-day-at-a-time approach to life. Compared to young adults, old people generally think about death more often but fear it less. Probably the fear is less because old people are "socialized" (taught, or led to believe by society) to expect death and to prepare for it, emotionally as well as financially. Death, even the thought of it, is disturbing to many young people. Perceptions of social desirability are also influential. Many older adults think they are expected to say wise and gracious things about life and death and consequently do so. Others may feel a need to review their attitudes toward death and revise and transform the relevant beliefs and attitudes. A full and satisfying life appears to further reduce anxiety about death in old people, but among the young and middle-aged, it probably increases one's fears. Death at the end of a life well lived is acceptable, but death in the midst of such a life is viewed as something like a tasteless joke played by inscrutable fate.

Kastenbaum (2000) suggested that useful clues to adults' orientation toward death can be derived by studying their practical decisions as well as their expressed attitudes. Has a person made a will and revised it to keep up with changing circumstances? Has a person changed exercise, dietary, or drinking habits out of concern over his or her longevity? Does a person visit or avoid seriously ill friends and relatives? Does a person turn first to the obituary pages of the newspaper or purposely skip over them? Faced with the probable death of her husband, does a wife take practical steps to adjust?

Nevertheless, it remains difficult to predict the causes and discover the correlates of anxiety about death. A survey of a random sample of older American adults, however, informs us on some of the factors to which it is not related. These include the respondent's activity level, purpose in life, and tendency toward repression. Surprisingly, anxiety about death does not seem to be related to chronological age (Lonetto and Templer, 1986; Thorson and Powell, 1994). It appears that death anxiety may be a function of past experience rather than current life circumstances (Tomer, 1992; 1994).

A few correlates of death anxiety are known. Religious beliefs, as might be expected, are generally associated with less than average anxiety about death. Thus strengthening these beliefs in the face of death, provided they also raise self-esteem, should be expected to reduce anxiety (Harmon-Jones et al., 1997). But those subjects who usually show the highest death anxiety are not atheists or agnostics; instead they are the irregular churchgoers, those people who are inconsistent in their beliefs and practices (Rosik, 1989; Thorson and Powell, 1994), Most of the studies of correlates of death anxiety assume that there is a linear relationship with the other variables studied. However, it is quite possible that these relationships hold only for certain extreme levels of death anxiety. (cf. Neimeyer, 1997–1998).

The Process of Dying

Thus far, we have been discussing the general fears that people have in anticipation of their death, but what of people who know they are dying? What do they experience?

The process of dying, for many individuals, may be more fearful than the recognition that life is about to end. Many dying persons are burdened by the expectation that they should participate in a ritual process that involves denial and pretense in relation to those around them. The dying person is often trained to assume an expected role by those providing the final care (Kastenbaum, 1998; Strauss and Glaser, 1985). The "good" dying person is expected to pretend that improvement is at hand, turn over treatment decisions to others, and talk only about neutral topics or the immediate future. Perhaps the objective of this role is to shield the living from what they, too, must eventually endure at the ends of their lives (Corr, Doka, and Kastenbaum, 2000; Weenolsen, 1988).

The best-known research on the process of dying is by Elisabeth Kübler-Ross (1969, 1981, 1991), a psychiatrist who has observed and interviewed several hundred dying patients. Kübler-Ross suggests that each person's response to dying expresses four dimensions essential to human beings: physical, emotional, intellectual, and spiritual-intuitive. She identified five stages of dying, each characterized by a certain attitude. The first stage is *denial:* "Oh, no! Not me! It can't be true!" Obvious symptoms of impending death are ignored or treated as if they were unimportant. Denial is followed by *anger,* in which the approaching death is acknowledged, but with rage: "Why me? Why now?" *Bargaining* is the third stage, in which the person pleads with God or Satan or Fate for a pardon or at least a postponement. The patient often becomes compliant, hoping to win some extra time on earth "for good behavior." In the fourth stage, *depression,* death is perceived as unavoidable. This hopeless sorrow is perhaps preparation for the fifth and final stage, *acceptance.* Acceptance is not a happy stage, but neither is it a sad one. "It is almost void of feelings. It is as if the pain had gone, the struggle is over" (Kübler-Ross, 1969, p. 100).

Kübler-Ross's work has awakened interest in the psychological aspects of dying and has undoubtedly helped some people who are trying to understand the feelings of a loved one whose death is imminent. As a scientific theory, however, it leaves much to be desired (Shneidman, 1982; Kastenbaum, 2000). Her interviews were not very systematic; instead of statistical analyses, she offers examples and anecdotes. Other researchers do not find the same five stages. Of the five, only depression is consistently reported (Schulz and Alderman, 1974). Kübler-Ross herself has stated that not everyone expresses each stage, that the stages do not always occur in the same order, and that, in fact, the patient may exhibit two or even three stages at the same time (Kübler-Ross, 1974). Thus, we should not consider Kübler-Ross's ideas as a stage theory of the dying process, as it is so often described, but as a rather insightful discussion of attitudes that are often displayed by people who are dying.

Denial. Of the five attitudes, denial is one of the most frequently discussed. But what is often called denial may actually represent other kinds of control strategies that include selective attention, selective response, compartmentalization, deception, and resistance. Some of these mechanisms may well have adaptive qualities (Kastenbaum, 1998). In some patients and their loved ones, however, denial can take an extreme form. The idea of impending death is denied access to consciousness, and the opposite is asserted, often vehemently: "I am *not* dying!" The patient (or loved one) denies even the obvious symptoms: "I am *not* having trouble breathing!" Or, denial breaks the link between symptom and implication: "So I'm having a little trouble breathing. That means *nothing!*" Other people admit the symptoms and implications, but blithely maintain that they are exceptions: "Untreatable lung cancer does *not always* mean death, you know."

Outright denial is common in some form at some time in the process of dying. Most common, however, is the conscious avoidance of talk about death in the presence of the person who is dying. Societal standards of etiquette require that if one person involved in the process—patient, loved one, doctor, nurse—does not want to talk about it, no one should. Death then becomes a taboo topic. Also, no one is permitted to discuss major symptoms or the future. Someone who breaks the code (for instance, by crying) must be ignored; discussions of the weather, the quality of hospital food, and how to sleep in a hospital environment must continue unabated (Kastenbaum, 1998; Shneidman, 1982).

Refusing to discuss someone's death and dying is typically motivated by humanitarian concerns, but sparing someone's feelings has a price. The patient, as well as his or her loved ones, might actually benefit from a sharing of sorrow. Inevitably, problems arise when a family member dies; these problems could and should be discussed and possible solutions could be formulated. Many times, the dying person has "unfinished business" (a will needs to be drawn up, a petty argument with a friend or family member needs to be made up), and the denial that life is ending prohibits him or her from successfully tying up these loose ends.

Anger. Anger is a common response to news that one will die soon. People feel cheated and frustrated, and they "do not go gentle into that good night." They rail against God, Nature, their doctor, and whatever other scapegoat they can imagine. Their loved ones, feeling the same sense of loss, sympathize and may feel anger themselves (Young, 1984).

Anger can be a valuable experience, a way of integrating death with the rest of one's life. Two common examples come to mind. One is the death of a young adult. The sense of being cheated out of a full measure of life is particularly strong, but the search for meaning that results can add immeasurably to the remaining life of the dying and the survivors, as many parents of children with cancer can attest (Rando, 1991; Tebbi et al., 1989). But such anger can also have negative long-term consequences to the survivors' long-term personal adjustment (Arbuckle and de Vries, 1995). Anger in an older person may represent important values. One young woman spoke of her father, an atheist, who raged against a priest whom she called in to administer last rites. In his last effort, he rose in bed and said to the priest, "Go to hell!" The woman was embarrassed, of course, and half-afraid that he had alienated God. But she was also half-pleased that he had managed to keep to his own values to the end.

Alternative Viewpoints. Further clarification of the process of dying is provided by views that compete with stage theory. A prime example of such an alternative view is the work of Edwin Shneidman (1974, 1982), whose research on death and dying is almost as famous as that of Kübler-Ross and considerably more scientific.

Shneidman sees death as imposing burdens of two kinds. First, one must prepare oneself for one's own death. Second, one must deal with the interpersonal aspects of death that will affect one's loved ones. People must prepare themselves to be survivors. The process of confronting these two burdens, he says, involves continual alternation between pervasive emotional states, including grief, anguish, anger, anxiety, and denial. Shneidman describes dying people, for example, who shock a listener one day with their candor in expressing their profound acceptance of imminent death and then shock the same listener the next day with their unrealistic talk of leaving the hospital and going on a trip. This interplay between acceptance and denial, understanding and disbelieving, reflects a deeper dialogue in which the person's knowing that death is imminent is balanced with the need to "not know" in order to survive the final ordeal.

Coping with dying has more recently been conceptualized as a life-span developmental task. Two psychologists, Charles Corr and Kenneth Doka, have pioneered this approach. They suggest that there are four challenges that must be faced by the dying. First, it is necessary to deal with the physical aspects of satisfying bodily needs and reducing pain and distress. Secondly, the dying must satisfy the psychological needs of feeling secure, being in control, and having some sort of remaining life to live. Third is the social dimension of trying to keep valued attachments to other individuals and groups. Finally there is the spiritual need of finding or affirming meaning (Corr, 1992). In addition, Doka (1993) describes phase-specific requirements that accompany the dying process.

The developmental approach considers death to be a normative rather than a pathological event. Dying persons still try to accomplish final life tasks (cf. Schaie & Willis, 2000a). The developmental approach also considers the dying person in a holistic manner and thus counteracts the medicalization of dying. This approach is consistent with the productivity-oriented character of Western societies, in that people who have been achievement-oriented throughout life will find a task-oriented approach as a meaningful way of living the end of their lives.

Unanswered Questions. Research on dying needs to be expanded to investigate a greater variety of influences. For example, the nature of the disease probably affects the way a person dies; dying of cancer, many physicians report, is different from dying of emphysema or heart disease. As one reviewer states, the mere mention of the word *cancer* strikes terror into the hearts of patients (Kaplowitz, Osuch, Safron, and Campo, 1999). Cancer elicits images of violence and sadism and the idea, sometimes unconscious, that the patient ("victim") is being forced to submit passively to a merciless killer.

The relationship between physical and mental states also requires further exploration. As an example of this complex interaction, one study of terminally ill patients who appeared to be in a stage of quiet acceptance (as defined by Kübler-Ross) found that 75 percent were suffering from organic brain disorders, many no doubt induced by the life-threatening illness itself (Spikes, 1980). Also, there are likely to be sex differences and almost certainly ethnic differences in the style of dying. A teenager dies differently than someone very old, and dying at home is different from dying in a hospital.

TREATMENT OF THE DYING

The Hospice Movement

Over the last decade, there have been major developments in the effort to improve the humane treatment of the dying. While the hospital remains a good place for treating diseases amenable to cure or amelioration, it may not be the best place to die. Indeed, the heroic methods of life preservation practiced in many hospitals may be contrary to the desires of the patient. Many of the recent developments in the care of the dying have grown out of the hospice movement, which developed in England and in recent years has been spreading in the United States (Gilmore and Gilmore, 1988). The hospice movement emphasizes the individuality of patients as well as the needs and rights of families and caregivers. Hospices provide an alternative to a final stay in the hospital for terminal patients. The goal is to relieve the pain and preserve the dignity of the dying person, not to use technology in every way possible to prolong a person's life in circumstances that may prove to be destructive to the dying patient and his or her family (Hayslip and Leon, 1992; Littlewood, 1992). In 1991, there were 951 hospices in the United States (Jones, 1994). In 1993, these hospices and home health-care agencies provided hospice services to approximately 257,000 persons in institutions or in the community (Strahan, 1994; see also Kramarow et al., 1999).

A hospice, however, is more than just a shelter for the dying. It is expected to provide a supportive environment in a professional manner. This means that a full-service hospice program is expected to have a professional staff that includes physicians, nurses, social workers, pastoral counselors, and psychologists; to provide continuity of care for the patient at home, in the hospital, or in the hospice; to use all of the primary caregivers—the patient's family, friends, and neighbors; and to use carefully selected, trained, and supervised community volunteers. Modern hospices also provide out-patient services that permit dying people to be cared for in their home, and they provide support services for bereaved people.

Hospices are expected to deliver a "safe" death, one that is dignified and private. This expectation may, however, be unrealistic in some instances, such as people dying from AIDS, for whom a "safe" sociocultural context for dying may not be possible (Kastenbaum, 1988, 2000; Littlewood, 1992; Ogden 2000).

It has been recognized that, in addition to the well-recognized pattern of gradual decline, there is often a more discontinuous pathway to death. For example, sudden falls that are not in themselves serious may signal rapid terminal deterioration. A traditional hospital would discharge the patient after he or she recovered from the fall, not recognizing that continuing support is often needed because the fall signals a broader systematic decline. Hospices are designed to provide such supportive care. They can also respond appropriately when a patient

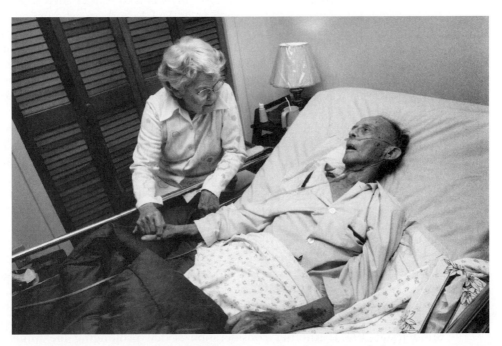

The hospice movement has provided alternative settings for dying with dignity.

expresses a wish to die at home. Hospices may reverse the trend toward providing less than first-rate care to dying older patients.

Two different patterns have developed in the United States—the hospice based in the home or the community, and the hospice operated as part of a hospital. After a rocky beginning, hospice care has now become part of the health-care industry, particularly because benefits for hospice care are included in the Medicare program (Mor, 1987a). The growth of hospice services has produced a new group of compassionate and skillful caregivers, including many older people, whose maturity and coping skills make them valuable volunteers (Mor, 1987b). Hospice research has also added new dimensions to our knowledge of the dying process (Kastenbaum, 1985, 2000).

The Right to Die

A hotly debated issue is whether people should be allowed to die naturally when keeping them alive through heroic efforts will bring them only unmitigated suffering or give them only a vegetative existence (Emanuel, 1994). This issue is often discussed under the rubric of "death with dignity" (Wong and Stiller, 1999). Associated with the right to die is the issue of rational suicide for the terminally ill (Hook, 1987; Lenzer, 1999). The debate on this issue has become even more heated as the voters of one American state (Oregon) have passed a referendum permitting physician-assisted suicide in the terminally ill, even though federal regulations currently would make it illegal for physicians to render such assistance. In the news also have been physicians such as Dr. Jack Kevorkian, who defied the laws of Michigan and other states and helped terminal patients commit suicide (Kaplan, Lachenmeier, O'Dell, and Uziel, in press). Public opinion on this issue remains strongly divided among old people as well as organizations representing the elderly (Clark and Liebig, 1996). Physician-assisted suicide has recently been sanctioned by law, and had previously been tolerated and practiced by physicians in the Netherlands (Van der Wal et al., 1994).

Many people would abhor "active" euthanasia, in which those who are presumed to be hopelessly sick or disabled are killed. However, the issue is far less clear with regard to "passive" euthanasia, in which case extraordinary medical care that might prolong life is specifically withheld (Kassirer, 1997; Wekesser, 1995). Some would perceive medical technology to be cruel when it unnecessarily prolongs the life of a person who would die soon in any event. On the other hand, a similar argument could be used to justify withholding medical care for the old because such care might be considered wasteful, and indeed there is some evidence for de facto health care rationing for the very old (cf. Kapp, 1998). There is also the problem that the outcome of many medical interventions in the severely ill is not reliably predictable in advance. For one terminally ill cancer patient, major surgery may be nothing more than an ordeal; for another, it might have life-enhancing effects, permitting greater mobility, for example (Butler, Lewis, and Sunderland, 1991). Another consideration is that prolonging life unnecessarily may have severe psychological and economic consequences for the family of the dying person as well as reducing the economic resources available to society for providing better health care in general. In the United States these discussions are complicated by diverging religious approaches to these issues (for a Christian perspective see Rowell, 2000).

When should medical efforts cease? Some patients really are the living dead: they breathe and their hearts beat, but they are incapable of any response that we would characterize as being "human." For this reason, modern definitions are coming to recognize death as the irreversible destruction of the brain. Matters become even more complicated when we are dealing with a critically ill person who has expressed a wish to die. Should individuals be allowed to make that decision? There has been much discussion of "living wills" or "advance directives," formal documents in which physicians and family are directed to refrain from so-called heroic and life-sustaining treatments when all hope of potential recovery is gone. Thoughtful discussion of such directives must involve other members of the family, and often the participation of a religious counselor may be helpful (Brown and Kayashima, 1999).

Although the expression of the wish to die is legally recognized in a number of states in the United States, there remain problems. Some states require that the "living will" be updated in case people change their minds, and the validity of such wills requires evidence that the person executing the will was competent to consider the consequences carefully. It should be noted that advanced directives, in any event, will work only when the patient is indeed close to death. An additional precaution for avoiding unwanted treatment may therefore be a health-care power of attorney, appointing a relative or friend to make surrogate health-care decisions when one is cognitively incapacitated from making such decisions oneself (cf. Smyer, Kapp, and Schaie, 1996).

THE SURVIVORS: BEREAVEMENT AND GRIEF

Death may end the suffering of the dying, but the family often faces a long period of adjustment. We refer to the family collectively as "the bereaved"—those who have been deprived of someone dear. The name that we give to what they are feeling is grief. We generally expect some instability, until the survivors adapt to life without the one who "passed away."

Throughout this book, we have described the family as a system of interdependent relationships. The death of a family member disrupts that system of relationships. Adjustment to the death of a loved one, in family terms, is the attempt to restore equilibrium to the system; roles and tasks must be reassigned, and power alignments must be revised. If the deceased was the family leader and the primary source of income, adjustment obviously can be radical and pervasive, but even the loss of the youngest child requires considerable adaptations and change. Sometimes people even engage in antipatory grief in the expectation of the loss of a loved one (Fulton, Maden, and Minichiello, 1996).

How pervasive are these effects? Interestingly enough, reactions to loss do not necessarily affect all areas of function. For example, a study of the impact of bereavement on the survivors in a sample of 309 families in Leyden in the Netherlands found that strong loss reactions among the bereaved were indeed related to impaired health, but also that the effective maintenance of social functioning was relatively independent of the severity of the loss (Cleiren, 1993).

There are three components that are thought to be part of the bereavement process: loss, grief, and, recovery (Mullan, Pearlin, and Skaff, 1992). *Loss* represents distancing oneself from a part of one's life to which one was emotionally attached; *grief* involves the emotional, cognitive and perceptual reactions that go with the loss of a loved one; and *recovery* involves the survivor's restructuring their lives and calling upon supportive resources that permit going on without the person who is being mourned.

Coping Techniques

Many different methods are employed by the survivors to cope with their loss; these mechanisms differ with the life-stage of the bereaved (Stroebe, Stroebe, and Hanasson, 1988). For example, in a study of several thousand college students, La-Grand (1986) found that the most frequently reported means of coping were talking about the loss, gradually accepting it, crying, support of friends, and the passage of time. Less frequent, but still reported by at least a fourth of LaGrand's sample, were the coping mechanisms of keeping busy, or thinking of all the other good things in their relationships. Religious and philosophical beliefs, developing new interests, and "replacement" of the loved one were mentioned by less than one out of five in this study. Among older persons experiencing loss through death, mourning and reminiscence may play a more central role (Viney, Benjamin, and Preston, 1989). Religion is also more important to older survivors, but it seems to be an intrinsic religious orientation, rather than religious participation, that has the most stress-reducing quality (Lehman et al., 1999).

A number of self-help approaches have been advocated to cope with the aftermath of the death of a loved one. It is rarely possible to cope with grief alone, and it is therefore important for the grieving person to let others know that he or she is feeling hurt and to allow them to help. Likewise it is important for the grieving person to accept feelings that seem abnormal as appropriate during the mourning period. It is important also to express feelings and thoughts related to the personal loss and the consequent emotional experiences. Eventually, the grieving person needs to rise above the bitterness and resentment felt about the loss. Equally important is the endeavor to deal with immediate problems, make decisions, and keep up one's physical strength (Leming and Dickinson, 1994). In the Dutch study referred to above, it was found that if there were still strong reactions four months after the death of the loved one, then future problems could be expected to be reported in the one-year longitudinal follow-up (Cleiren, 1993).

Rituals

Following the death of a family member, most families engage in a set of rituals or ceremonies that simultaneously help them handle their grief and express certain societal values and beliefs about death (Littlewood, 1992). Saying goodbye

Funeral rites not only honor the departed, but offer a context for expression of grief by the survivors. But the manner of grieving may be determined by the cultural context.

to a loved one is a common theme in literature (Schulman, 1996). Often, the deceased may have expressed detailed wishes as to their last rites; sometimes having made their own provisions as early as midlife (Hayslip, Servaty, and Guarnaccia, 1999). Pre-need funeral arrangements and particularly prepayment may remove a great deal of stress for the survivors (Bern-Klug, Ekerdt, and Nakashima, 1999).

A funeral service is usually the keystone of this ritualistic structure; the deceased's better qualities are praised, and the beliefs of his or her religion about death and life after death are stated. Funeral rites reflect a view of death as sorrowful and important although the extent of rites will vary across different cultures and ethnic groups (see Barrett, 1993, for an excellent account of funeral rites and attitudes on death of African Americans). The family is kept busy with details (making decisions about arrangements, contacting relatives, and so on), while friends and community organizations offer their support (e.g., preparing food). Wakes, "sitting shiva," and other rituals complement the funeral service. After burial (or other ceremonies, if the body is cremated or donated to medical research), there is often a ritualistic social gathering, which is not always an unhappy occasion, where the bereaved and their friends can further work out their feelings. In even the simplest of cases, more detail work follows the funeral. If there is a will, it is read and executed. Old clothing must be distributed, old photo albums must be examined, thank-you notes must be written. One need not concern oneself with decisions about dress; in Western societies, black or dark attire is traditional. But note that many rituals of death often require expending scarce economic resources and thus may not be available to the very poor (Bern-Klug, Ekerdt, and Nakashima, 1999).

Research evidence on the effect of rituals is lacking, but most psychologists believe the ceremonial behaviors lessen the effect of severe grief. By giving the bereaved some easy work to do, the rituals prevent rumination and wallowing. They also muster community support for people who very much need support at this time. The rituals include formal opportunities for the bereaved to consider their relationships with the deceased and their lives without him or her. And they state facts, values, and beliefs (belief in an afterlife, for example) that promote positive thinking. Funeral rituals are also time-limited, thus setting temporal boundaries for the duration of expressions of intense grief (Marris, 1986). Even the cemetery plays a role; it is, as one sociologist called it, "the city of the dead," a symbolic replica of the living community (Warner, 1965). The cemetery is an expression of the belief that the "social personality" of the deceased is still with us, though the physical body is without life. One's influence on others remains; it is a sort of eternal life.

Nevertheless, perhaps in reaction to the commercialization of death by the funeral industry, there has been an increasing trend in the United States to think of the departed as not placebound in cemeteries or to be commemorated by physical monuments. This has lead to a dramatic increase in the use of cremation followed by memorial services and/or other nonphysical ways of honoring the dead.

In fact, it is estimated that by 2010 more than 30 percent of those dying will leave instructions to be cremated (Bern Klug, Ekerdt, and Nakashima, 1999; Gill, 1996).

Grieving

As there seem to be stages in the acceptance of one's own death, there are what appear to be stages in the acceptance of the death of a loved one. One theorist has proposed three broad stages, which, he claims, are observable not only in humans but in many species of animals as well (Bowlby, 1974). In the first, the bereaved yearn for the deceased; they feel anger born of the inevitable frustration of their craving. The second stage is characterized by apathy and disorganized behavior. Finally, the bereaved reorganize their life. In other terms, these stages might be called denial and anger, depression, and acceptance and readjustment (Spikes, 1980). So put, the stages of grieving are quite similar to the stages of dying proposed by Kübler-Ross.

The severity of these reactions and the time span over which they endure vary, depending on factors such as the individual's closeness to the deceased, the social support available, and the degree to which the death was expected (Kastenbaum, 2000; Littlewood, 1992). Grieving reactions are even observed in children as young as 1 year of age. When placed with strangers, such children make determined efforts to recover their lost mothers. For days, the children cry loudly, throw themselves about, and search eagerly for any sight or sound that might prove to be their missing mothers (Bowlby, 1980). For a week or so, hopeful looking about alternates with periods of urgent distress. Somewhat older children may have visual experiences in which the departed person is reported as an apparition (cf. LaGrand, 1986, p. 93). But eventually despair sets in. The child continues to long for the mother's return, but with less and less hope that she actually will come back. Ultimately, the child's demands cease, and he or she becomes apathetic and withdrawn. At this stage, the child cries intermittently in a state of great misery.

A similar pattern of response is also observed in people who clearly do know that they have suffered bereavement. Indeed, it is a familiar sight among institutionalized geriatric patients. This behavioral response, then, is associated with a perception of critical loss (Kastenbaum, 1985, 2000).

Of course, all deaths do not have the same meaning or result in the same level of social disruption. It has been suggested that the death of aged people has relatively little influence on society. Several studies have found that the death of an older parent is less disruptive, less emotionally debilitating, and generally less significant for adult children than either the death of a spouse or the death of a child (Littlewood, 1992; Owens, Fulton, and Markusen, 1983). The survivors of the death of a parent are less likely to have a traditional funeral ritual and less likely to become ill in subsequent months.

The impact of the death of an older parent may be diminished by its predictability and by the factors that have diminished the influence of the nuclear family. Another factor may be that the adult child repeatedly considers and rehearses the death of a parent; there is certainly less of a taboo associated with anticipating the death of a parent than with anticipating the death of a spouse or a child. By anticipating the death of a parent over many decades, the adult child is prepared for it when it comes (Fulton, Madden, and Minichello, 1996). The process may also involve subtle preparation for one's own death.

The above comments also could be interpreted as a devaluation of the death of the older person and as the final expression of ageism (Kastenbaum, 2000). On the other hand, the death of an older person with a long productive life may become an occasion for reminiscence and a celebration of a life well-lived. Sometimes death is actually romanticized. The dying person is pictured as grasping control of the death scene and exerting his or her will to use this final opportunity to forgive, admonish, and instruct loved ones. A person dying with calmness and composure was, at least in Victorian times, thought to inspire relatives and friends with final signs of inward grace and fortitude, thus setting an example to the survivors (Boyle and Morriss, 1987).

Older individuals are more at risk than younger persons for most, if not all, of the grief-inducing losses (Lopata, 1999; Mullan, Pearlin, and Skaff, 1995). It is not surprising, therefore, that some people find the loss of a loved one—spouse, child, or parent—so unbearably painful for such a prolonged time that the grief can be described as pathological. Such grief may involve feelings of self-hatred and loss of self-esteem; in some cases, mourners may even attempt to take their own lives. During pathological grief, self-images and modes of interacting with others that were held in check by the existence of the deceased person may reemerge.

Health

The health of people who are grieving over the loss of a loved one seems to suffer. Compared to people of the same age, recently widowed people have more physical complaints and visit their doctors more often (Cleiren, 1993; Parkes, 1972). The death rate of bereaved persons is generally found to be higher than one would expect, at least for the first six months following the death. However, some studies report a rise in death rate only for bereaved people under 65, with no such increase among the those above 65.

These data have been explained in many ways: (1) the stress of bereavement makes illness and death more likely; (2) removal of the person with whom the bereaved's inner clock was synchronized leads to physical discomfort and dissynchronization (Hofer, 1984); (3) the stress of bereavement leads to life-threatening behaviors, such as smoking, drinking, a lack of interest in exercise, and poor sleep habits; (4) bereaved people were understandably unwilling to do much about their own medical problems before their loved one died, and thus an increase in visits to doctors represents an averaging-out of medical complaints between the pre- and postdeath periods (untreated problems, of course, can become more serious and even increase the chances of death). Perhaps all these factors are present in some degree or another. Also, some reviewers are sharply critical of the research that underlies these data (Stroebe, Stroebe, and Hansson, 1988). Perhaps there is no real increase in illness or death to interpret!

Therapy

People who have lost a loved one usually can benefit from supportive psychotherapy or counseling; some are in desperate need of such help (Butler, Lewis, and Sunderland, 1991). Religion is a source of comfort for many, and a good friend or another family member can provide emotional support for some (Brown and Kayshima, 1999; Kalish and Reynolds, 1976).

One of the major problems faced by widows is the inferior status of older women in society. The widows cannot (or think that they cannot) function well without their husbands, who provided the bulk of the income and who escorted them to various activities (Lopata, 1996a, 1996b; see also Chapter 7). Thus, it is not surprising that women's consciousness-raising groups are among the most effective forms of therapy for grieving widows. In these groups, the widows consider sex-role stereotypes—the woman as passive, dependent, incompetent—and discuss the ways in which these stereotypes affect their adjustment as widows. They may also be given "assertiveness training" to provide them with the confidence to lead independent lives in a male-oriented, youth-oriented, and couple-oriented society (DeBallis et al., 1986; Lopata, 1999).

SUMMARY

1. Most people have a certain amount of conscious or unconscious anxiety about death. Old people, who expect death soon, are less anxious than young people. Young children often personify death as a being who takes people away. The most fundamental feature of death, to both the dying and the survivors, is loss—loss of self, loss of a loved one.

2. Kübler-Ross sees the process of dying in five stages: denial, anger, bargaining, depression, and acceptance. Although Kübler-Ross has done much to stimulate interest in the emotional life of dying individuals, her stage theory has not received much empirical support. If a stage theory is appropriate at all, it will probably have to be modified to account for age, sex, ethnic, and other differences in the process of dying. Other approaches recognize similar attitudes. Denial or avoidance of the topic of death in the presence of dying is common and understandable, although it can prevent the dying person from carrying out important last-minute duties. Anger results from frustration and imminent loss. Bargaining may take the form of changes in behavior that the individual hopes will allow a few more days or weeks of life, perhaps until some important event, like a birthday. Depression, as we might imagine, is the most common emotion among the dying.

3. Shneidman sees death as imposing two kinds of burdens: one must prepare for one's own death and one must deal with the effects of one's death on one's loved ones. Corr and Doka conceptualize death as a developmental task. Four challenges faced by the dying are re-

ducing pain and distress, feeling secure and in control, trying to keep valued attachments, and finding or affirming meaning.

4. The hospice movement provides an alternative to hospital care for terminally ill patients. Hospices emphasize the comfort and dignity of patients rather than the use of elaborate and expensive technology to prolong the lives of suffering patients as much as possible. The question of whether an individual should have the "right to die" remains controversial. "Passive" euthanasia, in which medical care that might prolong life is withheld, is a complex issue, especially when the patient has expressed a wish to die.

5. The term "bereavement" is used in reference to the family and friends of the person who died. Grief, the extreme sadness most bereaved people feel, is helped by rituals, such as the funeral, which give the bereaved something to do and time to sort out their thoughts and feelings. Stage theories of the grieving process are similar to those of the dying process—from denial and anger to depression to acceptance and readjustment. Grieving reactions have been noted even in very young children. All deaths do not have the same meaning or result in the same level of social disruption; the deaths of aged people, for example, may have relatively little influence on society. Some people, on the other hand, experience such extreme grief that it can be considered to be pathological.

SUGGESTED READINGS

Braun, K. L., Pietsch, J. H., and Blanchette, P. L. (2000). *Cultural issues in end-of-life decision making*. Thousand Oaks, CA: Sage. A collection of essays on how different cultures approach decisions that must be made at the end of life, written by psychologists, social workers, and lawyers.

Kastenbaum, R. (2000). *The psychology of death* (3rd ed.). New York: Springer Publishing Co. Provides a comprehensive discussion of psycological perceptions of death and dying from the perspectives of children, adolescents, and adults.

Kothari, M. L., and Mehta, L. A. (1986). *Death: A new perspective on the phenomena of disease and dying*. New York: Marion Boyars. An alternative account of death from the viewpoint of two physicians with non-Western philosophical perspectives.

Littlewood, J. (1992). *Aspects of grief: Bereavement in adult life*. New York: Routledge. Heavily documented coverage of the topics summarized in this chapter, illustrated with many individual accounts of the grieving process.

General Resources

HANDBOOKS

Bengtson, V. L.,and Schaie, K. W. (Eds.). (1999). *Handbook of theories of aging*. New York: Springer Publishing Co.

Binstock, R. H., and George, L. (Eds.). (1996, 2001). *Handbook of aging and the social sciences* (4th and 5th eds.). San Diego, CA: Academic Press.

Birren, J. E., and Schaie, K. W. (Eds.). (1996, 2001). *Handbook of the psychology of aging* (4th and 5th eds.). San Diego, CA: Academic Press.

Birren, J. E ., Sloane, R. B., Cohen, G. D., Hoyman, N. R., Lebowitz, B., Wykle, M. H., and Deutchman, D. E. (Eds.) (1992). *Handbook of mental health and aging* (2nd ed.). San Diego, CA: Academic Press.

Carstensen, L. L., and Edelstein, B. A. (1988). *Handbook of clinical gerontology*. New York: Pergamon.

Cassel, C. K., Riesenberg, D. E., Sørenson, L. B., and Walsh, J. R. (Eds.) (1990). *Geriatric medicine* (2nd ed.). New York: Springer-Verlag.

Maddox, G. L. (Ed.). (2001). *The encyclopedia of aging* (3rd ed.). New York: Springer Publishing Co.

Masoro, E., and Austad, S. (Eds.) (2001). *Handbook of the biology of aging* (5th ed.). San Diego, CA: Academic Press.

Schneider, E. L., and Rowe, J. A. (Eds.). (1996). *Handbook of the biology of aging* (4th ed.). San Diego, CA: Academic Press.

SERIALS

Annual Review of Gerontology and Geriatrics. New York: Springer, 1980 to 2001 (Volumes 1 to 21).

Life-span Development and Behavior. New York: Academic Press, 1978–1986. Hillsdale, NJ: Erlbaum, 1987–1989 (Volumes 1 to 10).

RECENT VOLUMES WITH BROAD COVERAGE OF TOPICS

Adams-Price, C. E. (Ed.). (1998). *Creativity and successful aging*. New York: Springer Publishing Co.

Atchley, R. C. (2000). *The social forces in later life* (9th ed.). Belmont, CA: Wadsworth.

Baltes, P. B., and Baltes, M. M. (Eds.) (1990). *Successful aging: Perspectives from the behavioral sciences*. Cambridge, UK: Cambridge University Press.

Baltes, P. B.,and Mayer, K. U. (Eds) (1999). *The Berlin Aging Study: Aging from 70 to 100*. Cambridge, UK: Cambridge University Press.

Bengtson, V. L., Schaie, K. W., and Burton, L. (Eds.) (1995). *Adult intergenerational relations: Effects of societal changes*. New York: Springer Publishing Co.

Bergener, M., Hasegawa, K., Finkel, S. I., and Nishimura, T. (Eds.) (1992). *Aging and mental disorders: International perspectives*. New York: Springer Publishing Co.

Birren, H., Kenyon, G., Ruth, J. E., Schroots, J. J. F., and Swensson, T. (Eds.) (1996). *Aging and biography: Explorations in adult development*. New York: Springer Publishing Co..

Cavanaugh, J. C., and Whitbourne, S. K. (Eds.) (1999). *Gerontology: An interdisciplinary perspective*. New York: Oxford University Press.

Cohen, G. D. (1992). *The brain in human aging*. New York: Springer Publishing Co.

Cohen, S. H., and Reese, H. W. (Eds.) (1994). *Life-span developmental psychology: Theoretical issues revisited*. Hillsdale, NJ: Erlbaum.

Craik, F. I. N., and Salthouse, T. A. (Eds.), (1999). *Handbook of aging and cognition* (2nd ed.). Mahwah, NJ: Erlbaum.

De Vries, B. (Ed.) (1999). *End of life issues.* New York: Springer Publishing Co.

Dixon, R.A., and Bäckman, L. (Eds.) (1995). *Psychological compensation: Managing losses and promoting gains.* Hillsdale, NJ: Erlbaum.

Hersen, M., and Van Hasselt, V. B. (Eds.) (1996). *Psychological treatment of older adults.* New York: Plenum.

Hultsch, D. F., Hertzog, C., Dixon, R. A., and Small, B. J. (1998). *Memory changes in the aged.* New York: Cambridge University Press.

Kastenbaum, R. (2000). *The psychology of death.* New York: Spring Publishing Co.

Knight, B. G., Teri, L., Wohlford, P., and Santos, J. (Eds.) (1995). *Mental health services for older adults: Implications for training and practice in geropsychology.* Washington, DC: American Psychological Association.

Magnusson, D., and Caesar, P. (Eds.) (1995). *Longitudinal research on individual development, present status and future perspectives.* New York: Cambridge University Press.

Park, D. C., Morell, R. W., and Shifren, K. (Eds.) (1999). *Processing of medical information in aging patients: Cognitive and human factors perspectives.* Mahwah, NJ: Erlbaum.

Park, D. C., and Schwarz, N. (Eds.) (1999). *Cognitive aging: A primer.* Philadelphia, PA: Psychology Press.

Puckett, J. M. and Reese, H. W. (Eds.) (1993). *Mechanisms of everyday cognition.* Hillsdale, NJ: Erlbaum.

Riley, M. W., Kahn, R. L., and Foner, N. (Eds.) (1995). *Age and structural lag.* New York: Wiley..

Schaie, K. W. (1996). *Intellectual Development in Adulthood: The Seattle Longitudinal Study.* New York: Cambridge University Press.

Schaie, K. W., and Achenbaum, W. A. (Eds.) (1993). *Societal impact on aging: Historical perspectives.* New York: Springer Publishing Co.

Schaie, K. W., Blazer, D., and House, J. (Eds.) (1992). *Aging, health behavior and health outcomes.* Hillsdale, NJ: Erlbaum.

Schaie, K. W., Campbell, R. C., Meredith, W. A., and Rawlings, S. A. (Eds.) (1988). *Methodologi-* cal issues in the study of aging. New York: Springer Publishing Co.

Schaie, K. W., and Hendricks, J. (Eds.). (2000). *Evolution of the aging self: Societal impacts.* New York: Springer Publishing Co.

Schaie, K. W., Leventhal, H., and Willis, S. L. (2001). *Social structures and health behavior in the elderly.* New York: Springer Publishing Co.

Schaie, K. W., & Pietrucha, M. (Eds.) (2000). *Mobility and transportation in the elderly.* New York: Springer Publishing Co.

Schaie, K. W., and Schooler, C. E. (Eds.). (1998). *Impact of the work place on older persons.* New York: Springer Publishing Co.

Schulz, J. H. (1995). *The economics of aging* (6th ed.). Westport, CT: Auburn House.

Smyer, M. A., Kapp, M., and Schaie, K. W. (Eds.) (1996). *Impact of the law on older adults' decision-making capacity.* New York: Springer Publishing Co.

Sprott, R. L., Huber, R. W., and Williams, T. F. (Eds.) (1993). *The biology of aging.* New York: Springer Publishing Co.

Willis, S. L., and Dubin, S. S. (Eds.) (1990). *Maintaining professional competence.* San Francisco, CA: Jossey-Bass.

Willis, S. L., and Reid, J. (Eds.) (1999). *Aging in the middle.* San Diego, CA: Academic Press.

Willis, S. L., Schaie, K. W., and Hayward, M. (1997). *Impact of social structures on decision making in the elderly.* New York: Springer Publishing Co.

Wisocki, P. A. (Ed.) (1991). *Handbook of clinical behavior therapy with the elderly client.* New York: Plenum Press.

Zarit, S. H., Pearlin, L. I. and Schaie, K. W. (Eds.). (1993). *Caregiving systems: Informal and formal helpers.* Hillsdale, NJ: Erlbaum.

JOURNALS

Aging and Health Research
Ageing and Society
Aging, Neuropsychology, and Cognition
Australian Journal on Ageing
Canadian Journal on Aging
Developmental Psychology
Educational Gerontology
Experimental Aging Research

Gerontologist
Human Development
International Journal of Aging and Human Development
International Journal of Behavioral Development
Journal of Adult Development
Journal of Clinical Geropsychology
Journal of the American Geriatric Society
Journals of Gerontology

A: Biological and Medical Sciences
B: Psychological and Social Sciences
Journal of Marriage and the Family
OMEGA, The International Journal of Death and Dying
Psychology and Aging
Research on Aging
Zeitschrift für Gerontologie

References

Aaronson, A. L., Dent, O. B., Webb, J. T., and Kline, C. D. (1996). Graying of the critical items: Effects of aging to MMPI-2 critical items. *Journal of Personality Assessment, 66,* 169–176.

AARP (1994). *Aging baby boomers: How secure is their economic future?* Washington DC: AARP Research Division.

AARP (1998). *Boomers approaching midlife: How secure a future?* Washington, DC: AARP Public Policy Institute.

AARP (1999, August). *AARP/Modern Maturity Sexuality Study.* Washington, DC: AARP Research Group (available at www.aarp.org).

Abeles, R. P., and Riley, M. W. (1987). Longevity, social structure and cognitive aging. In C. Schooler and K. W. Schaie (Eds.), *Cognitive functioning and social structure over the life course* (pp. 161–175). Norwood, NJ: Ablex.

Abramson, L. Y., Seligman, M. E. P., and Teasdale, J. (1978). Learned helplessness in humans: Critique and reformulation. *Journal of Abnormal Psychology, 87,* 49–74.

Achenbaum, W. A. (1993). (When) did the papacy become a gerontocracy? In K. W. Schaie and W. A. Achenbaum (Eds.), *Societal impact on aging: Historical perspectives* (pp. 204–231). New York: Springer Publishing Co.

Ackerman, P. L., and Heggestad, E. D. (1997). Intelligence, personality and interests: Evidence for overlapping traits. *Psychological Bulletin, 121,* 219–245.

Acock, A. C. (1988). The impact of divorce on children. *Journal of Marriage and the Family, 50,* 619–648.

Adami, H. O., Bergstrom, R., and Sparen, P. (1993). Increasing cancer risk in younger birth cohorts in Sweden. *Lancet, 341,* 773–777.

Adams, B. N. (1979). Mate selection in the United States: A theoretical summarization. In W. Burr, R. Hill, I. Nye, and R. Reiss (Eds.), *Contemporary theories about the family* (vol. 1). *Research-based.* New York: Free Press.

Adams, D. (1954). *The anatomy of personality.* New York: Doubleday.

Adams, J. M., and Hoffman, L. (1994). Implications of issues in typographical design for readability and reading satisfaction in an aging population. *Experimental Aging Research, 20,* 61–69.

Adams, R. A., and Blieszner, R. (1995). Aging well with friends and family. *American Behavioral Scientist, 39,* 209–224.

Adams, R. A., and Blieszner, R. (1998). Structural predictors of problematic friendship in later life. *Personal Relationships, 5,* 439–447.

Adams, S. H., Cartwright, L. K., Ostrove, J. M., Stewart, A. J., and Wink, P. (1998). Psychological predictors of good health in three longitudinal samples of educated midlife women. *Health Psychology, 17,* 412–420.

Adams-Price, C. (1998). Aging, writing, and creativity. In C. Adams-Price (Ed.), *Creativity and successful aging* (pp. 269–287). New York: Springer Publishing Co.

Adkins, G., Martin, P., and Poon, L. W. (1996). Personality traits and states as predictors of subjective well-being in centenarians, octogenarians, and sexagenarians. *Psychology and Aging, 11,* 408–416.

Agronick, G. S., and Duncan, L. E. (1998). Personality and social change: Individual differences, life path, and importance attributed to the women's movement. *Journal of Personality and Social Psychology, 74,* 1545–1555.

Aguilar, S. M., and Hardy, A. M. (1993). AIDS knowledge and attitudes for 1991: Data from the National Health Interview Survey. *Advance Data, No. 225.* Washington, DC: National Center for Health Statistics.

Ainlay, S. C., and Smith, R. (1984). Aging and religious participation. *Journal of Gerontology, 39,* 357–363.

Aizenberg, R., and Treas, J. (1985). The family in the late life: Psychosocial and demographic considerations. In J. E. Birren and K. W. Schaie (Eds.), *Handbook of the psychology of aging* (2nd ed.). New York: Van Nostrand Reinhold.

Alan Guttmacher Institute (1998). *Into a new world: Young women's sexual and reproductive lives.* New York: Guttmacher Institute.

Albert, M. (1994). Brief assessments of cognitive functions in the elderly. In M. P. Lawton and J. A. Teresi (Eds.), *Annual review of gerontology and geriatrics* (vol. 14, pp. 93–106). New York: Springer Publishing Co.

Aldous, J., Mulligan, G. M., and Bjarnason, T. (1998). *Journal of Marriage and the Family, 60,* 809–820.

Aldwin, C. M., and Brustrom, J. (1997). Theories of coping with chronic stress: Illustrations from the health psychology and aging literatures. In B. H. Gottlieb (Ed.), *Coping with chronic stress* (pp. 75–103). New York: Plenum.

Aldwin, C.M., and Levenson, M.R. (1994). Aging and personality assessment. In M. P. Lawton and J. A. Teresi (Eds.), *Annual review of gerontology and geriatrics* (Vol. 14, pp. 182–209). New York: Springer Publishing Co.

Aldwin, C. M., Spiro, A., Levenson, M. R., and Bossé, R. (1989). Longitudinal findings from the Normative Aging Study: I. Does mental health change with age? *Psychology and Aging, 4,* 295–306.

Alexander, C., and Langer, E. J. (Eds.) (1990), *Beyond formal operations: Alternative endpoints to human development.* New York: Oxford University Press.

Allport, G. W. (1937). *Personality.* New York: Holt, Rinehart and Winston.

Altman, W. M., Parmelee, P. A., and Smyer, M. A. (1992). Autonomy, competence and informed consent in long term care: Legal and psychological perspectives. *Villanova Law Review, 37,* 1671–1704.

Alwin, D. F. (1998). The political impact of the baby boom: Are there persistent generational differences in political beliefs and behavior? *Generations, 22,* 46–54.

Alzheimer, A. (1987). About a peculiar disease of the cerebral cortex (Translation of the original 1907 article by L. Jarvik and H. Greenson).

Alzheimer's Disease and Associated Disorders, 1, 7–8.

Amato, P. R., and Booth, A. (1996). A prospective study of divorce and parent–child relationship. *Journal of Marriage and the Family, 58,* 356–365.

Amato, P. R., and Keith, B. (1991). Parental divorce and the well-being of children: A meta-analysis. *Psychological Bulletin, 110,* 26–46.

Amato, P. R., and Rogers, S. J. (1997). A longitudinal study of marital problems and subsequent divorce. *Journal of Marriage and the Family, 59,* 612–624

American Academy of Neurology AIDS Task Force. (1991). Nomenclature and research case definitions for neurologic manifestations of human immunodeficiency virus-type 1 (HIV-1) infection. *Neurology, 41,* 778–785.

American Psychiatric Association. (1987). *Diagnostic and statistical manual of mental disorders* (3rd rev. ed.). Washington, DC: American Psychiatric Association.

Anastasi, A. (1976). *Psychological testing* (4th ed.). New York: Macmillan.

Anderson, A., Russell, C., and Schumm, W. (1983). Perceived marital quality and family life cycle categories: A further analysis. *Journal of Marriage and the Family, 45,* 127–139.

Anschutz, L., Camp, C., Markley, R., and Kramer, J. (1987). Remembering mnemonics: A three-year follow-up on the effects of mnemonics training of elderly adults. *Experimental Aging Research, 13,* 141–143.

Anstey, K., Stankov, L., and Lord, S. (1993). Primary aging, secondary aging, and intelligence. *Psychology and Aging, 8,* 562–570.

Antonucci, T. C., and Akiyama, H. (1996). Social support and the maintenance of competence. In S. L. Willis, K. W. Schaie, and M. Hayward (Eds.), *Societal mechanisms for maintaining competence in old age.* New York: Springer Publishing Co.

Aquilino, W. (1990). The likelihood of parent-child coresidence: Effects of family structure and parental characteristics. *Journal of Marriage and the Family, 52,* 405–419.

Araujo, A. B., Durante, R., Feldman, H. A., Goldstein, I., and McKinlay, J. B. (1998). The relationship between depressive symptoms and male erectile dysfunction: Cross-sectional results from the Massachusetts male aging study. *Psychosomatic Medicine, 60,* 458–465.

Arbuckle, N. W., and de Vries, B. (1995) The long-term effects of later life spousal and parental bereavement on personal functioning. *Gerontologist, 35,* 637–647.

Arbuckle, T. Y., Gold, D. P., Andres, D., and Schwartzman, A. (1992). The role of psychosocial context, age, and intelligence in memory performance of older men. *Psychology and Aging, 7,* 25–36.

Arbuckle, T. Y., Maag, U., Pushkar, D., and Chaikelson, J. S. (1998). Individual differences in trajectory of intellectual development over 45 years of adulthood. *Psychology and Aging, 13,* 663–675.

Arbuckle, T. Y., Pushkar, D., Chaikelson, J., and Andres, D. (1999). Coping and control processes. Do they contribute to individual health in older adults? *Canadian Journal on Aging, 18,* 285–312.

Arenberg, D. (1990). Misclassification of "probable senile dementia of the Alzheimer's type" in the Baltimore Longitudinal Study of Aging. *Journal of Clinical Epidemiology, 43,* 105–107.

Ash, P. (1966). Pre-retirement counseling. *Gerontologist, 6,* 127–128.

Astin, A W., Green, K., Korn, W., and Schalit, M. (1987). *The American freshman: National norms for fall 1987.* Los Angeles: Higher Education Research Institute, University of California.

Astin, A. W., Korn, W., Sax, L. J., and Mahoney, K. M. (1994). *The American freshman: National norms for fall 1994.* Los Angeles, CA: Higher Education Research Institute, University of California at Los Angeles.

Atchley, R. C. (1976). *Sociology of retirement.* New York: Halsted.

Atchley, R. C. (1982). The aging self. *Psychotherapy: Theory, Research and Practice, 19,* 338–396.

Atchley, R. C. (1989a). A continuity theory of normal aging. *Gerontologist, 29,* 183–190.

Atchley, R. C. (1989b). Demographic factors and adult psychological development. In K. W. Schaie and C. Schooler (Eds.), *Social structure and aging: Psychological processes* (pp. 11–34). Hillsdale, NJ: Erlbaum.

Atchley, R. C. (1991). The influence of aging or frailty on perceptions and expressions of the self: Theoretical and methodological issues. In J. E. Birren and J. Lubben (Eds.), *The concept and measurement of quality of life in the frail elderly* (pp. 207–225). San Diego, CA: Academic Press.

Atchley, R. C. (1993). Continuity theory and the evolution of activity in later adulthood. In J. R. Kelly (Ed.), *Activity and aging.* Beverly Hills, CA: Sage.

Atchley, R. C. (1994). *Social forces and aging* (6th ed.). Belmont, CA: Wadsworth.

Atchley, R. C. (1995). Continuity of the spiritual self. In M A. Kimble (Ed.). *Aging, spirituality and religion: A hand-*book (pp. 68–73). Minneapolis, MN: Fortress Press.

Atchley, R. C. (2000). *Social forces and aging* (9th ed.), Belmont, CA: Wadsworth.

Atchley, R. C., and Miller, S. J. (1983). Types of elderly couples. In T. H. Brubaker (Ed.), *Family relationships in later life.* Beverly Hills, CA: Sage.

Atkinson, J. W., and Birch, D. (1978). *Introduction to motivation* (2nd ed.). New York: Van Nostrand Reinhold.

Avis, N. E. (1999). Women's health at midlife. In S. L. Willis and J. E. Reid (Eds.), *Life in the middle: Psychological and social development in middle age* (pp. 105–147). San Diego, CA: Academic Press.

Avis, N. E., Brambilla, D., McKinlay, S. M., and Vass, K. (1994). A longitudinal analysis of the association between menopause and depression. *Annals of Epidemiology, 4,* 214–220.

Avis, N. E., Crawford, S. L., and McKinlay, S. M. (1997). Psychological, behavioral, and health factors related to menopause symptomatology. *Women's Health: Research on Gender, Behavior, and Policy, 3,* 103–120.

Avis, N. E., Kaufert, P. A., Lock, M., McKinlay, S. M., and Vass, K. (1993). The evolution of menopausal symptoms. In H. Burger (Ed.), *Baillere's Clinical Endocrinology and Metabolism,* (Vol. 7, pp. 17–32). London, England: Bailliere Tindall.

Avis, N. E., and McKinlay, S. M. (1991). A longitudinal analysis of women's attitudes towards the menopause: Results from the Massachusetts Women's Health Study. *Maturitas, 13,* 65–79.

Avolio, B. J. (1991). Levels of analysis. In K. W. Schaie (Ed.), *Annual Review of Gerontology and Geriatrics* (pp. 239–260). New York: Springer Publishing Co.

Avolio, B. J., and Waldman, D. A. (1990). An examination of age and cognitive test performance across job complexity and occupational types. *Journal of Applied Psychology, 75,* 43–50.

Avolio, B. J., Waldman, D. A., and McDaniel, M. A. (1990). Age and work performance in non-managerial jobs: The effects of experience and occupational type. *Academy of Management Journal, 33,* 407–422.

Axinn, W. G., and Thornton, A. (1992). The relationship between cohabitation and divorce: Selectivity or causal influence? *Demography, 29,* 357–374.

Bäckman, L. (1989a). Effects of pre-experimental knowledge on recognition memory in adulthood. In A. F. Bennett and K. M. McConkey (Eds.), *Cognition in individual and social contexts* (pp. 267–281). Amsterdam, The Netherlands: Elsevier.

Bäckman, L. (1989b). Varieties of memory compensation by older adults in episodic remembering. In L. W. Poon, D. Rubin, and B. Wilson (Eds.), *Everyday cognition in adulthood and late life.* Cambridge, MA: Cambridge University Press.

Bäckman, L. (2001). Learning and memory. In J. E. Birren and K. W. Schaie (eds.). *Handbook of the psychology of aging* (5th ed.). San Diego, CA: Academic Press.

Bäckman, L., and Forsell, Y. (1994). Episodic memory functioning in a community-based sample of old adults with major depression: Utilization of cognitive support. *Journal of Abnormal Psychology, 103,* 361–370.

Bäckman, L., and Herlitz, A. (1992). The relationship between prior knowledge and face recognition memory in normal aging and Alzheimer's disease. *Journal of Gerontology: Psychological Sciences, 45,* P94–100.

Bäckman, L., Josephsson, S., Herlitz, A., Stigsdotter, A., and Vitanen, M. (1991). The generalizability of training gains in dementia: Effects of an imagery-based mnemonic on face-name retention duration. *Psychology and Aging, 6,* 489–492.

Bäckman, L., Mantyla, T., and Herlitz, A. (1990). The optimization of episodic remembering in old age. In P. B. Baltes and M. M. Baltes (Eds.), *Successful aging: Perspectives from the behavioral sciences.* (pp. 118–163). New York: Cambridge University Press.

Bäckman, L., Small, B. J., and Larson, M. (2000). Memory. In G. Evans (Eds.), *Oxford textbook of geriatric medicine.* 2nd Ed. Oxford, UK: Oxford University Press.

Bäckman, L., Small, B. J., Wahlin, A., and Larsson, M. (1999). Cognitive functioning in very old age, In F. I. M. Craik and T. A. Salthouse (Eds.), *Handbook of aging and cognition* (2nd ed.). Mahwah, NJ: Erlbaum.

Bagby, M. R., Costa, P. T., Jr., McCrae, R. R., Livesley, W. J., Kennedy, S. H., Levitan, R. D., Levitt, A. J., Joffe, R., and Young, L. T. (1999). Replicating the five factor model of personality in a psychiatric sample. *Personality and Individual Differences, 27,* 1135–1139.

Bahrick, H. P. (1984). Semantic memory content in permastore: Fifty years of memory for Spanish learned in school. *Journal of Experimental Psychology: General, 113,* 1–26.

Bahrick, H. P. (1998). Loss and distortion of autobiographical memory content. In C. P. Thompson and D. J. Herrmann, (Eds.), *Autobio-*

graphical memory: Theoretical and applied perspectives. (pp. 69–78). Mahwah, NJ: Lawrence Erlbaum.

Bahrick, H. P., and Phelphs, E. (1987). Retention of Spanish vocabulary over eight years. *Journal of Experimental Psychology: Learning, Memory and Cognition, 13,* 344–349.

Bailey, J. M., Bobrow, D., Wolfe, M., and Mikach, S. (1995). Sexual orientation of adult sons of gay fathers. *Developmental Psychology, 31,* 124–129.

Baker, L., Cesa, I. L., Gatz, M., and Mellins, C. (1992). Genetic and environmental influences on positive and negative affect: Support for a two-factor theory. *Psychology and Aging, 7,* 158–163.

Balducci, L., Schapira, D. V., Cox, C. E., Greenberg, H. M., and Lyman, G. H. (1991). Breast cancer of the older woman: an annotated review. *Journal of the American Geriatrics Society, 39,* 1113–1123.

Ball, K., and Owsley, C. (1992). The useful field of view: A new technique for evaluating age-related decline in visual function. *Journal of the American Optometric Association, 63,* 71–79.

Ball, K., and Owsley, C. (2000). Increasing mobility and reducing accidents of older drivers In K. W. Schaie and M. Pietrucha (Eds.), *Mobility and transportation in the elderly* (pp. 213–250). New York: Springer Publishing Co.

Baltes, M. M. (1996). *The many faces of dependency in old age.* New York: Cambridge University Press.

Baltes, M. M., and Carstensen, L. L. (1992). Possible selves across the life span: Comment. *Human Development, 34,* 256–260.

Baltes, M. M., and Carstensen, L. L. (1996). The process of successful

ageing. *Ageing and Society, 16,* 397–422.

Baltes, M. M., and Carstensen, L. L (1999). Social-psychological theories and their application to aging: From individual to collective. In V. L. Bengtson and K. W. Schaie (Eds.), *Handbook of theories of aging* (pp. 209–226). New York: Springer Publishing Co.

Baltes, M. M., and Horgas, A. L. (1996). Long-term care institutions and the maintenance of competence. In S. L. Willis, K. W. Schaie, and M. Hayward (Eds.), *Societal mechanisms for maintaining competence in old age.* New York: Springer Publishing Co.

Baltes, M. M., and Reichert, M. (1992). Successful ageing: the product of biological factors, environmental quality, and behavioral competence. In J. Gerorge and S. Ebrahim (Eds.), *Health care for older women* (pp. 236–256). Oxford, UK: Oxford University Press.

Baltes, M. M., and Reisenzein, R. (1986). The social world in long-term care institutions: Psychosocial control toward dependency. In M. M. Baltes and P. B. Baltes (Eds.), *Psychology of control and aging* (pp. 315–343). Hillsdale, NJ: Erlbaum.

Baltes, M. M., and Silverberg, S. B. (1994). The dynamics between dependency and autonomy: Illustrations across the life span. In D. L. Featherman, R. M. Lerner (Eds.), *Life-span development and behavior* (Vol. 12, pp. 41–90). Hillsdale, NJ: Erlbaum.

Baltes, M. M., and Wahl, H. W. (1987). Dependency in aging. In L. L. Carstensen and B. A. Edelstein (Eds.), *Handbook of clinical gerontology.* New York: Pergamon.

Baltes, M. M., and Wahl, H. W. (1992). The behavior system of dependence in the elderly: Interaction with the social envirnoment. In M. Ory, R. P. Abeles, and P.D. Lipman (Eds.), *Aging, health, and behavior* (pp. 83–106). Beverly Hills, CA: Sage

Baltes, P. B. (1979). Life-span developmental psychology: Some converging observations on history and theory. In P. B. Baltes and O. G. Brim, Jr. (Eds.), *Life-span development and behavior* (Vol. 2). New York: Academic Press.

Baltes, P. B. (1987). Theoretical propositions of life-span developmental psychology: On the dynamics between growth and decline. *Developmental Psychology, 23,* 611–626.

Baltes, P. B. (1993). The aging mind: Potential and limits. *Gerontologist. 33,* 580–594.

Baltes, P. B. (1997). On the incomplete architecture of human ontogenesis: Selection, optimization and compensation as foundations of developmental theory. *American Psychologist, 52,* 366–381.

Baltes, P. B., and Baltes, M. M. (1990). Psychological perspectives on successful aging: The model of selective optimization with compensation. In P. B. Baltes and M. M. Baltes (Eds.), *Successful aging: Perspectives from the behavioral sciences* (pp. 1–34). Cambridge, UK: Cambridge University Press.

Baltes, P. B., Cornelius, S. W., and Nesselroade, J. R. (1979). Cohort effects in developmental psychology. In J. R. Nesselroade and P. B. Baltes (Eds.), *Longitudinal research in the study of behavior and development.* New York: Academic Press.

Baltes, P. B., and Kliegl, R. (1987). On the dynamics of growth and decline in the aging of intelligence and memory. In K. Poeck, H. J. Freund, and H. Ganshirt (Eds.), *Neurology* (pp. 1–17). Heidelberg, Germany: Springer-Verlag.

Baltes, P. B., and Kliegl, R. (1992). Further testing of limits of cognitive plasticity: Negative age differences in a mnemonic skill are robust. *Developmental Psychology, 28,* 121–125.

Baltes, P. B., Kliegl, R., and Dittmann-Kohli, F. (1988). On the locus of training gains in research on the plasticity of fluid intelligence in old age. *Journal of Educational Psychology, 80,* 392–400.

Baltes, P. B., and Labouvie, G. V. (1973). Adult development of intellectual performance: Description, explanation, and modification. In C. Eisdorfer and M. P. Lawton (Eds.), *The psychology of adult development and aging.* Washington, DC: American Psychological Association.

Baltes, P. B., and Lindenberger, U. (1988). On the range of cognitive plasticity in old age as a function of experience: 15 years of intervention research. *Behavior Therapy, 19,* 283–300.

Baltes, P. B., and Lindenberger, U. (1997). Emergence of a powerful connection between sensory and cognitive functions across the adult life span: A new window to the study of cognitive aging. *Psychology and Aging, 12,* 12–21.

Baltes, P. B., and Mayer, K. F. (Eds.) (1999). *The Berlin Aging Study: Aging from 70 to 100.* Cambridge, UK: Cambridge University Press.

Baltes, P. B., Mayer, K. U., Helmchen, H., and Steinhagen-Thiessen, E., (1993). The Berlin Aging Study (BASE): overview and design. *Ageing and Society, 13,* 483–533.

Baltes, P. B., Schaie, K. W., and Nardi, A. H. (1971). Age and experimental mortality in a seven-year longitudinal study of cognitive behavior. *Developmental Psychology, 5,* 18–26.

Baltes, P. B., and Smith, J. (1990). The psychology of wisdom and its ontogenesis. In R. J. Sternberg (Ed.), *Wisdom: Its nature , origins and development* (pp. 87–120). New York: Cambridge University Press.

Baltes, P.B., and Smith, J. (1997). A systemic-holistic view of psychological functioning in very old age: Introduction to a collection of articles from the Berlin Aging Study. *Psychology of Aging, 12,* 395–409.

Baltes, P. B., and Smith J. (1999). Multilevel and systemic analyses of old age: Theoretical and empirical evidence for a fourth age. In V. L. Bengtson and K. W. Schaie (Eds.), *Handbook of theories of aging* (pp. 153–173). New York: Springer Publishing Co.

Baltes, P. B., Smith, J., and Staudinger, U. (1992). Wisdom and successful aging. In T. Sonderegger (Ed.), *Psychology and aging: Nebraska symposium on motivation, 1991* (pp. 123–167). Lincoln, NE: University of Nebraska Press.

Baltes, P. B., Sowarka, D., and Kliegl, R. (1989). Cognitive training research on fluid intelligence in old age: What can older adults achieve by themselves? *Psychology and Aging, 4,* 217–221.

Baltes, P. B., Staudinger, U. M., and Lindenberger, U. (1999). Life-span psychology: Theory and application to intellectual functioning. *Annual Review of Psychology, 50,* 471–507.

Baltes. P. B., Staudinger, U. M., Smith, J., and Maercker, A. (1995). People nominated as wise: A comparative study of wisdom-related knowledge. *Psychology and Aging, 10,* 155–166.

Baltes, P. B., and Willis, S. L. (1978). Life-span developmental psychology, cognition and social policy. In M. W. Riley (Ed.), *Aging from birth to death.* Washington, DC: American Association for the Advancement of Science.

Baltes, P. B., and Willis, S. L. (1982). Enhancement (plasticity) of intellectual functioning: Penn State's Adult Development and Enrichment Project (ADEPT). In F. I. M. Craig and S. Trehub (Eds.), *Aging and cognitive processes.* New York: Plenum.

Bandura, A. (1977). *Social learning theory.* Englewood Cliffs, NJ: Prentice-Hall.

Bandura, A. (1988). Reflections on non-ability determinants of competence. In J. Kolligian, Jr., and R. J. Sternberg (Eds.), *Competence considered: Perceptions of competence and incompetence across the lifespan.* New Haven, CT: Yale University Press.

Bandura, A. (1997). *Self-efficacy: The exercise of control.* New York: Freeman.

Banner, C. (1993). Recent insights into the biology of Alzheimer's disease. In R. L. Sprott, R. W. Huber and T. F. Williams (Eds.), *The biology of aging* (pp. 53–62). New York: Springer Publishing Co.

Barefoot, J. C., Siegler, I. C., Nowlin, J. B., Peterson, B. L., Haney, T.L., and Williams, R. B., Jr. (1987). Suspiciousness, health, and mortality: A follow-up study of 500 older adults. *Psychosomatic Medicine, 49,* 450–457.

Barnett, R. C., and Marshall, N. L. (1992a). Worker and mother roles, spillover effects and psychological distress. *Women and Health, 18,* 9–40.

Barnett, R. C., and Marshall, N. L. (1992b). Men's job and partner roles: Spillover effects and psychological distress. *Sex Roles, 27,* 455–472.

Barnett, R. C., Marshall, N. L., and Sayer, A. (1992). Positive-spillover effects from job to home: A closer look. *Women and Health, 19,* 13–41.

Barrett, R. K. (1993). Psycho-cultural influences on African-American attitudes towards death, dying and funeral rites. In J. D. Morgan (Ed.), *Personal care in an impersonal world: A multidimensional look at bereavement* (pp. 216–230). Thousand Oaks, CA: Baywood Publishing Co.

Barrett-Connor, E., Chang, J. C., and Edelstein, S. L. (1994). Coffee-associated osteoporosis offset by daily milk consumption. *Journal of the American Medical Association, 271,* 280–283.

Bartel, A., and Sicherman, N. (1993). Technological change and retirement decisions of older workers. *Journal of Labor Economics, 11,* 162–183.

Bastian, L. A., Couchman, G. M., Nanda, A. and Siegler, I. C. (1998). Hormone replacement therapy: Benefits, risks, and management. *Atlas of Office Procedures, 1,* 79–86.

Bazargan, M., and Hamm, W. P. (1995). The relationship between chronic illness and depression in a community of urban black elderly persons. *Journal of Gerontology: Social Sciences, 50B,* S219–S127.

Bearon, L. B. (1989). No great expectations: The underpinning of life satisfction for older women. *Gerontologist, 29,* 772–778.

Beattie, V. (1992). *Analysis of the results of a survey on sexual violence in the U.K.* Cambridge, UK: Women's Forum.

Beck, R. W., and Beck, S. H. (1989). The incidence of extended households among middle-aged black and white women: Estimates from a 5-year panel study. *Journal of Family Issues, 10,* 147–168.

Becker, P., and Moen, P. (1999). Scaling back: Dual-career couples' work-family strategies. *Journal of Marriage and the Family, 61,* 995–1007.

Beland, F. (1987). Multigenerational households in a contemporary perspective. *International Journal of Aging and Human Development, 25,* 147–166.

Bell, S. E. (1990). Sociological perspectives on the medicalization of menopause. *Annals of the New York Academy of Sciences, 592,* 173–178.

Bellak, L. (1975). *The Thematic Apperception Test, the Children's Apperception Test and the Senior Apperceptive Technique in clinical use* (3rd ed.). New York: Grune and Stratton.

Bellantoni, M. F., and Blackman, M. R. (1995). Menopause and its consequences. In E. L. Schneider and J. W. Rowe (Eds.). *Handbook of the biology of aging* (pp. 415–426). San Diego, CA: Academic Press.

Belsky, J. (1990). Children and marriage. In J. Fincham and T. Bradsury (Eds.), *The psychology of marriage.* New York: Guilford.

Belsky, J., and Rovine, M. (1990). Patterns of marital change across the transition to parenthood. *Journal of Marriage and the Family, 52,* 109–123.

Belsky, J., Rovine, M., and Fish, M. (1989). The developing family system. In M. Gunnar (Ed.), *Systems and development. Minnesota symposia on child psychology* (Vol. 22, pp. 119–166). Hildsdale, NJ: Erlbaum.

Bem, S. L. (1978). Beyond androgyny: Some presumptuous prescriptions for a liberated sexual identity. In J. Sherman and F. Denmark (Eds.), *Psychology of women: Future directions of research.* New York: Psychological Dimensions.

Bengtson, V. L. (1975). Generation and family effects in value socialization. *American Sociological Review, 40,* 358–371.

Bengtson, V. L. (1985). Diversity and symbolism in grandparent roles. In V. L. Bengtson and J. Robertson (Eds.), *Grandparenthood* (pp. 11–26). Beverly Hills, CA: Sage.

Bengtson, V. L., and Achenbaum, W. A. (1993). *The changing contract across generations.* New York: Aldine de Gruyter.

Bengtson, V. L., and Black, K. D. (1973). Intergenerational relations and continuities in socialization. In P. B. Baltes and K. W. Schaie (Eds.), *Life-span developmental psychology: Personality and socialization.* New York: Academic Press.

Bengtson, V. L., and Giarrusso, R. (2001). The aging self in social context. In R. H. Binstock and L. K. George (Eds). *Handbook of aging and the social sciences* (5th ed.). San Diego, CA: Academic Press.

Bengtson, V. L., Reedy, M. N., and Gordon, C. E. (1985). Aging and self-conceptions: Personality processes and social contexts. In J. E. Birren and K. W. Schaie (Eds.), *Handbook of the psychology of aging* (2nd ed.). New York: Van Nostrand Reinhold.

Bengtson, V. L,, Rice, C. J., and Johnson, M. L. (1999). Are theories of aging important? Models and explanation in gerontology at the turn of the century. In V. L. Bengtson and K. W. Schaie (Eds.), *Handbook of theories of aging* (pp. 3–20). New York: Springer Publishing Co.

Bengtson, V. L., Rosenthal, C., and Burton, L. (1990). Families and aging: Diversity and heterogeneity. In R. H. Binstock and L. K. George (Eds.), *Handbook of aging and the social sciences* (3rd ed.). San Diego: Academic Press.

Bengtson, V. L., and Schaie, K. W. (Eds.) (1999). *Handbook of theories of aging.* New York: Springer Publishing Co.

Benninger, W. B., and Walsh, W. B. (1980). Holland's theory and non-college-degree working men and women. *Journal of Vocational Behavior, 17,* 18–88.

Benton, A. L. (1994). Neuropsychological assessment. L. Porter (Ed.) *Annual Review of Psychology, 45,* 1–23.

Berg, C. A. (1990). Efficacy and cognitive functioning. In J. Rodin, C. Schooler, and K. W. Schaie (Eds.), *Self-directedness and efficacy: Causes and effects throughout the life course.* Hillsdale, NJ: Erlbaum.

Berg, C. A., and Klaczynski, P. A. (1996) Practical intelligence and problem solving: Searching for perspectives. In F. Blanchard-Fields and T. Hess (Eds.), *Perspectives on cognitive change in adulthood and aging* (pp. 323–357), New York: McGraw Hill.

Berg, C. A., Klaczynski, P. A., Calderone, K. S., and Strough, J. (1994). Adult age differences in cognitive strategies: Adaptive or deficient? In J. Sinnott (Ed.), *Interdisciplinary handbook of adult life-span learning* (pp. 371–388). Westport, CT: Greenwood.

Berg, C. A., and Sternberg, R J. (1985). A triarchic theory of intellectual development during adulthood. *Developmental Review, 5,* 334–370.

Berg, C. A., and Sternberg, R. J. (1992). Adults' conceptions of intelligence across the adult life span. *Psychology and Aging, 7,* 221–231.

Berg. C. A., Strough, J., Calderone, K. S., Sansome, C., and Weir, C. (1998). The role of problem definitions in understanding age and context effects on strategies for solving everyday problems. *Psychology and Aging, 13,* 29–44.

Berg, S. (1996). Aging, behavior and terminal decline. In J. E. Birren and K. W. Schaie (Eds.), *Handbook of the psychology of aging* (4th ed., pp. 323–337). San Diego, CA: Academic Press.

Bergman, L. R., and Magnusson, D. (1997). A person-oriented approach in research on developmental psychopathology. *Development and Psychopathology, 9,* 291–319.

Bergman, M., Blumenfeld, V. G., Casardo, D., Dash, B., Levitt, H., and Margulies, M. K. (1976). Age-related decrement in hearing for speech: Sampling and longitudinal studies. *Journal of Gerontology, 31,* 533–538.

Bergstrom, T. C., and Bagnoli, M. (1993). Courtship as a waiting game. *Journal of Political Economy, 101,* 185–202.

Bergstrom-Walan, M., and Nielsen, H. (1990). Sexual expression among 60–80 year-old men and women: A sample from Stockholm, Sweden. *The Journal of Sex Research, 27,* 289–295.

Bernheim, K. F., and Lewine, R. R. (1979). *Schizophrenia.* New York: Norton.

Bern-Klug, M., Ekerdt, D. J., and Nakashima, M. (1999). Helping families understand final arrangement options and costs. In B. De Vries (Ed.), *End of life issues* (pp. 245–262). New York: Springer Publishing Co.

Bertman, S. L. (1991). Children and death: Insights, hindsights, and illuminations. In D. Papadatou, and C. Papadatou (Eds.) *Children and death* (pp. 311–332). New York: Hemisphere.

Besharov, D. J., and Gardiner, K. N. (1993). The truth and consequences of teen sex. *The American Enterprise,* 52–59.

Betz, N. E., and Hackett, G. (1997). Applications of self-efficacy theory to the career assessment of women. *Journal of Career Assessment, 5,* 383–402.

Bibby, R. W. (1993). Religion in the Canadian 90s: The paradox of poverty and potential. In D. A. Roozen and C. K. Hadaway (Eds.), *Church and denomiational growth.* Nashville, TN: Abingdon Press.

Bielby, D., and Papalia, D. (1975). Moral development and perceptual role-taking: Their development and interrelationship across the life-span. *International Journal of Aging and Human Development, 62,* 93–308.

Bieman-Copland, S., and Ryan, E. B. (1998). Age-biased interpretation of memory successes and failures in adulthood. *Journal of Gerontology: Psychological Sciences, 53B,* P105–P111.

Binet, A., and Simon, T. (1905). Méthodes nouvelles pour le diagnostic du niveau intellectuel des anormaux. *L'Année Psychologique, 11,* 191.

Birkhill, W. R., and Schaie, K. W. (1975). The effect of differential reinforcement of cautiousness in the intellectual performance of the elderly. *Journal of Gerontology, 30,* 578–583.

Birren, J. E. (1961). A brief history of the psychology of aging (Part II). *Gerontologist, 1,* 127–134.

Birren, J. E. (1974). Translations in gerontology—from lab to life. Psychophysiology and speed of response. *American Psychologist, 29,* 808–815.

Birren, J. E. (1988). A contribution to the theory of aging: As a counterpart of development. In J. E. Birren and V. L. Bengtson (Eds.), *Emergent theories of aging* (pp. 153–176). New York: Springer Publishing Co.

Birren, J. E. (1990). Creativity, productivity, and potentials of the senior scholar. *Gerontology and Geriatrics Education, 11,* 27–44.

Birren, J. E. (1993). Understanding life backwards: Reminiscing for a better old age. In R. N. Butler and K. Kiikuni (Eds.), *Who is responsible for my old age* (pp. 18–32). New York: Springer Publishing Co.

Birren, J. E., and Birren, B. A. (1990). The concepts, models and history of the psychology of aging. In J. E. Birren and K. W. Schaie (Eds.), *Handbook of the psychology of aging* (3rd ed., pp. 3–20). San Diego: Academic Press.

Birren, J. E., Cunningham, W. R., and Yamamoto, K. (1983). Psychology of adult development and aging. In M. R. Rosenweig (Ed.) *Annual Review of Psychology, 34,* 543–575.

Birren, J. E., and Fisher, L. M. (1992). Aging and slowing of behavior: Consequences for cognition and survival. In T. Sonderegger (Ed.), *Psychology and aging: Nebraska Symposium on Motivation, 1991* (pp. 1–37). Lincoln, NE: University of Nebraska Press.

Birren, J. E., Kenyon, G. M., Ruth, J. E., Schroots, J. F., and Swensson, T. (Eds.) (1995). *Aging and biography: Explorations in adult development.* New York: Springer Publishing Co..

Birren, J. E., and Perlmutter, M. A. (1990). Measuring our psychological performance. In R. N. Butler, M. R. Oberlink, and M. Schechter (Eds.),

The promise of productive aging: From biology to social policy (pp. 48–69). New York: Springer Publishing Co.

Birren, J. E., and Schaie, K. W. (Eds.). (2001). *Handbook of the psychology of aging* (5th ed.). San Diego, CA: Academic Press.

Birren, J. E., and Schroots, J. F. F. (1996). History, concepts, and theory in the psychology of aging. In J. E. Birren and K. W. Schaie (Eds.), *Handbook of the psychology of aging* (4th ed.). San Diego, CA: Academic Press.

Birren, J. E., and Schroots, J. J. F. (2001). On the origins of geropsychology. In J. E. Birren and K.W. Schaie (Eds.), *Handbook of the psychology of aging* (5th ed.). San Diego, CA: Academic Press.

Bischof, L. J. (1976). *Adult psychology* (2nd ed.). New York: Harper and Row.

Blackburn, J. A., Papalia-Finley, D., Foye, B. F., and Serlin, R. C. (1988). Modifiability of figural relations performance among elderly adults. *Journal of Gerontology: Psychological Sciences, 43,* P87–P89.

Blanchard-Fields, F. (1996). Social cognitive development in adulthood and aging. In F. Blanchard-Fields and T. M. Hess (Eds.), *Perspectives of cognitive change in adulthood and aging* (pp. 454–487). New York: McGraw-Hill,

Blanchard-Fields, F., and Abeles, R. (1996). Social cognition and aging. In J. E. Birren and K. W. Schaie (Eds.), *Handbook of the psychology of aging* (4th ed., pp. 150–161). San Diego, CA: Academic Press.

Blanchette, P. L., and Valcour, V. G. (1998). Health and aging among baby boomers. *Generations, 22,* 76–80.

Blandford, G. (1998). Eating disorders. In R. Tallis, H. Fillit, and J. C. Brocklehurst. (Eds.), *Brocklehurst's textbook of geriatric medicine and gerontology,* (5th ed.). Edinburgh, Scotland: Churchill Livingstone.

Blazer D. (1992). *Later life depression: The importance of interdisciplinary understanding.* Washington, DC: Association for Gerontology in Higher Education.

Blazer, D. G., Bachar, J. R., and Manton, K. G. (1986). Suicide in late life: Review and commentary. *Journal of the American Geriatric Society, 34,* 519–525.

Blazer, D. G., Federspiel, C. F., Ray, W. R., and Schaffner, W. (1983). The risk of anticholinergic toxicity in the elderly: A study of prescribing practices in two populations. *Journal of Gerontology, 38,* 31–35.

Blazer, D. G., George, L., and Landerman, R. (1986). The phenomenology of late life depression. In P. E. Babbington and R. Jacoby (Eds.), *Psychiatric disorders in the elderly.* London, UK: Mental Health Foundation.

Blazer, D. G., Hughes, D. C., and George, L. K. (1987). The epidemiology of depression in an elderly community population. *Gerontologist, 27,* 281–287.

Blazer, D. G., and Williams, C. D. (1980). Epidemiology of dysphoria and depression in the elderly populations. *American Journal of Psychiatry, 137,* 439–444.

Blieszner, R. (1995). Friendship processes and well-being in the later years of life: Implication for interventions. *Journal of Geriatric Psychiatry, 28,* 105–182.

Blieszner, R., and Hamon., R. (1992). Filial responsibility: Attitudes, motivataions and behaviors. In J. W. Dwyer and R. T. Coward (Eds.), *Gender, fami-* lies and elder care. (pp. 105–119). Newbury Park, CA: Sage.

Blieszner, R., McAuley, W. J., Newhouse, J. K., and Mancini, J. (1987) Rural-urban differences in service use by older adults. In T. H. Brubaker (Ed.), *Aging health, and family: Long-term care* (pp.162–174). Beverly Hills, CA: Sage

Blieszner, R., Willis, S. L., and Baltes, P. B. (1981). Training research in aging on the fluid ability of inductive reasoning. *Journal of Applied Developmental Psychology, 2,* 247–265.

Block, J. (1978). *The Q-sort method.* Palo Alto, CA: Consulting Psychologists Press.

Blueband-Langner, M. (1996). *In the shadow of illness.* Princeton, NJ: Princeton University Press

Blumenthal, J. A., Emery, C. F., Madden, D. J., Schniebolk, S., Riddle, M. W., Cobb, F. R., Higginbotham, M., and Coleman, R. E. (1991). Effects of exercise training and bone density in older men and women. *Journal of the America Geriatrics Society, 39,* 1065–1070.

Blumenthal, J. A., and Gullette, E. C. D.(2001). Exercise interventions and aging. In K. W. Schaie, H. Leventhal, and S. L. Willis (Eds.), *Societal impact on health behaviors in the elderly.* New York: Springer Publishing Co.

Blumstein, P., and Schwartz, P. (1983). *American couples.* New York: Morrow.

Bokemeier, J. L., and Lacy, W. B. (1987). Job values, rewards, and work conditions as factors in job satisfaction among men and women. *Sociological Quarterly, 28,* 189–204.

Booth, A., and Amato, P. R. (1994). Parental marital quality, parental divorce, and relations with parents. *Journal of Marriage and the Family, 56,* 21–34.

Borawski, E. A., Kinney, J. M., and Kahana, E. (1996). The meaning of older adults' health appraisals: Congruence with health status and determinant of mortality. *Journal of Gerontology: Social Sciences, 51B,* S157–S170.

Bossé, R., Aldwin, C., Levenson, M., and Workman-Daniels, K. (1991). How stressful is retirement? Findings from the Normative Aging Study. *Journal of Gerontology: Psychological Sciences, 46,* P9–P14.

Bosworth, H. B., and Schaie, K. W. (1997). The relationship of social environment, social networks, and health outcomes in the Seattle Longitudinal Study: Two analytic approaches. *Journal of Gerontology: Psychological Sciences, 52B,* P197–P205.

Bosworth, H. B., and Schaie, K. W. (1999). Survival effects in cognitive function, cognitive style, and sociodemographic variables in the Seattle Longitudinal Study. *Experimental Aging Research, 25,* 121–139.

Bosworth, H. B., Schaie, K. W., and Willis, S. L. (1999). Cognitive and sociodemographic risk factors for mortality in the Seattle Longitudinal Study: *Journal of Gerontology: Psychological Sciences, 54B,* P273–P282.

Bosworth, H. B., Schaie, K. W., Willis, S. L., and Siegler, I. C. (1999). Age and distance to death in the Seattle Longitudinal Study. *Research on Aging, 21,* 723–738.

Botwinick, J. (1977). Intellectual abilities. In. J. E. Birren and K. W. Schaie (Eds.), *Handbook of the psychology of aging.* New York: Van Nostrand Reinhold.

Bould, S., and Longino, C. F. Jr (1997). Women survivors: The oldest old. In J. Coyle (Ed.), *Handbook on women and aging* (pp. 110–222). Westport, CT: Greenwood Press.

Bould, S., Smith, M. H., and Longino, C. F. Jr. (1997). Ability, disability and the oldest old. *Journal of Aging and Social Policy, 9,* 13–31.

Bowlby, J. (1974). Psychiatric implications in bereavement. In A. H. Kutscher (Ed.), *Death and bereavement.* Springfield, IL: Charles C. Thomas.

Bowlby, J. (1980). *Loss.* New York: Basic Books.

Boyd, S. H., and Weissman, M. M. (1982). Epidemiology. In E. S. Paykel (Ed.), *Handbook of affective disorders.* New York: Guilford Press.

Boyle, J. M., and Morriss, J. E. (1987). *The mirror of time: Images of aging and dying.* New York: Greenwood Press.

Bradley, C. L., and Marcia, J. E. (1998). Generativity-stagnation: A five-category model. *Journal of Personality, 66,* 39–64.

Brambilla, D. J., and McKinlay, S. M. (1989). A prospective study of factors affecting age at menopause. *Journal of Clinical Epidemiology, 42,* 1031–1039.

Branch, L. G., Horowitz, A., and Carr, C. (1989). The implications for everyday life of incident self-reported visul decline among people over age 65 living in the community. *Gerontologist, 29,* 359–366.

Brandtstädter, J., and Greve, W. (1994). The aging self: Stabilizing and protective processes. *Developmental Review, 14,* 1–29.

Brandtstädter, J., and Renner, G. (1990). Tenacious goal pursuit and flexible goal adjustment: Explication and age-related analysis of assimilive and accommodative strategies of coping. *Psychology and Aging, 5,* 58–67.

Brandtstädter, J., and Wentura, D. (1995). Ajustment to shifting possibility frontiers in later life: Complementary adaptive modes. In R. A. Dixon and L. Bäckman (Eds.), *Compensating for psychological deficits and declines: Managing losses and promoting gains* (pp. 83–106). Mahwah, NJ: Erlbaum.

Brandtstädter, J., Wentura, D., and Greve, W. (1993). Adaptive resource of the aging self: Outlines of an emergent perspective. *International Journal of Behavioral Development, 16,* 333–349.

Brant, L. J., and Fozard, J. L. (1990). Age changes in pure-tone hearing thresholds in a longitudinal study of normal aging. *Journal of the Acoustical Society of America, 88,* 813–820.

Brant, L. J., and Pearson, J. D. (1993). Variability in longitudinal patterns of aging: Hearing loss. In D. Crews and R. Garruto (Eds.), *Biological anthropology and aging: An emerging synthesis.* New York: Oxford University Press.

Braun, K. L., Pietsch, J. H. and Blanchette, P. L. (2000). *Cultural issues in end-of-life decision making.* Thousand Oaks, CA: Sage.

Bray, D. W., and Howard, A. (1983). The AT&T longitudinal studies of managers. In K. W. Schaie (Ed.), *Longitudinal studies of adult psychological development.* New York: Guilford Press.

Brent, S. B., Speece, M. W., Lin, C., Dong, Q., and Yang, C. (1996). The development of the concept of death among Chinese and U.S. children 3–17 years of age. From binary to "fuzzy" concepts? *Omega, Journal of Death and Dying, 33,* 67–84.

Bressler, R. (1987). Drug use in the geriatric patient. In L. L. Carstensen and B. A. Edelstein (Eds.), *Handbook of clinical gerontology* (pp. 152–174). New York: Pergamon.

Brim, O. G., Jr. (1988). Losing and winning. *Psychology Today, 9,* 48–52.

Brinton, L. A. (1990). Menopause and the risk of breast cancer. *Annals of the New York Academy of Sciences, 592,* 357–363.

Bristol, M., Gallagher, J., and Schopler, E.(1988). Mothers and fathers of young developmentally disabled and nondisabled boys: Adaptation and spousal support. *Developmental Psychology, 24,* 441–451.

Broderick, C. (1982). Adult sexual development. In B. B. Wolman (Ed.), *Handbook of developmental psychology.* Englewood Cliffs, NJ: Prentice-Hall.

Brody, E. M. (1985). Parent care as a normative family stress. *Gerontologist, 25,* 19–29.

Brody, E. M. (1990). *Women-in-the-middle: Their parent care years.* New York: Springer Publishing Co.

Brody, E. M., Hoffman, D., Kleban, M., and Schoonover, C. (1989). Caregiving daughters and their local siblings: Perceptions, strains and interactions. *Gerontologist, 29,* 529–538.

Brody, E. M., Kleban, M., Johnsen, P., Hoffman, C., and Schoonover, C. (1987). Work status and parent care: A comparison of four groups of women. *Gerontologist, 27,* 201–208.

Brody, J. E. (1993). Early action is crucial in combating heart failure. *New York Times,* September 29.

Bronstein, P. (1988). Father-child interaction: Implications for gender role socialization. In P. Bronstein and C. Cowan (Eds.), *Fatherhood today: Men's changing role in the family* (pp. 107–124). New York: Wiley.

Brooks-Gunn, J., Phelps, E., and Elder, G. H., Jr. (1991). Studying lives through time: Secondary data analyses in developmental psychology. *Developmental Psychology, 27,* 899–910.

Brown, K. L., and Kayashima, R. (1999). Death education in churches and temples: Engaging religious leaders in the development of educational strategies. In B. De Vries (Ed.), *End of life issues* (pp. 319–335). New York: Springer Publishing Co.

Brown, R., and Kulick, J. (1977). Flashbulb memories. *Cognition, 5,* 73–99.

Brown, S. L., and Booth, A. (1996). Cohabitation versus marriage: A comparison of relationship quality. *Journal of Marriage and the Family, 58,* 668–678.

Brun, A., and Gustafson, L. (1993). The Lund Longitudinal Dementia Study: A 25-year perspective on neuropathology, differential diagnosis and treatment. In B. Corin, K. Iqbal, M. Nicolini, B. Windblad, H. Wisniewski, and P. Zatta (Eds.), *Alzheimer's disease: Advances in clinical and basic research* (pp. 1–18). New York: Wiley.

Brush, J. A., and Camp, C. J. (1998). Using spaced retrieval as an intervention during speech-language therapy. *Clinical Gerontologist, 19,* 51–64.

Buchner, D. M., Cress, M. E., Wagner, E. H., De Lateur, B. J., Price, R., and Abrass, I. B. (1993). The Seattle FICSIT/MoveIt Study: The effect of exercise on gait and balance in older adults. *Journal of the American Geriatrics Society, 41,* 321–325.

Buehler, C. (1968). The general structure of the human life cycle. In C. Buehler and F. Masarik (Eds.), *Human life: A study of goals in human perspective.* New York: Springer Publishing Co.

Bumpass, L. L. (1984). Children and marital disruption: A replication and update. *Demography, 21,* 71–81.

Bumpass, L. L. (1990). What's happening to the family? Interactions between demographic and institutional change. *Demography, 27,* 483–498.

Bumpass, L. L., and Aquilino, W. S. (1995). *A social map of midlife: Family and work over the middle life course.* Madison, WI: University of Wisconsin-Madison, Center for Demography and Ecology.

Bumpass, L. L., and Sweet, J. A. (1991). *Family experiences across the life course: Differences by cohort, education, and race/ethnicity.* National Survey of Families and Households Working Paper No. 42. Madison, WI: University of Wisconsin–Madison, Center for Demography and Ecology.

Bumpass, L. L., Sweet, J. A., and Castro-Martin, T. (1990). Changing patterns of remarriage. *Journal of Marriage and the Family, 52,* 747–756.

Bumpass, L. L., Sweet, J. A., and Cherlin, A. (1991). The role of cohabitation in declining rates of marriage. *Journal of Marriage and the Family, 53,* 913–920.

Burg, A. (1968). Lateral visual field as related to age and sex. *Journal of Applied Psychology, 52,* 10–15.

Burgio, K. L., and Burgio, L. D. (1991) The problem of urinary incontinance. In P. A. Wisocki (Ed.), *Handbook of clinical behavior therapy with the elderly client* (pp. 317–336). New York: Plenum.

Burgio, K. L., Locher, J. L., Goode, P. S., Hardin, J. M., McDowell, B. J., Dombrowski, M., and Candib, D. (1998). Behavioral vs. drug treatment for urge urinary incontinence in older women: A randomized controlled trial. *Journal of the American Medical Association, 280,* 1995–2000.

Burgio, L. D., McCormick, K. A., Scheve, A. S., Engel, B. T., Hawkins, A., and Leahy, E. (1994). The effects of changing prompted voiding schedules in the treatment of incontinence in nursing home residents. *Journal of the American Geriatrcs Scoiety, 42,* 315–320.

Burgio, L. D., Scillen, K., Hardin, J. M. Hsu, C., and Yancey J. (1996). Environmental "white noise": An intervention for verbally agitated nursing home residents. *Journal of Gerontology: Psychological Sciences, 51B,* P364–P373.

Burke, D. M., and Harold, R. (1988). Automatic and effortful semantic processes in old age: Experimental and naturalistic approaches. In L. L. Light and D. M. Burke (Eds.), *Language, memory and aging.* New York: Cambridge University Press.

Burt, M. R., and Albin, R. S. (1981). Rape myths, rape definitions, and probability of conviction. *Journal of Applied Social Psychology, 11,* 212–230.

Burton, L. C., German, P. S., Rovner, B. W., and Brant, L. J. (1992). Physical restraint use and cognitive decline among nursing home residents. *Journal of the American Geriatrics Society, 40,* 811–816.

Burton, L. M. (1995). Intergenerational patterns of providing care in African-American families with teenage childbearers: Emergent patterns in ethnographic study. In V. L. Bengtson, K. W. Schaie, and L. M. Burton (Eds.). *Adult intergenerational relations: Effects of societal change* (pp. 79–96). New York: Springer Publishing Co.

Burton, L. M., and Bengston, V. L. (1985). Black grandmothers: Issues of timing and continuity of roles. In V. L. Bengston and J. Robertson (Eds.), *Grandparenthood.* Beverly Hills, CA: Sage.

Burton, L. M., and Dilworth-Anderson, P. (1991). The intergenerational family roles of aged black Americans. *Marriage and Family Review, 16,* 311–330.

Bush, T. L. (1990). The epidemiology of cardiovascular disease in postmenopausal women. *Annals of the New York Academy of Science, 592,* 263–271.

Buskirk, E. R. (1985). Health maintenance and longevity: Exercise. In C. E. Finch and E. L. Schneider (Eds.), *Handbook of the biology of aging* (2nd ed., pp. 894–931). New York: Van Nostrand Reinhold.

Buskirk, E. R., and Hodgson, J. L. (1987). Age and aerobic power: The rate of change in men and women. *Federation Proceedings, 46,* 1824–1829.

Buss, D. M. et al. (1990). International preferences in selecting mates: A study of 37 cultures. *Journal of Cross-Cultural Psychology, 21,* 5–47.

Busse, E. W. (1993). Duke longitudinal studies of aging. *Zeitschrift für Gerontologie, 26,* 123–128.

Butcher, J. N., Aldwin, C. M., Levenson. M. R., and Ben-Porath, Y. S. (1992). Personality and aging: A study of the MMPI-2 among older men. *Psychology and Aging, 6,* 362–370.

Butler, R. N. (1975). *Why survive?* New York: Harper and Row.

Butler, R. N., and Kiikuni, K. (Eds.) (1993). *Who is responsible for my old age.* New York: Springer Publishing Co.

Butler, R. N., Lewis, M., and Sunderland. T. (1991). *Aging and mental health: Positive psychosocial and biomedical approaches* (4th ed.). New York: MacMillan.

Cacioppo, J. T., Berntson, G. G., Klein, D. J. and Poehlmann, K. M. (1998).

Psychophysiological emotion across the life span . In K. W. Schaie and M. P. Lawton (Eds.). *Annual review of gerontology and geriatrics: emotion and adult development* (Vol. 17, pp 27–74). New York: Springer Publishing Co.

Callahan, C. M. (1993). Psychiatric symptoms in elderly patients due to medications. In J. W. Rowe and J. C. Ahronheim (Eds.), *Annual review of gerontology and geriatrics* (Vol. 12, pp. 41–75). New York: Springer Publishing Co.

Camp, C. (1999). Memory interventions for normal and pathological older adults. In R. Schulz, G. Maddox, and M. P. Lawton (Eds). *Annual review of gerontology and geriatrics: interventions research with older adults* (Vol. 18, pp. 155–189). New York: Springer Publishing Co.

Camp, C. J., Bird, M. J., and Cherry, K. E. (in press). Retrieval strategies as a rehabilitation aid for cognitive loss in pathological aging. In R. D. Hill, L. Bäckman, and A. Stigsdotter-Neely (Eds), *Cognitive rehabilitation in old age.* New York: Oxford University Press.

Camp, C. J., Foss, J. W., O'Hanlon, A. M., and Stevens, A. B. (1996). Memory interventions for persons with dementia. *Applied Cognitive Psychology, 10,* 193–210.

Camp, C. J., and Mattern, J. M. (1999). Innovations in managing Alzheimer's disease. In D. Biegel and A. Blum (Eds.), *Innovations in practice and service delivery across the lifespan* (pp. 276–294). New York: Oxford University Press.

Camp. C. J., and McKitrick, L.A. (1989). The dialectics of forgetting and remembering across the adult lifespan. In. D. A. Kramer and M. Bopp (Eds.), *Transformation in clinical and developmental psychology.* New York: Springer-Verlag.

Campbell, A. J., Borrie, M. J., and Spears, G. F. (1989). Risk factors for falls in a community-based prospective study of people 70 years and older. *Journal of Gerontology: Medical Sciences, 44,* M112–M117.

Campbell, D. T., and Stanley, J. C. (1963). Experimental and quasi-experimental designs for research in teaching. In N. L. Gage (Ed.), *Handbook of research on teaching* (pp. 171–246). Skokie, IL: Rand McNally.

Campisi, J. (1997). Aging and cancer: The double-edged sword of replicative senescence. *Journal of the American Geriatrics Society, 45,* 482–488.

Cantor, M. H. (1983). Strain among caregivers: A study of experience in the United States. *Gerontologist, 23,* 597–604.

Caporael, L. R., and Culbertson, G. H. (1986). Verbal response modes of baby talk and other speech at institutions for the aged. *Language and Communication, 6,* 99–112.

Caporael, L. R., Lukaszewski, M. P., and Culbertson, G. H. (1983). Secondary baby talk: Judgements by institutionalized elderly and their caregivers. *Journal of Personality and Social Psychology, 44,* 746–754.

Capp, M. B. (1996). Enhancing autonomy and choice in selecting and directing long-term care services. *The Elder Law Journal, 4,* 56–97.

Carabellese, C., Apollonio, I., Rozzini, R., Bianchetti, A., Frisoni, G. B., Frattola, L., and Trabucchi, M. (1993). Sensory impairment and quality of life in a commuity elderly population, *Journal of the American Geriatrics Society, 41,* 401–407.

Carmody, D. (1988). Freshmen found stressing wealth. *New York Times,* January 14, p. 55.

Carp, F. (1994). Assessing the environment. In M. P. Lawton and J. A. Teresi (Eds.), *Annual review of gerontology and geriatrics* (Vol. 14, pp. 302–323). New York: Springer Publishing Co.

Carr, D. B., Jackson, T. W., Madden, D. J., and Cohen, H. J. (1992). The effect of age on driving skills. *Journal of the American Geriatrics Society, 40,* 567–573.

Carr, D. B., LaBarge, E., Dunnigan, K., and Storandt, M. (1998). Differentiating drivers with dementia of the Alzheimer type from healthy older persons with a traffic sign naming test. *Journal of Gerontology: Medical Sciences, 53A,* M135–M139.

Carroll, J. B. (1993). *Human cognitive abilities: A survey of factor-analytic studies.* New York: Cambridge University Press.

Carstensen, L. L. (1992a). Selectivity theory: Social activity in life-span context. In K. W. Schaie (Ed.), *Annual review of gerontology and geriatrics* (Vol. 11, pp. 195–217). New York: Springer Publishing Co.

Carstensen, L. L. (1992b). Social and emotional patterns in adulthood: Support for socioemotional selectivity theory. *Psychology and Aging, 7,* 331–338.

Carstensen, L. L. (1993). Motivation for social contact across the life span: A theory of socio-emotional selectivity. In J. Jacobs (Ed.), *Nebraska symposium on motivation: Developmental perspectives on emotion* (pp. 209–254). Lincoln, NE: University of Nebraska Press.

Carstensen, L. L., Gross, J. J., and Fung, H. H. (1997). The social context of emotional experience. In K. W. Schaie and M. P. Lawton (Eds.), *Annual review of gerontology and geriatrics, 17,* 325–352.

Carter, H. B., Pearson, J. D., Metter, E. J., Brant, L. J., Chan, D. N., Andres, R., Fozard, J. L., and Walsh, P. C. (1992). Longitudinal evaluation of prostate-specific antigen levels in men with and without prostate disease. *Journal of the American Medical Association, 257,* 2215–2220.

Carter, J. H. (1982). The effects of aging upon selected visual functions: Color vision, glare sensitivity, field of vision and accommodation. In R. Sekuler, D. Kline, and K. Dismukes (Eds.), *Aging and human visual function.* New York: Alan R. Liss.

Caskie, G., Schaie, K. W., and Willis, S. L. (1999, November). *Individual differences in the rate of change in cognitive abilities during adulthood.* Gerontological Society of America, San Francisco, CA.

Caspi, A. (1987). Personality in the life course. *Journal of Personality and Social Psychology, 53,* 1203–1213.

Caspi, A. (1995). Personality development across the life course. In W. Camon and N. Eisenberg (Eds.), *Handbook of child psychology, Vol. 3: Social, emotional, and personality development* (5th ed., pp. 311–388). New York: Wiley.

Caspi, A., and Bem, D. A. (1990). Personality continuity and change across the life course. In L. A. Pervin (Ed.), *Handbook of personality: Theory and research* (pp. 550–575). New York: Guilford.

Caspi, A., Bem, D. J., and Elder, G. H., Jr. (1989). Continuities and consequences of interactional styles across the life course. *Journal of Personality, 57.*

Caspi, A., and Herbener, E. S. (1990). Continuity and change: Assortative marriage and the consistency of personality in adulthood. *Journal of Personality and Social Psychology, 58,* 250–258.

Caspi, A., Herbener, E. S., and Ozer, D. J. (1992). Share experiences and the similarity of personalities: A longitudinal study of married couples. *Journal of Personality and Social Psychology, 62,* 281–291.

Castro-Martin, T., and Bumpass, L. (1989). Recent trends and differentials in marital disruption. *Demography, 26,* 37–51.

Catalyst (1998a). *Fact Sheet: Labor Day, 1998.* New York: Catalyst Organization.

Catalyst (1998b). *Fact Sheet: Happy Mother's Day from Catalyst.* New York: Catalyst Organization.

Catalyst (1998c). *Two careers, one marriage: Making it work in the workplace.* New York: Catalyst Organization.

Catalyst (1998d). *Women of color in corporate management: Dynamics of career advancement.* New York: Catalyst Organization.

Cate, R. M., and Lloyd, S. A. (1992). *Courtship.* Newbury Park, CA: Sage

Cattell, R. B. (1971). *Abilities: Their structure, growth and action.* Boston, MA: Houghton Mifflin.

Cavanaugh, J. C. (1996). Memory self-efficacy as a moderator of memory change. In F. Blanchard-Fields and T. M. Hess (Eds.), *Perspectives on cognitive change in adulthood and aging* (pp. 488–508). New York: McGraw-Hill.

Center for Disease Control and Prevention (1998, November 20). *Morbidity and mortality weekly report: Osteoporosis among estrogen-deficient women, U.S., 1988-1994,* 45.

Center for International Statistics. (1992). International data base: 1991 Eurostat, Ireland and 2020 figures. *Europlink Age Bulletin,* November.

Cerella, J. (1990). Aging and information-processing rate. In J. E. Birren and K. W. Schaie (Eds.), *Handbook of the psychology of aging* (3rd ed., pp. 201–221). San Diego: Academic Press.

Cerella, J., Poon, L., and Fozard, J. (1982). Age and iconic read-out. *Journal of Gerontology, 37,* 197–202.

Challis, B. H., Velichovsky, B. M., and Craik, F. I. M. (1996). Levels-of-processing effects on a variety of memory tasks: New findings and theoretical implications. *Consciousness and Cognition: An International Journal, 5,* 142–164.

Chappell, N. L., and Badger, M. (1989). Social isolation and well-being. *Journals of Gerontology: Social Sciences, 44,* S169–S176.

Charles, D. C. (1970). Historical antecedents of life-span developmental psychology. In L. R. Goulet and P. B. Baltes (Eds.), *Life-span developmental psychology: Research and theory.* New York: Academic Press.

Charness, N. (1983). Age, skill, and bridge bidding: A chronometric analysis. *Journal of Verbal Learning and Verbal Behavior, 22,* 406–416.

Chatters, L. M., and Jackson, J. S. (1982). Health and older blacks. *NCBA Quarterly Contact, 5*(1), 7–9.

Chatters, L. M., and Taylor, R. J. (1998). Religious involvement among African Americans. *African American Research Perspectives, 4,* 83–93.

Cheng, T. (1989). Symptomatology of minor psychiatric morbidity: A cross-cultural comparison. *Psychological Medicine, 19,* 667–708.

Cherlin, A. J., and Furstenberg, F. F., Jr. (1998). Stepfamilies in the United States: A reconsideration. In S. J. Ferguson (Ed.), *Shifting the center: Understanding contemporary families* (pp. 448–467). Mountain View, CA: Mayfield.

Cherry, K. E., Park, D. C; Frieske, D. A ., and Smith, A. D. (1996). Verbal and pictorial elaborations enhance memory in younger and older adults. *Aging, Neuropsychology and Cognition. 3,* 15–29.

Cherry, K. E., and Smith, A. D. (1998). Normal memory aging. In M. Hersen and V. B. Van Hasselt (Eds.), *Handbook of clinical geropsychology* (pp. 87–110). New York, NY: Plenum.

Chesney, M. A., and Rosenman, R. H. (1985). *Anger and hostility in cardiovascular and behavioral disorders*. Washington, DC: Hemisphere.

Chiriboga, D. A. (1982). Adaptations to marital separation in later and earlier life. *Journal of Gerontology, 37,* 109–114.

Chiriboga, D. A. (1989). Mental health at the midpoint: Crisis, challenge, or relief? In K. Hunter and M. Sundel (Eds.), *Midlife myths: Issues, findings and practical implications* (pp. 116–141). Newberry Park, CA: Sage.

Choi, N. G. (1994). Patterns and determinants of social service utilization: Comparison of the childless elderly and elderly parents living with and apart from their children. *Gerontologist, 34,* 353–362.

Christopher, F. S., Madura, M., and Weaver, L. (1998). Premarital sexual aggressors: A multivariate analysis of social, relational and individual variables. *Journal of Marriage and the Family, 60,* 56–69.

Christensen, H., and Henderson, A. S. (1991). Is age kinder to the initially more able? A study of eminent scientists and academics. *Psychological Medicine, 21,* 935–946.

Clark, D. O., Maddox, G. L., and Steinhauser, K. (1993). Race, aging, and functional health. *Journal of Aging and Health, 5,* 536–553.

Clark, M., and Reis, H. (1988). Interpersonal processes in close relationships. *Annual Review of Psychology, 39,* 69–72.

Clark, N., and Liebig, P. S. (1996). The politics of physician-assisted death: California's Proposition 161 and attitudes of the elderly. *Politics and the Life Sciences, 15,* 273–280.

Clark-Plaskie, M., and Lachman, M. E. (1999). The sense of control in midlife. In S. L. Willis, and J. E. Reid (Eds.), *Life in the middle: Psychological and social development in middle age.* San Diego, CA: Academic Press.

Clausen, J. (1984). Mental illness and the life course. In P. B. Baltes and O. G. Brim, Jr. (Eds.), *Life-span development and behavior* (Vol. 6). New York: Academic Press.

Clayton, P. J., Halikes, J. A., and Maurice, W. L. (1971). The bereavement of the widowed. *Diseases of the Nervous System, 32,* 597–604.

Clayton, V. P. (1982). Wisdom and intelligence: The nature and function of knowledge in the later years. *International Journal of Aging and Human Development, 15,* 315–321.

Cleiren, M. P. (1993). *Bereavement and adaptation: A comparative study of the aftermath of death.* Washington, DC: Hemisphere.

Coberly, S. (1991). Older workers and the Older Americans Act. *Generations,* Summer/Fall, 27–30.

Cohen, D., Eisdorfer, C., Gorelick, P., Luchins, D., Freels, S., Semla, T., Pavezz, G., Shaw, H., and Ashford, S. H. (1993). Sex differences in the psychiatric manifestations of Alzheimer's disease. *Geriatrics, 41,* 229–232.

Cohen, G. D. (1990). Psychopathology and mental health in the mature and elderly adult. In J. E. Birren and K. W.

Schaie (Eds.), *Handbook of the psychology of aging* (3rd ed., pp. 359–374). San Diego: Academic Press.

Cohen, G. D. (1992). *The brain in human aging.* New York: Springer Publishing Co.

Cohen, J. (1957). The factorial structure of the WAIS between early adulthood and old age. *Journal of Consulting Psychology, 21,* 283–290.

Cohen-Mansfield, J., and Werner, P. (1997). Management of verbally disruptive behaviors in nursing home residents. *Journal of Gerontology: Medical Sciences, 52A,* M369–M377.

Cole, T. R. (1993). The prophecy of senescence: G. Stanley Hall and the reconstruction of old age in twentieth-century America. In K. W. Schaie and W. A. Achenbaum (Eds.), *Societal impact on aging: Historical perspectives* (pp. 165–181). New York: Springer Publishing Co.

Colligan, R, C., and Offord, K. P. (1992). Age, stage, and the MMPI: Changes in response pattern over an 85-year span. *Journal of Clinical Psychology, 48,* 476–493.

Colligan, R. C., Osborne, D., Swenson, W. M., and Offord, K. P. (1983). *The MMPI: A contemporary normative study.* New York: Praeger.

Collins, L. M. (1996). Measurement of change in research on aging: Old and new issues from an individual change perspective. In J. E. Birren and K. W. Schaie (Eds.), *Handbook of the psychology of aging* (4th ed., pp. 38–56). San Diego, CA: Academic Press.

Commons, M. L., Sinnott, J. D., Richards, F. A., and Armon, C. (Eds.) (1989). *Beyond formal operations. Vol. 2: Adolescent and adult development models.* New York: Praeger.

Commonwealth Fund (1991). *Case studies at major corporations show why employing workers over 50 makes good business sense.* New York: Author.

Commonwealth Fund (1993). *The untapped resource: Final report of the Americans over 55 at work program.* New York: Author.

Cook, T. C., and Campbell, D. T. (1979). The design and conduct of quasi-experiments in field settings. In M. D. Dunette (Ed.), *Handbook of industrial and organizational research.* Chicago, IL: Rand McNally.

Cooney, T. M., and Hogan, D. P. (1991). Marriage in a institutionalized life course: First marriage among American men in the twentieth century. *Journal of Marriage and the Family, 53,* 178–190.

Cooney, T. M., Pederson, F. A., Indelicato, S., and Palkovitz, R. (1993). Timing of fatherhood: Is "On-time" optimal? *Journal of Marriage and the Family, 55,* 205–215.

Cooney, T. M., Schaie, K. W., and Willis, S. L. (1988). The relationship between prior functioning on cognitive and personality variables and subject attrition in longitudinal research. *Journal of Gerontology: Psychological Sciences, 43,* P12–P17.

Cooney, T. M., Smyer, M. A., Hagestad, G. O., and Klock, R. (1986). Parental divorce in young adulthood: Some preliminary findings. *American Journal of Orthopsychiatry, 56,* 470–477.

Cooney, T. M., and Uhlenberg, P. (1990). The role of divorce in men's relations with their adult children after midlife. *Journal of Marriage and the Family, 52,* 677–688.

Cooney, T. M., and Uhlenberg, P. (1992). Support from parents over the life course: The adult child's perspective. *Social Forces, 71,* 63–84.

Cornelius, S. W., and Caspi, A. (1987). Everyday problem solving in adulthood and old age. *Psychology and Aging, 2,* 144–153.

Corr, C. A. (1992). A task-based approach to coping with dying. *Omega, Journal of Death and Dying, 24,* 81–94,

Corr, C.A., Doka, K. J., and Kastenbaum, R. (2000). Dying and its interpretation: A review of selected literature and some comments on the state of the field. *Omega, Journal of Death and Dying. 39,* 239–259.

Corso, J. F. (1987). Sensory-perceptual processes and aging. In K. W. Schaie (Ed.), *Annual review of gerontology and geriatrics* (Vol. 7, pp. 29–55). New York: Springer Publishing Co.

Costa, P. T., Jr., and McCrae, R. R. (1978). Objective personality assessment. In M. Storandt, I. C. Siegler, and M. P. Elias (Eds.), *The clinical psychology of aging.* New York: Plenum.

Costa, P. T., Jr., and McCrae, R. R. (1980a). Influence of extroversion and neuroticism on subjective well-being: Happy and unhappy people. *Journal of Personality and Social Psychology, 38,* 668–678.

Costa, P. T., Jr., and McCrae, R. R. (1980b). Still stable after all these years: Personality as a key to some issues in adulthood and old age. In P. Baltes and O. G. Brim, Jr. (Eds.), *Life span development and behavior* (Vol. 3). New York: Academic Press.

Costa, P. T., Jr., and McCrae, R. R. (1985a). Hypochondriasis, neuroticism and aging: When are somatic complaints unfounded? *American Psychologist, 40,* 19–28.

Costa, P. T., Jr., and McCrae, R. R. (1985b). *The NEO Personality Inventory manual.* Odessa, FL: Psychological Assessment Resources.

Costa, P. T., Jr., and McCrae, R. R. (1987). Neuroticism, somatic complaints, and disease: Is the bark worse than the bite? *Journal of Personality, 55,* 299–316.

Costa, P. T., Jr., and McCrae, R. R. (1988). Personality in adulthood: A six-year longitudinal study of self reports and spouse ratings on the NEO personality inventory. *Journal of Personality and Social Psychology, 54,* 853–863.

Costa, P. T., Jr., and McCrae, R. R. (1992a). Four ways five factors are basic. *Personality and Individual Differences, 13,* 654–665.

Costa, P. T., Jr., and McCrae, R. R. (1992b). Multiple uses for longitudinal personality data. *European Journal of Personality, 6,* 85–102.

Costa, P. T., Jr., and McCrae, R. R. (1992c). *Revised NEO Personality Inventory (NEO-PI-R) and NEO Five-Factor Inventory (NEO-FFI) professional manual.* Odessa, FL: Psychological Assessment Resources, Inc.

Costa, P. T., Jr., and McCrae, R. R. (1992d). Trait psychology comes of age. In T. Sonderegger (Ed.) *Nebraska Symposium on Motivation, 1991* (pp. 169–204). Lincoln, NE: University of Nebraska Press.

Costa, P. T., Jr., and McCrae, R. R. (1993). Stability and change in personality from adolescence through adulthood. In C. A. Halverson, G. A. Kohnstamm, and R. P. Martin (Eds.), *The developing structure of temperament and personality from infancy to adulthood.* Hillsdale, NJ: Erlbaum.

Costa, P. T., Jr., McCrae, R. R., de Lima, M. P., Simoes, A., Ostendorf, F., Angleitner, A., Marusic, I., Bratko, D., Caprara, G. V., Barbaranelli, C., Chae, J. H., and Piedmont, R. L.

(1999) Age differences in personality across the adult life span: Parallels in five cultures. *Developmental Psychology, 35,* 466–477.

Costa, P. T., Jr., McCrae, R. R., and Holland, J. L. (1984). Personality and vocational interests in an adult sample. *Journal of Applied Psychology, 42,* 390–400.

Costa, P. T., Jr., McCrae, R. R., Martin, T. A., Oryol, V. E., Senin, I.. G., Rukavishnikov, A. A., Shimonaka, Y., Nakazato, K., Gondo, Y., Takayama, M., Allik, J., Kallasmaa,T., and Realo, A. (1999). Personality development from adolescence through adulthood: Further cross-cultural comparisons of age differences. In V. J. Molfese and D. Molfese (Eds.), *Temperament and personality development across the life span.* Hillsdale, NJ: Erlbaum.

Costa, P. T., Jr., Zonderman, A. B., and McCrae, R. R. (1991). Personality, defense, coping, and adaptation in older adulthood. In E. M. Cummings, L. Greene, and K. H. Karraker (Eds.), *Life-span developmental psychology: Perspectives on stress and coping* (pp. 277–293). Hillsdale, NJ: Erlbaum.

Coward, R. T., Horne, C., and Dwyer, J. W. (1992). Demographic perspectives on gender and family caregiving. In J. W. Dwyer and R. T. Coward (Eds.), *Gender, families and elder care* (pp. 18–33). Newbury Park, CA: Sage.

Coward, R. T., and Cutler, S. J. (1991). The composition of multi-generational households that include elders. *Research on Aging, 13,* 55–73.

Cowdry, E. V. (1942). *Problems of aging.* Baltimore, MD: Williams and Wilkins.

Craik, F. I. M. (1990). Changes in memory with normal aging: A functional view. In R. J. Wurtman (Ed.), *Advances in neurology* (Vol. 51: Alzheimer's Disease; pp. 201–205). New York: Raven Press.

Craft, S., Teri, L., Edland, S. D., Kukull, W. A., Schellenberg, G., McCormick, W. C., Bowen, J. D., and Larson, E. B. (1998). Accelerated decline in Apolipoprotein E-e4 homozygotes with Alzheimer's disease. *Neurology, 51,* 149–153.

Craik, F. I. M., Anderson, N. D., Kerr, S. A., and Li, K. A. H. (1995). Memory changes in normal ageing. In A. D. Baddeley, B. A. Wilson, and F. N. Watts (Eds.). *Handbook of memory disorders* (pp. 211–241). New York: John Wiley and Sons.

Craik, F. I. M., Byrd, M., and Swanson, J. M. (1987). Patterns of memory loss in three elderly samples. *Psychology and Aging, 2,* 79–86.

Craik, F. I. M., and Jennings, J. M. (1992). Human memory. In F. I. M. Craik and T. A. Salthouse (Eds.), *Handbook of aging and cognition.* Hillsdale, NJ: Erlbaum.

Craik, F. I. M., and McDowd, J. M. (1998) Age differences in recall and recognition. In M. P. Lawton and T. A. Salthouse (Eds.), *Essential papers on the psychology of aging.* (pp. 282–295). New York: New York University Press.

Craik, F. I. M., and Salthouse, T. A. (Eds.) (1999). *The handbook of aging and cognition* (2nd ed.). Mahwah, NJ: Lawrence Erlbaum.

Crimmins, E. M., and Hayward, M. (1996). Active life expectancy. In S. L. Willis, K. W. Schaie, and M. Hayward (Eds.), *Societal processes that affect decision making in older adults.* New York: Springer Publishing Co.

Crimmins, E. M., and Saito, Y. (1993). Getting better and getting worse: Transitions in functional status among older Americans. *Journal of Aging and Health, 5,* 3-36.

Cristofalo, V. J., Tresini, M., Francis, M. K., and Volker, C. (1999). Biological theories of senescence. In V. L. Bengtson and K. W. Schaie (Eds.), *Handbook of theories of aging* (pp. 98–112). New York: Springer Publishing Co.

Crockett, W. H., and Hummert, M. L. (1987). Perceptions of aging and the elderly. In K. W. Schaie (Ed.), *Annual review of gerontology and geriatrics* (Vol. 7, pp. 217–242). New York: Springer Publishing Co.

Crook, T. H., Larrabee, G. J., and Youngjohn, J. R. (1989). Age associated memory impairment: Definition and assessment. In A. Agnoli and G. Bruno (Eds.), *Mental decline of elderly people* (pp. 21–28). Rome, Italy: CIC Edizioni Internatioali.

Crook, T. H., and West, R. (1990). Name recall performance across the adult life-span. *British Journal of Psychology, 81,* 335–349.

Crook, T. H., Youngjohn, J .R. and Larrabee, G. (1990). TV News Test: A new measure of everyday memory for prose. *Neuropsychology, 4,* 135–145.

Crose, R., Leventhal, E. A., Haug, M. R. and Burns, E. A. (1997). The challenges of aging. In S. Gallant, G. P. Keita, and R. Royal-Schaler (Eds.), *Psychosocial and behavioral factors in women's health care* (pp. 221–232). Washington, DC: American Psychological Association.

Cross, S., and Markus, H. R. (1991). Possible selves across the life course. *Human Development, 34,* 230–255.

Crowder, R. G. (1980). Echoic memory and the study of aging memory systems. In L. W. Poon, J. L. Fozard, L. S. Cermak, D. Arenberg, and L. W. Thompson (Eds.), *New directions in memory and aging: Proceedings of the George A. Talland memorial conference.* Hillsdale, NJ: Erlbaum.

Cui, X. J., and Vaillant, G. E.(1996). Antecedents and consequences of negative life events in adulthood: A longitudinal study. *American Journal of Psychiatry, 153,* 21–26.

Cumming, E., and Henry, W. (1961). *Growing old: The process of disengagement.* New York: Basic Books.

Cumming, R. G., and Klineberg, R. J. (1994). Fall frequency and characteristics and the risk of hip fractures. *Journal of the American Geriatrics Society, 42,* 774–778.

Cunningham, D. J., and Antill, J. K. (1984). Changes in masculinity and femininity across the family life cycle: A reexamination. *Developmental Psychology, 20,* 1135–1141.

Cunningham, W. R., and Owens, W. A., Jr. (1983). The Iowa State Study of the adult development of intellectual abilities. In K. W. Schaie (Ed.), *Longitudinal studies of adult psychological development.* New York: Guilford Press.

Curcio, C. A., Buell, S. J., and Coleman, B. D. (1982). Morphology of the aging central nervous system: Not all downhill. In J. A. Mortimer, F. J. Pirozzola, and G. L. Maletta (Eds.), *Advances in neurogerontology: The aging motor system.* New York: Praeger.

Cutler, N. E ., Gregg, D. W., and Lawton, M. P. (Eds.) (1992). *Aging, money, and life satisfaction: Aspects of financial gerontology.* New York: Springer Publishing Co.

Csikszenmihalyi, M (1991). An investment theory of creativity and its development: Commentary. *Human Development, 34,* 32–34.

Czaya, S. (2001). Technological change and the older worker. In J. E. Birren and K. W. Schaie (Eds.), *Handbook of the psychology of aging* (5th ed.). San Diego, CA: Academic Press.

Czaja, S. J., and Sharit, J. (1998a). Ability performance relationships as a function of age and task experience for a data entry task. *Journal of Experimental Psychology: Applied, 4,* 332–351.

Czaja, S. J., and Sharit, J. (1998b). Age differences in attitudes toward computers. *Journal of Gerontology: Psychological Sciences, 53B,* P329–P340.

Dai, X., Xie, Y., and Zheng, L. (1993). Age, education and intelligence declining in adulthood. *Chinese Mental Health Journal, 7,* 215–217.

Dale, A., Evandrou, M., and Arber, S. (1987). The household structure of the elderly population in Britain. *Ageing and Society, 7,* 37–56.

Danielson, K. K., Moffitt, T. E., Caspi, A., and Silva, P. H. (1998). Comorbidity between abuse of an adult and DSM-III-R mental disorders: Evidence from an epidemiological study. *American Journal of Psychiatry, 155,* 131–133.

Dansky, K. H., Brannon, D., Shea, D. G., Vasey, J., and Dirani, R. (1998). Profiles of hospital, physician, and home health service use by older persons in rural areas. *Gerontologist, 38,* 320–330.

Datan, N., Rodeheaver, D., and Hughes, F. (1987). Adult development and aging. In M. Rosenzweig (Ed.) *Annual Review of Psychology, 38,* 153–180.

DaVanzo, J., and Rahman, M. O. (1993). American families: Trends and correlates. *Population Index, 59,* 350–386.

Davis, D. L., Dinse, G. E., and Hoel, D. G. (1994). Decreasing cardiovascular disease and increasing cancer among whites in the United States from 1973 to 1987: Good news and bad news. *Journal of the American Medical Association, 271,* 431–437.

Dawson, D. A., and Hardy, M. (1989). AIDS knowledge and attitudes of black Americans. *Advance Data, Nr. 165.* Washington, DC: National Center for Health Statistics.

DeAlberto, M. J., McAvay, G. J., Seeman, T., and Berkman, L. (1997). Psychotropic drug use and cognitive decline among older men and women. *International Journal of Geriatric Psychiatry, 12,* 567–574.

DeBallis, R., Marcus, E., Kutscher, A. H., Torres, C. S., Barrett, V., and Siegel, M. (1986). *Suffering: Psychological and social aspects in loss, grief and care.* New York: Hayworth Press.

Deci, E. L. (1992). On the nature and functions of motivation theories. *Psychological Science, 3,* 167–171.

Deeg, D. J. H., Kardaun, W. P. F., and Fozard, J. L. (1996). Health behavior and aging. In J. E. Birren and K W. Schaie (Eds.), *Handbook of the psychology of aging* (4th ed., pp. 129–149). San Diego, CA: Academic Press.

DeHaan, L. G., and Schulenberg, J. (1997). The covariation of religion and politics during the transition to young adulthood: Challenging global identity assumptions. *Journal of Adolescence, 20,* 537–552.

DeKeseredy, W., and Kelly, K. (1993). The incidence and prevalence of woman abuse from Canadian university and college dating relationships. *The Canadian Journal of Sociology, 18,* 137–159.

Denney, N. W. (1974). Classification abilities in the elderly. *Journal of Gerontology, 29,* 309–314..

Denney, N. W. (1981). Adult cognitive development. In D. S. Beasley and

G. A. Davis (Eds.), *Aging: Communications processes and disorders*. New York: Grune and Stratton.

Denney, N. W. (1982). Aging and cognitive changes. In B. B. Wolman (Ed.), *Handbook of developmental psychology*. Englewood Cliffs, NJ: Prentice Hall.

Denney, N. W., and Heidrich, S. M. (1990). Training effects on Raven's Progressive Matrices in young, middle-aged, and elderly adults. *Psychology and Aging, 5,* 144–145.

Dennis, W. (1966). Creative productivity between the ages of 20 and 80 years. *Journal of Gerontology, 21,* 1–8.

Dennis, W. (1968). Creative productivity between the ages of 20 and 80 years. In B. L. Neugarten (Ed.), *Middle age and aging*. Chicago, IL: University of Chicago Press.

DeSpelder, L., and Strickland, A. (1992). *The last dance: Encountering death and dying* (3rd ed.). Mountain View, CA: Mayfield.

Deutsch, H. (1945). *The psychology of women*. New York: Grune and Stratton.

Diamond, M. C., Johnson, R. E., Protti, A. M., Ott, C., and Kajisa, L. (1985). Plasticity in the 904-day-old male rat cerebral cortex. *Experimental Neurology, 87,* 309–317.

Diehl, M. (1998). Everyday competence in later life: Current status and future directions. *Gerontologist, 38,* 422–433.

Diehl, M., Lago, D., Ahern, F., Smyer, M. A., Hermanson, S., and Rabatin, V. (1992). Examination of priorities for therapeutic drug utilization review. *Journal of Geriatric Drug Therapy, 6,* 65–85.

Diehl, M., Willis, S. L., and Schaie, K. W. (1995). Everyday problem solving in older adults: Observational assessment and cognitive correlates. *Psychology and Aging. 10,* 478–491.

Digman, J. M. (1990). Personality structure: Emergence of the five-factor model. *Annual Review of Psychology, 41,* 417–440.

Dilworth-Anderson, P. (1998). Emotional well-being in adult and later life among African Americans: A cultural and sociocultural perspective. In K. W. Schaie and M. P. Lawton (Eds.). *Annual review of gerontology and geriatrics: emotion and adult development* (Vol. 17, pp. 282–303). New York: Springer Publishing Co..

Dion, K. K. (1995). Delayed parenthood and women's expectations about the transition to parenthood. *International Journal of Behavioral Development, 18,* 315–333.

Dion, K. K., and Dion, K. L. (1996). Cultural perspectives on romantic love. *Personal Relationships, 3,* 5–17.

Dion, K. L., and Dion, K. K. (1988). Romantic love: Individual and cultural perspectives. In R. J. Sternberg and M. Barnes (Eds.), *The psychology of love* (pp. 264–289). New Haven, CT: Yale University Press.

Dion, K. L., and Dion, K. K. (1993). Gender and ethnocultural comparisons in styles of love. *Psychology of Women Quarterly, 17,* 463–473.

Dittmann-Kohli, F., and Baltes, P. B. (1990). Toward a neofunctionalist conception of adult intellect. In C. Alexander and E. Langer (Eds.), *Higher stages of human development: Perspectives on adult growth* (pp. 54–78). New York: Oxford University Press.

Dittmann-Kohli, F., Lachman, M. E., Kliegl, R., and Baltes, P. B. (1991). Effects of cognitive training and testing on intellectual efficacy beliefs in elderly adults. *Journals of Gerontology: Psychological Sciences, 46,* P162–P164.

Dixon, R. A. (1999). Concepts and mechanisms of gains in cognitive aging. D. C. Park and N. Schwarz (Eds.), *Cognitive aging: A primer* (pp. 23–41). Philadelphia, PA: Psychology Press.

Dixon, R. A., and Lerner, R. M. (1984). A history of systems in developmental psychology. In M. H. Borenstein and M. E. Lamb (Eds.), *Developmental psychology: An advanced textbook* (pp. 1–35). Hillsdale, NJ: Erlbaum.

Doherty, W. J., Kouneski, E., and Erickson, M. (1998). Responsible fathering: An overview and conceptual framework. *Journal of Marriage and the Family, 60,* 277–292.

Doka, K. J. (1993). *Living with lifethreatening illness.* Lexington, MA: Lexington Books.

Dolce, J., and Dickerson, P. C. (1991). Pain management. In P. A. Wisocki (Ed.), *Handbook of clinical behavior therapy with the elderly client* (pp. 383–399). New York: Plenum.

Doosje, B., Rojahn, K., and Fischer, A. (1999). Partner preferences as a function of gender, age, political orientation and level of education. *Sex Roles. 40,* 45-60.

Douglas, K., and Arenberg, D. (1978). Age changes, cohort differences, and cultural change on the Guilford-Zimmerman Temperament Survey. *Journal of Gerontology, 33,* 737–747.

Drachman, D. A. (1993). New criteria for the diagnosis of vascular dementia: Do we know enough yet? *Neurology, 43,* 246–249.

Dreher, G. F., and Ash, R. A. (1990). A comparative study of mentoring among men and women in managerial, professional and technical positions. *Journal of Applied Psychology, 75,* 539–546.

Dudek, S. Z., and Croteau, H. (1998). Aging and creativity in eminent architects. In C. Adams-Price (Ed.), *Creativity and successful aging* (pp. 117–152). New York: Springer Publishing Co.

Dudek, S. Z., and Hall, W. B. (1991). Personality consistency: Eminent architects 25 years later. *Creativity Research Journal. 4,* 213–231.

Duke University Center for the Study of Aging and Human Development. (1978). *Multidimensional functional assessment: The OARS methodology.* Durham, NC: Duke University Medical Center.

Duncan, L, E., and Agronick, G. S. (1995). The intersection of life stage and social events: Personality and life outcomes. *Journal of Personality and Social Psychology, 69,* 358–368.

Duncan, P. W., and Studenski, S. (1994). Balance and gait measures. In M. P. Lawton and J. A. Teresi (Eds.), *Annual review of gerontology and geriatrics* (Vol. 14, pp. 76–92). New York: Springer Publishing Co.

Dunkle, R. E., Roberts, B., Haug, M., and Raphelson, M. (1992). An examination of coping resources of very old men and women: Their association to the relationship between stress, hassles and function. *Journal of Women and Aging, 4,* 79–103

Dunn, G. (1989). *Design and analysis of reliability studies.* New York: Oxford University Press.

Dutta, R. (1992). *The relationship between flexibility-rigidity and the Primary Mental Abilities.* Unpubl. doctoral dissertation. University Park, PA: The Pennsylvania State University.

Dweck, C. S. (1992). The study of goals in psychology. *Psychological Science, 3,* 165–167.

Dykstra, P A. (1995). Loneliness among the never and formerly married: The importance of supportive friendships and a desire for independence. *Journal of Gerontology: Social Sciences, 50B,* S321–S329.

Dykstra, P. A. (1997). The effects of divorce on intergenerational exchanges in families. *Netherlands' Journal of Social Sciences, 33,* 77–93.

Earle, J. R., Smith, M. H., Harris, C. T., and Longino, C. F. (1998). Women, marital status, and symptoms of depression in a midlife national sample. *Journal of Women and Aging, 10,* 41–57.

Earles, J. L., and Salthouse, T. A. (1995). Interrelations of age, health, and speed. *Journal of Gerontology: Psychological Sciences, 50B,* P33–P41.

Easterbrooks, M. A., and Emede, R. N. (1986, April). *Marriage and infant: Different systems' linkages for mothers and infants.* Paper presented at the International Conference on Infant Studies, Beverly Hills, CA.

Easterlin, R. A. (1987). *Birth and fortune: The impact of numbers on personal welfare,* (2nd ed.) Chicago, IL: University of Chicago Press.

Easterlin, R. A., Schaeffer, C. M., and Macunovich, D. J. (1993). Will the baby boomers be less well off than their parents? Income, wealth and family circumstances over the life cycle in the United States. *Population and Development Review, 19,* 497–523.

Educational Testing Service. (1977). *Basic skills test: Reading.* Princeton, NJ: Educational Testing Service.

Eichorn, D. H., Clausen, J. A., Haan, N., Honzik, M. P., and Mussen, P. H.

(Eds.) (1981). *Present and past in middle life.* New York: Academic Press.

Eisdorfer, C. (1968). Arousal and performance: Experiments in verbal learning and a tentative theory. In G. A. Talland (Ed.), *Human aging and behavior.* New York: Academic Press.

Eisdorfer, C., Nowlin, J., and Wilkie, F. (1970). Improvement of learning in the aged by modification of autonomic nervous system activity. *Science, 170,* 1327–1329.

Ekelof, E. (1988). New Volvo plant in Uddevalla: More than just assembly. *Working Environment 1988* (Arbetmiljö International), 6–7.

Ekerdt, D. (1987). Why the notion persists that retirement harms health. *Gerontologist, 27,* 454–457.

Ekerdt, D., Bossé, R., and LoCastro, J. (1983). Claims that retirement improves health. *Journal of Gerontology, 38,* 231–236.

Ekerdt, D. J., and DeViney, S. (1990). On defining persons as retired. *Journal of Aging Studies, 4,* 211–229.

Ekerdt, D. J., and DeViney, S. (1993). Evidence for a preretirement process among older male workers. *Journal of Gerontology: Social Sciences, 48,* S35–S43.

Elder, G. H., Jr. (1979). Historical change in life patterns and personality. In P. B. Baltes and O. G. Brim, Jr. (Eds.), *Life-span development and behavior* (Vol. 2). New York: Academic Press.

Elder, G. H., Jr. (1998a). The life course as developmental theory. *Child Development, 69,* 1–12.

Elder, G. H., Jr. (1998b). The life course and human development. In R. M Lerner (Ed.), *Handbook of child psy-*

chology, Volume 1: Theoretical models of human development. New York: Wiley.

Elder, G. H., Jr., and Caspi, A. (1990). Studying lives in a changing society: Sociological and personological explorations. In A. I. Rabin, R. A. Zucker, and S. Frank (Eds.), *Studying persons and lives* (pp. 201–247). New York: Springer Publishing Co.

Elder. G. H. Jr., and O'Rand, A. M. (1994). Adult lives in a changing society. In K. Cook, G. Fine, and J. S. House (Eds.), *Sociological perspectives on social psychology.* New York: Basic.

Elder, G. H. Jr., Shanahan, M. J., and Clipp, E. C. (1997). Linking combat and physical health: The legacy of World War II in men's lives. *American Journal of Psychiatry, 154,* 330–336.

Elias, M. F., D'Agostino, R. B., Elias, P. K., and Wolf, P. A. (1995). Neuropsychological test performance, cognitive functioning, blood pressure and age: The Framingham Heart Study. *Experimental Aging Research, 21,* 369–391.

Elias, M. F., Elias, J. W., and Elias, P. K. (1990). Biological and health influences on behavior. In J. E. Birren and K. W. Schaie (Eds.), *Handbook of the psychology of aging* (3rd ed., pp. 80–102). San Diego: Academic Press.

Elias, M. F., and Elias, P. K. (1977). Motivation and activity. In J. E. Birren and K. W. Schaie (Eds.), *Handbook of the psychology of aging.* New York: Van Nostrand Reinhold.

Elias, M. F., Robbins, M. A., Elias, P. K., and Streeten, D. H. P. (1998). A longitudinal study of blood pressure in relation to performance on the Wechsler Adult Intelligence Scale. *Health Psychology, 17,* 486–493.

Elias, M. F., Wolf, P. A., D'Agostino R. B., Cobb, J. and White, L. R. (1993). Untreated blood pressure level is inversely related to cognitive functioning: The Framingham Study. *American Journal of Epidemiology, 138,* 353–364.

Elinson, J. (1988). Defining and measuring health and illness. In K. W. Schaie, R. T. Campbell, W. Meredith, and S. C. Rawlings (Eds.), *Methodological issues in aging research* (pp. 231–248). New York: Springer Publishing Co.

Ellison, C. G. (1998). Religion, health, and well being among African Americans. *African American Research Perspectives, 4,* 94–103.

Emanuel, E. J. (1994). The history of euthanasia debates in the United States and Britain. *Annals of Internal Medicine, 121,* 793–802.

Emery, C. F., Burker, E. J., and Blumenthal, J. (1992). Psychological and physiological effects of exercise among older adults. In K. W. Schaie (Ed.), *Annual review of gerontology and geriatrics* (Vol. 11, pp. 218–238). New York: Springer Publishing Co.

Erber, J. T., Szuchman, L. T., and Prager, I. G. (1997). Forgetful but forgiven: How age and life style affect perceptions of memory failure. *Journal of Gerontology: Psychological Sciences, 52B,* P303–P307.

Erikson, E. H. (1963). *Childhood and society* (2nd ed.). New York: Norton.

Erikson, E. H. (1964). *Insight and responsibility.* New York: Norton.

Erikson, E. H. (1979). Reflections on Dr. Borg's life cycle. In E. H. Erikson (Ed.), *Adulthood.* New York: Norton.

Erikson, E. H. (1980). *Identity and the life cycle.* New York: Norton.

Erikson, E. H. (1982). *The life cycle completed: A review.* New York: Norton.

Erikson, E. H. (1984). Reflections on the last stage—and the first. *Psychoanalytic Study of the Child, 39,* 155–165.

Erikson, E. H., Erikson, J. M., and Kivnick, H. Q. (1986). *Vital involvement in old age.* New York: Norton.

Ershler, W. B. (1993). Cancer biology and aging. In R. L. Sprott, R. W. Huber and T. F. Williams (Eds.), *The biology of aging* (pp. 45–52). New York: Springer Publishing Co.

Evans, L. K., Strumpf, N. E., Allen-Taylor, S. L., Capezutti, E., Maislin, G., and Jacobsen, B. (1997). A clinical trial to reduce restraints in nursing homes. *Journal of the American Geriatrics Society, 45,* 675–681,

Evans, W. J. (2000). Effects of exercise on body composition and functional capacity of elderly persons. In K. W. Schaie and M. Pietrucha (Eds.), *Mobility and transportation in the elderly* (pp. 71–90). New York: Springer Publishing Co.

Falk, P. (1989). Lesbian mothers: Psychosocial assumptions in family law. *American Psychologist, 44,* 941–947.

Farkas, J. (1992). *Kin assistance and labor force participation of midlife women.* Paper presented at the Annual meeting of the Population Association of America, Denver Colorado.

Farr, J. L., Tesluk, P. E., and Klein, S. R. (1998). Organizational structure of the workplace and the older worker. In K. W. Schaie and C. Schooler (Eds.), *Impact of work on older adults* (pp. 143–185). New York: Springer Publishing Co..

Farran, C. J. (1997). Theoretical perspectives concerning positive aspects of caring for elderly persons with dementia: Stress/adaptation and existentialism. *Gerontologist, 37,* 250–256.

Farrell, M. P., and Rosenberg, S. (1981). *Men at midlife.* Boston: Auburn House.

Featherman, D., and Petersen, T. (1986). Markers of aging: Modeling the clocks that time us. *Research on Aging, 8,* 339–365.

Feher, E. P., Mahurin, R. K., Inbody, S. B., Crook, T. H., and Pirozzolo, F. J. (1991). Ansognosia in Alzheimer's disease. *Neuropsychiatry, Neuropsychology, and Behavioral Neurology, 4,* 136–146.

Feingold, A. (1992). Gender differences in mate selection preferences: A test of the parental investment model. *Psychological Bulletin, 112,* 125–139.

Feingold, A. (1993). Cognitive gender differences: A developmental perspective. *Sex Roles, 29,* 91–112.

Feist, G. J. (1993). A structural model of scientific eminence. *Psychological Science. 4,* 366–371.

Feldman, H., Goldstein, I., Hatzichristou, D. G., Krane, R,. and McKinlay, J. B. (1994). Impotence and its medical and psychosocial correlates: Results of the Massachusetts Male Aging Study. *Journal of Urology, 151,* 54–61

Feldman, S. S., Biringen, Z. C., and Nash, S. C. (1981). Fluctuations of sex-related self-attributions as a function of stage of family life cycle. *Developmental Psychology, 17,* 24–35.

Fernie, G. (1994). Technology to assist elderly people's safe mobility. *Experimental Aging Research,* 219–228.

Ferraro, K. F., Farmer, M. M., and Wybraniec, J. A. (1997). Health trajectories: Long-term dynamics among black and white adults. *Journal of Health and Social Behavior, 38,* 38–54.

Ferster, C. B. (1973). A functional analysis of depression. *American Psychologist, 29,* 857–870.

Feychting, M., Pedersen, N. L., Svedberg, P., Floderus, B., and Gatz, M. (1998). Dementia and occupational exposure to magnetic fields. *Scandinavian Journal of Work Environment Health, 24,* 46–53.

Field, D. (1999). Continuity and change in friendships in advanced age: Findings from the Berkeley Older Generation Study. *International Journal of Aging and Human Development, 48,* 81–83.

Field, D., and Milsap, R. E. (1991). Personality in advanced old age: Continuity or change? *Journals of Gerontology: Psychological Sciences, 46,* P299–P308.

Field, D., and Minkler, M. (1988). Continuity and change in social support between young-old and old-old, and very-old adults. *Journal of Gerontology, 43,* P100–P106.

Field, D., and Minkler, M. (1993). The importance of family in advanced old age: The family is "forever." In P. A. Cowan, D. Field, D. A. Hansen, A. Skolnick, and G. E. Swanson (Eds.), *Family self, and society: Toward a new agenda for family research.* Hillsdale, NJ: Erlbaum.

Field, D., Schaie, K. W. and Leino, V. (1988). Continuity in intellectual functioning: The role of self-reported health. *Psychology and Aging, 3, 385–392.*

Field, D., Schaie, K. W. and Leino, V. (1991). Continuity in intellectual functioning: The role of personality. *Mensa Research Journal, 30,* 6–19.

Field, D., and Weishaus, S. (1992). Marriage over half a century: A longitudinal study. In M. Bloom (Ed.), *Changing Lives* (pp. 269–273). Columbia, SC: University of South Carolina Press.

Filipp, S. G. (1996). Motivation and emotion. In J. E. Birren and K. W. Schaie (Eds.), *Handbook of the psychology of aging* (4th ed.). San Diego: Academic Press.

Finch, C. E. (1988). Neuronal and endocrine approaches to the resolution of time as a dependent variable in the aging process of mammals. *Gerontologist, 28,* 29–42.

Finch, C. E. (1990), *Longevity, senescence, and the genome.* Chicago, IL: University of Chicago. Press.

Finch, C. E. (1991). Middle age: An evolving frontier in gerontology. *Neurobiology of Aging, 12,* 1–2.

Finch, C. E. (1996). Biological bases for plasticity during aging of individual life histories. In D, Magnusson (Ed.), *The lifespan development of individuals: Biological and psycho-social perspectives, a synthesis* (pp.488–512). Cambridge, UK: Cambridge University Press.

Finch, C. E. (1998). Variations in senescence and longevity include the possibility of negligible senescence. *Journal of Gerontology: Biological Sciences, 53A,* P235–P239.

Finch, C. E., and Rose, M. R. (1995). Hormones and the physiological architecture of life history evolution. *Quarterly Review of Biology, 70,* 1–52.

Finch, C. E., and. Seeman, T. E. (1999). Stress theories of aging. In V. L. Bengtson and K. W. Schaie (Eds.). *Handbook of theories of aging* (pp. 81–97). New York: Springer Publishing Co.

Finch, C. E., and Tanzi, R. E. (1997). Genetics of aging. *Science, 278,* 407–411.

Finch, N. J., Hayes, L., Mason, J., Masson, J., and Wallis, L (1996). *Wills, inheritance and families.* London, UK: Clarendon

Fincham, J. (1988). Patient compliance in the ambulatory elderly: A review of the literature. *Journal of Geriatric Drug Therapy, 2,* 31–52.

Finkel, D., and Pedersen, N. L. (2000). Contribution of age, genes, and environment to the relationship between perceptual speed and cognitive ability. *Psychology and Aging, 15,* 56–63.

Fiske, M. (1980). Tasks and crises of the second half of life: The interrelationship of commitment, coping, and adaptation. In J. E. Birren and R. B. Sloane (Eds.), *Handbook of mental health and aging.* Englewood Cliffs, NJ: Prentice-Hall.

Fitzgerald, J. M. (1978). Actual and perceived sex and generational differences in interpersonal styles: Structural and quantitative issues. *Journal of Gerontology, 33,* 394–401.

Flavell, J. H. (1963). *The developmental psychology of Jean Piaget.* New York: Van Nostrand.

Flavell, J. H. (1970). Cognitive changes in adulthood. In L. R. Goulet and P. B. Baltes (Eds.), *Life-span developmental psychology: Research and theory.* New York: Academic Press.

Fleeson, W., and Baltes, P. B. (1998). Beyond present-day personality assessment: An encouraging exploration of the measurement properties and predictive power of subjective lifetime personality. *Journal of Research in Personality, 32,* 411–430.

Fleeson, W., and Heckhausen, J. (1997). More or less "me" in past present and future: Perceived lifetime personality during adulthood. *Psychology and Aging, 12,* 125–136.

Fletcher, G. J. O., Simpson, J. A., Thomas, G., and Giles, L. (1999). Ideals in intimate relationships. *Journal of Personality and Social Psychology, 76,* 72–89.

Flint, M. (1982). Male and female menopause: A cultural put on. In A. Voda, M. Dinnerstein, and S. O'Donnell (Eds.), *Changing perspective on menopause.* Austin, TX: University of Texas Press.

Folstein, M. F., Folstein, S. E., and McHugh, P. R. (1975). Mini-Mental State: A practical method of grading the cognitive state of patients for the clinician. *Journal of Psychiatric Research, 12,* 189–198.

Foot, D. K., and Stoffman, D. (1996). *Boom, bust and echo: How to profit from the coming demographic shift.* Toronto, Canada: Macfarlane, Walter and Ross.

Ford, M., and Lowery, C. (1986). Gender differences in moral reasoning: A comparison of the use of justice and care orientations. *Journal of Personality and Social Psychology, 50,* 777–783.

Foster, J. M., and Gallagher, D. (1986). An exploratory study comparing depressed and non-depressed elders' coping strategies. *Journal of Gerontology, 41,* 91–93.

Fox, R. H., MacGibbon, R., Davies, L., and Woodward, P. M. (1983). Problem of the old and the cold. *British Medical Journal, 7,* 21–24.

Fozard, J. L. (1990). Vision and hearing in aging. In J. E. Birren and K.W. Schaie (Eds.), *Handbook of the psychology of aging* (3rd ed., pp. 150–171). San Diego: Academic Press.

Fozard, J. L. (2000). Sensory and cognitive changes with age. In K. W. Schaie and M. Pietrucha (Eds.), *Mobility and transportation in the elderly* (pp. 1–61). New York: Springer Publishing Co.

Fozard, J. L., and Gordon-Salant, S. (2001). Sensory and perceptual changes with aging. In J. E. Birren and K. W. Schaie (Eds)., *Handbook of the psychology of aging* (5th ed.). San Diego, CA: Academic Press.

Franz, C. E., McClelland, D. C., and Weinberger, J. (1991). Childhood antecedents of conventional social accomplishment in midlife adults: A 36-year prospective study. *Journal of Personality and Social Psychology, 60,* 586–595.

Franzoi, S. L., and Koehler, V. (1998). Age and gender differences in body attitudes: A comparison of young and elderly adults. *International Journal of Aging and Human Development, 47,* 1–10.

Fredrickson, B. L., and Carstensen, L. L. (1990). Choosing social partners: How old age, and anticipated endings make people more selective. *Psychology and Aging, 5,* 335–347.

Freud, A. (1946). *The ego and the mechanisms of defense.* New York: International Universities Press.

Freund, A. M. (1997). Individual age salience: A psychological perspective on the salience of age in the life course. *Human Development, 40,* 287–293.

Freund, A. M., and Baltes, P. B. (1998). Selection, optimization and compensation as strategies of life management: Correlations with subjective indicators of successful aging. *Psychology and Aging, 13,* 531–543.

Fries, J. F. (1985). Separating death from disease. *New York Times,* February 17, p. E5.

Fries, J. F., and Crapo, L. M. (1981). *Vitality and aging.* San Francisco, CA: Freeman.

Froehling, S. (1974). *Effects of propranolol on behavioral and physiological measures of elderly males.* Unpublished doctoral dissertation. Coral Gables, FL: University of Miami.

Fulton, G., Madden, C., and Minichiello, V. (1996). The social construction of anticipatory grief. *Social Sciences and Medicine, 43,* 1349–1358.

Fry, C. L. (1985). Culture, behavior and aging in the comparative perspective. In J. E. Birren and K. W. Schaie (Eds.), *Handbook of the psychology of aging* (2nd ed.). New York: Van Nostrand Reinhold.

Furchtgott, E., and Busemeyer, J. R. (1981). Age preferences for professional helpers. *Journal of Gerontology, 36,* 90–92.

Furstenberg, F. (1989). Good dads— bad dads: Two faces of fatherhood. In A. J. Cherlin, (Ed.), *The changing American family and public policy* (pp. 192–218). Washington, DC: Urban Institute Press.

Galinsky, E., Bond, J. T., and Friedman, D. E. (1993). *The national study of the changing workforce: Highlights.* New York: Families and Work Institute.

Gall, T. L., Evans, D. R., and Howard, J. (1997). The retirement adjustment process: Changes in the well-being of male retirees across time. *Journals of Gerontology: Social Sciences, 52B,* P110–P117.

Gallagher, D. E., and Thompson, L. W. (1981). *Depression in the elderly: A behavioral treatment manual.* Los Angeles, CA: University of Southern California Press.

Gallagher, D. E., and Thompson, L. W. (1983). Effectiveness of psychotherapy for both endogenous and nonendogenous depression in older adult outpatients. *Journal of Gerontology, 38,* 707–712.

Gallagher-Thompson, D., and Thompson, L. W. (1996). Applying cognitive-behavioral therapy to the psychological problems of late life. In S. H. Zarit, and B. G. Knight (Eds.) (1996). *A guide to psychotherapy and aging: Effective clinical interventions in a life-stage context* (pp. 61–82). Washington, DC: American Psychological Association.

Gallo, J. J., Cooper-Patrick, L., and Lesikar, S. (1998). Depressive symptons of whites and African Americans aged 60 years and older. *Journal of Gerontology: Psychological Sciences, 53B,* P277–P286.

Gallup Organization (1997a). *Global Study of Family Values.* Princeton, NJ: The Gallup Organization.

Gallup Organization (1997b, October). *Many women cite spousal abuse: Job performance affected.* Princeton, NJ: Gallup Organization.

Gallup Organization (1999a). *Long-term Gallup Poll Trends: A Portrait of American Public Opinion Through the 20th Century.* Princeton, NJ: Gallup Organization.

Gallup Organization (1999b). *Some change over time in American attitudes toward homosexuality but negativity remains.* Princeton, NJ: Gallup Organization.

Galton, F. (1883). *Inquiries into human faculty and its development.* New York: Macmillan.

Gang, A. (1991). Ergonomics and the older worker: An overview. *Experimental Aging Research, 17,* 143–155.

Ganong, L., Coleman, J., McDaniel, A. K., and Killian, T. (1998). Attitudes regarding obligations to assist an older parent or stepparent following later life remarriage. *Journal of Marriage and the Family, 60,* 595–610.

Gardner, J. (April, 1995) Worker Displacement: A decade of change. *Monthly Labor Review,* pp. 45–57.

Garfein, A. J., and Herzog, A. R. (1995). Robust aging among the young-old, old-old, and oldest-old. *Journal of Gerontology: Social Sciences, 50B,* S77–S87.

Garfein, A. J., and Smyer, M. A. (1991). P-technique factor analyses of the multiple affect adjective check list (MAACL). *Journal of Psychopathology and Behavioral Assessment, 13,* 155–171.

Gaskill, L. R. (1991). Same-sex and cross-sex mentoring of female proteges: A comparative analysis. *Career Development Quarterly, 40,* 48–63.

Gatz, M., (1989). Clinical psychology and aging. In M. Storandt and G. R. VandenBos (Eds.), *The adult years: Change and continuity* (pp. 79–114). Washington, DC: American Psychological Association.

Gatz, M., Bengtson, V. L., and Blum, M. J. (1990) Caregiving families. In J. E. Birren and K. W. Schaie (Eds.), *Handbook of the psychology of aging* (3rd ed., pp. 405–426). San Diego: Academic Press.

Gatz, M., Fiske, A., Fox, S. L., Kaskie, B., Kasl-Godley, K., McCallum, T., and Wetherell, J. (1998). Empirically-validated psychological treatments for older adults. *Journal of Mental Health and Aging, 4,* 9–46.

Gatz, M., Karel, M. J., and Wolkenstein, B. (1991). Survey of providers of psychological services to older adults. *Professional Psychology: Research and Practice, 22,* 413–415.

Gatz, M., Kasl–Godley, J. E., and Karel, M. J. (1996). Aging and mental disorders. In J. E. Birren and K. W. Schaie (Eds.), *Handbook of the psychology of aging* (4th ed., pp. 365–382). San Diego, CA: Academic Press.

Gatz, M., Pedersen, N. L., Berg, S., Johansson, B., Johnasson, K., Mortimer, J. A., Posner, S. F., Viitanen, M., Winblad, B., and Ahlbom, A. (1997). Heritability for Alzheimer's disease: The study of dementia in Swedish twins. *Journal of Gerontology: Medical Sciences, 53A,* M117–M125.

Gatz, M., Pedersen, N. L., and Harris, J. (1987). Measurement characteristics of the mental health scale from the OARS. *Journal of Gerontology, 42,* 332–335.

Gatz, M., and Smyer, M. A. (1992). The mental health system and older adults in the 1990s. *American Psychologist, 47,* 741–751.

Gatz, M., and Smyer, M. A. (2001). Mental health and aging at the outset of the twenty first century. In J. E. Birren and K. W. Schaie (Eds.), *Handbook of the psychology of aging* (5th ed.). San Diego, CA: Academic Press.

Gatz, M., VandenBos, G., Pino, C., and Popkin, S. (1985). Psychological interventions with older adults. In J. E. Birren and K. W. Schaie (Eds.), *Handbook of the psychology of aging* (2nd ed., pp. 755–785). New York: Van Nostrand Reinhold.

Gavey, N. (1991). Sexual victimization prevalence among New Zealand university students. *Journal of Consulting and Clinical Psychology, 59,* 464–466.

Gaylord, S. A., and Zung, W. W. K. (1987). Affective disorders among the aging. In L. L. Carstensen and B. A. Edelstein (Eds.), *Handbook of clinical gerontology* (pp. 76–95). New York: Pergamon..

Geary, D. C., Hamson, C. O., Chen, G. P., Liu, F., Hoard, M. K., and Salthouse, T. A. (1997). Computational and reasoning abilities in arithmetic: Cross-generational change in China and the United States. *Psychonomics Bulletin and Review, 4,* 425–430.

Geller, M. M., and Simpson, P. (1999) In search of late career: A review of contemporary social science research applicable to the understanding of late career. *Human Resource Management Review, 9,* 309–349.

Gendell, M. and Siegel, J. S. (1996). Trends in retirement age in the United States 1955–1993 by sex and race. *Journal of Gerontology: Social Science, 51B,* S132–S139.

George, L. K. (1993). *Financial security in later life: The subjective side.* Philadelphia, PA: Boettner Institute of Financial Gerontology.

George, L. K. (2000). Well being and sense of self: What we know and what we need to know. In K. W. Schaie and J. Hendricks (Eds.), *Evolution of the aging self: Societal impacts* (pp. 1–35). New York: Springer Publishing Co.

George, L. K., Fillenbaum, G., and Palmore, E. (1984). Sex differences in the antecedents and consequences of retirement. *Journal of Gerontology, 39,* 364–371.

Gergen, K. J., and Gergen, M. M. (2000). The new aging: Self construction and social values.In K. W. Schaie and J. Hendricks (Eds.), *Evolution of the aging self: Societal impacts* (pp. 281–306). New York: Springer Publishing Co.

Gergen, M. M., and Gergen, K. J. (1987). The self in temporal perspective. In R. Abeles (Ed.), *Life span perspective and social psychology* (pp. 121–137). Hillsdale, NJ: Erlbaum.

Geringer, E. S., Perlmuter, L. C., Stern, T. A., and Nathan, D. M. (1988). Age and diabetes related changes in verbal fluency. *Journal of Geriatric Psychiatry and Neurology, 1,* 11–15.

Gerner, R., and Jarvik, L. F. (1984). Antidepressant drug treatment in the elderly. In E. Friedman, F. Mann, and S. Gerson (Eds.), *Depression and antidepressants: Implications for consideration and treatment.* New York: Raven Press.

Giarusso, R., Feng, D., Silverstein, M., and Bengtson, V. L. (2000). Self in the context of the family, In K. W. Schaie and J. Hendricks (Eds.), *Evolution of the aging self: Societal impacts* (pp. 63–97). New York: Springer Publishing Co.

Giarusso, R., Stallings, M., and Bengtson, V. L. (1995). The "intergenerational stake" hypothesis revisited: Parent-child differences. In V. L. Bengtson, K. W. Schaie and L. M. Burton (Eds.), *Adult intergenerational relations: Effects of social change* (pp. 227–276). New York: Springer Publishing Co.

Gibson, R. C. (1987). Reconceptualizing retirement for black Americans. *Gerontologist, 27,* 691–698.

Gibson, R. C. (1991). The subjective retirement of black Americans. *Journal of Gerontology, 46,* S204–S209.

Gibson, R. C., and Jackson, J. S. (1992). The black oldest old: Health, functioning, and informal support. In R. M. Suzman, D. P. Willis, and K. G. Manton (Eds.), *The oldest old* (pp. 321–340). New York: Oxford University Press.

Gilewski, M. J. (1986). Group therapy with cognitively impaired older adults. *Clinical Gerontologist, 5,* 281–294.

Gilewski, M. J., and Zelinski, E. M. (1988). Memory Functioning Questionnaire (MFQ). *Psychopharmacology Bulletin, 24,* 665–670.

Gill, R. T. (1996). Whatever happened to the American way of death. *The Public Interest, Spring,* 105–117.

Gille, A. (1992). Living accommodations for the urban elderly. In M. Bergener, K. Hasegawa, S. I. Finkel,

and T. Nishimura (Eds.), *Aging and mental disorders: International perspectives* (pp. 56–64). New York: Springer Publishing Co.

Gilligan, C. (1982). *In a different voice: Psychological theory and women's development.* Cambridge, MA: Harvard University Press.

Gilligan, C. (1996). The centrality of relationship in human development: A puzzle, some evidence, and a theory. In G. Noam and K. W. Fischer (Eds.), *Development and vulnerability in close relationships. The Jean Piaget symposium series* (pp. 237–261). Mahwah, NJ: Lawrence Erlbaum Associates,

Gilligan, C. and Attanucci, J. (1988). Two moral orientations: Gender differences and similarities. *Merrill-Palmer Quarterly, 3,* 223–237.

Gilmore, A., and Gilmore, S. (1988). *Towards a safer death: Multidisciplinary aspects of terminal care.* New York: Plenum.

Gittings, N. S., and Fozard, J. L. (1986). Age related changes in visual acuity. *Experimental Gerontology, 21,* 423–433.

Gittings, N. S., Fozard, J. L., and Shock, N. W. (1987, November). *Age changes in stereopsis, visual acuity and color vision.* Paper presented at annual meeting of the Gerontological Society of America, Washington, DC.

Glantz M. (1981). Predictions of elderly drug abuse. *Journal of Psychoactive Drugs, 13,* 117–126.

Glass, T. A., Seeman, T. E., Herzog, A. R., Kahn, H., and Berkman, L. F. (1995) Change in productive activity in late adulthood: MacArthur studies of successful aging. *Journal of Gerontology: Social Sciences, 50B,* S65–S76.

Glenn, N. D. (1998a). The course of marital success and failure in five American 10-year marriage cohorts.

Journal of Marriage and the Family, 60, 569–576.

Glenn, N. D. (1998b). Values, attitudes and the state of American marriage. In S. J. Ferguson (Ed.), *Shifting the center: Understanding contemporary families* (pp 133–145). Mountain View, CA: Mayfield.

Glick, P. C. and Lin, S. (1986). More young adults are living with their parents: Who are they? *Journal of Marriage and the Family, 48*, 105–112.

Goetting, M. A., Martin, P., Poon, L. W., and Johnson, M. A. (1996). The economic well-being of community-dwelling centenarians. *Journal of Aging Studies, 10*, 43–55.

Gohm, C. L., Oishi, S., Darlington, J., and Diener, E. (1998). Culture, parental conflict, parental marital status, and the subjective well-being of young adults. *Journal of Marriage and the Family, 60*, 319–334.

Golant, S. M. (1992). *Housing America's elderly.* Newbury Park, CA: Sage.

Goldberg, L. R. (1993). The structure of personality traits: Vertical and horizontal aspects. In D. C. Funder, R. Parke, C. Tomlinson-Keasey, and K. Widaman (Eds.), *Studying lives through time: Approaches to personality and development* (pp. 169–188). Washington, DC: American Psychological Association.

Goldscheider, F. K., and Goldscheider, C. (1989). Family structure and conflict: nest-leaving expectations of young adults and their parents. *Journal of Marriage and the Family, 51*, 87–97.

Goldscheider, F. K., and Goldscheider, C. (1991). The intergenerational flow of income: Family structure and the status of black Americans. *Journal of Marriage and the Family, 53*, 499–508.

Goldscheider, F. K., and Goldscheider, C. (1994). Leaving and returning home in the twentieth century. *Population Reference Bureau Bulletin, 48*, 1–43.

Goldscheider, F. K., and Lawton, L. (1998). Family experiences and the erosion of support for intergenerational co-residence. *Journal of Marriage and the Family, 60*, 623–632.

Goldscheider, F. K. and Waite, L. (1991). *New families, no families? The transformation of the American home.* Berkeley, CA: University of California Press.

Goldstein, K. (1939). *The organism.* New York: American Book.

Goleman, D. (1988). Erikson, in his own old age, expands his view of life. *New York Times,* June 14, pp. C1, 14.

Gonyea, J. G. (1998). Midlife and menopause: Uncharted territories for baby boomer women. *Generations, 22*, 87–89.

Goodman, M. J. (1982). A critique of menopause research. In A. Voda, M. Dinnerstein, and S. O'Donnell (Eds.), *Changing perspective on menopause.* Austin, TX: University of Texas Press.

Gottman, J. M., Coan, J., Carrere, S., and Swanson, C. (1998). Predicting marital happiness and stability from newlywed interactions. *Journal of Marriage and the Family, 60*, 5–22.

Gough, H. G. (1987). *Manual for the California Psychological Inventory.* Palo Alto, CA: Consulting Psychologists Press.

Gough, H. G., Bradley, P., and Bedeian, A. G. (1996). *ACI scales for Tellegen's three higher-order traits.* Unpublished. Manuscript. Berkeley, CA: Institute for Personality Research, University of California.

Gould, E., Reeves, A. J., Graziano, M. S. A., and Gross, C. G. (1999). Neurogenesis in the neocortex of adult primates. *Science, 286,* 548–552.

Gould, R. L. (1978). *Transformations: Growth and change in adult life.* New York: Simon and Schuster.

Grant, H., and Dweck, C. S. (1999). Content versus structure in motivation and self-regulation. In R. S. Wyer, Jr. (Ed.), *Perspectives on behavioral self-regulation: Advances in social cognition* (Vol. XII, pp.161–174). Mahwah, NJ: Lawrence Erlbaum Associates.

Gratton, B. (1993). The creation of retirement: Families, individuals and the Social Security movement. In K. W. Schaie and W. A. Achenbaum (Eds.), *Societal impact on aging: Historical perspectives* (pp. 45–73). New York: Springer Publishing Co.

Green, S. K. (1981). Attitudes and perceptions about the elderly: Current and future perspectives. *Aging and Human Development, 13,* 95–115.

Greenfield, L. A., Rand, M. R., and Craven, D. (1998) *Violence by intimates: Analysis of data on crimes by current or former spouses, boyfriends, and girlfriends.* Washington, DC: Bureau of Justice Statistics, U.S. Department of Justice.

Greenough, W. T., and Green, E. J. (1981). Experience and the changing brain. In J. L. MacGaugh and S. B. Kiesler (Eds.), *Aging: Biology and behavior.* New York: Academic Press.

Greenwell, L., and Bengtson, V. L. (1997). Geographic distance and contact between middle-aged children and their parents: The effects of social class over 20 years. *Journal of Gerontology: Social Sciences, 52,* S13–S26.

Gribbin, K., and Schaie, K. W. (1979). Selective attrition in longitudinal studies: A cohort-sequential approach. In H. Orino, K. Shimada, M. Iriki, and D. Maeda (Eds.), *Recent advances in gerontology.* Amsterdam, The Netherlands: Excerpta Medica.

Gribbin, K., Schaie, K. W., and Parham, I. A. (1980). Complexities of life style and maintenance of intellectual abilities. *Journal of Social Issues, 36,* 47–61.

Grossberg, G., Manepalli, J., Hassan, R., and Solomon, K. (1992). Use of psychotropics in the elderly in the United States: An overview. In M. Bergener, K. Hasegawa, S.. I. Finkel, and T. Nishimura (Eds.), *Aging and mental disorders: International perspectives* (pp. 212–238). New York: Springer Publishing Co.

Grover, D. R., and Hertzog, C. (1991). Relationships between intellectual control beliefs and psychometric intelligence in adulthood. *Journal of Gerontology: Psychological Science, 46,* P109–P115.

Gruber-Baldini, A. L. (1991). *The impact of health and disease on cognitive ability in adulthood and old age in the Seattle Longitudinal Study.* Unpublished doctoral dissertation. University Park, PA: The Pennsylvania State University.

Gruber-Baldini, A. L., Schaie, K. W., and Willis, S. L. (1995). Similarity in married couples: A longitudinal study of mental abilities and flexibility-rigidity. *Journal of Personality and Social Psychology: Personality Processes and Individual Differences, 69,* 191–203.

Guilford, J. P. (1967). *The nature of human intelligence.* New York: McGraw-Hill.

Guilford, J. P., and Hoepfner, R. (1971). *The analysis of intelligence.* New York: McGraw-Hill.

Guillemard, A. M. (1992). Europäische Persecktiven der Alternspolitik [European perspectives on the politics of aging]. In P. B. Baltes and J. Mittelstrass (Eds.), *Zukunft des Alterns und gesellschaftlische Entwicklung* (pp. 614–639). Berlin, Germany: De Gruyter.

Gurland, B. J., and Meyers, B. S. (1988). Geriatric psychiatry. In J. A. Talbott, R. E. Hales, and S. C. Yudofsky (Eds.), *Textbook of psychiatry* (pp. 1117–1139). Washington, DC: American Psychiatry Press.

Gutmann, D. L. (1975). Parenthood: Key to the comparative psychology of the life cycle? In N. Datan and L. Ginsberg (Eds.), *Life-span developmental psychology: Normative life crises.* New York: Academic Press.

Gutmann, D. L. (1977). The cross-cultural perspective: Notes toward a comparative psychology of aging. In J. E. Birren and K. W. Schaie (Eds.), *Handbook of the psychology of aging.* New York: Van Nostrand Reinhold.

Gutmann, D. L. (1987). *Reclaimed powers: Toward a new psychology of men and women in later life.* New York: Basic Books.

Gutmann, D. L. (1992a). Culture and mental health in later life revisited. In J. E.. Birren, R. B. Sloane, G. D Cohen, N. R. Hoyman, B. Lebowitz, M. H. Wykle, and D. E. Deutchman (Eds.), *Handbook of mental health and aging* (2nd ed., pp. 75–97). San Diego, CA: Academic Press.

Gutmann, D. L. (1992b). Toward a dynamic geropsychology. In J. Barren, M. Eagle, and D. Welitzky (Eds.), *Interface of psychoanalysis and psychology* (pp. 284–295). Washington, DC: American Psychological Association.

Gutmann, D. L. (1997). *The human elder in nature, culture, and society.* Boulder, CO: Westview Press.

Haan, N., Milsap, R., and Hattka, E. (1986). As time goes by: Change and stability in personality over fifty years. *Psychology and Aging, 1,* 220–232.

Haas, L. (1991). Equal parenthood and social policy: Lessons from a study of parental leave in Sweden. In J. S. Hude and M. J. Essex (Eds.), *Parental leave and child care: Setting a research and policy agenda* (pp. 375–405). Philadelphia, PA: Temple University Press.

Haas, L. (1992). *Equal parenthood and social policy: A study of parental leave in Sweden.* Albany, NY: State University of New York Press.

Haber, C., and Gratton, B. (1994). *Old age and the search for security: An American social history.* Bloomington, IN: Indiana University press.

Hachinsky, V. (1992). Preventable senility: A call for action against the vascular dementia. *Lancet, 340,* 645–648.

Hackett, G. (1997). Promise and problems in theory and research on women's career development. *Journal of Counseling Psychology, 44,* 184–188.

Hagberg, B. (1995). The individual's life history as a formative experience to aging. In B. K. Haight and J. D. Webster (Eds.), *The art and science of reminiscing* (pp. 61-75). Washington, DC: Taylor and Francis.

Hagestad, G. O. (1985). Continuity and connectedness. In V. L. Bengtson and J. Robertson (Eds.), *Grandparenthood.* Beverly Hills, CA: Sage.

Hagestad, G. O. (1986). The family: Women and grandparents as kinkeepers. In A. Pifer and L. Bronte (Eds.), *Our aging society: Paradox and promise.* New York: Norton.

Hagestad, G. O., and Neugarten, B. L. (1985). Age and the life course. In R. Binstock and E. Shanas (Eds.), *Handbook of aging and the social sciences* (2nd ed., pp. 35–81). New York: Van Nostrand Reinhold.

Hagnell, O., Franck, A., Grasbeck, A., Ohman, R., Otterbeck, L., and Rorsman, B. (1993). Vascular dementia in the Lundby study. 2. An attempt to identify possible risk factors. *Neuropsychobiology. 27,* 210–216.

Haight, B. K., Coleman, P. and Lord, K. (1994). The linchpins of a successful life review: Structure, evaluation and individuality. In B. K. Haight and J. Webster (Eds.), *The art and science of reminiscing: Theory, research, methods and applications.* Washington, DC: Taylor and Francis.

Haight, B. K., and Webster, J. D. (Eds.) (1995). *The art and science of reminiscing: Theory, research methods, and applications.* Washington, DC: Taylor and Francis.

Hakeem, A., Sandoval, G. R, Jones, M., and Allman, J. (1996). Brain and life span in primates.In J. E. Birren and K. W. Schaie (Eds.), *Handbook of the psychology of aging* (4th ed.). San Diego, CA: Academic Press.

Hall, G. S. (1922). *Senescence, the last half of life.* New York: Appleton.

Haller, M., Hollinger, F., and Raubal, O. (1987). Levaithan or welfare state: Attitudes toward the role of government in six advanced western nations. In J. W. Becker, J. A. Davies, P. Ester, and P. Mohler (Eds.), *Attitudes to inequality and the role of government* (pp. 33–62). Rijswijk, The Netherlands: Social en Cultureel Planbureau.

Hambrick, D. Z., Salthouse, T. A., and Meinz, E. J. (1999). Prediction of crossword puzzle proficiency and moderators of age-cognition relations. *Journal of Experimental Psychology: General, 128,* 131–164.

Hamon, R. R., and Blieszner, R. (1990). Filial responsibility expectations among adult child-older parent pairs. *Journal of Gerontology: Psychological Sciences, 45,* P110–P112.

Hankin, B. L., Abramson, L. Y., Moffitt, T. E., Silva, P. A., McGee, R., and Angell, K. E. (1998). Development of depression from preadolescence to young adulthood: Emerging gender differences in a 10-year longitudinal study. *Journal of Abnormal Psychology, 107,* 128–140.

Hansen, L. A. (1994). Pathology of the other dementias. In R. D. Terry, R. Katzman and K. L. Blick (Eds.), *Alzheimer Disease* (pp. 123–166). New York: Raven Press.

Hansson, R. O., DeKoekkoek, P. D, Neece,W. M., and Patterson, D. W. (1997). Successful aging at work: Annual Review 1992–1996: The older worker and transitions to retirement. *Journal of Vocational Behavior, 51,* 202–233.

Hansson, R. O., Vanzetti, N. A., Fairchild, S. K., and Berry, J. O. (1999) The impact of bereavement on families. In B. De Vries (Ed.), *End of life issues* (pp. 99–118). New York: Springer Publishing Co.

Hareven, T. K. (1982). The life course and aging in historical perspective. In T. K. Hareven and K. J. Adams (Eds.), *Aging and life course transitions: An interdisciplinary perspective* (pp. 1–26). New York: Guilford Press.

Harker, L., and Solomon, M. (1996). Change in goals and values of men and women from early to mature adulthood. *Journal of Adult Development, 3,* 133–143.

Harkins, S. W., Price, D. D., and Martelli, M. (1986). Effects of age on pain perception. *Journal of Gerontology, 41,* 58–63.

Harlow, C. W. (1991). *Female victims of violent crime.* Washington, DC: U.S. Department of Justice: Bureau of Justice Statistics (NCJ–126826).

Harmon-Jones, E., Simon, L., Greenberg, J., Pyszcynski, T., Solomon, S., and McGregor, H. (1997). Terror management theory and self-esteem: Evidence that increased self-esteem reduces mortality salience effects. *Journal of Personality and Social Psychology, 72,* 24–36.

Harris, T. (1986). Aging in the eighties, prevalence and impact of urinary problems in individuals age 65 years and over. *NCHS Advance Data, 121,* 1–8.

Hasegawa, K. (1985). The epidemiology of depression in later life. *Journal of Affecive Disorders, Suppl. 1,* 3–6.

Hasher, L., and Zacks, R. T. (1979). Automatic and effortful processes in memory. *Journal of Experimental Psychology: General, 108,* 356–388.

Hassing, L., and Bäckman, L. (1997) Episodic memory functioning in population-based samples of very old adults with Alzheimer's disease and vascular dementia. *Dementia and Geriatric Cognitive Disorders, 8,* 376–383.

Hassmén, P., Ceci, R., and Bäckman, L. (1992). Exercise for older women: Training method and its influences on physical and cognitive performance. *European Journal of Applied Physiology, 64,* 460–466.

Hatch, N. O. (1989). *The democratization of American Christianity.* New Haven, CT: Yale University Press.

Haug, M. R., Musil, C. M., Warner C. D., and Morris, D. L. (1998). Interpreting bodily changes as illness: A longitudinal study of older adults. *Social Science and Medicine, 46,* 1553–1567.

Haug, M. R., and Ory, M. G. (1987). Issues in elderly patient-provider interaction. *Research on Aging, 9,* 3–44.

Havighurst, R. J. (1972). *Developmental tasks and education* (3rd ed.). New York: McKay.

Havighurst, R. J., and Albrecht, R. (1953). *Older people.* New York: Longmans Green.

Havighurst, R. J., Neugarten, B. L., and Tobin, S. S. (1968). Disengagement and patterns of aging. In B. L. Neugarten (Ed.), *Middle age and aging.* Chicago, IL: University of Chicago Press.

Haviland, J. M., and Kramer, D. A. (1991). Affect-cognition relationship in adolescent diaries: The case of Anne Frank. *Human Development, 34,* 143–159.

Hayes, B. C., and VanderHeuvel, A. (1994). Attitudes towards mandatory retirement: an international comparison. *Aging and Human Development, 39,* 209–231.

Hayflick, L. (1985). Theories of biological aging. *Experimental Gerontology, 20,* 145–159.

Hayflick, L. (1987). The cell biology and theoretical basis of human aging. In L. Carstensen and B. Edelstein (Eds.), *Handbook of clinical gerontology* (pp. 3–17). New York: Pergamon.

Hays, J. C., Fillenbaum , G. G., Gold, D. T., Shanley, M. C., and Blazer D. G. (1995). Black-white and urban-rural differences in stability of household composition among elderly persons. *Journal of Gerontology: Social Sciences, 50B,* S301–S311.

Hays, J. C., Gold, D. B., Flint, E. P., and Winer, E. P. (1999). In B. De Vries (Ed.), *End of life issues* (pp. 3–21). New York: Springer Publishing Co.

Hayslip, B., Jr. (1989). Alternative mechanisms for improvements in fluid ability performance among older adults. *Psychology and Aging, 4,* 122–124.

Hayslip, B. Jr., and Leon, J. (1992). *Hospice care.* Newbury Park, CA: Sage Publications.

Hayslip, B. Jr., Servaty, H. L., and Guarniaccia, C. A. (1999). Age cohort differences in the perception of funerals. In B. De Vries (Ed.), *End of life issues* (pp. 23–36). New York: Springer Publishing Co.

Hayward, M. D., Friedman, S., and Chen, H. (1998). Career trajectories and older men's retirement. *Journal of Gerontology: Social Sciences, 53B,* S91–S103.

Hayward, M. D., and Grady, W. R. (1990). Work and retirement among a cohort of older men in the United States, 1966–1983. *Demography, 27,* 337–356.

Health Care Financing Administration, Office of National Cost Estimates (1990). National health expenditures, 1988. *Health Care Financing Review, 11,* 1–41.

Heaton, T. B., and Blake, A. M. (1999). Gender differences in determinants of marital disruption. *Journal of Family Issues, 20,* 25–45.

Heaton, T. B., Jacobson, C. K., and Holland, K. (1999). Persistence and change in decisions to remain childless. *Journal of Marriage and the Family, 61,* 531–539.

Heckert, D. A., Nowak, T. C., and Snyder, K. A. (1998). The impact of husbands' and wives' relative earnings on marital disruption. *Journal of Marriage and the Family, 60,* 690–703.

Heckhausen, J., and Brim, O. G. (1997). Perceived problems for self and others: Self-protection by social downgrading throughout adulthood. *Psychology and Aging, 12,* 610–619.

Heckhausen, J., and Dweck, C. S. (Eds). (1998). *Motivation and self-regulation across the life span.* New York: Cambridge University Press.

Heckhausen, J., and Krueger, J. (1993). Developmental expectations for the self and most other people: Age-grading in three functions of social comparison. *Developmental Psychology, 29,* 539–548.

Heckhausen, J., and Lang, F. R. (1996). Social construction and old age: Normative conceptions and interpersonal processes. In G. R. Semin and K. Fiedler (Eds.), *Applied social psychology* (pp. 374–398). London, UK: Sage.

Heckhausen, J., and Schulz, R. (1995) A life-span theory of control, *Psychological Review, 102,* 284–304.

Heidemann, B., Suhomlinova, O., and O'Rand, A. M. (1998). Economic independence, economic status, and empty nest in midlife marital disruption. *Journal of Marriage and the Family. 60,* 219–231.

Helson, R. (1992). Women's difficult times and the rewriting of the life story. *Psychology of Women Quarterly, 16,* 331–347.

Helson, R. (1993). Comparing longitudinal studies of adult development: Towards a paradigm of tension beween stability and change. In D. Funder, R. Parke, C. Tomlinson-Kesey, and K. Widaman (Eds.), *Studying lives through time.* Washington, DC: American Psychological Association.

Helson, R., and Klohnen, E. C. (1998). Affective coloring of personality from young adulthood to midlife. *Personality and Social Psychology Bulletin, 24,* 241–252.

Helson, R., Mitchell, V., and Moane, G. (1984). Personality and patterns of adherence and non-adherence to the social clock. *Journal of Personality and Social Psychology, 46,* 1079–1096.

Helson, R., and Moane, G. (1987). Personality change in women from college to midlife. *Journal of Personality and Social Psychology, 53,* 176–186.

Helson, R., and Picano, J. (1990). Is the traditional role bad for women? *Journal of Personality and Social Psychology, 59,* 111–120.

Helson, R., and Wink, P. (1992). Personality change in women from the early 40s to the early 50s. *Psychology and Aging, 7,* 46–55.

Henderson. A. S., and Hasegawa, K. (1992). The epidemiolgy of dementia and depression in later life. In M. Bergener, K. Hasegawa, S. I. Finkel, and T. Nishimura (Eds.), *Aging and mental disorders: International perspectives* (pp. 65–79). New York: Springer Publishing Co.

Hendrick, C., and Hendrick, S. (1983). *Liking, loving, and relating.* Monterey, CA: Brooks/Cole.

Hendrick, C., and Hendrick, S. (1986). A theory and method of love. *Journal of Personality and Social Psychology, 50,* 392–402.

Hendrick, C., and Hendrick, S. (1988). Roles and gender in relationships. In S. Duck (Ed.), *Handbook of personal relationships: Theory, research and intervention* (pp. 429–448). New York: Wiley.

Hendricks, J., and Achenbaum, A. (1999). Historical development of theories of aging. In V. L. Bengtson and K. W. Schaie (Eds.), *Handbook of theories of aging* (pp. 21–39). New York: Springer Publishing Co.

Hendy, H. M., Nelson G. K., and Greco M. E. (1998). Social cognitive predictors of nutritional risk in rural elderly adults. *International Journal of Aging and Human Development. 47,* 299–327.

Henretta, J. C. (2001). Work and retirement. In R. H. Binstock and L. K. George (Eds.). *Handbook of aging and the social sciences* (5th ed). San Diego, Ca: Academic Press.

Henretta, J. C., Chang, C. G., and O'Rand, A. M. (1992). Retirement reason versus retirement process: Examining the reasons for retirement typology. *Journal of Gerontology: Social Sciences, 47,* S1–7.

Henretta, J. C., O'Rand, A., and Chan, C. G. (1993). Joint role investments and synchronization of retirement: A sequential approach to couples' retirement timing. *Social Forces, 71,* 981–1000.

Henry, J. P. (1985). Relation of psychosocial factors to the senile dementias. In J. E. Birren, M. L. Gilhooly, and S. H. Zarit (Eds.), *The dementias: Policy and management.* Englewood Cliffs, NJ: Prentice-Hall.

Herek, G., and Glunt, E. (1988). An epidemic of stigma: Public reactions to AIDS. *American Psychologist, 43,* 886–891.

Herlitz, A., and Bäckman, L. (1990). Recall of object names and colors of objects in normal aging and Alzheimer's disease. *Archives of Gerontology and Geriatrics, 11,* 147–154.

Herlitz, A., Lipinska, B., and Bäckman, L. (1992). Utilization of cognitive support for episodic remembering Alzheimer's disease. In L. Bäckman (Ed.), *Memory functioning in dementia* (pp. 73–96). Amsterdam: North Holland.

Herlitz, A., Nilsson, G,. and Bäckman, L. (1997). Gender differences in episodic memory. *Memory and Cognition, 25,* 801–811.

Herring, C. (1995). African Americans and disadvantage in the U.S. labor market. *African American Research Perspectives, 2,* 55–61.

Hertzog, C. (1996). Research design in studies of aging and cognition. In J. E. Birren and K. W. Schaie (Eds.), *Handbook of the psychology of aging* (4th ed., pp. 24–37). San Diego: Academic Press.

Hertzog, C., Dixon, R. A., and Hultsch, D. F. (1990). Metamemory in adulthood: Differentiating knowledge, belief, and behavior. In T. M. Hess (Ed.), *Aging and cognition: Knowledge organization and utilization.* Amsterdam, The Netherlands: Elsevier.

Hertzog, C., and Hultsch, D. F. (2000). Metacognition in adulthood and old age In F.I.M. Craik and T. A. Salthouse (Eds.), *Handbook of aging and cognition* (2nd ed., pp. 417–176). Mahwah, NJ: Lawrence Erlbaum.

Hertzog, C., Schaie, K. W., and Gribbin, K. (1978). Cardiovascular disease and changes in intellectual functioning from middle to old age. *Journal of Gerontology, 33,* 872–883.

Herz, D. E. (April, 1995). Work after early retirement: An increasing trend among men. *Monthly Labor Review.* pp. 13–20.

Herzog, A. R., Franks, M. M., Markus, H. R., and Holmberg, D. (1998). Activities and well-being in older age: Effects of self-concept and educational attainment. *Psychology and Aging, 13,* 179–185.

Herzog, A. R., House, J. S., and Morgan, J. N. (1991). Relation of work and retirement to health and well-being in older age. *Psychology and Aging, 6,* 202–211.

Herzog, A. R., and Markus H. R. (1999). The self-concept in life span and aging research. In V. L. Bengtson and K. W. Schaie (Eds.), *Handbook of theories of aging* (pp. 227–252). New York: Springer Publishing, Co.

Herzog, A. R., and Rodgers, W. L. (1999). Cognitive performance measures in survey research on older adults. In N. Schwarz, D. C. Park, B. Knaüper, and S. Sudman (Eds.), *Cognition, aging, and self-reports* (pp. 327–340). Philadelphia, PA: Psychology Press.

Hess, T. M., and Pullen, S. M. (1996). Memory in context. In F. Blanchard-Fields and T. M. Hess (Eds.), *Perspectives on cognitive change in adulthood and aging* (pp. 387–428). New York: McGraw-Hill.

Hetherington, E. M. (1989). Coping with family transitions: Winners, losers, and survivors. *Child Development, 60,* 1–14.

Hetherington, E. M. (Ed.) (1999). *Coping with divorce, single parenting, and remarriage: A risk and resiliency perspective.* Mahwah, NJ: Erlbaum.

Hetherington, E. M., Bridges, M,. and Insabella, G. M. (1998). What matters? What does not? Five perspectives on the association between marital transitions and children's adjustment. *American Psychologist, 53,* 167–184.

Hetherington, E. M., and Stanley-Hagan, M. (1999). The adjustment of children with divorced parents: A risk and resiliency perspective. *Journal of Child Psychology and Psychiatry and Allied Disciplines, 40,* 129–140.

Hetherington, M. M., and Rolls, B. J. (1996). Sensory-specific satiety: Theoretical Frameworks and central characteristics. In E. D. Capaldi (Ed). *Why we eat what we eat: The psychology of eating* (pp. 267–290). Washington, DC: American Psychological Association.

Hightower, E. (1990). Adolescent interpersonal and family precursors of positive mental health at midlife.

Journal of Youth and Adolescence, 19, 257–275.

Hill, R., Foote, N., Aldonus, J., Carlson, R., and MacDonald, R. (1970). *Family development in three generations.* New York: Schenkman.

Himes, C. L., Hogan, D. P., and Eggebeen, D. J. (1996). Living arrangements of minority elders. *Journal of Gerontology: Social Sciences, 50B,* S42–S48.

Hing, E. (1994). Characteristics of elderly home health patients: Preliminary data from the 1992 National Home and Hospice Care Survey. *Advance data, No. 247.* Washington, DC: National Center for Health Statistics.

Hirdes, J. P., and Forbes, W. F. (1992). The importance of social relationships, socioeconomic status and health practices with respect to mortality among healthy Ontario males. *Journal of Clinical Epidemiology, 45,* 175–182.

Hirdes, J. P., and Forbes, W. F. (1993). Factors associated with the maintenance of good self-rated health. *Journal of Aging and Health, 5,* 101–123.

Hirsch, K. (1990). Fraternities of fear: Gang rape, male bonding and the silencing of women. *Ms, 1,* 52–56.

Hite, S. (1976). *The Hite report.* New York: Dell.

Hofer, M. (1984). Psychobiological perspective on bereavement. *Psychosomatic Medicine, 46,* 183–197.

Hofer, S. M., Horn, J. L., and Eber, E. W. (1997). A robust five-factor structure of the 16PF: Strong evidence from independent rotation and confirmatory factorial invariance procedures. *Personality and Individual Differences, 23,* 247–269.

Hofferth, S., Kahn, J., and Baldwin, W. (1987). Premarital sexual activity among U.S. women over the past three decades. *Family Planning Perspectives, 19,* 46–53.

Hoffman, L. W., McManus, K. A., and Brackbill, Y. (1987). The value of children to young and elderly parents. *International Journal of Aging and Human Development, 25,* 309–322.

Hogan, D. (1985). Parental influences on the timing of early life transitions. In Z. Blau (Ed.), *Current perspectives on aging and the life cycle* (Vol. 1, pp. 1–59). Greenwich, CT: JAI Press.

Hogan, D., and Mochizui, T. (1988). Demographic transitions and the life course: lessons from Japanese and American comparisons. *Journal of Family History, 13,* 291–305.

Hogarth, T., and Barth, M. C. (1991). Costs and benefits of hiring older workers: A case study of B and Q. *International Journal of Manpower. 12,* 5–17.

Holland, J. L. (1966). *The psychology of vocational choice.* Waltham, MA: Blaisdell.

Holland, J. L. (1985). *Making vocational choices: A theory of vocational personalities and work environments.* Englewood Cliffs, NJ: Prentice-Hall.

Holland, J. L. (1996). Exploring careers with a typology: What we have learned and some new directions. *American Psychologist. 51,* 397–406.

Holstein, M.B. (2000). The "New Aging": Imagining alternative futures. In K. W. Schaie and J. Hendricks (Eds.), *Evolution of the aging self: Societal impacts* (pp. 319–332). New York: Springer Publishing Co.

Homma, A., Shimonaka, Y., and Nakazato, K. (1992). Mental function and health status of centenarians. In M. Bergener, K. Hasegawa, S. I. Finkel, and T. Nishimura (Eds.),

Aging and mental disorders: International perspectives (pp. 23–37). New York: Springer Publishing Co.

Hook, S. (1987). In defense of voluntary euthanasia. *New York Times,* March 1.

Hooker, K. (1992). Possible selves and perceived health in older adults and college students. *Journal of Gerontology: Psychological Sciences, 47,* P85–95.

Hooker, K., and Kaus, C. R. (1992). Possible selves and health behaviors in later life. *Journal of Aging and Health, 4,* 390–411.

Hooker, K., and Kaus, C. R. (1994). Health-related possible selves in young and middle adulthood. *Psychology and Aging, 9,*126–133.

Hooker, K., Monahan, D. J., Bowman, S. R., Frazier, L. D., and Shifren K. (1998). Personality counts for a lot: Predictors of mental and physical health of spouse caregivers in two disease groups. *Journal of Gerontology: Psychological Sciences, 53B,* P73–P85.

Hooker, K., Monahan, D., Shifren, K., and Hutchinson, C. (1992). Mental and physical health of spouse caregivers; The role of personality. *Psychology and Aging, 7,* 367–375.

Hooper, F., Fitzgerald, J., and Papalia, D. (1971). Piagetian theory and the aging process: Extensions and speculations. *Aging and Human Development, 2,* 3–20.

Hooper, F. H., Hooper, J. O., and Colbert, K. C. (1984). *Personality and memory correlates of intellectual functioning.* Basel, Switzerland: S. Karger.

Horgas, A. L., Wahl, H. W., and Baltes, M. M. (1995). Dependency in late life. In L. L. Carstensen, B. A. Edelstein, and L. Dornbrand (Eds.), *The practical handbook of clinical gerontology* (pp. 54–75). Thousand Oaks, CA: Sage.

Horn, J. L. (1978). Human ability systems. In P. B. Baltes (Ed.), *Life-span developmental psychology* (Vol. 1). New York: Academic Press.

Horn, J. L. (1982). The theory of fluid and crystallized intelligence in relation to concepts of cognitive psychology and aging in adulthood. In F. I. M. Craik and S. Trehub (Eds.), *Aging and cognitive processes.* New York: Plenum.

Horn, J. L., and Hofer, S. M. (1992). Major abilities and development in the adult period. In R. J. Sternberg and C. A. Berg (Eds.), *Intellectual development* (pp. 44–99). Cambridge: Cambridge University Press.

Horn, J. L., and McArdle, J. J. (1992). A practical and theoretical guide to measurement invariance in aging research. *Experimental Aging Research, 18,* 117–144.

Hornblum, J. N., and Overton, W. F. (1976). Area and volume conservation among the elderly: Assessment and training. *Developmental Psychology, 12,* 68–74.

Horner, K. L., Rushton, J. P., and Vernon, P. A. (1986). Relation between aging and research productivity. *Psychology and Aging, 1,* 319–324.

Horton, A. M. Jr., and Fogelman, C. J. (1991). Behavioral treatment of aged alcoholics and drug addicts. In P. A. Wisocki (Ed.), *Handbook of clinical behavior therapy with the elderly client* (pp. 299–316). New York: Plenum.

Howard, A. (1986). College experiences and managerial performance. *Journal of Applied Psychology, 71,* 530–552.

Howard, A. (Ed). (1995). *The changing nature of work.* San Francisco, Ca: Jossey-Bass.

Howard, A. (1998). New careers and older workers. In K. W. Schaie and C.

Schooler (Eds.), *Impact of work on older adults* (pp. 235–244). New York: Springer Publishing Co.

Howard, A., and Bray, D. W. (1988). *Managerial lives in transition: Advancing age and changing times.* New York: Guilford Press.

Howard, A., and Bray, D. W. (1990). Predictions of managerial success over long periods of time: Lessons from the Management Progress Study. In K. E. Clark and M. B. Clark (Eds), *Measures of leadership.* (pp. 113–130). West Orange, NJ: Leadership Library of America.

Howard, J. H., and Howard, D. V. (1997). Learning and memory. In A. D. Fisk and W. A. Rogers (Eds.), *Handbook of human factors and the older adult.* (pp 2–26). San Diego: Academic Press.

Howe, G. R., and Rohan, T. E. (1993). The epidemiology of breast cancer in women. In J. Lorrain (Ed.), *Comprehensive management of menopause.* New York: Springer-Verlag.

Hoyer, W. J., and Hooker, K. (1989). Psychology of adult development and aging: New approaches and methodologies in the developmental study of cognition and personality. In N. J. Osgood and A. Sontz (Eds.), *The science and practice of gerontology.* Westport, CT: Greenwood Press..

Hoyert, D. L., Kochanek, K. D., and Murphy, S. L. (1999). Deaths: Final Data for 1997. *National Vital statistics reports,* Vol. 47, No. 19. Hyattsville, MD:National Center for Health Statistics.

Huang, L., Cartwright, W. S., and Hu, T. (1988). The economic cost of senile dementia in the United States, 1985. *Public Health Reports, 103,* 3–7.

Hull, C. L. (1943). *Principles of behavior: An introduction to behavior theory.* New York: Appleton-Century-Crofts.

Hultsch, D. (1985). Adult memory: What are the limits? In E. M. Gee and G. M. Gutman (Eds.), *Canadian gerontological collection V* (pp. 20–52). Winnipeg, Manitoba: Canadian Association on Gerontology.

Hultsch, D., and Deutsch, F. (1981). *Adult development and aging.* New York: McGraw-Hill.

Hultsch, D., and Dixon, R. (1984). Memory for text materials in adulthood. In P. B. Baltes and O. G. Brim, Jr. (Eds.), *Life-span development and behavior* (Vol. 6). New York: Academic Press.

Hultsch, D., and Dixon, R. (1990). Learning and memory and aging. In J. E. Birren and K. W. Schaie (Eds.), *Handbook of the psychology of aging* (3rd ed.). San Diego: Academic Press.

Hultsch, D. F., Hammer, M., and Small, B. J. (1993). Age differences in cognitive performance in later life: Relationships to self-reported health and activity life style. *Journal of Gerontology: Psychological Sciences, 48,* P1–P11

Hultsch, D. F., Hertzog, C., Dixon, R. A., and Small, B. J. (1998). *Memory changes in the aged.* New York: Cambridge University Press.

Hultsch, D. F., Hertzog, C., Small, B. J., McDonald-Miszlak, L., and Dixon, R. A. (1992). Short-term longitudinal change in cognitive performance in later life. *Psychology and Aging, 7,* 571–584.

Hummert, M, L., Garstka, T. A., Shaner, J. L., and Strahm, S. (1994). Stereotypes of the elderly held by young, middle-aged, and elderly adults. *Jour-*

nal of Gerontology: Psychological Sciences, 49, P240–P249.

Humphreys, L. G., and Parsons, C. K. (1979). Piagetian tasks measure intelligence and intelligence tests assess cognitive development: A reanalysis. *Intelligence, 3,* 369–382.

Humphreys, L. G., Rich, S. A., and Davey, T. C. (1985). A Piagetian test of general intelligence. *Developmental Psychology, 21,* 872–877.

Hussain, R. A. (1987). Wandering and disorientation. In L. L. Carstensen and B. A. Edelstein (Eds.), *Handbook of clinical gerontology* (pp. 177–188). New York: Pergamon.

Huston, P., McHale, S., and Crouter, A. (1984). When the honeymoon's over: Changes in the marriage relationship over the first year. In R. Gilmour and S. Duck (Eds.), *Key issues in personal relations.* Hillsdale, NJ: Erlbaum.

Huyck, M. H. (1989). Midlife parental imperatives. In R. A. Kalish (Ed.), *Midlife loss: Coping strategies* (pp 115–148). Newbury Park, CA: Sage.

Huyck, M. J., and Gutmann, D. L. (1999). Developmental issues in psychotherapy with older men. In M. Duffy (Ed.), *Handbook of counseling and psychotherapy with older adults* (pp. 77–90). New York: Wiley.

Hyde, J. S., Essex, M., and Horton, F. (1993). Fathers and parental leave: Attitudes and experiences. *Journal of Family Issues, 14,* 616–641.

Hyde, J. S., and Phyllis, D. E. (1979). Androgyny across the life span. *Developmental Psychology, 15,* 334–336.

Ikels, C. (1988). Delayed reciprocity and the support networks of the childless elderly. *Journal of Comparative Family Studies, 19,* 99–112.

Ikels, C. (1997). Long-term care and the disabled elderly in urban China. In J. Sokolovsky (Ed.), *The cultural context of aging: Worldwide perspectives* (2nd ed., pp. 452–471). Westport, CT: Berger and Garvey.

Ikels, C. (1998a). Aging. In S. Lowe (Ed.), *Handbook of immigrant health.* New York: Plenum.

Ikels, C. (1998b) The experience of dementia in China. *Culture, Medicine, and Psychiatry, 22,* 257–283..

Ikels, C., Keith, J., and Fry, C. L. (1988). The use of qualitative methodologies in large-scale cross-cultural research. In S. Reinharz and G. D. Rowles (Eds.), *Contemporary practice in cross-cultural research* (pp. 274–296). New York: Springer Publishing Co.

Ikels, C., Dickerson-Putman, J., Draper, P., Fry, C. L., Glascock, A, Harpending, H., and Keith J. (1995). Comparative perspectives on successful aging. In L. Bond, S. Cutler and A. Grams (Eds.), *Promoting successful and productive aging* (pp. 304–323). Thousand Oaks, CA: Sage.

Inkeles, A., and Usui, C. (1989). Retirement patterns in cross-national perspective. In D. I. Kertzer and K. W. Schaie (Eds.), *Age structuring in comparative perspective.* New York: Erlbaum.

Jackson, D. J., Longino, C. F., Jr., Zimmerman, R. S., and Bradsher, J. E. (1991). Environmental adjustments to declining functional ability. *Research on Aging, 13,* 289–309.

Jackson, G. R., Owsley, C., Cordel, E. P., and Finley, C. D. (1998). Aging and scotopic sensitivity. *Vision Research, 38, 3655–3662.*

Jackson, J. S. (1996a). A life-course perspective on physical and psychological health. In R. J. Resnick and R. H. Rozensky (Eds.), *Health psychology through the life span* (pp. 39–57). Washington, DC: American Psychological Association.

Jackson, J. S. (1996b). Aging productively: An economic network model. In M. M. Baltes and L. Montada (Eds.), *Produktives Leben im Alter* [Productive living in old age] (pp. 211–238). Frankfurt, Germany: Campus Verlag.

Jackson, J. S., Antonucci, T. C., and Gibson, R. C. (1990). Social relations, productive activities, and coping with stress in late life. In M. A. P. Stephens, J. H. Crowther, S. E. Hobfoil, and D. L. Tennenbaum (Eds.), *Stress and coping in later life families* (pp. 193–212. New York: Hemisphere.

Jackson, J. S., Chatters, L. M., and Neighbors, H. W. (1982). The mental health status of older black Americans: A national study. *The Black Scholar,* January/February, 21–35.

Jackson, J. S., Williams, D.R., and Gomberg, E. S. L. (1998). A life-course perspective on aging and alcohol use and abuse among African Americans. In R. A. Zucker and E. S. L. Gomberg (Eds.). *The epidemiology of elderly drinking problems: The backdrop of aging.* Washington, DC: U.S. Government Printing Office.

Janus, S. S., and Janus, C. L. (1993). *The Janus Report on sexual behavior.* New York: Wiley and Sons.

Jaques, E. (1965). Death and the midlife crisis. *International Journal of Psychoanalysis, 46,* 502–514.

Jaques, E. (1993). The midlife crisis. In G. H. Pollock and S. I. Greenspan (Eds.), *The course of life: Vol. 5. Early adulthood* (pp 201–231). Madison, CT: International Universities Press.

Jarvik, L. F., and Bank, L. (1983). Aging twins: Longitudinal aging data. In K. W. Schaie (Ed.), *Longitudinal studies of adult psychological development.* New York: Guilford Press.

Jarvik, L. F., and Perl, M. (1981). Overview of physiologic dysfunctions related to psychiatric problems in the elderly. In A. Levenson and R. C. W. Hall (Eds.), *Psychiatric management of physical disease in the elderly.* New York: Raven Press.

Jensen, E., Dehlin, O., Hagberg, B., Samuelsson, G., and Svensson, T. (1998). Insomnia in an 80-year-old population: Relation to medical, psychological and social factors. *Journal of Sleep Research, 7,* 183–189,

Johansson, B., Allen-Burge, R., and Zarit, S. H. (1997). Self-reports on memory functioning in a longitudinal study of the oldest old: Relation to current, prospective, and retrospective performance. *Journal of Gerontology: Psychological Sciences, 52B,* P139–P146.

Johansson, B., and Berg, S. (1989). The robustness of the terminal decline phenomenon: Longitudinal data from the digit-span test. *Journal of Gerontology: Psychological Sciences, 44,* P184–P186.

Johansson, B., and Zarit, S. H. (1995). Prevalence and incidence of dementia in the oldest old: A longitudinal study of a population-based sample of 84-90-year-olds in Sweden. *International Journal of Geriatric Psychiatry, 10,* 359–366.

Johannson, C. B., and Campbell, D. P. (1971). Stability of the Strong Vocational Interest Blank for men. *Journal of Applied Psychology, 55,* 34–36.

Johnson, C. L. (1994a). Differential expectations and realities: Race, socioeconomic status and health of the oldest old. *International Journal of Aging and Human Development, 38,* 13–27.

Johnson, C. L. (1994b). Introduction: Social and cultural diversity of the oldest-old. *International Journal of Aging and Human Development, 38,* 1–12.

Johnson, D. R., and Booth, A. (1998). Marital quality: A product of the dynamic environment or individual factors. *Social Forces, 76,* 883–904.

Johnson, H. A. (1985). Is aging physiological or pathological? In H. A. Johnson (Ed.), *Relation between normal aging and disease* (pp. 239–247). New York: Raven Press.

Johnson, M. P., Caughlin, J. P.. and Huston, T. L. (1999). The tripartite nature of marital commitment: Personal, moral, and structural reasons to stay married. *Journal of Marriage and the Family, 61,* 160–177.

Jones, A. L. (1994). Hospices and home health agencies: Data from the 1991 National Health Provider Inventory. *Advance Data, No. 257.* Washington, DC: National Center for Health Statistics.

Jung, C. G. (1960). The stages of life. In H. Reed, M. Fordham, and G. Adler (Eds.), *Collected works* (Vol. 8 pp. 387–403). Princeton, NJ: Princeton University Press. (Original work published in 1931).

Kagan, J. (1980). Perspectives on continuity. In O. G. Brim, Jr., and J. Kagan (Eds.), *Constancy and change in human development.* Cambridge, MA: Harvard University Press.

Kahana, B., and Kahana, E. (1982). Environmental continuity, discontinuity, futurity and adaptation of the aged. In G. Rowles and R. Ohta (Eds.), *Aging and milieu: Environmental perspectives on growing old.* New York: Academic Press.

Kahana, B., and Kahana, E. (1998). Toward a temporal-spatial model of cumulative life stress. In J.Lomranz (Ed.), *Handbook of aging and mental health* pp. 153–177). New York: Plenum.

Kahn, R. L. (1994). Social support: Content, causes and consequences. In R. P. Abeles, H. C. Gift, and M. G. Ory (Eds.), *Aging and quality of life.* New York: Springer Publishing Co.

Kahn, S., Zimmerman, G., Csikszentmihalyi, M., and Getzels, J. W. (1985). Relations between identity in young adulthood and intimacy at midlife. *Journal of Personality and Social Psychology, 49,* 1316–1322.

Kaldor, P. (1987). *Who goes where? Who doesn't care: Going to church in Australia.* Homebush West, NSW, Australia: Lancer Books.

Kalish, R. A. (1975). *Late adulthood.* Monterey, CA: Brooks/Cole.

Kalish, R. A. (1985). *Death, grief and caring relationships* (2nd ed.). Monterey, CA: Brooks/Cole.

Kalish, R. A., and Reynolds, D. K. (1976). *Death and ethnicity.* Los Angeles, CA: University of Southern California Press.

Kamen-Siegel, L., Rodin, J., Seligman, M. E. P., and Dwyer, J. (1991). Explanatory style and cell-mediated immunity in elderly men and women. *Health Psychology,* 10, 229–235.

Kalmijn, M. (1999). Father involvement in childrearing and the perceived stability of marriage. *Journal of Marriage and the Family, 61,* 409–421.

Kamo, Y, and Zhou, M. (1994). Living arrangements of elderly Chinese and Japanese in the United States. *Journal of Marriage and the Family, 56,* 544–558.

Kannisto, V. (1994). *Development of oldest-old mortality, 1950–1990: Evidence from 28 developed countries.* Odense, Denmark: Odense University Press.

Kapantais, G., and Powell-Griner, E. (1989). Characteristics of persons dying from AIDS: Preliminary data from the 1986 Mortality Followback Survey. *Advance data from vital and health statistics,* No. 173. Hyattsville, MD: National Center for Health Statistics.

Kaplan, K, J,, Lachenmeier, F., O'Dell, J. C., ande Uziel, O. (In press). Psychosocial versus biomedical risk factors in Kevorkian's first 47 "suicides." *Omega, Journal of Death and Dying.*

Kaplowitz P. B., and Oberfield, S. E. (1999). Reexamination of the age limit for defining when puberty is precocious in girls in the United States: Implications for evaluation and treatment. *Pediatrics. 104,* 936–41.

Kaplowitz, S. A., Osuch, J. R., Safron, D., and Campo, S. (1999). Physician communication with seriously ill cancer patients: Results of a survey of physicians. In B. De Vries (Ed.), *End of life issues* (pp. 205–227). New York: Springer Publishing Co.

Kapp, M. B. (1998). De facto health-care rationing by age: The law has no remedy. *Journal of Legal Medicine, 19,* 323–349.

Karasek, R. A., and Theorell, T. (1990). *Healthy work: Stress, productivity and the reconstruction of working life.* New York: Basic Books.

Kasper, J. D. (1988). *Aging alone: Profiles and projections.* New York: The Commonwealth Fund.

Kassirer, J. P. (1997). Competent care for the dying instead of physician-assisted suicide. *New England Journal of Medicine, January 2,* pp. 54–58.

Kastenbaum, R. M. (1985). Dying and death: A lifespan approach. In J. E. Birren and K. W. Schaie (Eds.), *Handbook of the psychology of aging* (2nd ed.). New York: Van Nostrand Reinhold.

Kastenbaum, R. M. (1988). Safe death in the post modern world. In A. Gilmore and S. Gilmore (Eds.), *A safer death: Multidisciplinary aspects of terminal care.* New York: Plenum.

Kastenbaum, R.M.(1992). The creative process: A life-span approach. In T. R. Cole, D. D. VanTassel, and R. Kastenbaum (Eds.), *Handbook of the humanities and aging* (pp. 285–306). New York: Springer Publishing Co.

Kastenbaum, R. M. (1998). *Death, society, and human experience* (6th ed.). Boston, MA: Allyn and Bacon.

Kastenbaum, R. M. (2000). *The psychology of death* (3rd ed.). New York: Springer Publishing Co.

Kastenbaum, R. M,, and Herman, C. (1997). Death personification in the Kevorkian era. *Death Studies, 21,* 115–130.

Kaszniak, A. W. (1990). Psychological assessment of the aging individual. In J. E. Birren and K. W. Schaie (Eds.), *Handbook of the psychology of aging* (3rd ed., pp. 427–445). San Diego: Academic Press.

Kaszniak, A. W. (1996a). Techniques and instruments for assessment of the elderly. In S. H. Zarit, and B. G. Knight (Eds.) (1996). *A guide to psychotherapy and aging: Effective clinical interventions in a life-stage context* (pp. 163–218). Washington, DC: American Psychological Association.

Kaszniak, A. W. (1996b). The role of clinical neuropsychology in the assessment and care of persons with Alzheimer's disease. In R. J. Resnick and R. H. Rozensky (Eds.), *Health psychology through the life span* (pp. 239–264). Washington, DC: American Psychological Association.

Kaszniak, A. W., Garron, D. C., Fox, J. H., Bergen, D., and Huckman, M. (1979). Cerebral atrophy, EEG slowing, age, education, and cognitive functioning in suspected dementia. *Neurology, 29,* 1273–1279.

Katz, S., Branch, L. G., Branson, M. H., Papsidero, J. A., Beck, J. C., and Greer, D. S. (1983). Active life expectancy. *The New England Journal of Medicine, 309,* 1218–1224.

Katzman, R. (1994). Apolipoprotein E4 as the major genetic susceptibility factor for Alzheimer disease. In R. D. Terry, R. Katzman, and K. L. Blick (Eds.), *Alzheimer Disease* (pp. 455–458). New York: Raven Press.

Katzman, R., Aronson, M., and Fuld, P. (1989). Development of dementing illnesses in an 80-year-old volunteer cohort. *Annals of Neurology, 25,* 317–324.

Katzman, R., and Kawas, C. H. (1994). The epidemiology of dementia and Alzheimer disease. In R. D. Terry, R. Katzman, and K. L. Blick (Eds.), *Alzheimer Disease* (pp. 105–122). New York: Raven Press.

Kaufert, P. A., Lock, M., McKinlay, S., Beyenne, Y., Coope, J., Davis, D., Eliasson, M., Gognalons-Nicolet, M., Goodman, M., and Holte, A. (1986). Menopause research: The Korpilampi workshop. *Social Science and Medicine, 22,* 1285–1289.

Kaufert, P. A. and McKinlay, S. M. (1985). Estrogen replacement therapy: The production of medical knowledge and the emergence of policy. In E. Lewin and V. Olesen (Eds.), *Women, health, and healing: To-ward a new perspective.* New York: Tavistock.

Kaufman, A. S., Kaufman, J. L., McLean, J. E., and Reynolds, C. R. (1991). Is the pattern of intellectual growth and decline across the adult life span different for men and women? *Journal of Clinical Psychology, 47,* 801–812.

Kausler, D. H. (1982). *Experimental psychology and human aging.* New York: Wiley.

Keith, J. (1988). Participant observation. In K. W. Schaie, R. T. Campbell, W. Meredith, and S. C. Rawlings (Eds.), *Methodological issues in aging research* (pp. 211–230). New York: Springer Publishing Co.

Kelly, J. (1977). The aging male homosexual: Myth and reality. *Gerontologist, 17,* 328–332.

Kelsey, J. L., and Horn-Ross, P. L (1993). Breast cancer: magnitude of the problem and descriptive epidemiology. *Epidemiologic Reviews, 15*(1), 7–16.

Kemper, S. (2001). Language. In J. E. Birren and K. W. Schaie (Eds.). *Handbook of the psychology of aging* (5th ed.). San Diego, Ca: Academic Press.

Kendall, K. E., Wisocki, P. A., and Pers, D. B. (1991). Nutritional factors in aging. In P. A. Wisocki (Ed.), *Handbook of clinical behavior therapy with the elderly client* (pp. 73–96). New York: Plenum.

Kennett, J., and Schaie, K. W. (1999, November). *Early psychometric indicators of possible dementia in later life: ApoE genotypes and cognitive performance in community-dwelling.* Paper presented at the annual meeting of the Gerontological Society of America, San Francisco, CA.

Kenyon, G., Ruth, J. E., and Mader W. (1999). Elements of a narrative gerontology. In V. L. Bengtson and K. W. Schaie (Eds.), *Handbook of theories of aging* (pp. 40–58). New York: Springer Publishing, Co.

Kerckhoff, A. C., and Davis, K. (1962). Value consensus and complementarity in mate selection. *American Sociological Review, 27,* 295–303.

Kessler, R. C., Crum, R. M., Warner, L. A., Nelson, C. B., Schulenberg, J., and Anthony, J. C. (1997). Lifetime co-occurrence of DSM-III-R alcohol abuse and dependence with other psychiatric disorders in the national comorbidity survey, *Archives of General Psychiatry, 54,* 313–321.

Kettle, P. (1997, October). Alzheimer's disease: An update. *Hospital Medicine,* 12–20.

Kettle, P. (1999). Management of Alzheimer's disease in the home care setting. *Home Health Care Consultant, 6 (5),* 1–6.

Keunen, J. E. E., Van Norren, D., and Van Meel, G. J. (1987). Density of foveal cone pigments at older ages. *Investigative Ophthalmology and Visual Science, 28,* 895–991.

Keuthen, N. (1991). Medication and the aging organism. In P. Wisocki (Ed.), *Handbook of clinical behavior therapy with the elderly client* (pp. 55–72). New York: Plenum.

Keuthen, N., and Wisocki, P. A. (1991). Behavioral medicine for the health concern of the elderly. In P. A. Wisocki (Ed.), *Handbook of clinical behavior therapy with the elderly client* (pp. 363–382). New York: Plenum.

Keyes, C. L. M, and Ryff, C. D. (1998). Generativity in adult lives: Social structural contours and quality of life consequences.In D. P. McAdams and E. de St. Aubin (Eds.), *Generativity and adult development* (pp. 227–263).

Washington, DC: American Psychological Association.

Keyes, C. L. M., and Ryff, C. D. (1999). Psychological well-being in midlife. In S. L. Willis and J. E. Reid (Eds.), *Life in the middle: Psychological and social development in middle age* (pp. 161–181). San Diego, CA: Academic.

Khachaturian, Z. S., Phelps, C. H., and Buckholz, N. S. (1994). The prospect of developing treatments for Alzheimer disease. In R. D. Terry, R. Katzman and K. L. Blick (Eds.), *Alzheimer Disease* (pp, 445–454). New York: Raven Press.

Kim, J. E., Nesselroade, J. R., and Featherman, D. L. (1996). The state component in self-reported world views and religious beliefs of older adults: The MacArthur Successful Aging studies. *Psychology and Aging. 11,* 396–407

King, E., Rimer, B. K., Balsheim, A., Ross, E., and Seay, J. (1993). Mammography-related beliefs of older women. *Journal of Aging and Health, 5,* 82–100.

King, V., and Elder, G. H., Jr. (1995). American children view their grandparents: Linked lives across three rural generations. *Journal of Marriage and the Family, 57,* 165–178.

King, V. and Elder, G. H., Jr.(1997). The legacy of grandparenting: Childhood experiences with grandparents and current involvement with grandchildren. *Journal of Marriage and the Family, 59,* 848–859.

King, V. and Elder, G. H., Jr. (1998) Perceived self-efficacy and grandparenting. *Journal of Gerontology: Social Sciences, 53B,* S249–S257.

Kinnunen, U., and Pulkkinen, L. (1998a). Linking economic stress to marital quality among Finnish marital couples. *Journal of Family Issues, 19,* 705.

Kinnunen, U., and Pulkkinen, L. (1998b). Linking job characteristics to parenting behavior via job-related affect. In J. R. M. Gerris (Ed.), *Dynamics of parenting.* Hillsdale, NJ: Erlbaum.

Kinsella, D., and Gist, Y.J. (1995) *Older workers, retirement and pensions: A comparative international chartbook.* Washington DC: U.S. Bureau of the Census.

Kinsey, A. C., Pomeroy, W. B., and Martin, C. E. (1948). *Sexual behavior in the human male.* Philadelphia, PA: Saunders.

Kinsey, A. C., Pomeroy, W. B., Martin, C. E., and Gebhard, P. H. (1953). *Sexual behavior in the human female.* Philadelphia, PA: Saunders.

Kivela, S. L, Pahkala, K, and Honkakoski, A (1986). Sexual desire, intercourse, and related factors among elderly Finns. *Nordic Sexology, 4,* 18–27.

Kivitt, V. R. (1991). Centrality of the grandfather role among older rural black and white men. *Journal of Gerontology: Social Sciences, 46,* S250–S258.

Kleban, M. H., Lawton, M. P., Nesselroade, J. R., and Parmelee, P. (1992). The structure of variation in affect among depressed and nondepressed elders. *Journal of Gerontology, 47,* P190–P198.

Kleemeier, R. W. (1962). Intellectual change in the senium. *Proceedings of the Social Statistics Section of the American Statistical Association,* 290–295.

Kliegl, R., Smith, J., and Baltes, P. B. (1989). Testing the limits and the study of adult age differences in cognitive plasticity of a mnemonic skill. *Developmental Psychology, 25,* 247–256.

Kline, D. W. (1994). Optimizing the visibility of displays for older observers.

Experimental Aging Research, 20, 11–23.

Kline, D. W., and Schieber, F. (1985). Vision and aging. In J. E. Birren and K. W. Schaie (Eds.), *Handbook of the psychology of aging* (2nd ed.). New York: Van Nostrand Reinhold.

Kline, D. W., and Scialfa, C. T. (1996). Visual and auditory aging. In J. E. Birren and K. W. Schaie (Eds.), *Handbook of the psychology of aging* (4th ed.). San Diego, CA: Academic Press.

Klohnen, E. C., Vandewater, E. A., and Young, A. (1996). Negotiating the middle years: Ego-resiliency and successful midlife adjustment in women. *Psychology and Aging, 11,* 431–442.

Knäuper, B., Belli, R. F., Hill, D. H., and Herzog, A. R. (1997). Question difficulty and respondents' cognitive ability: The effect on data quality. *Journal of Official Statistics, 13,* 181–199.

Knight, B. G. (1986). *Psychotherapy with older adults.* Beverly Hills, CA: Sage.

Knight, B. G. (1996). Psychodynamic therapy with older adults: Lessons from scientific gerontology. In R. T. Woods (Ed.), *Clinical psychology of aging* (pp. 546–560). New York: Wiley.

Knight, B. G., and McCallum, T. J. (1998). Adapting psychotherapeutic practice for older clients: Implications of the contextual, cohort-based, maturity, specific challenge model. *Professional Psychology: Research and Practice, 29,* 15–22.

Knight, B. G., Teri, L., Santos, J. and Wohlford. P. (Eds.) (1995). *Applying geropsychology to services for older adults: Implications for training and practice.* Washington, DC: American Psychological Association.

Koenig, H. G. (1995). Use of acute hospital services and mortality among religious and nonreligious copers with medical illness. *Journal of Religious Gerontology, 9*, 1–22.

Koeppi, P. M., Bolla-Wilson, K., and Bleecker, M. L. (1989). The MMPI: Regional difference or normal aging? *Journal of Gerontology: Psychological Sciences, 44*, P95–P99.

Koepsel, T. D., Wolf, M. E., McCloskey, L., Buchner, D.M., Louie, D., Wagner, E. H., and Thompson, R. S. (1994). Medical conditions and motor vehicle collision injuries in older adults. *Journal of the American Geriatrics Society, 42*, 495–700.

Kogan, N. (1990). Personality and aging. In J. E. Birren and K. W. Schaie (Eds.), *Handbook of the psychology of aging* (3rd ed., pp. 330–346). San Diego: Academic Press.

Kohlberg, L. (1973). Continuities in childhood and adult moral development revisited. In P. B. Baltes and K. W. Schaie (Eds.), *Life-span developmental psychology: Personality and socialization.* New York: Academic Press.

Kohlberg, L. (1981). *The philosophy of moral development: Moral stages and the idea of justice* (Vol. 1). San Francisco, CA: Harper and Row.

Kohlberg, L., and Kramer, R. (1969). Continuities and discontinuities in childhood and adult moral development. *Human Development, 12*, 93–120.

Kohli, M., and Von Kondratowitz, J. J. (1987). Retirement in Germany: Towards the construction of the citizen of the work society: Science, psychological, and health factors. In K. S. Markides and C. L. Cooper (Eds.), *Retirement in industrialized societies* (pp. 131–166). New York: Wiley.

Kohn, M. L. (1977). *Class and conformity: A study in values.* Chicago, IL: University of Chicago Press.

Kohn, M. L. (1989). Comments on Lachman's "Personality and Aging at the Crossroads." In K. W. Schaie and C. Schooler (Eds.), *Social structure and aging: Psychological processes* (pp. 199–205). Hillsdale, NJ: Erlbaum.

Kohn, M. L., and Schooler, C. (1983). *Work and personality: An inquiry into the impact of social stratification.* Norwood, NJ: Ablex.

Kohn, M. L., and Slomczynski, K. M. (1990). *Social structure and self-direction: A comparative analysis of the United States and Poland.* New York: Blackwell.

Kohn, R. R. (1985). Aging and age-related diseases: Normal processes. In H. A. Johnson (Ed.), *Relations between normal aging and disease.* New York: Raven Press.

Koretz, J. F., Cook, C. A., and Kaufman, P. L. (1997). Accommodation and presbyopia in the human eye. Changes in the anterior segment and crystalline lens with focus. *Investigative Ophthalmology and Visual Science. 38*, 569-578.

Koss, M. P., and Dinero, T. E. (1988). Predictors of sexual aggression among a national sample of male college students. *Annals of the New York Academy of Sciences, 528*, 133–147.

Koss, M. P., Dinero, T. E., Seibel, C. A., and Cox, S. L. (1988). Stranger and acquaintance rape: Are there differences in the victim's experience? *Psychology of Women Quarterly, 12*, 1–24.

Koss, M. P., and Gaines, J. A. (1993). The prediction of sexual aggression by alcohol use, athletic participation and fraternity affiliation. *Journal of Interpersonal Violence, 8*, 94–108.

Koss, M. P., Gidycz, C., and Wisniewski, N. (1987). The scope of rape: Sexual aggression and victimization in a national sample of students in higher education. *Journal of Consulting and Clinical Psychology, 55,* 162–170.

Kothari, M. L., and Mehta, L. A. (1986). *Death: A new perspective on the phenomena of disease and dying.* New York: Marion Boyars.

Kottler-Cope, S., and Camp, C. J. (1990). Memory and aging. In E. Lovelace (Ed.), *Aging and cognition: Mental processes, self-awareness, and interventions.* Amsterdam, The Netherlands: North Holland.

Kovar, M. G. (1980). Morbidity and health care utilization. In S. G. Haynes and M. Feinleib (Eds.), *Proceedings of the second conference on the epidemiology of aging.* Washington, DC: U.S. Government Printing Office.

Kraft, J. M., and Werner, J. S. (1999). Aging and saturation of colors. *Journal of the Optical Society of America, 16,* 223–234.

Kramarow, E., Lentzner, H., Rooks, R., Weeks, J., and Saydah, S. (1999). *Health and Aging Chartbook: Health, United States, 1999.* Hyattsville, MD: National Center for Health Statistics.

Kramer, D. A. (1983). Post-formal operations? A need for further conceptualization. *Human Development, 26,* 91–105.

Kramer, D. A., and Woodruff, D. S. (1986). Relativistic and dialectical thought in three adult age groups. *Human Development, 29,* 280–290.

Krause, N. (1988). Stressful life events and physican utilization. *Journal of Gerontology: Social Sciences, 43,* S53–S61.

Krause, N. (1991). Stress and isolation from close ties in later life. *Journal of Gerontology: Social Sciences, 46,* S183–194.

Krause, N. (1998). Stressors in highly valued roles, religious coping and mortality. *Psychology and Aging, 13,* 242–255.

Krause, N. (2001). Social supports. In R. H. Binstock and L. K. George (Eds.) *Handbook of aging and the social sciences* (5th ed.). San Diego, CA: Academic Press.

Krause, N., Jay, G., and Liang, J. (1991). Financial strain and psychological well-being among the American and Japanese elderly. *Psychology and Aging, 6,* 170–181.

Krauss, I. K. (1980). Between- and within-group comparisons in aging research. In L. W. Poon (Ed.), *Aging in the 1980s* (pp. 542–551). Washington, DC: American Psychological Association.

Kronenberg, F. (1990). Hot flashes: Epidemiology and physiology. *Annals of the New York Academy of Sciences, 592,* 52–86.

Krueger, J., and Heckhausen, J. (1993). Personality development across the adult life span: Subjective conceptions versus cross-sectional contrasts. *Journal of Gerontology: Psychological Sciences, 48,* pp. 100–108.

Krueger, R. F., Caspi, A., Moffitt, T. E., Silva, P. A., and McGee, R. (1996). Personality traits are differentially linked to mental disorders: A multi-trait-multidiagnosis study of an adolescent birth cohort. *Journal of Abnormal Psychology, 105,* 299–312.

Kruse, A., Lindenberger, U., and Baltes, P. B. (1993). The power of combining real-time, microgenetic, and simulation approaches. In D. Magnusson and P. Casaer (Eds.), *Longitudinal research on individual development, present status, and future perpectives.* New York: Cambridge University Press.

Kübler-Ross, E. (1969). *On death and dying.* New York: Macmillan.

Kübler-Ross, E. (1974). *Questions and answers on death and dying.* New York: Macmillan.

Kübler-Ross, E. (1981). *Living with death and dying.* New York: Macmillan.

Kübler-Ross, E. (1991). The dying child. In D. Papadatou, and C. Papadatou (Eds.), *Children and death* (pp. 147–175). New York: Hemisphere.

Kuczmarski, R. J., Flegal, K. M., Campbell, S. M., and Johnson, C. J. (1994). Increasing evidence of overweight among U.S. adults. The National Helth and Nutrition Examination Surveys, 1960–1991. *Journal of the American Medical Association, 272,* 205–211.

Kuhn, D., Pennington, N., and Leadbeater, B. (1983). Adult thinking in developmental perspective. In P. B. Baltes and O. G. Brim, Jr. (Eds.), *Life span development and behavior* (Vol. 5). New York: Academic Press.

Kuller, L. H. (2000). Hormone replacement therapy and coronary heart disease. A new debate. *Medical Clinics of North America, 84,* 181–198.

Kunkel, S. R. (1979). *Sex differences in adjustment to widowhood.* Unpublished master's thesis. Miami University, Oxford, OH.

Kurdek, L. A. (1988). Perceived social support in gays and lesbians in cohabiting relationships. *Journal of Personality and Social Psychology, 54,* 504–509.

Kurdek, L. A. (1993). The allocation of household labor in gay, lesbian, and heterosexual married couples. *Journal of Social Issues, 49,* 127–139.

Kurdek, L. A. (1998). Relationship outcomes and their predictors: Longitudinal evidence from heterosexual married, gay cohabiting and lesbian cohabiting couples. *Journal of Marriage and the Family, 60,* 553–568.

Kurdek, L. A., and Schmitt, P. (1986). Relationship quality of partners in heterosexual married, heterosexual cohabiting, and gay and lesbian relationships. *Journal of Personality and Social psychology, 51,* 711–720.

Kutza, E. A. (1998). A look at national policy and the baby boom generation. *Generations, 22,* 16–21.

Labouvie-Vief, G. (1985). Intelligence and cognition. In J. E. Birren and K. W. Schaie (Eds.), *Handbook of the psychology of aging* (2nd ed.). New York: Van Nostrand Reinhold.

Labouvie-Vief, G. (1990). Wisdom as integrated thought: Historical and developmental perspectives. In R. J. Sternberg, (Ed.), *Wisdom: Its nature, origins, and development.* Cambridge, UK: Cambridge University Press.

Labouvie-Vief, G. (1992). A neo-Piagetian perspective on adult cognitive development. In R. J. Sternberg and C. A. Berg (Eds.), *Intellectual development* (pp. 197-228). Cambridge, UK: Cambridge University Press.

Labouvie-Vief, G. (1999). Emotions in adulthood. In V. L. Bengtson and K. W. Schaie (Eds.). *Handbook of theories of aging.* (pp 253–270). New York: Springer Publishing Co.

Labouvie-Vief, G., and Chandler, M. J. (1978). Cognitive development and life-span developmental theory: Idealistic versus contextual perspectives. In P. B. Baltes (Ed.), *Life-span developmental psychology* (Vol. 1). New York: Academic Press.

Labouvie-Vief, G., and Hakim-Larson, J. (1989). Developmental shifts in adult thought. In S. Hunter and M. Sundel (Eds.), *Midlife myths: Issues, findings and practical implications* (pp. 69–96). Newbury Park, CA: Sage.

Lacey, J. I. (1967). Psychophysiological approaches to the evaluation of psychotherapeutic process and outcome. In E. A. Rubenstein and M. B. Parloff (Eds.), *Research in psychotherapy*. Washington, DC: American Psychological Association.

Lachman, M. E. (1989). Personality at the crossroads: Beyond stability versus change. In K. W. Schaie and C. Schooler (Eds.), *Social structure and aging: Psychological processes* (pp. 167–190). Hillsdale, NJ: Erlbaum.

Lachman, M. E., Howland, J., Tennstedt, S., Jette, A., Assmann, S., and Peterson, E. W. (1998). Fear of falling and activity restriction: The Survey of Activities and Fear of Falling in the Elderly (SAFE). *Journal of Gerontology: Psychological Sciences, 53B,* P43–P50.

Lachman, M. E., and James, J. B. (Eds.), (1997). *Multiple paths of midlife development.* Chicago: University of Chicago Press.

Lachman, M. E, and Leff, R. (1989). Perceived control and intellectual functioning in the elderly: A 5-year longitudinal study. *Developmental Psychology, 25,* 722–728.

Lachman, M. E., and Weaver, S. L. (1998a). The sense of control as a moderator of social class differences in health and well being. *Journal of Personality and Social Psychology, 74,* 763–773.

Lachman, M. E., and Weaver, S. L. (1998b). Sociodemographic variations in the sense of control by domain: Findings from the MacArthur studies of midlife. *Psychology and Aging. 13,* 553–562.

Lachman, M. E, Weaver, S. L, Bandura, M.,and Elliott, E. (1992). Improving memory and control beliefs through cognitive restructuring and self-generated strategies. *Journal of Gerontology: Psychological Sciences, 47,* P293–P299.

Lachman, M. E., Ziff, M. A., and Spiro, A. (1994). Maintaining a sense of control in later life. In R. P. Abeles, J. C. Gift, and M. G. Ory (Eds.), *Aging and quality of life.* New York: Springer Publishing Co.

LaGrand, L. E. (1986). *Coping with separation and loss as a young adult.* Springfield, IL: Charles C. Thomas.

Lamb, M. E. (Ed.) (1997). *The role of the father in child development* (3rd ed.). New York: Wiley.

Lammers, E. P. (1995). Children, death, and fairy tales. *Omega, 31,* 101–108.

Lang, F. R., and Carstensen, L. L. (1998). Social relationships and adaptation in late life. In A. S. Bellack and M. Hersen (Eds.), *Comprehensive clinical psychology* (pp. 55–72). London, UK: Pergamon.

Lang, F. R., Staudinger, U. M., and Carstensen, L. L. (1998). Perspectives on socioemotional selectivity in late life: How personality and social context do (and do not) make a difference. *Journal of Gerontology: Psychological Sciences, 53B,* P21–P30.

Langer, E. J. (1975). The illusion of control. *Journal of Personality and Social Psychology, 32,* 311–328.

LaRossa, R., and Reitzes, D. (1993). Continuity and change in middle-class fatherhood: 1925–1939. *Journal of Marriage and the Family, 55,* 455–468.

Larrabee, G. J., McEntee, W. J., Youngjohn, J. R., and Crook, T. H. (1992). Age-associated memory impairment: Diagnosis, research and treatment. In M. Bergener, K. Hasegawa, S. I. Finkel, and T. Nishimura (Eds.),

Aging and mental disorders: International perspectives (pp. 134–149). New York: Springer Publishing Co.

Larsson, M., and Bäckman, L. (1998). Modality memory across the adult life span: Evidence for selective age-related olfactory deficits. *Experimental Aging Research, 254,* 63–82.

LaRue, A. (1992). Neuropsychological assessment. In A. La Rue (Ed.), *Aging and neuropsychological assessment* (pp.79–119). New York: Plenum.

Lavin, C., and Doka, K. J. (1999). *Older adults with developmental disabilities.* Amityville, NY: Baywood Publishing Co.

Lavretsky, E. P., and Jarvik, L. F. (1994). Etiolgy and pathogenesis of Alzheimer's disease: Current concepts. In R. C. Hamby, J. M. Trunbull, W. Clark, and M. Lancaster (Eds.), *Alzheimer's disease: A handbook for caregivers* (2nd ed., pp. 80–92). St. Louis, MO: Mosby.

Lavretsky, E. P., Matsuyame, S. S., Gerson, S., and Jarvik, L. F. (1996). Genetics of geriatric psychopathology. In J. Sadavoy, L. W. Lazarus, L. F. Jarvik, and G. T. Grossberg (Eds.), *Comprehensive review of geriatric psychiatry-II* (2nd ed., pp. 43–79). Washington, DC: American Psychiatric Press.

Lawrence, B. (1980). The myth of the midlife crisis. *Sloan Management Review, 21,* 35–49.

Lawton, M. P. and Brody, E. M. (1969). Assessment of older people: Self-maintaining and instrumental activities of daily living. *Gerontologist, 9,* 179–185.

Lawton, M. P., DeVoe, M. R., and Parmelee, P. (1995). Relationship of events and affect in the daily life of an elderly population. *Psychology and Aging, 10,* 469–477.

Lawton, M. P., Van Haitsma, K., Klapper, J., Kleban, M. H., Katz, I. R., and Corn, J. (1998). A stimulation-retreat special care unit for elders with dementing illness. *International Psychogeriatrics, 10* (4).

Leadbeater, B. J. R., and Way, N. (Eds.). (1996). *Urban girls: Resisting stereotypes, creating identities.* New York, NY: New York University Press.

Lebowitz, B. D., and Rudorfer, M. V. (1998). Treatment research at the millennium: From efficacy to effectiveness. *Journal of Clinical Psychopharmacology, 18,* 1.

Lechner, F. J. (1989). Catholicism and social change in the Netherlands: A case of radical secularization? *Journal for the Scientific Study of Religion, 28,* 136–147.

Lee, D. J., and Markides, K. S. (1990). Activity and mortality among aged persons over an eight-year period. *Journal of Gerontology: Social Sciences, 45,* S39–S42.

Lee, G. R., Willetts, M. C., and Seccombe, K. (1998). Widowhood and depression: Gender differences. *Research on Aging, 20,* 611–630.

Lehman, D. R., Wortman, C. B., Haring, M. Tweed, R. G., de Vries, B. S., Longis, A., Hemphill, K. J., and J. H. Ellard. (1999). Recovery from the perspective of the bereaved: Personal assessments and sources of distress and support. In B. De Vries (Ed.), *End of life issues* (pp. 119–144). New York: Springer Publishing Co.

Lehman, H. C. (1953). *Age and achievement.* Princeton, NJ: Princeton University Press.

Lehmann, H. E. (1982). Affective disorders in the aged. In L. F. Jarvik and G. W. Small (Eds.), *The psychiatric clinics of North America.* Philadelphia, PA: Saunders.

Leigh, J. P., and Fries, J. F. (1993). Associations among health habits, age, gender, and education in a sample of retirees. *International Journal of Aging and Human Development, 36,* 139–155.

Leming, M. R., and Dickinson, G. E. (1994). *Dying, death and bereavement* (3rd ed.). New York: Holt, Rinehart and Winston.

Lemke, S., and Moos, R. H. (1986). Quality of residential settings for the elderly. *Journal of Gerontology, 41,* 268–276.

Lemon, B. W., Bengtson, V. L., and Peterson, J. A. (1972). An exploration of the activity theory of aging: Activity types and life satisfactions among in-movers to a retirement community. *Journal of Gerontology, 27,* 511–523.

Lenzer, A. (1999). Physician-assisted suicide: Policy dilemma. In B. De Vries (Ed.), *End of life issues* (pp. 281–296). New York: Springer Publishing Co.

Lerner, R. M. (1995). Developing individuals within changing contexts: Implications of developmental contextualism for human development, research, policy and programs. In T. A. Kindermann and J. Valsiner (Eds.), *Development of person-context relations.* Hillsdale, NJ: Erlbaum.

Levenson, H. (1975). Additional dimensions of internal-external control. *Journal of Social Psychology, 97,* 303–304.

Levenson, M. R., Aldwin, C, M., and Spiro A., III. (1998). Age, cohort and period effects on alcohol consumption and problem drinking: Findings from the Normative Aging Study. *Journal of Studies on Alcohol, 59,* 712–722.

Levenson, R. W. (1999). The intrapersonal functions of emotion. *Cognition & Emotion, 13,* 481–504.

Levenson, R. W., Carstensen, L. L., Friesen, W. V., and Ekman, P. (1991). Emotion, physiology, and expression in old age. *Psychology and Aging, 6,* 28–35.

Leventhal, H., Rabin, C., Leventhal, E. A., and Burns, E. A (2001). Health/risk, behavior and aging. In J. E. Birren and K. W. Schaie (Eds.), *Handbook of the psychology of aging* (5th ed.). San Diego, CA: Academic Press.

Leventhal, H., Patrick-Miller, L., Leventhal, E. A., and Burns, E. A. (1998). Does stress-emotion cause illness in elderly people? In K. W. Schaie and M. P. Lawton (Eds.), *Annual review of gerontology and geriatrics* (Vol. 17, pp. 138–184). New York: Springer Publishing Co.

Levin, J. S. (1996). How religion influences morbidity and health: Reflection on natural history, salutogenesis and host resistance. *Social Science and Medicine, 43,* 849–864.

Levin, C., Kohlberg, L., and Hewer, A. (1985). The current formulation of Kohlberg's theory and a response to critics. *Human Development, 28,* 94–100.

Levin, J. S. Taylor, R. J., and Chatters, L. M. (1994). Race and gender differences in religiosity among older adults: Findings from four national surveys. *Journal of Gerontology: Social Sciences, 49,* S137–S145.

Levin, J. S., Taylor, R. J., and Chatters, L. M. (1995). a multidimensional measure of religious involvement in black Americans. *The Sociological Quarterly, 36,* 157–173.

Levine, J. A. (1993). Involving fathers in Head Start: A framework for public policy and program development. *Families in Society, 74,* 4-21.

Levinson, D. J. (1978). *The seasons of a man's life.* New York: Knopf.

Levinson, D. J. (1986). A concept of adult development. *American Psychologist, 41,* 3–13.

Levinson, D. J. (1990). A theory of life structure development in adulthood. In C. N. Alexander and E. J. Langer (Eds.), *Higher stages of human development: Perspectives on adult growth* (pp. 35–53). New York,: Oxford University Press.

Levinson, D. J., Darrow, C., Klein, E. Levinson, M., and McKee, B. (1978). *The season's of a man's life.* New York: Knopf.

Levy, S. M., Derogatis, L. R., Gallagher, D., and Gatz, M. (1980). Intervention with older adults and the evaluation of outcome. In L. W. Poon (Ed.), *Aging in the 1980s.* Washington, DC: American Psychological Association.

Lewinsohn, P. M., Duncan, E. M., Stanton, A. K., and Hautzinger, M. (1986). Age at first onset for nonbipolar depression. *Journal of Abnormal Psychology, 95,* 378–383.

Lewinsohn, P. M., Steinmetz, J. L., Antonuccio, D., and Teri, L. (1985). Group therapy for depression: The coping with depression course. *International Journal of Mental Health, 13,* 8–33.

Li, S. H., Jordanova, M., and Lindenberger, U. (1999). From good senses to good sense: A link between tactile information processing and intelligence. *Intelligence, 26,* 99–122.

Liang, J., Bennett, J., Akiyama, H., and Maeda, D. (1992). The structure of the PGC morale scale in American and Japanese aged: A further note. *Journal of Cross-cultural Gerontology, 2,* 745–768.

Lichtenstein, P., Gatz, M. and Berg, S. (1998). A twin study of mortality after spousal bereavement. *Psychological Medicine. 28, 635–643.*

Lichtenstein, P., Gatz, M., Pedersen, N. L., Berg, S. and McClearn, G. E. (1996). A co-twin-control study of response to widowhood. *Journal of Gerontology: Psychological Sciences, 51B,* P279–P289.

Lichter, D. T., LeClere, A., and McLaughlin D. K. (1991). Local marriage markets and the marital behavior of black and white women. *American Journal of Sociology, 96,* 843–867.

Liden, R. C., Stilwell, D., and Ferris, G. R. (1996). The effects of supervisor and subordinate age on objective performance and subjective performance ratings. *Human Relations, 49,* 327–347.

Liebig, P. S. (1996). Area agencies on aging and the National Affordable Housing Act: Opportunities and challenges. *Journal of Applied Gerontology, 15,* 471–485.

Liebig, P. S., and Sheets, D. J. (1998). Ageism, disability and access to environmental interventions. *Technology and Disability, 8,* 69–84.

Light, L. L. (1990). Interactions between memory and language in old age. In J. E. Birren and K. W. Schaie (Eds.), *Handbook of the psychology of aging* (3rd ed.). New York: Academic Press.

Lincoln, J. R., and Kalleberg, A. L. (1990). *Culture, control, and commitment: A study of work organization and work attitudes in the United States and Japan.* Cambridge, MA: Harvard University Press.

Lindenberger, U., and Baltes, P. B. (1994). Sensory functioning and intelligence in old age. *Psychology and Aging, 9,* 339–355.

Lindsay, D. S. (1990). Misleading suggestions can impair eyewitnesses' ability to remember event details. *Journal of Experimental Psychology: Learning, Memory, and Cognition, 16,* 1077–1083.

Linsk, N. L., Hanrahan, P., and Pinkston, E. M. (1991). Teaching the use of community services to elderly people and their families. In P. A. Wisocki (Ed.), *Handbook of clinical behavior therapy with the elderly client* (pp. 479–504). New York: Plenum.

Linton, R. (1949). The natural history of the family. In R. N. Anshen (Ed.), *The family: Its function and destiny.* New York: Harper.

Lipinska, B., Bäckman, L., and Herlitz, A. (1992). When Greta Garbo is easier to remember than Stefan Edberg: Influences of prior knowledge on recognition memory in Alzheimer's disease. *Psychology and Aging, 7,* 214–220.

Lipset, S.M. (1990). The work ethic—Then and now. *The Public Interest, 98,* 61–69.

Littlewood, J. (1992). *Aspects of grief: Bereavement in adult life.* New York: Routledge.

Litwak, A., and Longino, C. F., Jr. (1987). Migration patterns among the elderly: A developmental perspective. *Gerontologist, 27,* 266–272.

Loehlin, J. C., McCrae, R. R., Costa, P. T. Jr., and John, O. P. (1998). Heritabilities of common and measure-specific components of the Big Five personality factors. *Journal of Research in Personality, 32,* 431–453.

Loftus, E. F. (2000). Suggestion, imagination, and the transformation of reality. In A. A. Stone and J. S. Turkkan (Eds.), *The science of self-report: Implications for research and practice* (pp. 201–210). Mahwah, NJ: Lawrence Erlbaum.

Loftus, E. F., Levidow, B., and Duensing, S. (1992). Who remembers best? Individual differences in memory for events that occurred in a science museum. *Applied Cognitive Psychology, 6,* 93–107.

Loftus, E. F., Schooler, J., Boone, S., and Kline, D. (1987). Time went by so slowly: Overestimates of event duration by males and females. *Applied Cognitive Psychology, 1,* 3–13.

London, M., and Greller, M. M. (1991). Demographic trends and vocational behavior: A twenty year retrospective and agenda for the 1990s. *Journal of Vocational Behavior, 38,* 125–164

Lonetto, R., and Templer, D. I. (1986). *Death anxiety.* Washington, DC: Hemisphere.

Longino, C. F., Jr. (1981). Retirement communities. In F. J. Berghorn and D. E. Schafer (Eds.), *The dynamics of aging.* Boulder, CO: Westview Press.

Longino, C. F., Jr. (1998). Geographic mobility and the baby boom. *Generations (Spring),* 60–64.

Longino, C. F., Jr., Jackson, D. J., Zimmerman, R. S., and Bradshear, J. E. (1991). The second move: Health and geographic mobility. *Journal of Gerontology: Social Sciences, 46,* S218–S224.

Longino, C. F., Jr., and Kart, C. S. (1982). Explicating activity theory: Formal replication. *Journal of Gerontology, 37,* 713–722.

Longino, C. F., Jr., Marshall, V. W., Mullins, L. C., and Tucker, R. D. (1991). On the nesting of snowbirds: A question about seasonal and permanent migrants. *Journal of Applied Gerontology, 110,* 157–168.

Longino, C. F., Jr., and Serow, W. (1992). Regional differences in the characteristics of elderly return migrants. *Journal of Gerontology: Social Sciences, 47,* S538–543.

Longino, C. F., Jr., and Smith, K. (1991). Black retirement migration in the United States. *Journal of Gerontology: Social Sciences, 46,* S125–S132.

Looft, W. R. (1972). Egocentrism and social interaction. *Psychological Bulletin, 78,* 73–92.

Lopata, H. Z. (1980). The widowed family member. In N. Datan and N. Lohmann (Eds.), *Transitions of aging.* New York: Academic Press.

Lopata, H. Z. (1986). Time in anticipated future and events in memory. *American Behavioral Scientist, 29,* 695–709.

Lopata, H. (1993). The support systems of American urban widows. In M. Stroebe, W. Stroebe, and R. Hanson (Eds.), *Handbook of bereavement: Theory, research and intervention.* New York: Cambridge University Press.

Lopata, H. (1996a). *Current widowhood: Myths and realities.* Thousand Oaks, CA: Sage.

Lopata, H. Z. (1996b). Grief and husband sanctification. In D. Klass, P. Silverman, and S. Nickman (Eds.), *Continuing bonds: New understanding of grief* (pp. 149–162). New York: Taylor and Francis.

Lopata, H. Z. (1999). Grief and the self-concept. In B. De Vries (Ed.), *End of life issues* (pp. 37–56). New York: Springer Publishing Co.

Lorence, J (1987). Subjective labor force commitment of U.S. men and women, 1973–1985. *Social Science Quarterly, 68,* 745–760.

Lorence, J., and Mortimer, J. (1985). *American Sociological Review, 50,* 618–638.

Lorenz, F., Simons, R., Conger, R., Elder, G., Johnson M., and Chao, W. (1997). Married and recently divorced mothers' stressful events and distress: Tracing change across time. *Journal of Marriage and the Family, 59,* 219–232.

Lougee, M., and Packard, G. (1981, April). *Conformity and perceived competence in adulthood.* Paper presented at the biannual meeting of the Society for Research in Child Development, Boston.

Lovelace, E. A., and Twohig, P. T. (1990). Healthy older adults' perceptions of their memory functioning and use of mnemonics. *Bulletin of the Psychonomic Society, 28,* 115–118.

Lubart, T. I., and Sternberg, R. J. (1998). Life span creativity: An investment theory approach. In C. Adams-Price (Ed.), *Creativity and successful aging* (pp. 21–41). New York: Springer Publishing Co.

Luchins, D. J., Cohen, D., Hanrahan, P., Eisdorfer, C., Pavez, G., Ashford, J. W., Gorelick, P., Hirschman, R., Freels, S., Levy, P., Semla, T., and Shaw, H. (1992). Are there clinical differences between familiar and nonfamilial Alzheimer's disease. *American Journal of Psychiatry, 149,* 1023–1027.

Lugaila, T. A. (1998). Marital status and living arrangements: March, 1998. *Current Population Reports,* P20–51. Washington, DC: U.S. Census Bureau.

Lund and Manchester Groups. (1994). Consensus statement: Clinical and neuropathological criteria for frontotemporal dementia. *Journal of Neurology, Neurosurgery, and Psychiatry, 57,* 416–418.

Lynch, G., and Gerling, S. (1981). Aging and brain plasticity. In J. L. McGaugh and S. B. Kiesler (Eds.), *Aging: Biology and behavior.* New York: Academic Press.

Macey, S. M. (1989). Hypothermia and energy conservation: A tradeoff for elderly persons. *International Journal of Aging and Human Development, 29,* 151–161.

Maciel, A. G., Heckhausen, J., and Baltes, P. B. (1993). A life-span perspective on the interface between personality and intelligence. In R. J. Sternberg and P. Ruzgis (Eds.), *Intelligence and personality.* Cambridge, UK: Cambridge University Press.

Madden, D. J., and Blumenthal, J. A. (1998). Interaction of hypertension and age in visual selective attention performance. *Health Psychology, 17,* 76–83.

Maddox, G. L., and Clark, D. O. (1992). Trajectories of functional impairment in later life. *Journal of Healthy and Social Behavior, 33,* 114–125.

Maddox, G. L., Clark, D. O., and Steinhauser, K. (1994). Dynamics of functional impairment in late adulthood. *Social Science and Medicine, 38,* 925–936.

Magai, C. (2001). Emotion over the life span. In J. E. Birren and K. W. Schaie (Eds.). *Handbook of the psychology of aging* (5th ed). San Diego, CA: Academic Press.

Magdol, M., Moffitt, T. E., Caspi, A., Newman, D. L., Fagan, J., and Silva, P. A. (1997). Gender differences in partner violence in a birth cohort of 21-year-olds: Bridging the gap between clinical and epidemiological approaches. *Journal of Consulting and Clinical Psychology, 65,* 68–78.

Magdol, M., Moffitt, T. E., Caspi, A., and Silva, P. A. (1998). Developmental antecedents of partner abuse: A prospective-longitudinal study. *Journal of Abnormal Psychology, 107,* 375–389.

Maggi, S., Minicuci, N., Martini, A., Langlois, J., Siviero, P., Pava N. M., and Enzi, G. (1998). Prevalence rates of hearing impairment and comorbid conditions in older people: The Veneto Study. *Journal of the American Geriatrics Society, 46,* 1069–1074.

Magnusson, D. (1998). The logic and implication of a person-oriented approach. In R. B. Cairns, L. R. Bergman, and J. Kagan (Eds.), *Methods and models for studying the individual* (pp. 33–64). Thousand Oaks, CA: Sage.

Mahoney, M. J. (1982). Psychotherapy and human change processes. In *Master Lecture Series on Psychotherapy Research and Behavior.* Washington, DC: American Psychological Association.

Maier, H. (1995). *Health behaviors in adults: Interrelationships and correlates.* Unpublished doctoral thesis. University Park, PA: The Pennsylvania State University.

Maitland, S. B., Intrieri, R. C., Schaie, K. W., and Willis, S. L. (2000). Gender differences in cognitive abilities: Invariance of covariance and latent mean structures. *Aging, Neuropsychology and Cognition, 7,* 32–53.

Maitland, S. B., Willis, S. L., and Schaie, K. W. (1993, November). *The effect of cardiovascular disease on personality and attitudinal factors.* Paper presented at the annual meting of the Gerontological Society of America, New Orleans, LA.

Mangiano, C. M., Marcantoni, E. R., Goldman, L., Cook, F., Donaldson, M. C., Sugarbaker, D. J., Poss, R., and Lee, T. H. (1993). Influence of age on measurement of health status in patients undergoing elective surgery. *Journal of the American Geriatric Society, 41,* 377–387.

Mannell, R. C., and Dupuis, S. L. (1994). Leisure and productive activity. In M. P. Lawton and J. A. Teresi (Eds.), *Annual review of gerontology and geriatrics* (Vol. 14, pp. 125–141). New York: Springer Publishing Co.

Manton, K. G., Siegler, I. C., and Woodbury, M. A. (1986). Patterns of intellectual development in later life. *Journal of Gerontology, 41,* 486–499.

Manton, K. G., Stallard, E., and Corder, L. (1995). Changes in morbidity and chronic disability in the U.S. elderly population. *Journal of Gerontology: Social Sciences, 50B,* S194–S204.

Marcia, J. E. (1988). Common processes underlying ego identity, cognitive/ moral development, and individuation. In D. K. Lapsley and F. C. Power (Eds.), *Self, ego and identity: Integrative approaches* (pp. 211–266). New York: Springer-Verlag.

Marcia, J. E. (1993) The relational roots of identity. In J. Kroger (Ed.), *Discussions on ego identity.* (pp. 101–120). Hillsdale, NJ: Lawrence Erlbaum.

Marcia, J. E. (1999). Representational thought in ego identity, psychotherapy, and psychosocial developmental theory. In I. E. Sigel (Ed.), *Development of mental representation: Theories and applications* (pp. 391–414). Mahwah, NJ: Erlbaum.

Marcus, E. R. (1999). Modern ego psychology. *Journal of the American Psychoanalytic Association, 47,* 843–871.

Markides, K. S., Levin, J., and Ray, L. (1987). Religion, aging, and life satisfaction: An eight-year, three-wave longitudinal study. *Gerontologist, 27,* 660–665.

Marks, N. (1998). Does it hurt to care? Caregiving, work-family conflict, and midlife well-being. *Journal of Marriage and the Family, 60,* 951–966.

Marks, N. F., and Lambert, J. D (1998). Marital status continuity and change among young and midlife adults. *Journal of Family Issues, 19,* 652–686.

Markus, H. R., and Herzog, A. R. (1992). The role of the self-concept in aging In K. W. Schaie (Ed.),The role of the self-concept in aging. *Annual review of gerontology and geriatrics* (Vol. 11, pp. 110–143). New York: Springer Publishing Co.

Markus, H. R., and Nurius, P. (1986). Possible selves. *American Psychologist, 41,* 954–969.

Marmor, M. F. (1992). Age-related eye diseases and their effects on visual function. In E. E. Faye and C. S. Stuen (Eds.), *The aging eye and low vision* (pp. 11–21). Washington, DC: The Lighthouse.

Marris, P. (1986). *Loss and change.* London, UK: Routledge and Kegan Paul.

Marsh, G. R., and Thompson, L. W. (1977). Psychophysiology of aging. In J. E. Birren and K. W. Schaie (Eds.), *Handbook of the psychology of aging.* New York: Van Nostrand Reinhold.

Marsiske, M., Klumb, P., and Baltes, M. M. (1997). Everyday activity patterns and sensory functioning in old age. *Psychology and Aging, 12,* 444–457.

Marsiske, M., Lang, F. R., Baltes, M. M., and Baltes, P.B. (1995). Selective optimization with compensation: Life-span perspectives on successful human development. In R. A. Dixon and L. Bäckman (Eds.), *Compensation for psychological defects and declines: Managing losses and promoting gains* (pp. 35–79). Hillsdale, NJ: Erlbaum.

Marsiske, M, and Willis, S. L. (1995). Dimensionality of everyday problem solving in older adults. *Psychology and Aging, 10,* 269–283.

Marsiske, M., and Willis, S. L. (1998). Practical creativity in older adults' everyday problem solving: Life span perspectives. In C. Adams-Price (Ed.), *Creativity and successful aging* (pp. 73–113). New York: Springer Publishing Co.

Martin, G. R., Danner, D. B., and Holbrook, J. (1993) Aging—causes and defenses. *Annual Review of Medicine, 44,* 419–429.

Martin, P., Hagberg, B., and Poon, L. W. (1997) Predictors of loneliness in centenarians. *Journal of Cross-Cultural Gerontology, 12,* 203–224.

Maslow, A. H. (1970). *Motivation and personality* (2nd ed.). New York: Harper and Row.

Masoro, E. J., and McCarter, R. J. (1991). Dietary restriction as a probe of mechanisms of senescence. In V. J. Cristofalo (Ed.), *Annual review of gerontology and geriatrics* (Vol. 13, pp. 183–197). New York: Springer Publishing Co.

Masters, W. H., and Johnson, V. E. (1966). *Human sexual response.* Boston, MA: Little, Brown.

Matire, L. M., Stephens, M. A. P., and Townsend, A. L. (1998). Emotional support and well-being of midlife women: Role-specific mastery as a mediational mechanism. *Psychology and Aging, 13,* 396–404.

Matthews, K. (1992). Myths and realities of the menopause. *Psychosomatic Medicine, 54,* 1–9.

Mayer, J. D., and Bower, G. H. (1986). Learning and memory for personality prototypes. *Journal of Personality and Social Psychology, 51,* 473–492.

Maylor, E. A., and Wing, A. M. (1996). Age differences in postural stability are increased by additional postural demands. *Journal of Gerontology: Psychological Sciences, 51B,* P143–P154.

McAdams, D. P., and de St. Aubin, E. (1992). Theory of generativity and its assessment through self-report, behavioral acts, and narrative themes in autobiography. *Journal of Personality and Social Psychology, 62,* 1003–1015.

McAdams, D. P. and de St. Aubin, E. S. (Eds.) (1998), *Generativity and adult development: How and why we care for the next generation.* Washington, DC: American Psychological Association.

McAdams, D. P., Hart, H. M., and Maruna, S. (1998). The anatomy of generativity. In D. P. McAdams and E. S. de St. Aubin (Eds.), *Generativity and adult development: How and why we care for the next generation.* (pp. 7–43). Washington, DC: American Psychological Association.

McAdoo, P. (1988). Changing perspectives on the role of the black father. In P. Bronstein and C. Cowan (Eds.), *Fatherhood today: Men's changing role in the family.* New York: Wiley.

McAneny, L. (1992). Number of drinkers on the rise again. *The Gallup Poll Monthly, February* 43–46.

McClearn, G. E., and Fogler, G. P. (2001). Gerontological behavior genetics. In J. E. Birren and K. W. Schaie (Eds.), *Handbook of the psychology of aging* (5th ed.). San Diego, CA: Academic Press.

McCrae, R. R., Arenberg, D., and Costa, P. T., Jr. (1987). Declines in divergent thinking with age: Cross-sectional, longitudinal, and cross-sequential analyses. *Psychology and Aging, 2,* 130–137.

McCrae, R. R., and Costa, P. T., Jr. (1982). The self-concept and the stability of personality: Cross-sectional comparisons of self-reports and ratings. *Journal of Personality and Social Psychology, 43,* 1282–1292.

McCrae, R. R., and Costa, P. T., Jr. (1984). *Emerging lives, enduring dispositions: Personality in adulthood.* Boston, MA: Little, Brown.

McCrae, R. R., and Costa, P. T., Jr. (1985). Updating Norman's "adequate taxonomy": Intelligence and personality dimensions in natural language and in questionnaires. *Journal of Personality and Social Psychology, 49,* 710–721.

McCrae, R. R., and Costa, P. T., Jr. (1997). Personality trait structure as a human universal. *American Psychologist, 52,* 509–516.

McCrae, R. R., Costa, P. T., Jr., and Busch, C. M. (1986). Evaluating comprehensiveness in personality systems: The California Q-sort and the five factor model. *Journal of Personality, 54,* 430–446.

McCrae, R. R., and John, O. P. (1992). An introduction to the five-factor model and its applications. *Journal of Personality, 60,* 175–215.

McCrea, F. (1983). The politics of menopause: The discovery of a deficiency disease. *Social Problems, 31,* 111–123.

McDowell, B. J., Engberg, S., Sereika, S., Donovan, N., Jubeck, M. E., Weber, E., and Engberg, R. (1999). Effectiveness of behavioral therapy to treat incontinence in homebound older adults. *Journal of the American Geriatrics Society. 47,* 309–318.

McEntee, W. J., and Crook, T. M. (1992). Cholinergic function in the aged brain: Implications for treatment of memory impairments associated with aging. *Behavioural Pharmacology, 3,* 327–336.

McEvoy, G., and Cascio, W. (1989). Cumulative evidence of the relationship between employee age and job performance. *Journal of Applied Psychology, 24,* 11–17.

McGinnis, J. M. (1982). Recent health gains for adults. *New England Journal of Medicine, 306,* 671–673.

McHale, S. M., and Crouter, A. C. (1992). You can't always get what you want: Incongruence between sex-role attitudes and family work roles and its implications for marriage. *Journal of Marriage and the Family, 54,* 537–547.

McIntosh, J. L. (1992). Epidemiology of suicide in the elderly. *Suicide and Life-Threatening Behavior, 22,* 16–35.

McIntosh, J. L., and Jewell, B. L. (1986). Sex difference trends in completed suicide. *Suicide and Life-Threatening Behavior, 16,* 16–26.

McKain, W. C. (1972). A new look at older marriages. *The Family Coordinator, 21,* 61–69.

McKinlay, J. B., McKinlay, S. M., and Brambilla, D. (1987). The relative contribution of endocrine changes and social circumstances to depression in mid-aged women. *Journal of Health and Social Behavior, 28,* 345–363.

McKinlay, S. M., Brambilla, D. J., Avis, N. E., and McKinlay, J. B. (1991). Women's experience of menopause. *Current Obstetrics and Gynecology, 1,* 3–7.

McKitrick, L. A., and Camp, C. J. (1993). Relearning the names of things: The spaced-retrieval intervention implemented by a caregiver. *Clinical Gerontologist, 14,* 60–62.

McLanahan, S., and Booth, K. (1989). Mother-only families: Problems, prospects and politics. *Journal of Marriage and the Family, 51,* 557–580.

McLanahan, S., and Casper, L. (1995). Growing diversity and inequity in the American family. In R. Farley (Ed.), State of the union, America in the 1990's (Vol. 2: Social trends; pp. 1–45). New York: Russell Sage Foundation.

McNaught, W., and Barth, M. C. (1992). Are older workers "good buys"? A case study of Days Inn of America. *Sloan Management Review, 33,* 53–63.

McNeal, C. (1998). Marital disruption and marital control among black

Americans. *African American Research Perspectives, 4,* 27–34.

Meade, T. W., and Vickers, M. R. (1999). HRT and cardiovascular disease. *Journal of Epidemiology and Biostatistics, 4,* 165–190.

Meinz, E. J., and Salthouse, T. A. (1998). Is age kinder to females than to males? *Psychonomics Bulletin and Review, 5,* 56–70.

Melichar, J., and Chiriboga, D. (1985). Timetables in the divorce process. *Journal of Marriage and the Family, 47,* 701–708.

Mellinger, J. C., and Erdwins, C. J. (1985). Personality correlates of age and life roles in adult women. *Psychology of Women Quarterly, 9,* 503–514.

Menaghan, E. G. (1991). Work experiences and family interaction process: The long reach of the job? *Annual Review of Sociology, 17,* 419–444.

Mendes de Leon, C. F., Seeman, T. E., Baker, D. I., Richardson, E. D., and Tinetti M. E. (1996). Self-efficacy, physical decline, and change in functioning in community-living elders: a prospective study. *Journals of Gerontology: Social Sciences, 51,* S183–S190.

Meredith, W. (1993). Measurement invariance, factor analysis and factorial invariance. *Psychometrika, 58,* 525–543.

Merrill, S. S., and Verbrugge, L. M. (1999). Health and disease in midlife. In S. L. Willis and J. E. Reid (Eds.), *Life in the middle: Psychological and social development in middle age* (pp. 78–104). San Diego, CA: Academic Press.

Mertens, D. M. (1998). *Research methods in education and psychology: Integrating diversity with quantitative and qualitative approaches.* Thousand Oaks, CA: Sage.

Meyer, B. J. F. and Talbot, A. P. (1998). Adult age differences in reading and remembering text and using this information to make decisions in everyday life. In M. C. Smith and T. Pourchot (Eds). *Adult learning and development: Perspectives from educational psychology.* (pp. 179–199). Mahwah, NJ: Erlbaum.

Meyer, B. J. F., Talbot, A., Stubblefield, R. A., and Poon, L. W. (1998). Interests and strategies of young and old readers differentially interact with characteristics of texts. *Educational Gerontology, 24,* 747–771.

Michael, R. T., Gagnon, J. H., Laumann, E. O., and Kolata, G. (1994). *Sex in America: A definitive study.* Boston, MA: Little Brown.

Middlekoop, H. A. M., Smide-van den Del, D. A., Neven, A. K., Kamphuisen, H. A. C., and Springer, C. P. (1996). Subjective self characteristics of 1485 males and females aged 50–93; Effects of sex and age, and factors related to self-evaluated quality of sleep. *Journal of Gerontology: Medical Sciences, 51A,* M108–M115.

Migdel, S., Abeles, R. P., and Sherrod, L. R. (1981). *An inventory of longitudinal studies of middle and old age.* New York: Social Sciences Research Council.

Miles W. R. (1931). Measures of certain human abilities through the lifespan. *Proceedings of the National Academy of Sciences, 17,* 627–632.

Miller, B. (1994). Cancer mortality by age. *Journal of the National Cancer Institute, 86,* 257.

Miller, J., Slomczynski, K. M., and Kohn, M. L. (1987). Continuity of learning-generalization through the life span: The effect of jobs on men's intellectual process in the United States and Poland. In C. Schooler and K. W. Schaie (Eds.), *Cognitive functioning and social structure over the life course* (pp. 176–202). Norwood, NJ: Ablex.

Miller, S. Z. (2001). A cognitive-affective analysis of cancer behavior in the elderly. In K. W. Schaie, H. Leventhal, and S. L. Willis (Eds.), *Societal structures and effective health behavior in the eldery*. New York: Springer Publishing Co.

Mindel, C. H., and Vaughan, C. E. (1978). A multidimensional approach to religiosity and disengagement. *Journal of Gerontology, 33,* 103–108.

Mintz, J., Steuer, J., and Jarvik, L. F. (1981). Psychotherapy with depressed elderly patients: Research considerations. *Journal of Consulting and Clinical Psychology, 49,* 542–549.

Missinne, L. E. (1980). Aging in Bakongo culture. *International Journal of Aging and Human Development, 11,* 283–295.

Mitchell, B., Wister, A., and Burch, T. (1989). The family environment and leaving the parental home. *Journal of Marriage and the Family, 61,* 605–613.

Mitchell, D. B. (1989) How many memory systems: Evidence from aging. *Journal of Experimental Psychology: Learning, Memory, and Cognition, 15,* 31–49.

Mitchell, J., Wilson, K., Revicki, D., and Parker, L. (1985). Childrens' perception of aging: A multidimensional approach to differences by age, sex, and race. *Gerontologist, 25,* 182–187.

Moen, P. (1998). Recasting careers: Changing reference groups, risks, and realities. *Generations, 22,* 40–45.

Moen, P. (1999). *The Cornell couples and careers study*. Ithaca, NY: Cornell University.

Moen, P. (2001). Gender, age and the life course. In R. H. Binstock and L. K. George (Eds). *Handbook of aging and the social sciences* (5th ed.). San Diego, CA: Academic Press.

Moen, P., Erickson, M. A., and Dempster-McClain, D. (1997). Their mother's daughters? The intergenerational transmission of gender attitudes in a world of changing roles. *Journal of Marriage and the Family. 59,* 281–293.

Moen, P., and Shin-Kap, H. (in press). Reframing careers: Work, family and gender. In V. Marshall (Ed.). *Restructuring work and the life course.*

Moen, P,. and Wethington, E. (1999). Midlife development in a life course context. In S. L. Willis and J. E. Reid (Eds.), *Life in the middle: Psychological and social development in middle age* (pp. 3–24). San Diego, CA: Academic Press.

Moen, P., and Yan Y. (1999). Having it all: Overall work/life success in two-earner families. In T. Parcel (Ed.), *Research in the sociology of work* (Vol. 7, pp. 107–137). Greenwich, CT: JAI Press.

Monti, D., Grassilly, E., Troiano, L., Cozzarizza, A. M., Salvioli, S., Barbicri, D., Agnesini, C., Bettuzzi, S., Ingletti, M. C., Corti, A., and Fransceschi, C. (1992). Senescence, immortalization and apoptosis: An intriguing relationship. *Annals of the New York Academy of Science, 673,* 70–82.

Mor, V. (1987a). *Hospice care systems: Structure, process, cost and outcome.* New York: Springer Publishing Co.

Mor, V. (1987b). Hospice: The older person as patient and caregiver. *Generations, 11*(3), 19–21.

Morgan, D. L. (1998). Facts and figures about the baby boom. *Generations, 22,* 10–15.

Morgan, S., Lye, D., and Condran, G. (1988). Sons, daughter, and divorce; Does the sex of children affect the risk of divorce. *American Journal of Sociology, 94,* 110–129.

Morrell, C. H., and Brant, L. J. (1991). Modelling hearing thresholds in the elderly. *Statistics in Medicine, 10,* 1453–1464.

Morrell, R. W., and Echt, K. V. (1997). Designing written instructions for older adults: Learning to use computers. In A. D. Fisk and W. A. Rogers (Eds.), *Handbook of Human Factors and the Older Adult* (pp 335–362). San Diego, CA: Academic Press.

Morris, J. C., Heyman, A., Mohs, R. C., Hughes, J. P., Van Belle, G., Fillenbaum, G., Mellits, E. D., and Clark, C. (1989). The consortium to establish a registry for Alzheimer's disease (CERAD). Part I. Clinical and neuropsychological assessment of Alzheimer's disease. *Neurology, 39,* 1159–1165.

Morris, J. C., Storandt, M., McKeel, Jr., D. W., Rubin, E. H., Price, J. L., Grant, E. A., and Berg, L. (1995). Cerebral amyloid deposition and diffuse plaques in "normal" aging: Evidence for presymptomatic and very mild Alzheimer's disease. *Neurology, 46,* 707–719.

Morse, C., and Wisocki, P. A. (1991). Residential factors in behavioral programming for the elderly. In P. A. Wisocki (Ed.), *Handbook of clinical behavior therapy with the elderly client* (pp. 97–120). New York: Plenum.

Mortimer, J. T., and Borman, K. M. (Eds.) (1988). *Work experience and psychological development through the lifespan.* Boulder, CO: Westview.

Mortimer, J. T., and Finch, M. D. (Eds.) (1996). *Adolescents, work, and family: An intergenerational developmental analysis.* Thousand Oaks, CA: Sage.

Mortimer, J. T., Finch, M. D., and Kumka, D. (1982). Persistence and change in development: The multidimensional self-concept. In P. B. Baltes and O. G. Brim, Jr. (Eds.), *Life span development and behavior* (Vol. 4). New York: Academic Press.

Mortimer, J. T., and Johnson, M. K. (1998). Adolescents' part-time work and educational achievement. In K. Borman and B. Schneider (Eds.), *The adolescent years: Social influences and educational challenges. Ninety-seventh Yearbook of the National Society for the Study of Education* (Part I, pp. 183–206). Chicago, IL: National Society for the Study of Education.

Mortimer, J. T., and Lorence, J. (1979). Occupational experience and the self-concept: A longitudinal study. *Social Psychology Quarterly, 42,* 307–323.

Mortimer, J. T., and Lorence, J. (1994). The social psychology of work. In K. Cook, G. Fine, and J. House (Eds.), *Sociological perspectives on social psychology* (pp. 497–523). New York: Allyn and Bacon.

Moss, M. B., Albert, M. S., Butters, N., and Payne, M. (1986). Differential patterns of memory loss among patients with Alzheimer's disease, Huntington's disease, and alcoholic Korsakoff's syndrome. *Archives of Neurology, 43,* 239–246.

Moss, M. S., and Moss, S. Z. (1989). The death of a parent. In R. A. Kalish (Ed.), *Midlife loss: Coping strategies* (pp. 89–114). Newbury Park, CA: Sage.

Mueller, J. H., Johnson, W. C., Dandoy, A., and Keller, T. (1992). Trait distinctiveness and age specificity in the self concept. In R. P. Lipka and T. M. Brinthaupt (Eds.), *Self-perspectives across the life span* (pp. 225–255). Albany, NY: State University of New York Press.

Mui, A. C., and Burnette, J. D. (1994). A comparative profile of frail elderly persons living alone and those living with others. *Journal of Gerontological Social Work, 21,* 5–26.

Mullan, J. T., Pearlin, L.I., and Skaff, M.M. (1995). The bereavement process: Loss, grief and recovery. In I. Corless, B. Germino and M. Ptittman-Lindeman (Eds.), *Dying, death and bereavement.* Boston, MA: Jones and Bartlett.

Mumford, M. D., and Gustafson, S. B. (1988). Creativity syndrome: Integration, application, and innovation. *Psychological Bulletin, 103,* 27–43.

Mumford, M. D., Wesley, S. S., and Shaffer, G. S. (1987). Individuality in a developmental context: II. The crystallization of developmental trajectories. *Human Development, 30,* 291–321.

Murphy, C. (1983). Age-related effects on the threshold psychophysical function, and pleasantness of menthol. *Journal of Gerontology, 38,* 217–222.

Murray, H. A. (1938). *Explorations in personality.* New York: Oxford University Press.

Murtagh, D. R. R., and Greenwood, K. M. (1995). Identifying effective psychological treatments for insomnia: A meta-analysis. *Journal of Consulting and Clinical Psychology, 63,* 79–89.

Mussen, P. H., Conger, J. J., Kagan, J., and Geiwitz, J. (1979). *Psychological development: A life-span approach.* New York: Harper and Row.

Mutchler, J. E., Burr, J. A., Pienta, A. M., and Massagli, M. P. (1997). Pathways to labor force exit: Work transitions and work instability. *Journal of Gerontology: Social Sciences, 52B,* S4–S12.

Mutran, E. J., Reitzes, D. C. and Fernandez, M. E. (1997). Factors that influence attitudes toward retirement. *Research on Aging, 19,* 251–273.

Myers, G. C., and Manton, K. G. (1984). Recent changes in the U.S. age at death distributions: Further observations. *Gerontologist, 24,* 571–575.

Myers, S. M. (1997). Marital uncertainty and childbearing. *Social Forces, 75,* 1271–1289.

National Academy on an Aging Society (1999, December). *Hearing loss: A growing problem that affects quality of life.* Washington, DC: National Academy on an Aging Society.

National Center for Health Statistics. (1989). The National Nursing Home Survey. *Vital and Health Statistics,* No. 97. Washington, DC: Government Printing Office.

National Center for Health Statistics. (1990). Advance report for final mortality statistics, 1988. *NCHS Monthly Vital Statistics Report, 39* (7, Suppl.).

National Center for Health Statistics (1993). Advance report of final mortality statistics, 1991. *Monthly Vital Statistics Report, 42,* No. 2, Suppl.

National Center for Health Statistics. (1994a). Detailed diagnoses and procedures, National hospital discharge survey, 1991. *Vital and Health Statistics, Series 13,* No. 115.

National Center for Health Statistics. (1994b). Health characteristics by geographic region. Large metropolitan areas, and other places of residence, United States, 1992. *Vital and Health Statistics, Series 10,* No. 189.

National Center for Health Statistics. (1994c). Prevalence of selected chronic disease, United States, 1990-1991. *Vital and Health Statistics, Series 2,* No. 120.

National Center for Health Statistics (1995). *Advance Report of final divorce statistics, 1989–1990.* Washington, DC: U. S. Department of Health and Human Services, March 22.

National Center for Health Statistics (1999). *Births, marriages, divorces, and deaths: Provisional data for 1998.* Washington DC: U. S. Department of Health and Human Services, July 6.

National Center for Victims of Crime. (1992). *Rape in America: A Report to the Nation.* Arlington, VA: National Center for Victims of Crime.

National Center for Victims of Crime (2000a). *Spousal rape laws: 20 years later.* Arlington, VA: National Center for Victims of Crime.

National Center for Victims of Crime (2000b). *Frequently requested statistics.* Arlington, VA: National Center for Victims of Crime.

National Commission on AIDS. (1993). *Behavioral and social sciences and the HIV/AIDS epidemic.* Washington, DC: Author.

National Institute on Aging (1998). *AgePage: Prostate problems.* Bethesda, MD: National Insitute on Aging.

National Opinion Research Center. (1991). *General Social Survey.* Chicago, IL: University of Chicago.

National Victims Center (1992). *Rape in America: A report to the nation.* Arlington, VA: Author.

Neimeyer, R. A. (1997–1998). Death anxiety research: The state of the art. *Omega, Journal of Death and Dying, 36,* 97–120.

Neisser, U. (1991). A case of misplaced nostalgia. *American Psychologist, 46,* 34–36.

Nelson, H. (1928). The creative years. *American Journal of Psychology, 40,* 303–311.

Nesselroade, J. R. (1988a). Sampling and generalizability: Adult development and aging research issues examined within the general methodological framework of selection. In K. W. Schaie, R. T. Campbell, W. Meredith, and S. C. Rawlings (Eds.), *Methodological issues in aging research* (pp. 13–42). New York: Springer Publishing Co.

Nesselroade, J. R. (1988b). Some implications of the trait-state distinction over the life-span: The case of personality. In P. B. Baltes, D. L. Featherman, and R. M. Lerner (Eds.), *Life-span development and behavior* (Vol. 8, pp. 163–189). Hillsdale, NJ: Erlbaum.

Nesselroade, J. R., Stigler, S. M., and Baltes, P. B. (1980). Regression towards the mean and the study of change. *Psychological Bulletin, 88,* 622–637.

Neugarten, B. L .(Ed.) (1964). *Personality in middle and late life.* New York: Atherton Press.

Neugarten, B. L. (1968). The awareness of middle age. In B. L. Neugarten (Ed.), *Middle age and aging.* Chicago: University of Chicago Press.

Neugarten, B. L. (1977). Personality and aging. In J. E. Birren and K. W. Schaie (Eds.), *Handbook of the psychology of aging.* New York: Academic Press.

Neugarten, B. L., Moore, J. W., and Lowe, J. C. (1968). Age norms, age constraints, and adult socialization. In B. L. Neugarten (Ed.), *Middle age and aging.* Chicago, IL: University of Chicago Press.

Neugarten, B. L., and Neugarten, D. A. (1986). Changing meaning of age in the aging society. In A. Pifer and L. Bronte (Eds.), *Our aging society: Paradox and promise* (pp. 33–51). New York: Norton.

Newman, D. L., Moffitt, T. E., Caspi, A., and Silva, P. A. (1998). Comorbid mental disorders: Implications for treatment and sample selection. *Journal of Abnormal Psychology, 107,* 305–311.

Newman, J. P. (1989). Aging and depression. *Psychology and Aging, 4,* 150–165.

Newman-Hornblum, J., Attig, M., and Kramer, D. A. (1980, August). *The use of sex-relevant Piagetian tasks in assessing cognitive competence among the elderly.* Paper presented at the annual meeting of the American Psychological Association, Toronto, Canada.

Newport, F. (1999, December 24). *Gallup Poll: Americans remain very religious, but not necessarily in conventional ways.* Princeton, NJ: Gallup.

Nieswiadomy, M., and Rubin, R. M. (1995). Change in expenditure patterns of retirees: 1972–1973 and 1986–1987. *Journal of Gerontology: Social Sciences, 50B,* S274–S290.

Nordin, S., Monsch, A. U., and Murphy, C. (1995). Unawareness of smell loss in normal aging and Alzheimer's disease: Discrepancy between self-reported and diagnosed smell sensitivity. *Journal of Gerontology: Psychological Sciences,* P187–P192.

Norris-Baker, C., and Scheidt, R. J. (1994). From 'our town' to 'ghost town'? The changing context of home for rural elders. *International Journal of Aging and Human Development, 38,* 181–202.

Nussbaum, P. D., Kaszniak, A. W., Allender, J., and Rapszak, S. (1995). Depression and cognitive decline in the elderly: A follow-up study. *Clinical Neuropsychologist, 9,* 101–11.

Nyberg, L., and Tulving, E. (1996). Classifying human long-term memory: Evidence from converging dissociations. *European Journal of Cognitive Psychology, 8,* 163-183.

Ogden, R. (2000). End-of-life issues in the HIV/AIDS community. In K. L. Braun, J. H. Pietsch, and P. L. Blanchette (Eds.), *Cultural issues in end-of-life decision making* (pp. 265–284). Thousand Oaks, CA: Sage.

Ogilvie, D. M. (1987). Life satisfaction and identity structure in late middle-aged men and women. *Psychology and Aging, 2,* 217–224.

Okun, M. A., Barr, A., and Herzog, A. R. (1998). Motivation to volunteer by older adults: A test of competing measurement models. *Psychology and Aging, 13,* 608–621.

Okun, M. A., Olding, R. W., and Cohn, C. M. G. (1990). A meta-analysis of subjective well-being interventions among elders. *Psychological Bulletin. 108,* 257–266.

Olsho, L. W., Harkins, S. W., and Lenhardt, M. (1985). Aging and the auditory system. In J. E. Birren and K. W. Schaie (Eds.), *Handbook of the psychology of aging* (2nd ed. pp. 332–377). New York: Van Nostrand Reinhold.

Ordy, J. M. (1981). Neurochemical aspects of aging in humans. In H. M. Praag, M. H. Lader, O. J. Rafaelson, and E. J. Sacher (Eds.), *Handbook of biological psychiatry.* New York: Dekker.

Osipow, S. H. (1990). Convergence in theories of career choice and development: Review and prospect. *Journal of Vocational Behavior, 36,* 122–131.

Ostermann, K., and Sprung-Ostermann, B. (1988). Cerebrovascular disease and the elderly. In D. Evered and J. Whelan (Eds.), *Research and the aging population* (pp. 58–64). New York: Wiley.

Over, R. (1989). Age and scholarly impact. *Psychology and Aging, 4,* 222–225.

Owens, G., Fulton, R., and Markusen, E. (1983). Death at a distance: A study of family survivors. *Omega, 13,* 191–226.

Owens, W. A. (1966). Age and mental abilities: A second adult follow-up. *Journal of Educational Psychology, 57,* 311–325.

Owsley, C., and Burton, K. B. (1991). Aging and spatial contrast sensitivity: Underlying mechanisms and implications for everyday life. In P. Bagnoli and W. Hodos (Eds.), *The changing visual system* (pp. 119–139). New York: Plenum.

Owsley, C., and Sloan, M. E. (1987). Contrast sensitivity, acuity, and the perception of "real-world" targets. *British Journal of Ophthalmology, 71,* 791–796.

Owsley, C., Stalvey, B., Wells, J., and Sloane, M.E. (1999). Older drivers and cataract: Driving habits and crash risk. *Journal of Gerontology: Medical Sciences, 54,* M203–211.

Pachana, N.M , Gallagher-Thompson, D., and Thompson L. W. (1994). Assessment of depresssion. In M. P. Lawton and J. A. Teresi (Eds.), *Annual review of gerontology and geriatrics* (Vol. 14, pp. 234–256). New York: Springer Publishing Co.

Pallas, A. M. (1993). Schooling in the course of human lives: The social context of education and the transition to adulthood in industrial society. *Review of Educational Research, 63,* 409–447.

Palmore, E. B. (1986). Trends in the health of the aged. *Gerontologist, 26,* 298–302.

Palmore, E. B., Nowlin, J. G., and Wang, H. S. (1985). Predictors of function among the old-old: A 10-year follow-up. *Journal of Gerontology, 40,* 244–250.

Pals, J. L. (1999). Is personality adaptively patterned? A controversy—Identity consolidation in early adulthood: Relations with ego-resiliency, the context of marriage and personality change. *Journal of Personality, 67,* 295–329.

Pamuk, E., Makuc, D., Heck, K., Reuben, C., and Lochner, K. (1998). *Socioeconomic status and health chartbook, health, United States, 1998.* Hyattsville, MD: National Center for Health Statistics.

Panek, P. E. (1997). The older worker . In A. D. Fisk and W. A. Rogers (Eds). *Handbook of Human Factors and the Older Adult* (pp. 363–394). San Diego,CA: Academic Press.

Papalia, D., and Bielby, D. (1974). Cognitive functioning in middle and old age adults: A review of research based on Piaget's theory. *Human Development, 17,* 424–443.

Park, D. C. (1992). Applied cognitive aging research. In F. I. M. Craik and T. A. Salthouse (Eds.), *Handbook of cognition and aging* (pp. 449–493). Hillsdale, NJ: Erlbaum.

Park, D. C. (1999). Aging and the controlled and automatic processing of medical information and medical intentions. In D. C. Park and R. W. Morrell (Eds.), *Processing of medical information in aging patients: Cognitive and human factors perspectives* (pp. 3–22). Mahwah, NJ: Lawrence Erlbaum.

Park, D. C., and Gutchess, A. H. (1999). Cognitive aging and everyday life. In D. C. Park and N. Schwarz (Eds.), *Cognitive aging: A primer* (pp. 217–232). Philadelphia, PA: Psychology Press.

Park, D. C., Hertzog, C., Kidder, D. P., and Morrell, R. W. (1997). Effect of age on event-based and time-based prospective memory. *Psychology and Aging, 12,* 314–327.

Park, D. C., and Mayhorn, C. B. (1994). Remembering to take medications: The importance of non-memory variables. In D. Herrmann, M. Johnson, C. McEvoy, C. Hertzog, and P. Hertel (Eds.), *Research on practical aspects of memory* (Vol. 2). Hillsdale, NJ: Erlbaum.

Park, D. C., Morrell, R. W., and Shifren, K. (1999). *Processing medical information in aging patients.* Mahwah, NJ: Erlbaum.

Park, D. C., Smith, A. D., Morrell, R. W., Puglisi, J. T., and Dudley, W. N. (1990). Effects of contextual integration on recall of pictures by older adults. *Journal of Gerontology: Psychological Sciences, 45,* P52–P57.

Parkes, C. M. (1972). *Bereavement.* New York: International Universities Press.

Parmalee, P. A. (1994). Assessment of pain in the elderly. In M. P. Lawton and J. A. Teresi (Eds.), *Annual review of gerontology and geriatrics* (Vol. 14, pp. 281–301). New York: Springer Publishing Co.

Parnes, H. S., and Sommers, D. G (1994). Shunning retirement: Work experience of men in their seventies and early eighties. *Journal of Gerontology: Social Sciences, 49,* S117–S124.

Parsons, T. (1949). The social structure of the family. In R. N. Anshen (Ed.), *The family: Its function and destiny.* New York: Harper.

Pasupathi, M., Carstensen, L. L., and Tsai, J. L. (1995). Ageism in interpersonal settings. In B. Lott and D. Maluso (Eds.), *The social psychology of interpersonal discrimination* (pp. 160–182). New York: Guilford Publications.

Patterson, R. L. (1996). Organic disorders. In M. Hersen and V. B. Van Hasselt (Eds.)., *Psychological treatment of older adults: An introductory text* (pp. 257–279). New York: Plenum Press.

Pavalko, E. K., and Artis, J. E. (1997). Women's caregiving and paid work: Causal relationships in late midlife. *Journal of Gerontology: Social Sciences, 52B,* S170–S179.

Payami, H., Schellenberg, G. D., Zareparsi, S., Kaye, J., Sexton, G. J., Head, M. A., Mattsuyama, S. F., Jarvik, L. F., McManus, D.Q., Bird, T. D., Katzman, R., Heston, L., Norman, D., and Small G. W. (1997). Evidence for association of HLA-A2 allele with onset age of Alzheimer's disease. *Neurology, 49,* 512–518.

Payer, L. (1991). The menopause in various cultures. In H. Burger, M. Boulet (Eds.), *Portrait of the menopause.* New York: Parthenon.

Payne, B. P., and McFadden, S. J. (1994). From loneliness to solitude. Religious and spiritual journeys in later life. In L. E. Thomas and S. A. Eisenhandler (Eds.), *Aging and the religious dimension* (pp. 13–37). New York: Auburn House.

Peacock, J. R., and Paloma, M. M. (1991). *Religiosity and life satisfaction across the life course.* Paper presented at the Annual meeting of the Society for the Scientific Study of Religion, Pittsburgh, Pennsylvania.

Pearlin, L. I. (1982). Discontinuities in the study of aging. In T. K. Hareven and K. J. Adams (Eds.), *Aging and life course transitions: An interdisciplinary perspective.* New York: Guilford Press.

Pearlin, L. I., and Mullan, J. T. (1992). Loss and stress in aging. In M. L. Wykle, E. Kahana, and J. Kowal (Eds.), *Stress and health among the elderly* (pp. 117–132). New York: Springer Publishing Co.

Pearlin, L. and Skaff, M. M. (1995). Stressors and adaptation in later life. In M. Gatz (Ed.), *Emerging issues in mental health and aging* (pp 97–123). Washington, D.C. American Psychological Association.

Pearson, J. D. (1992). Attitudes and perceptions concerning elderly Samoans in rural Western Samoa, American Samoa, and urban Honululu. *Journal of Cross-Cultural Gerontology, 7,* 69–88.

Pedersen, J. B. (1998). Sexuality and aging. In I. H. Nordhus, G. R. VandenBos, S. Berg, and P. Fromhold (Eds.), *Clinical geropsychology.* (pp. 141–145). Washington,DC: American Psychological Association.

Pedersen, N. L., and Reynolds, C. A. (1998). Stability and change in adult personality: Genetic and environmental components. *Europan Journal of Personality, 12,* 365–386.

Pedersen, N. L., Reynolds, C. A., and Gatz, M. (1996). Sources of covariation among min-mental state examination scores, education and cognitive abilities. *Journal of Gerontology: Psychological Sciences, 51B,* P55–P63.

Peek, C. W., Coward, R. T., Henretta, J. C., Duncan, R. P., and Dougherty, M. C. (1997). Differences by race in the decline of health over time. *Journal of Gerontology: Social Sciences, 53B,* S336–S344.

Pellegrino, J. W., and Glaser, R. (1979). Cognitive correlates and components in the analysis of individual differences. In R. J. Sternberg and D. K. Detterman (Eds.), *Human intelligence.* New York: Ablex.

Penick, N. I., and Jepsen, D. A. (1992). Family functioning and adolescent career development. Special Section: Work and family concerns. *Career Development Quarterly. 40,* 208–222.

Penning, M. J. (1998). In the middle: Parental caregiving in the context of other roles. *Journal of Gerontology: Social Sciences, 53,* S188–S197.

Perlmutter, M., Adams, C., Berry, J., Kaplan, M., and Person, D. (1987). Aging and memory. In K. W. Schaie (Ed.), *Annual review of gerontology and geriatrics* (Vol. 7). New York: Springer Publishing Co.

Perlmutter, M., and Nyquist, L. (1990). Relationships between self-reported physical and mental health and intelligence performance across adulthood. *Journals of Gerontology: Psychological Science, 45,* P145–P155.

Perron, J., Vondracek, F. W., Skorikov, V. B., Tremblay, C., and Corbiere, M. (1998). A longitudinal study of vocational maturity and ethnic identity development. *Journal of Vocational Behavior, 52,* 409–424.

Peterson, C., and Seligman, M. E. P. (1984). Causal explanation as a risk factor for depression: Theory and evidence. *Psychological Review, 91,* 347–374.

Peterson, J., and Bakeman, R. (1988). The epidemiology of adult minority AIDS. *Multicultural Inquiry and Research on AIDS, 2,* 1–5.

Peterson, S. A., and Maiden, R. (1992–1993). Personality and politics among older Americans: A rural case study. *International Journal of Aging and Human Development, 36,* 157–159.

Petrovich, H., Vogt, T.M., and Berge, K. G. (1992). Isolated systolic hypertension: Lowering the risk of stroke in older patients. *Geriatrics, 47,* 30–38.

Phares, V. (1996). Conducting nonsexist research, prevention, and treatment with fathers and mothers: A call for change. *Psychology of Women Quarterly, 20,* 55–77.

Piaget, J. (1967). *Six psychological studies.* New York: Random House.

Piaget, J. (1972). Intellectual evolution from adolescence to adulthood. *Human Development, 15,* 1–12.

Pienta, A. M., Burr, J. A., and Mutchler, J. E. (1994). Women's labor force participation in later life: The effects of early work and family experiences. *Journals of Gerontology: Social Sciences, 49,* S231–S239.

Pierce, R. C., and Chiriboga, D. A. (1979). Dimensions of adult self-concept. *Journal of Gerontology, 34,* 83–85.

Pifer, A. (1993). The public sector: "We the people" and our government's role. In R. Butler and K. Kiikuni (Eds.), *Who is responsible for my old age* (pp. 139–157). New York: Springer Publishing Co.

Pillemer, K., and Suitor, J. J. (1998). Baby boom families: Relations with aging parents. *Generations, 22,* 65–69.

Pleck, J. H. (1997). Paternal involvement: Levels, sources, and consequences. In M. E. Lamb (Ed.), *The role of the father in child development* (3rd ed., pp. 66–103). New York: Wiley.

Plomin, R., and Caspi, A. (1998). DNA and personality. *European Journal of Personality, 12,* 387–407.

Plomin, R., Pedersen, N. L., Nesselroade, J. R., and Bergeman, C. S. (1988). Genetic influence on childhood family environment perceived retrospectively from the last half of the life span. *Developmental Psychology, 24,* 738–745.

Plotkin, D. A., and Jarvik, L. F. (1986). Cholinergic dysfunction in Alzheimer's disease: Cause or effect? In J. M. van Ree and S. Matthysee (Eds.), *Progress in brain research* (Vol. 65, pp. 91–103). Amsterdam: Elsevier.

Poole, M., and Bornholt, L. (1998) Career development of academics, The Netherlands: Cross-cultural and life-span factors. *International Journal of Behavioral Development, 22,* 103–126.

Poon, L. W. (1985). Differences in human memory with aging: Nature, causes, and clinical implications. In J. E. Birren and K. W. Schaie (Eds.), *Handbook of the psychology of aging* (2nd ed.). New York: Van Nostrand Reinhold.

Poon, L. W., and Fozard, J. L. (1980). Speed of retrieval from long-term memory in relation to age, familiarity and datedness of information. *Journal of Gerontology, 35,* 711–717.

Poon, L. W., and Schaffer, G. (1982, August). *Prospective memory in young and elderly adults.* Paper presented at the meeting of the American Psychological Association, Washington, DC.

Poon, L. W., Sweaney, A. L., Clayton, G. M., and Merriam, S. B. (1992). The Georgia Centenarian study. *In-*

ternational Journal of Aging and Human Development, 34, 1–17.

Poon, L. W., and Welford, A. T. (1980). Prologue: A historical perspective. In L. W. Poon (Ed.), *Aging in the 1980s.* Washington, DC: American Psychological Association.

Popelka, M. M., Chruickshanks, K. J., Wiley, T. L., Tweed, T. S., Klein, B. E. K., and Klein R. (1998). Low prevalence of hearing aid use among older adults with hearing loss: The epidemiology of hearing loss study. *Journal of the American Geriatrics Society, 46,* 1075–1078.

Power, T. G., and Parke, R. D. (1982). Play as a context for early learning: Lab and home analyses. In I. E. Siegel and L. M. Laosa (Eds.), *The family as a learning environment.* New York: Plenum.

Pratt, M. W., Golding, G., and Hoyer, W. J. (1983). Aging as ripening: Character and consistency of moral judgments in young, mature, and older adults. *Human Development, 26,* 277–288.

Prinz, P., Dustman, R. E., and Emmerson, R. (1990). Electrophysiology and aging. In J. E. Birren and K. W. Schaie (Eds.), *Handbook of the psychology of aging* (3rd ed., pp. 135–149). San Diego: Academic Press.

Prosser, S., Turrini, M., and Arslan, E. (1990). Effects of different noises on speech discrimination by the elderly. *Acta Oto-Larungologica, 476 (Suppl.),* 136–142.

Prusiner, S. B. (1995). Prion biology. In S. B. Prusiner, J. Collinge, J. Powell, and B. Anderton (Eds.), *Prion diseases in humans and animals.* London, UK: Ellis Horwood.

Pulkkinen, L. (1996). Female and male personality styles: A typological and developmental analysis. *Journal of Personality and Social Psychology, 70,* 1238–1306.

Pulkkinen, L. (1998). Levels of longitudinal data differing in complexity and the study of continuity and personality characteristics. In R. B. Cairns, L. R. Bergman, and J. Kagan (Eds.), *Methods and models for studying the individual* (pp. 161–183). Thousand Oaks, CA: Sage.

Pulkkinen, L., Ohranen, M., and Tolvanen, A. (1998) Personality antecedents of career orientation and stability among women compared to men. *Journal of Vocational Behavior, 53,* 1–22.

Quayhagen, M. P., and Quayhagen, M. (1989). Differential effects of family-based strategies on Alzheimer's disease. *Gerontologist, 29,* 150–155.

Quintar, B., Lane, R. C., and Goeltz, W. B. (1998). Psychoanalytic theories of personality. In D. F. Barone and M. Hersen (Eds.), *Advanced personality: The Plenum series in social/clinical psychology* (pp. 27-55). New York: Plenum.

Rabbitt, P. (1993). Does it all go together when it goes? *Quarterly Journal of Experimental Psychology: Human Experimental Psychology, 46A,* 385–434.

Rabbitt, P., and Abson, V. (1991). Do older people know how good they are? *British Journal of Psychology, 82,* 137–151.

Radner, D. B. (1993). Economic well-being of the old old: Family unit income and household wealth. *Social Security Bulletin, 56,* 3–19.

Ragins, B. R. (1999). Gender and mentoring relationships: A review and research agenda for the next decade. In G. N. Powell (Ed.). *Handbook of gender and work* (pp. 347–370). Thousand Oaks, CA: Sage.

Ragins, B. R., and Scandura, T. A. (1999). Burden or blessing? Expected costs and benefits of being a mentor. *Journal of Organizational Behavior. 20,* 493–509.

Rahe, R. H. (1972). Subjects' recent life changes and their near-future illness susceptibility. *Advances in Psychosomatic Medicine, 8,* 2–19.

Rahe, R. H., and Arthur, R. T. (1978). Life changes and illness studies. *Journal of Human Stress, 4*(11), 3–15.

Rain, J. S., Lane, I. M, and Steiner, D. (1991). A current look at the job satisfaction/life satisfaction relationship: Review and future considerations. *Human Relations, 44,* 287–307.

Rainey, L. M., and Borders, L. D. (1997). Influential factors in career orientation and career aspiration of early adolescent girls. *Journal of Counseling Psychology. 44,* 160–172.

Rakowski, W., Fleishman, J. A., Mor, V., and Brynt, S. (1993). Self-assessment of health and mortality among older persons. *Research on Aging, 15,* 92–116.

Rando, T. A. (1991). Parental adjustment to the loss of a child. In D. Papadatou, and C. Papadatou (Eds.) *Children and death* (pp. 233–254). New York: Hemisphere.

Rango, N. (1985). The social epidemiology of accidental hypothermia among the aged. *Gerontologist, 25,* 424–430.

Rank, M. R., and Davis, L. E. (1996). Perceived happiness outside of marriage among black and white spouses. *Family Relations: Journal of Applied Family and Child Studies, 45,* 435–441.

Ranson, R. L., Sutch, R., and Williamson, S. H. (1993). Inventing pensions: The origins of the company-provided pension in the United States, 1900–1940. In K. W. Schaie and W. A. Achenbaum (Eds.), *Societal impact on aging: Historical perspectives* (pp. 1–38). New York: Springer Publishing Co.

Rao, G. B., and Rao, S. (1997). Sector and age differences in productivity. *Social Science International, 13,* 51–52.

Ravin, J. G., and Kenyon, C.A. (1998). Artistic vision in old age: Claude Monet and Edgar Degas. In C. Adams-Price (Ed.), *Creativity and successful aging* (pp. 251–267). New York: Springer Publishing Co.

Ray, W. A., Blazer, D. G., Schaffner, W., and Federspiel, C. F. (1987). Reducing antipsychotic drug prescribing for nursing home patients: A controlled trial of the effect of an educational visit. *American Journal of Public Health, 77,* 1448–1449.

Raykov, T. (1989). Reserve capacity of the elderly in aging sensitive tests of fluid intelligence: A reanalysis via a structural equation modelling approach. *Zeitschrift für Psychologie, 197,* 263–282.

Raynor, J. O., and Entin, E. E. (Eds.) (1982). *Motivation, career striving, and aging.* Washington, DC: Hemisphere.

Rebok, G. W., Rasmusson, D., and Brandt, J. (1997). Improving memory in community elderly through group-based and individualized memory training. In D. G. Payne and F. G. Conrad (Eds)., *Intersections in basic and applied memory research* (pp 327–343). Mahwah, NJ: Lawrence Erlbaum.

Regnier, V. (1996). The physical environment and maintenance of competence. In S. L. Willis, K. W. Schaie, and M. Hayward (Eds.), *Societal mechanisms for maintaining competence in old age* (pp. 232–250). New York: Springer Publishing Co.

Reid, B. (1984). An anthropological reinterpretation of Kohlberg's stages of moral development. *Human Development, 27,* 57–64.

Reifler, B. V. (1992). Depression versus dementia in the elderly. In M. Bergener, K. Hasegawa, S. I. Finkel, and T. Nishimura (Eds.), *Aging and mental disorders: International perspectives* (pp. 83–90). New York: Springer Publishing Co.

Reker, G. T., Peacock, E. I., and Wong, T. P. (1987). Meaning and purpose in life and well-being: A life-span perspective. *Journal of Gerontology, 42,* 33–49.

Rennemark, M., and Hagberg, B. (1997). Sense of coherence among the elderly in relation to their perceived life history in an Eriksonian perspective. *Aging and Mental Health, 1,* 221-229.

Rennison, C. M. (1999). *Criminal Victimization 1998: Changes 1997-98 with Trends 1993-98.* Washington: Bureau of Justice Statistics, U. S. Department of Justice.

Repetti, R. L. (1987). Individual and common components of the social environment at work and psychological well-being. *Journal of Personality and Social Psychology, 52,* 710–720.

Reuben, D. B., Walsh, K., Moore, A. A., Damasyn, M., and Greendale, G. A. (1998). Hearing loss in community-dwelling older persons: National prevalence data and identification using simple questions. *Journal of the American Geriatrics Society, 46,* 1008–1011.

Rexroat, C., and Shehan, C. (1987). The family life cycle and spouses' time in housework. *Journal of Marriage and the Family, 49,* 737–750.

Riegel, K. F. (1975). Adult life crises: A dialectical interpretation of development. In N. Datan and L. H. Ginsberg (Eds.), *Life-span developmental psychology: Normative life crises.* New York: Academic Press.

Riegel, K. F. (1976). From traits and equilibrium toward developmental dialectics. In W. Arnold (Ed.), *Nebraska Symposium on Motivation* (Vol. 24). Omaha, NE: University of Nebraska Press.

Riegel, K. F., and Riegel, R. M. (1972). Development, drop, and death. *Developmental Psychology, 6,* 306–319.

Riley, M. W. (1992). Cohort analysis. In E. F. Borgatta and M. L. Borgatta (Eds.), *Encyclopedia of sociology* (Vol. 1, pp. 227–237) New York: Macmillan.

Riley, M. W. (1994). Aging and society: Past, present and future. *Gerontologist,* 34, 436–446.

Riley, M. W., Foner, A., and Riley, J. W. Jr. (1999). The aging and society paradigm. In V. L. Bengtson and K. W. Schaie (Eds), *Handbook of theories of aging* (pp. 344–360). New York: Springer Publishing Co.

Riley, M. W., Kahn, R. L., and Foner, N. (Eds.) (1994). *Age and structural lag.* New York: Wiley.

Riley, M. W., and Loscocco, K. A. (1994). The changing structure of work opportunities toward an age-integrated society. In R. P. Abeles, H. C. Gift and M. G. Ory (Eds.), *Aging and quality of life* (pp. 236–252). New York: Springer Publishing Co.

Riley, M. W., and Riley, J. W., Jr. (1994). Age integration and the lives of older people. *Gerontologist, 34,* 110–115.

Rindfuss, R., Morgan, S. P., and Swicegood, G. (1988). *First births in America: Changes in the timing of parenthood.*

Berkeley and Los Angeles, CA: University of California Press.

Roberts, B. W., and Helson, R. (1997). Changes in culture, changes in personality: The influence of individualism in a longitudinal study of women. *Journal of Personality and Social Psychology, 72,* 641–651.

Roberts, E. E., Kaplan, G. A., Shema, S. J., and Strawbridge, W. J. (1997). Prevalence and correlates of depression in an aging cohort: The Alameda County Study. *Journal of Gerontology: Social Sciences, 52B,* S252–S258.

Roberts, M. A., and Caird, F. L. (1976). Computerized tomography and intellectual impairment in the elderly. *Journal of Neurology, Neurosurgery and Psychiatry, 39,* 986–989.

Robbins, M. A., Elias, M. F., Croog, S. H., and Clayton, T. (1994). Unmedicated blood pressure levels and quality of life in elderly hypertensive women. *Psychosomatic Medicine, 56,* 251–259.

Robins, R. W., John, O. P., and Caspi, A. (1994). Major dimensions of personality in early adolescence: The big five and beyond. In C. F. Halverson, G. A. Kohnstamm, and R. P. Martin (Eds.), *The developing structure of temperament and personality from infancy to adulthood* (pp. 267–291). Hillsdale, NJ: Erlbaum.

Rodeheaver, D., Emmons, C., and Powers, K. (1998). Context and identity in women's late life creativity. In C. Adams-Price (Ed.), *Creativity and successful aging* (pp. 195–234). New York: Springer Publishing Co.

Rodin, J. (1983). Behavioral medicine: Beneficial effects of self-control training in the aged. *International Review of Applied Psychology, 32,* 153–181.

Rodin, J., and Langer, E. J. (1980). Aging labels: The decline of control and the fall of self-esteem. *Journal of Social Issues, 36,* 12–29.

Rodin, J., Schooler, C., and Schaie, K. W. (Eds.) (1990). *Self-directedness: Cause and effects throughout the life course.* Hillsdale, NJ: Erlbaum.

Rogers, C. (1972). *The coming partners: Marriage and its alternatives.* New York: Dell.

Rogers, S. J., and White, L. K. (1998). Satisfaction with parenting; the role of marital happiness, family structure, and parents' gender. *Journal of Marriage and the Family, 60,* 293–308.

Rogers, S. L., Friedhoff, L. T. et al. (1996). The efficacy and safety of donepezil in patients with Alzhheimer's disease: Results of a U.S. multicentre, randomized, double-blind, placebo-controlled trial. *Dementia, 7,* 293–302.

Rogosa, D., Brandt, D., and Zimowsky, M. (1982). A growth curve approach to the measurement of change. *Psychological Bulletin, 92,* 726–748.

Rollins, B. C. (1989). Marital quality at midlife. In S. Hunter and M. Sundel (Eds.), *Midlife myths.* Newbury Park, CA: Sage.

Rollins, B. C., and Feldman, H. (1970). Marital satisfaction over the life cycle. *Journal of Marriage and the Family, 32,* 20–28.

Rosenberg, S. D., Rosenberg, H. J., and Farrell, M. P. (1999). The mid-life crisis revisited. In S. L. Willis and J. E. Reid (Eds.), *Aging in the middle: Psychological and social development in middle age* (pp. 47–77). San Diego, CA: Academic Press.

Rosik, C. H. (1989). The impact of religious orientation in conjugal bereavement among older adults.

International Journal of Aging and Human Development, 28, 251–260.

Rosow, I. (1974). *Socialization in old age.* Berkeley, CA: University of California Press.

Rossi, A. (1980). Aging and parenthood in the middle years. In P. B. Baltes and O. G. Brim, Jr. (Eds.), *Life-span development and behavior* (Vol. 3). New York: Academic Press.

Rott, C. (1993). Intelligenzentwicklung im Alter [Development of intelligence in old age]. *Zeitschrift für Gerontologie, 23,* 252–261.

Rovner, B. W., German, P. S., Brant, L. J., Clark, R., Burton, L., and Folstein, M. F. (1991). Depression and mortality in nursing homes. *Journal of the American Medical Association, 265,* 993–996.

Rowell, M. (2000).Christian perspectives on end-of-life decision making: Faith in a community. In K. L. Braun, J. H. Pietsch, and P. L. Blanchette (Eds.), *Cultural issues in end-of-life decision making* (pp. 147–164). Thousand Oaks, CA: Sage.

Rubin, D. C. (1999). Autobiographical memory and aging: Distributions of memories across the life-span and their implications for survey research. In N. Schwarz and D. C. Park, (Eds.), Cognition, aging, and self-reports. (pp. 163–183). Hove, UK: Psychology Press/Erlbaum.

Rubin, D. C., Rahhal, T. A., and Poon, L. W. (1998).Things learned in early adulthood are remembered best. *Memory and Cognition, 26,* 3–19.

Rubin, E. H., Storandt, M., Miller, J. P., Kinscherf, D. A., Grant, E. A., Morris, J, C., and Berg. L. (1998). A prospective study of cognitive functions and onset of dementia in cognitive healthy elders. *Archives of Neurology, 55,* 395–401.

Rudinger, G., and Minnemann, E. (1997). Conditions of life of elderly women and men in East- and West-Germany: First results from the Interdisciplinary Long-Term Study of Adulthood and Aging (ILSE). *Zeitschrift für Gerontopsychologie und Psychiatrie, 10,* 205–212.

Ruesch, H. (1959). *The top of the world.* New York: Pocket Books.

Ruggles, S. (1994). The origins of African-American family structure. *American Sociological Review, 59,* 136–151.

Ruhm, C. (1989). Why older Americans stop working. *Gerontologist, 29,* 294–299.

Ruth, J. E., and Coleman, P. (1996). Personality and aging: Coping and management of the self in later life. In J. E. Birren and K. W. Schaie (Eds.), *Handbook of the psychology of aging* (4th ed., pp. 308–322). San Diego, CA: Academic Press.

Rybash, J. M., Roodin, P. A., and Hoyer, W. J. (1983). Expressions of moral thought in later adulthood. *Gerontologist, 23,* 254–260.

Ryff, C. D. (1989). In the eyes of the beholder: Views of psychological well-being. *Psychology and Aging, 4,* 195–210.

Ryff, C. D. (1996). Psychological well-being: Meaning, measurement and implications for psychotherapy research. *Psychotherapy and Psychosomatics, 65,* 14–23.

Ryff, C. D., Kwan, C. M. L. and Singer, B. H. (2001). Personality and aging: Flourishing agendas and future challenges. In J. E. Birren and K. W. Schaie (Eds.), *Handbook of the psychol-*

ogy of aging (5th ed.), San Diego, CA: Academic Press.

Ryff, C. D., and Baltes, P. B. (1976). Value transition and adult development in women: The instrumentality-terminality hypothesis. *Development Psychology, 12,* 567–568.

Ryff, C. D., and, Essex, M. J. (1992). Psychological well-being in adulthood and old age: Descriptive markers and explanatory processes. In K. W. Schaie (Ed.), *Annual review of gerontology and geriatrics* (Vol. 11, pp. 144–171). New York: Springer Publishing Co.

Ryff, C. D., Lee, Y. H., Essex, M. J., and Schmutte, P. S. (1994). My children and me: Midlife evaluations of grown children and self. *Psychology and Aging, 9,* 195–205.

Ryff, C. D., Schmutte, P. S., and Lee, Y. H. (1996). How children turn out: Implications for parental self evaluation. In C. D. Ryff and M. M. Seltzer (Eds), *The parental experience in midlife* (pp. 383–422). Chicago, IL: University of Chicago Press.

Ryff, C. D., and Seltzer, M. M. (Eds), (1996). *The parental experience in midlife.* Chicago, IL: University of Chicago Press.

Ryff, C. D., and Singer, B. (1998). The contours of positive human health. *Psychological Inquiry, 9,* 1–28.

Ryff, C. D., Singer, B., Love, G. D., and Essex, M. J. (1998). Resilience in adulthood and later life: Defining features and dynamic processes. In J. Lomranz (Ed.), *Handbook of aging and mental health* (pp. 69–96). New York: Plenum.

Sacktor, N., Gray, S., Kawas, C., Herbst, J., Costa, P. T., Jr., and Fleg, J. (1999). Systolic blood pressure within an in-termediate range may reduce memory loss in an elderly hypertensive cohort. *Journal of Geriatric Psychiatry and Neurology, 12,* 1–6.

Safford, F. (1993). Differential assesment of dementia and depression in elderly people. In F. Safford and G.I. Krell (Eds.), *Gerontology for health professionals: A practice guide* (pp. 51–67). Washington, DC: NASW Press.

Salthouse, T. A. (1979). Adult age and the speed-accuracy tradeoff. *Ergonomics, 22,* 811–821.

Salthouse, T. A. (1984). Effects of age and skill in typing. *Journal of Experimental Psychology: General, 113,* 345–371.

Salthouse, T. A. (1985). Motor performance and speed of behavior. In J. E. Birren and K. W. Schaie (Eds.), *Handbook of the psychology of aging* (2nd ed., pp. 400–426). New York: Van Nostrand Reinhold.

Salthouse, T. A. (1987). Age, experience, and compensation. In C. Schooler and K. W. Schaie (Eds.), *Cognitive functioning and social structure over the life course* (pp. 142–157). New York: Ablex.

Salthouse, T. A. (1990) Working memory as a processing resource in cognitive aging. Special issue: Limited resource models of cognitive development. *Developmental Review, 10,* 101–124.

Salthouse, T. A. (1993). Speed mediation of adult age differences in cognition. *Developmental Psychology, 29,* 722–738.

Salthouse, T. A. (1994). The nature of the influence of speed on adult age differences in cognition. *Developmental Psychology, 30,* 240–259.

Salthouse, T. A. (1996). The processing-speed theory of adult age differences in cognition. *Psychological Review, 103,* 403–428.

Salthouse, T. A. (1997). Psychological issues relevant to competence. In S. L. Willis, K. W. Schaie, and M. Hayward (Eds.), *Societal mechanisms for maintaining competence in old age* (pp. 50–93). New York: Springer Publishing Co.

Salthouse, T. A. (1998). Independence of age-related influences on cognitive abilities across the lifespan. *Developmental Psychology, 34,* 851–864.

Salthouse, T. A. (1999). Theories of cognition. In V. L. Bengtson and K. W. Schaie (Eds.), *Handbook of theories of aging* (pp. 196–208). New York: Springer Publishing Co.

Salthouse, T. A., and Babcock, R. L. (1991). Decomposing adult age differences in working memory. *Developmental Psychology, 27,* 763–776.

Salthouse, T. A., Hambrick, D. Z., and McGuthry, K. E. (1998). Shared age-related influences on cognitive and non-cognitive variables. *Psychology and Aging, 13,* 486–500.

Salthouse, T. A., Hancock, H. E., Meinz, E. J., and Hambrick, D. Z. (1996). Interrelations of age, visual acuity, and cognitive functioning. *Journal of Gerontology: Psychological Sciences, 51B,* P317–P330.

Salthouse, T., and Maurer, T. J. (1996). Aging, job performance, and career development. In J. E. Birren and K. W. Schaie (Eds.), *Handbook of the psychology of aging* (4th ed.). San Diego, CA: Academic Press.

Salthouse, T. A., and Mitchell, D. R. (1990). Effects of age and naturally occurring experience on spatial visualization performance. *Developmental Psychology, 26,* 845–854.

Salzman, C. (Ed.) (1992). *Clinical geriatric psychopharmacology* (2nd ed.). Baltimore, MD: Williams and Wilkins.

Samuelsson, G., and Dehlin, O. (1989). Social class and social mobility—effects on survival: A study of an entire birth cohort during an 80-year life span. *Zeitschrift für Gerontologie, 18,* 260–265.

Samuelsson, S. M., Alfredson, B. B., Hagberg, B., Samuellson, G., Nordbeck, B., Brun, A., Gustafson, L., and Risberg, J. (1997). The Swedish centenarian study: A multi-disciplinary study of five consecutive cohorts at the age of 100. *International Journal of Aging and Human Development, 45,* 223–253.

Sanders, R. E., and Sanders, J. C. (1978). Long-term durability and transfer of enhanced conceptual performance in the elderly. *Journal of Gerontology, 33,* 408–412.

Sands, L. P., Terry, H., and Meredith, W. (1989). Change and stability in adult intellectual functioning assessed by Wechsler item responses. *Psychology and Aging, 4,* 79–87.

Sapolsky, R. M. (1993). Stress and neuroendocrine changes during aging. In R. L. Sprott, R. W. Huber and T. F. Williams (Eds.), *The biology of aging* (pp. 63–72). New York: Springer Publishing Co.

Sasser-Coen, J. R. (1993). Qualitative changes in creativity in the second half of life: A life-span developmental perspective. *Journal of Creative Behavior. 27,* 18–27.

Sax, L. J., Astin, A. W., Korn, W. S., and Mahoney, K. (1999). *The American Freshman: National Norms for Fall 1999.* Los Angeles, CA: Higher Education Research Institute, University of California Los Angeles.

Scandura, T. A. (1992). Mentorship and career mobility: An empirical investigation. *Journal of Organizational Behavior, 13,* 169–174.

Schaefer, J. A., and Moos, R. H. (1998). The context for posttraumatic growth: Life crises, individual and social resources, and coping. In R. G. Tedeschi, C. L. Park, and L. G. Calhoun (Eds.), *Post-traumatic growth: Positive changes in the aftermath of crisis* (pp. 99–125). Mahwah, NJ: Lawrence Erlbaum.

Schaie, K. W. (1965). A general model for the study of developmental change. *Psychological Bulletin, 64,* 92–107.

Schaie, K. W. (1977). Quasi-experimental research designs in the psychology of aging. In J. E. Birren and K. W. Schaie (Eds.), *Handbook of the psychology of aging.* New York: Van Nostrand Reinhold.

Schaie, K. W. (1977–1978). Toward a stage theory of adult cognitive development. *Aging and Human Development, 8,* 129–138.

Schaie, K. W. (1979). The primary mental abilities in adulthood: An exploration in the development of psychometric intelligence. In P. B. Baltes and O. G. Brim, Jr. (Eds.), *Lifespan development and behavior* (Vol. 2). New York: Academic Press.

Schaie, K. W. (1981). Psychological changes from midlife to old age: Implications for the maintenance of mental health. *American Journal of Orthopsychiatry, 51,* 199–218.

Schaie, K. W. (1982). Longitudinal data sets: Evidence for ontogenetic development or chronicles of cultural change? *Journal of Social Issues, 38,* 65–72.

Schaie, K. W. (Ed.) (1983a). *Longitudinal studies of adult psychological development.* New York: Guilford Press.

Schaie, K. W. (1983b). The Seattle Longitudinal Study: A twenty-one year exploration of psychometric intelligence in adulthood. In K. W. Schaie (Ed.), *Longitudinal studies of adult psychological development.* New York: Guilford Press.

Schaie, K. W. (1984a). Historical time and cohort effects. In K. A. McCluskey and H. W. Reese (Eds.), *Life-span developmental psychology: Historical and generational effects.* New York: Academic Press.

Schaie, K. W. (1984b). Midlife influences upon intellectual functioning in old age. *International Journal of Behavioral Development, 7,* 463–478.

Schaie, K. W. (1985). *Manual for the Schaie-Thurstone Adult Mental Abilities Test (STAMAT).* Palo Alto, CA: Consulting Psychologists Press.

Schaie, K. W. (1986). Beyond calendar definitions of age, period, and cohort: The general developmental model revisited. *Developmental Review, 6,* 252–277.

Schaie, K. W. (1988a). Ageism in psychological research. *American Psychologist, 43,* 179–183.

Schaie, K. W. (1988b). Internal validity threats in studies of adult cognitive development. In M. L. Howe and C. J. Brainerd (Eds.), *Cognitive development in adulthood: Progress in cognitive development research* (pp. 241–272). New York: Springer-Verlag.

Schaie, K. W. (1988c). Variability in cognitive function in the elderly: Implications for societal participation. In A. Woodhead, M. Bender, and R. Leonard (Eds.), *Phenotypic variation in populations: Relevance to risk management* (pp. 191–212). New York: Plenum.

Schaie, K. W. (1989a). The hazards of cognitive aging. *Gerontologist, 29,* 484–493.

Schaie, K. W. (1989b). Individual differences in rate of cognitive change in adulthood. In V. L. Bengtson and K. W. Schaie (Eds.), *The course of later life: Research and reflections* (pp. 68–83). New York: Springer Publishing Co.

Schaie, K. W. (1989c). Perceptual speed in adulthood: Cross-sectional and longitudinal studies. *Psychology and Aging, 4,* 443–453.

Schaie, K. W. (1993a). Ageist language in psychological research. *American Psychologist, 48,* 49–51.

Schaie, K. W. (1993b). The Seattle Longitudinal Study: A thirty-five year inquiry of adult intellectual development. *Zeitschrift für Gerontologie, 26,* 129–137.

Schaie, K. W. (1994a). The course of adult intellectual development. *American Psychologist, 49,* 304–313.

Schaie, K. W. (1994b). Developmental designs revisited. In S. H. Cohen and H. W. Reese (Eds.), *Life-span developmental psychology: Theoretical issues revisited.* (pp. 45–64). Hillsdale, NJ: Erlbaum.

Schaie, K. W. (1996a). Generational differences. In J. E. Birren (Ed.), *Encyclopedia of gerontology,* (pp. 567–576). San Diego, CA: Academic Press.

Schaie, K. W. (1996b). *Intellectual development in adulthood: the Seattle longitudinal study.* New York: Cambridge University Press.

Schaie, K. W. (1998). Advances in longitudinal research methodology. *Australian Journal on Ageing, 17*(1, Suppl.), 78–81.

Schaie, K. W. (2000). The impact of longitudinal studies on understanding development from young adulthood to old age. *International Journal of Behavioral Development, 24,* 257–266.

Schaie, K. W., and Baltes, P. B. (1975). On sequential strategies and developmental research. *Human Development, 18,* 384–390.

Schaie, K. W., Dutta, R., and Willis, S. L. (1991). The relationship between rigidity-flexibility and cognitive abilities in adulthood. *Psychology and Aging, 6,* 371–383.

Schaie, K. W., Gonda, J. N., and Quayhagen, M. (1981). The relationship between intellectual performance and perception of everyday competence in middle-aged, young-old, and old-old adults. *Proceedings of the XXIInd International Congress of Psychology.* Leipzig, Germany: International Union of Psychological Sciences.

Schaie, K. W., and Hendricks, J. (Eds.) (2000). *Evolution of the aging self: Societal impact.* New York: Springer Publishing Co.

Schaie, K. W., and Hertzog, C. (1985). Measurement in the psychology of aging. In J. E. Birren and K. W. Schaie (Eds.), *Handbook of the psychology of aging* (2nd ed.). New York: Van Nostrand Reinhold.

Schaie, K. W., and Hertzog, C. (1986). Toward a comprehensive model of adult intellectual development: Contributions of the Seattle Longitudinal Study. In R. A. Sternberg (Ed.), *Advances in human intelligence* (Vol. 3, pp. 79–118). Hillsdale, NJ: Erlbaum.

Schaie, K. W., and Hofer, S. (2001). Longitudinal studies of the adult life course. In J. E. Birren and K. W. Schaie (Eds.), *Handbook of the psychology of aging* (5th ed.). San Diego, CA: Academic Press.

Schaie, K. W., Labouvie, G. V., and Barrett, T. J. (1973). Selective attrition effects in a fourteen-year study of adult intelligence. *Journal of Gerontology, 28,* 328–334.

Schaie, K. W., and Lawton, M. P. (1998) (Eds.). *Annual Review of Gerontology and Geriatrics: Emotion and Adult development* (Vol. 17). New York: Springer Publishing Co.

Schaie, K. W., Maitland, S. B., Willis, S. L. and Intrieri, R. L. (1998). Longitudinal invariance of adult psychometric ability factor structures across seven years. *Psychology and Aging, 13,* 8–20.

Schaie, K. W., Nguyen, H. T., Willis, S. L., Dutta, R., and Yue, G. A. (2000). Environmental factors as a conceptual framework for examining cognitive performance in Chinese adults. *International Journal of Behavioral Development, 24.*

Schaie, K. W., and Parham, I. A. (1974). Social responsibility in adulthood: Ontogenetic and sociocultural changes. *Journal of Personality and Social Psychology, 30,* 483–492.

Schaie, K. W., and Parham, I. A. (1976). Stability of adult personality traits: Fact or fable? *Journal of Personality and Social Psychology, 34,* 146–158.

Schaie, K. W., & Pietrucha, M. (Eds.). (2000). *Mobility and transportation in the elderly.* New York: Springer Publishing Co.

Schaie, K. W., Plomin, R., Willis, S. L., Gruber-Baldini, A., and Dutta, R. (1992). Natural cohorts: Family similarity in adult cognition. In T. Sonderegger (Eds.), *Psychology and aging: Nebraska Symposium on Motivation, 1991* (pp. 205–243). Lincoln, NE: University of Nebraska Press.

Schaie, K. W., and Schooler, C. (Eds.) (1998). *Impact of work on older adults.* New York: Springer Publishing Co.

Schaie, K. W., and Stone, V. (1982). Psychological assessment. *Annual Review of Gerontology and Geriatrics, 3,* 329–360.

Schaie, K. W., and Strother, C. R. (1968). A cross-sequential study of age changes in cognitive behavior. *Psychological Bulletin, 70,* 671–680.

Schaie, K. W., and Willis, S. L. (1986). Can intellectual decline in the elderly be reversed? *Developmental Psychology, 22,* 223–232.

Schaie, K. W., and Willis, S. L. (1991). Adult personality and psycho-motor performance: Cross-sectional and longitudinal analyses. *Journal of Gerontology: Psychological Sciences, 46,* P275–P284.

Schaie, K. W., and Willis, S. L. (1993). Age difference patterns of psychometric intelligence in adulthood: Generalizability within and across ability domains. *Psychology and Aging, 8,* 44–55.

Schaie, K. W., & Willis, S. L. (1995). Perceived family environments across generations. In V. L. Bengtson, K. W. Schaie, & L. Burton (Eds.), *Adult intergenerational relations: Effects of societal change,* (pp. 174–209). New York: Springer Publishing Co.

Schaie, K. W., and Willis, S. L (1999). Theories of everyday competence and aging. In V. L. Bengtson and K. W. Schaie (Eds.), *Handbook of theories of aging* (pp. 174–195). New York: Springer Publishing Co.

Schaie, K. W., and Willis, S. L. (2000a). A stage theory model of adult cognitive development revisited. In R. Rubinstein, M. Moss, and M. Kleban (Eds.), *The many dimensions of aging:*

Essays in honor of M. Powell Lawton, (pp. 175–193). New York: Springer Publishing Co.

Schaie, K. W., and Willis, S. L. (2000b). Towards implementation of empirical findings on human aging. In H. Reents (Ed.), *Handbuch der Gerontotechnik.* [Handbook of gerotechnology] (2nd ed.). Iserlohn, Germany: Ecomed.

Schaie, K. W., Willis, S. L., Jay, G., and Chipuer, H. (1989). Structural invariance of cognitive abilities across the adult life span: A cross-sectional study. *Developmental Psychology, 25,* 652–662.

Schaie, K. W., Willis, S. L., and O'Hanlon, A. M. (1994). Perceived intellectual performance change over seven years. *Journal of Gerontology: Psychological Sciences. 49,* P108–P118.

Schaie, K. W. and Zuo, Y. L. (2001). Family environments and cognitive functioning. In R. J. Sternberg and E. Grigorenko (Eds.), *Cognitive development in context* (pp. 337–361). Hillsdale, NJ: Erlbaum.

Schappert, S. M. (1992). Office visits for diabetes mellitus: United States, 1989. A*dvance Data, No. 211.* Washington, DC: National Center for Health Statistics.

Schappert, S. M. (1993a). Office visits to cardiovascular disease specialists: United States, 1989–90. A*dvance Data, No. 226.* Washington, DC: National Center for Health Statistics.

Schappert, S. M. (1993b). Office visits to psychiatrists: United States, 1989-90. *Advance Data, No. 237.* Washington, DC: National Center for Health Statistics.

Scheibel, A.B. (1996). Structural and functional changes in the aging brain. In J. E. Birren and K. W.

Schaie (Eds.), *Handbook of the psychology of aging.* (4th ed.). San Diego, CA: Academic Press.

Scheidt, R. J., and Schaie, K. W. (1978). A situational taxonomy for the elderly: Generating situational criteria. *Journal of Gerontology, 33,* 848–857.

Schieber, F. (1992). Aging and the senses. In J. E. Birren, R. B. Sloan, and G. Cohen (Eds.), *Handbook of mental health and aging,* (2nd ed., pp. 251–306). San Diego, CA: Academic Press.

Schieber, F., Fozard, J. L., and Gordon-Salant, S. (1991). Optimizing sensation and perception in older adults. *International Journal of Industrial Ergonomics, 7,* 133–162.

Schieber, F., Kline, D. W., Kline, T. J. B., and Fozard, J. L. (1992). *The relationship between contrast sensitivity and the visual problems of older drivers.* SAE Technical Paper Series, Nr. 920613. Warrendale, PA: The Engineering Society for Advancing Mobility.

Schiffman, S. S., and Warwick, Z. S. (1988). Flavor enhancement of foods for the elderly can reverse anorexia. *Neurobiology of Aging, 2,* 24–26.

Schmidt, R. M. (1994). Preventive healthcare for older adults: Societal and individual services. *Generations, 18* (1), 33–36.

Schmitt-Rodermund, E., and Silbereisen, R. K. (1998). Career maturity determinants: Individual development, social context, and historical time. *Career Development Quarterly, 47,*16–31.

Schmitt-Rodermund, E., and Vondracek, F. W. (1999). Breadth of interests, exploration, and identity development in adolescence. *Journal of Vocational Behavior, 55,* 298–317.

Schmitz-Scherzer, R., and Thomae, H. (1983). Constancy and change of behavior in old age: Findings from the Bonn Longitudinal Study of Aging. In K. W. Schaie (Ed.), *Longitudinal studies of adult psychological development* (pp. 191–221). New York: Guilford Press.

Schmutte, P. S., and Ryff, C. D. (1997). Personality and well-being: Reexamining methods and meanings. *Journal of Personality and Social Psychology, 73, 549–559.*

Schneider, E. L. (1993). Biological theories of aging. In R. L. Sprott, R. W. Huber and T. F. Williams (Eds.), *The biology of aging* (pp. 3–12). New York: Springer Publishing Co.

Schooler, C. (1984). Psychological effects of complex environments during the life span: A review and theory. *Intelligence, 8,* 259–281.

Schooler, C. (1987). Cognitive effects of complex environments during the life span: A review and theory. In C. Schooler and K. W. Schaie (Eds.), *Cognitive functioning and social structure over the life course* (pp. 24–49). Norwood, NJ: Ablex.

Schooler, C., Kaplan, L., and Oates, G. (1998). Aging and work: An overview. In K. W. Schaie and C. Schooler (Eds.), *Impact of work on older adults* (pp. 1–10). New York: Springer Publishing Co.

Schooler, C., Mulatu, M. S., and Oates, G. (1999). The continuing effects of substantively complex work on the intellectual functioning of older workers. *Psychology and Aging, 14,* 483–506.

Schroots, J. J. F., and Birren, J. E. (1990). Concepts of time and aging in science. In J. E. Birren and K. W. Schaie (Eds.), *Handbook of the psychology of aging* (3rd ed., pp. 45–66). San Diego: Academic Press.

Schulkind, M. D., Hennis, L. K., and Rubin, D. C. (1999). Music, emotion, and autobiographical memory: They're playing your song. *Memory and Cognition, 27,* 948–955.

Schulman, S. (1996). "Good night, sweet prince": Saying goodbye to the dead in Shakespeare's plays. *Death Studies, March/April,* 185–192.

Schultz, K. S., Morton, D. R., and Weckerle, J. R. (1998). The influence of push and pull factors on voluntary and involuntary early retirees' retirement decision and adjustment *Journal of Vocational Behavior, 53,* 45–57.

Schultz, N. R., Elias, M. F., Robbins, M. A., and Streeten, D. H. (1989). A longitudinal study of the performance of hypertensive and normotensive subjects on the Wechsler Adult Intelligence Scale. *Psychology and Aging, 4,* 496–499.

Schulz, J. H. (1995). *The economics of aging* (6th ed.). Westport, CT: Auburn House.

Schulz, R., and Alderman, D. (1974). Clinical research and the "stages of dying." *Omega, 5,* 137–144.

Schulz, R., and Heckhausen, J. (1998). Emotion and control: A life-span perspective. In K. W. Schaie and M. P. Lawton (Eds.), *Annual review of gerontology and geriatrics* (Vol. 17, pp. 185–205). New York: Springer Publishing Co.

Schulz, R., O'Brien, A T., and Tompkins, C. A. (1994). The measurement of affect in the elderly. In M. P. Lawton and J. A. Teresi (Eds.), *Focus on assessment: Annual review of gerontology and geriatrics* (Vol 14). New York: Springer Publishing Co.

Schutte, K. K., Brennan, P. L., and Moos, R. H. (1998). Predicting the development of late-life late-onset drinking problems: A 7-year prospective study. *Alcoholism Clinical and Experimental Research, 22,* 1349–1358,

Schwartz, P., and Blumstein, P. (1983). *American couples: Money, work and sex.* New York: William Morrow.

Schwarz, N. (1999). Self-reports: How the questions shape the answers. *American Psychologist, 54,* 93–105.

Schwarz, N., and Knäuper, B. (1999). Cognition, aging, and self-reports. In D. C. Park and N. Schwarz (Eds.), *Cognitive aging: A primer* (pp. 233–252). Philadelphia, PA: Psychology Press.

Schwarz, N., and Park, D.C. (Eds.), (1999). *Cognition, aging, and self-reports.* Hove, UK: Psychology Press/Erlbaum.

Scialfa, C. T., Kline, D. W., and Lyman, B. J. (1987). Age differences in target identification as a function of retinal location and noise level: Examination of the useful field of view. *Psychology and Aging, 2,* 14–19.

Scogin, F. (1998). Anxiety in old age. In K. H. Nordhus, G. R. VandenBos, S. Berg, and P. Fromholt (Eds.), *Clinical geropsychology.* Washington, DC: American Psychological Association.

Scogin, F., and McElreath, L. (1994). Efficacy of psychosocial treatments for geriatric depression: A quantitative review. *Journal of Consulting and Clinical Psychology, 62,* 69–74.

Sczomak, J. (1989, November). *Prospective memory in the elderly: Efficacy of mnemonic strategies in naturalistic settings.* Paper presented at the annual meeting of the Gerontological Society of America, Minneapolis, MN.

Seale, C. (1998). *Constructing death: The sociology of dying and bereavement.* Cambridge, UK: Cambridge University Press.

Segraves, R. T., and Segraves, K. B. (1995). Human sexuality and aging. *Journal of Sex Education and Therapy, 21,* 88–102.

Seelbach, W. C. (1984). Filial responsibility and the care of aging family members. In W. Quinn and G. Hughston (Eds.), *Independent aging: Family and social system perspectives* (pp. 92–105). Rockville, MD: Aspen.

Seibert, S. (1999). The effectiveness of facilitated mentoring: A longitudinal quasi-experiment. *Journal of Vocational Behavior. 54,* 483–502.

Seligman, M. E. P. (1981). A learned helplessness point of view. In L. P. Rehm (Ed.), *Behavior therapy for depression: Present status and future directions.* New York: Academic Press.

Selko, D. J., Ihara, Y., and Salazar, F. J. (1982). Alzheimer's disease: Insolubility of partially purified paired helical filaments in sodium dodecyl sulfate and urea. *Science, 215,* 1243–1245.

Selzer, J. A. (1991). Relationships between fathers and children who live apart: The father's role after separation. *Journal of Marriage and the Family, 53,* 79–101.

Selzer, M. M., and Ryff, C. D. (1994). Parenting across the life span: The normative and non-normative cases. In D. L. Featherman, R. M. Lerner, and M. Perlmutter (Eds.), *Life-span development and behavior* (Vol. 12, pp. 1–40). Hillsdale, NJ: Erlbaum.

Shanan, J. (1993). Die Jerusalemer Langsschnittuntersuchungen der mittleren Lebensjahre und des Alterns—JESMA [The Jerusalem Longitudinal Study on mid-adulthood and aging]. *Zeitschrift für Gerontologie, 26,* 251–255.

Shanas, E., Townsend, P., Wedderburn, D., Friis, H., Milhoj, P., and Stehouwer, P. (Eds.) (1968). *Old people in three industrial societies.* London, England: Routledge and Kegan Paul.

Shapiro, A. and Lambert, J. D. (1999). Longitudinal effects of divorce on the quality of the father-child relationship and on fathers' psychological well-being. *Journal of Marriage and the Family, 61,* 397–408.

Sharma, S. K., Tobin, J. D., and Brant, L. J. (1986). Factors affecting attrition in the Baltimore Longitudinal Study of Aging. *Experimental Gerontology, 21,* 329–340.

Sharps, M. J., and Price-Sharps, J. L. (1996). Visual memory support: An effective mnemonic device for older adults. *Gerontologist, 36,* 706–708.

Shaw, R. J., and Craik, F. I. M. (1989). Age differences in predictions and performance on a cued recall task. *Psychology and Aging, 4,* 131–135.

Sheehy, G. (1976). *Passages.* New York: Dutton.

Sheikh, J., Hill, R., and Yesavage, J. (1986). Long-term efficacy of cognitive training for age-associated memory impairment: A six-month follow-up study. *Developmental Neuropsychology, 2,* 413–421.

Shifren, K., Hooker, K., Wood, P., and Nesselroade, J. R. (1997). Structure and variation of mood in individuals with Parkinson's disease: A dynamic factor analysis. *Psychology and Aging, 12,* 328–339.

Shimizu, M. (1992). Depression and suicide in late life. In M. Bergener, K. Hasegawa, S. I. Finkel, and T. Nishimura (Eds.), *Aging and mental disorders: International perspectives* (pp. 91–101). New York: Springer Publishing Co.

Shinn, Y. (1992, June). *Sexual violence against women in Korea: A victimization survey of Seoul women.* Paper presented at the conference on International Perspectives: Crime, Justice, and Public Order. St. Petersburg, Russia.

Shneidman, E. S. (1974). *Deaths of man.* New York: Penguin.

Shneidman, E. S. (1982). *Voices of death.* New York: Bantam.

Shock, N. W. (1985). Longitudinal studies of aging in humans. In C. E. Finch and L. Hayflick (Eds.), *Handbook of the biology of aging* (2nd ed., pp. 721–743). New York: Van Nostrand Reinhold.

Shock, N. W., Greulick, R. C., Andres, R., Arenberg, D., Costa, P. T., Lakatta, E. G., and Tobin, J. D. (1984). *Normal human aging: The Baltimore Longitudinal Study of Aging.* Washington, DC: U.S. Government Printing Office. NIH Publication No. 84-2450.

Siegler, I. C. (1983). Psychological aspects of the Duke longitudinal studies. In K. W. Schaie (Ed.), *Longitudinal studies of adult psychological development.* New York: Guilford Press.

Siegler, I. C. (1989). Developmental health psychology. In M. Storandt and G. R. VandenBos (Eds.), *The adult years: Continuity and change* (pp. 115–142). Washington, DC: American Psychological Association.

Siegler, I. C., Blumenthal, J. A., Barefoot, J. C., Peterson, B. L., Saunders, W. B., Dahlstrom, W. G., Costa, P. T. Jr., Suarez, E. C., Helms, M. J., Maynard, K. E., and Williams, R. B. (1997). Personality factors differentially predict exercise behavior in men and women. *Women's Health: Research on Gender, Behavior and Policy, 3,* 61–70.

Siegler, I. C., and Botwinick, J. (1979). A long-term longitudinal study of intellectual ability of older adults: The matter of selective attrition. *Journal of Gerontology, 34,* 242–245.

Siegler, I. C., George, L. K., and Okun, M. A. (1979). Cross-sequential analysis of adult personality. *Developmental Psychology, 15,* 350–351.

Siegler, I. C., McCarthy, S. M., and Logue, P. E. (1982). Wechsler Memory Scale scores, selective attrition and distance from death. *Journal of Gerontology, 37,* 176–181.

Siegler, I. C., Peterson, B. L., Barefoot, J. C., and Williams R. B. (1992). Hostility during late adolescence predicts coronary risk factors at mid-life. *American Journal of Epidemiology, 136,* 146–154.

Silverberg, S., and Steinberg, L. (1990). Psychological well-being of parents with early adolescent children. *Developmental Psychology, 26,* 658–666.

Silverstein, M., and Angelelli, J. J. (1998). Older parents' expectations of moving closer to their children. *Journal of Gerontology: Social Sciences, 53B,* S153–S163.

Silverstein, M., and Long, J. (1998). Trajectories of grandparents' perceived solidarity with adult grandchildren: A growth curve analysis over 23 years. *Journal of Marriage and the Family, 60,* 912–923.

Silverstein, M., and Zablotsky, D. (1996). Health and social precursors of later life retirement-community migration. *Journal of Gerontology: Social Sciences, 51B,* S150–S156.

Simon, R. W., and Marcussen, K. (1999). Marital transitions, marital beliefs, and mental health. *Journal of Health and Social Behavior, 40,* 111–125.

Simon, S. L., Walsh, D. A., Regnier, V., and Krauss, I. K. (1992). Spatial cognition and neighborhood use: The relationship in older adults. *Psychology and Aging, 7,* 389–394.

Simoneau, G. G., and Leibowitz, H. W. (1996). Posture, gait, and falls. In J. E. Birren and K. W. Schaie (Eds.), *Handbook of the psychology of aging.* (4th ed.) San Diego, CA: Academic Press.

Simonton, D. K. (1977). Creative productivity, age, and stress: A biograph-ical time series analysis of 10 classical composers. *Journal of Personality and Social Psychology, 35,* 791–804.

Simonton, D. K. (1988). Age and outstanding achievement: What do we know after over a century of research? *Psychological Bulletin, 104,* 251–267.

Simonton, D. K. (1989). The swan song phenomenon: Last works effects for 172 classical composers. *Psychology and Aging, 4,* 42–47.

Simonton, D. K. (1990a). Creativity in the later years: Optimistic prospects for achievement. *Gerontologist, 30,* 626–631.

Simonton, D. K. (1990b). Creativity and wisdom in aging. In J. E. Birren and K. W. Schaie (Eds.), *Handbook of the psychology of aging* (3rd ed., pp. 320–329). San Diego: Academic Press.

Simonton, D. K. (1991a). Career landmarks in science: Individual differences an interdisciplinary contrasts. *Developmental Psychology, 27,* 119–130.

Simonton, D. K. (1991b). Emergence and realization of genius: The lives and works of 120 classical composers. *Journal of Personality and Social Psychology, 61,* 829–840.

Simonton, D.K. (1992). Leaders of American psychology, 1879–1967: Career development, creative output, and professional achievement. *American Psychologist, 62,* 5–17.

Simonton, D. K. (1998). Career paths and creative lives: A theoretical perspective on late life potential. In C. Adams-Price (Ed.), *Creativity and successful aging* (pp. 3–18). New York: Springer Publishing Co.

Simonton, D. K. (1999). Creativity from a historiometric perspective. In R. J. Sternberg (Ed.), *Handbook of creativity* (pp. 115–133). New York: Cambridge University Press.

Sinnott, J. D. (1984). Postformal reasoning: The relativistic stage. In M. L. Commons, F. A. Richards, and C. Armon (Eds.). *Beyond formal operations: Late adolescent and adult cognitive development* (pp. 298–325). New York: Praeger.

Sinnott, J. D. (1993). Creativity and postformal thought: Why the last stage is the creative stage. In C. Adams-Price (Ed.), *Creativity and aging: Theoretical and empirical approaches.* New York: Springer Publishing Co.

Sinnott, J. D. (1996). The developmental approach: Post formal thought as adaptive intelligence. In F. Blanchard-Fields and T. Hess (Eds.), *Perspectives on cognitive change in adulthood and aging* (pp. 358–383). New York: McGraw Hill.

Sinnott, J. D., and Johnson, L. (1997). Complex postformal thought in skilled research administrators. *Journal of Adult Development, 4,* 45–53.

Sirocco, A. (1988). Nursing and related care homes as reported from the 1986 inventory of long-term care places. *NCHS Advance Data, 147,* 1–11.

Skinner, B. F. (1983). Intellectual self-management in old age. *American Psychologist, 38,* 239–244.

Skoe, E. E., and Marcia, J. E. (1991). A measure of care-based morality and its relation to ego identity. *Merrill-Palmer Quarterly, 37,* 289–304.

Skoog, I. (1988). Sexualitet hos aldre [Sexuality in the elderly]. In *Medicinsk Sexologi.* Stockholm, Sweden: Svenska Läkaresallskapet and Spri.

Skorikov, V. B., and Vondracek, F. W. (1997). Longitudinal relationships between part-time work and career development in adolescents. *The Career Development Quarterly, 45,* 221–235.

Skorikov, V. B., and Vondracek, F. W. (1998). Vocational identity development: Its relationship to other identity domains and to overall identity development. *Journal of Career Assessment, 6,* 13–35.

Sliwinski, M., Lipton, R. B., Buschke, H., and Stewart, W. (1996). The effects of preclinical dementia on estimates of normal cognitive functioning in aging. *Journal of Gerontology: Psychological Sciences, 51B,* P217–P225.

Small, B. J., Basun, H., and Bäckman, L. (1998). Three-year changes in cognitive performance as a function of Apolipoprotein E genotype: Evidence from very old adults without dementia. *Psychology and Aging, 13,* 80–87

Small, B. J., Herlitz, A., Fratiglioni, L., Almquist, O., and Bäckman, L. (1997). Cognitive predictors of incident Alzheimer's disease: A prospective longitudinal study. *Neuropsychology, 11,* 413–430.

Smider, N. A., Essex, M. J., and Ryff, C. D. (1996). Adaptation to community relocation: The interactive influence of psychological resources and contextual factors. *Psychology and Aging, 11,* 362–372.

Smith, A. D. (1996). Memory. In J. E. Birren and K. W. Schaie (Eds.), *Handbook of the psychology of aging* (4th ed.). San Diego, CA: Academic Press.

Smith, B. L., Martin, J. A,, and Ventura, S. J. (1999). Births and deaths: Preliminary data for July 1997–June 1998. *National vital statistics reports;* (Vol 47, No. 22). Hyattsville, MD: National Center for Health Statistics.

Smith, D. B., and Moen, P. (1998). Spouse's influence on the retirement decision: His, her, and their perceptions. *Journal of Marriage and the Family, 3,* 44–64.

Smith, J., and Baltes, P. B. (1990). A study of wisdom-related knowledge:

Age/cohort differences in responding to life planning problems. *Developmental Psychology, 26,* 494–505.

Smith, J., Fleeson, B., Geiselmann, B, Settersten, T. S. Jr., and Kunzmann, U. (1999). Sources of well-being in very old age. In P. B. Baltes and K. U. Mayer (Eds.), *The Berlin Aging Study: Aging from 70 to 100* (pp. 450–471). Cambridge, UK: Cambridge University Press.

Smith, J., Staudinger, U. M, and Baltes, P. B. (1994). Occupational settings facilitating wisdom-related knowledge. *Journal of Consulting and Clinical Psychology, 62,* 989–999.

Smith, J. P. (1997). *The changing economic circumstances of the elderly: Income, wealth, and social security.* Policy Brief No. 8/1997. Syracuse, NY: Syracuse University Center for Policy Research.

Smith, K. J., Longino, C. F., Jr., and Leeds, D. (1992). Roots: Black return migration to the south. *Humanity and Society, 16,* 40–53.

Smyer, M. A. (1995). Formal support in later life: Lessons for prevention. In L. A. Bond, S. J. Cutler, and A. Grams (Eds.), *Promoting successful and productive aging* (pp. 186–202). Thousand Oaks, CA: Sage.

Smyer, M. A., Brannon D., and Cohen, M. (1992). Improving nursing home care through training and job redesign. *Gerontologist, 32,* 327–333.

Smyer, M. A., and Downs, M, G, (1995).Psychopharmacology: An essential element in educating clinical psychologists for working with older adults. In B. G. Knight, L. Teri, P. Wohlford, and J. Santos (Eds.), *Mental health services for older adults* (pp. 73–83). Washington, DC: American Psychological Association.

Smyer, M. A., Kapp, M., and Schaie, K. W. (1996). *Impact of the law on older adults' decision-making capacity.* New York: Springer Publishing Co.

Snarey, J., Son, L., Kuehne, V. S., Hauser, S., and Vaillant, G. (1987). The role of parenting in men's psychosocial development: A longitudinal study of early adulthood infertility and midlife generativity. *Developmental Psychology, 21,* 568–584.

Social Security Administration. (1985). The 1982 new beneficiary survey: No. 3. Health status of new retired-worker beneficiaries. *Social Security Bulletin,* 48(2).

Social Security Administration (1994). *Fast facts and figures about social security.* Washington, DC: Government Printing Office.

Social Security Administration (1998), Annual statistical supplement, 1998. *Social Security Bulletin.*

Sodei, T. (1993). Old age policy as a women's issue. In R. N. Butler and K. Kiikuni (Eds.), *Who is responsible for my old age* (pp. 73–95). New York: Springer Publishing Co.

Solano, L., Battisti, M., Coda, R, and Stanisci, S. (1993). Effects of some psychosocial variables on different disease manifestations in 112 cadets: A longitudinal study. *Journal of Psychosomatic Research, 37,* 621–636.

Soldz, S., and Vaillant, G. E. (1999). The Big Five personality traits and the life course: a 45-year longituindal study. *Journal of Research in Personality, 33,* 208–232.

Solomon, D. H. (1999). The role of aging processes in aging-dependent diseases. In V. L. Bengtson and K. W. Schaie (Eds.), *Handbook of theories of aging* (pp. 133–150). New York: Springer Publishing Co.

Solomon, D. H. (2001). Major issues in geriatrics. In J. E. Birren and K. W. Schaie (Eds.), *Handbook of the psychology of aging* (5th ed.). San Diego, CA: Academic Press.

Somers, A. R., and Spears, N. L. (1992). *The continuing care retirement community.* New York: Springer Publishing Co.

Sondik, E. J. (1994). Cancer incidence by age. *Journal of the National Cancer Institute, 86,* 169

Spence, K. W. (1958). A theory of emotionally based drive (D) and its relation to performance in simple learning situations. *American Psychologist, 13,* 131.

Spielberger, C. D. (1972). Conceptual and methodological issues in anxiety research. In C. D. Spielberger (Ed.), *Anxiety: Current trends in theory and research* (Vol. 2). New York: Academic Press.

Spikes, J. (1980). Grief, death, and dying. In E. W. Busse and G. D. Blazer (Eds.), *Handbook of geriatric psychiatry.* New York: Van Nostrand Reinhold.

Spirduso, W. W., and MacRae, G. P. (1990). Motor performance and aging. In J. E. Birren and K. W. Schaie (Eds.), *Handbook of the psychology of aging* (3rd ed., pp. 184–200). San Diego: Academic Press.

Spiro, A. III, Aldwin, C. M., Ward, K. D., and Mroczek, D. K. (1995). Personality and the incidence of hypertension among older men: Longitudinal findings from the Normative Aging Study. *Health Psychology, 14,* 563–569.

Spore, D. L., Horgas, A. L., Smyer, M. A., and Marks, L. N. (1992). The relationship of antipsychotic drug use, behavior, and diagnoses among nursing home residents. *Journal of Aging and Health, 4,* 514–535.

Stanford, E. P., Happersett, C. J., Morton, D., Molgaard, C., and Peddecord, K. M. (1991). Early retirement and functional impairment from a multiethnic perspective. *Research on Aging, 13,* 5–38.

Starr, B., and Weiner, M. (1981). *The Starr-Weiner report on sex and sexuality in the mature years.* New York: McGraw-Hill.

Starratt, C., and Peterson, L. (1997). Personality and normal aging. In P. D. Nussbaum (Ed.), *Handbook of neuropsychology and aging* (pp. 15–31). New York: Plenum.

Staudinger, U. M. (1996). Wisdom and the social-interactive foundation of the mind, In P. B. Baltes and U. M. Staudinger (Eds.), *Interactive minds* (pp. 276–315). New York: Cambridge University Press.

Staudinger, U. M. (1999). Older and wiser? Integrating results on the relationship between age and wisdom-related performance/ *International Journal of Behavioral Development, 23,* 641–664.

Staudinger, U. M., and Baltes, P. B. (1996). Interactive minds: A facilitative setting for wisdom-related performance? *Journal of Personality and Social Psychology, 71,* 746–762.

Staudinger, U. M., and Fleeson, W. (1996). Self and personality in old and very old age: A sample case of resilience? *Development and Psychopathology, 8,* 867–885.

Staudinger, U. M., Fleeson, W., and Baltes, P. B. (1999). Predictors of subjective physical health and well-being: Similarities and differences between the United States and Germany. *Journal of Personality and Social Psychology, 76,* 305–319.

Staudinger, U. M., Freund, A. M., Linden, M., and Maas, I. (1999). Self, personality, and life regulation: Facets of psychological resilience in old age. In P. B. Baltes and K. U. Mayer (Eds.), *The Berlin Aging Study: Aging from 70–100* (pp. 302–328). Cambridge, UK: Cambridge University Press.

Staudinger, U. M., Lopez, D. F., and Baltes, P. B. (1997). The psychometric location of wisdom-related performance; Intelligence, personality, and more? *Personality and Social Psychology Bulletin, 23,* 1200–1214.

Staudinger, U. M., Maciel, A. G., Smith, J., and Baltes, P. B. (1998). What predicts wisdom-related performance? A first look at personality, intelligence, and facilitative experiential contexts. *European Journal of Personality, 12,* 1–17.

Staudinger, U. M, Marsiske, M, and Baltes, P. B. (1995). Resilience and reserve capacity in later adulthood: Potentials and limits of development across the life span. In D. Cicchetti and D. Cohen (Eds.), *Manual of developmental psychopathology.* New York: Wiley.

Staudinger, U. M., Smith, J., and Baltes, P. B. (1992). Wisdom-related knowledge in life review tasks: Age differences and role of professional specialization. *Psychology and Aging, 7,* 271–281.

Stearns, P. (1975). Interpreting the medical literature on aging. In Newberry Library, Family and Community History Colloquia: *The Physician and Social History.* Chicago, IL, Oct. 30, 1975.

Steen, B. (1992). Psychosocial and cultural aspects of dementia. In M. Bergener, K. Hasegawa, S. I. Finkel, and T. Nishimura (Eds.), *Aging and mental disorders: International perspectives* (pp. 124–133). New York: Springer Publishing Co.

Steen, B., and Djurfeld, H. (1993). The gerontological and geriatric population studies in Gothenburg, Sweden. *Zeitschrift für Gerontologie, 26,* 163–169.

Steinberg, L. (1981). Transformations in family relations at puberty. *Developmental Psychology, 17,* 833–840.

Steinberg, L. (1987).The impact of puberty on family relations: Effects of pubertal status and pubertal timing. *Developmental Psychology, 23,* 451–460.

Steinberg, L., and Silverberg, S. (1987). Influences of marital satisfaction during the middle stages of the family life cycle. *Journal of Marriage and the Family, 49,* 751–760.

Stenmark, D. E., and Dunn, V. K. (1982). Issues related to the training of geropsychologists. In J. F. Santos and G. R. VandenBos (Eds.), *Psychology and the older adult.* Washington, DC: American Psychological Association.

Stern, Y., Gurland, B., Tatemichi, T. K., Ming, X. T., Wilder, D., and Mayeux, R. (1994). Influence of education and occupation on the incidence of Alzheimer's disese. *Journal of the American Medical Association, 271,* 1004–1010.

Sternberg, R. J. (1984). Toward a triarchic theory of human intelligence. *Behavioral and Brain Sciences, 7,* 269–315.

Sternberg, R. J. (1990). *Wisdom, its nature, origins, and development.* New York: Cambridge University Press..

Sternberg, R. J. (1998a). A balance theory of wisdom. *Review of General Psychology, 2,* 347–365.

Sternberg, R. J. (1998b). *Cupid's arrow: The course of love through time.* New York, NY: Cambridge University Press.

Sternberg, R. J., and Barnes, M. L. (Eds.) (1988). *The psychology of love.* New Haven, CT: Yale University Press.

Sternberg, R. J., and Berg, C. (1987). What are theories of adult intellectual development theories of? In C. Schooler and K. W. Schaie (Eds.), *Cognitive functioning and social structure over the life course* (pp. 3–23). Norwood, NJ: Ablex.

Sternberg, R. J., and Horvath, J. A. (Eds.) (1999). *Tacit knowledge in professional practice: Researcher and practitioner perspectives.* Mahwah, NJ: Lawrence Erlbaum Associates.

Sternberg, R. J., and Lubart, T. I. (1991). An investment theory of creativity and its development. *Human Development, 34,* 1–31.

Sternberg. R.J., and Lubart. T. I. (2001). Wisdom and creativity. In J. E. Birren and K. W. Schaie (Eds.), *Handbook of the psychology of aging* (5th ed.). San Diego, CA: Academic Press.

Stevens, J. C., Cruz, A., Marks, L. E., and Lakatos, S. (1998). A multimodal assessment of sensory thresholds in aging. *Journal of Gerontology: Psychological Sciences, 53B,* P263–P272.

Stigsdotter, A., and Bäckman, L. (1989a). Multifactorial memory training with older adults: How to foster maintenance of improved performance. *Gerontology, 35,* 260–267.

Stigsdotter, A., and Bäckman, L. (1989b). Comparisons of different forms of memory training in old age. In M. A. Luszca and T. Nettelbeck (Eds.), *Psychological development: Per-* spectives across the life span. Amsterdam, The Netherlands: Elsevier.

Stigsdotter, A., Neely. A., and Bäckman, L. (1993). Maintenance of gains following multifactorial and unifactorial memory training in late adulthood. *Educational Gerontology, 19,* 105–117.

Stigsdotter-Neely, A. (1994). *Memory training in late adulthood: Issues of maintenance, transfer, and individual difference.* Doctoral dissertation, Section of Geriatric Medicine, Department of Clinical Neuroscience and Family Medicine, Karolinska Institute, Section of psychology, Stockholm Gerontology Research Center, Stockholm, Sweden.

Stiver, L, S., and O'Leary, V. (Eds.) (1990) *Storming the tower: Women in the academic world.* East Brunswick, NJ: Nichols/GP Publishing.

Strahan, G. V. (1988). Characteristics of registered nurses in nursing homes. *NCHS Advance Data, 152,* 1–8.

Strahan, G. V. (1994). An overview of home health and hospice care patients: Preliminary data from the 1993 National Home and Hospice Care Survey. *Advance Data, No. 256.* Washington, DC: National Center for Health Statistics.

Straka, G. A., Fabian, T., and Will., J. (1990). "Berufsverbot" mit 65 [Mandatory retirement at 65]. *Psychologie und Gesellschaftskritik, 14,* 1–16.

Straker, M. (1982). Adjustment disorders and personality disorders in the aged. In L. F. Jarvik and G. W. Small (Eds.), *The psychiatric clinics of North America.* Philadelphia, PA: Saunders.

Strauss, A., and Glaser, B. (1985). Awareness of dying. In S. Wilcox and M. Sutton (Eds.), *Awareness of dying.* Palo Alto, CA: Mayfield.

Strawbridge, W. J., Cohen, R. D., Shema, S. J., and Kaplan, G. A. (1997). Frequent attendance at religious services and mortality over 28 years. *American Journal of Public Health, 87,* 957–961.

Strawbridge, W. J., Shema, S. J., Balfour, J. L., Higby, H. R., and Kaplan, G. A. (1998). Antecedents of frailty over three decades in an older cohort. *Journal of Gerontology: Social Sciences, 53B,* S9–S16.

Stroebe, M. S., Stroebe, W., and Hansson, R.O. (1988). Bereavement research: An historical introduction. *Journal of Social Issues, 43,* 1–18.

Strong, E. K., Jr. (1955). *Vocational interests 18 years after college.* Minneapolis, MN: University of Minnesota Press.

Sturgis, E. T., Dolce, J. J., and Dickerson, P. C. (1988). Pain management in the elderly. In L. L. Carstensen and B. A. Edelstein (Eds.), *Handbook of clinical gerontology* (pp. 190–203). New York: Pergamon.

Sundström, G . (1994). Care by families: An overview of trends. *Social Policy Studies, No. 14,* 15–55. Paris, France: OECD.

Sundström, G., and Thorslund, M. (1994). Caring for the frail elderly in Sweden. In L. K Olson (Ed.), *The graying of the world, who will care for the frail elderly* (pp. 59–85). Binghamton, NY: Haworth.

Super, D. (1992). Toward a comprehensive theory of career development. In D. Montross and C. Shinkman (Eds.), *Career development: Theory and practice.* (pp 35–64). Springfield, IL: Charles C. Thomas.

Suzman R., and Riley, M. W. (1985). Introducing the "oldest old." *Milbank Memorial Fund Quarterly: Health and Society, 63, 177–185.*

Svensson, T. (1996). Competence and quality of life: Theoretical views of biography. In J. E. Birren, G. M. Kenyon, J. E., Ruth, J. J. F. Schroots, and T. Svensson (Eds.), *Aging and biography: Explorations in adult development* (pp. 100–116) New York: Springer Publishing Co.

Svensson, T., Dehlin, O., Hagberg, B., and Samuelsson, G. (1993). The Lund 80+ study: Some general findings. In J. J. F. Schroots (Ed.), *Aging, health and competence: The next generation of longitudinal research.* Amsterdam, The Netherlands: Elsevier.

Swenson, M. W., Pearson, J. S., and Osborne, D. (1973). *An MMPI source book.* Minneapolis, MN: University of Minnesota Press.

Szinovacz, M. E.(1996a). Couples' employment/retirement patterns and perceptions of marital quality. *Research on Aging, 18,* 243–268.

Szinovacz, M. E. (1996b). Living with grandparents: Variations by cohort, race and family structure. *International Journal of Sociology and Social Policy, 16,* 89–123.

Szinovacz, M. E. (1997). Adult children taking parents into their homes: Effects of childhood living arrangements. *Journal of Marriage and the Family, 59,* 700–717.

Szinovacz, M. E. (1998). Grandparents today: A demographic profile. *Gerontologist, 38,* 37–52.

Szinovacz, M. E., and Harpster, P. (1994). Couples' employment/retirement status and the division of household tasks. *Journal of Gerontology: Social Sciences, 49,* S125–S136.

Szinovacz, M., and Washo, C. (1992). Gender differences in exposure to life events and adaptation to retirement. *Journal of Gerontology: Social Sciences, 47,* S191–S196.

Tamir, L. (1989). Modern myths about men at midlife: An assessment. In S. Hunter and M. Sundel (Eds.), *Midlife myths.* Newbury Park, CA: Sage.

Tamm, M. E. (1996). Personification of life and death among Swedish health care professionals. *Death Studies, 20,* 1–22.

Tatemichi, T. K., Sacktor, N., and Mayeux, R. (1994). Dementia associated with cerebrovascular disease, other degenerative diseases, and metabolic disorders. In R. D. Terry, R. Katzman, and K. L. Blick (Eds.), *Alzheimer Disease* (pp. 167–178). New York: Raven Press.

Tavris, C., and Offir, C. (1977). *The longest war: Sex differences in perspective.* New York: Harcourt Brace Jovanovich.

Tavris, C. and Sadd, S. (1975). *The Redbook report on female sexuality.* New York: Delacorte.

Taylor, R. J. and Chatters, L. M. (1991). Extended family networks of older black adults. *Journal of Gerontology: Social Sciences, 46,* S210–S217.

Taylor, R. J., Chatters, L. M., Jayakody, R., and Levin, J. S. (1996). Black and white differences in religious participation: A multi-sample comparison. *Journal for the Scientific Study of Religion, 35,* 403–410.

Taylor, R. J., Chatters, L. M., Tucker, M. B., and Lewis, E. (1990). Developments in research on black families: A decade review. *Journal of Marriage and the Family, 52,* 993–1014.

Teachman, J., Day, R., Paasch, K, Carver, C., and Call, V. (1998). Sibling resemblance in behavioral and cognitive outcomes: The role of father presence. *Journal of Marriage and the Family, 60,* 835–848.

Teachman, J. D., and Paasch, K. (1998). The family and educational aspirations. *Journal of Marriage and the Family, 60,* 704–714.

Tebbi, C. K., Zevin, M. A., Richards, M. E., and Cummings, K. M. (1989). Attribution of responsibility in adolescent cancer patients and their parents. *Journal of Cancer Education, 4,* 135–142.

Tellegen, A. (1985). Structures of mood and personality and their relevance to assessing anxiety with an emphasis on self report. In A. H. Tuma and J. D. Maser (Eds.), *Anxiety and the anxiety disorders* (pp. 681–706). Hillsdale, NJ: Erlbaum.

Teresi, J. H., and Holmes, D. (1994). Overview of methodological issues in gerontological and geriatric measurement. In M. P. Lawton and J. A. Teresi (Eds.), *Annual review of gerontology and geriatrics* (Vol. 14, pp. 1–22). New York: Springer Publishing Co.

Teri, L. (1991). Behavioral assessment and treatment of depression in older adults. In P. A. Wisocki (Ed.), *Handbook of clinical behavior therapy with the elderly client* (pp. 225–244). New York: Plenum.

Teri, L., Curtis, J., Gallagher-Thompson, D., and Thompson, L. W. (1994). Cognitive-behavior therapy with depressed older adults. In L. S. Schnedier, C. F. Reynolds, B. Liebowitz, and A. J. Friedhoff (Eds.), *Diagnosis and treatment of depression late life* (pp. 279–292). Washington, DC: American Psychological Association.

Teri, L., Ferretti, L., Gibbons, L. E., Logsdon, R. G., McCurry, S. M., Kukull, W. A., McCormick, W. C., Bowen, J. D., and Larson, E. B. (In press). Anxiety in Alzheimer's disease: Prevalence and comorbidity. *Journal of Gerontology: Medical Sciences.*

Teri, L., Logsdon, R., and Truax, P. (1997). Behavior and caregiver burden: Behavioral problems in patients with Alzheimer disease and its association with caregiver distress. *Alzheimer Disease and Associate Disorders, 11, (Suppl. 4),* S35–S38.

Teri, L., Logsdon, R., and Yesavage, J. (1997). Measuring behavior, mood, and psychiatric symptoms in Alzheimer's disease. *Alzheimer Disease and Associated Disorders, 11 (Suppl. 6),* 50–59.

Terry, R. D. (1978). Aging, senile dementia, and Alzheimer's disease. In R. Katzman, R. D. Terry, and K. L. Bick (Eds.), *Alzheimer's disease: Senile dementia and related disorders.* New York: Raven Press.

Tesch-Römer, C. (1997). Psychological effects of hearing aid use in older adults. *Journal of Gerontology: Psychological Sciences, 52B,* P127–P138.

Tesch-Römer, C., and Wahl, H. W. (1998). Rehabilitation in old age: Psychosocial issues. In A. Hersen and M. Bellack (Eds.), *Comprehensive clinical psychology* (Vol. 7, pp. 525–550). Oxford, UK: Elsevier.

Tett, R. P., Jackson, D. N., and Rothstein, M. (1991). Personality measures as predictors of job performance: A meta-analytic review. *Personnel Psychology, 44,* 703–742.

Thal, L. J., Grundman, M., and Klauber, M. R. (1988). Dementia: Characteristics of a referral population and factors associated with progression. *Neurology, 38,* 1083–1090.

Theriault, J. (1994). Retirement as a psychosocial transition: Process of adaptation to change. *International Journal of Aging and Human Development, 38,* 153–170.

Thoits, P. A. (1982). Conceptual, methodological and theoretical problems in the study of social support. *Journal of Health Social Behavior, 23,* 145–159.

Thomas, L. E., and Eisenhandler, S. A. (Eds.) (1999). *Religion, belief, and spirituality in late life.* New York: Springer Publishing Co.

Thompson, E. E., and Krause, N. (1998). Living alone and neighborhood characteristics as predictors of social support in later life. *Journal of Gerontology: Social Sciences, 53B,* S354–S364.

Thompson, I. (1994). Woldenberg Village: An illustration of supportive designs for older adults. *Experimental Aging Research,* 239–244.

Thompson, L. W., Davies, R., Gallagher, D., and Krantz, S. E. (1986). Cognitive therapy with older adults. *Clinical Gerontologist, 5,* 245–279.

Thompson, L. W., and Gallagher, D. E. (1985). Treatment of depression in elderly outpatients. In G. Maletta (Ed.), *Advances in neurogerontology, Vol. 5: Treatment of the elderly neuropsychiatric patient.* New York: Praeger.

Thompson, L. W., Gantz, F., Florsheim, M., DelMaestro, S., Rodman, J., Gallagher-Thompson, D., and Bryan, H. (1991). Cognitive/behavioral therapy for affective disorders in the elderly. In W. A. Meyers (Ed.), *New techniques in the psychotherapy of older patients* (pp. 3–19). Washington, DC: American Psychiatric Press.

Thompson, P., Itzin, C., and Abendstern, M. (1990), *I don't feel old: The experience of later life.* Oxford, UK: Oxford University Press.

Thompson, R. A., and Amato, P. R. (Eds.). (1999). *The postdivorce family: Children, parenting, and society.* Thousand Oaks , CA: Sage.

Thomson, E., and Colella, U. (1992). Cohabitation and marital stability:

Quality or commitment? *Journal of Marriage and the Family, 54,* 259–267.

Thornton, A. (1989). Changing attitudes toward family issues in the United States. *Journal of Marriage and the Family, 51,* 873–893.

Thornton, A., and Camburn, D. (1987). The influence of the family on premarital sexual attitudes and behavior. *Demography, 24,* 323–340.

Thorson, J. A., and Powell, F. C. (1994). A revised death anxiety scale. In R. A. Neimeyer (Ed.), *Death anxiety handbook* (pp. 31–44). Washington, DC: Taylor and Francis.

Thurstone, L. L., and Thurstone, T. G. (1941). Factorial studies of intelligence. *Psychometric Monographs,* No. 2.

Timiras, P. S. (1985). Physiology of ageing: Aspects of enuroendocrine regulation. In M. S. J. Pathy (Ed.), *Principles and practice of geriatric medicine* (pp. 105–130). New York: Wiley.

Timko, C., and Moos, R. H. (1990). Determinants of interpersonal support and self-direction in group residential facilities. *Journal of Gerontology: Social Sciences, 45,* S184–S192.

Timko, C., and Moos, R. H. (1991). A typology of social climates in group residential facilities for older people. *Journal Gerontology: Social Sciences, 46,* S160–S169.

Timko, C., and Rodin, J. (1985). Staff-patient relationships in nursing homes: Sources of conflict and rehabilitation potential. *Journal of Rehabilitation Psychology, 30,* 93–108.

Tjaden, P., and Thoennes, N. (1998). *Prevalence, incidence and consequences of violence against women. Findings from the National Violence Against Women Survey.* Washington, D.C.: National Institute of Justice, U.S. Department of Justice.

Tobin, S. S., and Neugarten, B. L. (1961). Life satisfaction and social interaction in aging. *Journal of Gerontology, 16,* 344–346.

Tolbert, P. S., and Moen, P. (1998). Men's and women's definitions of "good" jobs: Similarities and differences by age and across time. *Work and Occupations. 25,* 168–194.

Tomer, A. (1992). Death anxiety in adult life: Theoretical perspectives. *Death Studies, 16,* 475–506.

Tomer, A. (1994). Death anxiety in adult life—Theoretical perspectives. In R. A. Neimeyer (Ed.), *Death anxiety handbook* (pp. 3–30). Washington, DC: Taylor and Francis.

Tosti-Vasey, J. L., Person, D. C., Maier, H., & Willis S. L. (1992, November). *The relationship of game playing to intellectual ability in old age.* Paper presented at the annual meeting of the Gerontological Society of America, Washington, DC.

Treloar, A. E. (1974). Menarche, menopause, and intervening fecundability. *Human Biology, 46,* 89–107.

Treloar, A. E. (1982). Predicting the close of menstrual life. In A. Voda, M. Dinnerstein, and S. O'Donnell (Eds.), *Changing perspective on menopause.* Austin, TX: University of Texas Press.

Triplett, G., Cohen, D., Reimer, W., Rimaldi, S., Hill, C., Roshdieh, S., Stanczak, E, M., Sisco, K., and Templer, D. I. (1995). Death discomfort differential. *Omega, Journal of Death and Dying, 31,* 295–304.

Tross, S., and Blum, J. E. (1988). A review of group therapy with the older adult: Practice and research. In B. W. MacLennan, S. Saul, and M. B.

Weiner (Eds.), *Group psychotherapies for the elderly* (pp. 3–32). Madison, WI: International Universities Press.

Trull, T. J., Useda, J., Costa, P. T., Jr., and McCrae, R. R. (1995). Comparison of the MMPI-2 Personality Psychopathology Five (PSY-5), the NEO-PI, and the NEO-PI-R. *Psychological Assessment, 7,* 508–516.

Tuch, S. A., and Martin, J. K. (1991). Race in the workplace; Black/white differences in the sources of job satisfaction. *Sociological Quarterly, 32,* 103–116.

Tucker, D. M., and Desmond, R.E., Jr. (1998). Aging and the plasticity of the self. In K. W. Schaie and M. P. Lawton (Eds.), *Annual review of gerontology and geriatrics* (Vol. 17, pp. 266–281). New York: Springer Publishing Co.

Tulving, E. (1972). Episodic and semantic memory. In E. Tulving and W. Donaldson (Eds.), *Organization of memory.* New York: Academic Press.

Tulving, E. (1991). Memory research is not a zero-sum game. *American Psychologist, 46,* 41–42.

Tulving, E. (1993). What is episodic memory? *Current Directions in Psychological Science, 2,* 67–70.

Turban, D. B., and Dougherty, T. W. (1994). Role of protege personality in receipt of mentoring and career success. *Academy of Management Journal. 37,* 688–702.

Turner, L. W., Taylor, J. E., and Hunt, S. (1998). Predictors for osteoporosis diagnosis among postmenopausal women: Results from a national survey. *Journal of Women and Aging, 10,* 80–95.

Udry, J. R. (1971). *The social context of marriage* (2nd ed.). New York: Lippincott.

Udry, J. R. (1974). *The social context of marriage* (3rd ed.). New York: Lippincott.

Umberson, D., Wortman, C. B., and Kessler, R. C. (1992). Widowhood and depression: Explaining long-term gender differences in vulnerability. *Journal of Health and Social Behavior, 33,* 10–24.

Unger, R. K. (1979). *Female and male.* New York: Harper and Row.

U.S. Bureau of the Census. (1983). Persons in institutions and other group quarters. *1980 Census of Population: Subject Reports* (Vol. 2). Washington, DC: U.S. Government Printing Office.

U.S. Bureau of the Census. (1989a). *Current Population Reports.* Series P-25, No. 1018. Washington, DC: U.S. Government Printing Office.

U.S. Bureau of the Census. (1989b). *National data book and guide to sources: Statistical abstract of U.S. 1989.* Washington, DC: U.S. Government Printing Office.

U.S. Bureau of the Census (1990). *Education in the United States.* Washington, D.C.: U. S. Government Printing Office.

U.S. Bureau of the Census. (1992a). Age, sex, race and Hispanic origin information from the 1990 Census. *Report 1990 CPH-L-74.* Washington, DC: U.S. Government Printing Office.

U.S. Bureau of the Census. (1992b). *Current Population Reports.* Series P-25, No. 1092. Washington, DC: U.S. Government Printing Office.

U.S. Bureau of the Census (1993a). Marital Status and Living Arrangements. *Current Population Reports.* Washington, DC: U. S. Government Printing Office.

U.S. Bureau of the Census (1993b). Money income of the households, families and persons in the United States: 1992. *Current Population Reports.* Washington, DC: U.S. Government Printing Office.

U.S. Bureau of the Census (1994). *The diverse living arrangements of children: Summer, 1991.* Washington, DC: U.S. Government Printing Office.

U.S. Bureau of the Census, (1995). Current population reports, Series P20-514. Washington, DC: U.S. Government Printing Office.

U.S. Bureau of the Census (1996). Population projections of the United States by age, sex, race, and hispanic origin: 1995 to 2050. *Current Population Reports,* P25–1130. Washington, DC: U.S. Government Printing Office.

U.S. Bureau of the Census (1997). Percent of Persons aged 18 to 24 reported voted by race and hispanic origin: November 1964 to present. *Current Population Reports, Series P20-466.* Washington, DC: U.S. Government Printing Office.

U.S. Bureau of the Census (1998a). *Current Population Reports,* Series P20–514. Washington, DC: U.S. Government Printing Office.

U.S. Bureau of the Census (1998b). *Current Population Reports,* Series P20–515. Washington, DC: U.S. Government Printing Office.

U.S. Bureau of the Census (1998c). Income: 1997. *Current Population Reports,* P-60, No. 200. Washington, DC: U. S. Government Printing Office.

U.S. Bureau of the Census (1998d). Poverty, 1997. *Current Population Reports,* P-60, No.201. Washington, DC: U. S. Government Printing Office.

U.S. Bureau of the Census (1999). Money income in the United States, 1998. *Current Population Reports,* P-20, No, 206. Washington, DC: U. S. Government Printing Office.

U.S. Bureau of Labor Statistics (1994). *Employment and earnings.* Washington, DC: U. S. Government Printing Office.

Vaillant, G. E. (1977). *Adaptation to life.* Boston, MA: Little, Brown.

Vaillant, G. E. (1995a). *The natural history of alcoholism revisited.* Cambridge, MA: Harvard University Press.

Vaillant, G. E. (1995b). *The wisdom of the ego.* Cambridge, MA: Harvard University Press.

Vaillant, G. E., Bond, M., and Vaillant, C. O. (1986). An empirically validated hierarchy of defense mechanisms. *Archives of General Psychiatry, 43,* 786–794.

Vaillant, G. E., and Hiller-Stumhoefel, S. (1996). The natural history of alcoholism. *Alcohol Health and Research World, 20,* 152–161.

Vaillant, G. E., and McCullough, L. (1998). The role of ego mechanisms of defense in the diagnosis of personality disorders. In J. W. Barron (Ed.), *Making diagnosis meaningful: Enhancing evaluation and treatment of psychological disorders* (pp. 119–158). Washington, DC: American Psychological Association.

Valiant, G. E., Meyer, S. E., Mukamal, K., and Soldz, S. (1998). Are social supports in late midlife a cause or a result of successful physical aging? *Psychological Medicine, 28,* 1159–1168.

Vaillant, G. E., and Perry, J. C. (1980). Personality disorders. In H. Kaplan, A. Freedman, and B. Sadock (Eds.), *Comprehensive text on psychiatry* (3rd ed.). Baltimore: Williams and Wilkins.

Vaillant, G. E., and Vaillant, C. O. (1990). Determinants and consequences of creativity in a cohort of gifted women. *Psychology of Women Quarterly, 14,* 607–616.

Van der Wal. G.. Muller, M. T., Christ, L. M., and Ribb. M. W. (1994). Voluntary active euthanasia and physician-assisted suicide in Dutch nursing homes: Requests and administration. *Journal of the American Geriatrics Society, 42,* 620–623.

Van Doorn, C., and Kasl, S. V. (1998). Can parental longevity and self-rated life expectancy predict mortality among older persons? Results from an Australian cohort. *Journal of Gerontology: Social Sciences, 53B,* (pp. 528–534).

Van Manen, K., and Whitbourne, S. K. (1997). Psychosocial development and life experiences in adulthood: A 22-year sequential study. *Psychology and Aging, 12,* 239–246

Van Tilburg, T. (1998). Losing and gaining in old age: Changes in personal network size and social support in a four-year longitudinal study. *Journal of Gerontology: Social Sciences, 53B,* S313–S323.

Vaughan, N. E., and Letowski, T. (1997). Effects of age, speech rate, and type of test on temporal auditory processing. *Journal of Speech, Language and Hearing Research, 40,* 1192–1200.

Verbrugge, L. M., Gruber-Baldini, A. L., and Fozard, J. (1996). Age differences and age changes in activities: Baltimore Longitudinal Study of Aging. *Journal of Gerontology: Social Sciences, 51B,* S30–S41.

Viney, L. L., Benjamin, Y. N., and Preston, C. (1989). Mourning and reminiscence: Parallel psychotherapeutic processes for elderly people. *International Journal of Aging and Human Development, 28,* 239–249.

Vinick, B. H., and Ekerdt, D. J. (1991). Retirement: What happens to husband wife relationships? *Journal of Geriatric Psychiatry, 24,* 16–23.

Vollhardt, B. R., Bergener, M., and Hesse, C. (1992). Psychotropics in the elderly. In M. Bergener, K. Hasegawa, S.I. Finkel, and T. Nishimura (Eds.), *Aging and mental disorders: International perspectives* (pp. 194–211). New York: Springer Publishing Co.

Volling, B. L., and Belsky, J. (1991). Multiple determinants of father involvement during infancy in dual-earner and single-earner families. *Journal of Marriage and the Family, 53,* 461–474.

Vondracek, F. W. (1992). The construct of identity and its use in career theory and research. *Career Development Quarterly, 41,* 130–144.

Vondracek, F. W. (1998). Career development: A lifespan perspective (Introduction to the Special Section). *International Journal of Behavioral Development, 22,* 1–6.

Vondracek, F. W., Lerner, R. M., and Schulenberg, J. E. (1986). *Career development: A life-span developmental approach.* Hillsdale, NJ: Erlbaum.

Von Dras, D. D., and Siegler, I. C. (1997). Stability in extraversion and aspects of social support at midlife. *Journal of Personality and Social Psychology, 72,* 233–241.

Wagner, E. H., LaCroix, A. Z., Grothaus, L. C., and Hecht, J. A. (1993). Responsiveness of health status measures to change among older adults. *Journal of the American Geriatrics Society, 41,* 241–248.

Wahl, H. W. (1994). Visual impairment in later life: A challenge for environmental gerontology. *Aging and Vision News, 6,* 1–2.

Wahl, H. W. (1998). Age-related visual impairment as life crisis and challenge for compensating resources. *Zeitschrift für Klinische Psychologie, 27,* 111–117.

Wahl, H. W., and Baltes, M. M. (1990). Die soziale Umwetl alter Menschen: Entwicklungsanregende oder hemmende Pflegeinteraktionen [The social environment of the elderly: Caregiver interactions that enhance or inhibit positive development]. *Zeitschrift für Entwicklungspsychologie und Pädagogische Psychologie, 22,* 266–283.

Wahl, H. W., and Oswald, F. (2000). The person/environment perspective of visual impairment. In B. Silverstone, M. A. Long, B. Rosenthal, and E. Faye (Eds.), *The Lighthouse handbook of vision and rehabilitation.* New York: Oxford University Press.

Walker, A. J., Acock, A. C., Bowman, S. R., and Li, F. (1996). Amount of care given and caregiving satisfaction: A latent growth curve analysis. *Journal of Gerontology: Psychological Sciences, 51,* P130–P142.

Walker, L. (1984). Sex differences in the development of moral reasoning: A critical review. *Child Development, 55,* 677–691.

Walker, L. (1986). Experiential and cognitive sources of moral development in adulthood. *Human Development, 29,* 113–124.

Walker, S. N. (1994). Health promotion and prevention of diseases and disability among older adults: Who is responsible? *Generations, 18* (1), 45–50.

Wallin, A., Brun, A., and Gustafson, L. (1994). Swedish consensus on dementia diseases. *Acta Neurolologica Scandinavica, 90,* Supplement No. 157.

Wallston, K. A., and Wallston, B. S. (1981). Health related locus of control scales. In H. M. Lefcourt (Ed.), *Research with the locus of control construct: Assessment methods* (Vol. 1, pp. 189–243). New York: Academic Press.

Walsh, D. A., Till, R. E., and Williams, M. V. (1978). Age differences in peripheral perceptual processing: A montropic backward masking investigation. *Journal of Experimental Psychology: Human Perception and Performance, 4,* 232–243.

Warner, W. L. (1965). The city of the dead. In W. L. Warner (Ed.), *The living and the dead.* New Haven, CT: Yale University Press.

Warr, P. (1998). Age work and mental health. In K. W. Schaie and C. Schooler (Eds). *The impact of work on older adults* (pp. 252–296). New York: Springer Publishing Co.

Wass, H. (1991). Helping children cope with death. In D. Papadatou, and C. Papadatou (Eds.) *Children and death* (pp. 11–32). New York: Hemisphere.

Waterman, A. S. (1982). Identity development from adolescence to adulthood: An extension of theory and a review of research. *Developmental Psychology, 18,* 341–358.

Waterman, A. S. (1999). Identity, the identity statuses, and identity status development: A contemporary statement. *Developmental Review, 19,* 591–621.

Waterman, A. S., and Archer, S. L. (1990). A life-span perspective on identity prevention: Development in form and process. In P. B. Baltes, D. L. Featherman and R. M. Lerner

(Eds.), *Life-span development and behavior*. Hillsdale, NJ: Erlbaum.

Watzke, J. and Smith, D. B. D. (1994). Concern for and knowledge of safety hazards among older people: Implications for research and prevention. *Experimental Aging Research, 20,* 177–188.

Weale, R. A. (1988). Age and the transmittance of the human crystalline lens. *Journal of Physiology, 395,* 577–587.

Weatherford, M. J. (1981). *Tribes on the hill.* New York: Rawson, Wade.

Wechsler, D. (1972). "Hold" and "Don't Hold" tests. In S. M. Chown (Ed.), *Human aging.* New York: Penguin.

Weenolsen, P. (1988). *Transcendence of loss over the life span.* New York: Hemisphere.

Weg, R. B. (1983). Changing physiology of aging: Normal and pathological. In D. W. Woodruff and J. E. Birren (Eds.), *Aging: Scientific perspectives and social issues* (2nd ed.). Monterey, CA: Brooks/Cole.

Weiffenbach, J. M., Tylenda, C. A., and Baum, B. J. (1990). Oral sensory changes in aging, *Journal of Gerontology: Medical Sciences, 45,* M121–M125.

Weiss, R. S. (1979). The emotional impact of marital separation. In G. Levinger and O. C. Moles (Eds.), *Divorce and separation.* New York: Basic Books.

Weisz, J. R. (1983). Can I control it? The pursuit of veridical answers across the life span. In P. B. Baltes and O. G. Brim, Jr. (Eds.), *Life-span development and behavior* (Vol. 5). New York: Academic Press.

Wekesser, C. (Ed.) (1995). *Euthanasia: Opposing viewpoints.* San Diego, CA: Greenhaven.

Welch, D. C., and West, R. L. (1995). Self-efficacy and mastery: Its application to issues of environmental control, cognition, and aging. *Developmental Review, 15,* 150–171.

Welsh, K., Butters, N., Hughes, J., Mohs, R., and Heyman, A. (1991). Detection of abnormal memory decline in mild cases of Alzheimer's disease using CERAD neuropsychological measures. *Archives of Neurology, 48,* 278–281.

Werner, D. (1981). Gerontocracy among the Mekranoti of Central Brazil. *Anthropological Quarterly, 54,* 15–27.

West, R. L. (1989). Planning practical memory training for the aged. In L. W. Poon, D. Rubin, and B. Wilson (Eds.), *Everyday cognition in adulthood and late life.* Cambridge, UK: Cambridge University Press.

West, R. L. (1995). Compensatory strategies for age-associated memory impairment. In A. D. Baddeley and B. A. Wilson (Eds.), *Handbook of memory disorders* (pp. 481–500). Chichester, UK: John Wiley & Sons.

West, R. L., and Crook, T. H. (1990). Age differences in everyday memory: Laboratory analogues of telephone number recall. *Psychology and Aging, 5,* 1990, 510–529.

West, R. L., Crook, T. H., and Barron, K. L. (1992). Everyday memory performance across the life span: Effects of age and noncognitive individual differences. *Psychology and Aging, 7,* 72–82.

West, S. K., Muoz, B., Rubin, G. S., Schein, O. D., Bandden-Roche, K., Zeger, S., German, P. S., and Fried, L. P. (1997). Function and visual impairment in a population-based study of older adults. *Investigative Ophtal-*

mology and Visual Sciences, 38, 72–82.

Westerhof, G. J., and Dittman-Kohli, F. (2000). Work status and the construction of work-related selves. In K. W. Schaie and J. Hendricks (Eds.), *Evolution of the aging self: Societal impacts* (pp. 123–157). New York: Springer Publishing Co.

Whelan, E. A., Sandler, D. P., McConnaughey, D. R., and Weinberg, C. R. (1990). Menstrual and reproductive characteristics and age at natural menopause. *American Journal of Epidemiology, 131,* 625.

Whitbourne, S. K. (1985a). *The aging body: Physiological changes and psychological consequences.* New York: Springer-Verlag.

Whitbourne, S. K. (1985b). The psychological construction of the life span. In J. E. Birren and K. W. Schaie (Eds.), *Handbook of the psychology of aging* (2nd ed.). New York: Van Nostrand Reinhold.

Whitbourne, S. K. (1986). *The me I know: A study of adult identity.* New York: Springer-Verlag.

Whitbourne, S. K. (1989). Comments on Lachman's "Personality and aging at the crossroads." In K. W. Schaie and C. Schooler (Eds.), *Social structure and aging: Psychological processes* (pp. 191–198). Hillsdale, NJ: Erlbaum.

Whitbourne, S. K. (1996). Psychosocial perspectives on emotion: The role of identity in the aging process. In C. Magai and S. H. McFadden (Eds), *Handbook of emotion, adult development, and aging* (pp. 83–98). San Diego, CA: Academic Press.

Whitbourne, S. (1998). Physical changes. In I. H. Nordhus, G. R. VandenBos, S. Berg, and P. Fromhold (Eds.), *Clinical geropsychology.* (pp 79–108). Washington, DC: American Psychological Association.

Whitbourne, S. K., and Collins, K. J. (1999). Identity processes and perceptions of physical functioning in adults: Theoretical and clinical implications. *Psychotherapy, 35,* 519–530.

Whitbourne, S. K., and Connolly, L. S. (1999). The developing self in midlife. In S. L. Willis and J. D. Reid (Eds.), *Life in the middle: Psychological and social development in middle age* (pp. 25–45). San Diego, CA; Academic Press.

Whitbourne, S. K., Zuschlag, M. K., Elliot, L. B., and Waterman, A. S. (1992). Psychosocial development in adulthood: A 22-year sequential study. *Journal of Personality and Social Psychology, 63,* 260–271.

White, L., Booth, A., and Edwards, J. (1986). Children and marital happiness: Why the negative correlation. *Journal of Family Issues, 7,* 131–147.

Whitely, W. T., and Coetsier, P. (1993). The relationship of career mentoring to early career outcomes. *Organization Studies, 14*(3), 419–441.

Whitely, W., Dougherty, T. W., and Dreher, G. F. (1992). Correlates of career-oriented mentoring for early career managers and professionals. *Journal of Organizational Behavior, 13,* 141–154.

Whiting, W. L. IV, and Smith, A. D. (1997). Differential age-related processing limitations in recall and recognition tasks. *Psychology and Aging. 12,* 216–224.

Wigdor, B. (1980). Drives and motivation with aging. In J. E. Birren and R. B. Sloane (Eds.), *Handbook of mental health and aging.* Englewood Cliffs, NJ: Prentice-Hall.

Wiggins, J. S., and Pincus, A. L. (1992). Personality: Structure and assessment. In M. R. Rosenzweig and L. W. Porter (Eds.), *Annual review of psychology* (vol. 43, pp. 473–504). Palo Alto, CA: Annual Reviews.

Wilkie, J. R., Ferree, M. M., and Ratcliff, K. S. (1998). Gender and fairness: Marital satisfaction in two-earner couples. *Journal of Marriage and the family, 60,* 577–594.

Willett, J. B., and Sayer, A. G. (1994). Using covariance structure analysis to detect correlates and predictors of individual change over time. *Psychological Bulletin, 116,* 363–381.

Willett, W., Stampfer, M. J., Bain, C., Lipnick, R., Speizer, F. E., Rosner, B., Cramer, D., and Hennekens, C. (1983). Cigarette smoking, relative weight, and menopause. *American Journal of Epidemiology, 117,* 651–658.

Williams, R. B., Barefoot, J. C., Blumenthal, J. A., Helms, M. J., Luechen, L, Pieper, C., Siegler, I C., and Suarez, E. (1997). Psychosocial correlates of job strain in a sample of working women. *Archives of General Psychiatry, 54,* 543–548.

Williams, T. F. (1993). Aging versus disease: Which changes seen with age are the result of "biological aging"? In R. L. Sprott, R. W. Huber and T. F. Williams (Eds.), *The biology of aging* (pp. 35–44). New York: Springer Publishing Co.

Willis, S. L. (1985). Towards an educational psychology of the older adult learner: Intellectual and cognitive bases. In J. E. Birren and K. W. Schaie (Eds.), *Handbook of the psychology of aging* (2nd ed.). New York: Van Nostrand Reinhold.

Willis, S. L. (1987). Cognitive training and everyday competence. In K. W. Schaie (Ed.), *Annual review of gerontology and geriatrics* (Vol. 7, pp. 159–188). New York: Springer Publishing Co.

Willis, S. L. (1989a). Cohort differences in cognitive aging: A sample case. In K. W. Schaie and C. Schooler (Eds.), *Social structure and aging: Psychological processes* (pp. 95–112). New York: Erlbaum.

Willis, S. L. (1989b). Improvement with cognitive training: Which old dogs learn what tricks? In L. Poon, D. Rubin, and B. Wilson (Eds.), *Everyday cognition in adulthood and late life* (pp. 545–569). Cambridge, MA: Cambridge University Press.

Willis, S. L. (1990). Contributions of cognitive training research to understanding late life potential. In M. Perlmutter (Eds.), *Late life potential* (pp. 25–42). Washington, DC: Gerontological Society of America.

Willis, S. L. (1993). *The Everyday Problems Test.* Unpubl. manuscript, The Pennylvania State University, University Park, PA.

Willis, S. L. (1996). Everyday problem solving. In J. E. Birren and K. W. Schaie (Eds.), *Handbook of the psychology of aging* (4th ed., pp. 287–307). San Diego, CA: Academic Press.

Willis, S. L. (1997). Everyday cognitive competence in the elderly: Conceptual issues and empirical findings. *Gerontologist, 36,* 595–601.

Willis, S. L., Blieszner, R., and Baltes, P. B. (1981). Intellectual training research in aging: Modification of performance on the fluid ability of figural relations. *Journal of Educational Psychology, 73,* 41–50.

Willis, S. L., and Dubin, S. (Eds.) (1990). *Maintaining professional competence.* San Francisco, CA: Jossey-Bass.

Willis, S.L., Jay, G. M., Diehl, M., and Marsiske, M. (1992). Longitudinal change and prediction of everyday task competence in the elderly. *Research on Aging, 14,* 68–91.

Willis, S. L. and Margrett, J. (in press). Aging and education. In N. J. Smelser and P. B. Baltes (Eds.), *International encyclopedia of the social and behavioral sciences.* Oxford, UK: Elsevier.

Willis, S. L., and Nesselroade, C. S. (1990). Long term effects of fluid ability training in old-old age. *Developmental Psychology, 26,* 905–910.

Willis, S. L., and Reid, J. E. (Eds.). (1999). *Life in the middle: Psychological and social development in middle age.* San Diego, CA: Academic Press.

Willis, S. L., and Schaie, K. W. (1986a). Practical intelligence in later adulthood. In R. J. Sternberg and R. K. Wagner (Eds.), *Practical intelligence: Origins of competence in the everyday world* (pp. 236–268). Cambridge, UK: Cambridge University Press.

Willis, S. L., and Schaie, K. W. (1986b). Training the elderly on ability factors of spatial orientation and inductive reasoning. *Psychology and Aging, 1,* 239–247.

Willis, S. L., and Schaie, K. W. (1988). Gender differences in spatial ability in old age: Longitudinal and intervention findings. *Sex Roles, 18,* 189–203.

Willis, S. L., and Schaie, K. W. (1993). Everyday cognition: Taxonomic and methodological considerations. In J. M. Puckett and H. W. Reese (Eds.), *Mechanisms of everyday cognition* (pp. 33–54). Hillsdale, NJ: Erlbaum.

Willis, S. L., and Schaie, K. W. (1994a). Assessing competence in the elderly. In C. E. Fisher and R. M. Lerner (Eds.), *Applied developmental psychology* (pp. 339–372). New York: MacMillan.

Willis, S. L., and Schaie, K. W. (1994b). Cognitive training in the normal elderly. In F. Forette, Y. Christen and F. Boller (Eds.), *Plasticité cérébrale et stimulation cognitiv*e [Cerebral plasticity and cognitive stimulation] (pp. 91–113). Paris, France: Fondation Nationale de Gérontologie.

Willis, S. L., and Schaie, K. W. (1999). Intellectual functioning in midlife. In S. L. Willis and J. Reid (Eds.), *Life in the middle* (pp. 233–349). San Diego, CA: Academic Press.

Wilson, B. A. (1997). Cognitive rehabilitation: How it is and how it might be. *Journal of the International Neuropsychological Society, 5,* 487–496.

Wilson, M. N. (1998). Parenting and parent-child interactions in African American families: A synopsis. *African American Research Perspectives, 4,* 27–34.

Wilson, W. J. (1987). *The truly disadvantaged.* Chicago, IL: University of Chicago Press.

Wingfield, A. (1996). Cognitive factors in auditory performance: Context, speed of processing, and constraints of memory. *Journal of the American Academy of Audiology, 7,* 175–182.

Wingfield, A. (1999). Speech perception and the comprehension of spoken language in adult aging. In D. C. Park and N. Schwarz (Eds.), *Cognitive aging: A primer* (pp. 175–195). Philadelphia, PA: Psychology Press.

Wingfield, A., Stine, A. L., Lahr, C. J., and Aberdeen, J. S. (1988). Does the capacity of working memory change with age? *Experimental Aging Research, 14,* 103–107.

Wink, P., and Helson, R. (1997). Practical and transcendent wisdom: Their nature and some longitudinal findings. *Journal of Adult Development, 4,* 1–14.

Winn, F. J. (1991). Preface for special issue on ergonomics and the older worker. *Experimental Aging Research, 17,* 139–141.

Winsborough, H. H., and Bumpass, L. L. (1991). *The death of parents and the transition to old age.* National Survey of Families and Households Working Paper No. 39. Madison, WI: University of Wisconsin Center for Demography and Ecology.

Wisocki, P. A. (1998). Behavior therapy and cognitive behavior therapy interventions for anxiety disorders in older adults. *Journal of Geriatric Psychiatry, 31,* 173–192.

Wisocky, P. A., and Powers, P. A. (1997). Behavioral treatments for pain experienced by older adults. In D. I. Mostofsky and J. Lomranz (Eds.), *Handbook of pain and aging* (pp. 365–382). New York: Plenum.

Wissler, C. (1901). *The correlation of mental and physical tests.* New York: Columbia University Press.

Wohlwill, J. F. (1973). *The study of behavioral development.* New York: Academic Press.

Wolf, D. A., and Pinnelli, A. (1989). Living arrangements and family networks of older women in Italy. *Research on Aging, 11,* 354–373.

Wolinsky, F. D., Stump, T. E., and Callahan, C. M. (1996). Nursing home placement and subsequent morbidity and mortality. In S. L. Willis, K. W. Schaie, and M. Hayward (Eds.), *Societal mechanisms for maintaining competence in old age.* New York: Springer Publishing Co.

Wolk, R. L., and Wolk, R. B. (1971). *The Gerontological Apperception Test.* New York: Behavioral Publications.

Wong, P. T. P., and Stiller, C. (1999). Living with dignity and palliative counseling. In B. De Vries (Ed.), *End of life issues.* (pp. 97–94). New York: Springer Publishing Co.

Wong, Y. I., Garfinkel, I., and McLanahan, S. (1993). Single-mother families in eight countries: Economic status and social policy. *Social Service Review, 67,* 177–197.

Woodruff, D. S. (1983). The role of memory in personality continuity: A 25-year follow-up. *Experimental Aging Research, 9,* 31–34.

Woodruff, D. S. (1985). Arousal, sleep, and aging. In J. E. Birren and K. W. Schaie (Eds.), *Handbook of the psychology of aging* (2nd ed., pp. 261–295). New York: Van Nostrand Reinhold.

Woodruff, D. S., and Birren, J. E. (1972). Age changes and cohort differences in personality. *Developmental Psychology, 6,* 252–259.

Woodruff-Pak, D. S. (1989). Aging and intelligence: Changing perspectives in the twentieth century. *Journal of Aging Studies, 3,* 91–118.

Woodruff-Pak, D. S. (1997). *The neuropsychology of aging.* Malden, MA: Blackwell.

Woods, R. T. (1996). Psychological "therapies" in dementia. In R. T. Woods (Ed.), *Handbook of the clinical psychology of ageing* (pp. 575–600). Chichester, UK: John Wiley and Sons.

Woodworth, R. S. (1920). *The personal data sheet.* New York: Stoelting.

World Health Organization (1991). *World health statitstics annual 1990.* Geneva, Switzerland: Author.

Wray, L. A., Herzog, A. R., Willis, R. J. and Wallace, R. B. (1998). The impact of education and heart attack on smoking cessation among middle-aged adults. *Journal of Health and So-*

cial Behavior, 39, 271–294.

Wurtman, R. J. (1985). Alzheimer's disease. *Scientific American, January,* 62–74.

Wyatt-Brown, A. M. (1992). Literary gerontology comes of age. In T. R. Cole, D. D. VanTassel, and R. Kastenbaum (Eds.), *Handbook of the humanities and aging* (pp. 331–351). New York: Springer.

Xiaohe, X., and Whyte, M. K. (1998). Love matches and arranged marriages: A Chinese replication. In S. J. Ferguson (Ed.), *Shifting the center: Understanding contemporary families.* (pp. 115–132). Mountain View, CA: Mayfield.

Yang, J., McCrae, R. R., and Costa, P. T. Jr. (1998). Adult age differences in personality traits in the United States and the People's Republic of China. *Journal of Gerontology: Psychological Sciences, 53B,* P375–P383.

Yanik, A. J. (1994). Barriers to the design of vehicles for mature adults. *Experimental Aging Research, 20,* 5–10.

Yerkes, R. M. (Ed.) (1921). Psychological examining in the United States Army. *Memoirs of the National Academy of Sciences, 15,* 1–890.

Yesavage, J. (1982). Degree of dementia and improvement with memory training. *Clinical Gerontologist, 1,* 77–81.

Yesavage, J., Lapp, D., and Sheikh, J. A. (1989). Mnemonics as modified for use by the elderly. In L. W. Poon, D. Rubin, and B. Wilson (Eds.), *Everyday cognition in adulthood and late life.* Cambridge, UK: Cambridge University Press.

Yesavage, J. A., Westphal, J., and Rush, L. (1981). Senile dementia: Combined pharmacologic and psychologic treatment. *Journal of the American Geriatrics Society, 29,* 164–171.

Yost, E. B., Beutler, L. E., Corbishley, M. A., and Allender, J. R. (1986). *Group cognitive therapy: A treatment approach for depressed older adults.* New York: Pergamon.

Young, J. E., Beck, A. T., and Weinberger, A. (1993). Depression. In D. Barlow (Ed.), *Clinical handbook of psychological disorder* (3rd ed., pp. 240–277). New York: Guilford.

Young, V. (1984). *Working with the dying and grieving.* Davis, CA: International Dialogue Press.

Youngjohn, J. R., Larrabee, G. J., and Crook, T. H. (1992). Discriminating age-associated memory impairment from Alzheimer's disease. *Psychological Assessment, 4,* 54–59.

Yu, E. S., Liu, W. T., and Levy, P. (1989). Cognitive impairment among elderly adults in Shanghai, China. *Journal of Gerontology, 1989,* S97–106.

Zacks, R. T., Hasher, L. and Li, K. Z. H. (1999). Human memory. In F .I. M. Craik and T. A. Salthouse (Eds.), *Handbook of aging and cognition* (2nd ed.). Mahwah, NJ: Erlbaum.

Zarit, S. H. (1980). *Aging and mental disorders.* New York: Free Press.

Zarit, S. H. (1982). Affective correlates of self-report about memory in older adults. *International Journal of Behavioral Geriatrics, 1,* 25–34.

Zarit, S. H., Cole, K., and Guider, R. (1981). Memory training strategies and subjective complaints of memory in the aged. *Gerontologist, 21,* 158–164.

Zarit, S. H., Eiler, J., and Hassinger, M. (1985). Clinical assessment. In J. E. Birren and K. W. Schaie (Eds.), *Handbook of the psychology of aging* (2nd ed.). New York: Van Nostrand Reinhold.

Zarit, S. H., Zarit, J., and Reever, K. (1982). Memory training or severe memory loss: Effects of senile dementia. *Gerontologist, 22,* 373–377.

Zautra, A. J., Potter, P. T., and Reich, J. W. (1998). The independence of affects is context-dependent: An integrative model of the relationship between positive and negative affect. In K. W. Schaie and M. P. Lawton (Eds.). *Annual review of gerontology and geriatrics:* (Vol. 17., pp. 75–103) New York: Springer Publishing Co.

Zeiss, A. M., and Lewinsohn, P. M. (1986). Adopting behavioral treatment for depression to meet the needs of the elderly. *Clinical Psychologist, 39,* 98-100.

Zelinski, E. M and Burnight, K. P. (1997). Sixteen-year longitudinal and time lag changes in memory and cognition in older adults. *Psychology and Aging, 12,* 503–513

Zelinski, E. M, Crimmins, E., Reynolds, S., and Seeman, T. (1998). Do medical conditions affect cognition in older adults? *Health Psychology, 17,* 504–512.

Zelinski, E. M., Gilewski, M. J., and Schaie, K. W. (1993). Individual differences in cross-sectional and 3-year longitudinal memory performance across the adult life span. *Psychology and Aging, 8,* pp. 176–pp. 186.

Zelinski, E. M., and Stewart, S. T. (1998). Individual differences in 16-year memory changes. *Psychology and Aging, 13,* 622–630.

Zilboorg, G., and Henry, G. W. (1941). *A history of medical psychology.* New York: Norton.

Zimberg, S. (1987). Alcohol abuse among the elderly. In L. L. Carstensen and B. L. Edelstein (Eds.), *Handbook of clinical gerontology* (pp. 57–65). New York: Pergamon.

Zollar, A., and Williams, J. (1987). The contribution of marriage to the life satisfaction of black adults. *Journal of Marriage and the Family, 49,* 87–92.

PHOTO CREDITS

AUTHOR INDEX

SUBJECT INDEX